Show Thyself a Man

Southern Dissent

UNIVERSITY PRESS OF FLORIDA

Florida A&M University, Tallahassee
Florida Atlantic University, Boca Raton
Florida Gulf Coast University, Ft. Myers
Florida International University, Miami
Florida State University, Tallahassee
New College of Florida, Sarasota
University of Central Florida, Orlando
University of Florida, Gainesville
University of North Florida, Jacksonville
University of South Florida, Tampa
University of West Florida, Pensacola

SHOW THYSELF A MAN

Georgia State Troops, Colored, 1865–1905

Gregory Mixon

Stanley Harrold and Randall M. Miller, Series Editors

University Press of Florida
Gainesville · Tallahassee · Tampa · Boca Raton
Pensacola · Orlando · Miami · Jacksonville · Ft. Myers · Sarasota

Copyright 2016 by Gregory Mixon
All rights reserved
Published in the United States of America

First cloth printing, 2016
First paperback printing, 2024

29 28 27 26 25 24   6 5 4 3 2 1

Library of Congress Cataloging-in-Publication Data
Names: Mixon, Gregory, author.
Title: Show thyself a man : Georgia State troops, colored, 1865–1905 / Gregory Mixon.
Other titles: Southern dissent.
Description: Gainesville : University Press of Florida, [2016] | Series: Southern dissent | Includes bibliographical references and index.
Identifiers: LCCN 2016004177 | ISBN 9780813062723 (cloth) | ISBN 9780813080628 (pbk.)
Subjects: LCSH: Georgia. Militia—History. | African American soldiers—Georgia—History. | African Americans—Civil rights—Georgia—History. | Georgia—Race relations—History.
Classification: LCC UA159 .M59 2016 | DDC 355.3/708996073075809034—dc23
LC record available at http://lccn.loc.gov/2016004177

The University Press of Florida is the scholarly publishing agency for the State University System of Florida, comprising Florida A&M University, Florida Atlantic University, Florida Gulf Coast University, Florida International University, Florida State University, New College of Florida, University of Central Florida, University of Florida, University of North Florida, University of South Florida, and University of West Florida.

University Press of Florida
2046 NE Waldo Road
Suite 2100
Gainesville, FL 32609
http://upress.ufl.edu

CONTENTS

List of Illustrations and Tables vii

Preface ix

Acknowledgments xiii

Introduction 1

1. The Search for Freedom: Black Militiamen in Nineteenth-Century North America 23

2. "We Called It 'The Band of Brothers'": Black Independent Militia Formation and the Johnson County Insurrection of 1875 40

3. Creating the Georgia Militia: Blacks and the Road to State Militia Companies, 1865–1880 81

4. "Any Person Capable of Doing Military Duty": The Georgia Volunteers, 1878–1890s 126

5. "Be Thou Strong Therefore and Show Thyself a Man": Georgia Volunteers, Colored, 1889–1895 186

6. The Road to Disbandment, 1896–1899 249

7. The New Era, 1899–1905 296

Conclusion 337

Notes 343

Bibliography 391

Index 405

ILLUSTRATIONS AND TABLES

Figure 1. Captain Jesse Jones 2

Figure 2. "Private Jimmy" 4

Figure 3. "At Manassas" 5

Map 1. Georgia Counties and County Seats 58

Table 1. Roster of Colored Companies, Georgia, 1878 93

Table 2. Roster of White Infantry Companies, Georgia, 1878 129

Table 3. Report of White Cavalry Squadrons, Georgia, 1878 133

PREFACE

This study began in 1996, with the commentary and suggestion of John Haley, emeritus history professor at the University of North Carolina (UNC) at Wilmington, at a meeting of the Southern Historical Association in Little Rock, Arkansas, just as Governor William Jefferson Clinton began his candidacy for the presidency of the United States. I presented a paper at that meeting on the Atlanta riot and the Georgia militia as part of a session at which Haley served as commentator.[1] Just as we were wrapping up the session, Haley suggested that no one had studied African American militiamen in the United States South historically. The political scientist Charles Johnson Jr., also present at this session, reinforced this idea and noted his own work, *African American Soldiers in the National Guard: Recruitment and Deployment During Peacetime and War*.[2] Their suggestions and discussion of the topic stayed with me as I developed my work on the Atlanta race riot of 1906 as a book. The evolution of the work on the Atlanta riot and my professional career took me away from New Jersey to a new home in Charlotte, North Carolina, in 1999. Research on the Georgia militia began in 2000 with a University of North Carolina at Charlotte Faculty Research Grant. The original study was to have been an exploration of black militia companies in Georgia, North Carolina, South Carolina, and Virginia. This plan proved to be overly ambitious in light of the responsibilities of teaching, service, research, workload policies, and deadlines that define an academic career in the twenty-first century. Further, Georgia's archival collection on the Georgia Volunteers and Georgia Volunteers, Colored, proved to be much more extensive than anticipated, leading me eventually to change the focus of the book to Georgia. This decision occurred only after several research trips to archives in North Carolina, South Carolina, and Virginia and a need to meet the deadlines of academia.

Intellectually, this study has also evolved as a result of examining the sources and reading secondary materials. Originally, I was impressed and wondered why and how Virginia's African American militiamen managed, despite white supremacy, to successfully mount a northern tour, visiting such places as Providence, Rhode Island? As the research and teaching continued after the publication of the Atlanta riot monograph, my focus changed to how African Americans defined freedom, both at the moment of emancipation and beyond that into the nineteenth century, and the part the militia unit played in that process. The black militia company, I found, was part of the search for freedom that defined the moment at which slavery ended and freedom, citizenship, autonomy, and national belonging began. These ideas were reinforced by my exploration of the African descendant militiaman in Latin America, as my secondary reading and discussions with colleagues evolved to a more inclusive examination of not only the United States South but also the Western Hemisphere in the nineteenth century. It is because of these discussions that I utilize the term "African-descendant people" to illustrate the broader and more inclusive description of black people outside of the United States while also examining the broad panorama of those who lived in the Western Hemisphere. The work of Ben Vinson III, Jane Landers, Michele Reid-Vazquez, George Reid Andrews, Matt Childs, and Christopher Leslie Brown and Philip D. Morgan explained the importance of the militia to African-descendant people in the Western Hemisphere. My colleagues in Latin American studies at the University of North Carolina at Charlotte, Jerry Davila, Erika Edwards, Lyman Johnson, and Jurgen Buchenau, were each instrumental in introducing me to this literature and listening as well as reading my meandering thinking on the connections between race and militia service, African-descendant militiamen, freedom, and citizenship. The work of Michael Fitzgerald, Jeffrey Kerr-Ritchie, Roger Cunningham, and Eleanor Hannah were also critical to my thinking about the black militia in the United States as the project evolved. My thanks also go to Jeffrey Kerr-Ritchie for our early conversations.

The UNC Charlotte History Department's Brown Bag Seminar also provided collegial support and suggestions for revisions of parts of the book. My thanks go to the entire department for making professional development, collegiality, and research the way it should be: a collaborative, supportive activity, where each enjoys the success and evolution of the other. Thanks to David Goldfield for suggesting that I apply to Charlotte. My thanks and congratulations, further, go to Jim Hogue and Jurgen

Buchenau, members of the class of 1999. We have journeyed together at UNCC for a decade and a half. My colleague John David Smith has also offered his time to listen and suggest as the project evolved. Thank you, Mark Wilson, for your advice and for taking the time to read my fellowship applications, even though the efforts did not yield the hoped-for results.

Africana Studies at UNCC was equally important in my exploration of these ideas; Akin Ogundiran, department chair, Felix Germain, the annual Africana Studies Symposium, the Africana Studies Brown Bag Seminars, organized by Dorothy Ruiz-Smith and Debra Smith, and Oscar de la Torre provided opportunities both to discuss the book project in public venues and to develop an article-length examination of African-descendant militiamen in the Americas, published in *Boletín Americanista*. The Center for the Study of the New South, led by Jeffrey Leak, also provided a moment to share my work with colleagues in the Center's New South in the Afternoon series. The Charlotte Area Historians also read parts of the manuscript. Their comments were instrumental in reorganizing chapter 1, creating the introduction, and revising chapters 2 and 3 as I prepared the manuscript for publication. Colleagues Christopher Cameron and Cheryl Hicks provided additional suggestions, both as Charlotte-area historians and as History Department colleagues.

The work is a social and political history of an institution created in Western Europe and transported across the Atlantic Ocean to the Americas, where African-descendant people became members of that institution, making it, in part, their own. Black people in the Americas utilized the militia company as a vehicle for becoming integral members of the newly emergent colonial and nation-state societies that defined the process of colonization in the Americas, from the fifteenth century through the nineteenth century. The all-black militia company also played a vital role in Western Hemisphere nation-state formation in the nineteenth century. Race, citizenship, national belonging, and militia service were intertwined in many nineteenth-century communities. Post–Civil War Georgia was one of those communities, and these issues were part of the effort there to reconstruct a society within the postbellum United States. Emancipation in the United States was not a single moment when the nation committed to a full embrace of black people as citizens. The United States South was where much of that process of incorporation would be played out between blacks and whites. The militia company would serve as one of the institutions directly involved in the transition from slavery to freedom and the creation of the nation after the Civil War. It was within this context that African Americans in Georgia pursued militia membership as a means of presenting their credentials for full citizenship. White Georgians at the same time engaged a conflicted and conflicting vision that embraced, questioned, and rejected black claims to citizenship. White Georgians also wrestled with defeat in war, as well as the nature of their ongoing relationship with the national government. Their view of the militia as a local institution controlled by the state's governor was to evolve during the late nineteenth century, as whites resolved their defeat and their membership in the Union of states.

The introduction and chapter 1 provide a brief history of the militia in the Western Hemisphere and North America before the Civil War. African-descendant people joined local militia companies hoping to use the institution both as a platform to access greater freedom and membership within the societies they inhabited and as a means of self-defense. Chapters 2 and 3 define the two significantly separate forms of militia that black Georgians embraced during and after Reconstruction: the independent militia and the state-sponsored militia. These chapters also define the black and white visions of the militia. Chapter 4 examines black Georgians' efforts to utilize the militia company as an instrument of citizenship during public celebrations. Black Georgians defined citizenship as a public declaration of manhood, racial progress, and access to public rights. Chapter 5 explores the evolution of the Georgia Volunteers, Colored, as black Georgians coped with the reorganizations initiated by state government that were intended to manage the size of the Georgia Volunteers. Chapters 6 and 7 present a decade-long debate by whites and blacks over the definition of the militia as a state organization. Just as the legacy of the Civil War helped bring the Georgia Volunteers, Colored, into existence, war on a global scale against Spain in Cuba and the Philippines would be instrumental in deciding the membership of the early twentieth-century National Guard. The story of black militiamen in Georgia is a local, regional, and national story. It chronicles the evolution of black claims making for citizenship and national belonging, as well as the history of one of several African-descendant militias in nineteenth-century America.

ACKNOWLEDGMENTS

My work on this project was supported and encouraged by individuals and institutions. The University of North Carolina at Charlotte's Junior Faculty Summer Fellowship Grant and four Faculty Research Grants provided the financial base to conduct research in Georgia, North Carolina, South Carolina, and Virginia. These small grants allowed me to travel to archives, acquire primary sources, and secure lodging. A semester-long Reassignment of Duties Leave, sponsored by the College of Liberal Arts and Sciences, and two one-semester Cotlow Leaves from the History Department at UNC Charlotte provided the funding and time away from teaching to read secondary material and write portions of the manuscript. These opportunities came at critical times in the writing and revision process. My thanks go to Nancy Gutierrez, dean of the UNCC College of Liberal Arts and Sciences, and to Jurgen Buchenau, chair of the History Department, for these opportunities. Research support also came from two Virginia Historical Society Andrew W. Mellon Research Fellowships and a Watson-Brown Fellowship from the University of South Carolina.

The staff at the Georgia Department of Archives and History welcomed my research visits on numerous occasions. They provided research leads, suggestions, and new sources that have enhanced this project in more ways than one. The great recession and state budget cuts, however, ended the archival careers of many members of this supportive staff. This book is in part dedicated to the archivists, from Virginia to Georgia, who welcomed me into their facilities. Thank you for your support, assistance, suggestions, and friendships.

Two National Endowment for the Humanities Summer Institutes—"African American Freedom Struggles and Civil Rights, 1865–1965," at the Du Bois Institute at Harvard University, in 2011, and "Slaves, Soldiers, and Rebels: Currents of Black Resistance in the Tropical Atlantic, 1760–1880," at Johns Hopkins University, in 2009—provided collegiality and new sources that enhanced the project. I am grateful to Dr. Patricia Sullivan, Dr. Waldo Martin, and Dr. Ben Vinson III for these opportunities and brief but important months during which they opened these institutions for my use and time to read, digest, and rethink my project in a different locale. I also give my thanks to the Institute's participants, who made life in Cambridge and Baltimore creative, fun, and a learning experience. Thanks for allowing me to join each of you in the discussions of the readings, teaching, and research.

In 2012, as the presidential debates attracted the nation's attention, my mentor, Herbert Shapiro, passed. His patience and guidance ensured my matriculation through graduate school at the University of Cincinnati. Shapiro's advice led to my work on the Atlanta riot of 1906. His inspiration in the classroom and his mentorship outside of class have been a part of me since I left Cincinnati, in 1988 and 1989. This book therefore is dedicated to Herbert Shapiro, the one who believed in me throughout it all. Thank you.

My thanks also go to Glen N. and Marlene Jones. Our journey together began at Virginia Military Institute (VMI) and has continued since my departure from VMI. The Joneses welcomed me into their home on my research trips to Richmond. Our friendship has grown as a result of their hospitality and our ongoing conversations.

This book is additionally dedicated to my sister Deborah and her late daughter, Jonelle, as well as to my grandchildren, Raheem, Rahmel, Ja-Lyn, Zymir, Ervin, Tyshawn, Jamal, and Azyre and my first great-grandchild, Emury. It is also dedicated to my daughters, Rozetta and Mesha, and to Mesha's partner, Ervin Sr. All but one of the great-grand and grandchildren was born during the research, writing, and completion of this book. They have tolerated the isolation and ongoing persistence of my working all the time. Equally tolerant has been Nellie Holloway-Mixon, who has taken this journey with me for some thirty-seven years. Thank you, Nellie, for keeping me laughing, calm, and present when the grandkids came calling. Also thank you for your practicality and sense of humor. They have carried us on this road together.

INTRODUCTION

On May 7, 1904, Benjamin Davis, the African American owner and editor of the newly established *Atlanta Independent,* placed a picture of Captain Jesse Jones on the front page of his weekly newspaper. Davis used his paper to inspire, teach, direct, politicize, and inform blacks locally, regionally, and nationally about the achievements of African Americans. He further sought to prove to whites that black Americans were more than "buffoons" unworthy of admittance to positions of power, authority, manhood, and citizenship. The placement of a respected and long-serving black militiaman on the front page of the *Independent* was intended first to energize black Atlantans to shake off their "lethargy" and embrace the "military spirit" still alive in the distinguished personage of Captain Jesse Jones. Second, Davis sought to stir African Americans especially, and also whites, "to give encouragement to [Jones's] . . . deserving company," Atlanta's Fulton Guards. Third, Davis appears to have wanted to prove through this photograph, along with the supporting brief article, that African Americans still had white allies in a community that was increasingly embracing white supremacy, legislating Jim Crow segregation and disfranchisement, and endorsing as well as perpetrating antiblack violence. White supporters, Davis implied, recognized that there were blacks who embodied respectability, service, commitment, manliness, and dignity: characteristics blacks had pursued since the end of the Civil War and hoped to have demonstrated by participating in the Spanish-American War, the Cuban War of Independence, and the Philippine-American War, which were fought between 1898 and 1902.[1]

Exercising and living daily such characteristics, as well as incorporating them into the standards of militia membership, made these African Americans ready for inclusion in southern society as full citizens. Furthermore, being a militiaman was directly associated with manly and responsible citizenship. Davis both covertly and directly, with this page-one

Figure 1. Captain Jesse Jones, Fulton Guards, May 7, 1904, *Atlanta Independent*.

display and photograph of Jesse Jones, promoted the characteristics of manhood and citizenship that white supremacists sought to deny African Americans. The photograph of Captain Jesse Jones of the Fulton Guards, erect and immaculately uniformed, presented a gallant, respectable, and fine physical specimen of a black man. Jones's physically fit black persona highlighted for the public an important nineteenth-century characteristic of the American militiaman: the strong male body. The healthy body assured the public that their investment of financial resources in militiamen was well spent and indicated that the militia had a secure link to the community it served. Yet the new twentieth century marked a significant change in how the militiaman would be connected to the community he served and in the place of black militiamen in the nation's militia. These changes began in the 1890s, as militiamen's commitment to community gave way to the individualized twentieth-century militiaman, who was incorporated within the national reorganization of the nation's military defense force in 1903. This reorganization was followed three years later by antiblack violence in Atlanta, with the 1906 riot. The disfranchisement of blacks in Georgia followed a year later.[2]

Yet the image Captain Jones conveyed contradicted nineteenth- and early twentieth-century stereotypes of black racial inferiority, which whites used to justify their racism. Jones and his fellow African American militiamen had spent the last quarter of the nineteenth century engaged in activities, actions, and professionalization intended to challenge stereotypical charges of racial inferiority that had plagued African Americans at least since emancipation. Jones's twentieth-century appearance was an attempt to forestall the ever-rising tide of white supremacy manifested in Jim Crow segregation on public conveyances, abortive statewide disfranchising proposals, lynching, and antiblack rural and urban violence. The militia captain's public persona also represented the range of capabilities black people had acquired since the end of slavery in the United States, in 1865. Black Georgians had declared themselves to be citizens of the nation and the state. As militiamen in the nineteenth century they were members of that century's state-sponsored militia, the Georgia Volunteers, and the twentieth century's new state militia and National Guard, the Georgia State Troops.[3]

Jones, a veteran of the early-twentieth-century Georgia State Troops, Colored, the segregated black component of the state's National Guard organization, had been a member of the nineteenth-century state-sponsored militia, the Georgia Volunteers, Colored, since 1888. From his initial militia membership, Jones had risen through the ranks to his position of command through a dogged dedication to maintaining a black presence in the Georgia Volunteers, Georgia's official military. Beginning in 1888 as a private in another Atlanta-based black militia company, the Governor's Volunteers, Jesse Jones, within a year, was elected by his peers to officer rank as second lieutenant. According to the *Independent*, Jones continued as a member of the Governor's Volunteers, serving "with credit to the soldiery of Georgia and his race in particular until the disbandment of the company in 1900." By August 1901, Jones was affiliated with the Fulton Guards as a second lieutenant. He joined former members of the Governor's Volunteers who changed their affiliation to the Fulton Guards upon the demise of that militia company. Two years later, in 1903, the Fulton Guards elected Jones as their captain and commanding officer. This honor

4 · Show Thyself a Man

was celebrated with the support of "a host of friends . . . throughout the state both white and black who desire[d] to see him succeed."[4]

Conflicting Black Militia Images

By August and September 1904, white supremacy's advocates were attacking the integrity and capabilities of black militiamen. At a national encampment of National Guard units that included white regiments from Georgia, South Carolina, and Texas and black militiamen from Connecticut, a white Georgia subaltern refused to salute an African American

Figures 2 and 3. Contrast these caricatures of black militiamen with the image of Captain Jones. *Atlanta Constitution*, September 1904.

captain. Caricatures of black militiamen followed in the *Atlanta Constitution*, portraying black militiamen as unkempt, clown-like incompetents with overly large protruding lips who simply played at being a soldier. In contrast, white subalterns, privates, and corporals were in the same cartoon portrayed as qualified to serve in the militia because they wore the uniform smartly and correctly and possessed the proper manly military bearing.[5]

Whites had questioned black militia service since Reconstruction. Conservative white supremacist and South Carolina attorney Theodore D. Jervey authored a monograph, *The Slave Trade: Slavery and Color*,[6] that

LIEUT. VANDERBILT WAS OVERCOME BY THE HEAT

THE ATLANTA CONSTITUTION THURSDAY, SEPTEMBER 8, 1904

critiqued Reconstruction and black South Carolina's militiamen. Jervey presented three photographic images from the 1890s of what he claimed were black South Carolina militiamen. Two of the three militiamen had carved out highly public and active political careers inside the state. A third was a black militiaman-politician noted for his collaboration with white antiblack Reconstruction. In spite of his efforts at accommodation and his display of a manly military bearing, he was denied the respectability he had earned.[7] This third photograph, on the contrary, caricatured the black militiaman, who was pictured mounting a cow in a disheveled military uniform. This imagery depicted the militiaman as more farmer than military personage.

The farming image confirmed the attitudes whites espoused during the last four decades of the nineteenth century. The proper place for blacks, according to such thinking, was on the farm being subservient to whites. Specifically, the antiblack Nashville, Tennessee, *Union and Dispatch* and Atlanta's New South promoter Henry W. Grady argued that blacks needed to go "back to the cornfield where they belong!" Grady also urged young white men eligible for militia duty and employment in the emerging commercial-industrial economy to rise up and meet the challenges of a rapidly approaching new century that would include removing black men from positions of responsibility. By implication, Grady suggested that the new openings would be filled by white men in need of a job and enhanced status. Blacks, according to these white newspaper editors, needed to be controlled as they had been during slavery. Such a restoration of white supervision over black labor could re-create a lost moment of racial harmony during the tumultuous days of change that defined the post–Civil War South, Reconstruction, and the last decades of the nineteenth century. Black militiamen in the United States South, especially Georgia, nevertheless nurtured a counter image: They publicly marched, drilled, and sustained themselves as citizens, soldiers of the state, and voters sharing in local- and state-level governance and public policy decisions.[8]

Historiography

The militia was integral to black Georgians' collective search for freedom, citizenship, and belonging after the Civil War. African American Georgians ultimately participated in that search through two kinds of militia companies: independent companies and state-sponsored companies. Separately and collectively the black independent and state-sponsored militia companies defined the search for freedom in post–Civil War Georgia. The black militia company at the end of the Civil War simplified an institution heavily tied to a new ruling regimen in the South, the Republican Party. Yet the historiography describing these militiamen presents a biracial, and sometimes racially and physically segregated, state-sponsored militia struggling to find its way as the bloodshed of civil war ended and the brutal political and military combat over who would rule the South began. This process, as described in Otis Singletary's *Negro Militia and Reconstruction* (1957), defined the field and continues to set the parameters of black militia studies in the United States into the twenty-first century.[9] *Show Thyself a Man* challenges the narrow range of this study and suggests that we broaden our examination of black militia service, within both the confines of Reconstruction politics and the remaining three and a half decades of the nineteenth century. Singletary presented black militiamen and their companies as a failed experiment with an "inconsiderable amount" of "angry . . . racial violence" that was "directly connected with the Negro militia movement." The "Negro militia movement" was also part of the "ensuing program" that "contained the seeds of social revolution for the South."[10] While these assertions come close to blaming black militiamen for the violence levied by white conservative opponents of the new governing structures proposed by the Republican Party, Singletary contended that the primary functions envisioned for the Negro militia had been "defensive" and "protective": The military force was to defend Republican Party post–Civil War governance in the United States South.[11]

Negro Militia and Reconstruction appeared during the early stages of another social revolution, the post–World War II civil rights movement, specifically, in the wake of the United States Supreme Court's *Brown v. Board* decision and the Montgomery Bus Boycott, 1955–1956. Singletary, as a result, had "reason for fear[ing] a [white] resurgence of racial violence in the South" similar to the white response to black militiamen and the African American vision of freedom almost a hundred years earlier. Singletary's black militia study focused on mixed-race and racially segregated, state-sponsored, Republican Party–legislated militia companies. These units were created by Radical Republicans "to fill the power vacuum that resulted from the withdrawal of Federal troops when the [southern] states had complied with the conditions [readmission to the Union] set forth in the Reconstruction Acts."[12]

While Singletary's *Negro Militia and Reconstruction* is a state-by-state study of violent white southerners' responses to Radical Reconstruction governments that established black and white militia companies to defend the newly formed post–Civil War state governments, it is not a study of black expressions of freedom, citizenship, autonomy, political empowerment, and community building that *Show Thyself a Man* seeks to examine. Singletary's work focuses on the white response to the presence of a military force defending a "foreign" governing body, the Republican Party, in a postwar South. This white southern response, aimed at the restoration of white home rule, was violent. It fabricated black militia abuses of helpless white civilians and created a public image of black militiamen as aggressive, abusive, aberrant, and an "affront" to white public visions of the post–Civil War South. The affront was so severe that "this protective force caused so violent a reaction that it guaranteed the obstruction of the very thing it was created to protect," namely, Republican Party governance.[13]

The black militiaman, Singletary argued, joined these southern state militias for "a personal defense of his freedom." Yet very little of this important work examines African American conceptions of militia service and citizenship. Singletary instead contends that black field hands, bored with their obligations as plantation workers, sought relief from this "drudgery" by pursuing monetary rewards through militia service. Blacks found militia service attractive because of the "perennial appeal of the uniform." They also liked the "plume or feathers" adornments and the public allure of "the drills, parades, barbecues, and speeches" that broke "the monotony" of daily life. Black women additionally shamed "suspected [black male] shirkers" into militia service. Essentially black militiamen were engaged in "a delightful game" of "'playin sogers.'"[14]

In fact post–Civil War black militiaman in Georgia pursued militia service for other, more concrete reasons. African Americans who joined militia companies in Georgia after the Civil War pursued multiple aims, not least of which was the defense of their personal freedom. While Georgia's Radical Republicans did not legislate any defense force into existence, as happened in Tennessee and North Carolina, African Americans formed county-level independent militia companies that served not only to defend black and white Republicans but also to be an instrument of what historians Elsa Barkley Brown and Jeffrey R. Kerr-Ritchie have characterized as "collective responsibility." Black men in Georgia were part of an independent militia tradition whose roots extended back to the antebellum black collective defense of the race against slavery. These two scholars present black communal responsibility as an important African American ideal focused on common goals and shared responsibility for members of the race. An ideal developed within the antebellum and immediate post–Civil War lives of African Americans attempting to establish their collective right to citizenship and national belonging: a personal and communal vision of political, economic, and social freedom far different from the individualized worldview "of the larger white society."[15]

Brown and Kerr-Ritchie's work informs the central tenets of *Show Thyself a Man*: Georgia's black militiamen hoped to utilize the militia company as one of their key instruments in the collective search for racial freedom.[16] Black militia studies of the United States South, in such states as Tennessee, North Carolina, and Louisiana and written at the end of the twentieth century and beginning of the twenty-first century, present state-sponsored African American militiamen as an arm of the Republican Party responding to white violence against the state and local communities. Ben H. Severance, Samuel B. McGuire, James Hogue, and Rebecca J. Scott each examine the role of black and white militia units as peacekeepers in these three southern states against the backdrop of white conservative political violence. These studies not only affirm Singletary's focus on Reconstruction, with regard to the Republican Party governments' military defense needs, but also note the failure of white governors to utilize their militias to challenge white violence. The studies, with the exception of Scott's, end with Reconstruction and the triumph of antiblack white violence.[17]

Militia scholarship, including Scott's work, in the twenty-first century has moved beyond its previous focus on Reconstruction and on white-male military history and constitutional debates over the place of the militia within the nation's military structure.[18] This study joins the expanded effort to examine black militia service beyond the end of Reconstruction the focus of *Show Thyself a Man*. New scholarship transcends the earlier focus on the militia as a military force only. My study is more a political and social history. It joins Eleanor Hannah's *Manhood, Citizenship and the National Guard: Illinois, 1870–1917*, which combines race, gender, and social and political change in the late nineteenth-century United States. Hannah's work outlines the importance of masculinity, manhood, and community for all militiamen regardless of race. The militia was an evolving institution throughout the nineteenth century. Its late nineteenth-century position was subject to changes initiated by the Civil War and capital industrialization that defined race, gender, citizenship, and "freedom, liberty, and equality." These changes also sparked the rise of Jim Crow segregation, as southern whites sought a new system and culture that might regulate "the modern forces of capitalism." Georgia's militiamen wrestled with the transformative forces of the late nineteenth century, inside the state, the region, and the nation. These forces included debate about the militia's role in a changing American context of imperial expansion, race and racism, and definitions of citizenship, manhood, and inclusion within the social, political, and economic fabric of freedom.[19]

Late nineteenth-century state politics in the context of national, regional, and local change also shaped the post–Civil War and Reconstruction state-sponsored militia. Roger D. Cunningham's case study of Kansas's African American communities and black militia formation connects black state-sponsored militiamen to the ebb and flow of local community development, state politics, and the rise and fall of black political power. Cunningham also chronicles African American efforts to be citizens of the state. African American votes did have an, albeit limited, impact on Kansas's late nineteenth-century governors, who controlled militia company formation and determined militia leadership locally. Black enlistment and access to military training were also key experiences that made the difference between white militiamen's abilities to lead men and the obstacles that denied African Americans leadership experiences as militiamen. The paucity of black political power in Kansas in turn restricted how blacks could participate in the activities of state-sponsored militia, including leadership training: two circumstances that kept black Kansans from accessing mainstream militia training from the Civil War to the dawn of the twentieth century. In North Carolina and Illinois, on the other hand, black political power had a significant role in shaping the evolution of the state-sponsored militia and in mobilizing and securing resources for the Spanish-American War.[20]

Black people's post–Civil War search for freedom in Georgia involved efforts to transcend restricted political power, inadequate militia funding, and a one-party rule that defined Georgia's late nineteenth-century state militia politics. Georgians debated whether they wanted a militia, who should fund state units, and the shape of federal financing and control of the state's military. These issues determined how African Americans participated in post-Reconstruction politics. The Georgia Volunteers, Colored, survived federal, state, and militia politics for over thirty years, from 1872 to 1905. This book tells that story alongside that of the broader African American search for freedom and inclusion in Reconstruction and post-Reconstruction Georgia society as citizens of the state, region, and nation.

The Western Hemisphere and the Militia

Black Georgians additionally belonged to a broader story concerning African-descendant people in the Western Hemisphere. Late nineteenth-century black Georgia militiamen's search for freedom was part of a Western Hemisphere–wide and transnational effort by African-descendant people to find freedom, citizenship, and belonging and to secure the end of slavery. Black militiamen serving in wars in defense of Western European colonial possessions and in civil wars for independence in the Americas offered their military service in exchange for freedom and the recognition of their status as citizens within a newly emergent nation-state or as subjects of a colonizing imperial power. Black militiamen also fought during the early to mid-nineteenth century's Age of Revolution, directly contributing to the creation of nation-states in the Western Hemisphere in such places as Argentina, Brazil, Cuba, Haiti, and the United States. Their combat service in each of these emergent nation-states contributed to the creation of new nations, new forms of republican governance, and the abolition of slavery. Blacks served in anticipation of the rewards of freedom, citizenship, and inclusion in nation building and a seat at the table of governance. Their actions shaped the societies they sought to serve.[21]

Black militiamen in the Western Hemisphere operated within the confines of European transatlantic military systems that changed as colonial needs evolved, both in Western Europe and within their American colonies. African descendant militiamen served European states' colonial domestic needs against Native Americans, runaway and revolting slaves, civil disorder by laborers of all colors, and white independence movements. Wars for independence and slave revolts, sometimes led by black militiamen, were important events that affected the function and position of black militiamen in the Americas. Such service, Ben Vinson III, has argued, dates the black militiaman to Mexico's defense system, as early as the 1550s. The "free-colored militia," a group of *pardo*, *moreno*, and mulatto soldiers who were both volunteers and conscripted draftees, served the Spanish monarchy in Mexico. In exchange for their military service to the colony, free-colored militiamen could secure rights, "access a host of government officials," and leverage the system of colonial governance to benefit not only themselves but also, in some cases, the people in the communities they served.[22]

That said, members of Mexico's free colored military were defined by Spanish society as the "lowest members of the colonial racial matrix," and free blacks never attained the status of full citizenship, despite their militia service. From the 1550s to the completion of Spain's thirty-year Bourbon military reform/reorganization at the end of the eighteenth century, free black men defended Mexico's coastal region from external and internal incursions, meeting the needs of rural and urban communities. In 1556 colonial authorities, albeit reluctantly, integrated free-colored militiamen into the regular army as auxiliaries in Mexico, and free-colored militiamen served throughout the Spanish Empire under similar circumstances: in Havana (Cuba) in 1555, in Puerto Rico two years later, in Cartagena (Colombia) twice, in 1560 and 1572, and in Santo Domingo in 1583.[23]

Free-colored militiamen became critical to Mexico's defense system in 1683, when pirates raided for an entire week. Additional mobilizations of the black militia between 1685 and 1725 reinforced its importance. During these years African-descendant militiamen secured additional responsibilities, training, and a definitive public presence as the legal arm of colonial authorities or state-sponsored militia service. Free-colored militia power also encompassed involvement in local politics and the exercising of black rights. But royal reorganization and restructuring by the Spanish Crown, known as the Bourbon Reforms, reflected Spain's attempt to have an efficient global-colonial military. Bourbon reform undermined free-colored militia autonomy by reducing the number of black militiamen, from 1300 to 500; by whitening militia leadership; by standardizing military training with white regulars who controlled the process; by curtailing black legal rights; and by empowering poor, fragmented, and racist colonial leadership to make policies that negatively affected African-descendant militiamen and people. By 1795, Vinson notes, "for all intents and purposes, the era of widespread free-colored service had ended" in Mexico. Nevertheless, it appears that from the 1670s through the 1750s, free-colored militiamen persistently pursued ways "to determine the exact social impact that the militia would have upon their lives." During these years, blacks defined and controlled the militia as an institution that served African-descendant people.[24]

Mexico's African-descendant militiamen earned economic and political autonomy, a driving force among Georgia's post–Civil War independent black militiamen, before the Bourbon Reforms. Seventeenth-century free-colored militia companies could act with a significant degree of freedom: They controlled their own money, black officers led the militia companies, and they attained the legal rights conveyed to all of Spain's military personnel. Yet "blacks were called to duty . . . reluctantly." This reluctance was based on authorities' uncertainty about arming blacks and about recognizing all African-descendant people as having full status equal to whites. Some worried that blacks would use their equal status to overthrow the colonial administration. Indeed, free-colored people in Mexico joined slaves on several occasions in the sixteenth century to overturn colonial rule. These concerns would remain for hundreds of years throughout the Spanish Empire.[25]

More broadly, militias with African descendant militiamen were among the early institutional structures developed by blacks to address their needs in the Americas. Free blacks and mulattos, George Reid Andrews has asserted, used their free status to "organize collectively," just as nineteenth-century Georgia's black independent militiamen would mobilize African Americans at the county level in the late 1860s into the early 1870s for collective political action. Outside the United States African descendant militiamen participated in building such institutions as the militia, "Catholic religious brotherhoods, extended families, African based mutual aid societies and religious organizations" to organize and mobilize black people for collective and communal action. As Andrews notes, "Militia service in particular paved the way for extensive black participation in the [Western Hemisphere's] wars of independence, which in most of Spanish America were fought and won in large part by soldiers and officers of color." As a result, Andrews noted, the militia provided Afro-Latin Americans with opportunities for "black initiative and advancement," as well as secured for blacks access to the machinery of governance elevating black militias to be the "balance of power" in deciding the major political shifts in Latin American society at the local and national levels. Independence for Afro-Latin Americans mirrored the national commitment of early postcolonial black Americans to black freedom. According to Benjamin Quarles: "The Negro's role in the [American] Revolution can best be understood by realizing that his major loyalty was not to a place nor to a people, but to the principle. . . . Whoever invoked the image of liberty . . . could count on a ready response from blacks." This idea, Andrews contends, also defined black freedom in Latin America, because "whichever side, colonials or rebels," made "the clearest commitment to striking down" slavery and racial discrimination and championing "full racial equality" received Afro-Latin militia support. Such was the case in nineteenth-century Colombia, Venezuela, Argentina, and Cuba.[26]

A similar case arose in nineteenth-century Brazil. Hendrik Kraay asserts that black officers and enlisted militiamen struggled to get white elite colonial Brazilians in Salvador to recognize their capabilities, status, leadership, and loyalty. Black Salvadorian militiamen between 1798 and 1831 and Georgia's Captain Jesse Jones seventy years later found themselves engaged in an ongoing struggle by all black people in the Western Hemisphere to maintain a black presence in state-sponsored militias—a presence often, and especially in the nineteenth century, directly tied to citizenship, freedom, and autonomy for African-descendant people in the Americas. By the first quarter of the nineteenth century, whites, despite black militiamen's consistent service to the Portuguese colonial mission in the eighteenth century, followed by their participation in creating a Brazilian nation-state in the nineteenth century, debated black status in the new nation of Brazil. Black Brazilian militia officers, like Captain Jones in Jim Crow Georgia, walked a fine line. For black Brazilian militiamen, their forty-plus year challenge was negotiating the fine line between the two major political and ideological poles of Brazil's independence movements: liberal and conservative. Within this political maelstrom, the ultimate objective of black militia officers was to carve out a place for themselves in an independent Brazil where freedom meant they held "a special role as leaders and representatives of Afro-Brazilians." Their socio-political place was shaped by their persistent pursuit of "integration into the state apparatus, just as the [Portuguese] colonial regime . . . confirmed their status within the military." After 1824 and the battles for Brazilian independence, blacks and mulattos in the militia outnumbered whites 1,500 to 483 and possessed the battlefield and patriotic credentials that qualified them for leadership and command. As a result, they expected "to emerge as one of the pillars of the new regime," because militia service carried with it "an essential attribute of citizenship." Black militiamen also felt that "reward and recognition for services" rendered was due them as a "debt of gratitude."[27]

Brazilian independence, however, ushered in a host of negative results for black Brazilian militiamen. Republican governance resulted in military reorganization, marginalization of free black militiamen, their economic ruin, and conflicting political visions that were incompatible with liberalism. According to Kraay, to counter these challenges and changes in status, African descendant militiamen attempted to justify their existence by publicizing their long history of service. Afro-Brazilian militiamen, as most if not all black militiamen in the nineteenth-century Western Hemisphere, "had no idiom other than the language of service and reward" to make their case for continuing as militiamen and sustaining requests for citizenship. Thus the white "debt of gratitude" to black militiamen for their service became Afro-Brazilian militiamen's primary justification for a position in the new Brazilian government in 1829. The debate among whites culminated with the conclusion that black militiamen had no place in the newly emergent nation-state; the militia was abolished in 1831 and twenty-two of the thirty-one black militia officers were executed.[28] The United States moved in a similar direction more than sixty years later. In both of these instances in the Western Hemisphere, post–civil war nation building adversely affected state-sponsored black militia companies and inclusive citizenship. Black efforts to get their history of service recorded and recognized, too, became a hemisphere-wide contest between those whites who supported black militia service and those who opposed such service and the lengths to which each side would go to state their case.

Afro-Cubans and the Militia

Afro-Cuban freedom would be a much more complicated process. In Cuba in the early nineteenth century, militiamen utilized both the militia and the cabildo, as Philip Howard has argued, to organize slaves and free people of color. These two institutions—the militia, initiated by whites for defense of the colony, and the cabildo, a brotherhood–mutual aid institution operated and controlled by Afro-Cubans—functioned to preserve African language, ethnicity, and religious practices. It also provided financial assistance to its members, both slave and free, to purchase freedom, if need be, to invest in black businesses, and most importantly to acquire land. The cabildo, for Afro-Cubans, also performed a political function, as the independent militia company would do in post–Civil War Georgia. Afro-Cubans and black Georgians used the cabildo in Cuba and the independent militia company in North America, respectively, as the institution for organizing and mobilizing African-descendant people for political action.[29]

Matt Childs contends that Afro-Cubans came together in 1812 to challenge the existence of slavery, which was expanding with the commitment to sugar as a plantation crop at the end of the eighteenth century. Slavery's expansion in Cuba, like Spain's Bourbon Reform and Jim Crow in Georgia, undermined free black rights. This erosion of rights within Cuban-Spanish society encouraged nineteenth-century antiblack discrimination, especially by public officials. In response to their loss of status several black militiamen, including José Antonio Aponte, used their military training and service to unite the free black and slave communities in protest. Aponte and other militiamen, Howard asserts, organized Afro-Cubans through the cabildos representing such African slave and free black ethnic communities as Mandinga, Carabali, Ashanti, and Mina Guagui. Their combined objectives were terminating slavery and the transatlantic slave trade, which fed the expansion of Cuban slavery. In this vein they also hoped to "overthrow colonial [governmental] tyranny," which protected slavery's exponential growth. In its place they proposed "substitut[ing] the corrupt and feudal regime with another [government that would be] Cuban in nature, and without odious discriminations." Aponte called for Africans to see themselves as one people united so that Afro-Cubans could acquire freedom. Howard further argues that the militia and cabildo became instruments for black political organizing and blacks' search for freedom. Both institutions also helped create a black commitment to a national Cuban identity that would define nineteenth-century Cuban independence movements, wherein Afro-Cubans played a definitive role in shaping the nation's profile as a unified nation-state.[30]

Spanish officials in Cuba just over a generation and a half later, in 1844, accused black militiamen of once more organizing against slavery and colonial rule. According to Michele Reid-Vazquez' study, the "Conspiracy of La Escalera" combined the protests, revolts, and insurgencies of creoles, British abolitionists, and slaves in the 1840s in resistance to plantation society, especially slavery's nineteenth-century encroachment on free rights and status for all people of color. All three groups sought to establish Cuba as a free society. In response, authorities pursued policies that increased the restrictions on Afro-Cubans regardless of status. The Conspiracy nevertheless had a major impact on the future of black service in the militia.

The black militia company, under Spain's tutelage up to the mid-nineteenth century, had enabled African-descendant people to carve out positions of "honor and imperial loyalty" while accessing through military service "upward mobility" within Cuban and Spanish colonial society. The Age of Revolution in the Western Hemisphere "circulated [ideals concerning freedom] throughout the Atlantic" world, creating "the language of freedom and equality." Late eighteenth-century black militiamen "had clearly incorporated military service as a core part of their personal and group identity," particularly because militia duty had yielded to free blacks more rights and elevated their status. As a result, Jane G. Landers and Reid-Vazquez both note, free blacks appreciated the exemptions and privileges military service provided blacks, both slave and free, within the Spanish colonial system. These advantages of freedom also encouraged them and other blacks to begin "demanding rights beyond those tied to military service." From 1812 onward, however, and into the 1830s, Spain's attempts to control discussions of and white colonists' efforts to attain freedom, liberalism, and independence from Spain "chipped away at free blacks' previous colonial recognition for proven fidelity to the empire." Specifically black rights within the system had been under attack since the late eighteenth century's introduction of sugar and the plantation slave economy. Collectively these policies, which were intended to regulate, constrict, and control black rights, undermined the colonial militias and led to revolts in the 1830s spearheaded by militia officers.[31]

The repression perpetrated by the colonial government following the Conspiracy of La Escalera, in 1844, brought to an end black volunteer militia service in Cuba. The colonial response, Reid-Vazquez has concluded, caused Afro-Cubans to no longer view militia service as a beneficial institution that offered blacks a viable avenue to freedom and citizenship within the Spanish Empire. In response Afro-Cubans, ten years later, in 1854, declined to participate in colonial administrative attempts to restore "*pardo* and *moreno* militia units" that colonial officials had terminated in the wake of the alleged 1844 conspiracy. In that context, from 1854 onward, the effort to restore the militia as a component of the Cuban defense system met both white and black resistance. Whites raised concerns "about the risks of arming men of African descent" who might challenge slavery and the slave trade as they had done in the past not only in Cuba but also in other Spanish colonies. Afro-Cubans, in the wake of the colonial administration's destruction of the black militia companies in 1844 and the ensuing assault on free people of color's public and citizenship rights, no longer viewed the militia as a black-friendly institution promoting, securing, and protecting the participatory rights of African-descendant membership in Spanish society.

Further, as Reid-Vazquez writes, "The Escalera repression and its social and economic aftershocks, combined with the expansion of [white] peninsular [Spain-based military] forces in Cuba, forced militiamen of color and [the] free black community at large to recast militia service as a low priority." The collective Afro-Cuban refusal to embrace the militia after 1844 makes a case for wholesale black resistance against the attack on black rights, which included "foreign-born expulsion orders, coerced emigration, and prohibitive urban employment codes," all of which were part of a discriminatory antiblack structure. In response to these impositions and curtailed rights, black "resistance to colonial policies [was] informed by the politics of race, freedom, and empire."[32]

By 1865 Cuban colonial administration (Havana's Consejo de Administracion/Administrative Council) had entered a new phase in its assessment, acceptance, and acknowledgment of the attributes of "the militia of color." The decade-long effort to reconstitute the militia had failed because ten years, 1854 to 1865, of official anti-Afro-Cuban discrimination inside and outside of Cuba and extending to Mexico had undermined Afro-Cuban loyalty to Spain. Economic restrictions and attempts to force blacks to serve in a reconstituted militia also destroyed Afro-Cuban confidence in Spain's Empire as a place conducive to black freedom and citizenship. Debate among colonial officials was focused on finding a way to encourage and resurrect black militia enlistment, even to the point of making militia membership voluntary, as it had been during the more positive eighteenth-century days of black militia service, with the added incentive of "raising the militia's status and restoring it as an 'honorable force'" before 1844.

Yet colonial administration was not a monolithic entity. Colonial officials were divided, as "the detractors on the Council" countered the proposal for restoration with the hemisphere-wide white fear of blacks with guns. Officials, while acknowledging the decades-long black militia service to the colony and empire, argued that arming blacks had been a futile exercise. Instead of recalling black militiamen's successful defense of the colony over time, detractors in essence rewrote black militia history by claiming that "the militias of color are more dangerous than useful." Black militia utility was at an end, the detractors argued, because Spain had increased the number and presence of white troops in Cuba and had enhanced police protection. These constabulary forces made the "militia of color" of "no 'great necessity,'" especially since black militia units "had become a financial drain." As a result, in "September 1865, the committee voted unanimously to minimize and, ultimately, dissolve the *pardo* and *moreno* militias."[33]

Thus came to an end the "militia of color" in Cuba for a second time in twenty years. Its demise, Reid-Vazquez asserts, had been caught up in a continuous debate "throughout the late eighteenth and nineteenth centuries" about the wisdom of arming blacks against the backdrop of the expanding plantation economy in Cuba. This debate also encompassed how the colonial administration should deal with black "[m]ilitiamen's demands for fairer treatment" and "the impact of revolutions in Haiti and Spanish America," and "the exclusion of *libre de color* from Spanish citizenship heightened officials' fears of social and political upheaval at the hands of soldiers of color."[34]

Nineteenth-Century Black Militia Parallels

Nineteenth-century Western Hemisphere government officials, regardless of their ethnicity, contested the viability of black militiamen. They separately utilized the same glossary of justifications when officials terminated the existence of black militia companies within their jurisdictions. In Cuba and in Georgia, officials debated whether to maintain black state-sponsored militia companies when they questioned the utility of blacks with guns, the cost effectiveness of black units, and African-descendant militiamen's reliability during a domestic crisis. Black contributions to Spanish colonial or southern U.S. society over the years disappeared from the record as history was rethought, reconceptualized, and rewritten. Justifications for termination of black militias proceeded in both cases over nearly a decade of white debate, and black challenges to retain the militia, signs of inclusion, and discussions around potential disbanding made the fate of black militia service a difficult process to predict. This process coincided with social, political, and economic assaults on the rights of black people as members of colonial Cuba and of post–Civil War southern societies embracing Jim Crow and, as Grace Elizabeth Hale has concluded, an exclusive "culture of segregation." Antiblack repression in Cuba occurred over a thirty-year period, between 1812 and 1844, with increased repression in the wake of the Conspiracy of La Escalera, which initiated the disbanding of Cuba's black militia units, and a second dismantling of the *pardo* and *moreno* militia companies in 1865. While the emergent Cuban nationalism, championed by Afro-Cubans, in the second half of the nineteenth century offered a place for blacks in Cuban society up to the Spanish-American War, the Cuban War of Independence, and the Philippine-American War, all fought between 1898 and 1902, Afro-Cuban citizenship and inclusion, Ada Ferrer finds, was a casualty of that final nineteenth-century war and the process of early twentieth-century independence. Blacks were excluded from Cuban citizenship in the early twentieth century despite major black leadership and military contributions to Cuban nation building dating from the mid-nineteenth century to the first decade of the twentieth century.[35]

The ideas and concepts presented here and the impact of postconflict nation building reflect the duality of the black militia experience in the Americas. African-descendant people across the Americas pursued a self-defining persona that reflected their positive self-image as productive, self-confident representatives of black people. African descendant militiamen, who endeavored to serve the society that acknowledged them as citizen soldiers and empowered them with the right to bear arms, the right to self-defense, and the right to defend the colony or nation-state, were part of the process of being a citizen in the nineteenth-century Western Hemisphere, whether in the United States or elsewhere. At the same time black militiamen implemented their personal agendas and sometimes those of the broader community of black Americans using the institution of the militia to carve out a political, economic, and social place for themselves and the race within the colony, state, or nation-state.

Black Militias Reimaging: Disfranchisement, Defense, and Status

In Georgia and in other black militia traditions in the United States, black militia service was notable for its direct association with the state governmental revocation of the black right to vote, the rise of white assaults on black rights, and antiblack violence. This occurred during the early and late nineteenth and early twentieth centuries. Disfranchisement in the 1820s in Rhode Island, for example, coincided with a violent assault upon black home-ownership rights, political participation, and status within the state. The service of the black militia in the 1840s, which restored order in Rhode Island after white laborers revolted, resulted in the restoration of black suffrage rights and status. In the late nineteenth-century South nearly sixty years later, North Carolina black militiamen and African American volunteers rallied to defend the nation during the Spanish-American War, the Cuban War of Independence, and the Philippine-American War. Black political power in North Carolina had resulted in the election of Republican governor Daniel Russell. His "political debts to African Americans ran deep and wide," to the point that "he wanted to include black volunteer troops in the state's [war] mobilization quotas." Russell more than successfully lobbied the federal government "for authorization to create a black battalion" commanded by black officers. This circumstance was repeated in only two other states, Kansas and Illinois, where black political power also successfully influenced the thinking and actions of the governors to authorize the marshaling of black troops and to sanction black officers to lead the units. The resulting black troop recruiting campaign in North Carolina created the Third North Carolina Volunteer Regiment.[36]

While North Carolinians of all races celebrated the valor and commitment of the Third North Carolina in the spring of 1898, by the fall of 1898, with the Democratic Party controlling state government, the rationale for having black troops had dramatically changed. Members of North Carolina's Democratic Party "invert[ed] the patriotic symbolism of a black man in uniform" from a gallant patriot to the threatening specter of "imposters as sheep in wolves' clothing." Further, in "October, when the [Democratic Party's] white supremacy campaign centralized the party line and asserted that blacks were incapable of voting and office holding," black political influence was no longer a positive in the state and instead constituted a threat to the Democratic Party's commitment to whiteness. To cement the power of white supremacy "[w]hites infantilized" the black soldiers of the Third North Carolina Volunteer Regiment as "children in cowboy costumes" playing at soldiering.[37] White supremacy's political triumph and rewriting of militia history was followed, in November 1898, by an antiblack race riot in Wilmington, North Carolina, disfranchisement, and the dismantling of the black militia. Each of these antiblack acts occurred as the twentieth century dawned and as Jim Crow segregation emerged as the new system and culture intended to regulate the industrial capitalism now triumphant across the South and the United States. In parallel, white Georgians had also begun what would be a ten-year discussion concerning whether black militiamen were cost effective, reliable, and worthy of the title and whether black officers' rank made them soldiers deserving of white respect. In Cuba, North Carolina, and Georgia, black political recognition, power, and presence in their communities had helped bring the militia into existence. Detractors with official power and political clout questioned black power and African descendant militia service in a changing late nineteenth-century and early twentieth-century world.

The nineteenth century had nurtured black militia service across the Western Hemisphere. African-descendant people had used the black militia—an institution created by whites to defend whites in the absence of the regular military—as one way to secure black freedom. The search for freedom within nineteenth-century slave societies had been opened by black militia service. Throughout the Americas, black militiamen used sustained militia service as the vehicle that would, first, secure them recognized citizenship and a more stable place in society; second, provide them with access to respectability and status within white-controlled institutional structures; and third, help black men realize their definitions of manhood, through military service to the state and to their race, with an accompanying feeling of belonging as a member of the colony or new nation-state. African-descendant militiamen viewed themselves as real men, even as white authorities debated whether to disband black militia companies. In late nineteenth-century Georgia, the search for freedom would be performed by two kinds of militia units: independent units and state-sponsored units. The Civil War and black military service had transformed a divided state into a nation in search of its self, and black people mobilized to be a part of that search.

1

THE SEARCH FOR FREEDOM

Black Militiamen in Nineteenth-Century North America

This book explores how black Georgians utilized the institution of the militia company as an instrument of freedom as the transformations initiated by the Civil War evolved into the political and social issues of the late nineteenth century for black and white Georgians. It is less a military history than a political and social one, although the militia did constitute a distinct part of the nation's nineteenth-century military experience. Yet the utilization of the militia as a political and social institution was part of the struggle over who would rule post–Civil War Georgia and what status African Americans were to have as citizens of the United States and of Georgia. The militia was at the center of this effort at self-definition and at local, state, regional, and national belonging, which included claims on political and social status and the right to economic and political autonomy, central pillars of freedom in the United States.[1]

The black companies of the independent militia and of the state-sponsored Georgia Volunteers, Colored, and Georgia State Troops, Colored, were more than military units focused on learning military tactics and drill routines. These martial skills were important especially for the development and evolution of the state-sponsored companies—Georgia Volunteers, Colored, and Georgia State Troops, Colored—serving Georgia during the last thirty years of the nineteenth century and the early years of the twentieth century. State-sponsored units also embraced black political and social objectives, as defined by their primary role in organizing public celebrations of African American freedom over the same thirty-year period. Black militiamen also used the state-sponsored militia to demonstrate the quality and character of their race in response to white accusations of inferiority and unworthiness to participate in local, state, and national governance, national defense, and the use of economic and political power for black community development and individual autonomy. Georgia's black militia companies helped build community in the tradition in which African-descendant people utilized the militia across the Western Hemisphere. Georgia's black militiamen were not just citizen soldiers; they were key participants in the economic and political life of their communities.[2]

Community building also defined the black independent companies. They functioned as one of the institutions that defended black public rights to buy land, to vote, and to exercise political and economic autonomy. The independent units served a political and self-defense function that was perhaps parallel to the white paramilitary or independent militia units that defined southern white male resistance to Reconstruction. White antiblack and anti–Republican Party violence was sponsored and supported by the Democratic Party, Ku Klux Klan, and independent militia companies in Georgia during the late 1860s and into the mid-1870s. Both races mobilized their respective populations for political action during these years, with the militia company serving as a centerpiece in that effort. Violence, intimidation, and restored white dominance, however, became principal planks of the white paramilitary/independent militia and of political Redemption activities in the United States South and Georgia. White paramilitary groups sought to destroy black and Republican political activity as well as intimidate both groups. They also used violence to coerce white people to support their attempts to prevent black people and Republican Party members from exercising political power in the state. Whites also used the militia to force and enforce the development of white supremacy. African Americans, in contrast, viewed the militia as a tool and institution that would allow them to collectively "enjoy freedom by working for themselves" and to "live without the constraints and abuse" that had defined their antebellum lives. Blacks used the independent militia company as a vehicle for political mobilization, self-defense, and rights protection.[3]

Three Militias

In Georgia there were at least three distinct militia units. Race defined their differences and functions. African Americans utilized two militia formats as platforms for black post–Civil War efforts to define freedom, autonomy, and citizenship. The first, the independent militia company, defined the late 1860s into the mid-1870s. The independent militia unit had roots in the northern antebellum protest against slavery and in self-defense traditions developed by free blacks and slaves in the United States and Canada. Black self-defense traditions involved antebellum efforts to defend free blacks and escaped slaves from the respective threats of kidnapping and reenslavement by slave traders and slave catchers. The antebellum independent militia unit was also a medium by which free blacks established their claim as citizens of the nation and northern states. In the post–Civil War United States South, self-defense expanded to a defense not only of black peoples but also of African American political, citizenship, and property ownership rights. Post–Civil War blacks therefore used the militia company as a way of declaring that they belonged and were members of the national polity.[4]

The second militia platform combined the mass politics and street protests of the antebellum era that independent black militiamen had engaged in when they paraded in public venues.[5] This public tradition of parading would be incorporated within the official obligations of the African American citizen soldiers who joined the postbellum militia company as citizens of Georgia. They served as members of the military who officially represented, and served as a recognized agency of, the state government of Georgia. In this context, the post–Civil War black militiaman also pursued admission, acceptance, and inclusion within the official organization that had been established as the legally authorized state-sponsored defense force. These state-sponsored, state-supported, and state-acknowledged militia units would serve Georgia and African Americans for more than thirty years, from 1872 to 1905.

The state-sponsored black militia company was not unique to Georgia. This type of militia unit served the Western Hemisphere imperial and nation-state needs for local defense beginning in the sixteenth century and terminating, in some places and especially in the United States South, as the twentieth century dawned.[6] Throughout the hemisphere black militiamen volunteered to be citizen soldiers—men with daily employment obligations who took time out after work to learn military tactics, who drilled, and who in many cases supplied their own firearms in defense of the community in a time of military distress. These African-descendant people used the Western European institution of the militia as an instrument to define the race's right to belong and declare their citizenship of the imperial empire or nation. African-descendant militiamen used the militia to secure personal and community liberties, to build institutions serving the black community, and to mobilize for political rights and the abolition of slavery.[7] Georgia's black men utilized both the independent militia company and the state-sponsored militia unit to define African American post–Civil War freedom, citizenship, identity, and autonomy as the nation wrestled with the same concepts and the place that black Americans would hold as citizens of the southern states and the United States.

An Instrument of White Freedom

For Georgia whites the militia before the Civil War existed as a locally based set of citizen soldiers who, when called on, brought their guns and ammunition to defend the colony and state from invasion, insurrection, slave revolts, and civil disorder. After Reconstruction these citizen soldiers served the state and received and utilized weapons, ammunition, and accoutrements distributed by the state government from federal sources. Georgia's white militiamen were part of a colony and state military tradition wherein white citizen soldiers served as a defense force and army representing states' and planters' rights from the colonial era to the end of the Civil War.[8] This commitment to the local community's governance and to social control would continue through Reconstruction and into the eighth decade of the nineteenth century. During and after the 1880s white Georgians embraced their place as citizens of the United States, relinquishing their state militia to incorporation within the national militia effort, where it would be a component of the nation's twentieth-century defense network.[9]

The militia for late nineteenth-century white Georgians also served as an instrument of white freedom. Whites envisioned both independent militia companies—units not accepted for membership in the state militia but operating as a military unit at the county and municipal levels—and state-sponsored militia units as the key to local/county-level political dominance in post-Reconstruction Georgia. Whites further viewed the militia as a tool for resisting the overwhelming post–Civil War presence of federal power as centralized governance became a national reality. Yet even Georgia's state government would, in the late nineteenth century, embrace government's centralizing role in ruling the state. The role of the militia, too, would change, in the last two decades of the nineteenth century, as Georgia's General Assembly reorganized the state militia.

The twentieth century dawned with the triumph of white supremacy, and the nation embraced imperialism abroad and the subordination of people of color globally. Georgia's white militia also evolved. White militia companies became a part of the national defense system and accepted more federal resources and training, by which the early twentieth century's Georgia State Troops were incorporated within the National Guard. Just as, in the 1880s, Georgia's whites had recommitted themselves to celebrating the Fourth of July, as a sign of their national citizenship and of their submission to centralized federal authority, they now exchanged sovereignty over the militia for more federal money, United States Army regulars as trainers, and conformity to national military standards. White Georgians became U.S. citizens as they reconciled the end of the Civil War with national belonging in the wake of the Spanish-American War.[10]

The Georgia Militia: Key to Citizenship

The militia in Georgia provided both whites and blacks with an opportunity to embrace national citizenship as the nation rebuilt after the Civil War. Militia service continued to be an important part of defining citizenship, even as nineteenth-century definitions were embracing more race-based conceptions of national belonging.[11] White antiblack violence during Reconstruction and into the 1870s undermined the place and status of the black independent militia. White Redemption—the return of whites to political power and governance at the county and state levels at the end of Reconstruction—was not stable enough to prevent the federal government from insisting on the presence of the state-sponsored black militia in Georgia, even as Reconstruction passed into nonexistence and Redemption came to dominate the late nineteenth century. Whites would spend the rest of the nineteenth century searching for ways to accommodate federal authority and race relations until national white reconciliation was secured in the wake of the three wars that the carried the nation into the twentieth century: the Spanish-American War, the Cuban War of Independence, and the Philippine-American War. The Spanish-American War of 1898 led to the erosion of black military forces at the state and national levels. Despite these obstacles, black militiamen—both independent and state-sponsored—built African American communities after the Civil War. These militia companies provided blacks with opportunities to be autonomous citizens. They were not failures or instruments of destruction, as previous scholarship has contended.[12] The following pages explore the evolution of blacks as militia members in the British colonial and nation-building efforts in the Western Hemisphere.

Colonial Militia Experience

The presence of black militiamen in the northern part of the Western Hemisphere was conditional on "the price of nation-building and the making of independent states." That process was critical in determining "the exclusion of blacks from citizenship rights including the right to armed self-defense," even though the "right to armed self-defense against external aggression emerged as one of the central planks of natural rights philosophy in the American Republic." Questions about blacks' right to self-defense and their concurrent right to bear arms in the British North American colonies date to as early as 1639, when white Virginia colonials made public policy prohibiting blacks the right to armed self-defense. This law, titled Act X, initiated a confusing policy wherein blacks were sometimes welcomed into and other times excluded from full membership in British colonial life, including the right to bear arms. During those moments of inclusion, blacks, whether slave or free, offered their bodies and service as militiamen in exchange for freedom and status within the British North American colonies. White British North Americans did occasionally arm black slaves in defense of individual members of the thirteen colonies, with the reward of freedom offered in exchange for military service. The black militia experience within British North America and during the Western Hemisphere's Age of Revolution also established a baseline connection "between killing and freedom." Black military service for colonial and plantation defense could result in freedom; Georgia offered such terms in exchange for desperately needed militia service to free blacks in the early to mid-1760s.[13]

But the image and potential actions of blacks with guns disturbed whites in colonial America. It also raised the more vexing question of empowering slaves with firearms, as whites recruited and armed black bondsmen to supplement a colony's militia and defense structure. Black and white militia forces were utilized to repel invading and competing Western European military forces intent on making the colony one of their imperial possessions. Would such a commitment to the defense of white colonists against another white intruder cause slaves to reach the next logical conclusion about the use of firearms to attain freedom: "Would liberty be more certain if he killed that owner?" This circumstance led Georgia's neighboring colony, South Carolina, to "amend its militia laws so that a slave who killed or captured one of the enemy received not his freedom but a cash award." Yet the role of the colonial militia was to "defend settlements," be a police force, and "provide a trained pool from which a colony could draw soldiers for extended campaigns and wars" both within and outside the colony.

To fulfill this mission, British imperial authorities between 1795 and 1815 purchased African slaves solely for what would be "twenty years of arduous imperial military service" with the purpose of creating a twelve-regiment army (9,000 men). The units were created over the objections of fragmented white Caribbean planters. Organized to defend planters from external and internal threats during the Napoleonic Wars in the Caribbean, the West India Regiments served British colonial authority with distinction as a "reliable and efficient corps." The British government "from . . . the first West Indian Regiments . . . wisely committed . . . to a policy of equality in the governance of its black and white soldiers." As a result, the West Indian Regiments' black troops considered themselves free, "enjoyed a special status" over slaves, and "believed [themselves] the equal of white soldiers in every aspect of military services." African troops in the West Indies "served the King" until they were disbanded at the end of the decade (1817) in the Caribbean and throughout Africa in the wake of the abolition of British involvement in the transatlantic slave trade. Some attained land and settled in Trinidad, British Honduras, and Sierra Leone as free people. More importantly militia companies and the West India Regiments "became centralized agents of social cohesion in many settlements much like the local church or congregation," as well as an "informal social control mechanism that helped regulate class relationships and bonded county to country." The militia helped its members bond and belong; it made militiamen part of a community.[14]

Yet Georgia, like the rest of the colonies that became the United States, harbored mixed feelings about African-descendant people. Black labor helped to make Georgia prosperous, but equality and citizenship were denied even to free blacks. As a result, the right to armed self-defense was not extended to blacks. That said, as one scholar has asked, "Did collective self-defense around fugitive slaves constitute an informal expression of military preparedness led by black people in North America?" This question would be critical in determining the status of blacks as citizens from the colonial era forward, because it forced African Americans to wrestle with the accusation that they were unworthy of full citizenship. Militia membership was a declaration of worthiness and a definitive claim to full citizenship. While five thousand enslaved and free black people helped create the United States during the American Revolution, the nation and its states excluded "blacks from citizenship rights including the right to armed self-defence" as the thirteen colonies became the United States of America. Naturalization, as a part of early nation building in 1790, was also "limited . . . to white aliens" and culminated in 1792 with the federal government's definition of militia service as solely a white male obligation of citizenship.[15]

The Militia and Spanish Freedom

Scholars working on Atlantic Creoles, such as Jane Landers, have expanded the North American story of the first blacks' freedom in the Spanish North American colony of Florida at Fort Mose near St. Augustine. Seventeenth- and eighteenth-century slaves who successfully left the British North American southern colonies made their way to Florida. These escaped slaves won freedom and a degree of acceptance as they joined and served the Spanish Empire as militiamen. They also embraced the Catholic Church, which offered additional protective status that reinforced their sense of belonging and secured for them a position as free people within Spanish corporate institutions such as the church and military. The Age of Revolution in the Western Hemisphere made Spanish militiamen's existence much more complicated. American Revolutionary War and post-Revolution treaties helped push these militiamen and other former British North American slaves who joined the Spanish military out of North America as Spain lost its foothold in the region. Leading black militiamen, such as South Carolina's Prince Whitten, continued serving monarchial Spain because the Spanish offered them better guarantees of freedom and status than did the expanding United States republic. As a result, black militiamen such as Whitten went on to serve in Spain's Caribbean and South American nineteenth-century independence wars, civil wars, slave revolts, and militia-led slave revolts, because their service was rewarded with freedom.[16]

Canada

Both the independent and state-sponsored black militia companies played a significant role in Canada. Antebellum African-descendant militiamen extended the role of the militia beyond service to colonial/imperial government. They created militia companies to serve the needs of black people and their communities. Escaped slaves from the United States and freeborn blacks offered their loyalty and service to the British monarchy for reasons similar to those of Prince Whitten and the black militiamen who served the Spanish Crown a generation earlier, during the Age of Revolution. From 1837 to 1850 black Canadians served as militiamen meeting state and imperial needs. Black militiamen helped put down the William Lyon Mackenzie rebellion. Following this service to the colonial government, black militiamen constructed a road and served as peacekeepers between Catholic and Protestant Irish laborers during the construction of the Welland Canal. Ultimately colonial authorities authorized "five black companies." With the rebellion suppressed, local whites felt more secure. As a result, they "became intolerant of local black military power," to the point that whites began to accuse black militiamen of causing "a great deal of mischief, [and] rioting" and finally "rejoiced at the removal of the [black] troops." The disbanding of black troops soon followed, thus ending their official tenure in 1850.[17]

Members of the black Canadian militia company aligned with the British monarchy and government because of the nineteenth-century "British colonial retreat from slavery." Emancipation was a colonial policy that "stood in marked contrast to the [parallel] expansion of American slavery" in the United States. Black loyalty to British imperial power was therefore predicated on Britain's comprehensive abolition of American slavery in its colonial possessions between 1833 and 1834. Black militiamen marched in Canadian streets "from the mid-1830s onwards" commemorating "West India Day," the "British emancipation" of West Indian slaves. These public celebrations also became increasingly vital to blacks in North America, as the United States committed to slavery with the Fugitive Slave Act of 1850. The British colonial government persisted in upholding the end of slavery, even though the United States and Spain viewed emancipation as a colossal failure and as a threat to slavery within their realms. British colonial administration also helped create an atmosphere wherein "blacks in Canada enjoyed a greater degree of legal equality" than blacks in the United States. Legal equality or public rights encompassed "basic civic rights like suffrage, jury service, and property ownership," as well as "the right to bear arms in self-defence." Each of these freedoms gave black Canadians a sense of citizenship and belonging. Black people as a result convened in 1855 in "a 'Mass Meeting,'" passing resolutions stating that their loyalty belonged to a government "'that shields [blacks] from oppression.'"[18]

Black Canadians organized militia companies for reasons other than their debt of gratitude to the British government for abolishing slavery and emancipating blacks. Militiamen who "settled throughout the Niagara region . . . often participated in the self-defence of fugitive slaves from the United States." They also used the militia to enhance black identity. Robert Jones, a Philadelphia-born African descendant barber like Prince Whitten, came to a crossroads about life in the United States and slavery. Contemplating a freer life than what he experienced in the United States, Jones considered moving to Liberia in the 1850s. In the end his emigration journey took him to Hamilton, Canada, where he assisted escaping slaves and organized a black militia unit. Jones committed to creating the militia company "in order to elevate 'the condition of the colored people in Canada.'"[19]

While the boundaries between the independent and state-sponsored militia companies were blurry in Canada, African-descendant Canadians and black emigrants from the United States joined together to use the militia for their collective well-being and status as citizens of Canada. Militia service, combined with public rights and slavery's abolition, directly connected black people to British imperial administration. The right to self-defense, especially against U.S. bondage, in contradistinction to the end of slavery in British colonial possessions, enabled black Canadians to publicly parade in celebration of black freedom and public rights. The militia in Canada also elevated black people's collective identity, providing them with a positive self-concept that defied the degradation of Western Hemisphere slavery and racism.

Rehearsing for War in the United States

In the United States, the confusion over the right of blacks to be militiamen created during the colonial era continued into the nineteenth century, as the new state-controlled militia became the sole purview of white men. Some states in the new nation, nevertheless, enrolled militiamen regardless of race. By 1803, however, even state enlistments in such places as Ohio, where suffrage was expanded to include white men of all walks of life, excluded blacks. Exclusion from the rewards of full citizenship and the antebellum fight against slavery helped shape the black independent militia company. Further, between 1833 and 1860, the purpose of the black independent militia company in the United States "was a rehearsal for war"—the Civil War. Blacks mobilized to organize independent militia companies in the wake of the British abolition of slavery in the West

Indies, in 1833, and the United States' Fugitive Slave Act of 1850. In this context of social, political, and economic decision making, "young black men [in the United States] . . . sought knowledge of military science in order to combat American slavery and its territorial spread." They celebrated the most important "annual event among black people in North America," West India Day.

African American antebellum efforts at "self-organization and political mobilization against slavery" are reflected in the organization of some twenty-eight independent black militia companies. Black-initiated militia organizing also challenged the denial of state and national citizenship, especially after the *Dred Scott* Supreme Court decision, in 1857, which asserted that blacks regardless of status—enslaved or free—had no citizenship rights in the United States. Young black men in the antebellum United States nevertheless organized militia companies to defend their communities and citizenship rights. They also organized to publicly project the race's "militancy through parades and guns, and political mobilization. Most importantly, they demonstrated an important link between bearing arms and rights of citizenship," extending the colonial-era association between "killing and freedom." The pre–Civil War U.S. black militia associated African American citizenship and public rights with armed militia service focused on defending the African-descendant community against slavery during the decade before the Civil War. It also established a tradition for the independent black militia company to function as the vehicle for mobilizing, organizing, and politicizing the black community, both before and after the Civil War.[20]

Black militia organizing, collective resistance against slavery, and the tradition of armed self-defense combined with African Americans' civic activities to establish their political vision. Black civic participation, as both enslaved and free people, began with public celebrations of Pinkster and Election Day. Parading in public was a vital part of mass celebratory colonial culture, and it continued during the postbellum emancipation period as an important component of black efforts to define the parameters of freedom in the southern United States. These efforts placed the black militia company at the center of defining freedom in public. Antebellum black mobilization for the organization of militias, from 1848 to the Civil War, coupled with their public drilling, bearing arms, and parading, engaged blacks in "a performative politics of the street." This was a public politics "designed to display resistance, militancy, and power. The spatial defence of communities, the projection of militancy through parades and guns, and political mobilization" were all part of an emerging mass politics "characterized by [urban] mass-based [political] parties, public meetings, and a popular press." The parade was a central public platform for mass-based "cultural performance" and a means of announcing the goals, values, vision, and self-image of black communities seeking opportunities of belonging in local, state, and national culture. This antebellum tradition would continue during emancipation, as Georgia's state-sponsored militiamen led commemorations of black freedom as they paraded on city streets.[21] Independent black militiamen mobilized for political organizing and for the militant defense of black labor, land rights, and political power. These independent militiamen sought to protect black communities, as both federal and state governments failed to defend black and white Republican Party members from white antiblack political violence.

The antebellum militia, for both whites and blacks in North America, however, was one of the performers in the politics of the streets that empowered the masses before the Civil War. In the emerging context of black self-defense, mass black celebrations of emancipation in the British Caribbean, Canada, and parts of the United States, and the mobilization of African-descendant people against slavery in the Western Hemisphere, the African descendant militiaman, marching in public celebratory gatherings, embodied all of these elements. Black militiamen in Canada paraded as early as the mid-to-late 1830s, while blacks in the United States mobilized their resistance against the Fugitive Slave Act of 1850 by creating independent militia companies. Black militiamen then joined and initiated parades to celebrate emancipation events that had occurred outside the United States. Black militiamen in the antebellum United States marched in emancipation day parades in "Ohio, New Jersey, Michigan, Pennsylvania, and Connecticut." The African American militia's public presence inspired blacks such as Frederick Douglass, who concluded that black militiamen "marched, halted, wheeled, and handled their arms just as you have seen well-drilled white soldiers do." According to Douglass, black militiamen favorably compared to white militiamen and regular troops, and he viewed his first encounter with two black militia companies in New Bedford, Massachusetts, in 1855 with "admiration." Further, Douglass asserted, "if a knowledge of the use of arms is desirable in any people, it is desirable in us."[22]

Black self-defense was a vital reason for the organizing of African descendant militia in both the United States and Canada before the Civil War. The independent black militia unit in the United States emerged in

1848. It came into being in response to a "combination of legal exclusion, the need for self-defence, and the expansion of American slavery." As a result, "young black men began to organize their own militias in the northern states." Five years later, in Massachusetts, machinist and abolitionist William J. Watkins asserted that blacks were "CITIZENS." As full citizens, he and the other blacks petitioning "for the right to form an independent [militia] company" defined themselves as "law-abiding, tax-paying, liberty-loving, NATIVE-BORN, AMERICAN CITIZENS."[23]

The United States' Civil War

The opportunity to earn full citizenship came with the Civil War. Four percent of the eligible black men between the ages of eighteen and forty-five, or 3,486 individuals, enlisted from Georgia as soldiers.[24] According to several scholars examining blacks and the Civil War, "enlistment not only strengthened the bondman's claim to freedom, it also enhanced the freeman's claim to equality." Black men therefore fought to end slavery and inequality in the United States just as their Western Hemisphere counterparts had done during the nineteenth century. African American men also fought in the Civil War to defend and preserve the Union, to combat discrimination by white troops on both sides of the Civil War, to prove their manhood, and to "demonstrate their worthiness for full citizenship."[25]

The Civil War was also a transformative moment for all of its participants. For African Americans, the Civil War countered the ideas of inferiority that slavery's taint had imposed on both enslaved and free blacks regardless of gender. In this context, the war and military service encouraged blacks to define themselves in a number of proactive ways. Specifically they were self-confident, equal to whites, liberators, people with a "new standing," and full participants in the nation's future. Service in the Civil War further empowered black Americans to seek a more intimate role in politics, institution and community building, and community leadership.[26]

Empowering blacks with guns was not the intended consequence that whites, both North and South, envisioned. According to Carole Emberton, black Union soldiers were to be trained as "obedient soldiers whose violence could be controlled and channeled to appropriate ends." Further "the recruitment of black men into the army would not result in a second" Haitian Revolution, because "slaves had to be violent enough to become good soldiers but not too violent." While black Civil War military service provided the nation with proof of black "worthiness to be included in the body politic as full citizens" with "respect, honor, and political enfranchisement," Emberton defined this service as "obscure[ing] the gendered politics of emancipation" by "reduc[ing] freedom to a violent struggle between men"—white and black men. The post–Civil War and Reconstruction experience "would come to depend . . . on black veterans and local militias for its grassroots survival," but the "narrative relied upon violent rituals of war and remembrance that created a highly gendered vision of freedom and citizenship" that was solely the purview of black males. Like Otis Singletary, Emberton blames the victim, black militiamen and soldiers, for the violence initiated by white men. Emberton concludes that "this militarization of freedom contributed to the explosion of racial and political violence that ultimately brought Reconstruction to such a dispiriting end."[27] Yet what brought the nation to civil war and the violence of Reconstruction that followed was white gendered violence that ignored the voices of white women and children.

Earlier scholarship on blacks and the Civil War noted that the Union army and federal government were "unreliable allies whose interests only occasionally coincided with those of the black community." This circumstance stressed the need for black autonomy and goal setting in which "black people [would] have to keep their own counsel." To keep their own counsel, black women, children, and men, Elsa Barkley Brown argues, set a collective vision of freedom defined by black women that transcended gender to include all black people—a lesson that independent black militiamen and emerging political leaders had to repeat often after the war. The Civil War and Union army service "politicized" black troops and their families, just as the antebellum independent militia had done for blacks in the United States and Canada. The Civil War and the mental breaks with slavery that Vincent Harding and Amrita Myers note, in their examination of antebellum black women who had a vision of freedom, prepared black people "for the larger struggle they would face at war's end," when all black people, as Elsa Barkley Brown tells us, came together in places such as Richmond, Virginia, to "Catch the Vision of Freedom."[28]

Postbellum

The northern antebellum and southern postbellum militia both served as platforms for black American public declarations of citizenship in the United States. The independent black militia company and the "militarization of black life was also reported [in] the countryside" after the Civil War. The independent black militia company had rallied black people before the Civil War to resist slavery and to publicly declare African American citizenship. It continued to function as a vehicle to mobilize black people in the assertion of their new public rights as citizens of the United States free of slavery. In coastal South Carolina in 1865–1866 former slaves along the Santee River "began organizing local [independent] military companies, drilling, and parading on large plantations." southern African-descendant people also marched, drilled, and went to political meetings with arms "for the purposes of self-defence and [exercising their] political rights." They used the militia in both urban and rural settings in "Alabama, South Carolina, Louisiana, North Carolina, Georgia, Virginia, and Mississippi throughout the Reconstruction era."[29]

The post–Civil War independent southern black militia was distinctly different from its northern antebellum counterparts, despite their working toward some similar aims. Southern black independent militia units after the Civil War mirrored those of their antebellum brothers because African-descendant people continued to contend with exclusion from state militia organizations, until Reconstruction legislatures made some of them part of state government. The right to self-defense, the right to bear arms, and other civil rights continued to be major concerns as post–Civil War white antiblack violence followed immediately on the heels of national peace in New Orleans, Memphis, and across the South, including Georgia, where white southerners resisted black attempts to exert their public rights. The southern black militia company was different because these independent units were more numerous and larger than their antebellum predecessors, and "they played a critical role in the mobilization of black communities for the implementation of civil rights at the local, state, and national levels."[30]

Two Militias

The black militia company in Georgia, the subject of this study, was both a reflection of and slightly different from these important conclusions. Rural and urban blacks embraced two forms of the militia's evolving service to black people and the emergent nation-state at the end of the American Civil War. The independent militia company of the antebellum era continued, for a brief period in Georgia, as the institution that mobilized rural blacks for self-defense, political mobilization, and public rights. In the wake of Reconstruction, parading and marching, which before the Civil War took place in both rural and urban settings, became a more urban-focused mission of Georgia's state-sponsored militia companies.

Public celebratory parading events were a central function of Georgia's state-sponsored African American urban militia companies after Reconstruction. Freedom, citizenship, and a sense of belonging also defined the direction and goals of the postbellum black militia. Nation building, too, molded how the militia would be defined in the United States as the Civil War ended and as Reconstruction, post-Reconstruction, and emancipation evolved with the end of sectionalism and the start of nation building during the late nineteenth century. The Old South and the New South, under a post–Civil War federal mandate to create and support state-sponsored militia companies with black membership, did sustain such units in Georgia throughout the postbellum decades of the nineteenth century. Black men marched and paraded in celebration of the Union's triumph over the South in the American Civil War, during which black men died to free the slaves and define themselves as citizens of a reconstituted nation, the United States. After the Civil War, blacks in the United States South, including those in Georgia, sometimes drilled in secret as members of independent militia companies dedicated to defending themselves from whites who attacked, beat, jailed, and murdered blacks for insubordination, contesting wages, rape, voting, and participation in the Republican Party's efforts to organize both black and white voters. Meanwhile, as the militia company became an instrument of post–Civil War political dominance, whites competed with blacks to have a militia company in their community.[31]

Blacks in parts of the United States South joined volunteer state militia organizations either during Reconstruction, as they did in South Carolina, North Carolina, and Tennessee, or after Reconstruction, as they did in Georgia and Virginia. These black units paraded in celebration of African American freedom, as African Americans in the northern states did during the antebellum period. The new day of celebration was "Emancipation Day" in the United States, which began with the signing of the Emancipation Proclamation, on January 1, 1863. State-sponsored black militia units throughout the late nineteenth century joined African-descendant people's new institutional networks—in churches, mutual aid societies, Masonic organizations, and merchants associations—in celebrating the end of slavery and the beginning of freedom, citizenship, and belonging in the United States.[32]

Black militiamen in the United States South, if Georgia can be used as a model for this study, continued the African-descendant people's Western Hemisphere tradition of organizing to attain status and citizenship within a country building a new nation. On April 27, 1872, 130 African American members of the "Lincoln Association" in Savannah called a meeting "for the Purpose of turning our Institution into a Militia Company." They nominated "permanent officers to command our new organization," "unanimously" making Mat Jackson Bradley chairman. The members collectively decided that the militia uniform would be "the United States [blue] uniform worn by us when [3,486 black male Georgians were] U. S. soldiers." These black men also proposed wearing "the Black casooth Hat with Blue Tassel, Black feather & Leaf Eagle" as an additional adornment to the uniform. They "unanimously" agreed to name their "company . . . [the] Lincoln Guards," in recognition of President Abraham Lincoln's association with emancipation and their new status as U.S. citizens. This unit, along with more than sixty others, became a member of the nineteenth-century Georgia Volunteers, Colored, the black contingent of the Georgia Volunteers, which was the official militia of the state of Georgia after the Civil War. Black militiamen were African Americans with stable employment as laborers, porters, carpenters, butchers, cooks, candy makers, painters, shoemakers, upholsterers, switchmen, and waiters. They, along with the independent black militia company in post–Civil War Georgia, used the militia to search for freedom at a time when white Georgians, too, sought a new place for themselves as citizens of the United States. Both races joined a hemisphere-wide endeavor to create the nation-state, and the militia company was an integral part of nation building. Freedom, citizenship, and the militia were all defined by the nation, and the nation determined who had citizenship and who did not. This was the search for freedom by black people in the United States South and the white mission to deny black people that freedom.[33]

"WE CALLED IT 'THE BAND OF BROTHERS'"

Black Independent Militia Formation and the Johnson County Insurrection of 1875

Black Georgians in Burke, Jefferson, Johnson, Laurens, Richmond, Washington, and Wilkinson Counties resisted planters' and local officials' desires to re-create bondage-like labor on the public roads in 1875 by declaring that "it was not right to work the road under a white overseer—[because] that was played out since Civil Rights." Blacks took this position in the wake of the spring passage of the Civil Rights Act of 1875. Operating under the assumption that their claim to autonomy stood under the protective umbrella of federal power, African Americans endeavored to redefine who controlled their labor after the Civil War. Black rural Georgians pursued this idea by mapping out the boundaries of equality arguing, "If a white man came around for you to work the road you musn't do it. If a white man would not work with a colored overseer then he must work his end of the road & let the colored people work theirs."[1]

African Americans objected to what they thought was an unfair selection process in assigning citizens to perform legislated labor duties on county construction projects. The politicization of labor in Georgia dated back to the restoration of local governance following the end of the racially transformative Civil War. Ironically, Georgia's first Reconstruction government passed the *Code of Georgia* of 1866 with the sanction of President Andrew Johnson under Presidential Reconstruction, which allowed state power to control black labor. The Georgia Legislature created a local official armed with post–Civil War powers equivalent to those of a judge. This official's mandate was to restore order and authority at the politically significant county level of governance. The Georgia Legislature's aim, according to Numan V. Bartley, was "to restore order to labor relations." This act of the General Assembly of 1865–1866 was one of many that Bartley describes as "the reestablishment of social services for whites while generally ignoring blacks." The legislatively created official, the Ordinary, was empowered by the Reconstructed Legislature to carry out an array of responsibilities that included calling grand juries for the purpose of investigating local issues and reviewing this official's work. The General Assembly additionally endowed the Ordinary with local authority to define, regulate, and control labor for public construction projects. Georgia legislators further conveyed to the Ordinary supervisory power over local governance, taxation, and planning. Operating in the realm of labor mobilization, this official would be charged with channeling, regulating, and distributing labor for the construction and maintenance of public roads: "The several managers and employers of male [persons of color] shall whenever required, furnish the overseers [Ordinary and Road Commissioners] of the road district with a list (in writing) of those [local citizens] who are liable to work on the public roads."[2]

Radical Congressional Reconstruction, which took place from 1867 through the early 1870s, introduced African American citizens to the political process in Georgia. Who dominated and controlled county government revolved around black people redefining their societal role from slave and second-class free person to full citizenship in the wake of the Civil War. African American access to public power challenged white definitions of which race possessed the right to rule. The resulting contest for power between blacks and whites occurred within such institutions as the county, the independent militia, and the appointment and election of officials between 1865 and 1875.

These Reconstruction and immediate post-Reconstruction years marked the climax of the independent militia company's presence in rural Georgia politics. The independent black militia companies in Georgia's central and eastern counties allegedly involved in what became known as the Johnson County Insurrection came into being at the moment of transition from Republican rule to the newly empowered Democratic Party's conservative triumph over Congressional Reconstruction in Georgia. Blacks in Burke, Jefferson, Johnson, Laurens, Richmond, Washington, and Wilkinson Counties during these years looked to the independent militia companies to protect them as they pursued land acquisition. They utilized the independent militia company to confront local white repression. How did the black men who organized the local independent militia companies mobilize black people generally to implement the values of freedom, independent labor, and masculinity as they created a political and economic organization to secure black autonomy? Was their defense of black labor a tax revolt? Why was the independent militia company the institution blacks used to organize black people and politically and economically? The independent militia company was also a tool whites utilized to counter black political and economic action. In this context, the Johnson County Insurrection captures both races' vision of freedom, the militia being the central institution for turning that vision into reality.[3]

Black Militias in Georgia

Georgia's late nineteenth-century African Americans participated in the formation of two types of militia companies. Independent companies generally operated outside of Georgia's state government, with some seeking official state recognition as an acknowledgement of black citizenship within both the state and the nation. State and federal officials denied blacks such recognition and refused African American independent militiamen state-supplied weaponry, accoutrements, and funding, whether from state or federal sources. The independent company was more intimately involved with black self-defense and political initiatives and was an extension of the independent company that emerged during the antebellum era. Black men organized and joined antebellum independent militia companies to defend African descendant communities and individuals against slavery. Black independent militiamen continued defending African Americans and pursuing citizenship in the post–Civil War world of the United States South. The postwar African American independent militia company remained a political institution that would be utilized to defend black labor, rights, and property, especially the right to acquire land. The independent postwar militia also functioned as a political organizing institution for unifying the black community for political action and mobilization. It would further be part of the black effort to acquire economic and political autonomy. This would be the independent militia company's role in rural Georgia after the Civil War.

Federal and state funding were the principle sources for a second type of black militia-company: the state-sponsored unit. State authorities during the late nineteenth century officially recognized this African American urban-based company as a legitimate governmental agency. Official state-recognized militia companies operated with the approval and regulation of state government, commanded by the adjutant general and governor, who allocated money, arms, and officer's commissions. These units not only served as an arm of state government but also represented the civic and community pride of the sponsoring urban communities. The African American men who marched in these units were central to the civic activities planned and organized by black residents. The companies existed to demonstrate the black community's public declarations of freedom, civic belonging, manhood, and state and national citizenship. In the case of both independent and state-sponsored militia companies, local citizens collectively created, founded, and organized these companies to serve the aims and desires of African Americans. Georgia's black independent companies operated in the late 1860s and early to mid-1870s, while state-sponsored units were active within Georgia from 1872 into the twentieth century.

Militias: "Contests for Power"

Independent and state-sponsored black militiamen engaged in "contests for power" with local whites, especially the planter class, over labor control and political autonomy across the South. These contests were especially evident in Georgia and Louisiana after the Civil War. Black independent militia companies in Georgia and Louisiana were "closely linked to electoral politics" and "functioned as a means of self-defense for African American voters." Rural Louisiana blacks, like Georgia's rural African Americans, mobilized to act collectively to form local militias "as on-the-ground counter weights" to whites' independent companies, paramilitary forces, and antiblack violence. Louisiana's rural so-called negro militia, however, had a closer official relationship to state government than did the independent black companies in Georgia, where such relations were distant and often nonexistent. The black Georgia independent companies during the late 1860s and into the 1870s appeared at times to be parallel institutions that may have cooperated with the politically focused Union and Loyalty Leagues associated with the Republican Party that educated the black populace about political power and attempted to counter white paramilitary groups organized by the Democratic Party and conservatives. At the same time black independent militias seemed to be autonomous operators that could work with Republican Party efforts to defend the black community and its efforts to exercise political power. Some members of the black independent militia companies did petition Georgia's governors between the late 1860s and the mid-1870s for permission to become part of the official state militia forces. The governors denied their applications while approving some white applications. Yet the independent black militia unit also served a distinctly political function that would be different from Georgia's state-sponsored urban black militia companies, whose longevity and continuous service to blacks and Georgia's state government exceeded thirty years.[4]

Throughout those thirty-plus years, from 1872 to 1905, Georgia's governors and its adjutant generals commanding the militia did approve black requests to organize a state-sponsored urban militia company. Admission to what would, for most of the post–Civil War and post-Reconstruction eras, come to be known as the Georgia Volunteers required a petition of at least sixty locally based community men. These local men came together to form a militia company, hoping to join the State of Georgia's military upon the adjutant general's recommendation and the governor's approval. Black units that received official permission to organize elected officers and then received officer's commissions. They also obtained state-supplied firearms and accoutrements, along with the license to function as the state's formal military institution, making them members of the Georgia Volunteers. Yet racial separation required that the units operate solely within the Georgia Volunteers, Colored. These were the late nineteenth-century state-sponsored black militia companies in Georgia.[5]

Reconstruction: Black Self-Defense

It is within the context of the turmoil, transformations, and at times continuities of post–Civil War America that Georgia's African Americans came together to create independent and state-sponsored volunteer militia companies between the late 1860s and 1880. While the Civil War confirmed the personhood of the African Americans who lived and died to set the race free and earn U.S. citizenship, Reconstruction opened the door for a reconsideration of black people possessing a collective right to protection as an essential component of American freedom and citizenship. In Georgia specifically, Reconstruction was a bloody process, despite the presence of federal troops, the Freedmen's Bureau, Congressional Reconstruction, and an active black political presence in state politics. Yet, as

Howard Rabinowitz argues, crucial to our understanding of Reconstruction under Republican rule is its length.[6] In Georgia, Republican rule was very short owing to a weak and fractured Republican Party that was unable to implement Reconstruction with any degree of consistency, stability, or permanence. More importantly, however, integration and equality had been the goal of neither the Presidential nor the Radical Congressional Reconstruction. Republicans "constantly reminded Negroes that they [the Republican Party] were responsible for removing restrictions on black legal rights, instituting universal black male suffrage, organizing Negro militia units, inaugurating Negro public education, opening state and local welfare institutions to them, and pressing for their admittance to public conveyances and accommodations."[7]

White Republicans in Georgia took credit for many Reconstruction and post-Reconstruction initiatives, but black self-defense and militia-unit creation appear not to have been white Republican initiatives or priorities. In the mid- to late 1860s African American self-defense efforts invoked white Republican political opposition and provoked general white antiblack violence. Each white group—Republican, Democrat, and conservative—rebuked black economic, social, and political initiatives that included the restoration of family, self-employment, social and political equality, and an autonomy that would have allowed black Georgians to live without fear and white supervision. With African American freedom goals in conflict with southern white attempts to restore the antebellum South and with white Republican objectives focused on preventing black exclusion from a Reconstructed Georgia, violence against blacks loomed large.[8]

During the summer of 1865, Confederate veterans, fresh from their defeat by Union forces at the close of the Civil War, organized themselves to attack and terrorize freedmen seeking wages and exercising their newly acquired freedom. Southern whites, especially those outside the Unionist centers in the northern Georgia hill country and marshy Wiregrass region in South Georgia, came together out of fear that white and black Union Leaguers, and African Americans in general, would unite politically and militarily to overwhelm white post–Civil War aspirations. For rural freedmen, landownership was the key to black freedom, because it secured blacks a chance to develop self-sufficiency and autonomy. Freedmen, however, did not experience land as a resource willingly shared with them by ex-Confederates and planters as they created a New South built on racial, social, political, and economic equality. According to at least one scholar, African Americans looked to the federal government for land and, I would assert, also for the protections of freedom.[9]

The federal government recognized the need to protect freedmen from Southern whites. It also comprehended rural freedmen's hope to have access to land and urban blacks' desire for free labor and wages in the cities. Despite the federal acknowledgement of the freedmen's goals, the Republican Party, the Freedmen's Bureau, and Union military leaders often sided with planters, ex-Confederates, and white employers against blacks. In response African Americans, between 1865 and 1868, began organizing their own institutions and organizations. The Georgia Equal Rights Association emerged as one avenue through which freedmen protested such statewide problems as access to health care and medicine. Blacks also met locally, regionally, and statewide to discuss labor issues including wages, working conditions, and labor contracts.[10]

Black Georgians additionally came together in multiple venues to address the question of self-defense. On November 5, 1865, blacks in Columbus, Georgia, petitioned the federal government to keep and sustain Union troops in the city, stating, "we know that there are men [Union troops] here who would protect us if they had the power." The 125 black petitioners also made freedom and self-defense central to their definition of African American liberty: "We firmly believe that the Almighty has ordained our freedom; but at the same time, we wish to inform you that if the Federal Soldiers are withdrawn from us, we will be left in a most gloomy and helpless condition. A number of freedmen have already been killed in this section . . . and from expressions uttered by prominent men in this community in civil life, we have every reason to fear that others will share a similar fate."[11] Their fears were confirmed when George Logan, of Columbus, Georgia, became the victim of antiblack political violence.[12]

Blacks in Griffin, Georgia, expressed similar concerns about their collective safety. Denied "the right of voting for who we prefer" and "afraid of those who are naturally prejudiced against us," it was their "faithful belief that we could not live in this country in safety." Griffin's blacks organized "to give our voices some weight" and to prevent the dismissal of Freedmen's Bureau official and former Union army officer Captain J. Clarke Swayze. Local whites had charged in their report to Swayze's superior, proplanter Major General Davis Tilson, that the captain was "unfair and dishonest." Blacks countered, arguing that Swayze "administered justice without regard to race." Such impartiality had endeared Swayze to the black community and made him "acceptable to our race." Blacks also embraced the captain as "our chosen protector" because he had defended "our freedom" and therefore stood as "our friend."[13]

The white response in the late 1860s was negative and often deadly. Whites inside and outside all levels of government opposed any scenario involving blacks with guns and political power. The Georgia Senate, for example, passed a resolution in February 1866 objecting to "placing our former slaves, with arms" and giving them the power "to arrest, fine . . . imprison . . . lord it over their former owners . . . maltreat our citizens and insult their wives [and] . . . daughters." While this resolution successfully attracted the support of General Ulysses S. Grant in regard to the stationing of black Union troops in Georgia, the Georgia legislature two years later mobilized to prevent one "hundred [Savannah] black Union veterans" from organizing a local militia company. White Republicans and Democrats acted collaboratively to prevent any legislation that would have enabled state-sponsored black militias. This despite the real need for blacks to defend themselves in the late 1860s against antiblack violence.[14]

Antiblack violence in the late 1860s targeted black political organizing, self-defense initiatives, autonomy, and control over their own labor. Organizing the black militia company was one of those acts whereby black people asserted their citizenship rights to determine what happened to them. The pursuit of full freedom involved accessing the tools for self-defense, autonomy, and black political power. In that context, 1868 proved to be an important political watershed in Georgia. Even though by the end of the year the Republicans controlled the state, white antiblack violence increased because Georgia's African Americans voted for the first time that year, a direct sign of black political potential. The stakes were high because blacks mobilized 98,507 registered voters, just 3,904 short of political parity with the 102,411 qualified white voters.[15]

The battle for political dominance led directly to antiblack violence, some of which was directed at African Americans organizing independent militia companies. For example, Calhoun County resident Ralph Jones was "suspected" of clandestinely "drilling colored people." Unknown assailants "shot . . . and wounded" Jones for leading an independent black militia unit. Jones was one of numerous black Americans who were attacked, injured, beaten, or killed for their political participation and militia organizing at the county level. Earl County "radical preacher" John Gibson, like Jones, was shot and beaten. Disguised whites killed Montgomery County's "Radical leader" Joseph Troup "in his own yard at night."[16]

The worst violence targeting black political activity and independent militia organizing occurred in Mitchell County. The County Sheriff joined armed whites in massacring at least twenty-six blacks in Camilla, Georgia. Armed whites attacked Camilla blacks who, hoping to prevent violence, had come to a Republican Party political rally armed. In Randolph County White Leaguers, a white independent militia organization, forced blacks to vote Democrat and salute their parade. Each case illustrated that when black people organized, white people targeted their leaders. White independent militiamen utilized antiblack violence to counter black political power at the county level. Yet in 1868 independent black militia organizing, combined with black attempts to vote, exercise power, and define the terms of their freedom, was just the beginning.[17]

Tunis Campbell and Black Political Power

A prime example of this organizing involved New Jersey–born African American justice of the peace and state senator Reverend Tunis Campbell, who came south to Georgia's Sea Islands as a Freedmen's Bureau official. His objective: to aid, organize, and empower African Americans. He organized blacks in the Sea Islands until the administrator of the bureau changed from General Rufus Saxton, who was sympathetic to black post–Civil War needs, to Major General Davis Tilson, who was proplanter.

Moving to McIntosh County on Georgia's Atlantic coast, Campbell converted his community organizing efforts into black political power. Black political power elevated Rev. Tunis Campbell to offices within Georgia's government: justice of the peace and state senator. Campbell's power in the late 1860s and early 1870s was reinforced by other blacks who held government positions in McIntosh County. Louis Jackson, a Campbell lieutenant, served as McIntosh County's Ordinary. He exercised his power as a public official by protecting black bodies from white abuse. Jackson and Campbell used their legal power to protect and release abused black sailors serving on a British ship in the Port of Darien in 1871. In this case, they challenged white power in three ways: first, by calling for the arrest of the white British captain accused of assaulting the sailors; second, by contesting British consular authority in the matter by calling for this arrest; and third, by exercising legal power to protect black labor, which local whites viewed as a threat to white governance. Campbell, as justice of the peace, and Jackson, as Ordinary, authorized armed blacks and an African American constable to arrest the ship's captain. Two black public officials exercised public power to protect blacks' rights, labor, and personage against the established power and authority of local whites, a white ship's captain, and the British consul.[18]

In June 1871 Jackson contested Justice of the Peace Joseph P. Gilson's arrest of Tunis Campbell. Gilson, Campbell's white political opponent and fellow justice hoped to use his power to curtail Campbell's authority over whites. As Ordinary, Jackson challenged the arrest by issuing a writ of habeas corpus. Blacks additionally questioned Gilson's ruling against Campbell when "a large number of [about 150 armed] colored men" mobilized, intending to insist on Campbell's release. These men were part of McIntosh County's black independent militia company, which was answerable to Campbell and was called to action in this case by Campbell and Jackson. Empowered with public office and its accompanying legal authority, Jackson secured Campbell's release from Atlanta's Fulton County jail, reinforced by armed black militiamen.[19]

In January 1872 Senator Tunis Campbell urged McIntosh County African Americans to resist what he described as an "unconstitutional" legislative act: the Georgia General Assembly's passage of the Commissioner's Bill for McIntosh County to create Commissions of Roads & Revenue. This act empowered whites to control all black labor commissioned to make public improvements such as county road construction.[20] Blacks, as a result, considered Tunis Campbell's political activities and public address as an ongoing effort to educate "the colored people to work steady and save their money so that they may buy homes for themselves and children" and have control over their labor and lives. Essentially, Campbell argued for and presented a plan for black economic autonomy and political empowerment. He considered himself to be a representative of the people, directed by their will and collective decisions, and he endeavored to secure for blacks a voice in Georgia politics. The bill's passage had the potential to restrict black autonomy.

Campbell argued that the proposed public policy and labor measure would be "passed with a view to abridge ['the black man's'] . . . rights and in every way give advantage and supremacy to the whites." In daring to counter the power of an increasingly antiblack legislature, Campbell had assurances from Republican Governor Benjamin Conley that the legislation would not be signed into law. H. W. Corker, however, a white observer, claimed that Campbell's January 1872 speech wrongly condemned the Georgia Legislature as "a partial and corrupt body" that sought to pass an "unjust and oppressive" road construction and labor law. Senator

Campbell, Corker claimed, outlined additional avenues of black resistance "should enforcement of the same be attempted in Darien," bypassing the governor's veto. Determined to represent "the people's" wishes, Campbell advised that McIntosh County African Americans join him in fighting the legislation, even to the point of "apply[ing] to General Grant for military aid if the citizens of this community required martial law." According to Corker, Campbell "declared [the Commission for McIntosh County to be] . . . the most iniquitous unjust and diabolical thing ever attempted on citizens of a free country." Campbell therefore "advised them ["ignorant" blacks] by all means not to submit to it" and, as a way to avoid imprisonment for broken labor agreements with whites, counseled African Americans not to sign any labor contracts.[21]

While Campbell's white opponents called him "evil," the "Hon. T. G. Campbell, Sr.'s" black defenders adamantly declared his influence "over the Col[ored] people" to be solely "for good & not evil." Further, Campbell's advocacy had uniformly focused on "obedience to the laws & a faithful performance of their duty" to society. Fundamentally, Darien, Georgia, and McIntosh County had only "a small portion" of its people "wrongfully and maliciously prejudiced against" Campbell. Yet whites persisted in calling Campbell "a demi-god," because, they claimed, his fundamental objective as "a minister of the gospel" and an ambitious "Negro judge" was to impose upon whites his "highest aspirations . . . to give the Negro the supremacy over the white man." Campbell, in the minds of whites, was a powerful black leader who would lead black "freemans" in a violent campaign against whites. Both Campbell and "freemans" embraced "strife and bloodshed" because they held the "*musket* and *Bayonet*" "dear to their . . . heart." Whites, as a result, interpreted black political action as violence, rather than as participation in a democratic society.[22]

Whites' criticism revealed their own primary objective: controlling black labor. This objective became clear in a critique of "Mr. Campbell's [January 1872] Speech." Specifically, "We [whites] consider [the speech] highly inflammatory tending to create estrangement and strife between the races," a circumstance that, whites claimed, disrupted racial peace. Campbell also threatened the restoration of the pre–Civil War status quo. Racial tranquility was possible only if "this man Campbell" was removed. In Campbell's absence "the races would at once [achieve] harmony . . . [that would] work well." More importantly, with Campbell's removal, "the Colored People of the County" would be transformed into an "orderly, civil, polite labor force exhibiting a commendable regard to labor." Through this argument against black political power, whites hoped to regain control over how, when, why, and where black people worked. Whites dreamed of a restored subservience in contradistinction to the goals of black political and economic autonomy advocated for by such African American leaders as Tunis Campbell.[23]

Black Political Power beyond McIntosh County

Black and white contests for power did not occur in McIntosh County alone. African Americans and whites in rural Georgia competed with each other for political dominance and representation. This conflict extended to control over black labor and to an arms race that would determine who had freedom and who did not. Campbell had constructed a political machine enforced and protected by an independent black militia company and supported by a cast of black public officials who regulated the political and economic climate in McIntosh County. They and other black Georgians endeavored to utilize the tools of citizenship and governance to protect black property, life, and labor as black people defined themselves citizens of Georgia and of the United States.

Blacks in seven rural counties in central and eastern Georgia—Burke, Jefferson, Johnson, Laurens, Richmond, Washington, and Wilkinson—organized with the intent of securing and exercising their political and economic autonomy. African Americans mobilized to carve out a place for themselves that allowed them to create, nurture, protect, defend, and define black freedom and citizenship during the waning years of Georgia's Reconstruction.[24] The independent militia company was central to this effort. Local whites, however, did not accept black's collective search for freedom as autonomous laborers, independent economic players, and full political participants in the commercial-industrial-capitalist economy. In 1875 they accused blacks in these counties who sought economic and political autonomy of insurrection. Blacks' approach to autonomy was not modeled on the effort in McIntosh County, yet they, like Campbell's supporters, utilized the independent militia company to rally and organize themselves.

Like Campbell, blacks in the alleged insurrectionary counties invoked the name and power of the federal government to leverage their efforts at making freedom real. These African Americans not only defined freedom as equality at the supervisory level, intending to regulate who labored to maintain county roads and local governance, but also determined the boundaries of freedom using the independent volunteer militia company to promote the Civil Rights Act of 1875, acquire land, and mobilize blacks to exercise their political power within the Republican Party. African Americans in these seven counties formed a "Band of Brothers" inside their local independent militia companies, hoping to attain stability in black life at the end of Reconstruction. They proceeded despite counter mobilizations by local white independent militia units seeking to demonstrate the range of their political and economic dominance, as well as regulate local labor and the use of violence.

Public Rights

Blacks in these seven counties attempted to define what Rebecca J. Scott has outlined more broadly as "public rights" and "struggles over values." Public rights were those rights through which African people in the Western Hemisphere used their experiences as slaves and as free people to define their place as citizens both locally and nationally. Ideas about these rights developed over time, from the colonial period forward, through the process of nation building across the hemisphere, and especially during Reconstruction in the United States, which was a specific moment of nation building. Public rights defined black humanity, personhood, and, in the case of African Americans in Georgia, their manhood and political rights in the public sphere. Public rights, while part of the period extending from transnational colonialism to the Haitian Revolution, also evolved in the Gulf of Mexico basin, both inside and outside the antebellum United States. This ideal of broad-based human rights in the public sphere also had its roots across the Atlantic Ocean, as free blacks crossed borders and an ocean during their sojourns in Western Europe before the American Civil War. The Civil War and Reconstruction periods helped refine the meaning of public rights, especially in Louisiana, where the 1868 Constitution broadly defined "equal public rights" as individual dignity, manhood, and respect in public venues both spatially and culturally. Blacks in Georgia, and specifically those in the seven counties, sought to carve out a place within the public arena, utilizing the public political rally, autonomy on public road construction crews, jury duty, land acquisition, and independent and state-sponsored militia company formation as the realm of public rights. Blacks in these counties also looked to the federal government as the enforcer of the Civil Rights Act of 1875—an additional avenue through which African Americans sought to establish their vision of what black freedom should be in Georgia.[25]

"Struggle over Values"

The "struggle over values" revolved around the black-white conflict over who would control black labor, the right to collective action, the right to organize politically and economically, and the right to regulate labor, wages, and political power. Individually and collectively, these values defined black freedom after slavery as a component of the nation-building process across the postbondage Western Hemisphere. The fight for control over black labor played out violently in both Georgia and Louisiana. In Louisiana the stakes involved free labor and its connections to "not only material well-being but social and cultural life and the possibility of [a] political voice." Black Georgians in 1875 wrestled with these same issues, because white Georgians contested blacks' exercise of the rights of citizenship and equality. In both states, this contestation included patterns of work and its organization, along with the nature and compensation of labor within the context of racially contested political and economic power.

The issue of who regulated and owned black labor affected African Americans' rights to mobility and public assembly. Both rights defined liberty and freedom as African Americans understood these concepts. Black freedom entailed being able to organize economically to impact wages and shape the nature of economic rewards, as well as to independently decide who to forge alliances with, both politically and economically. The Johnson County Insurrection was an attempt to define black freedom against the white insistence that white freedom required black economic and political submission.[26]

The white vision of freedom did not include any process of shared governance with blacks or public acceptance of black autonomy. White people hoped to use the independent and state-sponsored militia companies to define white freedom, political participation, and their racially based right to rule. They utilized the militia as a counter agent to rising black political participation. The white militia, whether independent or state-sponsored, was the vehicle that would restore the white right to rule at the county and state levels. The Johnson County Insurrection was part of the process of restoring white rule in Georgia while minimizing, if not eliminating, black independent economic and political actions, citizenship, and the right to rule.

Black Masculinity

Blacks utilized the militia company to publicly declare their manhood and citizenship, two ideas that defined political power in the form of the right to vote. A few black militiamen additionally recalled the camaraderie of their Civil War days. As they did for their white counterparts, African American memories of Civil War brotherhood extended into peace time. Wartime male bonding and fellowship encouraged men of both races to promote militia formation as another way of declaring their manhood.

Political power, citizenship, and the right to vote were key African American ideals after the Civil War. Black militiamen viewed themselves as "Citizens of the County," because militiamen "did not organize themselves together for the purpose of doing anything inconsistent with their duties as citizens of this State or of the United States, but to carry out what they are advised to believe and do believe in the true spirit of the Laws." The militia company was further a symbol of masculine respectability since "the members [were] personally known . . . as excellent and meritorious citizens, & the troop [was] a credit to the state of Georgia."

Masculine brotherhood drove black Union veterans in Savannah, Georgia, to organize a "benevolent association," as their white counterparts did before 1872. The federal government, in response to Georgia's black codes and antiblack violence, had in the mid-1860s prohibited Georgia from having a state-sponsored militia. Yet blacks in the Lincoln Association met in April 1872 in preparation for transforming the Association into "A Militia Company," their collective purpose being the re-creation of the gendered fellowship of men during the Civil War. Generally and more broadly, black militiamen envisioned themselves embracing "a just and becoming pride in the laws, customs and institutions of that section of the Union which they were born, and which is now the home of their manhood."[27] Manhood was also a function of where you lived, worked, and made a name for yourself as a member of the community.

Savannah and Augusta, Georgia, were important to this discussion. Black citizens in both communities developed militia companies that became part of the state-sponsored companies. In Savannah, the discussion of black masculinity and manhood was also publicly examined. These cities occupied the same geographical region as the seven counties where independent black militia companies had emerged to promote black political and economic autonomy.

In the 1870s black masculinity and manhood was on an upward historical trajectory of taking responsibility to learn, to serve, and to endure. Black masculinity and manhood was defined sometimes by a classism that reflected a commitment to God and "Christian citizenship," community and nation building, and refinement in "art, science, and literature," as well as business. In March 1876, Hon. John Emory Bryant, a white former Union and Freedmen's Bureau officer, Union/Loyalty League militia advocate, and Republican leader in Georgia who sometimes closely associated with blacks and their politics, described what he believed to be the aspirations of African Americans at the dedication of St. James Tabernacle, an African American–created and controlled institution in Savannah, Georgia. Bryant presented blacks as major contributors to the U.S. national narrative that presented Africans Americans as citizens of the nation and as men having played an integral part in the nation's history. Bryant contended that black men had the capacity to learn, because they "may be taught man's duty to man" and "be governed by [God] as men, rational men." Blacks further needed to take on the lessons of the "Good Samaritan" by endeavoring to have "compassion in [their] heart" for their neighbors.[28]

Bryant then turned to "public matters" whereby African American men could be involved, provided they were "governed by right motives and not wrong ones." Politics, because it was inherently dishonest yet central to nation building, especially required virtuous manhood. Blacks needed to follow the path of the "good politician [who] must be an honest man." To build a nation of solid citizens, Bryant compared black Americans to the enslaved biblical Israelites in Egypt who "even in bondage" had access to the "advantages of an existence among the most refined and enlightened nation then known and benefited to commence their own national existence under leaders trained in all the learning of the Egyptians." Out of that experience of nation building, and by implication the development of manhood, the Israelites produced "a model nation and a model church." Bryant asserted, "And so it is with us." Black Americans, too, were an emerging nation within the United States.[29]

Slavery stained the original thirteen colonies where "liberty was to have [had] a new birth and a new development" that was central to the "develop[ment of] a great nation." Bryant believed that whites and blacks would, in the future, create a Christian family, but this vision of nation building required "the strength and manliness of Puritanism," which "had crossed the Atlantic" flawed with "its bigotry and narrowness" and its lack of an inclusive sense of liberty. This liberty rewarded "men succeeding who are doing wrong" while "failing [men] who do right." Blacks therefore had to be prepared to deal with "those men who go to the cabin of the poor negro and drag him out and cut his throat" and who wished to deny black people liberty.[30]

In this context, some blacks hoped that the black militia organization, along with the ballot box, would protect their liberty, both personally and collectively. The militia and the ballot box held important positions in such public venues as political rallies and parades: those contested arenas of masculine dominance and sites of confrontations between blacks and whites in middle and eastern Georgia.[31] Additionally, in the 1870s the militia company for blacks and whites served as a symbol of power; it helped organize and mobilize a community politically, socially, and economically. For whites, it was an instrument of military superiority, and for blacks it was a symbol of citizenship, national belonging, and personal autonomy, all key to the definition of manhood, participation, equality, and authority. Both races looked to the militia as an institution for defining freedom, masculinity, and dominance at the county level, whether that militia unit was sponsored and financially supported by Georgia's state government or an independent militia company organized and operating without state funding and arms as a local institution determining power and governance at the county level.

Even though blacks and J. E. Bryant, by 1875–1876, no longer agreed upon the direction of the Republican Party, Bryant's address at St. James Tabernacle may not have been far removed from the broad conceptions African Americans possessed of antebellum and post–Civil War visions of masculinity, manhood, and freedom. According to Kathleen Ann Clark and William Beck, the antebellum and immediate postbellum ministers of the African Methodist Episcopal Church and black veterans who engaged in Emancipation Day commemorations endeavored to define black masculinity, manhood, and citizenship as the essence of what it meant for African American males to be free men with political, economic, and social autonomy. Similar to "public rights," Clark argued that blacks pursued the symbols of masculinity and manhood, freedom, and citizenship with the intention of eventually securing the full range of privileges that would make them complete citizens. In that context, African Methodist Episcopal (AME) ministers sought to publicly prove that African American men had acquired the behaviors and attained the qualifications that made them men, citizens, and fully qualified free Americans.

Specifically, Beck noted that black manhood was equated with leadership, a sense of mission, and citizenship, as well as the ability to guide the darker brothers to salvation within Western culture, even if it meant leaving the United States for Africa. In this context, antebellum and postbellum black men carried on a debate focused on "the nature of black citizenship." Evidence of their achievements as citizens and men occurred in public venues where men marched and paraded to demonstrate their military capabilities, presented speeches, and acted as independent men. African Americans were no longer slaves dependent upon white decisions. Freedom made them autonomous beings able to take their own destinies in hand and to carve out a place for themselves within the new American landscape of productive citizenship, respectable actions, and a self-directed life. These traits reflected a self-made man capable of working with others but also proud of achieving objectives as independent competent men who led their families and the race to self-sufficiency. This was the essence of black freedom after the Civil War. Black male Georgians in both the independent and state-supported militia companies endeavored to act as free autonomous men who were citizens of the county, state, and nation equal to their neighbors with uninterrupted access to power, decision making, and the levers of governance that ensured their citizenship and autonomy. African-descendant people exercised this ideal across the Western Hemisphere in the nineteenth century as a baseline definition of a free black society.[32]

Middle and eastern Georgia blacks pursued such merged traits of masculinity, manhood, freedom, and equality, as well as the independence of "self-ownership," that made economic autonomy a priority. Blacks in the seven counties sought land and control over their labor and citizenship, even as county road construction undermined their conceptions of economic and political equality and a parallel autonomy in each of these categories. These men were engaging in more than a tax revolt. They were engaging in the more comprehensive rights revolt, the process of accessing full citizenship in the contested atmosphere of Georgia's post–Civil

Map 1. Counties and county seats of Georgia during the nineteenth century. The seven "insurrectionary" counties in east and central Georgia all border each other, and some border the Savannah River and state of South Carolina. Courtesy of the University of Georgia Press.

War counties. They also believed that African Americans needed to demonstrate very distinctly their patriotism as a declaration of their national citizenship.

Some black Georgians also used militia service to assure white people that they were citizens not only of the county but also of the state and nation, the prosperity of which they were committed to. Black Georgians, similar to their fellow African Americans in Baltimore, Maryland, in 1864, wanted to "let the world see that [they were] men who love[d] [their] country" and had "higher aspirations than [being] hewers of wood and drawers of water." Georgia's black men used the militia to join a national and hemisphere-wide black effort to assert that the race had a "full-blown history of . . . independent manhood" that legitimated the black claim to not only economic security but also political rights, including the right to vote. In parallel with J. E. Bryant's nation-building assertions, black Georgians, including AME Bishop Henry M. Turner, projected that postwar blacks had at last "come into their own." African-descendant people in the Americas shared this vision of freedom, leadership, and self-assertion with blacks in the United States South, and black Georgians independently and collectively sought to put into operation an autonomous personhood, complete with the attendant public rights they had established both before and after the Civil War.[33]

Richmond County

According to the *Augusta Chronicle and Sentinel*, "The plot to kill the whites by the negroes" occurred in "part of Richmond" County.[34] The seven-county plot had rural roots. Richmond County's black militiamen, however, lived in Augusta, the county's largest city. Two groups, each comprising about sixty African American men, successfully petitioned Governor James Milton Smith to organize two state-sponsored militia companies, which they founded in 1873 and 1874. The Douglass Infantry in 1873 declared its collective membership to be "Citizens of the County," claiming a place in metropolitan Augusta beside their white neighbors. Additionally, the company was one of the few black militia units able to equip, uniform, and arm themselves without petitioning the state for these resources. Declaring themselves armed with Enfield rifles, the Douglass Infantry also suggested that they were economically independent, which may have given them the autonomy to name their unit after the black abolitionist, escaped slave, orator, and Union army recruiter Frederick Douglass.[35]

In 1874 sixty-two more black citizens, held "in high esteem among the [elite] white citizens of the County," petitioned Governor James M. Smith to form an infantry company. Invoking class as a distinguishing mark of achievement and distinction, these African American men certified their behavior as safe and reputable. They were august citizens who "at all times scrutinized the character [of their applicants and members] for quiet, peace and order . . . admitting only such persons as would insure, an honorable reputation for the company." Furthermore each member had been approved first by whites, because many were employed by elite Augusta whites, and second owing to their publicly "conspicuous . . . devotion to religious principles, and . . . the prosperity of their state and section." Additionally, these sixty-two black men viewed themselves as committed to law and order and manhood.[36]

Naming their company "The Georgia Infantry," men such as Joseph K. Williams, Peter Smith, Henry Johnson, Richard W. Matthews, James W. Wingfield, and W. Henry defined themselves as "colored citizens of Augusta" while declining to identify their company by race. Instead of embracing black leader Frederick Douglass, Georgia Infantry members were "actuated by a just and becoming pride in the laws, customs and institutions of that section of the union in which they were born, and which is now the home of their manhood." They were Georgians and citizens of Richmond County. As a result, the Georgia Infantry pursued avenues that assured whites that they were unique and, more significantly, safe for whites and Governor Smith to admit to the Georgia volunteer militia command with guns.

By 1878 these two units were serving as state-sponsored militia companies and black Augusta institutions. That year, they were joined by the Colquitt Zouaves, led by J. Tyler, whose name honored Confederate General and Georgia Governor 1877–1882, Alfred H. Colquitt. The Richmond Guards followed, naming the unit as a county institution. Led by Daniel Lamar, the Richmond Guards appear to have ceased to exist by 1878, which indicates how quickly a unit might rise, fall, and disband. None of these black companies appeared in press discussions as insurrectionary African American militia units, suggesting that class (in this case, middle and elite) and location (in this case, urban) superseded race in Richmond County in the mid-1870s.

The Augusta-based Georgia Infantry was urban and led by black elites and had been immediately accepted as a state-sponsored militia company. The nearby seven counties had rural black independent militia companies.

Governor James Milton Smith denied these independent black militia companies admission to, and its leadership commissions in, the Georgia Volunteers, despite their request for state recognition. The Georgia Infantry had apparently made peace with local white power, which exercised some degree of patronage, supervision, and recognition of the urban-based black militia company. The rural independent black militia units, in contrast, challenged white power, as blacks in the seven rural counties sought to secure their political and economic autonomy by acquiring land and defending their political and labor rights. Blacks in both the rural and urban communities pursued inclusion as citizens of their respective counties. They declared themselves citizens of Georgia.[37]

Local Memories

Black people in the seven rural counties had organized at least three independent militia companies by the mid-1870s. The independent militia company was an institutional way of organizing large numbers of rural African Americans in hopes of overcoming the absence of economic opportunity in the region and the resurgent white rule enabled by the terror of the Ku Klux Klan and of white paramilitary or independent militia companies. The black independent militia unit also provided a platform through which to mobilize blacks for political action at the county level. Blacks in these counties sought to use black independent militia companies as the organizing vehicle that would secure for them a respected citizenship, access to land and economic autonomy, and control over not only their daily labor but also when, how, and why they labored. Blacks wanted primary ownership over their bodies and labor to secure the goals and objectives of freedom promised by the Civil War and Reconstruction.

The Johnson County Insurrection occurred during the summer of 1875. It was one of multiple convergence points across the seven rural counties where white and black Georgians made the competition for organizing county-level independent militia companies more than a war of words. The summer reinforced a post–Civil War conflict that was ongoing at the county level over who was to rule Georgia's rural communities.[38] County histories characterize Georgia's Reconstruction period, from 1865 to 1875, as a trying time for whites, who valiantly overcame economic deprivation, corrupt black political influences, and out of control newly freed African Americans. These county histories also establish the severe disappointment felt by blacks, who expected to gain the vote, land, and a life free of slavery. While the stories of Georgia's postbellum counties reinforced racial stereotypes on both sides, no county historian reported on the Johnson County Insurrection as a relevant event. County historians did, however, record "black insurrections," such as Laurens County's 1872 "negro riot," Wilkinson County's Reconstruction race war, and Jefferson County's Cudjo Fye Insurrection.[39]

Bertha Sheppard Hart's *Official History of Laurens County Georgia* contended that "Todd Norris, a big vicious mulatto," led a "negro riot" that threatened the white restoration of antebellum normalcy in the early 1870s. Norris headed a revolt of some "hundred or so" African Americans against white paternalism's plantation tradition of "ole marse" and "my negroes" and the ascendancy of tenant farming. This group would be arrested, jailed, imprisoned, and executed. A small group went free.[40]

Laurens County blacks also elected George Linder for service in the Georgia Legislature between 1868 and 1872. Linder would be radicalized during his tenure in the General Assembly, as whites, Republicans, and Democrats expelled black legislators in 1868 and 1872. In response to the expulsion Linder stated: "Roust us from here [and] we will roust you."[41]

Wilkinson County, northwest of and contiguous to Laurens County, was where black Americans assembled in "lines near a quarter mile long" to vote for the first time, in 1868. Black political power was emergent as African Americans and the Republican Party triumphed with the election of a black state senator representing Wilkinson, Twiggs, and Jones Counties.[42] Blacks also rallied in 1872, utilizing the power of the federal government with an all-black federal grand jury and federal troops, to, albeit unsuccessfully, oppose Wilkinson County's Ku Klux Klan and thereby challenge local white power.[43]

Population demographics defined black political power in Jefferson County, northeast of Laurens County. Blacks had a two to one—7,943 to 4,247—advantage in 1870. Political and economic power shifted significantly between 1869 and 1870 as plantation agriculture ceased and black life "entirely changed" as a result.[44] In July and August 1870 a literate African American, Cudjo Fye, was at the center of black efforts to exercise their power. Fye and Jefferson County African Americans mobilized black political power with an independent militia company and "[political] 'clubs'" that whites described as a military organization. Blacks argued that these institutions—the militia and the political club—provided protection and gave African Americans group cohesion. The political club, as some characterized similar organizations, such as the Republican Union or Loyalty League, existed to educate blacks about their rights, political potential, and the parameters of freedom and autonomy. Fye mobilized Jefferson County blacks, first, by educating them about their rights "as members of the political club," and, second, by unifying them for collective action through economic autonomy via landownership and control over property and through the exercise of political power. Blacks met in mass public meetings in Jefferson County to organize and then march on Louisville, Georgia, to demand the release of a jailed "club" member, "Captain" Tom Brewer. The "Cudjo Fye Insurrection," as this political mobilization came to be called in Jefferson County, reflected that county's black vision of freedom and autonomy. Under Fye's leadership, African Americans used the independent militia and political club to educate and unify local blacks politically, to define their political and economic rights, to define equality, and to establish the right to vote and use political power to meet African American needs.[45] The acts of Jefferson County blacks in 1870 would be paralleled five years later at another political rally in the county sandwiched between Laurens and Jefferson Counties, Johnson County.

While blacks in the seven central and eastern counties of Georgia were not as organized as those in McIntosh County, where Tunis Campbell developed a political organization or machine, African Americans had been politically active in seeking to implement their vision of freedom. In Burke and Wilkinson Counties, Joseph Morris, like Fye, played an important role mobilizing blacks in 1875. Morris, politically active in both counties, led blacks as an elected official and political organizer. Whites, in 1875, assumed Morris to be the "General" who organized the black "insurrectionary" independent militias in Georgia's seven eastern and central counties. Morris had served in the state legislature with Laurens County's George Linder. They experienced the frustrations of losing elections and of white Republican and Democratic joint expulsions of black legislators from the General Assembly in 1868 and again in 1872.[46]

In 1872 Morris was thirty-two years old. He worked as a teacher in Gordon, Georgia, in Wilkinson County. Yet it was his political activities in Burke County before 1872 that got the attention of whites in the region. Morris, like Tunis Campbell and Cudjo Fye, had some success organizing blacks. According to the *Sandersville Herald and Georgian*, Morris had "gained complete control of the minds of the worst negroes in that neighborhood, and fired the hearts of his followers . . . [with] midnight barranges . . . against the whites." Morris apparently also had access to independent black militiamen. The *Herald and Georgian*, consistent with its claim of looming black violence resulting from black political mobilization, charged that Morris threatened Governor James Milton Smith with retribution if the governor "did not furnish him guns to arm his fellow Africans." Specifically, Morris "warned [that] . . . the bones of the negro race would rise up in judgment against him." Smith denied the request.[47]

Moving southwest, passing through Jefferson and Johnson Counties and on to Wilkinson County, Morris around 1872 pursued elective office where African Americans were already seeking federal support to challenge the Ku Klux Klan. Morris sought a legislative seat "against the Hon. W. C. Adams, the [white] democratic nominee." Morris, however, arrived in Wilkinson County during the Democratic Party's ascendancy not only in Klan-led Wilkinson County but across the state of Georgia.[48] Morris lost the election by "about 600 votes," and whites hoped he would retire quietly to his "African villa" in Gordon's suburb, Jacksonville. Morris, nevertheless, persisted in his political activism by contesting local white political dominance. First, he apparently successfully pursued work as a tax collector. This position may also have empowered Morris to refuse to submit to work on the county "road" construction crews authorized by Wilkinson County's Ordinary and road commissioners. Morris, Campbell, Fye, Linder, and Norris all sought to organize and lead blacks in using political and economic power to declare that blacks were citizens.[49]

African American and white Georgians competed in the seven rural counties for political and economic dominance. The white response to black political power would be fear and misconstruals of black political action as violent assaults on white people. African Americans had been actively engaged in their efforts to define freedom, citizenship, and autonomy. By the summer of 1875 blacks had won and lost political power at the county and state levels. Yet they had utilized the independent black militia company as a platform for political organizing, mobilization, and defense of black rights as political and economic citizens. These were the central tenets of black freedom in the seven counties as they engaged in claims making.

Claims Making

The political military theorist Ronald R. Krebs argues, "Rights are rarely granted [to minorities] without struggle with central authorities, and claims-making, particularly when aggressive, may bring repression." Blacks in the seven counties had been testing the boundaries and places of freedom since the end of the Civil War, weighing what Krebs describes as "whether to mobilize or remain quiescent" in the context of "how likely the state [was] to grant citizenship rights and how likely it [was] to crush the movement." African Americans continually balanced the "costs and benefits" of their economic and political actions and mobilizations in these communities against the unpredictability of the white response to black power and African American efforts to exert their citizenship rights. Blacks sought what Krebs called "strong signals" of inclusion or exclusion.

Strong signals "are *credible, clear,* and *available.*" At the same time, "minority leaders may fear state elites have revised the manpower policy to tempt them into protesting their group's subordinate status and thereby giv[e] the authorities an excuse to clamp down," forcing blacks to try to determine before acting what was "credible" evidence of inclusion and the "willingness to widen the boundaries of the political community" and what was not, because "inclusion can be converted back into exclusion." While Krebs contends that changes such as inclusion, citizenship status, and widening of boundaries of the political community can be tracked by shifts in "military manpower policies," this "holds only when populations perceive themselves as citizens, not as subjects." Citizenship, according to Krebs, involved "mutual obligations" between those who rule and the populations ruled. Such mutuality or citizenship allows for "claims-making."[50] African Americans in the seven rural counties and in the urban communities where state-sponsored militia came into being were "claims-making" and seeking confirmation of their "public rights" in the late 1860s, 1870s, and beyond. Savannah and Augusta's blacks found acceptance. Blacks in the seven rural counties encountered rejection and the crushing mobilization of white power as whites searched for the normalcy of white freedom.

A Mass Meeting in Washington County

On June 28, 1875, Washington County's Rev. Cordy (aka Corday) Harris, a leader in the independent militia movement in the seven counties, submitted a letter that the local white press did not note until July. Hoping to allay white fears of large numbers of black people gathering in a public place, Harris communicated blacks' plans for a Republican Party political rally at the Washington County Courthouse scheduled for July 24, 1875. The meeting was a nominating convention to select candidates for two local political positions. The first involved selecting a "proper and fit person as a Military General of the Second [Militia] District of Georgia."

Governor James Milton Smith would commission the nominee. Blacks also intended to determine "the Republican Party County Chairman of the Executive Committee of Washington County, Ga." The gathering also invited African Americans from nineteen surrounding counties, including armed independent and state-sponsored militia units from Georgia and South Carolina, respectively, and accompanying band musicians.[51]

The "militia district" was one means of institutionalized political organizing in Georgia that both political parties and races utilized. It did not serve as a way of creating militia units. The militia district functioned as a political platform representing a geographical region and the political units within the communities inside that region. Further, because the black political convocation would occur within the established structures recognized by all Georgians as legitimate mechanisms for public political organizing, Harris and Morris appear to have assumed that the governor of Georgia would sanction such a meeting and not consider it a violation of white sensitivities. The rally was an attempt by black people to participate in the political process as members of Georgia's political community operating within the state's political structure.[52]

The Republican Party's regional convention had the potential to attract some major black political personalities. The invitation to the state-sponsored black South Carolina militia raised the possibility that a major political figure might also attend. The black militia leader was Prince Rivers, a self-liberated and self-taught former slave, both articulate and literate. Rivers had also served in the Union army and attained general officer rank in the post–Civil War South Carolina militia. Further, Rivers represented the rising presence of black political power and manhood. By the time of the rally in Georgia, Rivers had been elected intendant/mayor of Hamburg, South Carolina, just across the border between Georgia and South Carolina. South Carolina's governor had also appointed Rivers as a trial judge, the equivalent of a magistrate and similar to the position Tunis Campbell held in Georgia.

Equally important, Rivers was a Civil War combat veteran with recognized leadership experiences in the First South Carolina Volunteers. The Thirty-Third United States Colored Troops, later renamed the First South Carolina regiment during the Civil War, had been led by the abolitionist and theologian Colonel Thomas Wentworth Higginson. Colonel Higginson held such a high regard for Rivers's leadership qualities that he believed him to be officer material. Rivers, a tall dark-skinned man with considerable dignity, like Tunis Campbell, used his power as justice to preside over local cases, including the jailing of whites who abused blacks and reneged on contractual agreements with blacks. Whites in both states viewed Rivers as a Radical Republican politician, a Union League member, "impudent," and the leader of a "once . . . flourishing cotton mart of Western Carolina," Hamburg. A black and white community, Hamburg in the mid-1870s, whites claimed, had become "the abode of the most consummate Radical thieves, plunders and curs [that] . . . ever cursed . . . this green earth of ours." According to the *Edgefield Advertiser*, the "few decent people who are residents [of Hamburg] . . . pray[ed] fervently" for Rivers's removal and the termination of Hamburg, South Carolina, a community where claims making occurred as African Americans pursued political power and economic opportunity.[53]

It was in the spirit of legitimate political organizing that Joseph Morris, Burke County's political and militia leader, sent a letter to Washington County "Sheriff Rube Mayer" (aka Ruben Mayo) requesting the scheduling of the county courthouse on July 24, 1875, for the nineteen-county mass political meeting. According to the *Sandersville Herald and Georgian*, Morris's request was really a "command" because the letter allegedly opened with "You command to have cort house sweped and all cleand" and ended with an equally assertive demand for white authorities to "have you all the said rodes keep opened from No 13 Station [Tennille, Georgia] to the court house and the keys in Your hand to put in My hands." With this "Sambo dialect" description of black power, the local white press suggested that a savage and uncivilized race threatened white authority with demands that whites hand over ownership of a public venue. Specifically the press contended that Morris attempted to order and even intimidate whites, bending them to the will of black hordes preparing to descend upon the white public space of Washington County's courthouse.

Insurrection

In the white mind, Georgia's Reconstruction had not ended in 1872, because black political power still loomed as a part of the political system. If African American Republicans could meet to organize politically in a public space in any Georgia county, then a black insurrection or race war loomed on the horizon.[54]

Whites assumed that African Americans were coming to Washington County to take control and overwhelm them. Additionally the most prominent building and symbol of white power, the courthouse, was under attack. The county courthouse, as whites viewed it across the South, was a white possession and not a public venue where all citizens regardless of color might convene. Whites also concluded that blacks did not intend to come in peace, since armed independent militia companies were part of the convention. These were the signposts of race war. Furthermore, that black militiamen were drilling in secret preordained a black assault on the county courthouse and the local white community. In response to the pending race war, "the [white] people got ready" to keep the county courthouse safe from "the polluting presence of disturbers of the peace at all hazards." Race war in Washington County was black "insurrection."[55]

The grand jury transcript for the "Johnson County Insurrection" contains black testimony that explains the actions, goals, visions, and aims of African Americans in the seven counties in 1875.[56] The *Savannah Morning News* published reports by its correspondent Sydney Herbert. He presented white concerns that included questions posed to blacks and confessions secured by white interrogators. According to Herbert, "General" Morris, Rev. Corday Harris, Ephriam Brantley, Rev. Jerry Simmons, and unit officers such as Francis Murkerson, Ben Davis, Jake Mooreman, Jerry Walters (aka Waters), and Harrison Tucker led the black militia. Black militia companies and their leaders organized, mobilized, and encouraged African Americans to use this institution to define the parameters of black political and economic organizing, which whites believed to be the focus of the "insurrection." Blacks in Herbert's estimation began organizing at the beginning of May 1875, but local support for the Civil Rights Act of 1875 suggests a much earlier date for black political organizing in the seven counties and explains why blacks looked to the federal government to substantiate their political and economic rights. Blacks mobilized to implement their rights in the spring of 1875.[57]

Captain Harrison Tucker led what African Americans James Wright, Tobe Morris, and Richard Smith of Laurens County described to their white interrogators as "a secret military organization," the independent militia company founded in local black churches in Johnson and Laurens Counties. According to John Chiles, Rev. Corday Harris founded the black militia movement in Washington County's Sandersville, Georgia. He was assisted by Frances Murkerson, a leading member of the Washington County movement. Harris and Murkerson were able to get "all the colored men in this section," that is, Washington County, to meet and unite black men in a "secret military organization" focused on securing for blacks equality and land.

Johnson County's independent black militia company, the Zion Hope Company, operated under the leadership of Captain Jerry Walters (aka Waters). Wright testified that he had been recruited by the captains of both companies, while Tobe Morris and Richard Smith joined the Laurens County company, the Buckeye Company. Wright accepted Walters's invitation. Tucker apparently recruited Tobe Morris to serve as the unit's secretary owing to his literacy, but Smith claimed to know why these men really had joined their county's independent black militia companies. According to Smith, "the object of the organization" was landownership and equality, because "if they, the white people, did not mind the negroes will have this land." More specifically, both Smith and Tobe Morris conveyed to Wright that the land was "government land" and "that the Negroes were justly entitled" to become property owners as a marker of citizenship, claims making, and autonomy. Tobe Morris also noted that "government land . . . must be cut up in government pieces," suggesting an equitable distribution to all American citizens.[58]

Having equal access to land and equitable distribution, the foundation for both economic and political power and autonomy in the United States, was especially important for blacks in the wake of the March 1875 passage of the Civil Rights Act. The Civil Rights Act of 1875 focused on public access to accommodations in hotels, restaurants, and jury duty, not on political and economic rights. Yet blacks viewed this law as critical in defining their public rights, citizenship, and economic foundation. The Act served as the endpoint to a series of Civil War and post–Civil War public and private rumors, assumptions, and promises to blacks, including the implied federal promise of land and empowerment to black citizens that reinforced their desire for autonomy. Black independent militiamen in the seven counties looked forward to federal officials enforcing their authority at the local level based on the tenets not only of the Civil Rights Act of 1875 but also of all federal efforts to support black citizenship.[59]

Land stood at the center of black claims making, public rights, and the struggle for values that shaped the process of emancipation and postemancipation black freedom in the Western Hemisphere. Economic viability, labor, citizenship, manhood, and violence also defined emancipation societies throughout the Western Hemisphere, where whites and blacks competed to determine the parameters of freedom and citizenship in the context of black claims making. Across the hemisphere the status and membership of blacks within the political community of their respective nation-states evolved as a point of contention between the races. The independent black militia companies involved in the Johnson County Insurrection were part of an ongoing hemisphere-wide contest over black and white conflicting visions of land ownership, labor, and control over black people. It also involved post–Civil War nation building, participation in governance, definitions of citizenship, and the contradictory atmosphere of claims making between blacks and whites. Government, too, evolved from the fragmented decentralized circumstances of local governance to centralized state and national governance.

These issues also defined Reconstruction and a post–Civil War United States South. Specifically, race, land redistribution, the federal role in governance, and political violence—all concerns since the summer of 1865 in North and South Carolina and since November 1865 in Georgia—were intimately connected. As Steven Hahn contends, "mutually reinforcing rumors of a world turned wholly upside down either by federal government fiat or armed black insurrection" reinforced what black freed people expected from emancipation and what whites feared. Hahn has asserted that this applies collectively to African Americans in the United States, and I would argue that this was true of blacks throughout the Western Hemisphere. Hahn notes that blacks "seemed to hold the rather vague belief that there would be 'some great change in the conditions of affairs.'" Southern whites, according to Hahn, also believed change was imminent, but their vision "warned of a race war, 'a negro Jubilee insurrection.'" Whites further worried about "a general division of property" whereby "'the Government [was] going to take the Planters land and other property from them and give it to the colored people,' or, failing that, . . . the blacks would carry out the deed themselves."[60] This was the context of Georgia's politics in the 1870s and of the 1875 Johnson County Insurrection.

Black militiamen Morris, Smith, and Wright provide evidence that this debate between the races in Georgia—wherein African Americans looked to the federal government as the defender of black public rights as well as of their vision and definitions of freedom—continued into the mid-1870s. Further, the coerced testimony from Johnson County's militiamen Ben Davis and Jake Mooreman seemed to confirm white fears that black power would overwhelm white power by force of arms. Smith and Morris, Wright asserted, believed that access to land was a right of black people "and they intended to have it or blood." Smith added that he "firmly believe[d] that the negroes intended to kill the white people and get their lands," and that their efforts would receive assistance "from the North or somewhere." These coerced statements reaffirmed white southern fears of federal intervention and black armed violence. Federal intervention, in the eyes of southern whites, included the centralizing and intrusive power of a national government bent on reshaping the South and empowering African Americans as citizens. Whites viewed federal power as antagonistic toward white dominance and restoration goals.

Wright claimed that "the tenor of the ... conversation [he had with Isaac Wright of Johnson County's independent black militia company] ... meant that whenever [blacks] got strong enough they would take the land—and take it by force if necessary." African American John Chiles's coerced statements reinforced this assertion, claiming that blacks joined the "secret military [independent militia] organization for the purpose of getting 'equality.'" According to Chiles, blacks meant "to take lands in this county by force and arms," even if doing so required them to "kill out the whites, beginning with the little babe in the crib, and killing all up." Chiles reinforced the standard white assertion that the intention of black political power was white annihilation.[61]

Morris addressed the question of land acquisition with black militiamen Andrea Peters and Tony Wright. He presented them with the vision "that each [African American] man should have a piece [of land]." "I believe that to be the impression of every man in the company," Morris continued. "From the language used ... they intended to take the land by force if necessary. At any rate ... to have the land, let what come that would."[62] Black violence, as these African American militiamen allegedly envisioned, would occur only "if necessary"; whites, on the other hand, concluded the exact opposite, namely, that black violence was lurking dangerously close. African Americans, however, had since the Civil War been anticipating gaining access to land, economic and political autonomy, and the acknowledgment of their citizenship. Their combined political and independent militia activity in 1875 was part of black claims making. This claims making occurred in a contradictory state after postwar and post-Reconstruction efforts at nation building by both black and white southerners.

White fears were reinforced by the coerced black descriptions of independent African American militia activities in which blacks met to organize and voice their agenda. They did this, white people believed, by drilling with arms and engaging in secret oath making. These actions taken together—but oath making specifically, whites thought—encouraged blacks to operate as a unified community against whites. Such unified military action triggered white fears of deadly slave insurrections such as the Haitian Revolution, wherein white property became black property and white governance came to an end.

Wright, Smith, and Morris each noted that militia meetings did not occur with any consistency; they also indicated that the militia companies at times failed to maintain a sustainable following. Wright reported that blacks in Laurens County met as a company but had limited opportunities for organized drilling. Morris, too, noted an irregular meeting schedule but also indicated that blacks met every, or every other, Saturday, suggesting some degree of regularity. The three eventually left their respective companies because of the alleged planned "mischief." Yet Johnson County militiamen Ben Davis and Jake Mooreman defined the independent black militia company as the military arm of a political organization tied directly to Joseph Morris and the summer political rally that held blacks united against whites with secret oaths and planned violence. Chiles reaffirmed the black desire for unity as Washington County's black militia, led by Corday Harris and Frances Murkerson, got unanimous African American participation. A correspondent for a white newspaper also reported that black collective action traversed age and gender, with black men, women, and children arming themselves with farm implements to prepare for a call to action against whites.[63]

The grand jury investigations pursued additional questions concerning the independent black militia company. White interrogators were persistent in attempting to determine exactly how the black militia unit operated: They wanted to know why these militia units came into being, who led them, and how they could separate leaders from followers. Georgia's solicitor general, John W. Robison, also served as prosecutor during the one-day Johnson County grand jury investigation. Robison assessed that the independent black militia company was not only "an organization" but "a secret organization in this county" that held "secret meetings." Mirroring antebellum investigations into slave insurrections, Robison, along with the Grand Juries in Johnson County and Washington County, focused on clandestine black behavior parallel to that of the Nat Turner rebellion forty-four years earlier in Virginia, the 1800 aborted slave conspiracy and revolt by Gabriel in Richmond, Virginia, and the initial stages of the Haitian Revolution nearly eighty years before the summer of 1875.

Robison looked to the past for answers to black behavior, but he also called African American John Chiles, a witness in the Cordy Harris case in Washington County, to testify against thirty-four African Americans. Chiles described how blacks in Johnson County organized for collective action. According to Chiles, militia leader Francis Murkerson journeyed to meet with Joseph Morris in Burke County at least once during the spring of 1875. In April 1875 he urged Johnson County black men to meet at Jake Mooreman's residence. Robison inquired of Chiles, "You say there was a secret meeting to organize—what was the Society called? I mean what were the men called who belonged to it—what was its name?" Chiles responded, "Well, Sir, the Society was called 'Brotheren.'" Robison asked, "What was the object of that Society?" Chiles hesitantly noted, "Well, Sir. It's hard to say. They 'was' to has something—a sort of equal rights . . . a civil rights bill—that the colored people were not [waiting?] to receive it & they was to make up some money & send three or four men [delegates] from each [militia] district to Waynesboro," in Burke County. Cordy Harris and Francis Murkerson "went together" to "see about this Civil Rights Bill" of 1875. In this context, Harris and Murkerson endeavored to promote a federally advocated new set of civil rights standards by making their "Society" the "Equal Rights Society" in Johnson County.[64]

With Jake Mooreman's home as their primary meeting place both before and after the Waynesboro meeting in the spring, more than twenty black men in Johnson County organized a militia company that also served as a militia district political organization, a civil rights advocacy group, and the vehicle for land ownership. The four-pronged independent militia company levied membership dues at a rigid fifty cents and required an oath of secrecy to keep their discussions within the black community. Murkerson led at least one meeting wherein members discussed obtaining access to land, including its division, distribution, and ownership. These black militiamen, as they sought to develop the independent militia company as a platform for local social, economic, and political power, also "raise[d] a 'treasury,'" anticipating that "if anything happened [they] would have money, if [they] wanted any protection." Chiles corrected Robison, stressing that Murkerson "didn't say whether [the land in question was] government land or this land" in Johnson County. Chiles contended that Murkerson "just said the land . . . 'was' [intended to allow blacks] to quit working the [county] roads under white overseers & such" and "to quit letting white folks sell [their] cotton." Blacks in the seven counties were seeking economic autonomy.

While Robison questioned Chiles in hopes of convicting blacks of insurrection, Chiles told a story of black men seeking self-mastery and pursuing economic and political autonomy and equality with their white neighbors. They also looked to federal civil rights legislation to prove their case for political and economic autonomy. Chiles and black people based their right to autonomy on the equally important right to organize themselves politically, and they utilized the independent militia company to achieve multiple economic and political aims.[65]

Contesting black desires for economic security and independence, Robison inquired, "What was to be done if there was any opposition to this division of the land?" Chiles asserted, "Nothing was said to the contrary. He just said we 'was' to divide the land." Robinson then countered, "Divide the land where? What land? In Kansas? . . . Did he say anything about your moving away from this County to get the land? . . . What did he say about property in this section of the County if he said anything?" In response, Chiles held his ground, arguing that Murkerson "didn't say anything particular about the property, only we 'was' to have 40 acres and a mule. He didn't say where we 'was' to get it from we 'was' to have it." Furthermore, Murkerson made no assertion "about [killing] the white people."[66]

Yet Chiles and Robison's discussion shifted to alleged black violence against whites during the insurrection. Robison claimed that Murkerson and colleagues sought to kill "white people & Democrat 'niggers'" and that they would do it "from the cradle up." Specifically the violence was to start as blacks "march[ed] down the road by Dr. Haines & through his yard & we 'was' to come to this place & they 'was' to kill from the cradle up when they started." The story conflicted here, as black masses were described as marching to Dr. Haines's to "plumb (illegible word) his yard," because "they didn't scept him," but Chiles claimed that he really "didn't know what" the purpose was, "except to Kill them I reckon." Robison, however, persisted, endeavoring to paint a picture of blacks threatening white property and profits. He asked Chiles, "After the white people were killed, what disposition was to be made of their crops, of the cotton, corn, [and] rice." According to Chiles, blacks were not just marching passed Dr. Haines's home but to the Johnson County seat in Wrightsville to "hold a mass meeting."[67] Robison then returned to the question of black people, work, and land, asking why Murkerson advised blacks to stop working under white supervision. There seemed to be two reasons. First, Murkerson encouraged blacks to control their own labor and productivity as an act of autonomy. Second, some of the black militiamen did not live independently. They resided with their employer and lacked economic and political autonomy.[68]

Colonel W. H. Wiley, a white militiaman with ties to Savannah, took over the prosecutorial questioning. He interrogated Jacob Mooreman, a primary witness before the Washington County grand jury called to testify in Johnson County. Wiley focused on the "secret military company or organization in this or adjoining counties among the colored people." He wanted to know who commanded the various black militia companies. Mooreman acknowledged that he had served as a first lieutenant in "our [Johnson County] company," a unit led by Captain Jerry Walker (aka Jerry Walters and Jerry Waters). In terms of who led blacks, Wiley inquired, "Was Jerry Walters under the [company—crossed out word] command of anybody? If so, whom?" Mooreman responded, "No more than Francis Murkerson and [Cordy] Harris," suggesting that local Johnson County blacks as well as African Americans in Laurens and Washington Counties formulated their own agendas and goals before meeting in Waynesboro to share political information. After the Waynesboro meeting, blacks proceeded to create the independent black militia companies, which served multiple economic and political objectives.[69]

Mooreman then contested "whether to call [the independent militia company] secret or not." He noted that those who joined the unit in Johnson County, including Jake Hicks, "called it The Band of Brothers." Their collective purpose was to support the Civil Rights bill of 1875. Specifically Mooreman reported, "When we first got up the Company—Murkerson & Harris said that the Radical men wanted to receive the Civil Rights Bill in Washington. If that was the case they were going to cut loose" by organizing politically with militia companies across the region, collecting money, and sending thirteen delegates from Laurens County, the lower end of Washington County and Johnson County to Burke County's principal municipality, Waynesboro. Political organizing apparently energized Murkerson, because on returning from Waynesboro, "He said he wanted to see the boys make up a Company" and "tell all that was done in Waynesboro." He focused on setting the parameters of black rights while stressing that "we could all have a military Company if we wanted to," because "we must all come together as a band of brothers." Out of that meeting apparently Company H was formed, under Jerry Walters. According to Mooreman, "The object of the military company . . . was only to drill &

have amusement." Murkerson, however, contended that there was more. Blacks joined the militia companies so that they could vote together. But such political solidarity had "no hostile designs" against whites "by force," or any intent to resist "any of the laws of the State of Georgia."[70]

Murkerson, Mooreman claimed, "made us a speech explaining why the Civil Rights Act of 1875" was important to blacks in Johnson County and the region. According to Mooreman, Murkerson "said it was not right to work the road under a white overseer—that was played out since Civil Rights," in March 1875, when the act became law. Murkerson advised, "If a white man [Sheriff or Ordinary] came around for you to work the road you mustn't do it. If a white man would not work under a colored overseer then he must work his end of the road & let the colored people work theirs." The Civil Rights Act of 1875 also empowered blacks to "ride on the train in the white folks car; if the conductor puts you off that is a fine. Then he goes on to say that if we made the crops ourselves we were to sell them ourselves." Additionally, "it was against the law for white men to sell your cotton without leave. That was your [black] privilege," which, Murkerson argued, extended to the right to vote. Murkerson told his fellow militiamen "how to vote," because "if we vote for [General Ulysses S.] Grant he would become King & all of this land would be his & instead of giving 1/3, 1/4 or 1/2 . . . to white men we would only give 1/10 to Grant." Further only Grant could assure forty acres of land to blacks at an affordable cost, along with the "time to pay for it."[71]

While Mooreman established blacks' desire for self-mastery and independent thinking in the region, he also described black initiative, in forming independent militia companies under the leadership of local blacks. Those who joined the independent militia units were not dupes of unscrupulous death-dealing demons. Both Murkerson and Mooreman affirmed the black goal to have economic autonomy as landowners and self-defined proprietors, as part of the promise of freedom and citizenship. Black economic autonomy, however, disturbed white assumptions about their own economic autonomy. As a result, Colonel Wiley expressed concern about the black abrogation of property and "any movement against the property of the whites in this section," by "any [black independent militia] order." Black militiamen such as Murkerson, Wiley contended, were "looking to injure or hurt the white people." Wiley was additionally aware of black out-migration to Kansas and other venues outside the South, suggesting that whites wanted to confine black labor in the region. Whites not only were disturbed by the black desire for land but also feared losing control over black labor and the autonomy that leaving the South offered African Americans.[72]

Mooreman's testimony and efforts to contradict white assumptions about the meaning, direction, and aims of the black militia company shifted to African American politics and the independent militia company as a political instrument. Meeting at Ben Davis's home, militia members learned the rudiments of militia drills and intended "to try the[ir] rights to [assemble publicly at] the Court House." They planned to convene for a thirty-five-delegate meeting in Washington County's primary community, Sandersville, on July 24, 1875. Murkerson stressed that black people must "never deny [their] profession," because any denial meant denying their rights. Following the July mass meeting, "orders" were issued from "Genl [Prince] Rivers & [Joe] Morris" for an August meeting. Murkerson and Harris also planned to have access to the Washington County Courthouse. In the wake of the July meeting, Murkerson and Harris intended to "succeed in [getting] the Court House," having apparently failed in July to obtain use of the facility. Success in Sandersville, they reasoned, would open the doors to each county seat and courthouse in the region, where blacks might "try [their] rights" first in Dublin in Laurens County and later in Wilkinson County, with Joseph Morris leading marches to four regional cities. Based on this testimony, it seemed that blacks intended to test their right to public meetings in public facilities such as the county courthouse—a central tenet of the Civil Rights Act of 1875.[73]

The key to the anticipated August mass meetings, however, was a letter ["not in evidence"] from Cordy Harris to Harrison Tucker that Jerry Walters was alleged to have lost around August 1. Murkerson's involvement suggests that blacks in Johnson County sought to be their own masters by "transact[ing] . . . business" and "not allow[ing]" any one or thing to prevent them from meeting their objectives. Mooreman, however, was never clear on what that goal was, except that they "would raise war & slay" at #11 station [Tennille railroad junction] in Johnson County. In cross-examination by defense attorney General R. W. Carswell, Mooreman testified that the business transaction involved only the militia company and that Murkerson was determined during his speech at the first organizational meeting to "transact . . . business even if [the company] had to kill others to do it." Yet Murkerson did not advocate "killing and slaying"; his principal aim "was telling [blacks] what . . . rights" they had "under the Civil

Rights Bill" of 1875, which included the right to vote, to elect General U. S. Grant "King," and to pay the federal government a tenth of their earnings in exchange for black landownership. But there was "nothing about killing [white] people." The grand jury adjourned after Carswell's cross-examinations. After deliberating "about an hour on Thursday Sept 9' 1875," the Johnson County grand jury found Jake Hicks and "all the defendants except Francis Murkerson, not guilty."[74]

While most blacks in the seven counties appear to have been freed after the grand jury investigations, blacks nevertheless paid a price for political and economic organizing. Corday Harris would be "convicted of the offense of Simple Larceny and sentenced therefore to twelve months in/on the Chain Gang" two or three years later. Despite petitions by Washington County's "best [white] citizens," who had served as jury members convicting Harris, and private citizens calling for judicial mercy while questioning the circumstantial evidence that convicted Harris, Rev. Corday Harris "served nearly the full period of his penalty." Governor Alfred Colquitt released Harris with clemency instead of a pardon because "a pardon will not shorten the punishment" and "clemency will not impune the public interest." Colquitt ended Harris's sentence owing to the power and request of Washington County's leading citizens and Harris's "good conduct before and since his conviction." Harris paid for organizing Washington County blacks, as did other African American political actors, including Tunis Campbell.[75] The *Savannah Tribune* bitterly asserted at the beginning of 1876 that Washington County had executed blacks captured during the alleged 1875 insurrection.[76]

Nevertheless, the 1875 Johnson County Insurrection was one of many emancipation and postemancipation attempts by Georgia's African Americans to shape the parameters of their freedom, which included public rights and the struggle for values, manhood, masculinity, self-mastery, claims making, and autonomy. Black efforts to acquire self-mastery, autonomy, and manhood occurred alongside efforts to control the new post–Civil War environment in which they sought to live as full citizens. Their objective was economic autonomy, the exercise of political rights, the right to free assembly, and a self-mastery of all it meant to be black, a person, and a citizen of the United States after the Civil War. Collectively, blacks sought to exercise public rights and make proper claim to their rightful participation in the reunited nation wherein the Thirteenth, Fourteenth and Fifteenth Amendments to the U.S. Constitution and the supporting

Civil Rights Acts of 1866 and 1875 defined the parameters of freedom, citizenship, and the struggle for values. The seven rural counties in middle and eastern Georgia were a hotbed of black political activity from the moment of emancipation into the twentieth century. Their efforts did not meet with much success, even when African Americans from these counties pursued emigration to Africa in 1894, nearly a generation after the 1875 insurrection. Yet blacks continually sought to establish their political and economic autonomy through claims making, despite white repression during the "insurrection" and across the generations that followed.[77]

The independent militia company lent itself to this process during the emancipation, Reconstruction, and the immediate post-Reconstruction years in Georgia. The independent militia company enabled rural black people to mobilize and organize. The independent militia company filled a gap for blacks at the county level. It provided a means of organizing African Americans to confront the absence of civil rights and economic opportunity. From the beginning of Reconstruction through the 1870s, it was a vehicle for black community advocacy and a platform for political participation. The independent black militia unit also offered African Americans a chance to demonstrate their commitment to a new governmental vision that seemed to anticipate their full participation and engagement as equals with their rural white neighbors. They further expected equality as state citizens. These ideals were expressed both in militia membership and in efforts to wield power as county level administrators and political officials. Black people in Burke, Jefferson, Johnson, Laurens, Richmond, Washington, and Wilkinson Counties envisioned the independent militia company as a military institution and political organization that yielded economic, political, and social autonomy and the power of self-mastery. It was one of their weapons of claims making.

The independent militia company also supported black manhood, as blacks in the seven rural counties sought in 1875 to be the masters of their fate, labor, ballot, bodies, and souls. They separately and collectively challenged white parallel institutions such as the independent militia company and the county-level political party as they staked their claim to citizenship in the United States and their allegiance to Georgia. For blacks, the independent militia company in rural Georgia and the emerging black state-sponsored militia companies in the cities met and organized not only to drill, muster, and conduct social activities but also to prove that African Americans, as citizens of Georgia and the United States, were armed with the right to vote, by federal authority, and with the right to use public facilities, according to the Civil Rights Act of 1875. Whites, meanwhile, also looked to the militia company, both independent and state-sponsored, to restore traditions that dated to the American Revolution, when white citizenship was defined by militia service, violence, and dominance at the local level.

3

CREATING THE GEORGIA MILITIA

Blacks and the Road to State Militia Companies, 1865–1880

Two events in January 1872 defined white male power. The first involved the white male right to firearms. Page one of the *Savannah Morning News*, in the "Affairs in Georgia" section, noted on January 8 the following incident in Columbus, Georgia: Mr. James Long "called upon Miss Mary Williams, wearing upon his warlike person the usual pistol," because the "young men of Columbus wear pistols." The *Morning News* did question why Mr. Long needed his firearm "when . . . call[ing] on young ladies . . . for what sanguinary purpose, current commentators do not presume to suggest." Long, nevertheless, wore his pistol that romantic evening with Miss Williams. Sometime during their socializing the gun "accidentally dropped to the floor and shot the young lady in the leg. Long didn't stay long after that. After the pistol went off, he went off too, and it is hoped that he will hereafter eliminate from his person all firearms." While James Long violated the protocols of courtship by wearing his pistol, he reconfirmed the white male right to be armed as a symbol of his collateral right to violent self-defense. Those, such as Charles Nordhoff, who observed the Reconstruction process and the South's post–Civil War evolution found that men and "even boys of fourteen" were armed in public. Having a pistol, as James Long demonstrated, "was an almost universal" part of a man's personal attire and was central to defining the male persona. According to Nordhoff, men resolved "every trifling dispute" with a firearm.[1] In Columbus, Georgia, armed whites made black life dangerous, as whites used force to reassert their right to rule.

The second event occurred on January 13, 1872. On that day, James Milton Smith was inaugurated governor before "Georgia's fair daughters to honor the dawning of the new era" of Democratic Party control of state government, a white triumph over African Americans and Radical

Reconstruction.[2] With this political victory, economic and political power formally shifted from the Republican Party to the Democratic Party. The passing of power from one political party to another had broader repercussions. The shift marked a looming change in how Georgians, black and white, defined the state's military, especially its independent militia units. Federal power also played a role in repositioning the militia. The U.S. Congress, a year after Smith's inauguration, authorized Georgia to organize, statewide, a state-sponsored militia, the Georgia Volunteers. Georgia could restore its militia with the caveat that the state militia would be open to both races. State authorities in 1873 also announced, "Any person capable of doing military duty (not under 16 years of age) may be enrolled as a volunteer." This race-neutral clause was countered with the legislative stipulation that "every [militia] company and battalion must be composed of men of the same race and color." With this edict Georgia officially segregated the state militia and initiated a county-level racial, military, and weaponry competition in the battle for political supremacy.[3]

The fight for political supremacy at the county level manifested itself within black and white efforts to construct local militia companies. For some white Georgia communities, political supremacy and independent and state-sponsored militia formation were critical to countering black independent militia organizing and African American petitions for state-sponsored militia companies. In at least seven Georgia counties, whites combined political dominance with economic supremacy. Whites in these communities found themselves in political combat with blacks. They fought over who would control African American labor, determine the local economy, and assert political supremacy at the county level. As a result, white citizens in Burke, Jefferson, Johnson, Laurens, Richmond, Washington, and Wilkinson Counties responded to black power in ways similar to how whites across the Western Hemisphere had separately defined black political action, namely, as Haitianization—the exercising of black economic and political power whereby blacks "might take over" a governing structure by force and turn a community into "a black republic," thereby effecting the Africanization of white life. Instead of seeing black citizens participating in the established political process, whites saw "insurrection"—the Johnson County Insurrection of 1875.[4]

This chapter examines the white and black competition for a state-sponsored militia company, the formation of black state-sponsored militia units, and the white conception of the Johnson County Insurrection, which involved whites' pursuit of the means to control the intrusion of change the Civil War initiated. Rural communities, such as the seven counties in central and eastern Georgia, wrestled with postwar change. The Civil War had eroded and sometimes destroyed the antebellum plantation traditions that had defined the rural South and white male dominance. The plantation economy and planter regulation of labor, politics, and autonomy served as the local community's prewar foundation. Local whites had hoped to continue these traditions after the Civil War. What whites did not see was that change had already arrived through initiatives that they themselves had introduced both before and after the war. Specifically, the railroads and newspapers both undermined and reinforced white efforts to impose white dominance in rural Georgia. These two institutions introduced changes that in turn initiated the transformation of white manhood and southern racial identity, as whites searched for order and the restoration of a lost antebellum culture, into what Grace Elizabeth Hale has called the "new culture of segregation"—an effort to control capital industrialization, urbanization, and the new consumer culture.[5]

Benevolent Associations

From 1872 to 1880 blacks and whites in Georgia's counties competed locally, first, to create an independent militia company and, then, after organizing such a unit, to secure the governor's attention by way of petition to establish a state-sponsored militia company. Such authorization by the governor translated into state permission to elect officers to lead the company and to utilize state-provided weaponry, thus making the unit a state-sponsored organization that agreed to utilize force under the command and leadership of Georgia's governors. The state of Georgia provided arms and ammunition, while members of the unit were responsible for their uniforms. Both races had been organizing military organizations from as early as the late 1860s as benevolent associations. Whites submerged their militia connection to the Civil War by claiming that after the war these units were benevolent associations that had no militia or military function. White men also sought to disconnect their organized Civil War militia service from a prewar independent militia tradition directly connected to controlling slaves with slave patrols. Some of these militia companies possessed legacies dating back to the American Revolution and prerevolutionary Georgia. White and black military veterans looked forward to a time in the early to mid-1870s when their benevolent groups could become independent militia companies. Whites also hoped to be recalled by the state to military duty as representatives of both county and state governmental power. That call came in 1872–73, when black and white men, in groups of fifty to sixty-five, organized independent militia companies without state initiative. With a state call for state-sponsored units, many companies petitioned the governor for official recognition and for permission to elect militia company officers, which would make the group a formal government agency.

While blacks formed state-sponsored and independent militia companies for different reasons—the former to prove their citizenship and the latter to defend black political and economic autonomy—they utilized both to define freedom and citizenship. Whites in the same communities organized to counter rising black political power that at times included a rural independent black militia company. Whites pursued the independent and state-sponsored militia company in hopes of preserving white dominance locally and statewide. In the case of the white state-sponsored unit in the 1870s and part of the 1880s, whites envisioned a state military controlled by the governor and a Democratic Party candidate and always independent of the federal government's centralizing power.

The year 1873 gave credence to former Confederates with concerns about federal power. These men had long inquired "whether there exists any Federal law forbidding the forming of volunteer companies in the Southern States?" The inquiry was in part a way to change the standing of "our *ante bellum* volunteer corps . . . maintained since the war, as benevolent associations" into militia units again. White queries also reflected the previous year's political power shift from biracial Republican Party governance to white-dominated Democratic Party rule over Georgia. The inquiry for militia restoration came from Macon and Savannah, Georgia—white political power centers in close proximity to the counties where African Americans challenged white dominance in 1875. White members of Savannah's and Macon's benevolent organizations were eager to reconstitute these community service institutions as militia companies recognized and supported by state government.[6]

Yet benevolent association members hesitated to openly transform the associations, since there was "a diversity of opinion as to the advisability of such a move on the part of the volunteer companies at present time." Doing so could invite federal intervention, despite Union League activity supporting the Republican Party and countering competing white paramilitary forces and benevolent associations. To alleviate what whites perceived to be federal concerns, at least one benevolent association argued that the white "volunteer companies of former times were never partisan in their character, and it is not probable ... in the future." Ex-Confederates contended that their desire to organize militia companies was for "personal and social" reasons of soldierly comradeship. In the spring of 1872, however, Georgia's Confederate veterans pointed to New Orleans, Louisiana, and Mobile, Alabama, as locations where "volunteer militia companies ... composed mainly of soldiers of the late Confederate army [were] commanded by ex-Confederate officers." These units, especially in Mobile, had been "reorganized and.... armed" and served a powerful white partisan function in state politics.[7]

What white Georgia militia advocates in 1872 did not acknowledge in the newspaper was that both New Orleans and Mobile were sites where ex-Confederates linked military comradeship, politics, and antiblack violence with white power and the restoration of white governance and dominance. White militiamen also withheld evidence of the militia's longstanding commitment to merge antebellum objectives with postbellum objectives of property protection, plantation and race management, race control, and insurrection prevention—all objectives of whites hoping to contest the involvement of black people in the Johnson County Insurrection. As a result, the antebellum southern militia had operated to maintain the boundaries of slavery and white control over enslaved black labor, while the postbellum white militia aimed to restore white rule and black subordination. Specifically, the antebellum militia protected slaves as property and operated in cooperation with the federal military and local slave patrols to deter slave insurrections that whites believed could spiral out of control. As an example, U.S. slaves, just as black slaves in Haiti had done in the 1790s, embraced the revolutionary and trans-Atlantic ideals of "liberty, equality, and fraternity"—the foundational principles of individual autonomy and self-rule across the Western Hemisphere that both races embraced in the nineteenth century.[8]

After the Civil War white Georgians in Macon and Savannah publicly claimed, despite the highly partisan and violent nature of Georgia and southern politics during Reconstruction, that the militia was a nonpartisan benevolent association. Whites subsumed the militia's antebellum responsibilities, which had not ceased to exist, within this proposed nonpartisan institution until a new militia could emerge with the permission of the federal government, which had prohibited the maintenance of post–Civil War militia from 1867 to 1873. That subsumed role would be revived with the new county-based independent and state-sponsored militia companies, whose responsibilities included maintaining white political dominance, managing blacks, preventing black insurrection, obstructing black political governance and power, and maintaining white control over the balance of violence, which was the primary function of the antebellum and postbellum white militia.[9]

Who Controls the County?

For Georgia whites, the militia would be a partisan and sometimes violent tool for imposing white political and economic dominance. As a result, white militiamen, in direct competition with blacks for permission to create a militia unit, made clear that their primary reason for forming a militia unit was to impose their will on the county. They envisioned continuing the militia's role in race control by "arrest[ing] . . . armed bod[ies] of negroes," removing blacks from public office, and "plac[ing white] officers of the law in their positions" to restore white governance. The white militia company was also intended to prevent "the attempt being made by the colored population to organize" using "the assistance of the state [in] thus giving them [blacks] a preponderance in strength over the white population, whom they already greatly outnumber." Further, the governor, who granted a white militia company permission to organize, ensured "harmony [and] tranquility," because "the reverse action [allowing the existence of a black militia company] may lead to disastrous consequences, inflating the pride and insolence of the other class."

For another set of whites, the militia company connected them to a past that continued unbroken from the American Revolution and until the closing days of the Confederacy and the early moments of Reconstruction. The postbellum white militia company constituted a clear link across time whereby a "distinguished reputation" as a white service institution and as an instrument of war was "closely [associated] with the prosperity of our county, its pride & boast." In this context the white militia unit became one of several post–Civil War institutions that whites used to resist the forces of change unleashed upon the South by the Civil War and Emancipation and to reorganize the white mechanisms that had defined pre–Civil War southern white society.[10]

In late July 1868 "twenty-odd" white men, probably former Confederate soldiers, answered a call to meet published in the *Savannah Morning News*. These men convened "to consider the feasibility of a reorganization of the old company," the Savannah Cadets. By early September, the "corps" membership discussed the need "for the mutual defense of our just rights." According to Savannah Cadets' member Private Weldrim, the initiator of this discussion at the September 8, 1868, meeting, white rights were "now in peril from the secret organizations of negroes and radicals in this section of the state." Weldrim called for the creation of a committee of three Cadets to reach out to "the other organizations in the city and consider the expediency of organizing for the mutual defense of our just rights." The threat came from black militia and African American political power. Even though Weldrim was only a private in the Savannah Cadets, his proposal earned him the committee chairmanship. Weldrim, now at the head of the effort to stem the tide of emerging black military and political power, contacted other white units in Savannah "to confer" and make policy concerning the black threat to white rights.

More problematic for Weldrim was Savannah's other white military organizations, who responded to his suggested white solidarity with silence. No one replied, despite the increasing presence of black militiamen in the region. Weldrim's influence, however, did not decrease. He led the unit's continuing efforts to communicate with fellow units and was responsible for widely distributing the company's by-laws across Savannah in an effort to increase membership. In the end the Savannah Cadets struggled with low membership, and in an effort to liven up dull meetings and lessen the pain of an "unwarrantable amount of dues" they made their meetings quarterly and their rifle practice monthly. The Cadets also debated whether they should equip themselves with rifles and uniforms in preparation for the celebration of Robert E. Lee's birthday. By 1872 these issues had been resolved and the unit solidified, with over sixty members. Weldrim, nevertheless, articulated for Savannah whites, especially some white militiamen, the fear of blacks with guns, equal status, and the benefits of citizenship.[11]

Four years after the organizational meeting of the Savannah Cadets in 1868, Reconstruction had been defeated and Democrat James Milton Smith was governor. Ironically, while federal power was not utilized to defend Reconstruction, federal dictates ended a six-year moratorium on Georgia operating a state-sponsored and -controlled militia responsible to the governor of Georgia. With Democratic rule replacing Republican in 1872, white Georgians were emboldened to challenge blacks for local political and military supremacy, even to the point of demanding number one status in county governance. Four days after celebrating Independence Day with a meeting to resuscitate "the Liberty Independent

Troops," forty-eight whites petitioned Governor Smith for the right to reorganize "the oldest" mounted volunteer cavalry company "South of Masons' & Dixon's line, & the oldest of any volunteer corps ever existing in the state of Georgia, the [Savannah, Georgia, area] Chatham Artillery excepted."

The members presented four reasons "why we desire this particular branch of the service (cavalry), as well as to forestall any attempts which may be made to anticipate our action & secure your favor." First, a cavalry unit in coastal Georgia could cover more geography more rapidly than an infantry unit could. Second, to counter "the attempt being made by the colored population to organize & sustain the assistance of the state thus giving them a preponderance in strength over the white population, whom they already greatly outnumber." Third, "the white population having been greatly reduced in pecuniary resources by the late war, & being despoiled of their arms, have not been able to supply the deficit, whereas outsiders (?) took occasion by our defeat, to supply the other class [blacks] with the same." Fourth, "the reorganization of the L.I. Troops with the assistance furnished by the state, is exceedingly appropriate & conducive to harmony [and] tranquility, and the reverse action may lead to disastrous consequences, inflating the pride and insolence of the other class."

Finally the petitioners added that the Liberty Independent Troops' traditions reached back nearly to the American Revolution and that it played a role in the Confederacy. More important, this cavalry unit possessed a "distinguished reputation . . . closely [associated] with the prosperity of our county, its pride & boast." For whites in Liberty County, the militia served as an institution that was important to the defense of tradition and provided clear evidence of which class considered its claim to leadership and power to be predicated on its members' political, economic, and social legacy within the county. The militia company was also an economic engine. Reestablishing the traditions and dominance of the Liberty Independent Troops was vital in the competition with newly freed African Americans. Being the first and perhaps only militia company sustained by the state of Georgia in Liberty County was vitally important to members of the white elite. This class made the militia a significant institution in securing political power at the county level of governance.[12] Liberty County's issue with African American power was not limited to the county only. Rev. Tunis Campbell, the rising power of black people, and the black independent militia in McIntosh County bordered Liberty County to the south. Chatham County and the city of Savannah, with their multiple developing state-sponsored black militia companies, were on Liberty County's northeast border.

Another cavalry petition came from Ogeechee County in 1872. Ogeechee whites organized a "posse of one hundred and fifty men." Their request included state defrayment of horse rentals to counter and "arrest . . . an armed body of negroes." Blacks, the telegram to the governor asserted, had "beaten & driven off" whites as well as usurped positions of authority in the county. Ogeechee whites additionally asked that Gov. Smith sanction white efforts to organize "a large [cavalry] mounted force" strong enough to "arrest [the black] offenders . . . and place officers of the law in their positions."[13]

Whites also counted on their whiteness to make their claim to a militia company more essential than black applications that predated white organizing efforts. Bartow, Georgia, "citizens" in Jefferson County who served in the Fourteenth Georgia Regiment of the Confederate States of America reminded Governor James Milton Smith about Republican proscriptions against white militia formation during Reconstruction. Specifically in August 1870 Republican Governor Rufus Bullock "commanded" Bartow whites "to cease organizing as such organizations would not be allowed" by federal authorities. But in June 1872, "seeing that companies [were] being organized in different parts of the state," Jefferson County's A. T. Harman thought he "would ascertain if we would be allowed to organize now?" Whites in Jonesboro, Georgia, south of Atlanta, in June 1872 petitioned Governor Smith for permission to "take the liberty . . . to raise a volunteer company of Whites in" Clayton County.

Whites in Thomas County on the Georgia-Florida border in Thomasville, Georgia, announced on July 13, 1872, their intention "to organize a volunteer company under the laws of Georgia." Claiming to have complied with the Georgia code that set the standards for how many men were needed to create a militia unit, be it state-sponsored volunteers or an independent militia company, Thomasville whites called upon the governor's professed white racial solidarity to better qualify their request to organize. Thomasville white men declared, "We are afraid however that the *Colored* portion of our community has taken like action and that their papers applying for organization will preceed ours by about 24 hours. We would ask if consistent with your duties that our organization be considered the senior one in Thomas Co."

Morgan County whites in central Georgia pursued a response from Governor Smith in June and July 1872. In both instances Morgan County "citizens" called upon Smith's white racial solidarity to make the difference between their application for a militia unit and that of Morgan County blacks. On June 11, 1872, "some . . . [white] citizens" in Morgan County wanted to know "whether or not the negroes of Morgan County ha[d] notified [the governor] of the organization of a Military Company." Concerned about the balance of weaponry, Morgan County whites demanded to know "what [would] be the Quota of Arms *that* Morgan County will be entitled to in the distribution? They desire[d] to know these facts in order to keep the Arms out of the hands of the negroes, in case there should not be more than enough for one Company. And on the other hand if there should be more Arms coming . . . than enough for one company . . . [their] object was to remain quiet and not stir them by example." Three weeks later, Seaborn Reese, the author of both letters, represented "the officers elect of the R. E. Lee Volunteers." Reese inquired as to why the officers' commissions "have never been sent them?" In the interim, "since [Morgan County's] election [of militia officers,] there has been a Negro company organized." Reese made it clear what the Lee Volunteers wanted from the governor: "Now what we desire is to supercede the negro organization as we are justly entitled to it whether we ever get any arms or not."[14]

White racial unity was not the sole measure of influence that whites utilized to guarantee the governor's acceptance of their militia applications. Whites in Culverton, Georgia, in Hancock County bordering Washington and Jefferson Counties, hoped to use the power of their voting strength to sway Smith's decision. At the end of their letter, Culverton whites inquired, "Is our county entitle[d] to two companies or more. We vote[d for you at] about 2200." The "citizens" of Bethany, Georgia, in Jefferson County, on July 18, 1872, convened together "for the purpose of organizing a Volunteer Cavalry Company." They contended, "Our object is . . . to organize and perfect ourselves in the use of the Sabre and to train ourselves and horses in the different moves and drills incident to this branch of the services and in case of a riot—similar to that of August 1870 [Cudjo Fye] in the suppression of which your petitioners took an active part." Further the suppression of Cudjo Fye caused "therewith [to] be no necessity of Federal intervention." Bethany citizens argued that they had used their personal weapons to bring peace and harmony to the community and therefore needed the state to "furnish such" so that the white military supremacy they had achieved with their personal weapons might continue.[15]

A few white units did not blatantly pursue race as their primary method of getting acceptance as official members of the Georgia Volunteers. In Atlanta and Augusta, Georgia, respectively, "the best young men of the city" and "young men of good standing, a credit to themselves and to the State," totaling nearly "some sixty strong," each met to form the "Atlanta Cadets" and "Oglethorpe Infantry" companies in July and June 1872. The Atlanta Cadets also elected Governor Smith to be "an honorary member of the Company," in part celebrating the triumph of the Democrats over Republican rule.[16]

One east Georgia unit hoped to use the power of the militia not only to certify their own existence but also to stand prepared to engage any opposition to Democratic Party rule. The Savannah Cadets, private Weldrim's company, in July 1872 asked Governor Smith to commission their officers for a parade and "in case of trouble with the blacks on the day on which you are to be elected the next Governor of Georgia." Claiming to be "the only . . . uniformed and thoroughly armed, equipped, and drilled" militia unit in Savannah, the seventy-member company pressed James Milton Smith for their commissions and for recognition as a state institution. The Cadets wanted the authority "to preserve the peace" and "go in lawfully as a regular part of the state forces acting under orders of the state officer in charge and not as a mob without any lawful officers to command us." If Savannah Cadet officers were not commissioned soon the unit "would have to go as a mob with no order or discipline." Further, such a failure of the governor-elect to act gave blacks an "excuse for raising a row."[17]

White leaders also promoted the formation of militia companies to forestall the emergence of black political and economic power, whether that power came from the ballot box, from wages and control over black labor, from freedom of movement, or from the competition for each county's military supremacy. Whites mobilized to take advantage of the re-emergence of white power after the Civil War "destroyed the labor system" and a way of life that justified white dominance. Georgia whites additionally sought to recall and re-create antebellum and early war years. One symbol of this time was the military uniform, which for white southerners held strong memories of antebellum times. White postwar militiamen, if given the choice, preferred "the gray [Confederate] uniform" in their effort to re-create the past as the new militia emerged as an important local institution.[18]

In some Georgia counties, creating a militia company meant privileging whiteness over blackness, even if African Americans had fairly utilized the postwar rules for militia formation and thereby secured the first right to create a company long before whites organized. Blacks combined politics, self-protection, the right to organize politically, and militia formation in an effort to define freedom and prevent white efforts to restore their dominance at the local level. For whites, a militia company meant preparing for the "anticipated [black American] insurrection" or race war in the contest over who was organized enough to rule at the county level.[19]

Black State-Sponsored Militia Formation

African Americans petitioned Georgia's Governors, James Milton Smith (1872–1877) and Alfred H. Colquitt (1877–1882), for official recognition of their companies as state-sponsored units. Black petitions came as the Democratic Party went about the work of consolidating its power over the Republican Party, both statewide and at the county level. Black militia petitions, from 1872 to 1880, downplayed race and instead emphasized citizenship, loyalty, character, adherence to the law, and acceptance by local whites, stressing black respectability and a nonthreatening posture focused on the interests of the greater society. Walter H. Johnson of Columbus, Georgia, despite the hazards to black life in that city, took the chance and petitioned Governor Smith in 1872 "for the purpose of organizing a military company." He "sent . . . a roll of names of [Columbus] colored people," but when Smith failed to respond, Johnson, in July 1872, requested of Smith, "Will you please be kind enough to return the roll?" Two years later, Walter Johnson no longer served as secretary for the "Columbus Volunteers," and Joseph Ferguson, the new Columbus Volunteers secretary, submitted "a list of names . . . and a petition asking for an official order from" Governor Smith "to hold and [sic] election for [company] officers." With fifty-nine members in 1874, the Columbus Volunteers survived to be one of the forty-two "colored companies" serving Georgia in 1878.[20]

The Savannah Chatham Light Infantry and Lincoln Association in Savannah, Georgia, created black militia companies three months before whites, in the Savannah Cadets and nearby Liberty Independent Troops, could officially mobilize and petition Governor Smith to authorize parallel but competing militia units. While the Liberty Independent Troops argued for a white militia company to counter the local black presence, the

Table 1. Roster of Colored Companies, Georgia, 1878

Name of Company	Name of Captain	Location in Georgia
1. Athens Blues	W. A. Pledger	Athens
2. Atlanta Light Infantry[a]	Jefferson Wyly	Atlanta
3. Butler Light Infantry	F. Fluker	Quitman
4. Bibb County Blues	Spencer Moseley	Macon
5. Bainbridge Guards	W. O. Crawford	Bainbridge
6. Columbus Volunteers[a]	W. Allbright	Columbus
7. Chatham Light Infantry[a]	J. H. Gardner	Savannah
8. City Blues	E. Ansley	Americus
9. Central City Light Infantry[a]	George Wallace	Macon
10. Colored Home Guard	Fred Reid	Madison
11. Columbus Light Infantry	G. P. Lewis	Columbus
12. Colquitt Blues[a]	W. H. DeLyon	Savannah
13. Capital Guards[a]	C. C. Wimbush	Atlanta
14. Colquitt Zouaves[a]	J. Tyler	Augusta
15. Douglass Infantry[a]	T. P. Beard	Augusta
16. Forest City Light Infantry (A)[a]	W. H. Woodhouse	Savannah
17. Forest City Light Infantry (B)[a]	E. J. Colvin	Savannah
18. Forest City Light Infantry (C)[a]	R. H. Burke	Savannah
19. Fulton Blues[b]	Smith Easley	Atlanta
20. Georgia Infantry[a]	John Stiles	Savannah
21. Griffin Light Infantry	L. W. Beeks	Griffin
22. Georgia Volunteers[a]	John C. Shelton	Atlanta
23. Grant Guards	Jasper Mitchell	LaGrange
24. Georgia Infantry[a]	Arthur S. Kimbles	Augusta
25. Glynn County Militia Guards	A. Braxton	Brunswick
26. Home Guards	Wade H. Green	Irwinton
27. Harrisburg Blues[a]	O. T. Adams	Midway
28. Lincoln Guards[a]	T. N. M. Sellers	Macon
29. Lone Star Cadets[a]	M. A. Grant	Savannah
30. Lincoln Guards	H. H. Hutchinson	Valdosta
31. Middle Georgia Volunteers[a]	R. Collins	Milledgeville
32. Putnam Blues	W. M. Adams	Eatonton
33. Reid Rifle (Boys)[a]	Walter Reid	Macon
34. Richmond Guards	Daniel Lamar (?)	Augusta
35. Savannah Light Infantry[a]	W. H. Royal	Savannah
36. Thomasville Independents[a]	J. S. Flipper	Thomasville
37. Union Blues[a]	E. Hamilton	Thomasville
38. Union Delmonico Guards[a]	C. Green	Savannah
39. Union Lincoln Guards[a]	M. J. Cumming	Savannah
40. Washington Guards[a]	T. Turner	Atlanta
41. Savannah Hussars; Cavalry Co.[a]	Capt. W. H. Bell	Savannah
42. Georgia Artillery; Artillery Co.[a]	Capt. George McCarty	Savannah

Source: Compiled by Sidney Herbert of the *Savannah Morning News*.
Notes: a. Active or live companies
b. Dead companies
Companies with no identifying mark have an unknown status—active or inactive—within the Georgia Volunteers and Georgia Volunteers, Colored.

Savannah Cadets, on March 22, 1872, entertained a motion to acquaint the governor by letter "with the fact that this company is regularly organized as a military body." The Cadets also wanted arms and "use of the state arsenal in conjunction with other military companies in the city" to drill. They also wanted to receive officers' commissions and the authority to put black militiamen in their place without a militia company. By early April the Cadets formed a three-person committee asking the governor to "prescribe a uniform and order an election" for company officers.

African Americans in the Savannah Chatham Light Infantry, in spite of white petitions and organizing, sought commissions and a pathway to avoid confrontations with whites. Applying for admission to the state militia on April 22, 1872, with "a prayer [ful]" petition and respect for the governor's office, the Chatham Light Infantry endeavored to prove that its sixty-seven members were law-abiding and loyal citizens of the nation. Specifically, "the petitioners met together and in accordance with the Laws of the Land organized themselves as a Volunteer Military Company." The members, represented by John Gardiner Jr., Stetson Law, Augustus Johnson, and David Ellison, reinforced their commitment to law and order by adopting "a Constitution and By-Laws in harmony with the Constitution of the United States and of this State and laws" for a Georgia militia company.

More important, these black petitioners "did not organize themselves together for the purpose of doing anything inconsistent with their duties as Citizens of this State or of the United States, but to carry out what they are advised to believe and do believe in the true spirit of the Laws . . . that they might thereby be enabled to inform themselves of the duties of Soldiers." This included "the general military Tactics of the Country" so that blacks in Savannah might be prepared "if needed . . . to respond" in defense of the nation. Like the white Savannah Cadets, the black Savannah Chatham Light Infantry petitioned to commission its officers, yet the African American militiamen also urged the governor to use his authority to "ensure justice" and "at the proper time to furnish the necessary arms and accoutrements."[21]

Five days later in Savannah, on April 27, 1872, the Lincoln Association, a black benevolent association with 130 African American members, met to transform the association into a state-sponsored militia company. Lincoln Association members nominated "permanent officers to command our new organization" and planned to model their uniforms on the blue Union army's Civil War uniform. They hoped to utilize militia status as another way to verify their "citizenship and connection to the Union victory."[22]

Both Governor James M. Smith and Governor Alfred Colquitt, in 1872 and 1878, respectively, received petitions to create a militia company of African Americans seeking to organize the Forest City Light Infantry in Savannah. Each petition carried with it the promise of white assistance or a supporting endorsement. In 1872 attorney A. W. Stone filed the petition for fifty-three "uniformed" African Americans who declared themselves "citizens of the United States and the state of Georgia and residents of Chatham County." The company, also like some white militia units in the South, included a membership category for six "Honorary" members. In 1878 membership in the Forest City Light Infantry had grown by thirty-two, to eighty-five militiamen. This second attempt at organization repeated the black claim to citizenship in the state of Georgia and Chatham County, but in 1878 U.S. citizenship was either assumed or not an issue that blacks felt it wise to publicly remind Governor Colquitt and other whites of.

Georgia militia colonel Clifford W. Anderson, the white commanding officer of Georgia's First Regiment of Volunteer white militiamen, endorsed the Forest City Light Infantry's 1878 application. Anderson "approved" the application because the "leading Spirits in this proposed organization are worthy colored Citizens" who "will reflect credit on the Volunteer force of Ga." Anderson's endorsement did not establish precedence since, on July 21, 1877, the Savannah Light Infantry came into being with white militia acceptance of "over fifty . . . all already well disciplined" black "residents and citizens . . . of Savannah" who sought to create "a military organization." The company, like the Forest City Light Infantry in 1878, gained white militia support from the commander of the First Regiment for the right to organize the unit and elect company officers. More specifically, the white commanding officer conveyed his support by "earnestly recommend[ing] that the petition be granted." Anderson's 1877 and 1878 endorsements as a high-ranking militia officer marked a significant shift in white attitudes, as reflected in those of private Weldrim and the Savannah Cadets. Anderson would join other white officials later in 1878 to remind the Savannah public of this change.[23]

Georgia's lone African American cavalry unit, the Savannah Hussars, was organized in the early 1870s. This solitary unit came into being against the backdrop of sixty-nine white mounted companies. The Hussars also earned endorsement from at least one white Savannah civic leader who vouched for the company's seventy-two black members, mostly local black butchers. The unit's commanding officer, William H. Bell, wrote the petition letter to Governor Alfred H. Colquitt on June 22, 1877. The proposed company "ask[ed the Governor's] *favor*" of official recognition. Bell characterized the black participants as having "united wishes" and "a desire of becoming duly organized . . . as all good citizens would" to be "formed into a Similar organization [a cavalry company]."

The Savannah Hussars also sought to use a positive public appearance to secure official acceptance as a company in the state militia, the Georgia Volunteers. The black cavalry unit's leadership pursued this public acknowledgment and elevation to official membership in the Georgia militia because the Hussars had paraded in Savannah's May 25, 1877, "Grand Review" with Governor Colquitt in attendance. As a result, the Hussars felt "assured" that Governor Colquitt had "an idea of" them: "[This] prompts me and my comrades in the name of good Citizens . . . to beg your Excellency to grant us the favor that we have the Honor of asking Your Honor . . . that this Petition will meet with your favor."

Robert H. Anderson, a leading white in Savannah, eleven days later "certified" the unit's membership based on his personal knowledge of the company's members. Anderson noted that "to the best of my knowledge and belief" the muster roll was both "correct and accurate." More specifically, "[a] large number of the members are personally known to me as excellent and meritorious citizens, & the troop is a credit to the state of Georgia." With Anderson's personal certification and Governor Colquitt's equally personal observation of the unit's quality, the Savannah Hussars were authorized to elect officers on July 5, 1877, thereby becoming an official state militia company.[24]

In September 1873 Richmond County blacks identified themselves "respectfully" as "citizens of the County," appropriating the citizen moniker that white militia applicants had hoped to reserve for themselves. With sixty active members this group of black citizens had "organized themselves into a Military Corps, with the name of the *Douglass Infantry*." The name suggests an attempt to align the company with Frederick Douglass, the noted black escaped slave, abolitionist, orator, and organizer of black Union troops. Douglass Infantry members obtained uniforms "in accordance with the law and regulations of similar [Georgia] organizations" and "provided themselves with the necessary arms . . . Enfield Rifles." Their letter petitioned for permission to elect company officers. The Douglass Infantry was one of the few black units able to equip themselves with uniforms and firearms independent of the state, which suggests that these men, like the Hussars, were economically secure enough to sustain their own company.

By the spring of 1874, Richmond County African Americans had also met to form another militia unit in Augusta, Georgia. On March 5, 1874, six "memorialists"—Joseph K. Williams, Peter Smith, Henry Johnson, Richard W. Matthews, James W. Wingfield, and W. Henry Miller—representing the proposed African American militia company, The Georgia Infantry, pursued a much more conciliatory tone toward whites than was evident in the name Douglass Infantry. The memorialists identified themselves as "colored citizens of Augusta" who "in accordance with the provisions of the statute laws of force in this state, . . . have associated themselves together for the purposes of forming a volunteer company . . . [and] enrolled the requisite number of [sixty-two] members and have adopted a imitable (?) uniform."

This group explicitly revealed their membership criteria: "They have at all times scrutinized the character [of potential members] for quiet, peace and order." The membership endeavored to admit "only such persons as would insure, an honorable reputation for the company." Further, "a very large majority of the members are in high esteem among the white citizens of the County, with whom many of them hold Employment." They claimed that Georgia Infantry members were "conspicuous for their devotion to religious principles, and . . . well wishers of the prosperity of their state and section." In contradistinction to the Douglass Infantry, Georgia Infantry members outlined in their petition the rationale for their name. According to the Georgia Infantry, "They were actuated by a just and becoming pride in the laws, customs and institutions of that section of the union in which they were born, and which is now the home of their manhood." They were Georgians.[25]

The members of the Georgia Infantry laid claim to class, citizenship, familiarity to whites, and black manhood as traits that separated them from other African Americans in Richmond County. Class made the memorialists black men of reputation, a trait that even white employers recognized. They were Georgia Christians committed to the prosperity of their region and state. Georgia Infantry members had white approval and declared themselves law abiding and therefore safe enough for white certification and acceptance as militiamen in Richmond County. Whites in nearby Johnson County and the surrounding communities that would encompass the 1875 "Johnson County Insurrection," however, felt threatened by "midnight [independent black] militia drills," black secret oath taking by these same men, and most distressing, the possibility that African Americans might organize and ruthlessly use independent black militia skills to "kill" all whites, including women and children.[26]

Georgia Infantry members tried hard to prove that the unit uniquely came together as an organization that was safe for whites and Governor Smith to admit to the Georgia volunteer militia command with guns. They were urban blacks living in Augusta, Georgia, employed by whites, which made them economically dependent upon the white elite for jobs and for approving the formation of the black militia company. As a result, Georgia Infantry members consciously sought ways in their application to allay local white fears of black "hostility" toward whites. This tactic succeeded in Richmond County, as the company attained membership in the Georgia Volunteers as a state-sponsored company.

Black Atlantans, more clearly than the rest of African American Georgia, demonstrated the connections that blacks established and maintained between state-sponsored militia company formation and political power. On August 27, 1873, black Atlantans, some of whom worked actively in the Republican Party, convened as "a body of men" ready to elect militia company officers. William Jefferson White served as chairman of the nearly seventy members who came together to form the Atlanta Light Infantry.

The creation of this infantry company opened the way for the emergence of a series of Atlanta-based black militia units who sought admission into the Georgia Volunteers between 1873 and 1880. Although not a viable unit by 1880, the Fulton Guards at their founding in 1874 garnered fifty-four African American members. The company would reemerge in 1883 and survive until 1900, during its second existence and membership within the Georgia Volunteers. In May 1877 the Atlanta Washington Guards came into being at the behest of fifty-three, "citizens of Fulton County . . . desirous of forming . . . a Military Company."

A year later, the Capital Guards followed Atlanta's Washington Guards in petitioning Governor Alfred H. Colquitt for authorization to form a militia company. For some Atlanta African Americans, militia service and influence in the Republican Party went hand in hand. Jackson McHenry, active in the Republican Party and a longtime militia leader, led the fifty-six-member company that included fellow young black Republicans, C. C. Wimbush and Henry Allen Rucker. Wimbush would go on to command his own Atlanta-based militia company. McHenry and Wimbush appear to have been the political and military mentors to Rucker. Both men, Wimbush and McHenry, served as militia company leaders in the 1870s, with Henry Rucker in the ranks. The three helped reshape Georgia's Republican Party at the beginning of the 1880s. Henry A. Rucker developed overlapping connections by joining his militia service with local and state Republican Party politics. Active political participation and militia service enabled Rucker to rise through the ranks of the Republican Party patronage structure. Rucker's political success resulted in his becoming Georgia's collector of internal revenue on the election coattails of President William McKinley.

Other black Atlantans formed additional militia companies with less clear political connections. In February 1879 fifty-nine black Atlantans formed the Georgia Cadets. They came together as "citizens" and "organized themselves into a military company" outfitted with their own armory on "Broad St near the bridge." Four months later, on June 19, 1879, fifty-three African American men met to form the Governor's Volunteers. Their announced purpose was that they had "banded themselves together & uniformed and equipped themselves and purchased arms" in anticipation of electing the company's commissioned officers. State approval came five days later. By 1880 Atlanta had five black militia companies. This number encouraged Atlanta's African Americans to petition Governor Colquitt for permission to organize a battalion commanded by black officers from the five units. Between June and the end of September 1880, Savannah's and Atlanta's black militia companies successfully petitioned to place their collective units in the First and Second Battalions, respectively, of the Georgia Volunteers, Colored.[27]

These black battalions, significantly, were organized following the splintering of the Republican Party along racial fault lines in April 1880. Several of Atlanta's black militia leaders and enlisted men participated in the black revolt to change the Republican Party, replacing the Reconstruction black and white leadership with a younger, more educated set of African Americans intending to lead Georgia Republicans. They based their revolt on the premise that blacks provided three quarters of the party's voting strength statewide, and yet black Georgians reaped very little in power, influence, rewards, and material well-being. Some Republicans had also twice joined the Democrats in ousting blacks from the Georgia Legislature. Several black militiamen, including thirty-six-year-old Jackson McHenry, who by 1880 had moved from the Capital Guards to captain the Governor's Volunteers, and C. C. Wimbush, of the same age and rank in 1880, had risen from the enlisted ranks to lead the Capital Guards. Twenty-eight-year-old militia private Henry Allen Rucker aligned himself politically with black Athens, Georgia, lawyer and newspaper-owner William A. Pledger. Rucker, as a result, was one of the young black Republicans who successfully overthrew the established party hierarchy that included black radical Reconstruction Republicans Aaron Bradley, Congressman Jefferson Long, who was to be Rucker's future father-in-law, and established party leaders Rev. Henry M. Turner and Rev. Tunis G. Campbell.[28]

By 1880 African Americans had envisioned the militia company as an institution necessary for the "contest for power." In the late 1860s, as the Freedmen's Bureau was dismantled, independent black militia companies functioned at times as the institution that mobilized mass black political organizing and self-defense under the leadership of local blacks, including Tunis Campbell, Cudjo Fye, Cordy Harris, Todd Norris, and Joseph Morris. The militia as a political organization perhaps reached its apogee in 1880, when young, educated, and urban-based black Georgians took the initiative to take control of the state Republican Party. They would rule that political party for a mere two years, from 1880 to 1882, after which the Republican Party in Georgia declined into a patronage distribution organization. Some of those revolting black Republicans also led the founding, in the 1870s, of African American militia companies in Atlanta and Savannah. While their efforts to transform politics did not yield permanent access to power and influence, these young men acted to carve out a better political position for African Americans in Georgia based on the power of black voting and the race's ability to be the main Republican voting bloc. Black militiamen also insisted upon public recognition as citizens qualified to serve the United States, the region, Georgia, and their county, city, and community. They organized militia companies and political organizations in a variety of ways, at times aggressively and at other moments in a conciliatory way. Black militiamen took the initiative to be the first in their communities to organize a militia company as an act of participatory citizenship, and not necessarily to frighten their white neighbors. Their efforts brought them in direct conflict with white neighbors who feared the emergence of black political, economic, and military power immediately after the Civil War and beyond the successful white counterrevolution of Redemption and Democratic Party hegemony throughout the 1870s.

Beginning in 1872 African American men petitioned for admittance to Georgia's militia service to be part of state-sponsored militia companies.

Their efforts culminated with the creation of the five companies needed to form black battalions in Atlanta and Savannah. Militia and Republican Party membership, along with young black political activism, resulted in 1880 in the black political revolt against the Republican establishment. While African American militiamen during these eight years competed with whites for coveted militia assignments at the county level as a function of citizenship, whites viewed this competition as a black mobilization in preparation for county-level race wars and recertification of white dominance. Blacks in contrast hoped that an urban-based black militia company would convey their creditability as citizens worthy of membership in the community of Americans, both black and white. This was reflected in the vision of both Savannah's Lincoln Association and Richmond County's Georgia Infantry. The Lincoln Guards in 1872 looked to the Civil War to validate their citizenship. The memorialists of Richmond County embraced the militia movement as an opportunity to define themselves as loyal, Christian gentlemen committed to the social harmony, political tranquility, and economic development of metropolitan Augusta, Georgia.

These African American men, including those in the Douglass Infantry, were willing to go so far as to invoke the distinguishing marker of class to highlight their commitment to a mission that would not only assert their manhood but also establish them as unique disciples of a broader definition of community. They were willing to concede some ties to blackness and form an alliance with the white elite in exchange for recognition of their manhood and citizenship. Membership in the Georgia Volunteers also prompted a more delineated separation between urban black political organizing and the militia company urban militiamen embraced, on the one hand, and the more rural communities, where militia membership represented African American social, economic, and political autonomy, on the other.[29]

White Memory, Change, and Restoration

Rural black people in Burke, Jefferson, Johnson, Laurens, Richmond, Washington, and Wilkinson Counties envisioned militia membership in 1875 as a key component to opposing white repression. They also wanted control over not only their daily labor but also when, how, why, and for whom they labored. Blacks desired control over their labor because of the promises of freedom earned during the Civil War and initiated as a right of citizenship in Reconstruction Georgia.

White people in the central counties of alleged insurrectionary activity insisted on retaining the right to set the parameters of black freedom. The Johnson County Insurrection, during the summer of 1875, was the convergence point where white and black Georgians made the competition for county militia companies more than a war of words. The independent and state-sponsored militia company was the symbol of white and black freedom. Both sides mobilized, intending that the militia serve as the institution that secured their freedom, especially their local political presence.

The Civil War, however, "shattered the old hierarchical structures of power," certainly throughout the South and nation but especially in the rural South. Grace Elizabeth Hale has argued in this context that post–Civil War southern whites sought to control the forces of change unleashed by the national conflict and the "trends toward centralization, standardization, urbanization, and mechanization" that followed, transforming the late nineteenth century and shaping the twentieth. These forces, along with capital industrialization, as other scholars have argued, "meant that American [national and southern] collective identity itself was anything but clear" after the war. Economic "changes [also] destabilized the categories of power" in the 1880s and 1890s.[30]

According to the white county historians writing about the Civil War's impact on the political and economic categories of power that had defined rural Georgia, the war "crushed" or "destroyed" white power. Whites experiencing these postwar challenges grappled with a failing societal order. Believing that blacks had not "earned the right to self-mastery," whites looked to forming a postwar racial identity as the "means of ordering the newly enlarged meaning of America." Establishing a national identity was one of the problems of nation building. That new identity, Hale has asserted, was driven by new technology that had already invaded the rural South as white southerners searched for a new system, "the culture of segregation," to mediate and provide some control over "modernity."[31]

Technology reshaped rural Georgia during the decade immediately after the Civil War. The railroads provided black Georgians from nineteen counties with the mobility and opportunity to visit and converge on Washington County's Courthouse in 1875 for a Republican Party convention. According to Hale, trains "broke down local southern racial settlements . . . during and after Reconstruction" and "visibly unhinged" as well as "disrupted local [rural] isolation." Trains "moved [people] beyond the reach of personalized local relations of class and racial authority."

Railroads transported local people to new experiences outside the boundaries of local white elite control. They brought strangers into communities that before the Civil War existed as self-contained units where white male elite authority—paternalism—reigned over every man, woman, and child, regardless of color. From 1865 on, trains "spread traveling pockets of anonymous social relations, more akin to" those of urbanization into rural communities. The railroads and train stations conveyed to the rural South the city, along with its anonymity, unpredictability, contradictions, and discomfort.[32]

While the railroad and train station conveyed urbanization, standardization, and strangers to rural Georgia, inexpensive newspapers opened a new mode of communication to a broader public who could thereby participate in discussions about the meaning of the militia, community involvement, and racial liberty. One reporter in the region used this medium to promote militia formation in some of the seven counties. Sydney Herbert, journalist and militia advocate, not only reported on independent and state-sponsored militia development but also tried to define the scope of insurrection and who white people believed black people were. The newspaper also revealed that white control was not absolute as blacks pursued political and economic autonomy, demonstrating that they were more than slaves. They were independent citizens, and each act contested the white position that "any space was" white space.[33]

In this context of the so-called invasion of white space by strangers, blacks "worked to retain and expand their freedom and citizenship." African Americans also sought "control over themselves and their hope of belonging to what would become a new American whole," a nation of equals. For white southerners, black freedom and identity "became unhinged for the first time from the taint of slavery," as former slaves collectively declared, "We are free; we are free!" White people in contrast "found it difficult to imagine African Americans as anything other than poor and uneducated," subservient, and powerless. Blacks challenged this stereotype locally as they pursued political and economic power inside the county. Meanwhile, "the white southern elite, planters . . . and other members of a [new and] growing white middle class" needed to find a solution to black freedom. They had to find out "how to reconstruct a powerful and collective definition of whiteness." Trains, Hale has contended, forced rural whites to realize that they had an additional need to seek the power of state government to help them forge a southern "racial order," a "culture of segregation." This would be a new cultural and racial order, intended as the mechanism that would allow whites to cope with a new national consumer culture open to whites of all classes, as well as to middle-class blacks. According to Hale, the racial order and cultures of segregation and consumerism were realized in 1890.[34] The local white response to the impact of the Civil War, in 1865, and the Johnson County Insurrection a decade later suggests that rural whites in Georgia's seven counties pursued these changes immediately after the Civil War.

Tensions surrounding the definitions of whiteness and blackness in the seven counties predated the Johnson County Insurrection. During Reconstruction economic issues of black access to the tools of success were noted in Burke County. Whites with plantations attempted to maintain their antebellum status as leaders and rulers of the community. Former slaves sought to earn a living for their families and establish their economic, social, and political independence. A planter in Wilkinson County backhandedly confirmed these black goals, arguing that voting in 1868 and African American participation in politics had ruined black workers locally even though he held the upper hand economically as sharecropping emerged in the county. Black sharecroppers, the planter argued, "did not want to work for wages. . . . [They] wanted to be furnished with land, mules, implements and provisions, and receive half of the products of the land." Blacks then strove to be independent, economic citizens.

In 1869 a group of six blacks attempted to construct an independent economic life. They saved their farming income to acquire new horses and buggies. The newspaper in Augusta, Georgia, complimented them for their "industry, good behavior, and thrift," arguing that these were three characteristics beneficial to "the colored man as well as white man." Plantation owners, nevertheless, including Charles Colcock Jones Jr., resisted such acts of autonomy, fearing first that he would have to break up his plantation to sell land to blacks and second that he would have to actually pay the African American wage earners he employed. Blacks, in response to Colcock's policies, undermined the plantation's productivity, marking the lines of friction between blacks and whites in rural Georgia. Land, labor, and black political and economic autonomy would be the central points of conflict for "the insurrection" seven years later.[35]

W. F. Cannon, Sheriff of Wilkinson County, writing from Toomsboro, Georgia, prepared for "war" with "negro [militia] troops." Cannon's letter to Governor James Milton Smith on July 31, 1872, was intended to serve multiple purposes. First, he sought to prevent the creation and mobilization of a black militia in Wilkinson County. Second, in light of such a threat, he felt that whites needed to organize "at once." Third, he argued that white mobilization was required to prevent the emergence of a black militia, because such a unit constituted the center of African American political organizing in the county. Perhaps foreshadowing events three summers later, Cannon argued that whites had to counter and terminate African American efforts to assert their political autonomy, especially when blacks met "for Charitable purposes in order that they may band themselves together." Mass meetings of African Americans, Cannon asserted, had negative consequences for whites. As a result, Cannon's fourth point warned whites that a race war would loom if black militiamen gained access to arms and were allowed to unify black people politically. Cannon, a veteran of the Confederate army, "had [seen] plenty of *war* having served nearly four years." The experience had been hell but Cannon urged whites to prepare for the next conflict, because blacks were becoming a political force.[36]

Sheriff Cannon wrote Governor Smith because he had "information . . . lately received that the colored People are organizing" a militia company. Further, Cannon wrote, "I think it prudent that if there is only a certain number [of militia companies] allowed [per Georgia county] that it should not be in the hands of ignorant blacks." Additionally, "if . . . there has been no effort made by the white People we will try to fix [it] up at once." Cannon noted, "In my opinion the organizing of the negroes is for an Electioneering Scheme under the pretence of organizing not only for the Militia But were into Societies which they claim are for Charitable purposes in order that they may band themselves together." In closing, Cannon acknowledged that "war" was a costly affair. The price for his nearly four years' service to the Confederacy was "coming out minus my right *arm*." Yet Sheriff Cannon wanted whites mobilized to meet the threat of an organized and state-sponsored black militia, or what he called "negro troops" in Wilkinson County. This was a prospect, Cannon noted, "I don't want see."[37]

Cannon was not alone in this view concerning the potential of black political, economic, and militia organizing. While Jefferson County whites and the county's grand jury declared "things in Jefferson County [to be] . . . 'perfectly quiet'" and cheerful in 1869, the following year, 1870, "trouble was brewing," because plantation agriculture died in the county. As a consequence black life "entirely changed"; African Americans outnumbered whites almost two-to-one, changing the county's political equation in favor of blacks under the leadership of Cudjo Fye. The transition, whites argued, resulted in "the rapid release [of blacks] into barbarism," with "a riot" and Cudjo Fye's insurrection. Whites in Bethany, Georgia, responded that year by founding a cavalry company, the Jefferson Dragoons. Two years later, Jefferson County whites petitioned Governor Smith to recognize their volunteer cavalry company as a state-sponsored militia unit based on their memories of how whites had collectively responded to the Fye Insurrection. In August 1870 whites used their personal weapons to put down black political mobilization. Their 1872 petition included a request for state-provided weaponry and instruction in cavalry tactics. The perceived need to counter black political power continued after 1872. Six years later, in 1878, the Savannah journalist Sydney Herbert, an avid Georgia militia supporter, published a comprehensive roster of Georgia's militia companies. The roster listed three white Jefferson County cavalry units: the Jefferson Hussars, located in Bartow, Georgia; the Jefferson Dragoons, located in Bethany, Georgia; and the Jefferson Sabres, located in Louisville, Georgia. Jefferson County was also the location of three infantry companies: the Light Infantry, in Bartow, Georgia, A. T. Harman's unit; the Jefferson Grays, in Bethany, Georgia; and the Jefferson Riflemen, in Louisville, Georgia, led by State Senator Captain J. H. Polhill. The Jefferson Dragoons and its commanding officer, Captain J. R. Murphy, patrolled Jefferson County, dispersing blacks during the August 1875 "insurrection" and thereby expanding their training in black control begun five years earlier.[38]

Whites organized additional independent infantry units across the seven counties in response to African American political activities. Laurens County was represented by the Laurens Guards of Bailey's Courthouse. Johnson County's militia came from Wrightsville, Georgia, the home of the Johnson Rangers. In Sandersville, Georgia, there were three infantry units, two cavalry companies, and one artillery battery. The Sandersville infantry companies included the Jack Smith Guards, the Tabernacle Guards, and the Washington Rifles, with Captain R. L. Rogers commanding the Washington Rifles during the "insurrection." Sandersville's two cavalry units and its solitary artillery unit were, respectively, Governor Smith's Horse Guards, the Washington Light Horse Guards, and Martin's Battery, "without guns." Tennille, Georgia, served as Washington County's rail center, the place where blacks had disembarked from trains before marching to the county courthouse for a Republican Party political rally in 1875, the convention that had frightened whites. Tennille had a white cavalry company. In Wilkinson County, the Irwinton,

Georgia, community supported three infantry companies and a cavalry unit: the Home Guards, the Oconee Grays, the Wilkinson Rifles, and the Wilkinson Grays, the cavalry company. Additionally Burke County served as the headquarters for two white cavalry companies: the Burke Hussars, in Waynesboro, Georgia, and the Burke Dragoons, in Midville, Georgia.[39] Whites organized militia companies to challenge and defeat black political and economic autonomy, as well as to restore white freedom in the face of the changes sparked by the Civil War.

Whites in Laurens County, according to its *Official History*, recalled Reconstruction as a time of "suffer[ing and post–Civil War] privations." Former Confederates came home from the war having to start all "over again," but did so "with determined hearts." Their work yielded "the latter part of the seventies restoration," with profitable cotton sales. The recovery appears to have begun with the 1872 Laurens County grand jury report that all was well in the county, because "the county is out of debt" and heading toward "purity, and prosperity with sister [Georgia] counties." Whites were also unified "in observing law and fostering good," as well as sustaining "friendly" relations between plantation owners and ex-slaves. Whites assumed this to be true, because "in most cases the negroes were unwilling to leave old masters and go out for themselves." Blacks, whites concluded, wanted to remain dependent on white largesse. Yet blacks did contest white paternalism's resurrection with "a negro riot" that Laurens County whites successfully put down with arrests, executions, and imprisonments in 1872. But, three years later, blacks were involved in the 1875 insurrection, and in 1876 the Laurens County grand jury recommended that the Ordinary create a chain gang to punish "criminals found guilty of minor offenses." Laurens County was a political battleground between blacks and whites for county dominance from the end of the Civil War onward, as whites sought to rule and control the power of the law and its punishment mechanisms.[40]

The Civil War "crushed . . . the [white] people" of Wilkinson County, yet, despite the privations of the postwar years, they "went to work with a will." Like Laurens County, a significant cotton harvest brought profits and ended post–Civil War economic problems in Wilkinson. Blacks were free but idle and crime ridden. In response Wilkinson whites, similar to those in Laurens County, came together, crossing such antebellum political divides as Whig and Democratic Party lines out of "fear of 'black heels on white necks.'" In 1868 African Americans won enough political offices to dominate county government. White Georgians countered black and

Republican Party governance by characterizing it as "an orgy of misrule," with "justice . . . broken down" and murder and mayhem over the election of a black state senator. According to Wilkinson County historian Victor Davidson, black political power caused the county to descend into a situation worse than "when [colonial and antebellum] Indian massacres . . . threatened" white Georgians. In 1870, "rumors of negro uprisings" were rampant. Whites near Toomsboro claimed to have discovered and intercepted black communication "notes," intended for distribution among African Americans during their alleged insurrection planning. Local whites charged that Republicans "unmistakably . . . incited" African Americans to the point of blacks "rising against the whites" and that "all the horrors of a racial war seemed imminent." Five years later, in July 1875, whites made a similar claim about intercepting black communication during the Johnson County Insurrection.[41]

According to these local histories, blacks and whites competed for political dominance in Jefferson, Wilkinson, and Laurens Counties immediately after the Civil War and continued to do so through Reconstruction. Whites defined and described black county-level governance as bloody, uncivilized, criminal, savage, and violently out of control, requiring the forceful intervention of "the people," that is, white people. Intervention encouraged white independent militia formation, with cavalry companies the unit of choice in some counties. Militia development, nevertheless, occurred in all seven counties, as whites mobilized to counter black political and economic autonomy. White men in Wilkinson County also responded by organizing the Ku Klux Klan, which targeted both whites and blacks. County Klansmen in and around Irwinton, Georgia, organized and mobilized to address "a very serious offense . . . by a negro," while blacks countered by seeking external support from the federal government in the form of troops and a grand jury. Black efforts fell apart in 1872 as the Democratic Party ascended to power in Wilkinson County and across Georgia.[42]

Insurrection

The Washington-Johnson County Insurrection of 1875 began as the Camilla Massacre of 1868 did, at the county courthouse where African Americans attempted to utilize a public building to conduct a large political meeting. Even though blacks defined their gathering as a convening to exercise political power like any other Georgian, whites viewed the gathering as a threat to white power locally. The local press would play a central role in characterizing the African American threat to all whites. The *Sandersville Herald and Georgian*, on July 19, 1875, alleged that Joseph Morris in Burke County composed an inflammatory and hostile letter to Burke County "Sheriff Rube Mayer" (aka Ruben Mayo) requesting the use of the Washington County Courthouse on July 24, 1875. Morris indicated that he and African Americans from several counties wanted to assemble "for a mass meeting ... fur [the] Republican Party ... [to] hon major General P. R. Rivers and, his [militia] staff from aiken SC and charmans, exicutive committee of 19 counties in Sandersville[,] Washington County." Morris allegedly began the letter by threatening and commanding Sheriff Mayo to have the courthouse cleaned and open for public use. The letter ended with the demand that all the roads from the rail junction in Tennille, Georgia, leading to the Washington County Courthouse be kept open for blacks to march and parade from the train station to the courthouse. Finally, Mayo was commanded to have the courthouse keys ready to put in Morris's hands. This was to be a meeting that included armed militia companies from Burke County, Georgia, and South Carolina's state-sponsored militiamen, joined by black Republican Party executive committee members from nineteen Georgia counties.[43]

The white response to the alleged threatening letter ranged from derision to abject fear. The *Herald and Georgian* published "an exact copy of this wonderful letter" in its July 29, 1875, edition, after the scheduled black political meeting. The letter sparked a broader white discussion about black competence, inferiority, capabilities, and status that the white press would engage in throughout the grand jury inquests at the end of the summer. The press established that white people were more competent and had more law-abiding intentions than black people, who were linked to images of black rage that would enter Washington County to harm whites. The *Herald and Georgian* did not regard the Morris letter as civil or respectful. It also bypassed an opportunity for civic boasting and community pride that would have welcomed the gathering of black Republicans from nineteen counties as a public honor that would bring needed revenue to the region. According to the *Herald and Georgian*, the letter, the black militia companies, and the mass political meeting were all "intended to overawe ... [and] scare" Sheriff Mayo and a "thousand others in the county just like him." The Sandersville newspaper concluded that, after "putting 'this and that' together, matters began to look a little war like." To whites, black militia organizing constituted clear signs of "race war." Specifically, "those midnight [black militia] drills, mysterious [secret] meetings and roll calls in the still hours of the night" were signs of black desires to take over the county.

Additionally, the presence of the black "Generals" Joseph Morris and South Carolina's state-sponsored militia leader, Prince Rivers, prompted the white conclusion that armed black militiamen "would attempt to take possession of the Court-house by force. In fact it had been intimated that they would have it or *blood*." In white eyes, African Americans were coming to Washington County to forcefully overthrow white rule by overwhelming local whites and the most prominent building and symbol of white power, the courthouse. The building, as Grace Elizabeth Hale has described it, stood "tall in the sky and central, fixing a town as an axle pierces a wheel"; the courthouse was a symbol of white power. Each of these signposts made it clear to whites that blacks were preparing for war, bloodshed, and domination as the nineteen counties produced African Americans determined to use force to impose their will on local whites. In response, "the [white] people got ready" to keep the county courthouse safe from "the polluting presence of disturbers of the peace at all hazards."[44]

"The people" mobilized to defend two local institutions from black threats: Washington County's Courthouse and white elected officials, namely, the sheriff and "the venerable and beloved Ordinary," Hon. Haywood Brookins. Whites united to resist the black invaders. Sandersville whites William Warthen and W. H. Wiley, temporarily acting as Solicitor General, the *Atlanta Daily Constitution* reported, contacted Governor James Milton Smith for assistance. Yet, bypassing the governor, Captain Peacock, leading the Washington Rifles, an all-white independent militia company, telegraphed the all-white state-sponsored second battalion in Macon, Georgia. Peacock requested a thousand additional rounds of ammunition from the state-sponsored unit. White Macon militia authorities sent the cartridges and offered their assistance "in suppressing any outbreak," effectively subsuming state power to an independent militia unit not yet recognized as a state militia unit.

Governor James Milton Smith, the *Daily Constitution* reported, "sent the orders" to Sandersville's sheriff and militia commanders to be prepared for insurrection. However, Smith denied a request for state militia mobilization in Augusta, despite the city being "in a perfect uproar of excitement." Yet members of Augusta's white militia units also ignored the governor. They "volunteered and went anyhow, taking with them their guns and ammunition." Further, as the *Herald and Georgian* reported, "Any number of [additional white] men could be had at the word to go and aid in squelching this fiendish uprising." In Sandersville, Captain Weedon commanded a biracial police force composed of "appointed white and colored." The *Herald and Georgian* asserted that this integrated force symbolized how white people possessed "the best feeling" for Washington County African Americans, concluding that if "they [were] let alone there never would be any disturbance. But we did not know what [Prince] Rivers and his crowd might incite them to do."[45]

This contradictory statement suggested that local whites wanted to believe that they securely lived in a racial utopia—one sealed off from eroding external forces that whites assumed would set the races in deadly opposition. All would be well, however, as long as local whites resumed holding the commanding position as the dominant force in Washington County. The courthouse, located at the center of a community, had a different function from that of the train station. The railroad line and train station, as Grace Elizabeth Hale has argued, brought disturbing change to the South's small towns. In contrast to the courthouse, the railroad line, along with the train station, was located a distinct distance from the center of white community activity. The train station was the portal that "broke down local" personalized "racial authority," which had defined slavery and the antebellum South. Trains also were becoming "the focus of late nineteenth-century racial conflicts," as blacks used their purchasing power to buy first-class accommodations and challenged attempts that prevented black use of that purchase. Asserting this emergent national right of consumption by purchasing and utilizing the railroad transformed southern race relations. Railroads brought to small towns blacks whose dress, deportment, and behavior, Hale asserted, belied any "notion of southern blacks' racial inferiority," especially as antebellum slaves. Trains conveyed black strangers across local boundaries and introduced them into communities where local whites had no personalized relationship with them. The Johnson County Insurrection was a white response to black strangers coming to visit Washington County for a political convention.[46]

On Saturday morning, July 24, 1875, a procession of several hundred blacks proceeded from the railroad junction and nearest telegraph in Tennille, Georgia. They marched and paraded from Tennille to Sandersville "between six and seven o'clock," accompanied by what the *Herald and Georgian* described as "the war like sound of many drums." Local black plantation workers were part of the procession, causing the paper to ask:

"O, ye hard working colored men and women of Washington county, why will you be misled by . . . scoundrels who . . . have you at enmity with the white race upon whom you are dependent for the homes that you occupy and the very bread that you eat."[47]

Despite the alleged "warlike" presence of "several hundred" blacks active in Republican Party politics, the procession to the courthouse was peaceful. The press reported the gathering as unorganized and claimed that Morris and Rivers abandoned the meeting, acting as do "all the Radical leaders: they tempt the poor negro into danger and then they are off." Yet Rev. Cordy (aka Caudy and Corday) Harris at ten o'clock led the participants to the courthouse yard and allegedly "suggested that the meeting be postponed." Having agreed to end the convocation, the amassed group re-formed "as militia companies and marched around for some time, and . . . gradually [began] to disperse for home." The *Herald and Georgian* asserted, "Better order we never saw anywhere. Not a profane word or an angry expression did we hear during the entire day, and there were hundreds congregated," suggesting that local blacks and African Americans from the surrounding nineteen counties did meet and conduct some business.[48]

Even though the mass meeting on July 24 occurred without incident, rumors persisted that "a second visitation from the negro insurrectionists Harris, Morris, Rivers, and their followers" lurked on the horizon. Whites debated rumors about what was to come until a letter composed by Rev. Cordy Harris, secretary to "Generals" Joseph Morris and Prince R. Rivers, "was found where a party of Negroes had been drinking at a country store in Johnson county," the reason why Johnson County was associated with black "insurrection." The alleged insurrection letter had been "written in a miserable hand, scarcely intelligible and . . . [was] evidently the work of the murderous villain" Harris, the *Herald and Georgian* contended. The newspaper endeavored to put the August 6, 1875, "letter in plain English" for its readers:

> To Jerry Waters [Walters]: You and your Company must start to killing the whites on August 20. Kill every one you can find, and tell Harrison Tucker to kill all the whites he can find, and go towards 11 Station, and there will meet Gen. Morris and staff and Gen. Rivers and his staff. You do as I tell you and Cap. Tucker. This must be secrete. You tell brother Jake to kill every white man and get every gun he can. Make out to the white men you are very sorry that they

think we want to hurt them. And if you know of any man that has got money make them give it to your Treasurer and we will divide it. Have all your Company nedes (?) Kill with axes, hoes, pitchforks, and get guns, powder and shot as you kill. So I close to depend on you.

Cordy Harris, Secretary.
By order of Gen. Morris and from Gen. Rivers.[49]

The paper then reported that the letter was conveyed to the Washington County sheriff, who issued warrants for the arrests of black militia captains, Waters (aka Walters) and Tucker's "brother" Jake. These black men were jailed in Sandersville, while the paper claimed that Cordy Harris, Joseph Morris, and Prince R. Rivers had all escaped. But by August 19, 1875, thirty-four African American men were being held in "the Hotel de Mayo," with the anticipated consequence that Sheriff Ruben Mayo would be supervising a very crowded Johnson County jail.[50]

While whites arrested African Americans, the Washington County Dragoons and the Washington County Rifles, both white independent militia companies, mobilized to guard the courthouse and jail where they detained African Americans. According to the *Herald and Georgian,* these "gallant companies . . . were ordered out and have been in camp and on duty." The white martial presence, in comparison to the "war drums" of the black conventioneers and militiamen marching to a political rally, reminded the press of the "bugle call and stirring drum, for drill, dress parade, guard, picket and other duties, [that] carry us back to the days of the bloody strife between the North and South." The Dragoons and Rifles may have resurrected Civil War memories in 1875 also as they mobilized to counter mass black political organizing. The white militia units stood ready to protect whites, because "without this organized military force, [whites] should have been in a deplorable condition indeed." White civilian volunteers also rode across the landscape, serving as advance scouts and spies, with one group allegedly being shot at by blacks. This vanguard was the advance warning system intended to further prevent whites from being caught unaware and unprepared for the "surprise insurrection." Middle Georgia whites organized to terminate the black threat by gathering a core group of white counter forces that included the unofficial militia companies, local police, armed whites, and post-insurrection grand jury investigations.[51]

The *Herald and Georgian* reported and shaped the narrative of insurrection. The newspaper constructed images of black-initiated race war—a war conducted by semiliterate blacks marching, drilling, organizing in secret, and threatening local whites with a massive armed invasion. According to the newspaper, blacks planned to take the courthouse, the public symbol of white power, first by intimidating local officials and then by overwhelming local white residents. The plan came close to surprising whites, but they mobilized independent militia companies just in time to end the emergency. Local blacks in each county were not the problem, even though they marched with visiting independent black militiamen, from Georgia and South Carolina, and Republican Party political organizations. According to the white press, black insurrection had been stirred by outsiders such as Prince Rivers, who mislead local black people and pitted harmonious locals of both races against each other in an unnecessary race war.

"Confessions"

For answers as to why the so-called insurrection occurred, whites turned to the local grand jury. There appear to have been at least two grand jury investigations between the end of August and the middle of September 1875. "Confessions" were elicited from blacks arrested between August 20 and 23, 1875. In an eerie parallel to the Nat Turner slave rebellion in 1831 and to the stereotypical assumptions surrounding slave insurrections generally, the alleged black violence in 1875 was chronicled as the mobilization of local African American farmworkers armed with agricultural equipment. The confessions were those of a white community stunned that black agriculturalists/slaves had issues with life in rural Georgia. Further, black farmworkers, according to the confessions, hoped to use their farm equipment to kill whites of all ages, genders, and status, just as slaves were accused of doing before the Civil War. In the 1875 context, though black farmworkers were organized as militiamen in military companies, they, oddly, armed themselves with farm implements rather than the lethal firearms Georgia militia companies hoped to access, whether through the federal government, the state, or private purchase by individual groups of militiamen in independent and state-sponsored companies. The black insurrectionists, the confessions revealed, would kill with hoes and pitchforks, not with the guns that had made the Civil War a bloodbath and made militiamen modern servants of local and state government.

White men such as Colonel W. H. Wiley assumed the role of solicitor general in the absence of the Solicitor John W. Robison. The "confessions"

Wiley and other local whites extracted immediately became public as front-page news in the *Savannah Morning News*. Sydney Herbert, a reporter for the weekday *Morning News* also wrote articles for the weekend supplement, *Savannah Weekly News*, while editing and writing the *Weekly News*' Military Department. The Military Department reflected Herbert's personal commitment to and advocacy for the state militia. As a self-proclaimed militia advocate, Herbert had publicly called for local militia formation while defending and championing Washington County's two white militia companies. He lauded their prompt mobilization during the crisis and commended them as peacekeepers assisting the county sheriff in arresting and then guarding blacks. It was within this context that Herbert went to Sandersville to observe and record "insurrection" news and then filed special reports on the confessions solicited from the thirty to fifty African Americans arrested by white militiamen and county sheriffs in Burke, Laurens, Washington, Johnson, and Jefferson Counties.[52]

On August 23, 1875, Herbert, working as a special correspondent for the *Morning News*, reported what had "transpired in this section during the past ten days," including the questions, examinations, and confessions whites secured from their black captives. According to Herbert, "All the testimony goes to confirm [Corday] Harris statements that this movement commenced about the first of May, and that 'Gen.' Morris was the agitator who caused the insurrection, with Rev Corday Harris, Ephriam Brantley, Rev. Jerry Simmons, and the officers [of the black militia] companies to assist him. The character of the organization can be gathered from the . . . statements freely made under oath and without intimidation." James Wright, Tobe Morris (aka Norris), and Richard Smith, of Laurens County; John Chiles, of Johnson County; Corday Harris, Jake Mooreman, and Ben Davis, of Washington County; and Eliza Young, of no county listed, each made statements. Wright, Tobe Morris, and Smith were "examined," while "confessions" came from Chiles, Mooreman, and Davis, letters and statements from Harris to Herbert and Governor James Milton Smith, and "testimony" from Young, the sole black female called by the grand jury.[53]

According to James Wright, Tobe Morris, and Richard Smith, "a secret military organization" led by Captain Harrison Tucker did exist in Laurens County. All three men were asked either to join Laurens County's company or to move on to serve under Captain Jerry Walters in Johnson County after rejecting Tucker's leadership in Laurens County. These men also eventually withdrew their membership, each being concerned about what Wright defined as "mischief" presumably aimed at whites. Morris was recruited because he could write, which resulted in him becoming the unit's secretary. Smith reported secret midnight meetings, while Wright indicated while there were meetings, very few times did the company drill—an act whites found disturbing when blacks performed it consistently. Morris noted that militia meetings occurred sometimes every Saturday or every other Saturday, stressing an inconsistency that may have alleviated white fears that blacks were conducting secret meetings, outside the purview of white supervision, that they combined with military drills. Blacks with guns who secretly met, organized, and planned white deaths reinforced white fears of the Haitian Revolution.

Smith, however, established that "the object of the [militia] organization" was to secure land for blacks. Wright in contrast vaguely understood this to be the goal, noting, "If they, the white people, did not mind the negroes will have this land." Specifically, Smith and Morris identified the land as "government land . . . that the Negroes were justly entitled to a part of . . . and they intended to have it or blood." According to Morris, "government land . . . must be cut up in government pieces." The objective of militia organizing was land ownership, not violent overthrow of white rule. Yet Wright, Morris, and Smith allegedly concluded that land acquisition meant blacks would use deadly force if their needs were not met. Smith, "firmly believe[d] that the negroes intended to kill the white people and get their lands" and "expected help from the North or somewhere." Morris got the "impression [from black militiamen Andrea Peters and Tony Wright] . . . that each man should have a piece, and I believe that to be the impression of every man in the company. From the language used . . . they intended to take the land by force if necessary." Wright asserted that "the tenor of the . . . conversation [with Issac Wright of Johnson County's militia company] . . . meant that whenever they got strong enough they would take the land—and take it by force if necessary." Whites assumed that blacks wanted white land in the counties. Morris explained that it was federally owned land that they hoped to access.[54]

The reported confessions by Chiles, Davis, and Mooreman and the testimony of Eliza Young focused on the black community's mobilization to kill whites. Although the evidence does not connect Young to any of the independent militia companies or even to the political and economic efforts to achieve autonomy, the press included her testimony about "the insurrection movement . . . in Washington County." She was alleged to have overheard several conversations, including one indicating "that the colored folks, both women and children and men are going to rise with pitchforks, hoes, etc., and kill *every white man woman and child*." She further indicated that her relatives were involved, asserting, "Tom Derassaw told me that my brother and Virgil Walker was in the fuss," as well as "I heard that Uncle John Hasty [in Tennille] a month or six weeks I inferred ... that the present troubles were what he had reference." Young also "heard the men from Jefferson [County] telling the colored folks in town the day of the big meeting ... if the colored folks would lean their heads together they could succeed," and "the colored folks saying ... they did not like the white folks; that there would be another war soon and if there were they would take their hoes, pitchforks, &c., to kill the whites."[55]

Two officers in Jerry Walters's company confessed. Davis, "Third Lieutenant of Jerry Walters's Company," acknowledged, "We was to organize the company ... and go down the road and start to killing out the whites," including some white women, suggesting assumed black behavior during slave revolts. General Joseph Morris "was to command us on the day when we commenced the killing." The company also had secret oaths and signs that were "binding," triggering white concerns dating back to slavery and slave insurrections. Jake Mooreman made a full confession about "the colored citizens of Washington, Laurens, Johnson, and *sixteen other counties*." A first lieutenant under Walters, Mooreman defined the militia chain of command, starting with Prince. R. Rivers, including Joe Morris, Corday Harris, Francis Murkerson, and preceding to Captain Walters. The militia company was a political organization, with Murkerson serving as first captain of the Eighty-eighth Militia District. On August 20, 1875, "all our companies and all black men were to meet at No. 11 Central Railroad [Tennille Station], to transact our business." They met to find ways of "carrying out the insurrection plans" to "KILL ALL THE WHITE MEN AND UGLY WHITE WOMEN AND TAKE THE PRETTY WHITE WOMEN FOR OURSELVES" on August 20, 1875.[56]

These confessions fed white fears and stereotypical assumptions about their conceptions of black insurrection and the potentiality of race war. Stressing a mythology of black violence that targeted white women, African American postbellum political organizing was transformed in the white mind into a throwback moment when whites feared slave insurrections. The confessions reflected the legacy of slave insurrections that combined in the post–Civil War world with the independent black militia company and African American efforts to challenge the stereotypes of slavery. The independent black militia company, as a vehicle for political mobilization and a platform for black self-defense and autonomy, prompted whites to recall the militarization of slaves through secret meetings, secret oaths, loss of white property, and black government. The coming together in the seven counties of each of these factors caused whites to assume that a race war was upon them.

The "confessions" Mooreman and John Chiles made on August 23, 1875, would make them key witnesses for a grand jury investigation a month later, but Chiles's August testimony also provided a more concrete portrait of the goals of black independent militiamen. These black church-based organizations brought black men together for a common purpose. As whites understood it, local black militiamen gathered in a "secret military organization for the purpose of getting 'equality.'" "By that I mean," Chiles stated, "to take lands in this county by force and arms—to kill out the whites, beginning with the little babe in the crib, and killing all up." Additional objectives included getting "all the money we could find and put[ting] it in our treasury; to divide all the personal property between us and to divide the lands into forty acre lots between us; and I suppose you know the intention was to kill all the whites along the line of march." In contrast black independent militiamen's "main object[ive was] . . . the enforcement of the [1875] civil rights bill representation in the jury box." They sought to use the militia to bring blacks together for a series of mass meetings. Local militia leaders Rev. Corday Harris and Joseph Morris also wanted the independent black militia units to become state-sponsored companies. Whites and blacks viewed and defined the purpose of the black independent militia unit in dramatically different ways. Whites concluded that black militiaman came to destroy everything they held dear. Blacks joined the militia so that the collective objectives of the race—namely, political and economic autonomy—might be realized, as was the promise of post–Civil War and post-Reconstruction Georgia.[57]

Grand Juries

Noting that rumors circulated as fact throughout the 1875 crisis in Washington and Johnson Counties, the *Sandersville Herald and Georgian* endeavored to restrain white eagerness to publish the insurrection confessions. Restraint was part of an overall effort to prove to northerners that blacks received fair treatment from southern whites. The grand juries of August 30 and September 15, 1875, were to be showcases of fairness.[58] Fairness, for the white South, would be an important component of a collective white effort to secure an economic and political place within the nation. This new nation was embracing a consumer economy in conjunction with capital industrialization, which sought to restrict black labor but include middle-class and elite African Americans within the looming new century. The South in the 1870s had just begun working on a process that might reincorporate the region into the national economic and political parameters. At the same time white southerners were not yet ready to concede their independence and desire to resist the centralizing power of the national economy and federal government. Proving that blacks and whites could cooperate with each other was a significant first step for the white South's return to a national white identity.[59]

On August 30, 1875, the Washington County grand jury convened under the direction of Herschel V. Johnson, a former governor, Washington County resident, and judge. Judge Johnson called for a fair and impartial grand jury of forty-eight "intelligent, upright, and conscientious citizens." Their task centered on defining attempted "insurrection through oath-bound organizations, the plain purpose of which was to burn the Court House, thereby destroying land titles, to murder the white people and take their property." Johnson also outlined the law and definition of "insurrection" under the Georgia legal code, which dated back to antebellum slavery. Section 4315–4316 of Georgia's *Code* characterized "insurrection and the attempt to incite insurrection" as "any combined resistance to the lawful authority of the State, with the intent to denial thereof, which the same is manifested, or intended to be manifested by acts of violence." Additionally, "Any attempt by persuasion or otherwise, to induce others to join in any combined resistance to lawful authority of the State, shall constitute an attempt to incite Insurrection." White Georgians directly linked insurrection with violence and made the penalty for insurrection death.[60]

Johnson further noted that the leaders of the insurrectionary plot were former "slaves of the white race" who were now "free and entitled to a fair and impartial trial." Given this legal assertion, blacks and whites were equal under the law and owed equal protection. Johnson, however, insisted that black status under the Georgia *Code* had not changed with emancipation, because slavery had awarded similar fair legal protections to slaves before the Civil War. Johnson advised Washington County's grand jury to "ignore the fact that they were ever slaves. Deal with them as free, and as if they were white and award to them their full legal right to your impartiality."[61]

An additional task of the grand jury involved "bring[ing] the accused ringleaders to trial." The *Savannah Morning News* declared that authorities had "a dozen ringleaders safe in jail." Deliberating most of Monday, the grand jury concluded its work late on Tuesday. True bills were filed against African Americans Rev. Corday Harris, General Joseph Morris, Asa Gilmore, General Prince R. Rivers, of South Carolina, Captain Francis Murkerson, Neal Houston, and Rev. Jerry Simmons. Former U.S. Attorney General Amos T. Ackerman, who was born in New Hampshire but moved to Georgia before the Civil War, was three years removed from his failed federal prosecution of South Carolina's Ku Klux Klan violence. In Georgia in 1875, Ackerman led the attorneys defending the accused African Americans, while Georgia's Attorney General Hammond prosecuted Morris, Rivers, and Murkerson in absentia since they had allegedly fled the county. The grand jury charged each of these black men with insurrection.[62]

Of the more than one hundred black men who had been arrested during the crisis, the grand jury released thirty. These thirty black men, according to the grand jury, lacked the ability to lead the insurrection, because jury members declared them "dupes" and "stupid plantation hands." Members of the grand jury also released the thirty black men because they hoped to reduce court costs and "promote the ends of justice." The rationale did not please members of the press. On September 4, 1875, correspondent Sidney Herbert reported that he was taken aback when the grand jury found Rev. Corday Harris not guilty due to insufficient evidence. Not convinced of this decision, Herbert argued that he thought "a feeling of opposition and hatred to the whites" existed "among the negroes of Laurens, Johnson, and other counties." He agreed that the bulk of blacks "were ignorant and stupid plantation hands," but the African Americans founding and organizing the independent militia companies possessed intelligence, ambition, energy, and organizational skills. Herbert also concluded that the African Americans who founded the independent black militia companies exercised control over the duped and ignorant blacks. Further, black men such as these possessed an ability to deceive and the capacity to threaten white life and property. Therefore, "these negroes were the leaders."

The leaders, as militiamen, constituted a "certain class of negroes" who alone exhibited "a feeling of hostility to the white race." Rev. Corday Harris, third in command behind ringleaders Murkerson, Morris, and Rivers, escaped the grand jury because he had not threatened Washington County and Sandersville whites. Harris additionally had sought the counsel of the mayor and supposedly dispersed the black political gathering on July 24, making him appear more conciliatory toward whites than did his warlike counterparts. As a result, Herbert reported, "In all this there was no testimony with which to secure an honest conviction." Herbert concluded, "I cannot see . . . the conviction of any but the real *instigators* of this movement, the ambitious."[63]

On Monday, September 6, 1875, the Washington County grand jury completed its work. Foreman Theophilus J. Smith released the grand jury's findings to the press, concluding, first, that "the eyes of our [white] people were opened [just] in time to stay the threatening demon's bloody hand." Second, Smith declared, despite "the atrociousness of the crime . . . we succeeded well . . . in dispelling all selfishness, all prejudices and bitterness." Third, since March 1875 the grand jury had made favorable reports on the general status of race relations in Washington County, where "our people [had experienced] . . . improved morals, the prosperity, peace, and good will that [has] reigned among us." The racial harmony, fairness, and justice that had defined the grand jury investigation, Smith felt, occurred due to Judge Johnson's "rigid administration." Previous grand juries had also noted and even "congratulated our people upon the good feeling that prevailed between the races and cautioned our colored people against those seeking to stir up strife and arraign the races in antagonism to each other." Fourth, Smith continued, "the colored people have seemingly allowed wicked and designing men to inflame their passions to such an extent that some had been inspired by the wicked one to take the lives of not only white men, but of innocent and unsuspecting women and children." Yet, despite the claims of black violence and hostility against every white person of all ages, the grand jury reported no insurrection-related white fatalities.

The insurrection, however, made it clear that Washington County's racial utopia had noticeable fractures, as unearthed by outsiders. According to the Washington County grand jury, blacks in Laurens and Johnson Counties were guilty of insurrection. Washington County's blacks were innocent but also "duped into these nefarious plots by a few wicked demons" outside of Washington County. The troublemakers were Joseph Morris of Burke County, Prince Rivers of South Carolina, and "a few others in this and adjoining counties." Washington County's grand jury also asserted that "the larger portion of our colored people knew nothing" and that such isolation allowed local blacks to "give a deaf ear to such abominable wickedness and co-operate with all good citizens in suppressing crime." More importantly, local white authorities had overreacted to these external influences in spite of their "best of motives." As a result, the mass "indiscriminate" arrests of Washington County blacks "was exceedingly unfortunate," "suicidal and hasty," and financially reckless, overtaxing the county's already strained monetary resources. Further, local officials had arrested the wrong blacks. They had captured black insurrectionists outside Washington County's jurisdictions. Under the strict guidance of Judge Johnson, the grand jury released thirty-one more "misguided, deceived and duped" African Americans. Grand Jury Foreman Theophilus Smith noted, finally, that whites had acted within the law with "wisdom and discretion" because "not a gun [had] been fired or a drop of blood split—whilst we were so much exasperated."[64]

The Johnson County grand jury convened in Wrightsville, Georgia, in September 1875. Its members also found themselves keenly aware of their collective responsibility to demonstrate to those outside the South that the local legal system treated blacks fairly. Grand jury members concluded that blacks had "contemplated" and sought to execute a series of "evils" and "crimes" that "would have delighted those who are the enemies of our State & . . . grieved those who are her true friends." The Johnson County grand jury delivered a "Bill of Indictment" against twenty-four African Americans, who, on July 24, 1875, "did combine & confederate themselves into a militia company oath bound to follow & [obey] all orders of their leaders and commanders." Johnson County's definition of insurrection reflected white fears of slave revolts. The binding oath taking and making was a universal cause for whites fearful of experiencing Haitianization in Georgia. The specter of Haiti cast in a negative light all blacks exercising economic and political power and autonomy that undermined white rule. Haitianization also informed Johnson County's assessment of insurrection, which, whites felt, had "the effect of binding" the black members of the "said military organization" to resist whites' "lawful authority" and perpetrate "acts of bloodshed, lawlessness, and violence" against defenseless whites.

The grand jury also charged that black independent militiamen took an unspecified number of white lives. Further, fourteen of the twenty-four black men charged "did then and there combine & confederate themselves to accomplish the subversion & abrogation of" Georgia's laws with "the indiscriminate unlawfully killing" of white citizens.[65] According to the Georgia *Code*, punishment was to be "death, or if the jury recommend . . . mercy, confinement in the penitentiary for . . . not less than five nor more than twenty years."[66]

While the Johnson County grand jury contemplated imposing severe penalties for insurrection, Judge Herschel V. Johnson continued to guide the investigation. Johnson County focused on local militia leader Jake Hicks, the first to be tried in the second search for ringleaders. Authorities, however, struggled to impanel a grand jury. It took three unsuccessful attempts to impanel the Johnson County grand jury. The investigation revealed that Hicks, like his colleagues in Washington County, envisioned black men getting land. This vision included a future where "each colored man would get his forty acres and a mule." Hicks was also presented as a militiaman holding his ground, and holding "his gun level," in anticipation of "fighting" between the races. Judge Johnson, however, brought the inquest to an abrupt end when he informed "the jury that the evidence was not sufficient to convict," and thus "no verdict against the prisoner should be rendered." As a result, Hicks, like Rev. Corday Harris, received a not guilty verdict owing to insufficient evidence. Judge Johnson's judgment also brought about the release of all the black prisoners in Johnson County.[67]

The press and grand juries told the story of the Washington-Johnson County Insurrection from the white perspective, that is, fear of black martial and political power. Both focused on the possibility of race war—a fear dating to the colonial and antebellum slave insurrection scares in the United States and elsewhere in the Western Hemisphere. In the 1870s the independent and state-sponsored black militia company reminded many white Georgians of their pre–Civil War fears of slaves with guns. Reconstruction and the immediate post-Reconstruction years of the 1870s opened a new world where blacks and whites met as equals and citizens. In reality, white paternalism, racism, and dominance continued, even as African Americans sought to prove their loyalty to the United States and to Georgia. These years also initiated a competition for power that directly affected the black militia company, regardless of its status as an independent unit or as a state-sponsored unit accepted as a member of the Georgia Volunteers and the Georgia Volunteers, Colored.

The Aftermath

As the grand jury "insurrection" investigations reached their climax in August and September, whites mobilized to create both state-sponsored and independent militia units. Reflective of the white and black political competition preceding the alleged insurrection, eighteen white companies received permission from Governor James Milton Smith to elect officers. The granting of elections denoted the creation, and official state acceptance, of white state-sponsored militia units. Militias formed in the immediate wake of the insurrection in August included Jefferson County's Bartow Light Infantry, Laurens County's Guards, and Johnson County's Rangers. They each elected commanding officers—captains and subalterns—between August 16 and 26, 1875.

In September, Washington County's Dragoons welcomed a new unit, Company B, the Light Horse Guards, as they, too, chose new leaders. Companies not championed by the press between July and October 1875 nor recorded by Sydney Herbert in 1878 appear to be new independent companies organized for the purpose of meeting any further black challenges in the seven counties. There were new companies organized in August 1875 in Laurens, Johnson, Washington, and Wilkinson Counties. They possessed such names as the Bay Springs Volunteers, organized at Washington County's Oconee Post Office, and the Laurens County Troup Grays, organized in Laurens Hill, Georgia. Oconee Post Office was also the site where Johnson County's Buckeye Guards were created along with Wilkinson County's Howe Guards. September also marked the emergence of new militia units in the same counties: Laurens's Turkey Creek Rangers, founded in Dublin, Georgia; Wilkinson's Oconee Rifles, in Toomsboro, Georgia; the Oconee Grays, in Irwinton, Georgia; Johnson's Gunn Logue Rifles; Washington's Blues; and the Stellarville Cavaliers and Gordon Cavalry, two cavalry companies added in Jefferson County. Only four of these companies did not exist by 1878, when Sydney Herbert published his official list of militia companies; the Stellarville Cavaliers, the Gordon Cavalry, the Howe Guards, and the Gunn Logue Rifles had all disbanded.[68]

The South's defeat in the Civil War, some rural whites admitted, marked the end of the plantation economy in their communities in Georgia. In the 1870s, railroads, train stations, and newspapers intruded on what rural whites believed was a utopian community marked by predictability, white male rule, and isolation from external intrusions. The Civil War ended slavery and provided blacks with new opportunities for autonomy and self-mastery, with the independent and state-sponsored militia companies serving as symbols of black freedom and new possibilities. This freedom for blacks to determine when, where, how, and why they labored was enhanced by their newfound mobility: riding a train to new communities. Newspapers brought stories of new places while penetrating the illusion of utopia. Trains and railway stations brought to Georgia's rural communities in the 1870s black strangers who were either no longer slaves or had a long history of freedom and participation in community activities. Tunis Campbell was one of those strangers who transformed Georgia's rural communities, as he elevated, educated, and enlisted black people in the service of self-mastery. Free people such as Campbell, Cudjo Fye, Joseph Morris, Todd Norris, and Corday Harris joined local African Americans in contesting the old utopian boundaries of slave labor and white economic and political dominance. They each used the independent militia company to help them defend and define black rights.

The carriers and conveyers of change forced local whites to seek new approaches to their postwar identities and sense of belonging as citizens of the United States and transformed their views and definitions of African Americans. The "culture of segregation," which whites used to try to control the impact of change, was in its infancy in the 1870s. Yet blacks' quest for political and economic autonomy challenged white conceptions of African Americans solely as slaves. Black militiamen who pursued membership in the Georgia Volunteers and participated in local, regional, and statewide Republican Party politics were neither slaves nor inferior. They were free citizens of the United States and Georgia.

"ANY PERSON CAPABLE OF DOING MILITARY DUTY"

The Georgia Volunteers, 1878–1890s

From the mid- to late 1860s through the mid-1870s the independent black militia functioned as a critical part of rural black efforts to define black political and economic autonomy. The independent militia company had been used to shape black freedom in multiple ways. Specifically, blacks used the militia company as a self-defense force, as a communication vehicle, and to defend black social, political, and economic rights. Further, the independent militia provided security and support for black elected officials and political organizers. Militiamen also helped enforce black authorities' power to protect African Americans from white abuses and mobilized the black community for unified political action, whether in physical defense of black elected officials or in bringing blacks together to defend, protect, and free local political leaders. The independent militia unit in the seven counties of central and eastern Georgia gave blacks a platform from which to organize rural blacks for collective economic and political autonomy. Rural blacks in the seven counties, empowered by the Civil Rights Act of 1875, sought to challenge white control over the use of labor and to secure the right to use public facilities for public meetings. The militia was also the central organizing institution for local collective economic autonomy, as rural African Americans pursued opportunities to acquire land and to reap the benefits and rewards that the land produced. Finally, the black independent militia and state-sponsored militia challenged local whites for the right to rule, because if "a political party without guns was no political party at all," then the inverse was also true.[1]

The all-black militia company continued to be important to Georgia's African Americans even as the rural independent militia unit ceased to exist after the Johnson County Insurrection. A limited set of state-sponsored urban black militia companies became the institution blacks utilized to mobilize the community to celebrate moments of black freedom. The units were administered by state officials. Their funding came from local fundraising and state distribution of federal money funneled to both white and black militia companies. These black militia companies represented and served the needs of their home cities and their state for the last two and a half decades of the nineteenth century. Black militia units persisted despite white political repression, which took a variety of forms including militia reorganizations, segregation, disfranchisement, and antiblack violence. The latter culminated in 1906 with the Atlanta race riot.

This chapter and the following three chapters explore the meaning and process of the state-initiated militia reorganization that extended from 1876 to the eve of the 1898 Spanish-American War, Cuban War of Independence, and Philippine-American War and culminated with the 1905 gubernatorial election. This chapter and the next reflect black efforts to establish their place as militiamen equal in all things to their white counterparts. The focus for the chapter is the fifteen years between 1876 and 1891, when the black state-sponsored militia became a key community institution and source of leadership in Atlanta and Savannah during the 1870s and 1880s. These black militia units endeavored to institutionalize local activities that made the companies community institutions. The local community and the state-sponsored militia company worked cooperatively to sustain the unit, as the Georgia Legislature reorganized the Georgia Volunteers in an attempt to manage and organize over 220 militia units. Racial segregation and reorganization would be key tools in managing the state militia.

The Georgia Legislature engaged in several militia reorganizations that impacted the presence of black militiamen as post-Reconstruction members of the Georgia Volunteers and of the early-twentieth-century organization, the Georgia State Troops. Black state-sponsored militiamen began joining the state militia in 1872. The General Assembly revived the Georgia militia at that time with the announcement to all Georgians that they could become members of the "first volunteer regiment," because "any person capable of doing military duty" was welcome to create a militia company in the state. While this invitation initially hinted at some measure of racial equality within the Georgia Volunteers, black militiamen immediately found themselves isolated from their white counterparts with the division of the militia into all-black and all-white units.[2] The physical separation of the races within the militia structure occurred as blacks and whites independently submitted applications requesting permission from the governor to create militia companies throughout the 1870s. These requests were part of the county-level competitions for political and racial hegemony that defined Reconstruction, the end of Reconstruction, and the beginning of white Democratic political supremacy in Georgia from 1872 onward. White political dominance would go essentially uncontested across the state for the rest of the nineteenth century and continue into the twentieth century.

The rise of white political violence during and after Reconstruction did not end black efforts to define freedom, autonomy, citizenship, and power through the institution of the militia company. The political power that militia companies conveyed to both white and black communities continued beyond the 1870s into the last two decades of the nineteenth century. In 1878, when *Savannah Morning News* journalist and militia advocate Sidney Herbert compiled a comprehensive roster of the Georgia Volunteers, there were forty-two black infantry units in Georgia. Twenty-three appeared to have been consistently active for six continuous years, since 1872, representing their communities and answering the need for a black political voice. Joining the infantry were solitary cavalry and artillery companies, both based in Savannah, Georgia. White infantry companies numbered a massive 175 companies, but only 52 units were classified as "continuously active" in Herbert's report. The remaining 106 operated less consistently. By 1878 a militia unit's official existence as a state institution was partially determined by how often a company complied with newly emerging state regulations and mandates concerning the monthly drills and quarterly, semiannual, and annual parades that were required by law. These rules of operation applied to every official unit that claimed membership in the Georgia Volunteers regardless of race. Yet segregation also defined the state militia, first by separating the companies by race and later by conducting annual training encampments that during the last decade of the nineteenth century would be reserved almost exclusively for white units.

There also were sixty-nine white cavalry units across the state and one artillery company in Washington County in 1878, three years after the 1875 insurrection. Between 1876 and 1878 it became clear, at least at the level of state government and in the popular press, that the 220-plus militia units across Georgia might be too many companies. It was assumed that these numbers would overtax state resources if all became state-sponsored militia units. Further, the governor, as militia commander in

Table 2. Roster of White Infantry Companies, Georgia, 1878

Name of Company	Name of Captain	Location in Georgia
1. Athens Guards[a]	T. W. Rucker	Athens
2. Albany Guards[a]	E. L. Wight	Albany
3. Atlanta Cadets[b]	E. S. McCandless	Atlanta
4. Austell Grays	J. W. Nelms	Fairburn
5. Aucilla Guards	T. J. Livingston	Grooversville
6. Americus Volunteer Rifles	J. R. McCleskey	Americus
7. Alexander Guards	(Disbanded)	Concord
8. Americus Guards	R. Key	Americus
9. Alexander Rifles	N. C. Munroe	Griffin
10. Appling Grays	J. P. McEachrin	Graham
11. Atlanta Home Guards	W. R. Page	Atlanta
12. Baldwin Blues[a]	B. R. Herty	Milledgeville
13. Beauregard Volunteers	J. M. Gray	Fort Valley
15. Bainbridge Independents	B. E. Russell	Bainbridge
16. Black Creek Volunteers	R. B. Bryan	Black Creek
17. Brunswick Riflemen	J. S. Blair	Brunswick
18. Brooks Rifles	J. E. Hanna	Quitman
19. Barnesville Blues[a]	E. J. Murphey	Barnesville
20. Belton Light Guards	W. W. Walls	Belton
21. Ben Hill Guards	E. Mobley	Hogansville
22. Buena Vista Guards	W. B. Butt	Buena Vista
23. Baldwin Volunteers	J. S. Pierce	Milledgeville
24. Buckeye Guards	J. A. Coleman	Oconee Post Office
25. Bartow Light Infantry	N. T. Hardman	Bartow
26. Branchville Independents	W. E. Davis	Camilla
27. Big Sandy Rangers	M. M. Sanders	Gordon
28. Bay Spring Volunteers	J. S. Wood	Oconee Post Office
29. Baker Fire Eaters	H. G. Lamar	Baker County
30. Columbus Guards	W. S. Shepherd	Columbus
31. Cuthbert Rifles	J. F. Kiddoo	Cuthbert
32. Clayton Volunteers	J. M. Smith	Jonesboro
33. City Light Guards[a]	R. J. Binford	Columbus

Captain W. L. Salisbury, City Light Guards, Assassinated, April 20, 1878

34. Clark Volunteers	C. W. Reynolds	Athens
35. Clinch Rifles[a]	Frank G. Ford	Augusta
36. Coweta Rangers	W. A. Turner	Newnan
37. Calhoun Rifles	J. H. Gardner	Morgan
38. Clayton Volunteers	J. M. Smith	Jonesboro
39. Cullers Volunteers	R. T. Culler	Lincolnton
40. County-Line Rangers	(Disbanded)	Harris County
41. Conyers Grays	J. C. Bartou	Conyers
42. Constitutional Guards[a]	J. L. Bird	Taylor's Creek
43. Centennial Light Guards	J. C. S. Timberlake	Gainesville
44. Clarke Light Infantry[a]	J. O. Clarke	Athens
45. Colquitt Guards	O. E. Finker	Union Point

(continued)

Table 2—*Continued*

Name of Company	Name of Captain	Location in Georgia
46. Cleburue Rifles[b]	John L. Conley	Atlanta
47. DuPont Light Infantry[a]	J. P. A. DuPont	DuPont
48. Dalton Guards	Thomas Hamilton	Dalton
49. Dooly Light Infantry	G. J. Lassiter	Vienna
50. Decatur Cadets	G. A. Ramspeck	Decatur
51. DeKalb Gordon Guards	W. R. Ragsdale	Lithonia
52. Dooly Grays	J. H. Evans	Drayton
53. Dawson Rifles	W. H. Andrews	Dawson
54. Dahlonega Cadets Co. A[a]	E. B. Earl	Dahlonega
55. Dahlonega Cadets Co. B[a]	J. R. Gray	Dahlonega
56. Emanuel Guards	M. B. Ward	Swainsboro
57. Early Guards[a]	J. D. Jones	Blakely
58. Etowah Infantry[a]	T. M. Milner	Cartersville
59. Floyd Rifles[a]	J. L. Hardeman	Macon
60. Fort Valley Volunteers	J. B. James	Fort Valley
61. Fort Gaines Guards[a]	M. T. Manderville	Fort Gaines
62. Fulton Blues[b]	J. G. Scrutchin	Atlanta
63. Gate City Guards[a]	J. F. Burke	Atlanta
64. Green Rifles	L. B. Willis	Greensboro
65. Glynn Guards	J. M. Cooper	Brunswick
66. Georgia Grays[b]	W. L. Salisbury	Columbus
67. German Volunteers[a]	John Schwarz	Savannah
68. Gibson Guards	J. J. McMahon	Gibson
69. Governor's Guards[a]	W. L. Heywood	Atlanta
70. Glasscock Independent Guards	W. R. Logue	Gibson
71. Griffin Light Guards[a]	W. H. Hartnett	Griffin
72. Gordon Rifles	J. H. Stephens	Ocklocknee
73. Gwinnett County Guards	W. B. Jackson	Dillard's
74. Gordon Cadets[a]	J. M. Moore	Brunswick
75. Georgia Zouaves[b]	John L. Conley	Atlanta
76. Hancock Guards	T. F. Pierce	Sparta
77. Hardwick Riflemen[b]	(Arms returned)	Bryan County
78. Hancock Vanguard	Geo. F. Pierce Jr.	Sparta
79. Hampton Guards	J. M. Williams	Hampton
80. Horse Creek Rangers	R. L. Miller	Scarboro
81. Harris County Light Guards	J. P. Hutchinson	Whiteville
82. Highland Rangers	J. L. Johnson	Rome
83. Home Guards	(no name recorded)	Irwinton
84. Hancock Blues	J. W. Weaver	Sparta
85. Herndon Volunteer Guards	E. L. Camp	Herndon
86. Irish Jasper Greens[a]	John Flannery	Savannah
87. Irish Volunteers[a]	Frank Smyth	Augusta
88. Jefferson Riflemen	J. H. Polhill	Louisville
89. Jack Smith Guards	D. H. Tucker	Sandersville
90. Johnson Light Infantry[a]	A. P. Adams	Savannah

Name of Company	Name of Captain	Location in Georgia
91. Jeff Davis Guards	J. L. Deadwyler	Elberton
92. James Rifles	J. G. Lister	Fayette county
93. Jasper County Grays	M. Pitts	Freeman's
94. Johnson Rangers	J. P. Kennedy	Wrightsville
95. Jefferson Grays	G. G. Johnson	Bethany
96. LaGrange Light Guards[a]	W. H. Huntley	LaGrange
97. Liberty Hill Volunteers	S. J. Heath	Pike County
98. Lee Guards	J. R. Anthony	Washington
99. Laurens Guards	J. L. Linden	Bailey's County
100. Lochrane Guards[b]	Jackson Boyd	Atlanta
101. Lowndes Volunteers	S. L. Varnedoe	Valdosta
102. Marietta Riflemen[a]	J. C. Lynes	Marietta
103. Macon Volunteers	W. W. Carnes	Macon
104. McIntosh Guards	J. G. Young	Darien
105. Macon Cadets[a]	T. L. Ross	Macon
106. Minute Men of 72	S. J. Fynt	Raytown
107. Muscogee Rifles[a]	Reese Crawford[c]	Columbus
108. Madison Rifles	S. H. Dye	Madison
109. Macon Guards[a]	Geo. L. Mason	Macon
110. Montezuma Guards	J. C. Ellington	Montezuma
111. Mountain City Guards	(Disbanded)	Rome
112. Morgan Rangers	C. W. Snead	Meriwether
113. Milledgeville Cadets[a]	L. L. Hunter	Milledgeville
114. Mitchell Light Guards[a]	J. O. McManus	Macon
115. Newnan Guards	L. R. Ray	Newnan
116. Newton Guards	R. Brown	Covington
117. Oglethorpe Infantry[a]	C. E. Coffin	Augusta
118. Ocklocknee Light Infantry	(No name recorded)	Boston
119. Oconee Rifles	T. B. Duggan	Watkinsville
120. Oglethorpe Light Infantry[a]	Robert Falligant	Savannah
121. Oconee Rifles	J. W. Johnson	Toomsboro
122. Oglethorpe Guards	J. D. Matthews	Lexington
123. Oconee Grays	V. S. Jeanes	Irwinton
124. Putnam Rifles[a]	I. H. Adams	Eatonton
125. Phoenix Riflemen[a]	R. E. Lester	Savannah
126. Pulaski Volunteers	Thos Henley	Hawkinsville
127. Polk County Guards	J. A. Peek	Cedartown
128. Piscola Volunteers	S. T. Kingsbury	Quitman
129. Powelton Guards	P. G. Veasey	Powelton
130. Pike Defenders	T. J. Irwin	Hallonsville
131. Palmetto Guards	J. K. Smith	Palmetto
133. Quitman Guards[a]	T. B. Cabaniss	Forsyth
134. R. E. Lee Volunteers	G. B. Knight	Madison
135. Republican Blues[a]	George A. Mercer	Savannah
136. Regulators	W. W. Kitchens	Glasscock

(continued)

Table 2—*Continued*

Name of Company	Name of Captain	Location in Georgia
137. Rome Light Guards[a]	E. J. Magruder	Rome
138. Savannah Cadets[a]	John W. Anderson	Savannah
139. Southern Rifles	W. E. Ragland	Talbotton
140. Stephens Light Infantry	B. M. Lannean	Crawfordville
141. Savannah Volunteer Guards (A)[a]	P. N. Raynal	Savannah
142. Savannah Volunteer Guards (B)[a]	T.F. Screven	Savannah
143. Savannah Volunteer Guards (C)[a]	H. C. Cunningham	Savannah
144. Sumter Light Guards	J. F. Pickett	Americus
145. Schley Guards	T. B. Myers	Ellaville
146. Southern Rights Guards[a]	J. G. Davis	Perry
147. Smith Rifles	J. M. Bowden	Henry County
148. Spalding Grays[a]	Seaton Grantland	Griffin
149. Salem Grays	W. Ennis	Milledgeville
150. Smith Volunteers	J. O. Knight	Crawford County
151. Stonewall Rifles[a]	W. A. Wilkins	Waynesboro
152. St. Mary's Guards	J. J. Rudolph	St. Mary's
153. Smith Guards	W. H. Brown	Thomaston
154. Thomasville Guards[a]	E. M. Smith	Thomasville
155. Troup County Guards	O. P. Autry	Harrisonville
156. Telfair Guards	T. J. Smith	McRae
157. Thomasville Cadets	E. M. Smith	Thomasville
158. Tatnall Guards	J.D. Bell	Reidsville

Capt. B. R. Herty, Baldwin Blues, Milledgeville, Died October 7, 1878

159. Troup Grays	(No name recorded)	Laurens Hill
160. Twiggs Volunteers	L. A. Nash	Gordon
161. Tabernacle Guards	R. P. Bynum	Sandersville
162. Turkey Creek Rangers	C. C. Stokes	Dublin
163. Twiggs Guards	J. E. McDonald	Jeffersonville
164. University Cadets Co. A[a]	S. T. Lake	Athens
165. University Cadets Co. B[a]	C. L. Floyd	Athens
166. Warren Light Infantry	J. Thompson	Warrenton
167. Walton Guards	W. S. R. Hardeman	Walton County
168. Washington Rifles[a]	R. L. Rogers	Sandersville
169. Wayne Rifles	W. H. Whaley	Wayne County
170. Walton County Volunteers	R. T. Bowie	Walton County
171. Warren Volunteers	J. C. Brinkley	Warrenton
172. Webster County Light Infantry	G. S. Rosser	Preston
173. W. T. Harris Guards	J. C. Fuller	Greenville
174. West Point Guards[a]	J. J. Smith	West Point
175. Wilkinson Rifles[a]	H. F. Carswell	Irwinton

Source: Compiled by Sidney Herbert of the *Savannah Morning News*.
Notes: a. Active or live companies
b. Dead companies
c. Military commander member of the present General Assembly of Georgia

chief, had exerted little if any control over the ever-growing number of militia companies. This seemed to be true in spite of Governor James Milton Smith's refusal to admit into the state military black rural independent militia companies from the seven counties involved in the alleged Johnson County Insurrection. Despite the governor's isolated and racially motivated effort to regulate the number of black militia companies, an effort that would continue, it was evident to state leaders and the press that the Georgia Volunteers badly needed pruning, reorganization, and better management if the size and operation of the state's military was to be controlled.[3]

Table 3. Report of White Cavalry Squadrons, Georgia, 1878

Name of Company	Name of Captain	Location in Georgia
1. Butler Dragoon	No name	Newton
2. Burke Hussars[a]	L. R. Fulcher	Waynesboro
3. Black-Horse Cavalry	No name	No location
4. Blue Ridge Mounted Infantry	T. W. Murray	Tunnel Hill
5. Barnett Horse Guards	No name	Barnett
6. Bullock Troop Cavalry	W. N. Hall	Cameron
7. Burke Dragoons	No name	Midville
8. Bullock Hussars	W. D. Brannon	No location
9. Boston Troop	A. B. Deyerle	Boston
10. Columbia County Cavalry	F. E. Eve	Appling
11. County-Line Hussars	J. W. Mays	Dougherty County
12. Dawsonville Troop	J. C. Coatney	Thomasville
13. DeKalb Dragoons	E. Cox	Decatur
14. Decatur Troop	J. D. Harrell	Bainbridge
15. Effingham Hussars[a]	E. Bird	Springfield
16. Etowali Dragoons	F. M. B. Young	Cartersville
17. Effingham Troop[a]	O. E. Smith	Egypt
18. Eureka Cavalry	W. A. Sales	Americus
19. Franklin Light Horse Cavalry	J. E. Pendergrast	Franklin
20. Georgia Hussars[a]	R. H. Anderson	Savannah
21. Governor's Troop	W. J. Oliver	Ward's Station
22. Georgia Troopers	J. E. Ritch	Athens
23. Gov. Smith Horse Guards	J. W. Robison	Sandersville
24. Governor's Dragoons	W. A. Branch	Carmak
25. Gordon Hussars	J. J. Thomas	No location
26. Hancock Troop	R. B. Baxter	Sparta
27. Hardeman Troopers	D. H. Holloman	Bryan Post Office
28. Houston Cavalry	J. Palmer	Perry
29. Hardwick Mounted Riflemen	R. Harvey	Eden
30. Jefferson Dragoons	J. L. Murphy	Bethany
31. Jasper Dragoons	J. W. Gray	Leakville

(continued)

Table 3—*Continued*

Name of Company	Name of Captain	Location in Georgia
32. Jefferson Hussars	J. R. Mixon	Bartow
33. Jones County Dragoons	J. J. Clay	Macon
34. Jefferson Sabres	G. T. Underwood	Louisville
35. Jackson Hussars	W. C. Howard	Jefferson
36. Lee Mounted Rifles	R. G. Hitt	Lee County
37. Liberty Independent Troop	W. A. Fleming	Liberty County
38. McDonough Dragoons	G. G. Green	McDonough
39. Milton Smith Dragoons	J. M. James	Douglassville
40. McDuffie Hussars	J. R. Wilson	Thomason
41. Morgan Cavalry	W. A. Broughton	Not Located
42. M. A. Candler Dragoons	C. B. C. Holeman	Fayetteville
43. McIntosh Light Dragoons	No name	Darien
44. Meriwether County Dragoons	J. T. Latimer	Grantville
45. Monroe Light Horse	A. O. Davis	Forsyth
46. Newton County Light Horse	No name	Brick Store
47. Madison County Light Dragoons	J. B. Eberhart	Paoli
48. Oglethorpe Cavalry	J. H. Pittard	Winterville
49. Richmond Hussars[a]	John W. Clark	Augusta
50. R. E. Lee Cavalry	P. M. Blakely	Meriwether
51. Smith Troop	No name	Red Bluff
52. Stonewall Cavalry	O. P. Hollis	Sumter County
53. Screven Troop	E. J. Sheppard	Haleyon Dale
54. Smith Cavalry	A. H. Smith	White Plains
55. Stellarville Cavalry	J. W. Brinson	Stellarville
56. Schley Cavalry	S. M. Cottle	Schley County
57. Smith Troop	W. M. Henderson	Red Clay
58. Stonewall Light Horse Company	H. C. Worthy	Greenville
59. Twiggs County Cavalry	W. B. Watts	Jeffersonville
60. Town Creek Dragoons	M. B. Talbird	Milledgeville
61. Twiggs County Dragoons	J. W. Trunell	Buzzard's Rock
62. Thomas Hussars[a]	W. D. Mitchell	Thomasville
63. Wilkes Hussars	C. A. Alexander	Washington
64. Washington Dragoons[a]	J. C. Harman	Tennille
65. Webster Light Horse Guards	G. W. Jennings	Preston
66. Wilkinson Dragoons	J. A. Shinholser	Toombsboro
67. Wilkins Cavaliers[a]	J. P. Thomas	Waynesboro
68. Washington Light Horse Guards	B. S. Boatright	Sandersville
69. Wilkinson Grays	A. A. Beall	Irwinton

Source: Compiled by Sidney Herbert of the *Savannah Morning News*.
Notes: a. Active or live companies
Others unknown

Reorganization: Georgia's Militia and Constitution and the National Guard

The first reorganization began in 1876, when "the attention of the Legislature was called to this matter," and was implemented in 1878, when the report calling for reorganization was presented to the General Assembly. During that two-year period and slightly before the study, the Georgia Militia's Board of Officers wrestled with changing the Georgia Volunteers from a freewheeling set of mostly independent units, where any group of citizens could convene and call themselves a militia company, to a group of militia companies whose number and nature would be regulated by the legislature, the militia leadership, and the governor. The Board of Officers—a whites-only group primarily located in middle Georgia, from Macon south and east to the Savannah and Augusta, Georgia, metropolitan areas—was formed to evaluate the loosely organized militia companies. Reorganization in Georgia reflected a national initiative to provide state militia organizations with direction and professionalization and to encourage lobbying for a steady stream of funding from the state and federal legislatures. The National Guard Association (NGA) endeavored to coordinate across state lines to press for federal assistance and uniformity in the administration of the militia as a national and state institution. The NGA encouraged states to create a "Board of Officers" to better regulate the militia at the state level and to provide a united and organized professional face to federal authorities. Georgia's Board of Officers ended up being a very informal committee of citizen soldiers that worked with the Military Committees of the Georgia General Assembly to effectuate the reorganization process and "make an earnest appeal for proper recognition [of the militia] by the State."[4]

The Georgia militia's reorganization in the late 1870s was part of a comprehensive dismantling of the Reconstruction constitution of 1868 and rewriting of the Georgia *Code*. Elite whites and Democrats, led by rabid anti-Reconstructionist and former Confederate secretary of state, General Robert Toombs, came together in 1877 to discard the Reconstruction document in favor of a new state constitution that enabled the restoration of local white elite and planter rule across Georgia. The white elite dominated the Georgia legislature in 1877 and condemned the 1868 constitution as a document "framed by foreigners, aliens, and adventurers." Further, it was "not a constitution of the people of Georgia," since it declared that "the State shall forever remain a member of the Union" and "that its people are part of the American nation" with "a paramount allegiance to the government of the United States." The new 1877 constitution needed to be "framed by the intelligence of Georgians," who would "baptize it as [their] own," and "owe allegiance to the State first and the general government afterwards." Fundamentally, it was felt that the "rights and interests should be left in the hands of Georgians, and Georgians alone."[5]

Clifford W. Anderson and Reorganization

Empowered by the new constitution, which restored home rule, the Georgia General Assembly in 1877 appointed a nine-member "committee of citizen soldiers" charged with the task of developing a "systematic plan for the reorganization of the volunteer soldiery of the state." From February 1877 to November 1878 the committee assessed the militia. Colonel Clifford W. Anderson from Savannah, leading the all-white First Regiment, chaired the Board of Officers in February 1877. The board was charged with revising the Georgia *Code* as it addressed the state's military. The central issues of reorganization involved the "actual operations" of the Volunteer force. Specifically, the Board of Officers indicated that the present system of governance was "inadequate and unadapted to our wants and purposes." Additionally, "deficiencies" that violated the *Code* had "been discovered through the actual operations of the volunteer military." All this needed to be corrected by "the substitution of better regulations" that outlined the mission and structure of the Georgia militia. Furthermore, reorganization was required to elevate state standards to make Georgia's military equal to that of "any other State in the Union." To meet that standard, the militia had to exist "under proper and effective regulation and discipline," which was missing from the large number of white militia companies, especially because the militia lacked a unifying chief operating officer who could both provide centralized authority and install overall harmony within the state military. The Georgia Volunteers needed an adjutant general similar to that of the other states with a centralized military organization. Georgia had not had an adjutant general since the end of the Civil War, when the federal government abolished all of the South's state militia units, primarily because of their service to the Confederacy. As a result, in the 1870s, when Georgia's militia was reauthorized by federal authorities, the governor was overwhelmed with having to manage the needs of an ever-growing restored militia institution and state government. To remedy this management problem, Georgia's newly created Board of Officers called for a new subordinate to the governor who would lead, administer, and manage the daily needs of the militia.

While Anderson's report identified the ills affecting the volunteer force, he also connected the militia to Civil War bravery and the Confederate "past and present," claiming a continuity that transcended the federal abolition of southern militia units. Anderson's "short and practical address" to white Georgians through this report on the state of the militia specifically noted that, while "the war is hushed" and the southern "military spirit has wholly died," the Georgia Volunteers both "past [and] present [are] *living* monuments of deeds of daring and acts of heroism, devotion, and self-sacrifice." Yet the Civil War had not been a victorious engagement for the South. It had been an unequivocal battlefield defeat. But defeat had not been spiritual, and so Anderson noted, "We too of Georgia can say we lost all save our honor." Anderson, nevertheless "thank[ed] God in preserving [honor]," because "untarnished we could afford to lose all else."[6]

Recommendations for Reorganization and Johnson County's Legacy

In November 1878 the committee reported to the legislature that the legal structure that defined the current glut of militia companies was "inadequate" and "impossible to amend." The recommendation was to create an entirely new code to define the militia, its mission, and its relationship to the state government. This recommendation would transform the Georgia militia. It changed the militia from a solely unregulated, locally focused institution created by local citizens obligated only to their collective local mission to a state militia organization representing not only the local community but also the state government under the command of the governor and adjutant general. Anderson's report noted that from 1872 to 1878 Georgia "considered her soldiery a plaything to be indulged in only so long as it did not cost anything," a charge that would also be made at the end of the nineteenth century. This assertion in the 1870s ignored the freewheeling county-level competition for political power still raging between black and white militiamen, because the Georgia Volunteers was assumed to be a nonpartisan institution representing state government and not a specific political party. Further militiamen in all of the independent companies regardless of race hoped to be funded by the state and thereby gain legitimacy, recognition, and better funding as representatives of state governance.[7]

Anderson reiterated this objective before a statewide convention of white militiamen in 1880: "Georgia is the only State in the country that cannot afford to appropriate a dollar for her volunteer force." This fact stood in contrast to South Carolina, which even during a budget crisis funded its militia, concluding that a well-funded militia was "the palladium of her security." But, "Georgia, the grand old keystone State of the South, is by her action crushing out the military spirit and with it the manhood of her sons."[8] Yet the militia was important in keeping the peace and harmony in a state fresh from Civil War defeat, a contested Reconstruction, and a state government rejoining a nation still recovering from civil war and the following decade's economic instability. This was clear in Georgia's "cities and counties" in the 1870s, as well as in "the labor riots [that] swept over the country like a tidal wave" during that decade. Both moments of instability had proven "that the volunteer troops had been of incalculable assistance in the preservation of order, in the sustenance of the civil authorities and in putting down riots and disorder" across the United States. Georgia's white militia officers hinted that locally the militia had forestalled the Johnson County Insurrection, in 1875, while encouraging the all-white citizen soldier's committee to create a more organized militia and declaring that it was time for the Georgia Legislature to give "some sort of aid to the volunteer soldiery."[9]

Specifically, the white citizen soldiers argued for a separate appropriation to organize, arm, equip, uniform, "and keep in shap[e] the military of the state." To fund the state's military, it was proposed that "a nominal tax of say .25 cents per annum, [be levied] on every male citizen of Georgia between the ages of 21 and 45." The citizen soldiers further recommended that the governor be relieved of administrative responsibility for the entire militia by restoring the position of adjutant general, which was federally abolished at the end of the Civil War. The committee also suggested lower and upper limits of how many men could constitute a militia company and encouraged legislation that granted commissioned officers lifetime commissions. To elevate the spirits of the state's volunteer soldiers, the committee urged the creation of a state flag as a symbol and signal of recognition that the Georgia Volunteers legitimately represented the state of Georgia as an official governmental institution.[10]

Segregation and Reconstruction

The press, citizen-soldier committee, and federal government debated and defined the place and position of African American militiamen. According to the *Savannah Morning Telegraph*, in March 1878 former United States Army General Henry C. Wayne asserted that in "the South, where Negroes are in large numbers, wisdom suggests that they be included in the militia law and be organized by themselves into regiments or battalions." He further noted that the black units were to be commanded "with the white organization under one common head." Implementing this organizational structure, in November 1878, the nine white Georgia citizen soldiers asserted, "There shall be no mixing of white and colored troops." Segregation, they argued, should begin at the company level and continue through the level of battalion to include "a white series and a colored series" in numbering and in recognizing each unit of the Georgia Volunteers. Careful not to invite federal intervention, the nine white citizen soldiers made it clear that "in every particular, . . . the colored troops have all the rights and privileges of the white troops." The key to making this new Georgia militia viable was "that the two races shall not be drilled or enlisted together. This is the wisest provision that could be made, and one that will be most agreeable to both classes of troops." With this mindset, the citizen soldiers defined separate as equal, making racial segregation the key to Georgia's racial harmony and an avenue for avoiding federal scrutiny.[11]

While elite white Georgians such as Howell Cobb objected to black troops of any ilk, post–Civil War arguments against incorporating black militiamen as "equal" members of the state military had political consequences that were tied to Reconstruction and post-Reconstruction Georgia. Some scholarship contends that "abuses of the militia function of black volunteer companies by Radical Republicans in South Carolina, Tennessee, and other Southern states was fresh in the minds of Conservative whites" and was the primary reason black units ceased to exist in these states. In this context of problems in neighboring states, both Georgia Radical Republicans and Democrats were hesitant in using the militia as a political weapon under the auspices of state government. More recent scholarship asserts that southern Radical Republicans failed to effectively utilize both black and white militias to implement and defend the Reconstruction program, as well as to utilize the state military to protect supporters of Reconstruction. Republicans also fragmented almost immediately after the Civil War, with moderate or centrist Republicans joining Democrats and conservatives in resisting Radical Reconstruction and with black state-sponsored militias serving as arms of Reconstruction governments.[12]

An all-white coalition defined Georgia's Reconstruction in 1868 and beyond into the early 1870s. Radical Republican Governor Rufus Bullock disbanded Georgia's militia because Congress decreed its dissolution in 1867 owing to the fact that white militias just coming out of the Civil War endangered societal order. Bullock from that point on had no official black or white militia to protect Radical Reconstruction in Georgia. Bullock's hopes that Congress, Union troops, and the president of the United States would exercise the power of the national government to make Radical Reconstruction a reality in Georgia further came to naught. Bullock was ousted, which ended Republican rule, in 1871/1872. Additionally, Georgia Democrats, white conservatives, and the Ku Klux Klan combined to use violence much more effectively than Georgia Republicans did, despite the presence of Union League, Loyalty League, and armed independent black militias that reinforced Republican political power.[13]

Even though the federal government ended military Reconstruction in Georgia in 1870 and opened the way for Georgia to reinstitute its white militia two-plus years later, the reorganized militia would not be a whites-only institution. Between 1870 and 1873 the Democratic Party sought first to destroy the Republican Party and Radical Reconstruction. Second, Democrats spent these years debating what could be and should be done with the militia in the context of focused federal oversight and potential federal intervention in state affairs. One commentator in 1870, calling themselves "Resurgum," projected that "the old militia system's" restoration loomed large on the horizon, with "a militia bill [aimed at] re-organizing the militia of Georgia." This was especially important since the "bill [would] provide for the enrollment by the sheriffs in their respective counties of all able-bodied citizens between the ages of eighteen and forty-five." Local control, presumably at the county level, Resurgum noted, reinforced the position of Georgia's militia districts as the foundation for the state's political system. According to Resurgum, the proposed bill [to end Reconstruction in Georgia] would authorize "the militia in each militia district to organize into companies, [and] elect officers." Under these conditions, Resurgum anticipated, with considerable fondness, the return of the "ancient militia muster, with all its fun, foibles, and" local focus as a clear indication the white militia was "about to be resumed."[14]

Despite political exhaustion at the congressional and presidential levels over Reconstruction, federal agencies imposed policies that transformed the Georgia militia from an all-white, state-sponsored, and informally organized institution into a biracial, segregated military organization. Both the War Department and Congress required that the new state militia include African Americans. The War Department in March 1873, with congressional approval, distributed arms and equipment to the states. The act stipulated that states receiving this 1873 appropriation had to avoid discriminating "on account of race, color, or former condition of servitude" when organizing and equipping militia companies with federal arms and equipment. This would be especially significant since the Georgia Legislature refused to allocate state resources to operate the Georgia Volunteers. Federal money, arms, and equipment became the sole method Georgia authorities used to operate the Georgia militia from the early 1870s restoration until the late 1880s. Within the context of federal stipulations, Georgia had to include black militia companies within the state governing structure at the rebirth of the Georgia militia. At the same time, segregating white from black and maintaining racially separate but parallel militia companies were also fundamental organizing principles that defined both the 1873 reinitiation and the 1878 reorganization of the Georgia Volunteers. Throughout this period Georgia's General Assembly, which was controlled by the Democratic Party, made a point of establishing that the legislature proposed, defined, and regulated the vision of the new state militia. Operating as the agency intending to direct the militia, the General Assembly utilized federal resources to sustain its military while claiming the militia's allegiance to the state of Georgia, not the federal government of the United States.[15]

The General Assembly's Vision

Georgia's General Assembly did not adopt the recommendations of the white citizen soldiers' committee without inserting its own vision and making modifications. The General Assembly rejected the military fund proposal. As a result, the fund would not be incorporated into any legislative appropriation until the late 1880s. The legislature also never taxed militiamen or Georgia's male citizens to operate the military service, but it did make commissioned officers lifetime members of the militia and it did institutionalize segregation to physically separate the races into all-white and all-black militia companies. Lifetime commissioning would survive until the turn of the century. But throughout most of the 1880s militia funding, equipping, and arming came solely from the federal government, at levels as low as $11,000 and as high as $16,000 annually. This funding formula would remain intact until the end of the 1880s.[16]

Black Militiamen: Power, Class, Race, and Leadership

Despite state authorities' neglect, throughout the late nineteenth century, of all state-supported and recognized militia companies nationally, Georgia's black militia from 1872 to 1905 was one center of African American political power. In 1880 young black militiamen who also held membership in the Republican Party mounted a successful coup that enabled them to take over Georgia's Republican Party for two years, from 1880 to 1882. Young black militiamen Jackson McHenry, Christopher C. Wimbish, Henry A. Rucker, and William A. Pledger helped lead the rebellion that challenged the party's established biracial leadership. Atlanta-based militiamen McHenry, Wimbish, and Rucker were ex-slaves, independent businessmen, laborers, and political activists whose political and economic careers endured into the early twentieth century. Their aim was to take control of the party to obtain more political power for African Americans, since African American voters in Georgia constituted 75 percent of the party's voting strength. They also challenged party leadership that limited black access to patronage rewards.[17]

Jackson McHenry, possibly a Civil War veteran who served in a heavy artillery unit, led Atlanta's all-black Capital City Guards in the 1870s. He wrote the letter that in 1878 petitioned Governor Alfred Colquitt for authorization to elect officers for the fifty-six-member company.[18] McHenry, in Atlanta, carved out a reputation as a race man whose "flame of anxiety . . . for the progress of his people" defined his "very existence." His commitment to the "elevation and welfare of the young of his race" was "an uncontrollable flood." A patron of the Freedman's Bank in the early 1870s, McHenry had the ability to mobilize people using the "power of speech," to "electrify and entertain any assembly of people, political or religious, ignorant or educated, as well as any man of superior attainments." McHenry accomplished this even though he was not "a man of letters." Nevertheless, McHenry utilized "common sense, wit and humor" to leverage institutional access for African Americans, a trait he applied less successfully with white militia authorities in the 1890s. His articulations in the 1870s, both verbally and in writing, were merged when he helped create the Capital City Guards as an extension of the Republican Party. His militia membership would ensure his public presence in Atlanta throughout the late nineteenth century. He became the face of Atlanta's black militiamen, despite the fact that other more educated African Americans would lead Atlanta's black battalion in the 1880s and 1890s.[19]

Jackson McHenry did not stop with the militia. A political activist, McHenry joined the late nineteenth-century black community effort to partially secure African American access to public education in Atlanta. Part of a cadre of working-class African American men, McHenry worked for the Republican Party at multiple levels while contending with its white supremacy and the limitations Jim Crow segregation imposed in the last twenty years of the century. While McHenry continually stood for public office, he reaped only a series of low-paying jobs and patronage positions that secured him employment as a janitor. Black Atlantans benefited from his attempts to get them access to politics and employment, yet political activism and militia service, spanning the decades from Reconstruction to the twentieth century, did not elevate McHenry to the ranks of wealth and high status. This despite his public persona as a major militia leader, if not *the* black militiaman of Atlanta.[20]

McHenry's protégé, Henry Allan Rucker, in contrast, found considerable reward as a black militiaman, businessman, and politician. The future collector of internal revenue in Georgia, from the end of the nineteenth century and through the first decade of the twentieth century, Rucker was a charter member of the Atlanta-based Capital City Guards two years before black Republicans, including members of this company, mobilized to transform and briefly take over Georgia's Republican Party. Rucker, between 1878 and 1880, was a private in the Capital City Guards, but the militia company also appears to have been Rucker's introduction to Republican Party politics. Jackson McHenry and C. C. Wimbish were Capital City Guards' officers and active Republicans. These two men could have recruited Rucker for membership in both the black militia company and Atlanta's Republican Party that participated in the brief takeover. Rucker was an up-and-coming young African American man who from the end of the Civil War to 1880 had carved out a secular education in Atlanta as a student of Storrs Congregational School, a night school, and, for two years, Atlanta University. Rucker also successfully began a barber business that gave him enhanced economic stability, in comparison to McHenry's dependence on patronage. The barber trade also provided Rucker with access to black and white politicians and businesspeople, sparking a political and business career that spanned four decades and included intimate relations with fellow black militiamen statewide and an active membership in the business and political communities throughout the late nineteenth century. While, unlike McHenry, Rucker does not appear to have been a lifelong militiaman, Rucker began his journey to political leadership in 1880, when black Republicans elected him to serve as a delegate to the Republican National Convention. He also joined fellow militiamen Pledger, Wimbush, and McHenry in turning black electoral power into the mastery of Georgia's Republican Party from 1880 to 1882.[21]

Militiamen Rucker and Christopher C. Wimbush and militiaman-to-be Floyd H. Crumbly belonged to a new generation of political activists in black Atlanta who were different from their mentor Jackson McHenry. According to Allison G. Dorsey, McHenry represented a working-class leadership cadre that lacked the educational foundation and access to business and property ownership that protégés Rucker and Wimbush, especially, attained along with Crumbly as a result of a broader education. Rucker and Wimbush in the early 1870s acquired normal school and collegiate educations. Their educations opened opportunities closed to McHenry. Rucker by the end of the nineteenth century had become collector of internal revenue and a Republican political boss, controlling patronage distributions to both blacks and whites and serving as collector longer than any white contemporary. Rucker's power extended to the national Republican Party, where he attempted to influence the party's platform on lynching. He also tried to keep African Americans in Georgia active in Republican Party politics throughout the late nineteenth century and into the new twentieth century. In Atlanta, Rucker amassed sufficient capital and business associates to initiate construction of the Rucker Building, the center of the black business district in downtown Atlanta at the beginning of the twentieth century. He also served as a lieutenant of Booker T. Washington and an organizer of one of the earliest meetings of the National Business League, a business organization founded by Washington for African American businesspeople. Wimbush reaped similar benefits from his educational training. In 1875 Wimbush was appointed "a black letter carrier." Education additionally provided Wimbush with credibility within black Atlanta as a leader in the elite First Congregational Church and a thirty-year career as a political activist representing African Americans in the patronage-focused Republican Party.[22]

Floyd H. Crumbly and Rucker together were late nineteenth-century black institution builders, entrepreneurs, and politicians. Born in Rome, Georgia, but a "leading young colored merchant" whose fortune grew as Atlanta developed, Crumbly's career could have mirrored those of his white contemporaries in the Chamber of Commerce, who like him migrated to Atlanta after the Civil War to take advantage of the city's and the community's economic growth and development. Unlike his white contemporaries, however, Crumbly, eighteen years old in 1876, enlisted in the United States Army. He spent five years in the West involved in cavalry service with the Tenth and Fourth Cavalries, rising each year to a new noncommissioned rank from sergeant and company clerk to, finally, "Sergeant Major of white and colored troops."

Crumbly was part of the continuing black quest, outlined by Frederick Douglass in 1863, that regarded African American military service as the direct path to full citizenship in the United States. Post–Civil War military service kept this promise alive, as black men enlisted in the military to "stake their claim to citizenship," serve in the country's "nation-building work," escape "the harsh realities of contract labor"—sharecropping—and find their place in the world. Crumbly was also part of what Elizabeth Leonard has characterized as the white "spread of civilization" west and "the final consolidation of America's nationhood," the national conquest of Native Americans. Floyd Crumbly enlisted and rose through the ranks in the postwar military, serving in the six-month "Victory [Victorio] Campaign of 1880 . . . commanded by Generals [Benjamin Henry] Grierson and [Edward] Hatch" against Native Americans.

Five years of military service provided Crumbly not only with an honorable military career but also with "a first-rate business education" and leadership skills that he brought back to Atlanta, working first as a grocery clerk and later, with assistance from two white merchants, as a successful grocer and entrepreneur. Participating in nation building and white settlement on the American frontier earned Crumbly a degree of success. According to Atlantan Rev. Edward R. Carter, Crumbly's "earnestness, honest business integrity and energy soon drew to him a good line of customers." Crumbly also endeavored to build his business with property investments, locating his primary enterprises on "one of the principal thoroughfares of the city." By the turn of the century, Crumbly had resumed his military career as a junior officer leading an all-black regiment in the Spanish-American War of 1898. American imperial expansion exported white supremacy, segregation, and racism overseas during this conflict. The war also marked the end of white nation building, closed the door on black citizenship, erased the history of black contributions to the nation's history, and defined the culture of segregation as a white American tradition.[23]

In the 1890s Rucker and Crumbly worked together in real estate. They founded the Georgia Real Estate Loan and Trust Company, which Rucker led. Together they controlled what was described as "more than twenty-five thousand dollars worth of Atlanta's valuable soil." Further, Crumbly, like several other black militia officers across the state, served as a Masonic leader, spending eight years as Secretary of the Grand Lodge of Freemasons of Georgia, where he initiated a benevolence program for the dependents of deceased lodge members. The combining of militia service, mutual aid society membership, and political activism was not just a function of black Georgia militiamen. Nineteenth-century Afro-Cubans used the militia, the mutual aid society known as the cabildo, and political activism to participate in political, social, and economic acts of inclusion similar to those that Crumbly and other Atlanta and Georgia black militiamen attempted in late-nineteenth-century Georgia. Black political efforts at defining freedom, inclusion, identity, and self-worth had parallels across the Western Hemisphere. E. R. Carter presented Crumbly in an effort to prove black worthiness and integrity. He assessed Crumbly as a military man who "possesses great military ability" and "is acknowledged by all as having no equal." In that context, Crumbly's resumption of a military career as a militiaman began with the early 1890s reorganization of the Georgia militia and included volunteer service at the end of the nineteenth century and beginning of the twentieth century, respectively, in Cuba and the Philippines. In January 1891 Populist Georgia Governor William J. Northen appointed Crumbly to be adjutant to newly commissioned African American Lieutenant-Colonel Thomas Grant, who commanded the Second Battalion of the Georgia Volunteers, Colored, which was based in Macon and incorporated Atlanta's militia companies. C. C. Wimbush also received a militia appointment, resuming his military career as commissary supervisor.[24]

Black militiamen throughout the late nineteenth century in Georgia would wear multiple hats. They were militiamen, Civil War and post–Civil War combat veterans, masons, members of the Republican Party, and holders of a variety of occupations. Some attained the status of independent entrepreneurs, which allowed them a significant degree of autonomy. This autonomy enabled them to challenge white supremacy and discrimination, on occasion publicly. These independently employed men worked as physicians, butchers, grocers, newspaper owners, and barbers in African American communities, sometimes serving white customers and at other times aware of their increasing obligation to serve black patrons, as segregation transformed their relationships with black and white clients alike.

In the militia, most of these men served as enlisted men, and a select few were elected officers of their units. Enlisted men worked in such jobs as laborer, porter, drayman, brick mason, barber, and carpenter—employment that provided a degree of stability. Collectively, the political power of black militiamen and blacks in general rose and fell with the declining fortunes of a racially fragmented Republican Party. From 1882 into the twentieth century, and culminating with the 1905 disbanding of the black militia, the Republican Party distributed only federal patronage and rarely if ever elected a black or white official to local, county, or state office. The year 1880 marked the high-water mark of black political power in Georgia. Federal patronage, not politically elected office, would set the narrow parameters of Republican Party power after 1882, making the party nearly invisible as a force that shaped public policy, sponsoring economic development, and deciding political and social issues. The black militia company retained a public presence lost to Republicans within the state governance structure because black militiamen were official members of the state of Georgia's military, the Georgia Volunteers. Further, they were the Georgia Volunteers, Colored, an institution that despite being segregated by race and saddled with obsolete equipment, marched, drilled, and attained some local public recognition as an arm of state government in their respective urban communities, a status that may have been more important than the steadily declining and racially fractured and segregated Republican Party in Georgia.

John H. Deveaux: Newspaper Owner and Militiaman

Across the state John H. Deveaux—Savannah black militia officer, Republican politician, businessman, customs house clerk, newspaper owner and editor, member of the black elite, and voice for the black community—chronicled the activities of Georgia's Volunteers, Colored, for much of the late nineteenth century. He utilized his newspaper to create an image of African Americans as worthy professional militiamen who were citizens of the United States and Georgia. Deveaux—like his fellow African-descendant leaders in Atlanta and elsewhere in the Western Hemisphere who utilized periodicals to promote racial unity, self-determination, self-reliance, activism, images of dignity and self-worth, and publicized behaviors that defined black people in the Americas as respectable citizens of their nation-state—wore many hats. These included, as it did with African-descendant people across the Western Hemisphere, the ability to organize collectively, to make demands on their government, and to insist on the right to free access to public places as citizens.

Further, Deveaux and other African-descendant leaders acted as purveyors of nationalism. They embraced both racial and patriotic nationalism, advancing the race while elevating their class as equal to that of their white counterparts making public policy decisions. Further, these black advocates for racial progress and participation in the larger society attempted to create a new model person that all black people might aspire to become. Such a person was a citizen whites might respect based on their compliance with Western cultural traditions and standards for middle- and upper-class behavior. They hoped by their example to convey the race to the status of full citizenship, earning all the rights and privileges that come with being a member of the nation.

Deveaux's primary objective as a newspaper owner was to construct a positive image of African Americans that blacks could believe in and whites might respect. With the *Savannah Tribune* Deveaux made it his mission to create "the best paper published in the interest of the race." From the mid-1870s into the twentieth century, he focused his newspaper on black competence that challenged white abuse and stereotypes against African Americans. The paper's coverage of public events demonstrated that blacks wrestled with "The Progress of the Negro [and how it] has not been commensurate with his opportunities."[25]

Transportation was one area of concern. Deveaux in 1872 helped lead a successful black streetcar boycott. In Savannah, public use of streetcars illustrated the contradictions surrounding the debate about black progress and access to public space. African Americans were the primary patrons of "each of the electric lines in the city. Yet the managers do not appreciate this enough to give employment to them." If black ridership was taken away, the *Tribune* projected, "these roads . . . [would] not make sufficient money to pay their white help." Further, "If we are forced to ride in separate car[s] let them be equally furnished. The same amount paid for tickets by whites, are also paid by us therefore give us equal accommodation." Whites meanwhile viewed such protests as "persistent attempts" by blacks "to force themselves into the street cars reserved to the whites." Whites also feared African American rejection of racially separate vehicles, a system they claimed "has worked sufficiently for a long time." Yet the "negroes of Savannah . . . refused to ride in their own cars and violently and insultingly obtruded themselves into" the streetcars reserved for whites only. According to whites, black objections to segregated public transportation had resulted in "a series of petty conflicts and assaults which culminated in a more serious street difficulty," specifically that black men with guns were being led by whites and "negroes of different wings of the Radical party" to disturb the peace of Savannah. Inside Savannah this group made "trouble for political effect," while those on the city's periphery, allegedly "unprovoked," fired into a white family gathering. White and black Savannahians, as a result, had a conflicting vision for the city about race and power.[26]

Race and public power across Georgia was also a question of local versus national authority, the former advancing white solidarity and states' rights and the latter promoting and protecting black rights. The chair of the Democratic Party's executive committee in 1872, militiaman T. Hardeman, contextualized this watershed year as "the perils of the times and the duties of the hour." According to Hardeman, elite white people were "engaged in a great contest" to determine whether constitutional government should be "return[ed] to the old landmarks of the fathers" or belong to the conveyors of enforcement acts, bayonet rule, and subordination of civil and military power to the federal government. The stakes, Hardeman argued, like those of the segregated transportation article, were high, as it was a contest with blacks for public power. The conflict was "between the friends of true government and the open enemies of Constitutional law and liberty."

To decide this competition for public power "the true men of the North and South, the East and West are preparing by forgetting the bitter memories of the [Civil War] past." Whites were no longer divided by the old sectional differences that had defined the Civil War but were reconciling "in the spirit of a noble brotherhood and a patriotic liberality." Whites transcended regionalism as they combined "to save the Government from overthrow and the people from the tyrannies of a centralized [federal] despotism." Like the segregated transportation author, Hardeman called for the restoration and maintenance of "Our State Government," because it was "the sheet anchor of our hopes" that "Democrats, [and] Liberal Republicans [become] collaborators in this work of reconciliation and reform." Governance, in many white minds, had to remain solely in the hands of whites, who wrestled with emancipation as a problem of Western liberalism. At stake was who would control black labor and define citizenship.[27]

For Deveaux, as a result, the *Tribune*'s mission was "devoted to the advancement and elevation of the colored race" with a focus on "the defence of the rights of the colored people and their elevation to the highest plane of citizenship." Deveaux also envisioned the *Tribune* as a vehicle "to effect reform in any department of the body politic." The newspaper belonged to black people. It was to be their "organ of communication one with the other and of speaking our sentiments to the country" in response to being "vilified with impunity by our enemies and misunderstood and despised by our friends." *The Colored Tribune* would in the end become "an advocate" for African Americans and their institutions.[28]

Founded in 1875 as the voice of African Americans—standing with friends and resisting foes who promoted negative images of blacks—*The Colored Tribune* claimed a year later to be "the only Republican paper now publishing in Georgia."[29] Deveaux not only opened the *Tribune* for blacks and Republicans, he also made the paper into an advocate for African American masons, mutual aid societies, and militiamen and a platform for celebrating Emancipation Day. The *Tribune* became the place where Republicans, militiamen, masons, the images and issues of black Americans, and their opponents intersected. The paper served as the source from which public announcements were released declaring each community group's activities, especially those of militiamen. Deveaux used the paper to encourage black people and promote black institutions. It was the site where a note of promotion encouraging public support came from. The pages of the *Tribune* also fleshed out the debate about the image and status of blacks in both the South and nationally, with the definition of citizenship constituting the primary contested issue.

On December 30, 1876, the Chatham Light infantry paid a final tribute to two African American members of the Georgia militia. The black "Board of Officers of the military of Savannah, Ga." announced in the *Tribune* that Captain William Yates of the Union Delmonico Guards and Lieutenant W. A. Harvey of the Savannah Light Infantry had died. They were recognized with resolutions announcing their deaths, but more importantly the resolutions purposely served as notes of "tribute and respect" that declared Yates and Harvey as "faithful officers" who deserved such fitting pronouncements. Death, however, had robbed the country of "useful citizens." Captain William H. Woodhouse of the Forest City Light Infantry and Board of Officers president, along with Lieutenant Frank A. Johnson, Board Secretary, made sure that Board minutes included the resolutions and "that these resolutions be published in the Savannah *Tribune*."[30]

Emancipation Day and Its Meaning

Two other articles on the same page of the December 30, 1876, issue highlighted the impending Emancipation Day celebration and registered an ongoing protest against the Hamburg Massacre, an attack on black citizenship and freedom. First was a white assault upon black citizenship and freedom, the Hamburg Massacre that occurred in South Carolina during the summer, and second, was Savannah's Emancipation Day, a verification of African American freedom and citizenship. The Hamburg Massacre article focused on the aftermath of this deadly white assault upon black South Carolina militiamen. The *Tribune* criticized the South Carolina Legislature for "reward[ing former Confederate General] M[atthew] C. Butler," as the leader of "the Hamburg slaughter, [and sending] him as their representative to the United States Senate." According to the *Tribune*, "when [Butler] gets in the Senate [it] will be about as honorable as the South Carolina penitentiary." In contrast, the *Tribune* noted that January 1, 1877, would be the "Fourteenth Anniversary of the Proclamation of Emancipation issued by Abraham Lincoln as President of the United States." This important event was to be "appropriately celebrated in Savannah on Monday [by] the military of our city," noting what would become a late nineteenth-century tradition of black militiamen setting the agenda for the commemoration.[31]

Unfortunately the January 1, 1877, issue is lost, but the *Tribune* opened the New Year, 1876, focused on black self-respect, a united nation transcending class and race, white respect for African Americans, and Emancipation Day as a key moment of black public display of collective citizenship. The articles, announcements, and reporting for this year could represent a set of annual traditions that the newspaper promoted, joining African Americans and black militiamen to publicly celebrate events and actions vital to defining black freedom and citizenship. The year 1876 also saw an extensive collection of *Tribune* articles focused on commemoration, militia activities, and defining black progress. According to the *Tribune*, the first day of a new year had been "from time immemorial always looked upon by mankind with the greatest hope and celebrated with the greatest rejoicing." It was an opportunity for a new start, a moment blacks viewed as the end of slavery and the beginning of freedom and full citizenship in both the nation and the state. With this vision the newspaper called for every U.S. citizen to "let every one be friendly and ask God to continue His mercies, and make this a year of plenty, and of good feeling and harmony among all people of our country."[32]

In that context, the *Tribune* noted that there were one hundred thousand black men in Georgia who needed to do a self-assessment and redefine what it meant to be African American. Significant numbers of these men, the newspaper contended, lacked "self-esteem" as well as "self-respect," because they "fanc[ied] themselves wise" and in possession of enough knowledge to be critical of "the efforts and labors of those who struggle to obtain a position of respect among their people and to elevate the masses to a higher plane of citizenship." Blacks accepting such false assertions about African American leadership from white men received "pats on the back" and were "told by white men, that they are 'good boy[s and], that they are respected by the whites as intelligent honest men." Blacks who acceded to this white critique "bow[ed] and scrape[d before] . . . white men and obey[ed] their bidding like slaves." By embracing white judgments, black men submitted to white aspersions and had "no respect for, or do anything to encourage their own leaders or people. They make a great mistake," since "no white man, of any principles whatever; has any respect for any man who has not self respect enough to love his race and do his part to advance its interests." To cement a relationship between blacks and their leaders, blacks had "respect [for them]selves," the newspaper declared: "[We must] respect our public enterprises—churches, schools, newspapers, and charitable institutions—and respect our educated leaders though they be as black as can be. Till we learn to do this, we may expect to be disrespected as we are." Leadership for blacks, the newspaper contended, was a two-way street, because "leaders must be true to the people in every respect, and the people must sustain those who are battling for the cause of human rights."[33]

With this critique Deveaux chastised blacks to support African American institutions. The *Tribune*, he noted, was "an experiment." The paper constituted a major risk, since "so many colored men have failed in the attempt to publish newspapers in the interest of our race." Deveaux had taken his chance by starting small. Success, Deveaux argued, enabled him to give his black audience "a paper twice the size of what it has been," and he promised that it would "continue to improve" if African Americans consistently supported the paper and other black institutions.[34]

While Deveaux attempted to mold a solid relationship between his paper and its audience, he also cemented black militiamen to Emancipation Day. The *Tribune*, throughout its run in the 1870s and from the late 1880s beyond the first decade of the twentieth century, consistently recorded and reported the militia's celebratory actions on this important day. In this context, Emancipation Day was a moment to celebrate and define black peoples' freedom, citizenship, power, and collective commitment. Savannah's African American militiamen were at the center of these commemorations.

The Thirteenth Anniversary, according to the *Tribune*, was an almost totally military event. Five all-black, state-sponsored, and recognized militia companies, constituting an unofficial battalion, "marched off at 11 o'clock," Saturday morning on January 1, 1876. Beginning on South Broad Street the disciplined units presented themselves in "a fine soldierly appearance creditable alike to themselves and our people." The African American cavalry company, the Savannah Hussars, led the parade. Black officers and noncommissioned officers followed with a procession consisting of infantry companies including the Forest City Light Infantry, the Chatham Light Infantry, the Union Delmonico Guards, the Savannah Light Infantry, and the Chatham Cadets, who completed the military contingent. The parade terminated in Savannah's most public park—the park extension—"where a large concourse of our people had assembled to do homage to the occasion." The Emancipation Proclamation was read, followed by prayer and speeches by Rev. Henry McNeal Turner and Judge J. M. Simms. The military rounded out the ceremony with a military salute and a series of skill competitions sponsored by the Hussars. With "our people in the best [of] humor" the celebration was perfect, as "nothing occurred to mar the joyousness of the occasion." In this moment blacks, both militiamen and members of the audience, demonstrated their ability to be sober independent citizens of the nation. Such a perfect moment might have reflected one scholar's comment about black militias marching on city streets: Parading black militiamen "must have infused African American onlookers" with a "chill . . . of pride and inspiration," because this moment marked a major change for former slaves, who were no longer under the "constant [white] monitoring of their actions." The marching armed militiamen enabled blacks to celebrate the "right to be men" and women—a fundamental part of citizenship in the black mind.[35]

The perfection of black militia public celebration on Emancipation Day, however, was challenged by advocates of an older southern martial tradition—the antebellum "patrol system" reborn in an article entitled "How to Treat the Colored People." Reprinted in the *Tribune* from the *Atlanta Independent* and *Atlanta Republican*, the article "How to Treat the Colored People" proposed solutions to public displays of African American freedom. According to the article's author, "the [Democratically controlled] government [of Georgia needed to] take steps to reinaugurate the patrol system all through those portions of Georgia where the negro abounds so largely." The newly re-created patrols in a world of constrained black freedom were intended to address black public gatherings and the African American leaders organizing such events. Public displays of "armed and uniformed black men marching in ranks through city streets or running through military drills on the celebration grounds" caused "chills of apprehension" among whites. A reinitiated patrol system was needed to "prescribe [to blacks] hours for going and coming." Blacks would be regulated by white "inspectors" armed with "the power to disperse" blacks who "habitually parad[ed]." The "inspectors" also should possess the power to punish "all violators of the regulations [with] prescribed" flogging, because African Americans taking up public space on their "thoroughfares . . . wedged in the throng in all their filth and villainous odors [was] too much to endure." In that context whites were "determined to rule" and "dictate the conduct and order, socially and politically," as well as "protect themselves" from public demonstrations of black freedom.[36]

Days of Freedom with Black Militiamen

African American militiamen also publicly paraded to celebrate events other than Emancipation Day. February 12, Abraham Lincoln's birthday, drew attention from blacks and their institutions. The *Tribune* profiled Lincoln's life, stressing his "humble origins," his endurance through the "greatest hardships," and his status as "an avowed opponent of slavery and injustice of every kind." The Emancipation Proclamation made Lincoln "immortal." It also "endeared his memory to our people and to all lovers of freedom and humanity everywhere." Black militiamen on Lincoln's birthday "turn[ed] out . . . in honor . . . of the illustrious son of America and benefactor of the colored race."[37]

Independence Day, July 4, was also important, as an opportunity to demonstrate black loyalty to the nation and that they were unquestioned citizens of the United States. The *Tribune* noted that the "(colored) military celebrated the 4th [of] July," while "the white military of Savannah did not celebrate the 4th," concluding, "Their patriotism has failed." White commemoration focused on Confederate and white southern events such as the centennial of Charleston, South Carolina, Confederate Memorial Day, on April 26, and exclusively white militia parades for George Washington's birthday and May Day. Georgia's white militiamen also paraded without black militiamen in celebration of the January 19 "anniversary of Gen. [Robert E.] Lee's birthday." For the Lee commemoration Savannah's "public schools were closed and business [was] very generally suspended" as "white citizens" marched in a "grand military parade" to honor Lee. Businesses also suspended operations on Confederate Memorial Day, which whites defined as "a worthy saints' day in the calendar of liberty!"

Blacks and whites partially blurred the boundaries of racial segregation when they marched separately in the same procession, either during a moment of shared community grief, as in 1879 for the funeral of Congressman Julian Hartridge, or during the visit of a mutually acceptable personality, such as the 1880 visit of General Ulysses S. Grant, reviled President of the United States to some white southerners, and, to others, a respected symbol of the Civil War. In 1885, however, the *Augusta Chronicle* declared that 1886 would be "a good time for the South to begin again to celebrate the Fourth of July," because "we of the South, [are] now living under a Democratic Administration [in Georgia and with President Grover Cleveland], guided by Jeffersonian principles." As a result, "we cannot too zealously and warmly proclaim, by a public holiday, our supreme loyalty to the Gospel of Freedom and Nationality."

But in the context of whites' continuing veneration of the Confederacy in the 1870s and early 1880s, with Lee's commemoration standing in contradistinction to the black celebration of Independence Day, the *Tribune* asserted that whites needed "a little more reconstruction," especially since "our Democratic friends say this is a white man's country." The *Tribune* asked, "Would it not be well for us to inform some of our patriotic friends who are so gloriously celebrating the 100th anniversary of American Independence [in 1876], that the first blood that was shed for American liberty was that of a negro, Crispus Attucks, who fell while nobly defending . . . Boston March 5th, 1770?" This important date, along with August 1, 1833, which marked the end of slavery in the British Caribbean, were clear symbols of why blacks had earned freedom and citizenship.[38]

In these contrasting cases of freedom celebrations, blacks marched to establish their status as loyal U.S. citizens. They also sought to declare their autonomy, competence, and capabilities by reminding audiences "of the importance of liberty." Further, each public gathering provided an opportunity to celebrate moments in black history that confirmed their patriotism and commitment both to freedom and to setting forth important dates. These racially separate public celebrations by both white and black militiamen additionally defined the racial battle lines "for [political] power," as the events they commemorated served as political rallies as well. Whites celebrated the Confederacy and southern commemoratory moments to cement white unity in direct opposition to African American attempts to exercise and declare their collective rights, freedom, and citizenship. Black parades with armed marching militiamen especially were events that "reinforce[d black] manhood," a collective vision of the race, and the hope of using politics to defend and expand black equality.[39]

For black militiamen, celebrating freedom extended beyond the beginning of the New Year. Veneration of the institutions of freedom also became a central part of militia commemorations. In May 1876 six black infantry companies and the Savannah Hussars turned out fully armed and in their best uniforms, making their "appearance . . . second to none in the State." The seven well-dressed companies convened for the sixth anniversary of the Fifteenth Amendment: the foundation of black political rights and defense of African American citizenship. Captain W. H. Woodhouse, "acting Major," certifying his responsibilities as leader of the combined units, led the disciplined companies. Collectively they "presented one of the finest military displays ever witnessed in our city." The companies paraded through Savannah's streets to the park extension, where they were met by a crowd similar in size to that of Emancipation Day. For this occasion the seven militia companies spent "several hours" drilling. Based on the physical appearance and discipline of the men, the precision of the drill routines, the relationship between the militiamen and black Savannah, and the significance of the event, the *Tribune*'s reporter concluded, "Our people have every reason to be proud of their military organization which is a credit to themselves, and an honor to the community."[40]

The Fifteenth Amendment celebration occupied a vital position in the white and black debate about black access to public space. The amendment's connection to and representation of federal power sustaining African American voting rights and citizenship also justified the black right to gather in public. Parading, drilling, celebrating, and exercising black power through the vote and black militiamen gave African Americans a reason to meet on urban thoroughfares, in parks, and within public buildings such as the county courthouse to plan and develop their visions of freedom, to exercise political power, and to conduct business as citizens. The utilization of public space to display black power was also an act of African American autonomy. The public celebrations of freedom's symbols—the Emancipation Proclamation, Abraham Lincoln's birthday, and the Fifteenth Amendment—announced that black bodies, their minds, and their attitudes belonged to black people. This was black freedom and the bedrock of African American citizenship.

Time, too, belonged to African Americans, who forsook the dictatorship of the clock and white control over black labor, recreation, spirituality, and community to march in Savannah's streets in 1876 or to gather at the Johnson County Courthouse a year earlier without white supervision. Dressing well and setting standards of military behavior and discipline declared that black bodies belonged to black people. Yet, even with federal power as the foundation of black public power, the *Tribune* and Deveaux made it clear that black ownership of self was fragile. It required constant nurturing, with blacks supporting African American leaders and institutions through their attendance, resources, and consistent defense of themselves as worthy citizens.[41]

Black Militia Celebrations

Individual African American militia companies also conducted their own specialized celebrations. In early January 1876, the Forest City Light Infantry, the Chatham Light Infantry, and the Savannah Hussars cavalry company convened as a "body in full uniform" and contributed "over one hundred dollars" to "commemorate the first spot in which a congregation of [black] people met to worship God" in Savannah. The First Bryan Baptist Church was the focal point of this week-long celebration, which included not only the militia companies but also seven other African American church congregations.[42]

Separately the Union Lincoln Guards and the Savannah Hussars, both founded four years before 1876, engaged in ceremonies reinforcing their respective public presences. The Hussars advertised the company's forthcoming "Fourth Grand Anniversary Pic-Nic" on August 7, 1876. The event was a fundraiser, with admission charges for both children and adults. A flag ceremony united the Union Lincoln Guards with a parallel organization, the United Daughters of Lincoln and the Hussars. The United Daughters of Lincoln convened at the home of the "venerable and patriotic lady Mrs. Georgia Kelly," who presented a flag containing symbols of black freedom to the Union Lincoln Guards. The gift was a blue silk flag with a "heavy gold" border that had on one side an armed "Goddess of Liberty" holding "a sword in her right hand" and in her left hand "scales containing the emancipation proclamation and the civil rights bill" (probably the Civil Rights Act of 1875). These two documents represented the bond between blacks and the federal government and set the parameters for African American freedom in the United States.

The Goddess of Liberty was encircled by the implements of industry, war, and peace. On the flag's opposite side were symbols of the nation, including the Nation's Capitol, stars to represent each state in the Union, and "a representation of the immortal [Abraham] Lincoln." The flag in its entirety reinforced the African American commitment to citizenship and the Union and reflected one united nation that black people had defended during the Civil War and continued to sustain as citizens. Speeches followed and a parade showing off the company's recently acquired uniforms; the flag presentation capped the social function sponsored by the Hussars.[43]

African American Women and Freedom Commemoration

Mrs. Georgia Kelly's donation represented broader themes that defined black women's post–Civil War aspirations and participation in public events. According to William A. Blair, "African American women had a political consciousness of their own and . . . black men recognized that their partners digested and conveyed information that helped them reach decisions on important issues of the day." As a result, "Black women supported [such] endeavors [as Emancipation Day, the Fifteenth Amendment Anniversary, and black militia events] and announced their own claim for citizenship on the public stage." African American women's contribution to black public events reflected an African American effort to attain status and respectability. In Mrs. Georgia Kelly's case the *Tribune* anointed her a "lady," "venerable," and "patriotic." These three accolades were indicators of middle-class status and respectability: two badges of racial progress with one of citizenship and loyalty to the nation. The donated flag represented what William Blair has characterized as "the activity of middle-class women . . . North or . . . South" who used the flag to portray the "abstract principles of the nation." Further, black women such as Mrs. Georgia Kelly used their public participation in black commemorations to "signal that they deserved the same treatment as white women" and to declare that "they were loyal to the United States," claiming a national citizenship first and then allegiance to the state of Georgia all couched within the status of ladyhood.[44]

Women, black and white, were also central to militia social functions and ceremonial events, especially flag presentations, which connected militiamen to patriotism and the defense of the nation. Eleanor Hannah further notes the presence of gender roles that stressed sexuality, romanticism, and the male body in uniform. The *Tribune*, however, devoted very little attention to the role of women in defining the militia tradition in Savannah, save for this special moment with the United Daughters of Lincoln and Mrs. Georgia Kelly's donation of the flag. There appears to have been an occasional acknowledgment of black women's assistance in decorating and organizing a major social event such as a grand ball, as women who supported militia fundraising for both races did. Reporters for the paper seem to have not covered any similar event where the role of black women in the militia was highlighted. Yet social functions were important to black militiamen as a fundraising mechanism, as a public relations and promotion vehicle, and most importantly as a key means of sustaining a militia company over time, and women generally provided critical assistance in making militia social events successful. Further, as Hannah contends, social functions and the presence of women at those events helped encourage militia membership. Gender further combined with militia membership to make potential militiamen think about the "social and national importance and value of the militia." Such consideration made the militia a desirable local institution whose membership needed to be respected and supported by the public, as militiamen endeavored to serve the nation while defining citizenship and manliness locally.[45]

Flag gifts, Hannah argues, tied the militia company to its local community and to the nation by defining the militia members as men of honor and as responsible citizens who exercised their obligations to duty, patriotism, and national defense. Militiamen also practiced an "adult manhood," suggesting a maturity that accompanied the men who became members of the militia. Further, Hannah asserts, "women also explicitly acknowledged and rewarded" militia members for their commitment to service and their devotion to making the militia a viable institution. Their mission as militiamen verified their manliness, citizenship, and willingness to learn the military skills needed to defend the nation. These were actions of mature manly men who donned the uniform, making them romantically and sexually attractive to women in the community.[46]

Savannah Hussars: "One Common Act of Responsible Citizenship and Disciplined Manhood"

One dashing unit that demonstrated what Hannah has called "one common act of responsible citizenship and disciplined manhood—the military parade"—was the Savannah Hussars. Comprising black Savannah butchers and businessmen primarily, the Hussars participated in Charleston, South Carolina's, annual "Grand Cavalry" parade and picnic. This community event celebrated by the South Carolina black militia attracted "several thousand" who watched an "imposing" procession of "soldiery bearing" by multiple African American cavalry companies. The uniforms, horsemanship, and military bearing of the Hussars "attracted much attention" from the crowd as the company paraded through Charleston's major streets, ending at the Belvidere Farm, where all the companies enjoyed a picnic and military drills. The Hussars proved to be a "promising company" whose actions at this event "looked superb," and the unit performed such that their "reminiscences . . . may last them through life."[47]

Responsible Citizens: Forest City Light Infantry and Other Militiamen

Captain William H. Woodhouse, president of the black Officer's Board, also commanded the Forest City Light Infantry and led the unofficial black battalion, with all the African American militia companies in Savannah under his direction. The *Tribune* reported that Forest City regularly engaged in target practice and drill routines, but the company also maintained connections to black Savannah and memorialized its leaders. Simon Mirault, an "esteemed honorary member," died in January 1876. A man possessing an unimpeachable character and "a well spent life," Mirault had "contribut[ed] most materially to the successful organization of this company." Additionally, he provided the members with both "wise" and "paternal counsel," making him a cherished personage whose "memory and good counsel" was "sacredly kept." Mirault, according to this description, embodied what Hannah has defined as "responsible citizenship." Such a definition of citizenship was part of an ongoing post–Civil War debate, induced by industrialization and urbanization, about citizenship and manhood where black men took their role as militiamen seriously. This debate was especially important as their representative lives made clear that they were U.S. citizens equal to whites who had stepped forward to defend the nation during its hour of need. Blacks therefore had earned their place as equal citizens. As such, they were ready and willing to meet their patriotic obligation in the new post–Civil War world. This made them "responsible citizens"—militiamen prepared to serve both local and national needs.[48]

In May 1876 the company publicly demonstrated its commitment to serious militia service by celebrating its fourth anniversary with shooting and drill exercises. Officers from the Chatham Light Infantry judged the shooting competition. The *Tribune* also asserted that the unit's drill routines "displayed much improvement," marking one rare occasion where the newspaper did not accord a militia unit automatic high praise. Woodhouse and the Forest City company went to Macon, Georgia, for an "excursion" and drill with Macon's Union Lincoln Guards in late August that carried over to September 1. The *Tribune*, noting the overnight train excursion from Savannah to Macon and the return, continued its evaluative assessment, contending that the Forest City Light Infantry was "a gallant corps" that ranked "among the best military companies in the State." Woodhouse additionally led the dedication of the newly created "hospital for colored persons." He was appointed superintendent of the facility, which was located in an old schoolhouse of questionable structural integrity. The appointment occurred during a yellow fever epidemic. Black militiamen in Savannah and Macon mobilized to meet the crisis as civic leaders. John H. Deveaux was part of black Savannah's yellow fever committee, which worked closely with Savannah's African American benevolent organizations in a citywide movement to contain the disease.

Woodhouse and Deveaux were also on the board of directors of a relief society that addressed the crisis. Macon's Lincoln Guards opened their city-owned armory to "colored citizens" who were organizing fund-raising and relief efforts for Savannah's victims. Lincoln Guards officers Frank Disroon and John H. Loving held leadership positions on the Macon committee while working with Savannah's Benevolent Association. Macon's militia officers, along with Savannah's Woodhouse and Deveaux, not only served as volunteer citizen soldiers but also worked as urban leaders coordinating yellow fever relief. Woodhouse and Deveaux were officers in Masonic and benevolent organizations, as well as political leaders in the Republican Party. Like Mirault, Woodson, Deveaux, and the Macon militiamen publicly exercised "responsible citizenship."[49]

Chatham Light Infantry: "Best Drilled"

The Chatham Light Infantry, like the Forest City company and the Hussars, had its own excursion activities. Chatham Infantry members, for example, went to Mulberry Grove for a daylong event. The *Tribune* assessed the unit as "look[ing] well" as they marched home to Savannah following the excursion, and their drilling at the company's armory led the newspaper to declare them "one of the best drilled companies in the State." The unit celebrated its fifth anniversary in April 1876. They had become noted for their "fine appearance" and their "discipline and soldierly bearing." Additionally, the *Tribune* asserted it would "put the Chathams [up] against any company in the South as far as the drill is concerned." Chatham's picnic fund-raiser occurred in early September and included a shooting competition with a nationally recognized cup as the primary prize. The Carolina Light Infantry company, of Charleston, South Carolina, attended the picnic as guests of the Chatham Light Infantry. For entertainment, a band played for the gathering. Chatham members wanted everyone in attendance to have fun, but their ad announcing the picnic also stressed, "Good order will be preserved, and no liquor . . . allowed" in Savannah's Woodlawn Park. In September, the company "enjoyed themselves hugely . . . at their pic-nic," which was followed the same night "with a fine supper at their hall." Black militiamen and their local patrons would be respectable upstanding citizens.[50]

Militiamen in Public Life: Responsible Citizens

In May 1876 the Lone Star Cadets paraded and drilled neatly dressed. They followed this performance with a picnic. Six days later they did something similar, by first parading and then meeting for a "Grand Supper" complete with a local band to entertain the militiamen and their guests. While these were positive celebratory events, the nation's centennial undercut four years of black organization, development, and a growing pride in their public presence. In June 1876 the Forest City Light Infantry and Chatham Light Infantry decided against participating in the national centennial for reasons the newspaper did not elaborate on, except to note that the companies had announced in another source the details of their withdrawal.[51]

Despite this disappointment, militia officers were increasingly involved in leading relief activities, political life, Masonic groups, and citizenship activities. The Hussars' commanding officer, Captain W. H. Bell, the Chatham Light Infantry commander, Captain John H. Gardner, and militiaman Lewis M. Pleasant, a customs inspector for the port of Savannah and later a railroad route agent and postal employee, joined Woodhouse and Deveaux as active members of the Chatham County Republican Party. Essentially, militia officers and enlisted men in Savannah and Atlanta were also active black Republican Party political leaders and Masonic officers. Deveaux, in 1876, was consistently elected, appointed, and asked to speak at Republican Party functions. At the May Georgia Republican Party convention in Atlanta, delegates "unanimously elected [Deveaux] temporary chairman." In July, Deveaux called on black people to register and vote. He chastised over five thousand Chatham County blacks who had failed to register and therefore destroyed any opportunity to determine the next governor of Georgia. Blacks were aligned with Republicans, Deveaux argued: "[The] party has given us our freedom and all the privileges which we enjoy." Furthermore, the Republican Party protected African American freedom by placing the ballot "in our hands." But the ultimate question, Deveaux charged, was whether blacks were going to use their ballot or watch the Democratic Party "fill every office" and "enact such oppressive laws as will render it impossible for colored men to live." Blacks needed to register to vote and exercise this right by making their voices heard through voting. Political participation by voting, Deveaux contended, was blacks' primary political weapon within Savannah politics.

In August Deveaux spoke before a mass audience, urging them to organize a club to elect Rutherford B. Hayes president of the United States. Deveaux warned these Republicans, "Eternal vigilance is the price of liberty." Additionally, Deveaux journeyed to Macon, Georgia, in Bibb County, to organize another Hayes contingent where his oratorical skills "won fresh laurels," but the local police interrupted the proceedings, forcing Deveaux to call for calm, order, and adjournment. By September Deveaux had been elected party chairman of the First District, reflecting his power and presence in Chatham County. This position led to Deveaux becoming a delegate to the national Republican convention. Aside from his political responsibilities, Deveaux led the St. John the Evangelist chapter of the Grand Lodge in Georgia. According to his lodge report, "the fraternity" was "rapidly spreading over the State." All the branches "with but one or two exceptions, [were] progressing finely." Deveaux headed the list of fourteen new officers as grand master. These elected positions and appointments made it clear that Deveaux was a responsible citizen serving his community as a political leader, a newspaper owner, a crisis leader, and a militiaman.[52]

Hamburg, South Carolina, and Responsible Citizenship

South Carolina militiamen were also important to Deveaux. The *Tribune* addressed the massacre of "innocent colored [militia] men at Hamburg, S. C." as they celebrated the nation's centennial on the Fourth of July. They were killed by "white men who crossed [the Savannah River directly across] from [Augusta,] Georgia" and joined local South Carolina whites the following day. The *Tribune* reported on the massacre from the Fourth of July to the beginning of the fall of 1876, focusing on the circumstances that sparked the violence: white objection to black militiamen. According to the *Tribune*, "the street in which the colored militia was marching in columns of 'fours' was about fifty feet wide." These measurements, the newspaper claimed, provided clear evidence that "the [two white men] in the buggy" who objected to the black militia's presence had "ample room to pass" the militiamen with ease. The *Tribune* concluded that this circumstance "leads one strongly to suspect that the whole matter had been prearranged" to "enrage" whites into attacking Hamburg's black militiamen, because parade etiquette should have forestalled any confrontation.

Further, street or parade etiquette, according to the Georgia statutes, had traditionally maintained that "the greatest courtesy and deference always [be] extended military companies while out on parade, no matter what race." In this context, blacks concluded, that regardless of race and state boundaries military courtesy universally took precedence over racism. Parading state-sponsored militiamen, blacks assumed, had earned the respect of all people, because the militia was an institution with a clear track record of service, manliness, citizenship, military preparedness, and commitment to duty at the local, state, and national levels, especially over the issues of patriotism and defending the nation. Hamburg challenged all of these ideals and made it clear that black citizenship was not secure or respected by whites, even on Independence Day, when all citizens come together to celebrate the birth of the United States.

The Hamburg, South Carolina, confrontation between two white men and a black militia company continued into the next day, July 5, when Hamburg became an armed camp of white men from both Georgia and South Carolina determined to "disarm the [black] company" and overthrow black political activity. The African American militiamen, "seeing the danger[,] repaired to a brick building," intending to defend themselves and maintain their rights as militiamen. Armed black self-defense, in conjunction with the militia as a symbol of black political power, "enraged" white South Carolinians and Georgians. Whites from Augusta, Georgia, secured a cannon and transported it across the Savannah River to Hamburg, South Carolina. They fired canister shot against the brick building where the black militiamen had taken refuge, forcing the militiamen to surrender. Despite the black militia's capitulation, armed whites from both states "butchered" many of the disarmed African American militiamen.[53]

White Georgians quickly joined white South Carolinians in challenging the credibility, citizenship, and right of the black South Carolina militiamen to march in a public space. The *Savannah Morning News* led that debate in Savannah. According to the *Morning News*, the two white men in the buggy were "eloquent gentlemen [who] should have known . . . that the negroes who caused the trouble by their defiant attitude were not organized militiamen." As a result, black militiamen "had no shadow of right[s] to arms," especially because armed, unorganized black men "threatened the safety of the white citizens of Hamburg. It was [the black militiamen's] refusal to surrender these arms that brought about the troubles." The *Tribune* contested the white press's charge by pointing to the Second Amendment and the right of all citizens to bear arms, stressing "that the negroes now are citizens" and that therefore armed black militiamen had engaged themselves in legitimate acts of responsible citizenship: armed militia drill. In the context of full black citizenship the black newspaper asked, "What right had [former Confederate] Gen. [Matthew C.] Butler [who led the Hamburg massacre] or any other white man to make the demand [that black militiamen surrender their arms]?" The answer: "None at all," because "the negroes done right to refuse" to give ground or relinquish their weapons to white civilians who did not meet their civic obligations to serve and defend the nation. Maintaining the dignity of black citizenship was therefore necessary despite the loss of life at the "hands of the Georgia Ku Klux." Hamburg's Black militiamen, the

African American paper argued, were to be avenged by "a just God [who] will sooner or later overtake" the white murderers who killed South Carolina's black militiamen.[54]

In August, the *Tribune* also condemned South Carolina's Republican governor, Daniel H. Chamberlain, for allowing "His state" to be "invaded by an armed force from Georgia" who shot "his soldiers down like dogs." The governor further failed "to vindicate the dignity of the State or protect the lives of its loyal citizens. Six hundred armed white men led by Matthew C. Butler, the human butcher interfered with and threatened and broke up a second Republican party meeting-in-Edgefield, South Carolina," around the same time as the Hamburg murders. Chamberlain failed to respond to either attack. He "issued no proclamation" condemning the violence, nor did the South Carolina governor attempt to validate and defend African American militiamen and their citizenship. The *Tribune* completed its scathing assessment by quoting the *Toledo Blade*, which argued that the Republican Party, along with northern and southern Democrats, needed to accept the fact "that every black man in the South is to be protected in all his rights as an American citizen." This was a citizenship that respected black people, acknowledged equality between the races, and endorsed militia membership as a rite of citizenship and manhood.[55]

The *Tribune* also lent its support to a black South Carolina laborers' revolt known as the "Combahee Strike." Reprinting a Charleston *Standard and Commercial* article by former slave, Civil War hero, post–Civil War politician, congressman, and South Carolina militia officer Robert Smalls, the paper noted that three hundred unarmed black men and women had "refused to work for checks payable in 1880," four years in the future. These black citizens "demanded money for their labor." Calling for fairness and equality, these African American citizens made two demands: They would call off the strike "if the planters would pay them in [cash] money [and] they would go to work at the usual prices." Being paid cash reinforced black freedom from control of the rice planters, who insisted upon compensating black labor in worthless checks. The planters additionally sought to bind black workers to a state of dependency, especially when African American workers attempted to "purchase medicines, or employ physicians or obtain anything except through the agency of the planter."[56] The *Tribune* supported the citizenship and respect of black workers beyond those involved in the militia.

Tunis Campbell: Liberalism and an Integrated State Militia

While the *Tribune* commended the Republican Party for defending black rights in 1876 with the ballot, the case of Tunis G. Campbell challenged that commendation, because Georgia justice contradicted the concepts of equality before the law and called into question the Republican commitment to the viability and validity of black political power. Further, blacks' ability to defend African Americans and the rights accompanying their autonomy was indeed fragile, because men such as Washington County's Rev. Corday Harris and McIntosh County's Tunis Campbell had paid a high price when they utilized the independent black militia company to organize, mobilize, instruct, and protect black people. Campbell symbolized the black vision of a cooperative citizenship wherein African Americans worked with white Georgians to create a state representing all the people. Campbell called for a universal definition of citizenship by proposing that there be an integrated state militia where race meant increasingly less as a point of division. As a result, the political life of Tunis Campbell was tied up intimately with the place and purpose of both the independent and state-sponsored militias. Both were platforms on which African Americans could found their power, freedom, and place as citizens of Georgia.

Tunis Campbell, exercising his power as justice of the peace, "sent an important white man to jail for a few days for contempt of his court" in 1876. In response, the *Savannah Morning News* and two white judges "at last succeeded in sending" the elderly but still politically active and powerful Campbell to jail. Collectively the press and judges "convicted [him] of false imprisonment." The punishment, "one year in the penitentiary," had an additional goal—the termination of Campbell's political career and power in Georgia. In comparison, a white man, W. H. Rainey, "convicted of the same offence," paid a ten-dollar fine. Such disparity in sentencing revealed that Georgia Democrats had finally developed a scheme to strip Campbell of his judicial power and thereby continue the destruction of black political power in Georgia on the heels of the Johnson County Insurrection. The assault on Campbell and the white response to the Johnson County Insurrection marked the public termination of the independent black militia company.[57]

The *Tribune*, nevertheless, endeavored to lend Campbell its public support with a petition for clemency. Petitioners based the call for clemency on Campbell's advanced age, his time served, and "the humiliation of being displaced by conviction from the position he once held in the affections and esteem of his race." Further, the newspaper and black petitioners ironically attempted to extricate Campbell from convict leased "hard labor in Washington County," Georgia, the center of the 1875 Johnson County Insurrection. African Methodist Episcopal churchman Henry M. Turner led the petitioners of "colored men." They signed the clemency document while endeavoring to represent "a large majority of the colored people of the State." Further, they claimed to also be "identified with all of the interests of Georgia," as citizens representing the collective will of the state. Establishing their citizenship credentials and loyalty to the state and their race, militiamen Deveaux, Lewis M. Pleasant, and William A. Pledger, of Athens, Georgia, signed the petition. Other black political activists and noted public and civic persons—including Judson Lyons, William Craft, J. M. Simms, E. R. Belcher, W. H. Harrison, Thomas Butler, W. D. Moore, George Wallace, James B. Deveaux, L. C. Belcher, J. A. Brown, and W. B. Higginbotham—added their names and prestige to the clemency request. Georgia Governor James Milton Smith, in response, denied Campbell clemency, contending that the law must be obeyed and enforced, even as he ignored black efforts to do just the same.[58]

Tunis Campbell had come south from New Jersey to organize African Americans in Georgia's Sea Islands, Sapelo and St. Catherine, at the end of the Civil War. According to Campbell's biographer, Russell Duncan, the fifty-year-old Campbell hoped to transform labor from a status of inequality to one of equality and autonomy—goals expressed by blacks in the seven so-called insurrectionary counties. In the island communities, Campbell helped organize independent all-black militia companies created in part to defend African American political and economic rights. These militia companies, like the units in the seven insurrectionary counties, were not recognized by Georgia's government as arms of state governance. Yet, in parallel to the militia units in the seven counties, the independent companies reflected the will of local blacks, and as Duncan argues, the independent African American militia provided blacks with "an esprit de corps that would lead to a sense of obligation to protect the commonwealth" of African American political and economic citizenship.[59]

The independent militia companies also served as the vehicles for educating blacks about "self-government [and] . . . teach[ing] citizens' responsibility," self-reliance, autonomy, and equality. Duncan notes that there were "approximately 275 citizen-soldiers" serving St. Catherine Island. These independent militiamen operated in cooperation with "a judicial system" intended "to defend [black Sea Islanders'] newly gained freedom and property." Campbell wanted to lead the Sea Island communities to a state of self-determination, economically and politically, and to a collective vision of community cooperation that prioritized black acquisition of both human and monetary capital.

He additionally developed public education and a Union League organization as a paramilitary arm of the Republican Party dedicated to physically defending black rights while educating and politicizing local African Americans about the scope of their rights as citizens. Educating the black electorate was a quest Campbell shared with all African American Georgians and African-descendant people in the Western Hemisphere, hoping for the realization of a liberal ideology focused on individual liberty, property holding, and the political power that shored up and made citizenship the promised reality. In Georgia and across the hemisphere these discussions focused on blacks gaining access to land and the political power to protect and defend their economic, political, and social citizenship. Tunis Campbell made the promise of empowerment clear when he noted, "The great cry of our people is for land. If they can be protected they will get on well enough. . . . They want to be freeholders, landholders, and to hold office like white men." Campbell as a result had come south to give voice to universally held black goals that also defined emancipation in Georgia, namely, the realization of liberalism, which was the foundation of liberty in the Western Hemisphere and the guarantor of property ownership and citizenship.[60]

From the Georgia Sea Islands Campbell moved, in 1866–1867, to McIntosh County. According to Duncan, Campbell worked in McIntosh County to "set-up a separate social and political [black] community with its own ideological base." Campbell encouraged blacks to resist white employers who abused them, arguing, as Deveaux would in his newspaper, "if [blacks] expected to be respected they must respect themselves." Campbell also "formed a citizens' [independent black] militia company headed by a captain and a sergeant to protect blacks' rights." The independent black militia further functioned as Campbell's communications apparatus, "pass[ing] the word throughout the county" for black citizens to leave whatever they were doing and convene "together for political meetings." Such convocations solidified community and racial unity and educated the community about the benefits of black self-determination and collective action as the foundation of black citizenship.

The independent black militia company became the foundation of Campbell's black political machine, allowing him to harness, focus, and exercise black political power in combination with his position as McIntosh County's justice of the peace. Enhancing his power were two black constables, a sheriff, and a deputy sheriff, who enforced Campbell's verdicts and protected the labor and land rights of African Americans in McIntosh County as he did the black sailors in Darien. Campbell created and consolidated a political machine that exercised black power in McIntosh County for the rest of the nineteenth century using the independent black militia, a grassroots political organization, and his work as a voter registrar and justice of the peace. Black political power was further enhanced by both Campbell and his son serving, respectively, in the Georgia Legislature as one of three black state senators and in the Georgia House of Representatives as one of twenty-nine African American representatives.[61]

As a state senator in 1868 and especially in 1870, Campbell served on the state senate's Military Committee and on three other committees, including a joint legislative advisory committee to the governor. He proposed legislation that would have empowered the governor "with the authority to raise and equip integrated militia companies," a measure rejected by Republican Governor Rufus Bullock and the Democrats who two years later seized state government and destroyed African American political power. Expelled from the legislature in 1872, Campbell returned to serve locally in McIntosh County, where the independent black militia continued on as "the core of his political operation" until his arrest and conviction in January 1876. The conviction was part of the statewide white assault on black political power intended to dismantle African American political ascendency in the 1860s and 1870s.[62]

Tunis Campbell had been successful in organizing African Americans in Georgia's coastal region. For over a decade the independent black militia was a central part of his efforts to organize blacks politically, socially, and economically while utilizing the independent militia unit as a protective defense force, a communication vehicle, and a defender of black social, economic, and political rights. Independent black militias' purpose in the South was threefold. First, it protected the black community. Second, as one scholar notes, militia companies served as political clubs, a function more distinct in Georgia with Cudjo Fye before 1882. Third, the militia company provided a springboard toward the creation of black institutions, groups, and fraternal societies. These independent militia units, which operated without state funding, also gave black office holders the security to run for office, get elected, and serve, with Tunis Campbell being almost the solitary beneficiary of this institution in Georgia. The independent companies existed in the late 1860s and early 1870s "to protect the political party that defended the rights of themselves and their families" and because "a political party without guns was no political party at all."[63] Campbell's career proved this axiom to be true in Georgia.

The integrated militia company, as an arm of state government, was also the inspiration of Campbell's sometime political ally, black Savannah lawyer and radical activist Aaron A. Bradley. Separately, both men envisioned an integrated state militia serving all Georgians regardless of race. Campbell proposed legislation in 1870, while Bradley, in the mid- to late 1860s through the early 1870s, publicly argued for integrated militia units as part of his more inclusive platform that also advocated for women's suffrage and an eight-hour workday for all laborers. The eight-hour workday was part of a national debate about citizenship and the utilization of government to implement social, economic, and political change. These national issues aimed at empowering working-class people were part of a collective political vision that transformed some white Radical Republicans, Nancy Cohen has noted, into "liberal reformers." Liberal reformers opposed the eight-hour workday and suffrage for women, and concluded that black political empowerment, a major Radical objective, had been a colossal mistake.[64]

Both Campbell and Bradley were forced to recommend that African Americans limit their association with whites in order to secure a collective black agenda intended to assure African American social, economic, and political autonomy. The all-black independent militia company was the key to that autonomy and development. At the same time, Campbell and Bradley's vision of blacks and whites working together in an integrated statewide Georgia militia dramatically contrasted with that envisioned by the white officials controlling state government. Specifically, decision makers, white militia officers, and white Democrats and Republicans embraced segregation as the only option they envisioned for the state militia in a racially bifurcated world. Segregation and white dominance took precedence over black proposals of equality for all citizens.

African American leaders understood the need for a dual-purpose militia: an independent local defense force and a state-sponsored institution where blacks worked with whites. This duality confirms Angela Hornsby-Gutting's contention that blacks "used multiple institutional spaces for distinct and at times parallel uses." Blacks in general utilized institutional space as "secular and sacred, public and private—to promote [a] personal and [a] racial agenda." At the same time black men, such as Campbell and

Bradley, had to balance the contradictory scenarios posed by their white colleagues and opponents, and the militia was one of their earliest efforts to achieve two public policy goals at once. Whites associated the militia with black office holding, race war, and violent local competition for political supremacy. The combination of black military power and political, economic, and labor power caused whites to fear black independent and state-sponsored militias as antiwhite, dangerous, violent, and potentially deadly.[65] For blacks, nevertheless, the militia, whether independent or state-sponsored, fostered black solidarity and a collective vision of African American autonomy, citizenship, status, and self-determination before 1882.

1876: Black Liberty—Wake-up Call or Idleness

The *Tribune* in 1876 reflected a broader African American mindset reflective of the black militia's mission in microcosm. Blacks in the states of Georgia and South Carolina at a minimum defined freedom as change. They envisioned that slavery's end in 1865 had opened the door to full participatory citizenship, a significant right that marked the change from slavery to freedom. More specifically, African Americans believed their bodies and labor belonged to themselves as a right of citizenship. The end of slavery meant that blacks would shape their environments to meet their collective and individual needs as they envisioned and defined themselves citizens of the United States first and Georgia second. Blacks also viewed citizenship nationally and statewide as autonomy: the ability to initiate and shape their circumstances as self-reliant free people. Self-defense—including armed self-defense, individually and as members of the local independent and state-supported militias—was another component of black citizenship after slavery. The right to self-defense was functional in a limited way during Reconstruction and more comprehensively after Reconstruction as a recognized state institution. Citizenship existed beside blacks' sense of justice and the growing parameters of freedom and autonomy. Assertiveness in an embrace of freedom additionally characterized black laborers, leaders, and even militiamen on both sides of the Savannah River, as they exercised black power as a full manifestation of citizenship.[66]

Tribune articles in 1876 reinforced these African American notions of citizenship in the United States and Georgia. The newspaper defined citizenship as equality by quoting a *Boston Congregationalist* article on its front page. The expectation was "that the negro shall be allowed the free exercise of every public right, exactly as white people are." Black self-defense, too, made the *Tribune*'s front page. Noting one of the numerous violent white assaults on black people that defined the United States South in the 1870s the paper reported a case covered by the Wilmington, North Carolina, *Post* and the Atlanta *Republican*. Five "white young men" whipped "an old colored man and woman" alleged to have killed hogs belonging to the white men. The couple was "stripped and the lash well laid on." A pregnant black woman "was [also] stripped upward to the waist and held to the floor" while this same group burned her with "sealing wax . . . in a hundred different places." The press called for quick action where the "ku-klux scoundrels" would be "dealt with in short metre." In this context, blacks needed the legal protections accorded all citizens. These protections were required if the race was to be defended "from the constant outrages committed upon them by these 'rash boys,'" even to the point where the perpetrators were "killed and destroyed." The use of violence to protect and defend black citizenship was necessary especially when "the law fail[ed] to administer . . . evenhanded justice." Fundamentally, the *Tribune* argued, violence was "a game at which both sides [could] play, and the whites ha[d] vastly more to lose than the negroes." The bottom line, however, required blacks to do two things: to "prepare to defend themselves . . . [their] wives and their families by every means at their command" and to warn "whites who have anything at stake, beware" that black men would exercise their right to self-defense.[67]

Autonomy and self-determination were also part of the definition of citizenship espoused by the African American newspaper, because blacks wanted to "Paddle [their] own Canoe." They recognized, "Color we cannot change," and further asserted, "We don't wish to change it" because "God gave it [to] us." At the same time what had to be transformed was the black condition emergent "from slavery" and "its demoralization," which "ought to change as fast as possible" toward the affirmation of black citizenship rights. Change had to be self-reliantly accomplished by African Americans, as "work we must do ourselves," with the assistance of friends of the race. Key institutions in that effort to secure autonomy and the re-creation of black people as full citizens were "the school, the pulpit and the press." These institutions constituted the major "canoes in which we may make a successful voyage to the haven of social recognition" as contributors to national development.[68]

Politically, Rev. Henry M. Turner, in Savannah, defined his expectations for citizenship as the result of blacks' relationship with the Republican Party. Turner expressed his regrets that since 1872 the Republican Party had not marshaled a viable set of candidates able to challenge the Democratic Party. He also expected that a strong Republican party would affirm black citizenship, status, autonomy, and liberty. Noting that Georgia blacks supplied the party with 90 percent of its electoral power, African Americans would "support that party while it continue[d] to advocate the cause of liberty, justice, and political and civil equality." The political relationship between blacks and the Republican Party also required the presence and representation of blacks' "ablest and best men" at every important party event, especially at statewide conventions. Black autonomy and leadership were equally vital, because "none but true men" would be allowed to focus on African American interests. Only leaders, be they white or black, would "be placed in leading positions" to loyally reflect the aims and goals of African Americans, but ultimately blacks needed to be responsible for their political aims and objectives. Foreshadowing the 1880 black militiaman–led political revolt against established party leadership, Turner argued that black men should "lead the party." Black leadership needed to also "thrust aside all mercenary time servers, who seek our support in conventions, and are ashamed or afraid of us" or "too mean and treacherous to work for the party before the people." African Americans wanted to be full and equal participants in the political process. They did not view themselves as part-time or inherently inferior party citizens. White Republican "leaders . . . who never make a speech, or go to a Republican meeting" proposed "throwing the negro over-board." Such betrayals forced Turner to call for black Republicans to be ready to challenge their party opponents: "If the gauntlet is thrown down before us, let us be prepared to take it up."[69]

Deveaux added his voice to the discussion about black autonomy, unity, and assertive political action. He encouraged Savannah African Americans to embrace the self-determined power of ethnic and racial nationalism. The Irish, Deveaux insisted, were a group blacks ought to emulate. Pointing to the public success of the city's growing Irish population in organizing and celebrating St. Patrick's Day, Deveaux offered the Irish as a model for black collective action. Hoping to secure for blacks the same degree of racial or group unity and self-reliant power that he believed the Irish exercised, Deveaux was convinced blacks needed to embrace the cohesion offered by the ideology of nationalism. He believed this because the Irish commemorated St. Patrick's Day as a racial obligation. Nationalism secured "the greatest credit" and "devotion to the cause" of freedom for "their dear old Ireland." Further, while a publicly unified Irish people successfully presented and enjoyed Saint Patrick's Day, the real secret to Irish power and commitment to the cause of group solidarity was "constant agitation and compact organization." Irish leaders were successful because they mobilized their followers and convinced them to do their "duty ... to perform in honor of the memory of St. Patrick." Such concrete moments of racial and ethnic unity on that day alone made "the Irishmen the best organized people in our city, and resulted in their powerful display of strength"; indeed, "this close organization" had enabled "the Irish race in this city [to advance] ninety percent in the last decade."[70]

What Deveaux did not mention concerning Irish success in Savannah was the incorporation of Irish militiamen within white Savannah's militia structure. The Irish Jasper Greens were part of the Savannah Volunteer Guards, the city's white militia battalion, and the Jasper Greens had participated in Confederate celebrations such as Confederate Memorial Day and Robert E. Lee's birthday. The company was also active in May Day celebrations, as well as white community-based picnics. Each cemented the Irish community a place among whites in Savannah. The Jasper Greens, however, did not appear to be an overt political power base challenging local elite whites for public power the way the white elite projected the image of blacks pursuing access to public space, autonomy, and inclusion as political equals and full citizens. While Deveaux seems to have concluded that Savannah's Irish community had successfully found ways to unite their people and attain some level of inclusion within Savannah society, Deveaux missed an opportunity to compare how blacks and the Irish, respectively, were labeled as inherently inferior, both by elite whites in the United States South and by British colonial policy makers.[71]

Deveaux, nevertheless, believed that blacks "may learn an important lesson from the Irishmen" through their commitment and actions. According to Deveaux, blacks in 1876 had been "hitherto incapable of making the display of strength" that might mirror the power and inclusion attained by the Irish. To meet the challenge, blacks needed to wake up "from their lethargy and be up and doing," mirroring Turner's demand for an active black citizenry. Respect and "recognition of their rights in this State" would be theirs if they were proactive about uniting to exercise their rights as citizens. Presently, Deveaux asserted, "every right you hold dear is being trampled upon"; this had been a problem for the "past five or six years," reflecting back to the white Democratic Party's successful overthrow of Republican power in Georgia in the early 1870s. All would not been lost, however, if blacks decided "to right your wrongs, organize yourselves and show your power."[72]

Whites, in contrast, especially the planter elite, mobilized to defuse any actions by African Americans that challenged white governance and public presence. Georgian Frances Butler claimed that "liberty meant idleness" when African Americans exercised their freedom as citizens. Butler claimed that black liberty could only be countered by coercive white power. In this context of who did and did not possess liberty and citizenship, planters and elite whites viewed post–Civil War blacks as out of control, a trait that contradicted liberty's association with white self-control and self-restraint. The solution for planters, according to Charles L. Flynn Jr., was to repress "the independent will of the black worker," because white leaders believed that black people should know their place in the society, namely, as dependents on white benevolence.

Blacks, however, sought and developed a voice in contradistinction to white desires for a deferential black laboring class by exercising the full range of their self-determined citizenship rights, which included declarations of autonomy, political activism, militia formation, and demonstrations of public power by parading militiamen. Black militiamen on parade, as Eleanor Hannah has noted, declared their public and full right to citizenship and inclusion as active members of the polity. Parading also verified that militia membership certified that they were responsible and orderly citizens exercising citizenship in a mature patriotic way with a solid commitment to the nation, the United States. In response, the state of Georgia and southern whites concluded that the black militia and a free public education would "be crushing and utterly ruinous to the State." This was true because African Americans persisted in pursuing citizenship and inclusion using institutions that were critical to the construction of the new nation, the United States.[73]

Blacks Making Traditions and Controlling Institutions

The year 1876 not only marked the nation's centennial and recognition of who was an American but also the African American effort to regularize their militia traditions as acts of citizenship and freedom. The *Tribune* ended the year by suggesting that an Emancipation Day ceremony for January 1, 1877, "should be celebrated." "We hope," the paper declared, "steps are being taken in that direction though we have heard nothing as yet." At the end of 1876 this annually commemorated militia-based event had yet to be institutionalized. By the 1890s the Emancipation Association, a committee of black militia officers and civic leaders, were responsible for the annual January 1 celebration. At the same time the *Tribune's* future clouded over. Three years after the newspaper's initial issue, white printers refused to print the paper, again raising the question of whether blacks were citizens and in control of their own institutions and destiny. As a result, the *Tribune* ceased publication in 1878. It slumbered until Deveaux, his staff, and black investors and supporters managed, in an act of self-determination, to place the newspaper in the hands of black printers. But that was eight years later, in 1886. Deveaux continued as owner, editor, and manager until 1889, when Deveaux took on the collectorship of Brunswick, Georgia. He turned over the editorship to his protégé, twenty-one-year-old Solomon C. Johnson. Sol Johnson would serve as editor into the sixth decade of the twentieth century. He completed the late nineteenth century and opened the new century with a membership in the Georgia Volunteers, Colored, a career as newspaper editor and owner, and a lifetime of community service in Savannah.[74]

"An Eventful Day in the History of the Colored People": May 28, 1878

While the *Tribune* slumbered, Georgia's state government, in 1878, honored the black militiamen and at the same time reorganized the Georgia Volunteers. Reorganization, although intended to install efficiencies within the militia structure, did not enhance the long-term presence of the Georgia Volunteers, Colored, as a component of the state militia. The year 1878, however, also presented possibilities for black inclusion as Georgia citizens. In that light, the *Savannah Morning News* claimed that May 28, 1878, "was an eventful day in the history of the colored people of Savannah," because the "occasion was the first State prize drill of colored companies ever witnessed in Georgia." Black militiamen from Augusta, Georgia, initiated the event by, first, securing funding from local citizens and, second, purchasing the drill prize, "an elegant sword and belt" to be awarded to "the best drilled company in the State."

The drill invitational occurred in Savannah, where the black militia competition involved two of Augusta's militia units, the Douglass Infantry and the Georgia Infantry; one of Macon's two units, the Lincoln Guards; and five black Savannah militia companies led by the black cavalry company, the Savannah Hussars: the Forest City Light Infantry, the Chatham Light Infantry, the Union Delmonico Guards, the Lone Star Cadets, and the Union Lincoln Guards. Georgia governor Alfred Colquitt, a former Confederate major general and part of the "Bourbon Triumvirate"—the probusiness Democratic Party group—that ruled the state from 1872 to 1890 and pushed through the 1877 state constitution, also attended. African Americans invited him based on their belief that he was a racial moderate. Colquitt's notoriety among blacks was also reflected by the black residents of Macon and Atlanta, who named a militia company in his honor: respectively, Macon's Colquitt Blues and Atlanta's Governor's Volunteers. Colquitt graced the path-breaking competition accompanied by a personal secretary and at least one representative from the adjutant general's office.[75]

Savannah's Hussars escorted the governor and his entourage from the Pulaski House to Savannah's park extension, where many black public militia functions regularly occurred. Captain William. H. Woodhouse served as "acting Colonel," leading the ten black infantry units that marched in parade behind the governor and Hussars. According to the *Morning News*, approximately seven thousand people "gathered on the [park] grounds." Five thousand blacks and five hundred whites were present, along with guests from Charleston, South Carolina, Macon and Augusta, Georgia, and "other cities."[76]

After the parade, a "fine collation had been spread" for an invitation-only gathering of black militia officers and white officials at the Forest City Light Infantry hall. Governor Colquitt and his private secretary, Colonel Isaac W. Avery, along with Savannah's Colonel Clifford W. Anderson of the all-white First Georgia Regiment, addressed the African American militia officers. According to the *Morning News*, Governor Colquitt's remarks "were very kind and warmly applauded by the colored officers." Perhaps the black officer corps applauded because Colquitt defined "the qualities that make the true soldier" and form "the basis of a worthy citizenship." Physical appearance and bearing, Colquitt noted, were a reflection of the true soldier's character, along with "chivalry and virtue." These virtues had to be combined with "subordination to law and exercise of manhood," which Colquitt argued made "a people prosperous, happy, and respected." Within this context Colquitt outlined the parameters of his support for black endeavors. He pledged "his warmest sympathy as a man and his influence as a public officer" if blacks "in their efforts to elevate their race, broaden[ed] their intelligence and extend[ed] their usefulness."[77]

Anderson's remarks defined "a true soldierhood," and he complimented the black militiamen "on their excellent discipline, and wished that in the coming prize drill, as in all contests, they might win the laurels due to martial worth." Avery, "an old Savannah citizen," was pleased "to see the colored people of this city making so creditable a military display." But the real importance of the drill competition, Avery asserted, was to establish publicly that "the interests of the two races were reciprocal and their relationship should be harmonious" because "whites and blacks should be friends in the fullest sense of the word. This review to-day ought to convince the colored people that the whites felt a profound interest in their welfare and extended to them confidence, recognition, and regard." Such friendship was especially important in light of the "alienation [that] existed on the part of the colored people" that Avery claimed occurred "a few years back." In 1878, a decade later, that racial division, Avery claimed, "was forever ended," because "in such scenes as occurred this day an overwhelming proof that the whites with whom they lived were their true friends." Anderson's and Avery's speeches "were [just as] vociferously applauded" by African American militia officers as was Governor Colquitt's address. All three white men set the standards of soldiering and citizenship before black militiamen striving to do exactly as their guests defined military duty and citizenship. Overall, the *Morning News* concluded, the day "was indeed a striking evidence of the good feeling and harmony existing between the races in the great Democratic State of Georgia."[78]

Savannah's Chatham Light Infantry "was the best drilled company," with Augusta's Douglass Infantry being "the next best." Anderson in the presence of the governor and his private secretary, along with Savannah's Mayor John F. Wheaton, made the announcement. Black militiaman and *Tribune* owner and editor John H. Deveaux was "selected to present the prize" and make the last speech of the day to "his comrades." After commending the Chatham Light Infantry for exhibiting "the greatest proficiency in the manual exercises" with "coolness and the machine-like" execution of a polished company, Deveaux acknowledged Augusta's "patriotic ladies and gentlemen" for providing the event's funding and drill prize. In that context, Deveaux wanted to make it very clear that this competition was important to black people. Specifically, he could not "resist the opportunity of saying to you, my people, that I trust you fully appreciate this occasion. It has no ordinary significance. It is an indication of progress in civilization, and we should be encouraged and benefited by its teachings."[79]

Deveaux also believed May 28, 1878, to be a vitally important moment, because "ten years ago the colored American was despised as a citizen and ridiculed as a soldier." A decade later, those "who despised us—your Commander-in-Chief and Chief Magistrate of the State, and the Colonel of Georgia's best regiment, the representative of one of the strongest political and military families in our State—and the other honorable judges have deemed us of sufficient importance, both as citizens and as soldiers, to be present, and encourage us in our onward march of intelligence." Blacks and whites were "friends" who had "confidence and respect" after being "too long estranged." With identical interests "the success of the one must necessarily improve the condition of the other" for "the glory" of Georgia. The "gallant military spirit" that has "so long [been] manifested in our State by the Anglo-Saxons, has been imbedded in our people to a great extent. As proof, witness the success of Georgia's young son, [Henry O.] Flipper, the first colored graduate of West Point, and our grand military display to-day," in which the Chatham Light Infantry had "attained the highest eminence attainable in time of peace namely: proficiency and discipline."

This display of black discipline, proficiency, civilization, and honor, Deveaux believed, had "never been surpassed, perhaps equaled by our people in any part of the country in point of gallant military bearing, efficiency, elegance of uniform and, above all, in the excellency of the drill." The competition's success and Deveaux's commemoration helped to establish what became, by the 1890s, the annual May Parade, where black Savannah, Macon, and perhaps Augusta militia units marched in review before their African American constituency; rarely, if ever again, did Georgia's governor join a black commemoration, yet Colquitt's presence on May 28, 1878, made it a unique day for black militiamen.[80]

The May 1878 drill invitational, nevertheless, serves as one example of black commemorative ceremonies that drew black militiamen and white elite civic participation. It was also an event that did not involve direct connections to federal proscriptions that defined black freedom. The drill invitational, however, possessed a parallel structure to many celebrations initiated by African Americans across the United States, such as Emancipation Day, Abraham Lincoln's birthday, and the anniversaries of the Thirteenth, Fourteenth, and Fifteenth Amendments. Speeches at these events and especially the drill competitions were critical moments in which white and black speakers attempted to set the parameters of race relations, black history, the future relationship between blacks and whites, and what William A. Blair has described as "the role of public activity in the structure of power."[81]

Governor Alfred Colquitt, Colonels Isaac Avery and Clifford Anderson, and the *Savannah Morning News* endeavored to set the limits of black autonomy and citizenship. Colquitt, Avery, and Anderson set a new public relationship with blacks, though they intended to set definitive boundaries between the races. Whites shifted their racial attitudes from the outright fear expressed by private Weldrim to a restricted acceptance of black militiamen as citizens of Savannah. John H. Deveaux in this context insisted on outlining the black march of progress and recognizing a potential moment of equality with whites. He affirmed that blacks had generally changed and that the ten black militia units had achieved this equality at the drill invitational. The speeches reflected both white and black traditions, debates, and assumptions concerning the use of public space as a platform for shaping race relations and political power. The brief presentations by Colquitt, Avery, and Anderson, as well as the reporting of the *Morning News*, reflected some of the limitations whites sought to impose on African Americans. By 1878 white supremacy had set the tenor of Georgia's 1877 constitution, which intended to certify the end of black political influence as it had been known during Reconstruction.

This same governing document institutionalized the militia by incorporating the Georgia Volunteers, Colored, as an arm of Georgia state government. Colquitt's message defined the true soldier as someone whose manhood submitted to law and order. His message implied that submission produced a prosperous, happy, virtuous, and respected soldier. The governor also evoked the mantle of civilization as the key to "true soldierhood." Soldiers had self-control and refinement and lacked the barbarism and inferiority that had been long implied as the major flaws in black personal and collective character. Despite blacks' embrace of true soldierhood, during the drill invitational, Colquitt did not encourage black militiamen to be socially, economically, nor politically active or autonomous. He additionally did not recognize the militia as a component of black political and economic power or a key to African American inclusion in Georgia politics. Nor did he acknowledge black equality with whites and a respected black citizenship. Submission and true soldierhood suggested that black militiamen were soldiers only and not a source of black power and equal citizenship.[82]

Colonel Anderson focused exclusively on the military competition. Colonel Avery and the *Savannah Morning News* pursued the imagery of racial harmony in Georgia for national consumption. Avery's speech reflected the ideals of a paternal antebellum South where blacks and whites met each other in an unequal utopian master-slave harmony of "true friendship." His thoughts harkened back to unnamed moments of disharmony between the races a decade earlier, in 1868, when blacks first voted and endeavored to define their position as political, social, and economic equals and as autonomous people exercising the tools of black power and citizenship. This was also a time when whites such as Weldrim struggled to construct a white militia unit. By 1878 whites had dominated militia creation. Avery claimed that this public meeting—the drill competition in which elite whites and African American militia officers broke bread together—marked the resolution of ill-feeling and the announcement that racial harmony reigned in the South.

All of this, Avery contended, was made possible when in May 1878 black people finally realized that white people cared for them. Avery noted that white people conveyed their friendly concern, genuine regard, and confidence that racial peace had been attained through their attendance at the drill invitational. The implication was that black autonomy and political actions promoting citizenship in 1868 had soured the relationship between the races. With the passing of a decade, the successful rise of white power, and black political power's simultaneous decline, the black-white dynamic changed, whereby white paternal regard and friendship reemerged with the abrogation of black suffrage, autonomy, and citizenship. Black political and economic power was subsumed under the power of white paternalism and the unmentioned new state constitution. The *Savannah Morning News* celebrated the drill invitational as clear evidence, for northern observers, especially federal officials, that black and white Georgians were harmonious neighbors able to share public space in the paradise of a "democratic" Georgia—suggesting no need for the Civil Rights Act of 1875.[83]

John H. Deveaux utilized the black-initiated public event to announce that black people had arrived at a level of achievement equal to their white counterparts. African American men used public gatherings, as Angela Hornsby-Gutting has noted, to "stake their claim to racial dignity and respectable manhood outside the manly realm of politics" and to "advance the race's claim that [black people] had evolved into the highest state of 'civilization.'" The drill competition was also an opportunity for African Americans and their militiamen to exhibit what Eleanor Hannah argues "was a tangible demonstration of independence and self-reliance"—two characteristics whites had claimed as theirs alone but African Americans hoped to attain as evidence of their equal status as full citizens. Black leaders such as Deveaux took the public gathering as an opportunity to "showcase the industrial, intellectual, and moral evolution of" black people since slavery. Black self-congratulation, however, occurred in an atmosphere where "whites were firmly opposed to black citizenship rights yet receptive to the [black] ideology of progress" while reserving "progress and morality as ultimately the preserve of white males." The bottom line was that the black man's position in southern society "was essentially fixed. He might well advance, but never so far as to threaten white men's claim to power and prestige." He might "not seek the vote, social equality, or threaten the New South." Nevertheless, Deveaux, like other black contemporaries, "placed faith in the ability of powerful whites to see the black race as its equal once given opportunities to witness its accomplishments." Collectively blacks sought to "elicit from [elite] white men a mix of sympathy, understanding, and acknowledgement of a shared vision of manhood and citizenship." The drill invitational confirmed that black militiamen had achieved the treasured plateau of manhood and citizenship as they defined these concepts. Without conceding the militia's role in defending black citizenship, public rights, and status, Deveaux persisted in arguing for achievement despite what many whites believed—namely, that the 1877 Constitution circumscribed black political and economic power.[84]

Black-initiated public events were also intended to present, determine, and shape the parameters of black history, tradition, and memory and to complete their arguments for inclusion as American citizens.[85] Deveaux specifically argued at the start of his address that blacks needed to document that this was "no ordinary" moment for the race. The drill invitational was "an indication of [black] progress in civilization," and he felt that African Americans "should be encouraged and benefited by its teachings." The militia competition and the skill of black militiamen contrasted distinctly with the "despised ... [black] ... citizen and ridiculed ... [black] solider" of a decade earlier. On May 28, 1878, representatives of Georgia's white elite, Deveaux asserted, "deemed us of sufficient importance, both as citizens and as soldiers ... in our onward march of intelligence." Further, the day "will remove very many erroneous opinions existing in certain sections as to the condition of society in our State." According to Deveaux, "the homgeneousness of our people in this State I regard as nearly established. With liberal education it will be fully so." In Deveaux's mind, a "homogeneous" Georgia meant that "the glory of either class is the glory of the State, and the glory of the State is the glory of the whole people, and none will contradict the statement that a secret gratification is felt by one class when the other develops extraordinary abilities," especially the "military spirit." For Deveaux, black militiamen embraced a "military spirit, so long manifested . . . by the Anglo-Saxons . . . [and now] imbedded in our people" such that it reached "the highest eminence attainable in time of peace . . . proficiency and discipline." Such an achievement ought to be celebrated, observed, and noted not only by African Americans but also by elite whites, who shared in the pleasure of seeing black people progress because it shed a positive spotlight on the state of Georgia, of which all Georgians could be proud.[86]

Deveaux's vision focused on black militiamen and African Americans attaining equal status next to their white elite neighbors. Henry O. Flipper, a recent West Point graduate, Deveaux contended, had come close to equaling the "military spirit" of the New South and thereby attaining manhood and citizenship equal to that of white Georgians. As Deveaux defined it, equality was not fully a reality, but the presence of the white elite at the drill invitational signaled the realization of citizenship and a true soldierhood at an important moment in black history: African Americans had advanced through their own initiative and elite whites had witnessed it. Deveaux and his black colleagues across the Western Hemisphere during the last half of the nineteenth century, "advance[d] their complimentary pursuits of racial uplift, rights activism, and full inclusion in the republic, infusing those pursuits with positive and functional interpretations of African American history."[87]

Roster of Georgia Volunteer Military Organizations

Black militiamen also wanted to be included in the general profile of the Georgia Volunteers. During the spring of 1878, Sidney Herbert, journalist, militia advocate, and editor of the "Military Department" in the weekend *Morning News*, noted that the "Military Department" received "frequent letters . . . from members of the colored military organizations in the State." Herbert appeared slightly surprised "that our paper is being read" by African American militiamen and "that they take a deep interest in this department." Granting little if any recognition to the black militia, Herbert contended, "we shall always be glad to serve them in any way that we can." Herbert included a list of black militia companies in Georgia in his *Roster of Georgia Volunteer Military Organizations* in 1878. Headed by a portrait of former Confederate general and usurping governor of South Carolina, Wade Hampton, was a two-page "Roster of Colored Companies" listing all forty-two African American militia companies, including the Savannah Hussars and the sole black artillery company in the United States, the Georgia Artillery. According to this twenty-four-page document, Georgia blacks were indeed members of the Georgia Volunteers, as the Georgia Volunteers, Colored. Unfortunately issues of the "Military Department," from which the roster emerged due to Herbert's enthusiastic devotion to reporting on the state military, did not survive, leaving a significant gap in the history of both black and white militiamen, as well as in the recording of black and white relations within the Georgia Volunteers and Georgia Volunteers, Colored.[88]

Black militiamen had found an avenue to inclusion and citizenship, the Georgia Volunteers, Colored. Militia membership presented African Americans with a mechanism to celebrate, commemorate, define, and regularly and publicly declare that they were citizens of the United States and Georgia. They made parading, militia drilling, and the mastery of military tactics and techniques a part of their march from slavery to full citizenship. By the end of the 1870s African American militiamen had established a series of public displays of freedom; most importantly they commemorated Emancipation Day and other moments where blacks could publicly and collectively declare their citizenship, freedom, and belonging in Georgia's urban communities. Yet Georgia's reorganization of the Georgia Volunteers, in the 1880s and 1890s, loomed on the horizon. The reorganizations would transform black militiamen and their ongoing quest to achieve parity with their white counterparts. Further, whites proceeded to attack and dismantle the black political presence, causing black people to wonder whether they were, in fact, citizens of Georgia and the United States.

5

"BE THOU STRONG THEREFORE AND SHOW THYSELF A MAN"

Georgia Volunteers, Colored, 1889–1895

The last two decades of the nineteenth century and the first five years of the twentieth century were marked by the Georgia General Assembly's reorganization initiatives specifically focused on the state militia. The legislative reorganizations would eventually transform the Georgia Volunteers and Georgia Volunteers, Colored, into the Georgia State Troops and the Georgia State Troops, Colored. The reorganizations created a distinct difference between the nineteenth-century Georgia Volunteers and the new century's Georgia State Troops. Jim Crow Segregation, antiblack violence, and nationalization of the Georgia militia for incorporation within the National Guard and the nation's defense system were additional significant factors that shaped how Georgians defined and redefined the Georgia militia from the end of the 1870s to the initial years of the twentieth century. The post-Reconstruction and late nineteenth-century years would be a mix of black inclusion and exclusion, within both the militia and broader Georgia society. This quarter century was notable because black militiamen took the initiative to carve out a place for themselves within the Georgia Volunteers. White authorities' moments of acceptance, however, contrasted with public questioning of the utility of African American militia service.

The Georgia General Assembly reorganized the state militia to give Georgia's state government control over the potentialities and use of violence for the maintenance of law and order within the state and to separate the state military from federal power. Reorganization also gave state government regulating power over the growing number of military units hoping to be granted governmental recognition as a branch of state governance. While Georgia officials centralized the leadership structure of the state militia and the General Assembly took the lead in setting policy, neither side found a way to fund, encourage, and reward militiamen of all races in Georgia. Reorganization would, by the 1890s, change that as well as begin to redefine the mission of the militia, with more attention placed on professionalizing the force. For blacks the militia continued to be an institution that represented what Eleanor Hannah has defined as "their desire to be political and cultural actors on the larger stage."[1] African American militiamen endeavored to prove themselves citizens of the nation and state worthy of inclusion, because blacks had achieved the virtues of freedom, citizenship, and manhood in the short time since the end of slavery.

At the beginning of the 1870s the state government had issued only one charge to Georgia's men: organize militia companies. As a result, from 1872 to 1878, local citizens at the county level gathered together fifty to sixty citizens of the same race to create a militia company. For the four years between 1872 and 1876, this haphazard endeavor evolved without state governmental regulation, and the number of units grew without restraint, threatening to outstrip governmental resources. Legislatively initiated reorganization began with the 1876 to 1878 citizen-soldier study "to provide for the better organization, government and discipline, of the volunteer troops of this State." The Georgia Legislature, in October 1879, accepted the recommendations of citizen soldiers to improve the organization and management of the state's military, yet, the militia, until the end of the 1870s, existed with minimal to no real vision or direction from state officials, save for Georgia's governor, who was increasingly overwhelmed by the scope of that responsibility. With legislative acceptance of citizen-soldier recommendations late in 1879, governmental authorities began implementing the proposed statewide militia reorganization in 1880.

This chapter examines the evolution of the reorganization of the militia in the 1880s and early 1890s. Georgia officials used state-initiated reorganizations as a means of gaining control over the state militias' size and governance structure. Segregating the militia was fundamental to this reorganization. The Georgia Legislature also centralized state government despite its simultaneous commitment to states' rights, in opposition to federal power and centralized national government. While white southerners tried to resist political, cultural, and economic nationalization, these forces helped push the South to embrace late nineteenth-century segregation. These were the forces of change that restructured the New South at the end of the nineteenth century and caused whites to seek a new system—segregation—to control the transformative forces of change. This was not just a southern policy directed at the militia. Federal control over militia administration after the Civil War included racially enforced segregation that physically separated blacks from white militiamen, and members of the American military and black troops from white civilians. Segregation within the military and the militia was, by the late 1860s, a state and federal policy, but it was debated by members of the federal government for the rest of the nineteenth century. Georgia meanwhile made segregation the foundation of militia organization.[2]

White Georgians also debated national belonging. Black Georgians, in contrast, defined national belonging as a critical part of their freedom. Georgia's white civic leaders were originally resistant to federal power and centralized governance, and this resistance continued into the 1870s as Georgians debated who controlled the militia. The Georgia militia belonged to the state, not the nation's president. State governments also debated the militia's role in the nation's military structure: Did, for example, the militia belong within the country's defense network? State militiamen across the nation began campaigning to incorporate each state's militia as an institution integral to the national defense system. While Georgia initially resisted joining this effort, the state did join the national militia movement in the 1880s and 1890s as militiamen across the country committed to professionalized military training in exchange for increased governmental funding for the militia, both in Georgia and nationwide.

Reorganization also raised questions of how constructively Georgia dealt with its state militia. African American militiamen were well aware of Georgia's universal neglect of every militiaman, regardless of color, but there were signs that black militiamen and the race in general was making significant strides toward recognition as citizens of the United States and Georgia. Yet state militia reorganizations did not result in black people belonging as citizens. Each militia reorganization further undermined the Georgia Volunteers, Colored. Black militiamen endured reorganization in the 1880s with little protest, but the 1890s brought a decade of black protest for parity and access, as the state militia received new resources. New funding also brought about a redefinition of the militia, which evolved from a social club to an institution of citizen soldiers trained by military professionals. Increased governmental support merged with the question of where the militia belonged, culminating with who was a militiaman.

Georgia Volunteers, 1878–1880

This effort to establish a formal structure for the Georgia Volunteers began with the re-creation and restoration of the adjutant general's position as chief militia administrator subordinate to Georgia's governor's authority. All three official representatives of Georgia government—the governor, legislature, and the citizen soldier's committee—also used the Georgia *Code* to establish a company-level command structure. The *Code* further entrenched a system of lifetime officer commissioning "until death, resignation, promotion or dismissal" that lasted until the end of the century. The General Assembly, at the end of the 1870s, continued to allow local citizens to come together and petition for state recognition of their militia company. It also granted existing companies the right to retain any "uniform already adopted . . . at the time of the passage of this Act." In that context, the 1879 Georgia Legislature acknowledged the existence but not state recognition of "fifty-two colored military companies in Georgia." Most of these companies lacked official affiliation with state government and operated independently of all authority. With the legislature seeking to manage the number of militia companies, officials proposed that all independent units be required to attach themselves to a state-sponsored battalion. The requirement for official attachment to an organized branch of state government marked the first stage of militia centralization under state control. State militia regulation also encompassed the governor and adjutant general distributing arms and accoutrements from resources coming from "the government of the United States."[3] The reign of the independent militia company, whether white or black, fell to the statewide initiative to place all militia companies under the control of the Georgia Legislature, the governor, and the adjutant general.

Essentially the 1879 law set in place the formal organizational structure of the Georgia militia, establishing a vision, direction, and order where none had existed. Part of the new system of organization and management required all state-recognized units to file annual reports and march in parade "at least four times in every year [as a company], and every battalion [consisting of six or more companies] at least once in every year." Georgia's militia companies were to always be ready to meet any emergency, defined as "invasion, rebellion, [and] insurrection." In this context the commitment to state military defense went first to defending Georgia from all threats, with a subsidiary obligation to national defense. The Georgia *Code* urged each battalion to "carry the flag of the State," a citizen-soldier request aimed at improving militiamen's morale and establishing the militia as a publicly recognized state agency. In contrast, the General Assembly fully embraced the citizen soldiers' recommendation that racial segregation be a foundational component of the state military, a position the federal government also had endorsed since the Civil War by shaping and directing the African American presence in the nation's military. Significantly, Georgia's black militias, like their white counterparts from 1872 to 1878, were accepted and not substantially challenged by the legislature, except that the governor denied state recognition to rural African American independent militia companies such as the alleged independent black militia companies involved in the Johnson County Insurrection. In this context of transforming independent militia companies outside of state control into state-sponsored militia units, Georgia joined its fellow states by first centralizing the governance structure even as it allowed for the continuation of some local independent organizing. In the end Georgia, like its sister states, appeared to sanction "the formation of volunteer units out of all proportion to public need." This would precipitate a financial problem that reorganizations in the 1880s resolved with troop reductions.[4]

In 1880 public need for a centralized militia governance structure appeared to be a hopeful sign of black inclusion and an extension of the success black militiamen encountered two years earlier with the Savannah invitational drill competition. While the creation of black battalions in the 1880s represented one of the steps the state took to centralize militia operations, battalion status for black militiamen reflected a new level of inclusion for the race. The opening year of the 1880s marked a positive end to black militiamen's three-year attempt to attain battalion status for regional clusters of black companies statewide. Savannah's six infantry companies and one cavalry unit would be the first to be organized as a battalion by Georgia authorities. William H. Woodhouse and John H. Deveaux, respectively, were elected lieutenant colonel and commanding officer in 1880 and staff officer and major in 1881 by African American members of the Savannah units. Together Woodhouse and Deveaux led the new "First Battalion Georgia Volunteers, Colored," authorized in July 1880. In September 1880 Atlanta's six companies were granted battalion status as the Second Battalion Georgia Volunteers, Colored, and five years later, the Third Battalion Georgia Volunteers, Colored, came into being, recognizing Macon's and Augusta's six companies.[5]

While the 1879 legislation provided Georgia's militia with a structure, all militiamen faced a series of challenges that contested why they should join such an organization. Authorities in Georgia wanted the militia to have a formal organization managed by the state: the General Assembly, the governor, and the adjutant general. These authorities may have managed the militia, but they did not secure state funding for black or white militia companies. The General Assembly obligated the governor through the adjutant general to "furnish annually the commander of each battalion . . . fixed ammunition to the volunteers . . . out of the supplies of ammunition received from the government of the United States." Georgia, however, made "no appropriation for [arms]" for or to any of its militia units. Militiamen were to be responsible for providing their own uniforms and equipment; even in annual encampments, where white Georgia units trained in 1880, there was "no provision [by state governmental authorities] for . . . bedding, meals, and transportation." These disparities endured by Georgia's black and white militia volunteers paralleled national trends wherein state governments failed to fund their militia units. What funding militiamen did receive was filtered through state governments from the federal government.[6]

Jerry Cooper has suggested that post–Civil War state militias across the United States were similar in many ways. Militiamen were motivated to participate in their state organization due to "popular interest," as well as "interest in martial spirit, drill, pomp, and ceremony." Eleanor Hannah contends that both white and black men pursued militia membership hoping to find as well as define what it meant to be manly and a citizen of their local, state, and national communities. Post–Civil War and late-nineteenth-century manhood and citizenship eroded under the onslaught of industrialization, capitalism, and urbanization. Men in the post–Civil War world could not achieve manhood or prove their citizenship as their immediate predecessors had done in the caldron of Civil War combat. This would be true until the Spanish-American War, the Cuban War of Independence, and the Philippine-American War of 1898–1902. In this context, wherein the nation did not engage in war except on the domestic western frontier, there were no opportunities for men to be challenged by violent combat. The late nineteenth century, nevertheless, offered men choices about whether they would be overwhelmed by the industrial-capitalist-urban forces of change transcending their personal control, or take the initiative and redefine what it meant to be a militiaman, man, and citizen.[7]

Cooper has generally asserted that black southerners were part of the Reconstruction, or "Negro Militia," from 1869 to 1875. These state units were integrated and involved in "bitter racial-political conflicts" wherein they defended Reconstruction governments against "white terrorism." The Negro militia, however, died with the destruction of black political power and the defeat of the Republican Party by the Democratic Party in the contest to control southern governments during the 1870s. According to Cooper, white "Democrats abolished the Reconstruction militias" and "returned to the traditional policy of reorganizing volunteer-companies organized through-local private initiative." Further, the "uniformed militia" operated "like . . . fraternal societies such as the Masons" and military clubs who funded themselves by hosting "balls, dinners, [excursions], and theatricals." Despite state governance, post-Reconstruction militia units were less than stable owing to recurring turnover in local leadership. Officers attained their positions based on their popularity, a corrosive force on unit cohesion, longevity, and institutional stability. The militia, Cooper concluded, was "essentially [a] private fraternal organization" with no access to state funding and no obligation or pressure to attain or meet any standard of military training. Yet, from 1866 to 1896, state militias would be transformed by a series of state-initiated centralizing reorganization efforts. Georgia's reorganizations in the 1880s and 1890s were part of that national effort to gain a vision, secure a place, and establish a purpose for the post–Civil War state militia nationwide.[8]

While Georgia's militia history during and after Reconstruction did not replicate Cooper's broad general assessment of state militias in their racial, regional, and national contexts, Georgia's uniformed militiamen at the beginning of the 1880s were members of "military clubs" loosely organized around a politically appointed adjutant general, who was subordinate to the Democratic Party's control of the legislature and governor's office. Each unit lacked state funding and had to engage in fund-raising in their local community. Their initial allegiance was local and political, and their obligation to state service was almost secondary. What slim amounts of government financial support and equipment the units received came from the governor and adjutant general, who were distributing federal resources. The last twenty years of the nineteenth century, however, marked a significant transformation of the Georgia militia, as it did for its counterparts across the United States. That process officially began with further development of racial segregation in 1882. Georgia's *Code* made much more explicit the difference between the races within the state militia. Specifically, the *Code* defined "persons subject to military duty" as "all able-bodied free white male citizens between the ages of twenty-one and forty-five years." This section contained an asterisk beside the word "white," which linked to the footnoted question: "How is this affected by the 14th amendment to [the] Constitution of United States?" The footnote raised the specter of federal intervention challenging this clause and a racially segregated militia. This had been a possibility, white Georgians argued, since "March 1862, [when] Congress had stricken 'white' from the basic militia statute," thereby undermining states' rights in the South. There was an assumption, reinforced later by historian John K. Mahon, that "Radical Republicans [during Reconstruction] intended to make the southern militia predominantly black"—a popular interpretation assumed to be true even though this never occurred in Georgia.[9]

The State Militia: A State or Federal Institution?

The *Savannah Morning News* at the beginning of the 1880s positioned the militia as a key component of states' rights. The *Morning News* alerted white Georgians to the House of Representatives debate on Bill 5638, on April 7, 1880, "for reorganizing, arming, and disciplining the militia," or, more specifically, what the federal government needed to do "to keep the militia in effective condition." Yet the *Morning News* contended that the state militia was the foundation of "Democratic Republicanism," an ideal whose historical roots reached back to the colonial era, the Articles of Confederation, and the creation of the Constitution of the United States.

Each document and tradition defined the militia as an instrument of states' rights and democracy. In this light, the newspaper's editorialist declared, the militia was "the people," because militiamen were "the military protectors of . . . [local peoples'] independence and liberties." The militia unit was the institution connecting citizen soldiers to the local community. The editorialist continued, "The war was an experience in our national progress that revealed to us our military strength and the necessity to foster it," including continuing "the Democratic faith" that "the improvement of 'the militia' [w]as the real power of this country." Fundamentally, the militia belonged to "the [white] people" of Georgia, who were protected by "the provisions of the tenth amendment," where "the power not delegated to the United States by the Constitution, nor prohibited by it to the States, are reserved to the States respectively, or to the people." Within this context, the writer claimed, the "basis of our present militia system . . . was . . . that every able bodied white male citizen" had been a member of the militia since the 1790s, following the ratification of the U.S. Constitution. Further, the constitution declares, "The governing of the militia and the command of them shall be with the States and their Governors."[10]

Under the doctrine of states' rights, the states and their governors alone had the right to train, command, and exercise "control over the military" in their state and to commission officers from lieutenant to colonel. State control was a crucial "attribute of [state] sovereignty," superseding federal authority except during national emergencies. House Bill 5638 reminded white southerners too much about their Civil War defeat. The bill threatened to "make the militia of the state" an extension of the "overwhelming military power behind the Federal Government" instead of sustaining the governor's "power behind the state governments" as stipulated by the Constitution. Georgia joined a movement defining the militia/National Guard as the only institution able to stand up to the federal government's post–Civil War power. Within this context of federal versus "states' rights," a protective curtain began to emerge, insuring white institutional control over and support for such antiblack activities as segregation, lynching, and violence. All of these activities increased across Georgia in the 1880s as segregation of the militia became an unchallenged entrenched part of the institution and remained so for the rest of the nineteenth century. By regulating the militia and advocating states' rights, white supremacy, and antiblack violence, white elite men who dominated local and state governments set the foundation for a segregated and white-dominated New South.[11]

Militia Reorganization: Creating the Military Advisory Board

Three years after the 1882 Georgia *Code* reinforced militia segregation, the legislature and governor reorganized the Georgia Volunteers and Georgia Volunteers, Colored. On October 13, 1885, Governor Henry D. McDaniel signed "an Act of the Legislature . . . calling in all arms from Military Companies, not embraced in said act recognizing the Volunteers and limiting the number of companies both White & Colored." This act also established "a 'Military Advisory Board' to whom powers were designated to determine which companies should compose said Volunteer forces." The governor was empowered to appoint the officers of the Military Advisory Board, which became the policy making and coordinating center for the Georgia volunteers. The board and its members advised the governor about the approval of new companies and monitored the newly created legal limits that restricted the number of companies in the state militia. The Military Advisory Board was also responsible for "smoothing down all the little angularities in the ranks here and there about the state." It further gave assistance to the adjutant general in planning statewide militia activities that included creating white militia–centered encampments, distributing funding and resources, and guiding the overall direction of an evolving institution. Additionally, the board developed legislative proposals about "what changes should be made in the laws relating to the said volunteer forces" to be put before the General Assembly. Board members, the adjutant general, and Georgia's governor were to work together in making the militia more efficient, professional, and functional. At the same time, the governor did not always utilize this board of leading citizen soldiers to make decisions about the state volunteers. By the early 1890s the Military Advisory Board and the governor did not see eye to eye. At the end of the decade Georgia's governor refused to summon the Military Advisory Board into session, forcing on the board a two-year hiatus.[12]

Militia Reorganization by the Georgia Legislature

Centralization, the rise of state control over the militia, was achieved in Georgia through the combination of expanding racial segregation within the militia structure and limiting the number of militia organizations statewide. Several issues shaped the debate within the General Assembly in 1885 that crafted the reorganization statute. There was a concern that "The State is doing nothing for the militia" and that state agencies were "kept up by private enterprise and at great expense" instead of by democratic rule. As a result, some legislators resisted funding the militia in 1885. These opponents of the militia purposely ridiculed the proposed legislation for reorganization because they "opposed giving $20,000 a year for a standing army." Other sources of opposition contended that the 1877 state constitution made no provision for a state-funded militia. Others supported "the bill [because it] gave the State security from insurrection and riot" while providing militiamen with "a wise encouragement of a desirable military spirit." In 1885 there were forty white and thirty black companies, with the white units "breaking up often, because of the expense" of sustaining a militia company primarily through local fundraising. The colored companies, according to this source, were "increasing" in number, especially in Augusta, where there was "a very [strong] military spirit among the colored people." Black Augustans supported at least one militia company that had taken the initiative to purchase their own weapons, which served as an additional sign of black commitment to militia service.[13]

The crafters of the act in the General Assembly proposed appropriating "aid to fifty white and ten colored companies." Countering this vision was "Mr. [Anthony] Wilson, colored, of Camden, [who appeared to have successfully] offered an amendment to have twenty colored companies instead of ten" while conceding to a reduction in the number of black units from thirty to twenty. Wilson, a three-term legislator and "a farmer and school teacher," had consistently sought to protect African American citizenship rights by promoting the passage of a "Civil Rights bill." The proposed civil rights bill was intended to address African American access to public accommodations by preventing "discriminations by hotel keepers and common carriers." Wilson also proposed "establish[ing] a technological school for colored people." Operating almost alone in the legislature, Wilson persisted in speaking for black Georgians. He did this despite being lampooned by his fellow white legislators, who claimed, "Every one knows the bill will not pass, and [Wilson's] speeches at this session . . . can affect nothing [because they are] a waste of time." Yet his compromise measure remained in the reorganization bill even as the General Assembly approved the "substitute [bill] from [the General Assembly's] Military Committee" that became the 1885 act, which reduced the number of militia companies for both races.[14]

The act of October 13, 1885, continued the separation of the races and set the ceiling determining the number of militia units recognized as members of the Georgia Volunteers. The act declared: "The volunteer forces of this State shall be the active militia of this State, shall consist of infantry, cavalry and artillery, of which the white commands shall be known and designated as the Georgia Volunteers, and the colored commands as the Georgia Volunteers, colored." The white companies "shall consist of not exceeding fifty companies of infantry, seven companies of cavalry, and three companies of artillery." Black militiamen of "the Georgia Volunteers, colored," were to be "not more than twenty companies of infantry, one of cavalry, [and] one of artillery." According to the *Atlanta Constitution*'s article in November 1886 on the militia's annual report, "all other companies have been disbanded, excepting those existing prior to 1880." The surviving companies "elected to maintain themselves" as independent units within the new militia structure. The 1885 act, nevertheless, required "the governor [to organize] the companies into a general military force." The reorganized militia was a limited force with 62 white companies located in the following communities: "Savannah, 8; Augusta, 13; Macon, 3; Eastman, 1; Sparta, 1; Milledgeville, 4; Griffin, 1; Columbus, 2; LaGrange, 1; Talbotton, 1; Albany, 2; Montezuma, 1; Fort Gaines, 1; Brunswick, 1; Taylor Creek, 1; Dawson, 1; Rome, 2; Matlock, 1; Monroe, 1; Atlanta, 4; Thomson, 1; Griswoldville, 1; Knoxville, 1; Springfield, 1; McIntosh, 1; Darien, 1; Johnson Station, 1; Gainesville, 1; Greensboro, 1; Marietta, 1; Waynesboro, 1; Forsyth, 1." The nineteen "Colored companies" operated in "Savannah, 8; Augusta, 4; Albany, 1; Macon, 3; Atlanta, 2; Rome, 1." There were seventeen companies unattached to a specific community. They, however, continued operating, despite state centralization, as independent companies now part of "the general [state militia] force." Ten of these units were white and seven African American.[15]

Encampment: With No Money

Within a year of the act's enforcement, the state disbanded eleven unidentified companies. The adjutant general, Colonel John A. Stephens, who authored the 1886 report, also made several recommendations including the installation of an annual six-day encampment. Stephens additionally wanted a permanent location for annual encampments, hoping that such a site would institutionalize encampments as a regularly occurring militia-training event. He further requested that the legislature "take measures to improve the condition of the companies," because every company had "to rely solely upon themselves" and was "either in need of new equipments or of additions to those already in use." Given this need, Stephens emphasized that the state did "not appropriate anything for the support and maintenance of her military organizations" especially since the annual federal appropriation of $5,500 was "utterly inadequate" since it only "partially equip[ped] a limited number of companies." The *Constitution* noted that one Georgia legislator, in response to this financial need, proposed a "bill appropriating $15,000 per year to be spent on the military as the advisory board may see fit."[16]

Reorganization: State and National

It appears that Georgia, like its fellow states, reorganized the state militia to decrease the number of militiamen the state endorsed, regulated, supplied, and financed while also centralizing the command structure to take it out of local control. Georgia reorganized its militia in the mid-1880s at the end of a national effort spanning the twenty-year period between 1865 and 1885 when "citizen soldiers [sought] to establish [their unit] as a permanent state-supported institution." The continuing presence of southern black units, Cooper has argued, "reflected the lingering power of the Republican party and desire of Southern politicians to deflect federal attention from the treatment of former slaves." Georgia and South Carolina, as a result, Cooper noted, "accepted more black volunteers" than other southern states, which in part could explain the thirty-year longevity that some black Georgia militia units enjoyed despite the state's ongoing public embrace of segregation and the contradictory need to reduce the number of black and white units starting in 1885. Furthermore, the federal government in 1885 remained the sole financial foundation of most state militia forces, including the Georgia militia. Militiamen at the same time were organizing at the state and national levels. They joined the emergent state military boards in their efforts to convince the federal and state legislative bodies, respectively, to appropriate more and new militia funding. This, however, did not mean an increase in the number of black militiamen, and especially not in Georgia. The decline in black militia companies was reinforced by the continuing decease in black political power that spanned the almost ten years since Republicans had held a dominant position in Georgia's legislature and governor's office. Moreover, 1885 and 1886 marked the third and fourth years since black politicians relinquished control of Georgia's Republican Party to whites.[17]

New Companies in the Georgia Volunteers: Double Standards

During the month of August 1886 the Military Advisory Board "instructed [Adjutant General John A. Stephens] to organize [five] ... companies upon application [and,] as the state's ability to provide [these new units] arms," for admission to the Georgia Volunteers. By implication, the new companies were to be white, reinforcing the continuing signs that militia-based racial segregation set a double standard between the Georgia Volunteers and Georgia Volunteers, Colored. As one example of this separation, in an October 1886 correspondence, a black petitioner inquired of Stephens about organizing a new African American militia unit in La Grange, Georgia. Stephens's reply was that "[a]t the last session of the Legislature the number of colored companies were limited to twenty. There are that many companies in existence and therefore the Governor cannot authorize the organization of any more [black companies] at present."[18]

Lieutenant Colonel John H. Deveaux, commanding the First Battalion after William Woodhouse's forced resignation, for malfeasance as justice of the peace, requested arms for the Chatham Light Infantry. In reply Stephens asserted, "just as . . . it is sometimes [within] my power I will forward your command with necessary arms I am sorry I cannot do so now." Stephens additionally acknowledged to prospective white militia organizations in 1886, "There are now several [white] companies in process of organization," including "the Gainesville [Georgia] Volunteers . . . approved by the [Military] 'Advisory Board.'" As a result, "it will take all the arms now on hand suitable for the purpose to equip them," suggesting that priority went to white units while black militiamen occupied a secondary position. Stephens, however, was not going to be able to gather "up arms from defunded organizations in different parts of the state. The outlook from this source is not encouraging, as the arms I am now receiving are older style."[19]

By 1887, in this context of material scarcity, obsolesce, and militia expansion, "the Ga. State Volunteers [had] not [yet] met its full number of [legally designated] companies." Early that year there were "only forty-seven [white companies] organized or in the process of organizing," as the Military Advisory Board "approved" the petition of the Sylvania Rifles to begin operation as members of the Georgia Volunteers. By mid-May, "the number of white companies in the State . . . [was] now complete," with a total of at least sixty infantry companies. But Civil War naval hero and new Adjutant and Inspector General John McIntosh Kell discovered at the end of the month that "the result of counting in one company twice" incorrectly enabled Kell to advance a Warrenton, Georgia, militia application by John W. Thompson to the Military Advisory Board for approval. Kell, like Stephens, juggled the distribution of arms. With the "reorganization of the Cuthbert [Georgia] Light Infantry" and the Military Advisory Board's approval, Kell noted, "[It is] my pleasure to furnish you with arms at the Earliest date which will not be before July next. The arms at present in my possession are not fit for issue, hoping to hear from you soon." By February 1887 the General Assembly had done nothing toward funding the volunteer companies. In June 1887, Kell "instruct[ed]" the "Augusta Light Infantry (colored)" to "make out requisition for arms and accoutrements required for your command." According to Kell, "I have arms now in hand they may be better than yours if you were here to select them." Meanwhile Kell declared, "The colored companies are full . . . [and] no others can be organized under the law." Thus began the decline of the Georgia Volunteers, Colored.[20]

Military Advisory Board: Inspections

Less than a year after the 1885 reorganization, the *Atlanta Constitution* reported in mid-August on an upcoming Military Advisory Board meeting that would "probably make a complete reorganization" of the volunteer troops. With this announcement the *Constitution* made "reorganization" a refrain that would define the Georgia volunteers for the rest of the nineteenth century. The paper declared that Military Advisory Board reorganization recommendations in 1886 would mark "important changes in the military law." This meeting opened the door to five new white companies and no new black companies, and the Advisory Board imposed a statewide "inspection of all the military of the state, both white and colored." The results of the comprehensive inspection, the newspaper contended, would enable "this board [to] prepare a petition to be presented to the next legislature . . . asking for an appropriation for the military of Georgia." Reorganization was also a way of attempting to convince legislators to value the Georgia volunteers.[21]

On October 15, 1887, the General Assembly implemented a new round of militia reorganizations. The Legislature decided that "for the better organization, government and discipline of the volunteer troops of this State," Georgia Legislators would "repeal" the 1885 ceiling restricting the number of troops in the Georgia Volunteers. The 1887 Legislature took the initiative "Amending [the] General Law as to [the] Volunteer Troops" by "conferring upon the Advisory Board, provided for in said Act, the power, by and with the approval of the Governor, to increase the number of companies allowed . . . beyond the number therein limited, according to the circumstances and exigencies of the case and when such increase may, in the discretion of such Advisory Board, be practicable and desirable." This certified the ongoing militia company admissions policies that both the adjutant general and Military Advisory Board appeared to already have engaged themselves: the increased presence of white militia companies and the strangulation of black ones. The enabling section of the new act indicated "that the numbers of companies comprising the volunteer forces may from time to time be increased . . . with the approval of the

Governor ... [and] in the discretion of said Advisory Board." This legislative opportunity also applied to "any or all of the classes of troops of the Georgia Volunteers, Colored, under the circumstances above named."[22]

Two years later, in 1889, the General Assembly "passed an Act making an annual appropriation of $7300.00 for support and maintenance of the militia of the State, which [was] the only appropriation ever made by Georgia for that purpose." Despite legislation and militia administrators implying that the 1887 reorganization would promote equality across the volunteer forces, new white companies were approved by the governor, the adjutant general, and the Advisory Board while the Volunteers, Colored, did not grow beyond the 1885 legislatively approved twenty companies.[23]

"Great Drills": Training for Leadership for Whites Only

Compounding the parameters of militia segregation and discrimination was the statewide "great drill" competitions. White units came together annually in 1889, 1890, 1891, and beyond, to engage in whites-only drill and skill contests, officers' conventions, and statewide encampments. White militiamen at these meetings gave the militia a public face and united militia members in lobbying the public and General Assembly for a permanent funding stream. The great drill, officer's conventions, and encampments for the ranks provided white militiamen with concentrated opportunities for training, leadership, and professionalization at both the officer and enlisted personnel levels. According to an 1887 Military Advisory Board report, encampment should involve "all the troops in the state" so that they can be "thoroughly instructed in the duties of soldier." The Advisory Board considered state funding absolutely crucial to militia operations. As a result, the board deemed it critical that the legislature appropriate "the sum of twelve thousand dollars for the maintenance and support of the military organizations." They hoped to utilize encampment training and legislative recognition to open the doors to a permanent funding stream from the General Assembly. The Board also argued that state funding would have a beneficial impact because collectively state soldiers "would double [their] efficiency ... [and] the ranks would be filled by crowds of generous youths that now stand aloof from military affairs." Further training, support, recognition, and a younger membership were the keys to making Georgia's militia companies "the pride and glory of the state."[24]

Each of these proposed activities for militia improvement excluded black militiamen, with one exception: an encampment for the Georgia Artillery. Excluding African Americans prevented them from accessing the tools for the better preparation of militiamen that state authorities increasingly expected. Yet militia leaders, the Advisory Board, the adjutant general, the governor, and the emerging national effort to organize militiamen to secure state and federal funding endeavored to make a case for training in exchange for government recognition, financial support, and oversight. Advanced training as soldiers, the acquisition of leadership capabilities, and professional development marked a reciprocal relationship wherein states provided funding in exchange for militiamen submitting to state governmental control, regulation, and standards of professionalization. Further, as Roger Cunningham has noted about militiamen in Kansas, denying black militia officers access to training placed them at a distinct disadvantage. Kansas officials discouraged, ignored, and excluded black militiamen from the leadership opportunities that white commissioned officers benefited from, especially during encampments and other state-endorsed developmental sessions.[25]

Leadership: For Whites Only

While three African American men attained command of one of the three battalions comprising six infantry companies each, no black militiamen were promoted to the level of regimental commander or invited to sit on the Military Advisory Board. The Advisory Board—which comprised ten or eleven members in the 1880s and 1890s and seventeen at the beginning of the twentieth century—included in the late nineteenth century lieutenants and captains of individual white companies and in the early twentieth century first and second lieutenants, making service on the board an additional training opportunity for junior officers. Majors and lieutenant colonels leading all-white battalions and lieutenant colonels and colonels who led white regiments were also appointed to Advisory Board service by the governor, while the quartermaster general, the president of the board, and the adjutant general held the status of colonel and a permanent seat on the Advisory Board. Board membership gave white officers access to community leaders, such as former Reconstruction Republican Governor Rufus B. Bullock, who led the Piedmont Exposition Company, and Atlanta-based economic leaders, such as Jack Spalding, Edward Peters, and *Atlanta Constitution* leaders Clark Howell and W. A.

Hemphill, who collectively but unsuccessfully sought to bring the annual white militia encampment to the city.[26]

Advisory Board membership worked in reverse, too. Atlanta's leaders viewed Military Advisory Board membership as part of the city's representation within state government. City and county leaders made sure that "Atlanta's choice," militiaman Captain A. J. West, filled one of two vacancies that had "existed for some time on the military advisory board." West's credentials included being "a prominent member of the Fulton County Confederate Veterans' Association," which "urged his appointment." By 1892 Atlanta's lobbying efforts paid dividends. The city's "military spirits" looked forward to the Advisory Board's transformation of the Third Georgia Battalion's ten companies into the Fifth Regiment, with Atlanta as the new regiment's geographical and administrative center. The change from battalion to regiment was projected to be "a great thing for the military companies" in Atlanta and the surrounding communities and something that would "greatly simplify military government." Rome, Georgia, also lobbied "for the appointment of Mayor [A. W.] Walton" as north Georgia's representative on the board. Southwest Georgia's "leading politicians" were reported as organizing to get two people from their region on the Advisory Board. They were successful, securing seats for Second Regiment member Major R. N. Holtzclaw and Colonel Edward K. Wight from Albany, Georgia.[27]

Military Advisory Board: "Weeding Out"

The effects of denying African American officers access to the Military Advisory Board were compounded by Georgia's militia, legislative, and executive leadership's commitment to white needs, by the inequitable allocation of funding, and by the ongoing demands for reorganization. Georgians pressured the board for new companies throughout 1889. For example, applications for new militia companies had come before the Advisory Board by the fall of 1889 from "Athens, Rockmart, Dalton and four other towns." Each applying company, the *Atlanta Constitution* reported, "were all favorably considered, and as soon as these new companies ... complied with the requirements of the law they [would] be received as state troops." In November 1889 the Advisory Board also examined the "cases of about a dozen white companies and half a dozen colored companies cited to show cause why they should not be disbanded." The eighteen or so companies, according to the *Atlanta Constitution*, were declared "deficient at the inspection" by militia inspection officers. Final disposition, the newspaper reported, was decided in a "secret [Military Advisory Board] session." New companies topped the board's agenda as it planned the new encampment, and discussion of a $7,000 budget rounded out the meeting. Applications came "from several new companies," including "some . . . white, some colored." The article continued, "It was stated pretty authoritatively last night that the colored quota was about full and that no new colored companies would be enrolled." In the end seven white companies were disbanded and five others, along with three black units, had to come to the board's next meeting to "show cause why they should not be disbanded for neglect of the 'fundamental principles.'" Six white companies and a similar number of black units, the "doubtful cases," were "continued subject to the spring inspection of 1890." The board found seven white and three black units to be "improved and [worthy of being] retained." One new application was accepted as the board sought to "rehabilitate and put in proper condition the companies already existing" as part of a wholesale "process of 'weeding out'" deficient companies. In 1889 reorganizing "the military system of the state" had "merely begun," and it would continue "until the militia of the state [was] the finest [in the] south."[28]

Military Advisory Board: Militia Applications and Johnson County's Legacy

The *Constitution* noted that white applications for militia companies continued into the 1890s. In 1890 fifteen new applications joined the thirty-two "unconsidered" requests from the previous year. By early April 1890 the Military Advisory Board faced a backlog of fifty outstanding applications awaiting their action. The Advisory Board, however, had "decided at the last meeting [in 1889] that no new companies should be admitted into the state militia until a vacancy was made by the disbandment of the ones now on the rolls." "In spite of this order," the board declared, "the military spirit has induced the formation of several new companies." A day later the newspaper reported that such an order was being undermined by "strong appeals . . . from the southern and middle counties of the state, showing that the colored people far out-numbered the whites." These counties rationalized that "an organized military force was necessary for the protection of life and property." This argument reinforced the local white view that the militia served as a political and race control vehicle that empowered local whites, reflecting a twenty-plus-year-old definition of the militia as a local institution. According to the *Constitution*, "Under these circumstances, the board considered it proper to suspend the rules, and the following companies were admitted to membership in the Georgia Volunteers; the Burke Light Infantry and the Burke Cavalry Troop, both of Waynesboro; the Dublin Light Infantry, the Americus Light Infantry, and Eastman Volunteers. In order to admit the Burke Cavalry Troop, the number of cavalry companies allowed to the state was increased from eleven to twelve," making "the force stand [at] forty-seven companies of infantry and twelve of cavalry" in 1890.[29]

If the *Constitution*'s anticipatory and contradictory reporting reflects some degree of accuracy, then white central and southern Georgians fifteen years after the Johnson County Insurrection continued to see blacks as a political and military threat, and the white desire to form militia units was driven by the attendant desire for racial and political domination. Waynesboro appears to have persistently pursued maintaining a militia presence in Burke County, as evidenced by its petition for two militia companies to replace the former militia companies of the late 1870s. In 1890 race also had an impact on militia discipline. White militiamen from Madison, in Morgan County in central Georgia, failed "to turn out and aid the sheriff" in protecting a suspect, Brown Washington, "from lynch law." The company refused to report and "enforce the majesty of the law" despite the orders and anger of ex-Confederate general, Governor John B. Gordon, who objected to such a breach of military discipline even though "everybody thoroughly sympathized with the lynchers." A month later, the second lieutenant of the Madison Home Guards resigned his commission. In late 1890 the General Assembly allocated $25,000 for "better organizing, training, arming, equipping, and maintaining the volunteer forces of Georgia," all to be expended by the Military Advisory Board "as the necessity of the volunteer forces demand[ed]." The bill was intended to bring Georgia in line with "nearly every state in the union" with an appropriation, as well as to do something to "sustain . . . young men in their patriotic purpose of giving our state a first-class volunteer force." The allocation was especially necessary since "it [would] not be very long . . . before [the] . . . military force [would] be composed of a few city companies only." Additionally, riots were "of frequent occurrence," especially in southwest Georgia, where "a vicious class of our citizens . . . delight to bear long-range guns and provoke disturbances by their insolence." The allocation not only reinvigorated the young white militiamen but also "bound [them to] obey orders of the proper authorities," in contrast to the actions of the militia in Madison, Georgia.[30]

Appropriation: "A Pro Rate Share"

State appropriations gave the General Assembly and Military Advisory Board increased control over militia operations. It also invited what would become an ongoing protest from black militiamen about the unfairness of the appropriation process. A hint of what was to come arrived in March 1891, at the board meeting where "the negro troops" were an agenda item. The Advisory Board made the Negro troops one of the "two things . . . not mentioned" at the meeting of Georgia's leading military men. By June "colored military troops [were] bound [and determined] to have an encampment." Assuming that "the appropriation [was] addressed to the militia of the state of Georgia," and that black militiamen were indeed "a part of the state's military force, and under the head of the militia," African Americans asserted that they were "entitled to a pro rata share of the money." One unnamed black Atlanta militia leader contended, "We are subject to the orders of the governor and advisory board the same as the white troops" and "the act says the money shall be used for the military of the state." The officer concluded, "I don't see why we should not be treated fairly and given our just dues." The need, the officer felt, was dire because his unit had not "had new uniforms in twelve years." Further, given the ongoing inspections ordered by the Military Advisory Board, governor, and adjutant general of his command, the old uniforms "would present so poor an appearance that we would be disbanded immediately." He asked, "Is that fair?"[31]

Black militiamen's complaints and efforts to alleviate the problem had "long [been] contemplated." The appropriation was the last straw. To resolve the long-term disparity that black militiamen had endured since at least 1879, they mobilized to create parallel institutions to those of their white counterparts. Not only did they propose organizing their own encampment, but black officers led by Savannah's corps also called for "a convention of the colored military of the state of Georgia" to meet in Atlanta on July 3, 1891. According to the "prominent member of one of the Atlanta companies," blacks would "make an issue of it in the next election," to the point of "stump[ing] all over the state": "The man or men who will pledge themselves to give us our rights in this matter will get our votes, whether he be democrat or republican. If necessary we will put a ticket of our own in the field." Black Atlantans had done exactly that in 1890, mounting a secret but complete mayoral, aldermanic, and city council slate in which militiaman to be Floyd. H. Crumbly was a candidate. While this effort had been uncovered, undermined, and defeated by Atlanta's white elite, black militiamen still had confidence in their ability to exert some influence in Georgia politics. According to the *Atlanta Constitution*, black militiamen seemed "confident that they [would] succeed when they present[ed] their case to the governor in full," believing "that [Populist Governor William J. Northen would] take the necessary initiative steps to give them what they term[ed] their rights." They wanted "Governor Northen to veto the expenditure of the fund until . . . their status in the affair" could be determined. The paper nevertheless concluded, "It is needless to say that this will not be done," because the governor and Advisory Board "refuse to talk of the proposed action of the negro committee."[32] Nevertheless, black militiamen mobilized to get their fair share of state militia appropriations, marking the 1890s as their decade of protest and self-promotion as equal in status with their white colleagues and deserving of treatment as such.

"Be Thou Strong"

One step toward blacks' hoped-for late nineteenth-century parity with whites occurred on June 22, 1891. Atlanta black militiaman Captain Jackson McHenry led the Governor's Volunteers to the Butler Street Episcopal Church, where the company celebrated its twelfth anniversary by hearing Elder R. E. Hart's sermon "The Black Regiment." According to the *Atlanta Constitution*, Hart's scriptural text came from 1 Kings 2:2: "Be thou strong therefore and show thyself a man." Utilizing this text, Hart noted that slavery caused some to question blacks' military capabilities: "Will it do to trust him with arms? Will the white man fight side by side with him? Has he (the negro) enough courage to defend his country?" While these questions of character and manhood challenged "the military qualifications of the negro," Hart claimed that black "courage and powers of endurance had always been applauded" by their white commanders. Specifically, American heroes and generals George Washington and Andrew Jackson had contended that "the colored troops fought so well that they received unstinted praise."[33]

Yet this record of "courage, loyalty and services rendered by the negro soldier" had gone "unsung in history and song." The main reason, Hart contended, was that "the war department at Washington" recorded and publicized only a few of "their deeds of arms." Despite these drawbacks, wherein the broader society failed to acknowledge black achievement and manhood, Hart advised the Governor's Volunteers to "be strong and brave [and present] yourselves, [as] men." He especially counseled black militiamen to avoid any perversion of "the liberty entrusted to [them] by joining any cursed mob or any class of traitors who would raise insurrection." Black military people needed to "be firm, stand still and wait for the call of your commander-in-chief," thereby affirming their loyal service to the nation and state. All of this, however, had to be contextualized: Black militiamen belonged "to a race that [did] not receive even common respect." So, Hart counseled, "before you prove a traitor, die a martyr. If this government descends from justice, perverts its liberty, oppresses its poor, kicks and banishes its worthy, though black, it shall report, . . . to God the reason; for the voice of your blood-drops will join the chorus with that of the red man and the yellow man, and cry unto Jehovah" for recognition.[34]

Elder Hart's message marked a change in the black self-concept. The end of slavery meant embracing middle-class respectability, a turning away from "any cursed mob" and "traitors who would raise insurrection." This perspective called for accommodating whites and rejecting the political autonomy pursued in the 1870s by people such as Aaron Bradley, Tunis Campbell, Cudjo Fye, Todd Norris, and Joseph Morris. Hart argued that blacks must "wait for the call" to service and participation by the president of the United States. Yet black protest had validity: African Americans had "not receive[d] even common respect" from whites, both locally and nationally, because their military service and deeds of citizenship had been ignored. Their loyalty and definitions of liberty, too, had been erased or too poorly publicized for whites to notice them. They had proven their loyalty to the United States "through their deeds of arms." Blacks joined peoples of color across the globe who experienced what Hart suggested might be white imperial expansion. African Americans in the 1890s were at a crossroads. They questioned whether they were citizens who had earned citizenship and national belonging after loyal and faithful service or were unworthy of national, state, and local citizenship and not part of the national narrative.

Crossroads: A History of "Responsible Citizenship"

Blacks at the end of the 1880s and beginning of the 1890s were both visible and invisible, apparently appreciated and unappreciated. Their efforts as militiamen were noticed yet also ignored. According to the *Savannah Tribune* in 1889, there was "no Negro question or problem." The key was to "treat the Negro as a man and a citizen who is entitled under the laws of the land to certain priveilges [sic] among which is the pursuit of life, liberty and happiness." In the mind of Georgia's black militiamen, black men had and were proving their worthiness daily, both locally and as soldiers in the U.S. military. As proof of black worthiness, the *Tribune* republished an article from the *Chicago Tribune* in 1889 titled "Traits of Colored Soldiers." Noting the comments of unnamed white officers serving in the U.S. military on the American frontier who had worked with black enlisted personnel, "colored soldiers" had taken "special pride in their profession." This was a major step in proving African American military skill and worthiness. Their notable traits, besides being "subordinate and cheerful" and "free from habits of intoxication," included their trustworthiness, their "God fearing" attitude, and their courteous service to white officers, "their wives and little ones[,] during the long and toilsome marches on the distant frontier."[35]

The black militia's advocates—namely, the *Savannah Tribune* and black Atlantan Floyd. H. Crumbly, "Late Sergeant Co. I. 10th U. S. Cavalry and Sergt. Major, Fort Stockton, Texas"—lauded the exemplary behavior of black soldiers in the U.S. military. Crumbly specifically responded to the January 1889 "Traits" article while the *Tribune* made note of a separate report on black troops. According to the *Tribune*, the United States Army's surgeon-general's annual report presented "a good record for the colored troops in our regular army." The surgeon-general also noted that "Colored regiments" had successfully served "in our army for over a quarter of a century." Blacks as a result constituted "more than one-tenth of the whole military force" nationwide and stood "nearly on a level with the whites in the service." African American military personnel who had earned accolades for exemplary behavior were equal to whites. Black soldiers had earned laudable comments about their good "health and general effectiveness." Such soldierly acts had additional positive implications for the definition of African Americans as citizens and men. Black military men, according to the surgeon general's assessment, were so proficient "in some lines of duty" that their work and skill generated considerable respect and demand from the broader society.[36]

Crumbly, an emerging black economic leader in Atlanta in the 1890s, read the "Traits" article "with pleasure." According to Crumbly, the article "was very creditable to the 'brother in black.'" With such a positive portrait, Crumbly offered his personal testimony concerning the African American presence in the "army of the United States from 1876 to 1881." To reinforce this endorsement, Crumbly noted his experiences, observations, and evaluations of black servicemen during his tenure in the nation's military. Crumbly indicated that initially "white and colored recruits drill[ed] together daily" at Jefferson Barracks in St. Louis, Missouri. The military experience, Crumbly explained, had been transformative. Specifically, "our colored men . . . [evolved] from the cotton fields of Georgia to the arms of the nation." While some recruits appeared "best fitted for the rear ranks," there were "a few [who] exercise[d their military] lessons." These black men, as a result, had been changed and elevated from a "cornfield hand" to a position of parity, because the military did not allow them to be "second to [their] brethren."

Compliments also came from white United States Army officers who led black troops in the field, including Major J. K. Mizner. In 1888 Colonel Mizner inherited command of Crumbly's former unit, the Tenth Cavalry, from General Benjamin Henry Grierson. Mizner and several other serving officers found "no better soldiers than the colored men." Crumbly asserted that "Georgians were considered the best at Forts Sill, Reno, Indian Territory; Forts Richardson, Cocho, Stockton, Davis and Griffin, Texas." At each fort black Georgians "had an opportunity to show . . . soldierly ability." These achievements occurred "side by side with the whites," and black men had "received . . . honors" for their "cleanliness and soldierly qualifications." In essence Crumbly recounted his highly successful five-year cavalry career, marked by a rapid rise through the ranks, as a constructive experience.

Discharged in November 1881, Crumbly had by then earned the rank of sergeant-major. Those years refined his ability to evaluate men. Crumbly wrote, "I had favorable opportunities of judging and acknowledging the ability of soldiers, white and black." Equipped with these leadership and firsthand experiences, Crumbly concluded, "The colored man can do." Black men also had "done and . . . [possessed] the ability of doing as much as any avocation" they encountered. Their capabilities were especially evident when "opportunities . . . [were] equal," enabling African Americans to act "as any man, race, or nationality the sun ever shown upon." In Crumbly's estimation and experience, black military men had achieved and earned their place as citizens of the United States, with black Georgians making notable contributions as defenders of the nation. Such achievements were important in defining late nineteenth-century manhood and citizenship. Militiamen, Eleanor Hannah has noted, pursued militia service as a means of defining both manhood and citizenship while utilizing military training to prepare them to defend the nation. These were the actions of real men, mature men who practiced what Hannah has called "responsible citizenship."[37]

"The Negro Ye Have With You Always"

In this context of black martial achievement, the *Savannah Tribune* endeavored to argue that African Americans were contributors to both the region and the nation. The *Tribune* then endeavored to prove that African Americans had done things that deserved recognition, especially of black manliness, citizenship, and military bearing. A January 1889 editorial, "The Negro Ye Have With You Always," took up the themes of acceptance and recognition, declaring: "The people of the South may as well make up their minds that they will have the Negro with them always, as they will the poor, according to the scriptures."

The *Tribune*'s editorial also responded to negative claims and dispersions by an Alabama senator. Senator John Tyler Morgan, a former Confederate general, a staunch states rights advocate, and a racial segregationist, mounted a campaign to "expel from Alabama every Negro." He promoted black removal so that "'the prices of land would run up to the prices greater than those in Wisconsin,'" suggesting that the absence of black bodies increased property values and white opportunities for economic success. Countering Senator Morgan's land redistribution and black expulsion aims, the newspaper argued that expelling blacks "will never" enhance "the price of lands in Alabama or any other State in the South," because "the South is the natural home of the Negro, and here he will stay." As a result, "Senator Morgan and that class of crustacean bourbons" should pursue "the manly way [which] would be to reconcile themselves to the inevitable and make the most of it." "The Negro," the editorial contended, "has been useful to the south in a great many ways." Southern blacks had contributed "a great deal of the actual labor in the construction of railroads" and in "operating mines and manufactories." Finally, Morgan and his supporters needed to "treat the colored man right, because he deserves to be, and what he don't know, teach him as far as possible. Do not look upon him as an enemy, but as a natural friend. Encourage him to do his best."[38]

Emancipation Day 1889

While the *Tribune* and black southerners continued to justify their place in the late nineteenth-century South, the twenty-fifth Emancipation Day celebration called attention to the black need to remain positive about their own self-definition. On January 1, 1889, the *Savannah Tribune*, in a rare instance, abandoned its traditional Emancipation Day exclusive focus on militiamen parading by publishing the text of Rev. L. B. Maxwell's "eloquent and constructive" Emancipation Day address. According to Maxwell, "We need to congratulate ourselves upon the occasion which has called us together here today. This first day of January of all days belongs distinctly to the American Negro for many reasons. It is the day that gave birth to our liberty." The first day in January was also "the day on which the prayers of our ancestors came up before God for recognition" and blacks "walked forth into a new existence" armed with "the protection" of the "American eagle['s] . . . outspread wings" and with the right to "sing that grand song—'My Country 'tis of Thee.'" Given these signs of earned citizenship, January 1 should "stand pre-eminent in the mind of every true American Negro" as "a day [of] universal rejoicing and public speaking," because black people were citizens of the United States who deserved to be recognized as such.[39]

Maxwell's focus was on "the Negro's History" before and after slavery. Specifically, Maxwell declared, "I am ashamed of American slavery, but thank God I am not ashamed of the American slaves, for a noble record they have made, both as slaves and citizens." Fundamentally, "There has not been a great movement in the country since the Negro has been on American soil—political or social—upon which he has had no influence." Whites and blacks were both "intimate and inseparable [in] that the history of one is the history of the other." Additionally, Maxwell contended, "Our record as soldiers . . . showed great military genius. They fought like men, like freemen and not like slaves." Beginning with the African American/Native American Crispus Attucks and military service in the American Revolution through the post–Civil War years, black soldiers had served the country bravely. Their courage was not because "Caucasian blood" flowed through their veins. Black courage had been evident during the Civil War as African American men were commended by General David Hunter as "the best soldiers . . . because [they were] docile, teachable, sober and enthusiastic." According to Maxwell, they were also "fearless." In the post–Civil War world, Maxwell concluded, "We desire no special and peculiar legislation, only respect us for what we are worth and according to the rights guaranteed by the Constitution of the United States. We do not ask to become pets of the nation, but we ask a chance to become men, that is all."[40]

Maxwell, the *Tribune,* and Crumbly, separately and collectively, had argued for whites, both nationally and regionally, to respect the abilities, capabilities, rights, and presence of black people generally and black men specifically. They also called for whites to remember blacks' military sacrifices, bravery, and service in defense of the nation. Blacks therefore had earned the right to full citizenship by giving their blood and lives in service to the country. Maxwell, like Atlanta's Elder Hart, sought to tell a comprehensive story of "the Negro's History" in the United States. Rev. L. B. Maxwell joined a growing crescendo of black voices seeking to keep the record of black citizenship and military acts of national belonging before white America. His Emancipation Day address joined Civil War veteran and politician George Washington Williams's three books on black history published in the 1880s—the two-volume work, *The History of the Negro Race in American from 1619 to 1880* and *Negroes as Slaves, as Soldiers, and as Citizens* (1882) and *A History of Negro Troops in the War of the Rebellion* (1887)—and Joseph T. Wilson's *The Black Phalanx* (1887). All were aimed at reminding a nation drifting away from its Civil War past that black men had served and died in the war. Blacks had earned their freedom by making the supreme sacrifice of a citizen. In addition to citizenship, Williams's biographer, John Hope Franklin, noted that the two-volume study "covered virtually every aspect of the Afro-American experience in the New World."[41] Williams, Maxwell, and Wilson asserted that knowledge of the complete story about blacks' contribution to the national narrative proved black citizenship.

Williams, Hart, Crumbly, and Maxwell each sought in his own way to combat the national amnesia that was erasing from the national story black Civil War service and other acts of belonging. Williams combated both northern and southern reconciliation, which erased black citizenship. He used his three books to challenge the Union army's post–Civil War soldiers' association, the Grand Army of the Republic, because the organization failed to oppose antiblack violence and embraced the postwar amnesia that the war had been solely about preserving the Union and not about black citizenship. This study and Williams's challenges against the GAR and national amnesia made him a public figure in the 1880s. He was nominated, confirmed, and commissioned the next minister to Haiti, until the newly elected Democratic president of the United States, Grover Cleveland, assumed office and cancelled the appointment. Williams unsuccessfully sued the United States for his salary.[42]

Maxwell's themes mirrored Williams's and Hart's efforts to publicly announce black militiamen's collective record as American citizens and as men who served the nation. Maxwell, like Williams and Hart, stressed that African Americans had been part of the American story since the nation's founding. Black Americans had also served alongside whites as citizens, patriots, and soldiers at every vitally significant moment in U.S. history. They had transcended the taint of slavery to become men of service, responsible citizens, and soldiers. These acts of national belonging had earned black people citizenship and the promised protection of the federal government to defend and sustain black rights—a promise earned by the shedding of black blood in defense of the nation from the American Revolution to the 1880s.

Blacks also were not "pets," a probable reference to the conquest and warehousing of Native Americans on reservations. Floyd Crumbly had a direct hand in subduing Native Americans as a regular army cavalry man. Crumbly could argue that black manhood had been won in the West defeating a fellow man of color. Maxwell placed the history of the Negro on the side of his white neighbor instead of on the side of Native Americans to remind whites that blacks had evolved from slavery to freedom in the land of liberty right beside whites.[43]

Whites, nevertheless, eroded black citizenship, autonomy, and office holding by rewriting history. Grace Elizabeth Hale and Evelyn Nakano Glenn, respectively, describe the 1880s and 1890s as decades in which whites reconceptualized the past and declared American citizenship to be for whites only. Both scholars note that the nineteenth-century years were rewritten as a pastoral plantation past where slaves adored their master and Reconstruction was a black civil revolt against defenseless whites who had never harmed blacks. Reconstruction violence was done not by whites but by black militia. The rewriting, Glenn notes, "erased black resistance, striving [and] . . . accomplishments" in exchange for white claims that black people were depraved, corrupt, dangerous, and violent, especially the men. According to Hale, white southerners rewrote the antebellum and postbellum years by transforming slavery into a utopian era of racial peace and harmony destroyed by Reconstruction, which "made segregation the only possible future and social solution. The present . . . mixed-race, [and black] middle-class figures [traveling to new places] on the train simply disappeared from view." Hale further contends that history defined the place and distance between the past and present, making time "a cultural space in which to craft a new southern order," namely, racial segregation, which offered whites better control over the change. Maxwell's Emancipation Day address was part of the late nineteenth-century battle over whose history and identity defined the national narrative. Northern whites were hearing less about the black narrative of one nation under God and more about history, citizenship, and labor meant for whites only. In the end the new history declared that blacks had made no contribution to the national, regional, or local experience.[44]

Benjamin Harrison's Inauguration

Black militiamen in 1889 in Atlanta and Savannah wanted to place themselves, the race, and their citizenship on the national stage. African Americans hoped to join the "train loads of troops . . . lauded and marched" through the streets of Washington, D.C., as they pursued ways to participate in General Benjamin Harrison's inauguration as president of the United States, on March 4, 1889. The nation's and Georgia's solitary black artillery company, the Georgia Artillery, with the Union Cornet Band, appealed to Savannah's citizens for financial contributions, hoping to reduce travel expenses to and from Washington. Both groups sponsored "a grand ball" as one of their fund-raisers. Atlanta's Governor's Volunteers and Georgia Cadets, led by Captains Jackson McHenry and M. H. Bentley, respectively, organized Atlanta's fund-raising "to attend the inauguration ceremonies." According to the *Tribune*, local whites were liberally assisting the effort. A month later Atlanta's Fulton Guards and Governor Guards agreed to a temporary merger so that they could attend the inauguration as the Governor's Volunteers.

It is unclear how successful any of the Atlanta and Savannah units were in attaining the financial resources for the trip to Washington, D.C. Black militia officer John H. Deveaux, however, did attend the inauguration. He went as a private citizen and as Georgia's Republican Party representative. Additionally a "delegation of colored men representing seven States, headed by Prof. J[ohn Mercer] Langston, of Virginia visited" the president-elect to urge "the appointment of a colored man as Attorney General of the United States who would zealously enforce the laws relating to protecting the ballot in the South." Militiaman Jackson McHenry, along with Rev. William Jefferson White and Rev. W. J. Dungee, also represented

Georgia with these petitioners. In the end, however, the *Tribune* reported that there were "nearly 200,000" people in attendance with a "distinctly Northern and Western" audience, while "the Southern people were conspicuous by their absence."[45]

Fading Militiamen

Each of these events marked the public presence of African Americans as citizens of the nation. These moments also were attempts to make highly public demonstrations of the martial capabilities of black men, both nationally and within Georgia. Black militiamen closed the 1880s seeking to maintain the significance of African American citizenship locally, statewide, regionally, and nationally. Locally, the Georgia Volunteers, Colored, continued to maintain a significant presence organizing Emancipation Day in Savannah. Jackson McHenry attained local celebrity status in Atlanta as both a militia officer and political leader. Regionally and nationally blacks continued their commitment to the Republican Party, hoping that federal power might break the rising tide of white supremacy and black erasure from the historical record. Statewide, however, black militiamen were fading from that scene, despite their efforts at maintaining a public presence. The problem of fading from the scene would define the last decade of the nineteenth century and first years of the twentieth century, the first five years of the 1890s being a critical time in the effort to forestall the erosion.[46]

In Savannah, blacks and African American militiamen aligned themselves with the city's new mayor, Major John Schwarz, by voting him into office in January 1899. Nine months later Schwarz convened a militia meeting involving officers of the "colored military" to coordinate emergency militia mobilization procedures. Schwartz called this conference only after black militiamen protested the preceding whites-only coordinating meeting, which had ignored the black militia. Colonel William Garrard, commander of the all-white Savannah Volunteer Guards battalion, also attended at the mayor's invitation. One critical question they discussed was who would command the local militia during a crisis. The mayor and white militiamen had decided earlier that the most senior white officer would command, even when a higher-ranking black officer was present. This decision undermined the black militiamen locally and statewide, as white militiamen and public officials questioned whether black militiamen were relevant.[47]

By November, black militiamen found themselves again excluded from another public all-militia function. Governor John B. Gordon and members of the legislature announced their intention to visit Savannah. The proposal compounded an already contentious relationship between Savannah's white and black newspapers: the white *Morning News* and the black *Tribune*. The *Morning News* publicly suggested that there be a military parade honoring state leaders visiting the city and focused its attention on Savannah's ten white militia companies, assuming that only white militiamen should march on parade before state authorities. The paper's proposal that there be solely a white militia parade ignored a tradition, established more than a decade earlier, wherein all of Savannah's militia companies, representing both races, marched in honor of the passing of a beloved Georgia congressman. Focusing solely on white militia units, the *Morning News* ignored Savannah's eight black companies and the First Battalion's members in Augusta and Macon, who had in May performed "a dress parade" celebrating the Fifteenth Amendment's anniversary. In July Savannah's black companies had marched in Charleston's Independence Day commemoration with South Carolina's First and Second National Guard Regiments. Georgia's and South Carolina's companies "paraded in full ranks and presented a handsome appearance." To be excluded when the state's commander in chief visited the city was too much to take, given several very public and successful black militia parades that showered favorable publicity on the militia companies and the cities they represented.

The *Tribune*, in redress, focused on full inclusion, a theme that characterized the last two decades of the Georgia Volunteers, Colored. This call for inclusion was reinforced by the refrain, "Well how about the Negro Soldiers." Black militiamen "too [were] part of the State troops . . . organized and commissioned by the State Authorities. They [bore] state arms and [were] held responsible in every particular" the same "as their white brethren." "In time of need," the newspaper argued, "they would not be exempt from military duty, because they are *black*." "The Governor . . . is commander in chief," the paper asserted, "therefore when a parade is to be made for inspection by the Chief Commander, let all the troops turn out." Yet, in the end, Savannah's white militia companies held a racially segregated, nonmilitary, and private reception that did not include Savannah's black companies.[48]

Team Player

Issues involving all militiamen, then, did not go unnoticed by the *Tribune*'s editorial staff. General Assembly activities involving the Georgia Volunteers were noted by the newspaper in 1889. The paper joined a statewide appeal by militiamen requesting that the Georgia legislature take positive actions that affirmed and recognized the state militia. Like other militiamen during the 1880s, the brain trust behind the *Tribune*, Deveaux and Solomon C. Johnson, both also black militiamen, argued that "Georgia should certainly be proud of her soldiery" because "it is second to none in the Union." In that context, the men asserted, "We hope that the Legislature will look at its present condition, and the limited manner in which it is taken care of by the State." There was a dire need for financial support. If pending funding were to be forthcoming, the paper asserted, "We are confident that the bill will become a law; and all that is required of our companies is to full up their ranks, be well drilled and disciplined in order to receive the benefits of the bill," namely, ample financial support and state recognition.[49] Black militiamen tried to be team players, advocating for the general militia in hopes that any benefits would be shared equally among all state militiamen.

Changing the Militia's Role

The bill referred to the 1889 legislative effort to find money for the militia. Governor John B. Gordon in September asked the Legislature to appropriate funding and pass laws "to better discipline and organize the volunteer forces." Gordon's executive message to the General Assembly cited the 1877 Constitution's Article 10 section one, paragraph one, which noted the "necessity of a 'well regulated militia.'" Armed with this idea, Gordon declared that militia "efficiency can be very much increased by rigid inspections. . . . Such inspections and 'annual encampments' are recognized as among the best methods for establishing and maintaining a well regulated militia." Gordon recommended that the legislature fund "an annual encampment and regular inspections of the volunteer troops of the state," supervised by the adjutant general.

The principles of this recommendation were incorporated within "Colonel Reilly's bill" and explained to the public by white militiaman and Bibb County legislator, Captain Hardeman. According to Hardeman, Georgia's military "absolutely need[ed] substantial aid from the state." Yet "the state furnishe[d] nothing to the military except the commissions of the officers." Georgia did "not give a dollar to teach the soldier boys how to use" federally provided arms, while "the policy of any state [was] to prepare its volunteers" for military service in defense of the state and nation. Georgia's militiamen were young men who had to provide their own arms and accoutrements while independently working very hard "night after night," hoping to perfect their military skills with very little guidance and training.

Further, Gordon conceded that operating a company was a "heavy expense," but reiterated that "the greatest burden [was] the loss of time that the members must submit to perfect themselves in the rudiments of the drill." Fundamentally, these young men could "ill afford to bear the expense of renting [an] armory, furnishing uniforms, furnishing ammunition, gaslight, [and] music." In addition, the men were "often times kept under orders and liable to leave home and business" to confront a crisis outside their local communities. In this context of meeting an emergency, preserving order, and placing fear in the hearts of the lawless, "the companies [were] not local organizations." Rather, "they [were] liable to be called out by the state into any county of the state," because "the military is the strong arm of the government." For all of these services, militiamen merely asked for "the expenses of an encampment in which these troops may be trained and thoroughly trained."[50]

Gordon, as the head of state government, was changing the role of the militia in Georgia. In exchange for state funding, he called for more inspections and the training opportunities encampments could offer militiamen. To justify the legislature's appropriation of financial support, militiamen had to commit to being trained. Militiamen no longer served the local community. To meet this challenge required the development of a militia with enhanced late nineteenth-century military training.

Acting as a team player, the *Savannah Tribune* supported the drive to train the militia to meet the new challenges outlined by Governor Gordon and Georgia's legislators. They also expected black militiamen to share in that process, with access to the training proposed in Colonel Reilly's 1889 bill. The newspaper went further, however, making a case for black militiamen because "the Negro pays his full share" as a state taxpayer. But black patience was wearing thin. The paper "call[ed] for a meeting to organize a National African-American League," intending "to successfully combat the denial of our constitutional and inherent rights so generally denied or abridged." This was also a call to represent the "8,000,000 . . . [black] souls having a common interest peculiar to themselves," with "their first duty to themselves . . . [being] to organize for the redress of grievances and use the power conferred upon them to compel the granting of equal privilege and opportunity to the Negro as a citizen." In either case, blacks were citizens of the state and nation and therefore justified in having equal access to the advantages offered white militiamen as the militia in Georgia began to change from a social club and locally focused institution to a professionalizing instrument of state government.[51]

Persistence

The militia changed with the state as Georgia government shifted toward centralization and state-level authorities: the legislature, governor, and adjutant general redefined the militia. Government would provide the state militia with more resources if militiamen trained to become soldiers and relinquished their commitment to their local community, thereby making the militia an instrument of state government and less the servant of local interests. This was especially evident in John B. Gordon's new vision for the Georgia Volunteers. Black militiamen, despite their attempts to advocate for all militiamen, were excluded from participating in what the new state militia might become. This was evident among Savannah's local black militiamen, as their status changed from inclusion to exclusion. Excluded from a public event that more than a decade earlier had included black militiamen, albeit in a racially segregated manner, the public face of the black militiaman was slowly being erased. Yet African American militiamen continued as a public institution as Savannah's black community persisted in sustaining the eight companies and the battalion that served as their organizational umbrella. The First Battalion's Board of Officers "authorized to be appointed by the chair" a twenty-one-person committee to coordinate the planning of "a grand military bazaar" fundraising and community event during the winter of 1889 and the spring of 1890. Their goal was to raise funds "for the benefit of the Armory Fund for the First Battalion." The committee included Solomon C. Johnson, incoming editor of the *Tribune* and the First Battalion's sergeant major. According to militia members, this was "the first time that the battalion ha[d] asked the aid of the citizens" to provide funding for the construction of the First Battalion's armory.[52]

During the spring of 1889 "various military companies assembled" and "marched to the Charleston and Savannah Railway depot to tender an ovation to the Hon. Fred Douglass," passing through Savannah to Jacksonville, Florida, on the way to his appointment as minister to Haiti. Did Douglass see and think about how far black citizen soldiers had come since his first antebellum encounter with "armed companies of young black men marching in public." At that time, thirty-four years earlier, black militiamen "were not officially sanctioned by federal and state authorities." Antebellum black independent militiamen had come together and organized to defend blacks against slavery, making "self-defense and national liberation" important pre–Civil War goals. In 1889 Douglass was reminded about a celebration in 1855 of the West Indian Emancipation Day (August 1, 1833) when he first saw black militiamen: "How did these companies look and act? . . . I answer, for all the world, just like soldier[s]." Black militiamen in 1855, by marching with a "soldierly bearing," challenged the idea that blacks were "objects of ridicule." These antebellum black militiamen impressed Douglass to the point that they "compelled [his] admiration"; they "deported themselves handsomely, and attracted much attention."

Nearly three and a half decades, almost a generation and a half, later in Savannah, black state-sponsored militiamen representing the state of Georgia publicly received Frederick Douglass, U.S. Minister to Haiti. The black militiamen honoring Douglass in 1889 had spent seventeen years working very hard to prove their worthiness as representatives of the city and state. They honored a black federal official on a mission cementing relations between the first republics in the Western Hemisphere. The black militia companies in 1889 were a reflection of how African American militiamen had evolved from official governmental invisibility to public visibility and recognition by state and federal governments. Yet their achievements were again being ignored, despite financial and popular support in the local community.[53]

Savannah's black militia units continued to serve their community in 1889. They comprised active, responsible citizens who received community support. The Forest City Light Infantry had its own week-long bazaar where the Chatham Light Infantry tendered its assistance by attending "in full uniform." The Chatham Light Infantry also organized "a military hop at their armory" and sponsored an excursion picnic accompanied by "a grand ball [also] at their armory" as the unit entertained Augusta's Georgia Light Infantry. The same company, the Chatham Light Infantry, in late May 1889, with "detachments from all the other Savannah companies, along with two or three thousand people," welcomed the Georgia

Light Infantry a second time, demonstrating that the First Battalion and the individual black companies continued to be connected to the African American communities of Savannah, Augusta, and Macon.

These units persisted in the face of the continuing pressure of "very rigid" inspections of "their arms and uniforms," which needed to be "in perfect order" according to the standards set by the Military Advisory Board, adjutant general, and the governor. These authorities, especially Adjutant General John McIntosh Kell, contended as Governor Gordon would also, that inspections produced "a fine condition of discipline amongst the [white] militia—[and] that the troops are in better condition today than ever before in the history of the state." Also, encampments and legislative appropriations "had a most salutary moral effect" upon white militiamen, who as a result were "beginning to feel that they [were] really a state institution, and . . . not altogether forgotten."[54]

"Mad"

By 1890, black militiamen, especially the men of the First Battalion, were "mad." They were mad because white cavalrymen and their mounts proceeded through Savannah to Augusta for a cavalry encampment and because white infantrymen departed Augusta after encampment training elsewhere in the state. The *Atlanta Constitution*'s headline read: "The Colored Troops of Savannah Claim that They Have Been Slighted." African American militiamen were "mad," the newspaper noted, "due to the fact that they cannot participate" in Augusta's encampment. The *Savannah Tribune* announced that it had become clear that racial exclusion was now a state policy, "as we expected," since Adjutant General John McIntosh Kell had informed the "commanding officers of the different [black] companies . . . that it [was] impossible to allow them to go in encampment this year, and of course, all of the whites [would] go." The newspaper continued, "This is not the first time that the colored troops have been slighted by the state, and it seems that if they bear the name of state troops they should not be treated accordingly." By comparison, the *Tribune* argued, black companies had long-standing traditions and a presence as old as that of the white units: "Yet, still [the black units] are more wretchedly equipped than those of the whites who have just been admitted. It is only wished that the authorities will deal square with the colored troops."[55]

After the whites-only encampment in June, black militiamen organized public activities in July and August that unified the community.

Atlanta and Macon companies in July conducted "a big day at [Atlanta's] Piedmont park," with a "grand prize drill and barbeque and various other amusements" so as to "give everybody an opportunity to spend a pleasant day at the fairgrounds." It was also a way for the black "companies . . . to have their friends, white as well as colored, to come out and patronize them" and to fund another event in Columbus, Georgia, on July 26. Across the state the First Battalion, led by John Deveaux, who had returned from New Brunswick, Georgia, after his recent federal appointment, joined South Carolina militiamen in a parade of seven hundred African American militiamen. They marched in August in "the largest colored military display . . . for years."[56]

While these events were not training moments like those annual encampment opportunities could have provided, African American militiamen and their parades, drill competitions, and social activities constituted proofs of black manliness and citizenship, and served as continuing declarations that they embraced the standards of militia service practiced by white and black companies alike. Eleanor Hannah has argued that parades were demonstrations of manliness and active citizenship and were evidence of both a heroic past and steady performance. In the visual culture of the 1870s, which continued into the 1890s, being seen by a newspaper reporter kept the black militia in the public eye. The press also evaluated the level of activity, appearance, and performance maintained by African American militiamen. Additionally, these events allowed local supporters to see exactly where their money and support was going in light of militia fund-raising. Each public and social activity served as proof that the militia company trained men who had a commitment to local service and the accompanying responsibility of being exemplary men. They were citizens of the community.[57]

For Whites Only: Encampments, Funding, Professionalization

Yet the comparison between the training experience white militiamen attained during an encampment and that of the black drill competition and social events suggests that a major change loomed in how militiamen of both races would be evaluated in Georgia. Governor Gordon, Captains Reilly and Hardeman, Adjutant General Kell, and the all-white members of the Military Advisory Board separated white militiamen from their black counterparts in both subtle and definitive ways beginning in the 1890s. Georgia's Volunteer leadership was also transforming the militia.

This was evident in Hardeman's description of the militia and its duties. No longer were the Volunteers an informal collection of white men whose loyalties belonged first to the local community in which the company was organized and second to the home county, with only peripheral loyalty accorded to state government. This had been the militia of the 1870s and 1880s.

The Georgia Volunteers in 1890 had to take on responsibilities that carried them beyond the familiar locales of the originating county. Militiamen, Hardeman contended, were peacekeepers in a turbulent late nineteenth-century world of disruptive laborers and unruly citizens. State legislators and militia leaders compared the Volunteer force with other states across the country. Their rhetoric compared Georgia's Volunteers with unnamed militias in other states that funded their militia companies with state and federal monies. Militia leaders also suggested that states that appropriated funding to their militias should also set standards for military training. Georgia had not yet embraced such a commitment to the professionalization of its military by designating a clear funding stream. Encampments and the state funding that accompanied such opportunities at the end of the 1880s and beginning of the 1890s offered white Georgia militiamen a chance to begin measuring up to their militia brethren in other states. This professional development shifted militiamen from a focus on local service to potential statewide and federal service. State leadership asserted that training through encampments also pushed Georgia's white militiamen beyond the frolic of the social club that some members of the public believed characterized the militia to the pinnacle of being professional soldiers seriously committed to militia service.

Encampments therefore provided clear benefits to white militiamen. According to the Military Advisory Board's annual report for 1891, written by Colonels William Garrard, S. P. Gilbert, and C. M. Wiley, the Georgia Volunteers were "in a poor condition." The adverse state of the volunteers, the report noted, "reflect[ed] no credit upon the commonwealth [of Georgia], but it [was] gratifying to note that the effects of the late encampment [at Chickamauga during June and July 1891] [were] of incalculable value." Even though this encampment did not service all of the fifty-one infantry companies and fourteen cavalry units in the white commands, because the state appropriation was exhausted midway through the encampment, white militiamen experienced "strict discipline" that perfected their ability to perform "guard and other camp duties" and "to obey as well as to command."

The Chickamauga encampment "engendered a fine military spirit throughout the force," specifically a desire "to learn the practical duties of a soldier in the field." More crucially, however, both officers and enlisted men experienced the difference between "display" and "hard work." Through their encampment experience, white militiamen found out how to "subordinate display to hard work and [learn] martial efficiency." The report affirmed, "No other mode of instruction can accomplish the same result"; encampments "will inure the force to hardship and equip it for any service the state may demand." The encampment training was not all "fun and frolic," despite the claims of some newspapers in 1891. The Military Advisory Board believed that the encampment had been "an arduous" challenge for white militiamen. It gave white militiamen "an object lesson of great value, demonstrating that the volunteers of Georgia [were] real and not play soldiers."[58]

Whites-only encampments may have been the intermediate step between what Eleanor Hannah has characterized as the militia focus from 1870 to 1890 on drill, parade, and social events to provide public proof of soldierly bearing, manliness, citizenship, and civic leadership. The citizen soldier embodied this tradition before the 1890s. This immediate post–Civil War operation of the militia contrasted with the late-nineteenth-century effort to create "real soldiers" during the 1890s encampments and with the emergence of an individualized National Guardsman in the early twentieth century, the sharpshooter. Encampment training coincided with and was driven by the triumph of militiamen across the United States gaining access to a consistent stream of governmental financial support at both the state and federal levels. State support contributed to the transformation and transitions that shifted focus from the drill routines of the 1870s and 1880s to the encampments of the 1890s.

Sharpshooter vs. States' Rights

In Georgia, 1889, 1890, and 1891 were pivotal years for white militiamen and their evolution into the twentieth-century National Guardsman: an individualized, disciplined, professional killing machine, the sharpshooter. The sharpshooter was an individual whose loyalty would be to the nation and federal government, not to a collection of fellow militiamen beholden to each other and focused on local community needs. The sharpshooter's standard of excellence lay in his individually focused and developed self-discipline. The disciplined soldier demonstrated his skill through his accuracy with long-range weaponry and his patriotic allegiance to national institutions: the National Guard, federal power, the United States, and those advocating transformation of the militia into the National Guards, and the United States Army. This early-twentieth-century soldier, the National Guardsman, became what some white Georgia leaders had feared in the 1870s: the militia as an institution that appeared to be drifting toward being an extension of the all-powerful Civil War and immediate postwar federal government, which threatened to overwhelm state and local power. The late nineteenth-century and early twentieth-century National Guardsman was securely a representative of the nation, a member of a reserve army that served as a support unit of the regular national army. The militiaman from 1870 to 1890, in contrast, was a community leader committed to serving the political, social, and economic needs of a single Georgia county, as well as the state's military needs.[59]

Georgia, by appropriating funding for encampments, joined other states in transforming nineteenth-century militiamen into the approaching twentieth-century National Guardsman. This also meant that the militiaman was no longer a servant of the local community or at times even the state. By the early twentieth century the National Guardsman was an agent of the federal government and part of the nation's military structure as a reserve army. The National Guardsman moved from being an instrument of the local community to being a component of the United States Army.[60] The Georgia militia was becoming a national institution despite white Georgia's desire to preserve the militia as the foundation of states' rights.

Equality

For African American members of the Georgia Volunteers, Colored, U.S. citizenship, and not states' rights, remained the bedrock of their vision of themselves and the militia. They envisioned militia membership also reflecting their commitment to Georgia as their home state and as giving them access to recognition, quality participation, and equality as Georgians. Any failure by Georgia to meet these components of citizenship forced blacks to seek redress from the federal government as the defender of their rights as citizens. The public face of the black militiaman, however, was one of the continuing hopes that efficient work and service as militiamen would secure for them and the race in general a status equal to that of their white neighbors. This agenda dated back to at least 1878, when elite white friends and patrons were asked to see value and racial progress in black militia endeavors. The militia continued to be the institution wherein black men, through the traditional publicly visible militia mainstays of the drill and parade and the newspaper reporting, could document the quality of their personhood, citizenship, and manliness and the advancement of the race from slavery to modernity. Black militiamen contended that they were a constituent part of the Georgia Volunteers with equal standing alongside white militiamen. This meant that African American militiamen served the state under the direction of the commander in chief, Georgia's governor, just as their white militia brothers in arms were doing.

In public black militiamen added their voices to the universal militia plea for resources and for acknowledgement of the militia's contribution to state governance. Specifically, black men had carved out a rich tradition of militia service as they defined it, working for their local communities. They contended that such service compared favorably with that of white militia units, whose foundations dated back to the American Revolution. More importantly, the black militia company had offered martial and community service to both their home county and the state since the early 1870s. The consistency of black militia service and the tradition of militiamen representing their local community provided African American militiamen with seniority over white companies that entered militia service long after black units. Blacks believed their seniority should have given them priority in terms of access to equipment, accoutrements, and the training opportunities encampments offered. Yet despite their post–Civil War and Reconstruction drilling, parading, community service, and public demonstrations of citizenship and manliness, black militiamen's loyalty and contributions to the advancement of Georgia's public image as a "democracy" was being ignored in the 1890s by the leadership of the state and by the Georgia Volunteers.

The black militia company also served as a vehicle for the expression of African American aspirations and definitions of autonomy, citizenship, and "our day of freedom." Atlanta's Emancipation Days in 1889 and 1890 were platforms for presenting the black commitment to citizenship. The 1889 commemoration was a mass celebration of "all sizes and shapes, colors and conditions, old and young," who crowded together in the old capitol building on January 1. The *Atlanta Constitution* declared the importance of Emancipation Day for black Atlantans even as it exposed its racism through the caricature of black people. The newspaper claimed, "Never since the bugle note of the plantation darkey, has Atlanta witnessed a more compactly, conglomerated crowd of people of color than that in the capitol." The paper continued, "There was an unusual stir among the negro population and every individual who could get out was on the streets . . . discussing the day which is of such large importance to them." Nine black Atlanta militiamen and two former militiamen served on the organizing committee, and the four Atlanta companies—the Fulton Guards, the Georgia Cadets, the Governor's Volunteers, and the Washington Guards—of the "one hundred [man] strong" Second Battalion marched as a central part of the commemorations. According to the *Constitution*, "the proceedings, indoors and out, were all of the most orderly description, and not a single episode occurred to cast a reproach on the celebration of . . . the colored race, most momentous of all occasions."[61]

In 1890, the four-company Second Battalion led "delegations from the various colored societies" to the Loyd Street Methodist Church to participate in the daylong events of Emancipation Day. While the ceremonies followed the traditional service, which included prayer and music, a reading of the Emancipation Proclamation, a eulogy for Abraham Lincoln, and an "oration" by Rev. E. R. Carter, this Emancipation Day in Atlanta was marked by protest resolutions "condemning the recent murder of colored men confined in jail" in Jesup, Georgia, and Barnwell, South Carolina. The four resolutions called for white pulpits across the region, but especially in Georgia, to mobilize "the moral sentiment of the best white people . . . to denounce, in the name of Christ, these crimes against human nature." The "white press, another organ of the best element of that race," was also called on "to denounce these outrages in the name of the constitution of this state, and of the United States."

The protest document concluded, "We counsel our people to further patience, forbearance, and long sufferings and devise them no resistance, except such as may be defensive and defensible." The appeal for adherence to the state and national constitutions mirrored a tradition that black leaders in Savannah and Augusta had established in the 1870s as they organized militia companies. These leaders declared their loyalty to the documents that protected black citizenship as their rationale for service to the state of Georgia and the nation. Black Atlantans renewed that tradition in 1890, reminding their white neighbors that they were citizens of Georgia and the United States who upheld the law and constitutional protections for black people. Unfortunately, while Georgia's 1877 constitution may have recognized African Americans as citizens, it did not protect black rights thirteen years later.[62]

The objects of black militiamen's protest in the 1890s were not limited to lynching and murder. The protests also included challenges to Jim Crow segregation, "debasing laws," and "infamous class legislation" against African American children. The *Savannah Tribune* called on blacks to challenge white assaults on their status. The paper asked, "What are the colored men doing to check the evil?" The demand for unified black male action included notices of events that required a male convocation. The *Tribune* noted that the "next large gathering of colored men," the National Baptist Convention, would convene during the summer of 1892. Yet an earlier, more publicly vital local coming together of black men was the effort to organize Savannah's Emancipation Day. In its commitment to Emancipation Day, The *Tribune* utilized a two-pronged approach to making the day a success and demonstrating black unity. First, the paper insisted that "all male institutions" in the city needed to gather together in the newspaper's offices so that they could plan the event. Second, this convening of the black male institutional leadership went hand in hand with the *Tribune*'s campaign to revive public enthusiasm for the day and spearhead preparation for the commemoration to prevent having to organize the celebration at the eleventh hour. It also provided a public platform for demonstrating to both races that blacks were citizens and united in their advocacy and defense of that citizenship.[63]

According to the newspaper, January 1 "aught to be celebrated and . . . handed down to ages unborn as the greatest day to the colored race in the United States." The vital date was "greater than the 'Fourth day of July" because blacks were not freed during America's Independence Day. January's first day constituted "great event," and "every man, woman and child with one-eighth of Negro blood in his veins should deck themselves in their very best attire and show their appreciation for the birthday of their American liberty." Further, the paper contended that black Savannah needed to mount "a movement on foot to have the coming day properly celebrated." To achieve this aim, "civic and secret societies, together with the military should turn out." The *Tribune* brought together every black male-led institution in the city to put their hands toward creating a suitably commemorated Emancipation Day. Near mid-December 1891 the newspaper announced that the call for all African Americans to rally to the "proper celebration of Emancipation Day" had been successful because "a movement was immediately started to carry it into effect." Led by James E. Whiteman, who "invite[d] all of the officers of male institutions to meet in [the] Tribune building," black men came together to "perfect [the] arrangements" for "a tremendous celebration." Black militiamen were to be "on time" and were "enjoined to . . . strictly obey orders and observe rigid military decorum" in celebration of the importance of black liberty.[64]

Gendered Respectability or Mass Democracy

This demand for black men to act and serve as the solitary leaders of the black community was not atypical of late nineteenth-century African American men across the nation. Before 1880 black women had a voice that black men heard. Collective consultations involving black men, women, and children were part of the immediate postwar experience in Richmond, Virginia, where black people came together as a community to define their freedom. This collective action was especially evident when black decision making involved consultation with all ages and both genders. Black people's use of public space and their definition of freedom as a community activity was in contradistinction to the white focus on individuality, middle-class etiquette, and civilized behavior. These differences produced conflicting visions of freedom. Black women during emancipation had participated in a variety of public events and forums, including parades, rallies, conventions, and other public mass meetings. For Richmond's black women in the 1870s, this participation included organizing their own militia company. The women's unit served as a ceremonial organization active primarily during Emancipation Day activities, but its presence pointed to what Elsa Barkley Brown has argued was a black rejection of "the liberal bourgeois ideal of a solely male civic domain" that was coupled to and insisted on black submission to white male authority and leadership. Additionally, all African Americans publicly spoke their peace with a volume that irritated white politicians to the point that they found ways to limit opportunities for mass expressions of black democracy. As a result, democracy and flexible conceptions of gender roles gave way in the 1880s to male and bourgeois definitions of leadership that emphasized a decorum that would exclude the varied voices of black women and children that had characterized the moment of freedom in 1865.[65]

Limiting mass black public debate paralleled the coming of late nineteenth-century antiblack violence, declining black economic opportunity, and black disfranchisement. These restrictions evolved in parallel with a decline in black access to public facilities and space, owing to white Republican and Democratic pressure, and with the United States Supreme Court's declaration of the Civil Rights Act of 1875 as unconstitutional in 1883. Political debate became more restricted as public space was gendered and confined within white male literary societies, ward meetings, fraternal organizations, newspapers, and saloons. These specialized and gendered spaces also had class designations and structures that restricted who spoke in these private and semi-private venues. Within increasingly restricted access to spaces for public debate, Brown asserts, working-class black people were disfranchised within the African American community while the black middle class lost its place in the greater public realm, which was dominated by their white counterparts.

Gender and class divisions solidified during the post-Reconstruction era as blacks across the gender and class spectrum sought to redefine their political, economic, and social standing in hopes of reacquiring the "political authority they once had—internally and externally" during Reconstruction. This effort in Georgia extended to the early 1880s, when young black militiamen ruled the Republican Party from 1880 to 1882. Finally, according to Brown, late nineteenth-century definitions of a "respectable" middle-class womanhood and manhood accompanied by class entitlement "became central to the arguments for political rights" for blacks nationally. Savannah's black male organizing in the early 1890s was an extension of what was happening throughout Virginia.[66]

Brown, Michele Mitchell, and Angela Hornsby-Gutting have also contended that black middle-class respectability was both a defensive and constructive attempt to redefine black access to the public arena. Yet, in the process, respectability's intended paternal protection of black women and the working classes and collective rehabilitation of blacks' public image solidified class, gender, and leadership barriers within the black community. Further, freedom, respectability, and urban life have had a longer negative history involving class and culture than did the short generation between late nineteenth-century emancipation and disfranchisement. Respectability, class, and the city appear to have overwhelmed mass democracy in the nineteenth century, as the loud slave celebrations of Pinkster and General Election Day gave way to the more sedate respectable parades that northern free blacks adopted with the coming of freedom. Respectability against a backdrop of white antebellum antiblack violence, segregation, and disfranchisement was couched in temperance, thrift, and reform. Additionally, class combined with race to determine the proper middle-class and elite dress and behavior, which served as the fundamental elements of individualized respectability.[67]

The *Tribune*'s short-term intent was to rally black people around Emancipation Day by utilizing the energy, dedication, and public power of black male-led urban institutions to convey the image of a united race. This was a shift from how the newspaper had reported Emancipation Day commemorations in the 1870s. During that decade of black public power and militia parades, the paper presented the black militia companies as the central feature of Emancipation Day. It was an event that black militiamen initiated, planned, and executed, and few descriptions of the day's celebrations included activities beyond the militia parades through Savannah's streets that culminated at the park extension, where thousands of blacks received the militiamen and gloried in their drill routines before ending the ceremonies defining "our day of freedom." The *Tribune*'s successful call for Savannah's black civic men to rally together and create a "properly celebrated" Emancipation Day in 1892 institutionalized an apparently new process that created the "Emancipation Association." This group, from the 1890s into the twentieth century, took it upon themselves to organize Emancipation Day as a community event where the militia would "make the usual . . . parade." In addition, a "citizens committee met . . . and adopted the . . . programme," which included not only the militia but the "Grand Army Republic, Workingmen Union Association, Morning Call club, Crescent Lodge K[nights of] P[ythias]; Olympia Lodge K. of P.; Feay Division K. of P.; Joshua Division K. of P.; Irene Social Club, Broads Aid and Social club, United Tie of Brotherhood Labor Union Association, Lumbermen Union, and other societies." By November 1892 Atlanta and Augusta, too, had "a standing organization for this purpose." Significantly, the expansion of Emancipation Day in Savannah included fraternal groups whose military traditions would become increasingly important as Georgia's white leadership undermined black militiamen. Emancipation Day in the 1890s continued to include the militia, but the *Tribune* also published the text of the day's major orator—something that had not been done in the promising days of 1870s freedom. With the 1890s a new day had dawned, as ominous shadows of streetcar segregation, murder, disfranchisement, gender and class divisions, and the declining relevance of the Republican Party all conspired to negatively define Georgia's African Americans.[68]

Lieutenant Charles B. Satterlee, USA

The luster of the Georgia Volunteers, Colored, was also tarnished under the increasingly critical glare of the Military Advisory Board, Georgia's governor, the adjutant and inspector general, and his new evaluator, Lieutenant Charles B. Satterlee of the Third Artillery, United States Army. The appointment aligned Georgia with other states that invited the federal military to instruct state-based militiamen. This was a change from the 1870s, when Georgia's elite citizens endeavored to isolate the state militia from the federal military and government. Satterlee's official assignment was to instruct Georgia's military. That included service as encampment adjutant, who was in charge of the instruction of both officers and noncommissioned officers and of inspecting the entire contingent of the Georgia Volunteers, regardless of race. Specifically, Adjutant General John McIntosh Kell informed Augusta's Third Battalion Georgia Volunteers, Colored, to "hold your battalion in readiness for inspection."[69]

Satterlee toured the state inspecting the Georgia militia from September 25, 1891 to April 5, 1892. In January 1892 the *Savannah Tribune* and the First Battalion, Georgia Volunteers, Colored, awaited Satterlee's arrival. The newspaper characterized Satterlee as "an able soldier and a strict disciplinarian." It also noted that "only [one] white company in the city [had been] inspected so far." This compared to the three black units inspected that January and the five other black companies scheduled to be presented to Satterlee during his Savannah tour, in January and February. In anticipation of a scrutinizing inspection, the *Tribune* contended that the lieutenant would "find the colored troops in good condition." This claim was made with a definitive caveat. The "good condition" had to be contextualized. Specifically when observers "consider[ed] the adverse circumstances which they are placed in, and the non-support of the State," black militiamen had achieved a great deal. Yet, despite these obstacles and governmental neglect, the "boys [were] preparing to meet" Satterlee, and at least one company, the Forest City Light Infantry, "made a creditable showing" at inspection.

By the end of February 1892 Satterlee's two-month inspection of Savannah's black and white militia units came to an end, and "all of the [black] companies," the *Tribune* reported, "made a splendid showing, and were given some wholesome instructions by the inspector." The newspaper continued, the "inspection will be the means of infusing renewed vigor into the members of the different companies and spur them up to the full letter of their duties," including to "keep up regular drills and endeavor to perfect themselves as far as possible in the rudiments of the tactics." With this inspection, militiamen regardless of race were informed that they had to learn new drill techniques. The United States Army had abolished Upton's tactics, and this change in a fundamental standard of military procedure and drilling was initiated by the federal armed forces. Notably Georgia embraced federal standards without objection in 1891–1892. The new policy was implemented in striking contrast to newspaper-endorsed resistance less than fifteen years earlier, when white Georgians asserted that state's rights trumped federal power, especially in the contest of who controlled the militia: the state of Georgia or the federal government of the United States.[70]

Satterlee's report to Adjutant General John McIntosh Kell contended that the Georgia Volunteers in general could "not be excelled" because of the enthusiasm exhibited by the militiamen. Specifically, Satterlee noted in a newspaper interview that white militiamen constituted "a remarkably fine body of men." This group was intelligent and constituted "the flower of the state—and they are all gentlemen." The *Atlanta Constitution* reiterated this observation, asserting that privates in the militia were "prominent men" among whose ranks were "statesmen, professional men and businessmen—politicians and millionaires." The members of Savannah's Volunteer Guards battalion were noted for their "aristocracy and wealth," and "near millionaire" militiaman G. P. Baldwin, who led "the great Baldwin Fertilizer Company," was noted in particular. Additionally, the newspaper reported that the militia's rank and file constituted "the flower of... [Georgia's] youth... while the higher officers [were] generally prominent and often eminent," with such leading lawyers as E. L. Wight and George A. Mercer attaining the rank of colonel.

According to Satterlee, the Georgia Volunteers' collective spirited participation in their individual units and unified commitment to service made them "perhaps the finest body of volunteer troops to be found in the United States." At the same time, Satterlee's report noted that camaraderie alone did not sustain a militia. In fact camaraderie would not suffice since "military inspiration and enthusiasm must lose their edge and keenness and grow dull unless whetted by stimulus and hope of recognition." State recognition continued to be a problem that Georgia state leaders failed to address. Georgia's Volunteers also lacked fundamental operational elements such as "knapsacks, haversacks, cups, [and] leggings," as well as "the practical part of the work," which included deficits in drill and in comprehending the purpose of inspection. Fundamentally, the Georgia Volunteers badly needed to be appreciated by the state of Georgia, especially the legislature. Substantiating his contention, Satterlee argued that if Georgia funded its militia, adopted a new military code that standardized the state force, and set consistent regulations, a modern force could emerge. Satterlee, however, had his own caveat: "Until these are given consideration other recommendations are useless."[71]

While this was Satterlee's broad-based assessment of the Georgia Volunteers, he also wrote a separate section on the Georgia Volunteers, Colored. According to Satterlee's inspection of the three black battalions, African American militiamen were a combination of incompetence and competence. The major deficits, however, were in equipment, knowledge, record keeping, tactics, and the absence of uniformity in their dress. At the inspection every black company, like their white colleagues, lacked knowledge about guard duty, skirmish exercises, and unit discipline. Record keeping was a problem because black company leaders had no concept of enlistment and discharge or the recommended duration of either for a militia member—an issue with which the entire militia wrestled. This problem was compounded by the fact that "men come and go at will," disrupting the "principles of discipline" by inconsistent attendance, enrollment, and participation. Black armories were "too limited for company evolutions." Black companies also utilized state militia property and weapons that for all intents and purposes were worn out, old, and useless.

Additionally, units had to wear their dress uniforms at the inspection owing to the absence of field uniforms for informal duties and, by implication, inspections. This problem, Satterlee noted, reflected the impoverished state of black militiamen and their units. Their commitment to militia service was undermined by a slim financial foundation, with each unit having to do its own fundraising and members personally paying for their individual uniform and equipment. Black militiamen did all of this since no monetary support came from the Georgia General Assembly. As a result, black militiamen had no platform upon which to purchase, maintain, or modernize their state-issued property necessary to make the militia company viable. While state-issued military equipment was essential in performing black militiamen's obligations to the State of Georgia, there were other issues. Some black officers could not read or write. Further Satterlee observed, "No command is provided with a field outfit or mess kit; none with blankets." Such oversights appeared to be the fault of Georgia's governmental leadership.[72]

All was not negative in Satterlee's estimation. He complimented both black officers and men in the three black battalions. Satterlee did not name names, but he implied that First Battalion commander, Lieutenant Colonel John Deveaux, was "a very good officer, and [took] a good interest in his command." Savannah's six black infantry companies received a mix of positive grades for execution of drill routines and deficits for undisciplined ranks. Two-thirds of the companies had rusty, worn, and broken weapons, while about one-third of the battalion's companies possessed arms rated as "generally very good; free from rust." The Second Battalion, based in Atlanta, with one of its five companies in Columbus, Georgia, faired less well. The unit's adjutant, the recently appointed black militiaman, military veteran, and grocer Floyd H. Crumbly, "a very good officer," maintained accurate and complete records, but the battalion's arms and drill experience was "ragged." Augusta, the home of the three-company Third Battalion, received accolades for having the best company among the black militiamen. Company A was well drilled with "very good officers" who led the unit's members with few flaws. The Battalion's Company B drilled the best among black militiamen, performing the manual of arms and firing their weapons. There were also three unattached black companies along with the sole black artillery company. The three unaffiliated infantry companies received a great deal of criticism from Satterlee, because these units possessed poorly maintained weapons. The Savannah-based Georgia Artillery, Satterlee noted, had achieved a great deal in light of the fact that "at its own expense [the unit's members had] . . . provided two six-pounder brass pieces and carriages and limbers; kept in good order."[73]

"To the Highest Standard"

Throughout 1892 black Georgians endeavored to prove themselves to be respected citizens. One way they pursued this goal involved rehabilitating the image of disgraced Colonel William H. Woodhouse, first commander of the First Battalion. At the end of January Woodhouse was "restored to citizenship" by the "indefatigable efforts" of black militiamen, including Captain L. M. Pleasant and Colonel John Deveaux and such leading African American men as Rev. William Jefferson White and Captain Judson W. Lyons. These men took the "evidence . . . [of Woodhouse's innocence] to Atlanta." They were assisted by local white judges and lawyers along with members of the white jury that originally convicted Woodhouse. While this collective Savannah community effort cleared Woodhouse's name, he apparently did not return to the militia. Restoring Woodhouse's respectability had additional ramifications for African Americans, for respectability included a measure of racial equality. The *Savannah Tribune* contended that Georgia would not be a prosperous state "until all classes of its citizens [were] extended like privileges." Equal standing did not mean social equality, but it did mean "equal rights before the law—political equality." As a result, the paper claimed, black and white cooperation, such as the restoration of Woodhouse's reputation as an honorable man, marked a "new generation of white men and black men" who worked together in "a changed environment stronger in intelligence and individuality" and less prone to the bait of white racism.[74]

The *Savannah Tribune* also focused on the entire militia as an institution that might give blacks respectability. The newspaper endorsed statewide efforts to secure funding for the 4,577 Georgia Volunteers (3,309 white militiamen and 1,268 black militiamen) by reprinting the *Atlanta Constitution*'s endorsement of state funding for the Georgia militia. According to the *Tribune*, "The need for a proper maintenance of a militia has been fully demonstrated in these columns . . . and it rests with the legislature, which now has the question under consideration, as to whether or not the state soldiery shall be supported in the manner it deserves as a state institution." There was additionally a sense of pride in black militiamen and service to Georgia. The paper reflected this with its celebration "of the election of Adjutant Floyd H. Crumbly to the colonelcy of the Second Battalion of Atlanta." Crumbly, the newspaper asserted, "is an excellent officer," an assertion certified by Satterlee's inspection comments. Furthermore, his selection as one of the leaders of the Second Battalion "added another star to shine in favor of the colored military of the State." Black militiamen in Augusta elected a third African American colonel, Isaiah H. Blocker, who joined senior colonel John Deveaux of Savannah and the new officer, Atlanta Adjutant, F. H. Crumbly. The three black colonels together provided African American Georgians with an opportunity to "make a greater stride, with more assistance from the State." Additionally, the *Tribune* made the election of two black colonels a recruiting tool. These men's ascendancy to the colonelcy appeared to be an ideal way to rally young black men to become militiamen. As a result, the *Tribune* proclaimed, "The commanders of the various companies" should "make it their indispensible duty to have their ranks filled up with young men and bring them up to the highest standard."[75]

The year 1892 ended in Georgia with Governor William J. Northen's plea to the General Assembly to fund the Georgia Volunteers more consistently and beyond the incomplete financing of encampments. Northen's message to the legislature stressed "the absolute necessity for an efficient and thoroughly organized militia," especially in light of mob violence that threatened to overwhelm civil authority in unnamed states across the United States. To forestall such an event and to prevent any violent mass outbreak, Northen argued, an efficient, organized, and reliable militia must be maintained. For Northen having a "reliable" military was the ounce of prevention Georgia needed, but such a force would not be possible if Georgia continued to "rely upon the patriotic sacrifices" of militiamen deprived of public recognition and steady state funding. The governor suggested that at the current funding for the militia, "less than $6 per capita per annum," "the state could well afford to double the appropriation for the security of the life and property of its citizens."[76]

In the wake of Satterlee's 1891–1892 inspection, six white companies had been disbanded by 1893. Adjutant General and Inspector General John McIntosh Kell recommended approving the admittance of nineteen white companies to the Georgia Volunteers. The annual report also noted the need to standardize the Georgia Volunteers' organization. Battalions, for example, were to have a standard number of companies statewide. The 1893 militia and its predecessors lacked unit uniformity and apparently existed at whatever organizational level the local customs and leaders determined. The Georgia militia at the regimental and company levels was inconsistently staffed and unevenly organized, with some white regiments having five companies while others maintained ten to twelve units. There were no regulations setting upper and lower limits of staffing and membership at the level of both the regiment and the battalion. Militia company selection and admission appeared to be devoid of any "idea of geographical location," and no company owned its own armory.

A month later, the *Atlanta Constitution* reported on Satterlee's observations concerning a new military bill before the Georgia Legislature. The bill proposed creating the Atlanta-based Fifth Georgia Regiment to geographically balance the distribution of white regiments across Georgia. According to the *Constitution*, regiments represented specific districts in the state, and thus their organization and presence gave the regiment an identity that merged with that of its region. Currently companies were "widely scattered" and therefore could not represent a region or offer balance in the distribution of militia units across Georgia. While the new military bill suggested that the legislature might reorganize the militia by balancing the Georgia Volunteers' regional organization, the *Constitution* additionally noted that the contemplated reorganization made "no changes among the colored troops." Generally, the Georgia Volunteers needed consistency across the organization instead of fiefdoms of Georgia's elite, while the Georgia Volunteers, Colored, continued to be acknowledged but not addressed as a component of the militia in need of assistance, balancing, and perhaps reorganization like their white counterparts.[77]

Lobbying for the Military Advisory Board

The established organization of the militia dating from 1892 into the 1870s had encouraged political lobbying both within and outside of the Georgia Volunteers. Southern and southwestern Georgians in 1891 mounted a letter-writing campaign to get Lieutenant Colonel Ed Wight appointed to the Military Advisory Board. Hoping to influence both Governor Northen and Adjutant General and Inspector General John McIntosh Kell, attorney and militia captain N. E. Wooten composed a letter of support for Wight's candidacy. Wooten contended that Wight possessed the "zeal in the cause of our volunteer service" needed to promote the interests of the state militia. He further argued that Wight represented a section of the state that had "never had a representative on the Advisory Board" because "past Governors . . . selected [Military Advisory Board] members from the larger cities." In contrast, Wooten believed that "a large portion of the State troops [were] maintained" in his region, around Albany, Georgia. As a result, southern Georgia needed "a personal representative" on the Military Advisory Board who would forcefully address "our needs, wishes, and desires." The region's representative especially must be its voice in deciding such essential militia issues as a permanent encampment, when events such as encampment occurred, and "admission of new companies." With these issues in mind Wooten noted that Adjutant General John McIntosh Kell appeared to be "thoroughly in sympathy with our purpose." North Georgians from La Grange put forth Captain John Barnard of the Troup Hussars as their candidate for the Military Advisory Board, while coastal Georgians from Brunswick, claiming "our section of the country ought to be represented on the Board," offered Captain J. S. Thomas of the Brunswick Light Horse Guards as their nominee. Meanwhile, three black colonels went unnoticed for Advisory Board membership.[78]

The militia by 1891 had also become the personal project of some officers who led significant units in the state. William Washington Gordon, a former Confederate states legislator, Savannah mayor, and both pre– and post–Civil War cotton merchant, was a colonel in the Savannah-based cavalry company, the Georgia Hussars. He played a major role in recreating the Georgia Volunteers in the 1870s and in reorganizing Georgia's militia, with the assistance of Colonel William Garrard, a Savannah attorney. In mid-October 1891 Governor Northen endeavored to appoint Gordon to the Military Advisory Board. Gordon declined the appointment in favor of reappointing Garrard as the sole returning member of the Advisory Board. Gordon encouraged the governor to reappoint Garrard, because he had been a key driving force "in formulating the present Military law" since the creation of the Military Advisory Board more than ten years earlier. Gordon believed Garrard should be the appointee to the Advisory Board because Garrard held the institutional memory of the Georgia Volunteers. This characteristic seemed critical; Garrard knew "more about what ha[d] been done in the past, and the reason why certain things ha[d] been done and others left undone." More importantly, Garrard needed to be on the Advisory Board "to aid the new Board in deciding . . . the future." Garrard understood the issues facing the Georgia Volunteers "better than anyone else in the State," and his reappointment, Gordon argued, provided geographical balance to the Military Advisory Board. Gordon concluded his letter to Governor Northen by revealing that Atlanta's newspapers, and not Savannah's, were the Georgia Volunteers' conduit to the public and a vital institution that white elite militiamen utilized to explain the actions of the Military Advisory Board, governor, adjutant general, and the Georgia Volunteers.[79]

"The Military Is Being Treated Shabbily by the Legislature"

Satterlee's inspections between late 1891 and May 1894, the *Atlanta Constitution* noted, had transformed the Georgia Volunteers. Specifically, the newspaper asserted, since 1893 the militia units had "been organized in good shape" and were ready for the rigors of another Satterlee-led encampment and strict inspection. The Volunteers in this context had "made big strides during the past year, and ha[d] attained a standard of general excellence unequaled by that of any other state." Despite these accolades the General Assembly did not allocate any funding for the Georgia Volunteers in 1894. The projected consequences of this lack of funding included disbanding many militia companies and the cancellation of encampment, all in contradistinction to the finding that the militia was the "strong arm of the law" and that militiamen, regardless of race, continued to absorb "considerable expense to themselves to keep up their organization."

In response, the *Thomasville Times* concluded that the State Legislature "should, in all fairness, treat them [the militiamen] liberally," and the *Griffin News* reiterated that "the military of Georgia was again needed to maintain order" against the threat of mob violence. Noting William Y. Atkinson's message as Georgia's new governor in 1894, the *Savannah Tribune* published segments of Atkinson's proposal to the legislature. The military section emphasized the need for better appropriations, recognition, domestic law and order, the militia's role in state government, and its responsibilities as a bastion of law, order, and peace. The *Tribune* added a degree of resentment by comparing the suffering of black militiamen with the 1894 Legislature's refusal to allocate funding for the year and its negative impact on the militia. According to the *Tribune*, "The military [was] being treated shabbily by the Legislature," referring to the recent action not to fund the militia. Such legislative abuse, the *Tribune* claimed, was not new for the "colored contingent" of the Georgia Volunteers because they "can afford it," implying that zero funding had been the norm for black militiamen for decades, and it at last had come time for "whites [to] feel some of the burdens that [blacks] ha[d] felt all along."[80]

The 1894 encampment and the annual reports heaped considerable praise on the improving Georgia Volunteers. No longer did the press claim that encampments were convocations for frolicking militiamen who occasionally also devoted time to military training. White militiamen between 1891 and 1894 had gotten serious about the duties and professionalism required of them. Blacks were mentioned only in terms of their numerical presence as militiamen. Specifically, more than one annual report noted that the Georgia Volunteers, Colored, "remain[ed] unchanged." For 1894 there was roughly a ten to one differential between the legal limit for the white Georgia Volunteers constituting the cavalry, infantry, Gatling gun units, and the naval companies of 10,258 officers and men and that of the 1,159 members of the infantry companies, single artillery company, and single cavalry unit of Georgia Volunteers, Colored. These numbers marked a significant increase over the previous three years, with militia membership more than doubling among whites, from the low of 3,950 white militiamen in 1892. The ranks of African American militiamen also increased, but black militiamen now had a case for publicly declaring that the state of Georgia cared very little for its dark skinned militiamen. Black access to encampments continued to be denied by Georgia officials. White participation in encampments in 1894 was limited to a mere 1,889 participants owing to increased opposition within the Georgia Legislature to funding the militia.[81]

Atlanta Cotton States Exposition: "A Very Creditable Display"

The year 1895 opened with the First Battalion of Georgia Volunteers, Colored, in their usual post, parading in Savannah's Emancipation Day celebration. The black cavalrymen of the Savannah Hussars, who were butchers by profession, led the militia parade onto the park extension grounds followed by the Georgia Artillery without its cannons. These two solitary and unique black units marched passed the African American infantry battalion line. Lieutenant Colonel John H. Deveaux had already drilled the infantrymen in the manual of arms before the cavalry and artillery entered the park. Assistant Adjutant and Inspector General Charles B. Satterlee and two members of the Georgia Volunteers, Major J. F. Brooks and Captain R. G. Gaillard, observed and critiqued each unit's performance. The three white officers "were present unofficially and witnessed the parade." According to the *Savannah Tribune*, the infantry's presentation of the manual of arms was a "very creditable display," with similar accolades going to the Hussars and Georgia Artillery, each "making a good appearance." All the units paraded past "the Inspector General[,] who expressed his appreciation and gratification at the general appearance." Always the inspector general, Satterlee also "called attention to some of the particular defects observed." The African American militiamen, nevertheless, welcomed and accepted the critique, because the black "military commands [had] great confidence and respect for Inspector General Satterlee and were glad to have him with them," even if unofficially.[82]

While African American militiamen appreciated constructive criticism, they did not find long-standing state neglect to be a positive. April proved to be an important month in assessing the place of black militiamen in Georgia. Anticipating the 1895 Atlanta Cotton States Exposition, where Booker T. Washington would ascend to national attention, the *Tribune* compressed a discussion of the exposition and militia activities into a single article, noting not only disparities in the treatment of white and black militiamen but also the need to present the best that black people had to offer in the upcoming September 1895 exposition. Two hundred and fifty leased convicts worked the 189-acre exposition site. Two hundred members of this work detail were African American boys between the ages of ten and seventeen. In contrast forty-three black Atlanta professionals constructed the $9,923.87 building that was to highlight thirty years of progress by "Negro Americans." The process of constructing the Negro Building and the exposition itself placed the contradictions of southern black life in sharp relief. The exposition's main grounds crew was a collection of incarcerated black males whose numbers far exceeded whites who ran afoul of the law. Another workforce, black skilled craftsmen and professional builders, endeavored to build a temporary monument showcasing the various avenues of African American achievement since slavery. By combining its reporting on the exposition with two sections on black militiamen, the *Tribune* added to the contrasting public images of black Georgians as convicted convicts, on the one hand, and as professional craftsmen and militiamen seeking acceptance as respectable citizens, on the other.[83]

"The Colored Troops will Get only Rigid Examination": The Challenge of the Three Colonels

In this context of marking the race's progress, African American militiamen in Atlanta mobilized to change their community. Atlanta's M. H. Bentley joined former militiaman Henry A. Rucker's wife and daughter to organize a nondenominational, community mission. The Ruckers organized a church with a one-hundred-person children's choir, secured a minister, and organized a Sunday school.[84] While black militiamen built a new institution to service the moral needs of an Atlanta neighborhood, the *Savannah Tribune* bluntly noted that white militiamen went to encampments "receiv[ing] some kind of equipment," that is, professional development, training, and new equipment. "The colored troops," on the other hand, would "get only a rigid examination" and endless inspections. The newspaper pointed out the ongoing contradiction between the evolving and improving white militiamen and the financially strapped and declining Georgia Volunteers, Colored. Georgia's African American militiamen in the 1890s did not have access to the training that encampment annually provided to their white colleagues, except for the occasional drill competitions sponsored by black militiamen statewide. Despite these efforts by African American militiamen to perfect their craft, the Military Advisory Board insisted on more inspections. While through these inspections, Lieutenant Satterlee sought to professionalize the Georgia Volunteers, black militiamen suffered inspections without the follow-up training, new equipment, and financial resources that might correct their individual and collective deficits.[85]

To address these problems, black militia commanders Lieutenant Colonel John H. Deveaux, Lieutenant Colonel Floyd H. Crumbly, and Lieutenant Colonel Isaiah H. Blocker, respectively leading the First, Second, and Third Battalions, went before the Military Advisory Board "in the interest of the colored troops." The three colonels "protested against the injustice with which they [the Georgia Volunteers, Colored] ha[d] been treated." To redress the neglect of black militiamen, the three black colonels "filed an application for improved arms, [and] a full [complement of supporting] accoutrements and equipments." Collectively these colonels were articulate enough to "supplement their demands by speeches" in which they asserted that for more than twenty years African American militiamen had been "loyal citizens and soldiers of the State" and had done their "duty to assist the authorities in preserving order." Further, "the race had always been faithful to every trust when confidence was reposed in them." Given such consistent commitment to duty and loyal service, Deveaux, Crumbly, and Blocker condemned Georgia for its "delay in properly equipping the colored troops" as "manifest[ly] wrong." Such neglect and delay and the absence of state support suggested that the state government harbored "doubt as to [the black militiamen's] loyalty and fitness" for service to Georgia's citizens. These African American militiamen, however, "had maintained their organizations for over twenty years" despite "never receiv[ing] a dollar from the state." The black militia's leaders "asked that the injustice under which the colored troops ha[d] labored be rectified as early as possible."[86]

The *Atlanta Constitution* reported on this meeting in less detail. According to the white-owned newspaper, "A delegation of field officers of the colored troops appeared before the advisory board and urged that steps be taken to put this branch of the state military on a better footing." Specifically, they called for access to equipment and "assistance in other ways more than camp duty and did not ask for the latter," suggesting that blacks were not insisting on access to encampment training with whites but did seek to improve the black militia.

This may have been an important concession, given that in 1891 African American militiamen were determined to have an encampment, as the *Constitution* had contended. The Military Advisory Board, after "discussing [the colonels' 1895 presentation] for some time [decided] that the first step necessary was the general inspection of the colored troops."

Following the new round of inspections, the board proposed more steps "toward bettering their condition and putting them on a more efficient footing."[87]

By May 1895 black troops were being inspected again by Lieutenant Charles B. Satterlee, inspector general, as the Military Advisory Board responded to the "complaint and protest by the colored troops regarding their treatment in the past." The Advisory Board wanted an inventory for the purpose of "better arranging and equipping the troops." The positive relationship that black units had established with Satterlee continued, because Satterlee demonstrated what the *Savannah Tribune* described as an earnest interest in the development of Savannah's African American companies. The inspector general again critiqued the companies and provided "valuable suggestions as to the details of the manual and drills, and administrative control." The *Tribune*, nevertheless, reminded African Americans that despite this inspection to redress the past, black militia companies had "all been organized bordering on a quarter of a century" and had "maintained themselves at great expense . . . without recognition by the state." Over these years Georgia had issued the black companies "guns without equipments," and the state had "never expended one dollar to aid them." The inspection, however, served as a symbol of hope for a future when "the proper recognition [would] be accorded" a loyal citizenry who were "certainly entitled to some consideration from the authorities." Twenty-plus years of neglect, however, generated in black militiamen and the newspaper a waning tolerance for disdain.[88]

Perhaps to justify what appeared to be a positive change in Military Advisory Board policy, the *Constitution* published a report on Alabama's July encampments. While segregation separated black from white Alabama militiamen, the state's black militia was invited to a segregated African American encampment that immediately followed an all-white encampment. While white merriment in the wake of putting down a Birmingham mining strike allowed for relaxed regulations at the white encampment, Alabama's black militiamen entered their July 1895 encampment expecting a week of professional military instruction. By the end, Alabama's black militiamen had successfully completed their encampment. White militia leaders conveyed compliments to the black battalion for the professionalism they exhibited during the week-long training session. African American militiamen had "excellent" drill routines and as a result "had gained the confidence and respect of their [white] superior officers" and had left "good impressions on the minds of all." The white officer making these statements also pledged his official power to advance their status as militiamen. The battalion surgeon, Dr. C. N. Dorsette, also "spoke in high praise" for Alabama's black militiamen's "deportment," especially their observance of good sanitation practices and subsequent avoidance of camp-related diseases.[89]

Lynchings

While Alabama complimented its black militiamen, Georgia's new governor sought in October and in December to rein in white lynchings of black men and, at the same time, to enhance white self-perceptions. His December message to the legislature concerning lynching earned him compliments from the *Savannah Tribune*. In his October message to the General Assembly, William Yates Atkinson noted that white militiamen had to be called out several times to deal with mass disruptions. The militia, Atkinson asserted, "borne themselves in commendable and soldierly manner," but whites had lynched five African Americans for rape in 1895. Claiming that Georgia had several "thinly settled" areas, where white women might be isolated and undefended by white men, wrongly encouraged white men to seek the immediate and unlawful punishment of alleged black culprits. The governor asserted, "Fully one-third of our population is composed of those who up to a few years ago were slaves, a large percentage of whom lack moral training and have not the proper respect for law or the rights of others." Atkinson requested new legislation to remove from office any law enforcement person who allowed a mob to take their prisoner from legal authorities and lynch them. He also hoped to mobilize the law-abiding white citizens to prevent lynching, since "our race has control of the legislature and of the courts, furnishing both judges and jury." Whites controlled society, Atkinson contended, and therefore there was no need to use lynching to punish African Americans.[90] The courts could achieve the same end legally.

Contradictions: The Cotton States Exposition

October and November 1895 highlighted the ongoing contradictions that defined black life. While Governor Atkinson pursued ways to curtail antiblack violence and an alleged wave of black rapes of white women, African American militiamen joined other black people in celebrating the opening of the Negro Building at the Atlanta Cotton States Exposition.

The building's exhibits attracted the interest of both local Atlantans and visitors from across the United States. Their comments were favorable and "reflect[ed] great credit upon the colored race." Such comments the *Atlanta Constitution* "regarded as an encouraging record of" black progress. In that vein, the paper also noted, "Thousands of respectable colored people have attended the big show, and they have been as well treated as their white neighbors." Equally important was local whites' awareness that national and international audiences were watching how they treated black people at the Exposition. The *Constitution* cautioned local white attendees to be mindful of their words and avoid "sectional and racial discrimination," because the white South was "proud of the splendid showing made by the blacks at our fair."

African Americans at the same time were exposed to the "object lessons in arts and industry," symbols of progress and modernity. Lieutenant Colonel Floyd Crumbly chaired the opening ceremonies, welcoming visitors to the Negro Building. Other militiamen assembled with the dignitaries at the opening were Savannah's Lieutenant Colonel John H. Deveaux, Atlanta's Captain C. C. Wimbish, and Athens's William Pledger. The Georgia Volunteers, Colored, paraded in other exposition festivities, and the December parade proved one of their best. Black people from Savannah, Atlanta, and South Carolina celebrated their day at the exposition and hoped that their rights and status would be respected by their white neighbors.[91]

Georgians in 1895 wrestled with some significant contradictions that defined race and race relations and the status of black militiamen. The Georgia Volunteers, Colored, were part of that contrast between African Americans described as the criminal class—mostly incarcerated black males at the age of puberty and youthful manhood—responsible for raping white women in isolated communities and respectable blacks who organized and helped construct the Negro Building at the Cotton States Exposition. The black militia, or at least its leadership, stood at and spoke out in public venues before whites, who sought to prove to the nation and the world that white southerners did not abuse law-abiding, respectable African American citizens.

In this context, the black men leading the Georgia Volunteers, Colored, banked on their respectability to obtain white recognition, vitally needed equipment and accoutrements, and funding from the Military Advisory Board. Black militiamen had won the respect of Georgia's inspector general, a regular soldier in the United States Army, and some recognition from the white press, which acknowledged the harm done by more than twenty years of state neglect. As the white militia's training improved in the 1890s, African Americans sought access to similar training that would enhance their militia companies. The hope of securing equipment, funding, and recognition appeared on the horizon in 1895 but only after another inspection. Was this a true opportunity for change? Or was past neglect going to define the rest of the nineteenth century, even as war and a broader reorganization loomed over the nation's entire military structure?

6

THE ROAD TO DISBANDMENT, 1896–1899

While 1895 offered black militiamen the illusion of inclusion in a changing Georgia militia structure, segregation's increasing importance would also influence the fate of the Georgia Volunteers, Colored. Segregation had been a significant part of the Georgia Volunteers from the beginning. It originally had suggested an equality of sorts, wherein Georgia's state government neglected all militiamen. Georgia allocated only federal resources to sustain the militia, with blacks receiving obsolete weaponry and accoutrements and whites receiving only slightly better versions of the same. Blacks in the 1870s and 1880s initially responded to segregation and neglect by being team players, but at the beginning of the 1890s they turned to protesting the disparities in resource allocation as new resources sparked a redefinition of the Georgia Volunteers. The structure and definition of Georgia's militia changed at the end of the 1880s and the beginning of the 1890s as state funding, while erratic, became permanent.

Financial resources and development went to white militiamen in the 1890s. State governmental authorities offered resources in exchange for militiamen committing to being trained and professionalized as soldiers. With new resources and a commitment to learning how to be professionalized soldiers, militia members found themselves redefined by state and federal authorities. Segregation, as a result, no longer meant mutual neglect. Rather, it became important to whites in general and state authorities in particular for distinguishing what was for whites only. The new resources of the 1890s enhanced the racial disparities between militiamen, but it did not erase or prevent black militiamen from persistently seeking to carve out their place within the state's military. Global war, however, would have a distinct role in highlighting racial discrimination within the state and the nation's military and would culminate in two crucial reorganizations that had ramifications for the Georgia Volunteers and for the national military.

This chapter and the final chapter examine the evolution of segregation, black protests, and the definition of the militia. While the "culture of segregation" played a major role in this process, ultimately it was war that redefined the militia. It transformed a local and state agency into a national institution. This chapter examines Georgia's redefinition process up to the end of nineteenth century as war destroyed the state militia.

Segregation: Two Incidents

Every January 1 since 1863 African Americans had publicly commemorated the Emancipation Proclamation, black liberty, and citizenship in the United States. The first day of 1896 began in a more complex way than blacks in Savannah had anticipated. That day not only did African Americans celebrate their freedom but two whites also contested African Americans' right to celebrate in public space. Captain J. H. Johnston, president of the City and Suburban Railway Company, would question the existence of black militiamen. By mid-January Johnston was offering a reward of one hundred dollars "for the arrest and proof to convict the member of the Georgia Artillery who assaulted" one of his white employees, "Motorman West." The charge: "inflicting a wound" in the motorman's neck on January 1, 1896. The alleged culprit was a black militiaman.

The *Savannah Tribune* declared Johnston's accusation "ill advised" and a violation of the "comity that has and should exist between the military and our street railway corporations." Mutual respect was the "comity" that black militiamen and African Americans in general assumed to exist between streetcar employees and members of the Georgia militia, as had been the case at least since South Carolina's 1876 Hamburg Massacre. The January incident, however, appeared to announce the end of this cooperative relationship, if such a relationship ever existed in the first place in the New South twenty years after Hamburg. Specifically, white streetcar operators and their corporate supervisor did not, in 1896, "appreciate" Georgia's customary and legal tradition of yielding the right of way to marching and parading black militiamen. According to the *Tribune*, streetcar operator West ran his vehicle into the assembled Georgia Artillery members preparing for the 1896 Emancipation Day parade. The collision occurred despite the efforts of Georgia Artillery commander Captain John C. Simmons to flag down the motorman. The vehicle's motorman claimed that the streetcar's "bad condition" caused the collision between it and the militiamen.[1]

Georgia artillerymen had assembled for a parade on January 1, 1896, with swords drawn when the streetcar crashed into the militia company and one of the unit's cannons. Some of the Georgia Artillery members leaped onto the streetcar to avoid being injured. It was when the machine plowed into the militia that motorman West was allegedly wounded. No one knew about the injury because West did not alert the militiamen that they had hurt him until "they saw it in the [Savannah] *Morning News*." The white press claimed that West reported the incident to the police "sometime afterward and was unable to give a satisfactory description of the men who assaulted him." Suburban Railway Company president, Captain J. H. Johnston, however, took it upon himself to speak for motorman West, contending that the streetcar operator had slowed and brought his vehicle to a complete stop when he encountered the parade. West, according to Johnston, resumed his route only after the parade had passed through the intersection. What happened next, Johnston reported, was that black militiamen at the procession's end "became very much excited." They "made an attack upon [West] with their sabers," striking "with the flat of the sabers" but "one [struck] [West] in the neck."

Both Johnston and Savannah's Police Chief McDermott "demanded of Col. John H. Deveaux [, Savannah's black battalion commander, and of Captain J. C. Simmons, Georgia Artillery leader, that they] . . . ascertain the names of West's assailants and report them to the police." Johnston added a layer of disrespect for black militiamen when he told the *Savannah Morning News* that he wanted "to find out whether citizens can be assaulted with deadly weapons by any crowd of men who happen to be in uniform and to take offense at their actions without redress." Johnston intended to make Simmons responsible for the behavior of the Georgia Artillery by reporting Simmons and the Georgia Artillery to the adjutant general. Johnston's public statement simultaneously contested whether black men were in fact militiamen, by calling them a "crowd" with "deadly weapons" in meaningless "uniforms," and who was a citizen: West, the working-class white male, or the legitimately parading black militiamen?[2]

The black press countered Johnston and the *Morning News*, arguing that the Georgia Artillery's leadership and enlisted men were all honorable men. The *Tribune* supported Captain Simmons's assertion with four arguments. First, the wounding had not been malicious. Second, it was an accident. Third, even if the wound had been deliberate, Captain Simmons, a man of honor, would investigate and then "pass on the matter" to the proper authorities. Fourth, as a group, black militiamen were men of honor eager to resolve the complaint. Simmons's report to Colonel John H. Deveaux affirmed the encounter as an accident. The *Tribune* noted that the black military took "great pride in their organizations and the responsibilities committed to them." African American militiamen also stood "ready to defend the law and aid the civil authorities in suppressing disorder whenever called upon to do so." Even though black militiamen were paragons of commitment to community service and citizenship, the *Tribune* charged that individuals and corporations "don't understand themselves, the law, nor what is best for the community." In the *Tribune*'s estimation, nevertheless, whites, namely, Johnston and West, and the corporations they owned and worked for maintained "an utter disregard for everything except themselves and their earnings."[3]

Four months later, at the end of April, during Confederate Memorial Day, members of the Confederate Veterans Association and Savannah's white militiamen registered their vigorous objections to the "intrusion," "indignities," and "interference" to a violation of white public space. This was a dramatic change in how militiamen regardless of race used public space. Whites redefined who could use the parade ground in the park extension by declaring the park "exclusively the property of the white military commands." They were upset that the Chatham Light Infantry and its band marched onto the park extension grounds in celebration of the black unit's anniversary. Marching and parading on the public park extension grounds had been something black units had done since the early 1870s. Blacks paraded to commemorate African American freedom and special black militia days.

The trouble over who could utilize this public park stemmed from the fact that white and black commemorations occurred around the same time, on the same day, in the same place, but for dramatically different, and racially defined, reasons. As the Chatham Light Infantry marched onto the park extension parade ground commemorating its anniversary, the Irish Jasper Greens, one of Savannah's white militia companies, joined white children and women in decorating Confederate graves as they commemorated Confederate Memorial Day. In the wake of the scheduling conflict, white Confederate veterans and white militiamen directed their objections at "the military authorities in charge of the grounds," because the black unit "had use of [the public park facilities] only by their courtesy." The white militia officers and Confederate Veterans Association responded by petitioning the military and park supervisors, hoping "to prevent the colored militia from going on the parade ground again."[4]

This incident also brought white Confederate veterans, some of Savannah's white militiamen, and a few city officials together at the Knights of Pythias's meeting hall a day later. They convened to discuss white solidarity, use of the park extension, and, as the press defined the issue, "the Status of the Military Parade Ground." The two-hour meeting, with the white press present, prompted a discussion of the history of the parade ground, Savannah's white military, and a new version of post–Civil War race relations history. Their first consideration, however, was whether "the reporters [should] be allowed to remain." After some deliberation, they permitted the press's attendance, provided the reporters "submit[ted] their reports to a committee appointed by the [Confederate Veterans Association's] president."

According to the *Morning News*, whites discussed the issue dispassionately. They defined the actions and members of the Chatham Light Infantry as ignorant, but the black intrusion, they commented, lacked malicious intent. The violation was caused by black ignorance and the race's inherently inferior characteristics. The meeting continued, nevertheless, focused on the park extension and "exclusive control [of that space] by white military companies." At issue was who owned and controlled the public parade ground. To address the question of ownership, the Confederate Veterans asked Savannah's municipal attorney, S. H. Adams, Esquire, for his counsel. Adams reported that the U.S. military had turned control over the grounds before the Civil War to local white militia companies, assuming that the military green space would remain in the possession of white militiamen in perpetuity. He noted that the Chatham Light Infantry had committed a "gross breach of propriety and decorum" but warned that whites need not feel offended. Reinforcing racial stereotypes, white paternalism, and white desires to declare blacks after slavery to be inferior people, the attorney urged his white colleagues "to recall the fidelity with which negroes served their [slave] masters' families during the [Civil] war, while the masters were at the front." He additionally argued that "even in the reconstruction period . . . the negroes acted remarkably well." Thereby, Adams initiated the telling of a new version of the post–Civil War story, which previously had stressed "Negro domination," black crime and antiwhite violence, white fear and anger, and white antiblack violence aimed at restoring white rule.[5]

While one speaker, a Mr. Appleton, acknowledged that "the negro military company believed they had a right [to be] on the ground[s]," Confederate veterans and white militiamen convened to find a way to declare the parade ground a whites-only domain. Colonel Screven, a fifty-year Savannah militia veteran, presented his records search that day as he outlined the history of the park extension. Screven affirmed but expanded on attorney Adams's history: The park extension had been a United States Army military barracks from the 1820s to the 1840s. In 1853 the site was designated forever a "public place" and a military parade ground and was "vested [by] . . . several military captains of the city" as an award to Savannah. The key to whites possessing and utilizing this public space was that "all [of Savannah's 1850s] military commands" were white and had "not supposed [in the 1850s] that there would ever be such a thing as a negro military company." Screven concluded that the Chatham Light Infantry members "probably knew no better," especially the correct protocol to defer to whites. Yet his concern focused on "not establishing a precedent which might have very serious results." He made it clear that "the status of the parade ground should be settled at once and forever."[6]

The Road to Disbandment

These incidents reflect the beginning of the end for Georgia's black militia companies. Even though Georgia's Legislature passed legislation in the mid-1880s giving militiamen the right of way on community streets, a streetcar employee with corporate support crashed his derelict vehicle into a black militia unit on parade. Perhaps this was done deliberately. Perhaps Motorman West was already angry about having to enforce segregation on public transportation, which put him in direct daily confrontation with African American patrons, citizens, and marching militiamen. Did this frustration with having to impose public policy mandated by the Populist Georgia Legislature of 1891 cause West to deliberately drive his vehicle into parading black militiamen? Was West empowered by state segregation policy designating that public transportation companies enforce racially segregated seating, or did he resent having to be the enforcer of the law and take his anger out on this black militia unit? Or was the January 1, 1896, incident merely an accident colored by race and violence against blacks that increasingly characterized the rise of Jim Crow segregation in the New South, complete with lynchings and urban streetcar combat? The evidence does not allow us to conclusively answer any of these questions. What is clear is that Jim Crow, the culture of segregation, was taking on new parameters that shaped white and black behavior in the 1890s. Jim Crow's antiblack influence continued into the first decade of the twentieth century and was made stronger by the force of law, which resulted in the permanent disbanding of Georgia's black militia companies by a new generation of Georgia Legislators.[7]

A few months later, in April 1896, Savannah's Confederate veterans, along with white militiamen empowered by the rise of Jim Crow, registered their objections to the all-black Chatham Light Infantry's attempt to march on public grounds and celebrate its anniversary. Their parade unfortunately coincided with Confederate Memorial Day, which commemorated antebellum white southern freedom and Civil War memories. Black militiamen over the past twenty years had, nevertheless, marched and drilled on the park extension's parade ground, independently celebrating days and events important to African American postbellum freedom and citizenship in the United States. The Chatham Light Infantry in that context operated as it had in the past, as free people and citizens of Savannah.

On rare occasions black militiamen in the late 1870s had also marched in parades with white militiamen. The most prominent event was a memorial service for a popular politician who was highly regarded by both races. What had changed in the two intervening decades? Over that time black men had attempted to establish a public commitment to the state of Georgia as militiamen and as citizens. During those two decades black militiamen had sought to evolve along with their white counterparts in embracing military professionalism. In both cases African American Georgians engaged in citizenship and military service, hoping for white public recognition and certification of their freedom as citizens. White militia authorities, however, had neglected the African American units. With the white militiaman's demand for funding, recognition, and professional development in the late 1880s and early 1890s realized, the status of black militia companies came into question in a much more public and official way than it had twenty years earlier, when legalized segregation had yet to become an effective tool of white supremacy. Segregation's legal parameters were in the 1890s increasingly certified by the Georgia Legislature, and public transportation was the most visible change in public exchanges between black and white Georgians.

While these two incidents occurred in isolation from each other, the year 1896 marks a significant change in attitude toward Georgia's black militiamen.[8] Disbanding black militia units became a policy the Military Advisory Board thought was worth discussing after the 1895 black colonels' petition requesting better treatment for the black militia companies. The termination of African American militia companies was, by then, an ongoing possibility that Advisory Board members debated, considered, and finally acted on during the nine years between 1896 and legislative disbandment in 1905. The debate coincided with the emerging power of legalized Jim Crow segregation, which conveyed to white Georgians, and especially to elite whites, an empowering culture for handling capital industrialization and national consumer culture. Segregation enabled the white South to become part of the national narrative.

The transformative impact of the Spanish-American War, the Cuban War of Independence, and the Philippine-American War, fought from 1898 to 1902, further encouraged the Military Advisory Board to disband the black militia units once and for all. This global conflict helped to recast what the Georgia Volunteers were and how they fit within the new National Guard as a federally funded military institution. War changed the state militia even though no officially organized Georgia militia unit participated in the conflict. Jim Crow segregation, global war, black disfranchisement, antiblack violence, and the disbandment of the Georgia Volunteers, Colored, went hand in hand to reinvigorate and empower white supremacy and certify the triumph of the physical separation of the races. This was the road to disbandment, a near decade's march to the termination of the late nineteenth-century Georgia Volunteers, Colored, and then of the early twentieth-century Georgia State Troops, Colored.

"Show Cause Why They Should Not Be Disbanded"

The year 1896 began and ended with African American militia leaders defending the companies in their command from disbandment by state authorities. Even though the spring and summer of 1895 had suggested that a positive change was on the horizon for black militiamen, one that promised recognition, funding, and inclusion in coveted training opportunities, the events of 1896 contradicted that vision of inclusion. This shift from potential inclusion to the threat of disbandment emerged in mid-February 1896, when the black militia companies of Augusta and Savannah were called before the Military Advisory Board to "show cause" as to why they should not be disbanded. Lieutenant Colonel John H. Deveaux and five captains in the First Battalion, along with a separate contingent of captains leading Augusta's three "crack colored companies" of the Georgia Volunteers, Colored, journeyed to Atlanta to address the Advisory Board.

According to the *Atlanta Constitution*, Augusta's renowned units had to "show cause why they should not be disbanded for inefficiency." While we know that Lieutenant Colonel Deveaux accompanied the First Battalion's units, there are no newspaper reports to indicate that Lieutenant Colonel Isaiah H. Blocker joined the members of his Augusta battalion in Atlanta. The eight black companies argued their case in front of a Military Advisory Board, led by longtime Savannah militiaman Colonel William W. Gordon. Major/Captain Jordan F. Brooks also served on the Advisory Board, extending his evaluation of black militiamen from his informal assessment, with United States Army Lieutenant Charles Satterlee, at the 1895 Emancipation Day celebration in Savannah to the formal Military Advisory Board hearing involving both Brooks and Satterlee as official evaluators.[9]

The rumored agenda for the upcoming annual Military Advisory Board meeting scheduled for February 1896 gave no indication that the black militia companies would be the main topic of discussion. The *Constitution* reported on the impending admission of Atlanta's Gate City Guard into the Georgia Volunteers. This company had operated independently of the state organization for a number of years and thereby challenged militia authority. Its admission, therefore, was an important event. In spite of this local interest story and the suggestion that other new companies, including a new naval company, would be considered for admission at the February board meeting, both the black and white press made no mention of how significant the ongoing 1895 inspections would be on the future of the black units. According to the *Constitution*, the meeting turned out to be "a busy day[,] with the Board" focused "primarily [on the] . . . condition of the colored companies through[out] the state."

The February 1896 "show cause" meeting was the result of two issues. First, the *Constitution* contended, "There are colored companies which have been allowed to run down," implying that responsibility for the problem lay with the black militiamen. Second, the poor state of the companies gained significance because the "colored companies [called to show cause were part of] a general investigation into the condition of the colored militia" dating back to 1895's black colonels' petition. The findings suggested "that some of the companies [were] in such condition that it [was] advisable to disband them." As a result, "the object of the [Military Advisory Board meeting was] . . . to disband those [black militia companies] which were in such condition as to show that they were of no value to the service." The units having a "desire to continue" service in the Georgia

Volunteers, Colored, were to be assisted in bringing their companies "up to a standard of usefulness."[10]

Three of the eight companies were directly under Deveaux's command: the Forest City Light Infantry, led by Captain E. A. Williams, the Lone Star Cadets, led by Captain L. A. Washington, and the Union Lincoln Guards, led by Captain Robert Simmons. These three companies were members of Savannah's First Battalion. Two other units not officially part of the First Battalion but also based in Savannah were the Savannah Hussars and Georgia Artillery, which were the sole black cavalry and artillery units, respectively, within the Georgia Volunteers. The Georgia Artillery also occupied the unique position of being the only black artillery unit in the United States. Captain F. F. Jones directed the Hussars, while Captain J. C. Simmons led the Georgia Artillery. Augusta's "crack colored companies"— the Augusta Light Infantry, led by John Lark, the Attucks Infantry, led by R. G. Cummings, and the Georgia Infantry, a company long associated with Augusta's black elite—operated under the leadership of Captain T. G. Walker. According to the *Constitution*, Augusta's captains went to Atlanta "to find out wherein their companies [fell] short" of militia regulations, suggesting that the negative report and disbandment proposal had caught the usually efficient Augusta units by surprise. In that light the Augusta captains were "determined to raise their companies up to the standard of efficiency required by the state"; thus they went before the Advisory Board with a plan to address the inspection issues Satterlee had raised.[11]

Deveaux attempted to preempt Military Advisory Board action by filing a counter report to Lieutenant Satterlee's inspection document. Deveaux stressed that "none of the colored companies should be disbanded." It is unclear whether Satterlee's report undermined the positive relationship he had previously enjoyed with black militiamen in light of the negative 1896 inspections. In any event Satterlee's report recommended that the eight black companies be disbanded; nevertheless, Satterlee did include Deveaux's counter report in the documents he presented to the Advisory Board. Satterlee's inspections were not limited to the black units. His evaluations "affected companies in all parts of the state, under consideration."[12]

The *Savannah Tribune* argued that the inspections' evaluative results were not aimed at the black units alone. First Battalion commander Deveaux made the same claim, trying to reassure black militiamen and the African American public that the inspections and accompanying evaluations were not racially motivated. Deveaux concluded "that none of his companies would be disbanded." According to Deveaux, Georgia's governor and the Advisory Board planned "no injustice" to any of the black militia companies, because "a full opportunity [would] be given them to prove their efficiency." Furthermore, Deveaux believed "it was evident" that the Advisory Board had not planned to "decrease the number of colored companies arbitrarily." The twenty-two black units serving the state since the reorganization in the 1880s might well survive in 1895 and 1896. Nevertheless, Deveaux warned that the Military Advisory Board thought "a reduction would greatly strengthen the remaining companies," suggesting that disbandment was something the Advisory Board would consider and implement.[13]

With his assessment of the Advisory Board's goodwill, Deveaux walked a fine line between what one scholar contends was the respect he had garnered for himself over the years from both the white community and the black militia as an efficient officer leading the First Battalion and his position as the unofficial leader of Georgia's twenty-two African American companies. At the same time the signs were clear that life for African Americans and black militiamen was changing for the worse. Deveaux in this uncertain climate did not pass up an opportunity to explain, in the *Savannah Tribune*, "the many reasons . . . why the standard of the colored troops should not be expected to be as high as the white troops." According to Deveaux, there were three reasons. First and second was the fact that black troops "received no aid and encouragement from the state." Specifically, Georgia had never provided the black troops with uniforms or funding to build armories. And despite this conscious state neglect, African Americans had maintained their companies out of their own pockets with local community support. Third, Deveaux affirmed, "We have not had the benefit of encampments that the white troops have had." This was a circumstance that directly and decisively separated white militiamen from black militiamen, despite clear evidence that African American militiamen took their responsibilities seriously and committed "great interest in their commands." Black dedication was especially evident in the financial outlay they had made since the 1870s, given the absence of state recognition, support, and encouragement. Collectively black militiamen viewed disbandment as a distasteful option "they would feel . . . deeply."[14]

Proposed disbandment was not a new experience for black militiamen. Frances Smith has noted that tragedy, death, and inadequate finances had threatened the existence of the Georgia Artillery in the 1880s. Founded in 1878 and awarded two ten-pound parrot guns by the United States, the Georgia Artillery, like the other twenty-one black companies, operated with no state funding from the late 1870s to the mid-1890s. The company's membership over these years had found ways to finance the construction and purchase of matching gun carriages for their cannons. They also purchased and sustained their uniforms without state support, even though the state recognized the unit as a state-sponsored company. In 1887 after nearly a decade without any safety problems with the parrot guns, a militia sergeant was killed when one of the guns misfired and completely severed his left arm. Two years later disappointment at being unable to raise enough funds to send the unit to President Benjamin Harrison's inauguration combined with a state-ordered disbandment that followed a negative inspection. According to Smith, Savannah's white elite petitioned the governor to reconsider disbanding the unit. Smith notes that white supporters of the unit argued "that the organization did not cost the state anything," and as a result Georgia Governor John B. Gordon overrode the disbandment recommendation.

In spite of this reprieve, a fire in 1891 destroyed the unit's equipment. This setback was followed the next year with another recommendation for disbandment, but unit members raised enough money to buy two new cannons from Philadelphia. Black militiamen and their relationship with Savannah's white police officers added another layer of white disdain that predated the streetcar affair in 1896. Relations between the police and black militiamen remained tense in the 1880s and 1890s. Two local gangs purposely drove their vehicles into the Colquitt Blues as Lieutenant Satterlee inspected the unit in the spring of 1895. The police sided with the gang against Colonel Deveaux, who pressed charges against the two police officers.[15]

The evolution of the Georgia Artillery reflected in microcosm the general attitude of white Georgians toward the Georgia Volunteers, Colored. Locally whites accepted and supported the company, while state leaders questioned the usefulness of the unit. The bottom line was that the black units did not cost the state anything. Nevertheless, the development of the white militia companies projected an increased cost to the state, which caused Georgia, as it did its fellow states with black units, to reconsider the cost-benefit analysis for black militias and to reduce the number of African American units in favor of professionalizing the training and status of white militiamen.[16]

"The Military Companies of Savannah Are All Right"

At the end of February 1896 the *Savannah Tribune* reported, "The military companies of Savannah are all right." Deveaux and Georgia Artillery leader Captain J. C. Simmons spent a week in north Georgia. During their sojourn they communicated with Governor William Yates Atkinson, who the *Tribune* would months later describe as "the humane and fearless executive," owing to his stand against white lynchings of African Americans. At the February meeting Atkinson gave Deveaux and Simmons the "assurance" that Savannah's black militia companies would not be disbanded. With this news the *Tribune* urged "the boys" in the black militia organizations to "go to work in building up the several companies better than ever." A week later the *Savannah Morning News* acknowledged Governor Atkinson's decision to continue the Georgia Artillery's membership in the state militia. The unit in celebration went to Captain Simmons's home with the Chatham Light Infantry and a band to serenade their leader. Simmons was away attending to Republican Party national convention preparations, but R. N. Rutledge stood in for the militia captain.

Despite Governor Atkinson's reprieve, however, all was not well, at least for Savannah's black militia units and perhaps for Augusta's, too. Conflict between streetcar employees and African American patrons continued in February. The *Tribune* urged "colored patrons" not to be "intimidate[d]" by "villainous" off-duty streetcar workers, who on a Saturday night in mid-February murdered a black passenger. The accused assailants were white men who boarded the crowded West End line car and "went out on the trip" intentionally "to intimidate the colored passengers." A member of the group cut the rope controlling the overhead wire, darkening the streetcar, which allowed his colleagues to threaten the black patrons with pistols, "ordering them to pay their fare" to the ruffian railway employees. Some patrons were forced to pay two fares: the one to ride and the extorted fare. African American Stephen Gibbons attempted to get off the vehicle when the robbery began, but "he was shot while leaving by the cowards." The electric railway company's white intimidators were arrested. The newspaper promised to follow the case, anticipating that "justice must be done" as black law-abiding citizens would be watching how the law dealt with this fatal attack on black people.[17]

The First Battalion, Georgia Volunteers, Colored, while grateful that disbanding had been averted, still had problems to confront. On top of antiblack violence and white harassment from the police and streetcar employees, black militias suffered a manpower shortage. Young black men were leaving Savannah's units. Two lieutenants from Company A, Joseph L. Mirault and Philip Y. Giles, resigned. The *Tribune* noted that the two black men were "among the most energetic in the battalion." The newspaper acknowledged their resignations with "much regret," marking another moment in the 1890s when the *Tribune* expressed its concerns about the need for young black men to become members of and leaders in the African American militia companies. Antiblack violence, Jim Crow segregation, the lack of opportunity, incarceration, and a sense of injustice were having a negative impact on young African Americans. Black males between the ages of fifteen and thirty-four had been leaving Georgia since the 1870s. The number of black men in the state decreased by 4 percent in the 1870s, by 3 percent in the 1880s, and by 8 percent in the 1890s. The black newspaper did not make a direct link between the inspection problems and officer exodus that sparked the threatened disbandment. With black male out-migration increasing, the future of the Georgia Volunteers, Colored, in doubt, and the ongoing inequities black militiamen sought to overcome, it was clear that the next few years were going to be challenging.[18]

May Military Celebrations

In May both black and white militiamen planned military celebrations. Black men organized a First Battalion military fair, while white men created May Week and the Military Interstate Association of Savannah to manage a multi-state rifle shooting competition and military exhibition endorsed by Adjutant General John McIntosh Kell. With $12,000 as the funding base for the Military Interstate Association, Savannah hoped to make the occasion "so interesting and attractive" that it would become Savannah's version of Mardi Gras.[19]

In the wake of both May militia celebrations, Georgia officials planned the June 1896 militia encampment. No black units were invited. More than eleven hundred white militiamen were scheduled to attend. These white militiamen received a per diem of seventy-five cents, an increase for white militiamen attending encampment training. Some members of the Georgia General Assembly viewed encampments as a definite benefit to the state militiamen's development. The encampments also served as a good recruiting tool. Specifically, encampments "encouraged the soldiers and ... resulted in a great increase in the ranks of the military." This statement indicates that white companies, too, had a recruiting problem, albeit likely less than the one the black units encountered. Further white militiamen no longer had to pay out of pocket for their uniforms, as the encampments required a universal service uniform paid for by the state. The militia's 1896 budget was now organized around the idea of "put[ting] the forces of the state on a practical and economical basis" with unified cooperation from militiamen. This change in state authorities' attitude toward organizing, arming, equipping, clothing, and training "the volunteer forces of the state, as provided by the act of 1889" did not end the bickering and instability surrounding how much Georgia allocated to maintain the Georgia Volunteers. At the end of the year, members of the General Assembly debated whether to give the Volunteers a budget of $48,800, $30,000, or $24,000 or lower, the latter figure being a cut to the existing appropriation. The General Assembly ultimately decided to allocate the militia less than $23,000, because, as the adjutant general noted in 1898, "the State appropriation has never been larger" than that amount.[20]

Making a Case for Support: Atlanta's Second Battalion

Lieutenant Colonel Floyd H. Crumbly in May 1896 mobilized his staff "to do all in their power to make the Second Georgia battalion of colored volunteers the leading battalion among our people in the state." H. R. Butler, reporting on "What the Negro is Doing" for the *Atlanta Constitution*, became an advocate for the black state militia. Butler's hope for the "Colored Volunteers" was that the battalion would be fully equipped with "overcoats, blankets, canteens, and all else that may be needed to complete" and meet the needs of "our [Atlanta] battalion." Butler also observed, apparently in light of the recent disbandment scares, that "it would be wise for all of our troops in the state to begin and improve themselves in order that they ... will be an honor to themselves and the state." He ended his article on black Atlanta's activities by reinforcing the black militia's plea for state funding. African Americans, Butler argued, needed to "ask the next legislature to appropriate a sum of money to aid all of the colored volunteers in the state to come together at some point next spring and have a three days' parade and a military carnival." With this proposal Butler called for funding and equipping black militiamen. While he did not seek parity with white militiamen, he did advocate for a funding level that would have brought all the state's black militia companies together for a statewide drill competition. Such a competition, he hoped, would prove that black militiamen were worth the investment.[21]

Colonel Crumbly meanwhile mobilized the Second Battalion's staff in preparation for an inspection tour he had planned for the entire battalion, including the Columbus, Georgia, unit. Crumbly found Columbus's Company E "in very good condition," especially in terms of its enlistment numbers and training proficiency. The company's arms and equipment, however, were another matter. The guns constituted a great danger to the militiamen because the weapons were "wholly unfit for service." Crumbly noted that the problem was compounded because "[t]his part of the state militia st[ood] in great need of attention." According to Crumbly, black militiamen had reached inside their pockets and funded the Colored Volunteer companies long enough. Such sacrifice clearly "demonstrated their willingness to serve the state," but not the state's commitment to black units. If Georgians were to recognize black militiamen's contributions to the state, "every fair-minded citizen . . . ought to come to their relief and give them arms and accoutrements, send them in camp and get them in such condition that they will not only be of use, but will be an honor to the state." Crumbly concluded, "I hope our next legislature will not only consider the fairness of this proposition, but the great necessity of it."[22]

National Colors for True Soldiers

During the early fall of 1896 the First Battalion received a unique honor: for the "first time . . . national colors were presented to colored troops by direction of the governor of a southern state." Although Colonel A. R. Lawton stood in for Governor William Yates Atkinson at the presentation of the American flag to the First Battalion, Atkinson had delegated Colonel Lawton and directed him, as "one of his highest officers," to convey the honor. According to Lawton, "the flag stood for law and order." The First Battalion's new honor reinforced this idea because the unit represented Georgia's commitment to "the maintenance of place and the preservation of the government." Lawton argued that Georgia's citizenry regarded the entire militia as the "government" when "trouble and riot" threatened community harmony. Impressed by the fact that the First Battalion assembled with "full ranks" in the rain, Lawton declared during the flag presentation their commitment was "a testimonial of the state's confidence in them as defenders of the public order and peace." They were true soldiers.[23]

At the same time, acceptance of the militia as a viable institution was not universal in Georgia. Specifically, Lawton stated, "There are men who decry the militia service of the state and seeks means of injuring it." These critics described the militia as a "hollow show of brass buttons, handsome uniforms and brass bands," but these same people "demanded [the] militia['s assistance] when the police failed to keep order." In that context, the militia nationwide stood ready to respond to disorder, especially since each unit serving under the American flag was both "a bulwark against the outbreak of riots and organized lawlessness" as well as a "symbolic [representative] of power and government." The First Battalion, Georgia Volunteers, Colored, had received a significant honor. The awarding of the American flag also served as a sign that Georgia's governor recognized blacks as citizens of the United States and Georgia and as members of the Georgia Volunteers.[24]

Lieutenant Colonel John H. Deveaux accepted the American flag for the First Battalion and joined Lawton in commemorating the event. He thanked Lawton for representing the governor and for being "the ranking officer of our branch of service in this community." Additionally, Deveaux noted, Lawton was a "highly respected and honored" person throughout Georgia. In this context of the acceptance of and, eventually, submission to white paternal authority, Deveaux presented the rest of his speech, assuring Lawton of black militiamen's loyalty to a white state establishment as well as to the United States. Specifically, Deveaux assured his white guest, "There are no anarchists; socialists, nor conspirators in our ranks." Black militiamen possessed common sense and were "law abiding." The American flag "could not be entrusted to a more devoted and loyal class of people," as the First Battalion's men had over time "made a record of fidelity and trustworthiness." They first proved themselves during the Civil War, when black slaves protected every white family, home, and fireside as white men such as Lawton went off to war. Black militiamen had emerged from this stock of "humble guards." Given this pedigree, Deveaux told Lawton, "Surely sir, then you can rely upon us as soldiers to take care of and safe guard this banner of our country." Black militiamen "recognize[d] this flag as the very embodiment of law and order," and "the preservation and protection of public and private property." Further, they vowed to protect "our state, nation, and the homes of the people" with "their honor and their lives," as each represented a pillar of American freedom.[25]

Despite his bending to the mythology of blacks defending southern whites and their homes during the Civil War and accepting the supremacy of private property, Deveaux took a swipe at the disparities between black militia companies and their white counterparts. The black militia leader made it clear that the First Battalion's companies "may not be up to the full standard in point of proficiency and knowledge," since it "doubtless is not expected now," hinting at the threatened disbandment. Yet "we are composed of law abiding men with abundant common sense to thoroughly understand the trust reposed in us in this imposing ceremony today." Lawton and Deveaux agreed on one point: Militiamen were underappreciated, even after answering the call to duty and service numerous times in Georgia.[26]

A Petition to the Legislature

In mid-December, as the General Assembly debated how much it would allocate to the Georgia Volunteers for the year, a committee of black militiamen and African American citizens from Augusta and Atlanta carried a petition to the Legislature's Military Committee chair. Lieutenant Colonel Isaiah Blocker, commanding Augusta's Third Battalion, Georgia Volunteers, Colored, and Lieutenant Colonel Floyd H. Crumbly, commanding the Second Battalion, led the group. Company captains, Captain John A. Lockhart, from Macon, and Captain Jackson McHenry, noted Atlanta political activist and militia leader, also were on the committee. Like John Deveaux, these men put their local reputations and standing with local whites on the line to advocate for the 1,125 African American militiamen and the "800,000 colored citizens of the state." Two former militiamen and active Republicans, Henry A. Rucker and Christopher C. Wimbush, were also committee members. Rucker had just successfully promoted William McKinley's candidacy for the nation's presidency. His work for the Republican Party would make him collector of internal revenue and patronage dispenser. Atlanta attorney T. H. Malone rounded out the committee, joining a set of black citizens that included Atlantans Professor E. L. Chew, A. A. Blake, S. W Easley Jr., R. Washam, and A. Brown—a leadership cadre combining old with the new.[27]

Colonel Blocker presented and read the petition to the General Assembly's Military Committee. Colonel Crumbly, H. R. Butler reported, "made the speech of his life," but neither Butler nor the *Atlanta Constitution* provided the details of this "noble effort and manly plea." Attorney Malone,

S. W. Easley, and other committee members also spoke, yet their words, too, went unreported. The press, however, noted and recorded Jackson McHenry's message. McHenry argued both on the basis of the nation's history and of the recurring national call for black troops when the country confronted a military emergency. He asserted that black "soldiers were needed in the past by America and they [would] be needed again." Georgia, in that context of American history and the need for trained military manpower, would sooner or later have a need for black troops. Given such circumstances, McHenry stated, "I think the state should see to it that her colored troops are so prepared that should she ever call on them they will march forth not only [performing in a way that will be] an honor to themselves and their race and a pride to the state." McHenry projected that blacks armed with such patriotic enthusiasm would "be prepared to do valiant service for their country and good old Georgia."[28]

With the Augusta and Atlanta petition, black militiamen for the second consecutive year and for the third time in the 1890s sought to convince Georgia authorities to fund the Georgia Volunteers, Colored. The Augusta and Atlanta committee claimed to represent not only the eleven hundred officers and black enlisted militiamen but also all of Georgia's African American citizens. The year 1896 began with black militiamen defending their right to exist and serve as members of the Georgia Volunteers. The year closed with Georgia's governor conveying a unique honor upon John Deveaux and Savannah's First Battalion: an American flag acknowledging black citizenship, black militiamen, and the advances of the race since slavery. Despite this very public accolade, the year also closed with another black plea for funding, training, equipment, and recognition. The year 1896 also marked the reiteration of a point that black militiamen in Augusta had made in the early 1870s and that Jackson McHenry had stressed that December: Black militiamen were, first, citizens of the United States and, second, citizens of Georgia. The militia linked 1,125 militiamen to national citizenship and certified them as Georgia citizens. In each case the militia allowed African Americans to declare themselves citizens.[29]

The Cost of Neglect

The black militiaman's opportunity "to protect the American fireside" loomed as a possibility at the end of 1896, but the sad state of training and development had taken its toll. H. R. Butler contended that war with

Spain appeared to be a distinct possibility, and while Georgia's "colored militia" possessed a "great love for and desire to protect" their nation and state, it presented "a pittable appearance." This would be especially clear for all to see, were the companies asked to march to Georgia's coastline to repel an invader. The black units would have marched with "tattered uniforms [and] old guns with no sights or bayonets." The state had additionally neglected to provide black militiamen with any of the "paraphernalia of war," including overcoats, blankets, and canteens. Training deficits also abounded, as the black troops had not been allowed to participate in encampments and thereby become proficient in any duties of the soldier, especially in the target practice that was now a preoccupation of white units. In spite of these deficits, Butler declared that black militiamen would still "willingly go forth to meet the enemy with such weapons and with such practice and preparation as they have received from the hands of the state."[30]

In 1897 the Georgia Volunteers' annual report described white units' fitness for service. The companies were manned by "the best" with "men of all professions and employment." While unit weapons lacked quality, white troops' martial spirit and discipline was "good." Georgia's Volunteers had an opportunity to improve the state militia, if and when $100,000 in federal funding became available for the militia's annual operation. To qualify, Georgia had already begun the process of standardizing militia training so that militiamen might meet federal military standards. Despite the remaining need to transform citizen soldiers into real soldiers, one commentator declared Georgia's militiamen ready for war. Georgia's white militiamen in 1896 were just as ready for combat as "the brave men of '61" had been thirty-six years before, when white men went north to beat the Yankees.[31]

Black militiamen, in contrast, maintained their commitment to service at the beginning of January 1897 when they marched in various Georgia communities celebrating Emancipation Day. Even though a full contingent of black militiamen paraded on the first day in January, by February the Military Advisory Board appeared ready to disband all the African American companies. The *Atlanta Constitution* presented the presumed Military Advisory Board agenda near the end of February. Disbanding militia units was again on the Advisory Board's potential agenda, partially owing to limitations imposed by the General Assembly's inadequate funding allocation. According to the *Constitution*, militia funding did not accommodate the current size of both black and white companies. Pointing to the estimated 4,500 black and white militiamen, some militia officers declared, "There are at present too many men enlisted in the service of the state." The number, they argued, could be halved. Such a reduction might alleviate the funding issues, because communities, such as Atlanta, Augusta, Macon, and Savannah, that had both black and white units would be asked to eliminate this duplication. Atlanta served as a model for consideration. Specifically, Atlanta had ten white and four black militia units. The city, some officers projected, needed less than half that number of companies. Five white units might meet Atlanta's basic needs, while "the negro companies could be dispensed with entirely."[32]

It is unclear where this debate went after February 1897. War with Spain did loom on the horizon and Georgia's militiamen, regardless of color, assumed that they would have a role in that confrontation. The *Constitution* followed the announcement of the upcoming Advisory Board meeting with two articles on the status and readiness of various white militia companies across the state. No black units received any parallel press coverage. Despite articles complementing white units on their readiness, funding was an ongoing problem. A year earlier, however, the state seemingly had accommodated 4,500 troops, except that African American militiamen suffered as precariously in both 1896 and 1897. The difference between the two years was that the 1896 "show cause" meeting focused on why militia administrators should disband almost half of the black units; this, before the governor intervened and saved the black militia. By 1897 black militia companies could be "dispensed with entirely."[33]

Fund-Raising

Black militiamen, within this unstable context, maintained their connection to local communities with fund-raising activities that sustained their companies. At the beginning of 1897 the First Battalion opened its Military Fair, which involved the battalion's "lady['s] committee" and Savannah's business establishments. Additional financial contributions came from local white militia officers in the range of five to ten dollars, respectively, from Colonels George A. Mercer and A. R. Lawton. Black militiamen at the end of January also asked "all the citizens [to] turn out in a body during the week and give the soldier boys a boost." The fair lasted two weeks, closing out January and ending the first week in February with a ball that drew strong support. Daily attendance despite cold nights was "fair," with a final evaluation suggesting that "attendance was good and the receipts a fairly average one."[34]

The Military Fair proved to be vitally important in the maintenance and enhancement of the First Battalion's units. While it is unclear how much the bazaar raised monetarily, it apparently was enough money to provide the Lone Star Cadets with "new regulation coats and caps" as they celebrated their twenty-first anniversary. Captain L. A. Washington led the newly uniformed unit in its public parade. The "improvement was noticeable and commented on by citizens." The First Battalion's annual May military parade drew accolades from the *Tribune*'s white adversary, the *Savannah Morning News*. The *Tribune* reprinted the *Morning News*'s favorable report in some detail. According to the *Morning News*, the May 22, 1897, parade constituted "one of the finest made in the history of the battalion." While the statement may have been embellished, the newspaper was clear that the "troops showed marked improvement in their general make-up"—an improvement the fund-raiser had made possible, as "a majority of the companies [had] the new caps and coats prescribed by the regulations." The battalion as a result "made a fine appearance," and its "excellent display" was due to the Military Fair, which "raised money enough to purchase their uniforms."

Surprisingly, at the park extension the Georgia Artillery fired "a salute" honoring the anniversary of the Fifteenth Amendment while black infantry drilled and African American cavalrymen "executed several maneuvers" on grounds that a year earlier had been racially contested urban and military space. African American military demonstrations at the park extension in celebration of the black right to vote challenged white demands in 1896 that the parade ground be an exclusively white domain. Jim Crow, nevertheless, had not yet triumphed in determining where and when black militiamen paraded.[35]

Black militiamen, despite twenty years of official neglect, continued unit by unit to fund-raise locally throughout 1897. Their fund-raising efforts over the past two decades had kept the African American militia companies going. In Savannah, specifically in 1897, the Lone Star Cadets' anniversary events included a nighttime "military hop" and supper "prepared by the [company's] ladies' branch." The Chatham Light Infantry in March put on "a grand dance" with a fifteen-cent admission fee. The Forest City Light Infantry organized "a grand Easter hop" in mid- to late April, charging couples seventy-five cents and single individuals fifty cents. In this context the black community sustained their militia companies all by themselves.

The *Tribune* in August lashed out at the state. According to the *Tribune*, there were twenty-two black militia companies. That number was set in stone by state law and the full complement of units was "completed" with no allowance for any new companies. In contrast white units in 1893 had increased in number as a result of the Georgia Legislature's reorganization that year. White units increased from fifty infantry units to seventy-two, and the cavalry complement exploded from seven to twenty-four companies. This expansion helped account for the funding problems and desires to reduce the size of the overall militia four years later. The more important issue for the newspaper in 1897, however, was the "past eight years." Since 1889 Georgia had done "naught to assist these [black] companies." During those years, "several white companies were sent into camps annually and all expenses paid." Access to encampments enabled the white companies "to be efficient in every respect." Black militiamen meanwhile had to be "efficient and up to date while . . . not allowed the chance" at development white militiamen received. The paper noted that such "discrimination [was] uncalled for." Like other black Georgians the *Tribune* put its hope in the General Assembly, pleading "that the legislature [would] include the colored troops in its appropriation so that they may be given a chance to learn of camp duties" in what was called "the school of the soldier."[36]

Black Encampment: The Georgia Artillery

The *Tribune* did not publicize the fund-raising activities of the Georgia Artillery in the winter and spring of 1897, yet the paper celebrated the unit's week-long August encampment. That celebration coincided with the newspaper's criticism of the state and its matching plea for funding and access to encampment opportunities. On August 9, 1897, the Georgia Artillery became the first "colored military . . . of its numbers to go into camps." The company's members went to camp "in service uniform, armed and equipped." This was reason to celebrate. The opportunity, nevertheless, came with a major problem. The Georgia Artillery entered camp proudly, but the "penurious manner" that had characterized the treatment of black militiamen continued. Encampment costs came out of the pockets of the Georgia Artillery and not the state of Georgia.[37]

For the thirty Georgia Artillery members that attended the encampment at Flowersville, Georgia, seven miles outside of Savannah, the experience was a clear success. The week involved instruction in "camp duties" that the *Tribune* claimed would "cause them to be more proficient in every respect." Despite being an undermanned unit, which made their training "laborious," Georgia Artillerymen worked hard and maintained "almost perfect" discipline without complaining, because dedicated work was essential in the minds of both the enlisted men and the company's officers. The unit's members' ultimate objective was to demonstrate to state militia leadership the high "degree of proficiency they could attain without the assistance of an army officer" who since the late 1880s had served as the major instructor at militia encampments not only in Georgia but also across the country. In contrast early white encampments had hands-on instruction by regular army officers. Despite the absence of United States Army training officers, the officers of the Georgia Artillery sought to prove their mettle by making sure that "every detail in camp life was fully carried out." Visitors observed and complimented the company on the camp's neat appearance, further proving black capabilities as competent military officers and men. Camp maintenance also fell under the supervision of volunteer surgeon Dr. T. James Davis, a first lieutenant of the First Battalion. At the end of eight days of hard work as soldiers and battery men, the company declared that they felt "proud of the success of our encampment."[38]

Members of Savannah's African American community visited the encampment. The visitors included black militiamen from the First Battalion's infantry companies and from the sole black cavalry unit in the state, the Savannah Hussars. Officers of the First Battalion, including Major William H. Royall, who was standing in for Deveaux as battalion commander, and *Savannah Tribune* managing editor and battalion adjutant Solomon C. Johnson, were among the black militia leaders who made their way to Flowersville and what was now called Camp Kell, after ailing Adjutant General John McIntosh Kell. The citizenry also joined the Georgia Artillery on Sunday, sharing a sermon delivered to the unit two days before the completion of their training. The black community in a variety of ways turned out to support the Georgia Artillery and helped make the encampment a success for the company and the African American community.[39]

The Georgia Artillery had done what it had set out to do: prove themselves worthy and trainable soldiers whose proficiency deserved both state recognition and funding for development and improvement. While most of the black community showed up to view the endeavors and achievements of the sole African American artillery unit in the United States, whites appeared to be absent from this moment of triumph for at least thirty members of the Georgia Volunteers, Colored. What was distinctive during the eight-day encampment was that despite the Georgia Artillery's professionalism no white officials came to see them. In 1878, nineteen years earlier, the governor had attended a major black militia event along with several local white city and militia officials. In the 1880s and 1890s Georgia's governors and the adjutant general consistently attended white encampments wherever they occurred across the state. In contrast major members of the white Savannah militia community in 1897 did not take the short journey to observe the Georgia Artillery's encampment. And finally the acting Adjutant General Oscar J. Brown failed to visit the first black encampment. Further neither he nor any militia official inspected the unit. This was particularly egregious in light of the American flag ceremony a year earlier that publicly declared black militiamen Georgia Volunteers. This absence of white officials was "the greatest regret of the battery." The white establishment failed to acknowledge a unique local, state, and national institution. Adding insult to injury, the Georgia General Assembly allocated no funding for the Georgia Artillery's encampment training and continued to neglect every African American militia unit.

Securing funding for training, development, improvement, and recognition had been the collective goal of every member of the Georgia Volunteers, Colored, the black communities they represented, and the African American citizens of Georgia. Nineteen years earlier the prize drill had been a noted marker of black progress, civilization, and above all military proficiency. That event brought the white elite and the black militia together in a moment where whites could publicly recognize black capabilities. In 1897 black militiamen attained public support from one source only, the local black community.[40]

Black militiamen across Georgia commemorated national holidays, conducted unit fund-raisers, and attended special celebrations outside Georgia. In 1897 these special celebrations included the centennial celebration of Nashville, Tennessee, and the inauguration of President William McKinley. Captain Jackson McHenry led one Atlanta unit to Nashville for the community's centennial. Thirty members of Macon's Lincoln Guards attended the inauguration, using their own money after being denied state funding. Locally, Macon's Bibb County Blues sponsored "a big picnic" in mid-July. Black Atlanta's Independence Day commemoration became a two-day event, with four black militia units helping to lead the celebration and visitors from surrounding states. Savannah's First Battalion went to Charleston, South Carolina, where South Carolina and Georgia black militiamen celebrated Labor Day. Captain J. L. Mirault, one of two young lieutenants who resigned in 1896, returned to the militia briefly to command the Forest City Light Infantry for this special day.[41] Each event demonstrated the black militia's vision of U.S. citizenship and service to their home communities. Their participation also provided opportunities to prove themselves proficient militiamen.

Weapons Exchanges

Despite these successful public events, 1897 ended with a new round of antiblack discrimination directed at the state's black militiamen. Acting Adjutant General Oscar J. Brown initiated and monitored weapons exchanges between black and white units, equipping the black militiamen with obsolete weapons formerly used by the white units. He sent better and new arms to white companies. Brown's correspondence in November and December arranged weapons transfers from white to black militia units. Brown ordered Macon's Lincoln Guards, commanded by Captain John "Sandy" A. Lockhart, "to clean and pack the 40 Springfield" .50-caliber rifles and ship them to Springfield, Massachusetts. He instructed Captain Bell, leading the all-white Second Infantry, to give Lockhart forty .45-caliber weapons "being the old guns now in your armory." Similar orders went to Savannah's Lieutenant Colonel John Deveaux and all-white First Infantry Captain Jordan F. Brooks. Captain Brooks was requested to "turn over the sixty old guns in your possession to Lt. Col. John H. Deveaux." Meanwhile "new guns" were "issued to the [white] companies of various regiments."[42]

War Readiness

The year 1898 began in Atlanta with black militiamen leaping for their lives just as Savannah's militiamen had done two years earlier. A white streetcar operator ran his vehicle into an African American funeral procession accompanied by Atlanta's black militiamen, who were providing "military honors" for a black barber named Allen. Captain Jackson McHenry contacted the police afterward and charged the motorman with cutting the funeral march in two "for several seconds." The motorman, unlike Savannah's incident, would be called before the police court a day after the incident.[43]

During the spring of 1898 the Georgia militia's combat readiness once again drew attention, because war with Spain appeared imminent. The *Atlanta Constitution*, anticipating martial conflict, declared, "Atlanta Negroes Are Ready To Fight Spain." Focusing on Captain Jackson McHenry, the paper's correspondent reported that when war commenced, the regular army's twenty-five thousand troops would be supplemented by state militiamen. This was an opportunity for "colored militia companies" to lend their services to the nation's defense. According to the newspaper, Jackson McHenry's eighty-member company, the Governor's Volunteers, were "anxious to go to war." McHenry added that his company was "in good condition and . . . all talking about the chances of war," in part because the company had "new improved guns" and "a fair supply" of new uniforms, suggesting that the exchange of weapons at the end of 1897 and beginning of 1898 had improved the quality of weaponry that black units possessed. The weapons were not new, but they appeared to be better than the arms Colonel Crumbly inspected in 1896. Further, new uniforms went to more than Savannah's black battalion, confirming that Atlanta's units own fund-raising had led to an improved appearance. Reinforcing these achievements in the face of potential war, McHenry committed himself to organizing another fund-raising fair to further improve his company in the "best style."[44]

While McHenry promoted his company, he also commented on Cuba, the United States's mission, and African American military capability. McHenry thought that "the citizens of the United States should go down and take Cuba" and that it "would be a good country for the colored man" because black troops "could stand the climate of Cuba better than the white man." In so doing, McHenry embraced several national stereotypes, including the mythology that black men were more durable in a tropical climate owing to their skin color. McHenry also assumed, as Congress did, that blacks previously exposed to yellow fever were immune and therefore viable troops for immediate deployment to Cuba and later the Philippines.[45]

Armed with these ideas McHenry announced that Georgia's African American militiamen were ready to fight: "Colored soldiers are ready to defend their country and they will be found good soldiers when the time comes." Speaking for the more than one thousand black militiamen, McHenry claimed that they "would be the best soldiers for Cuba."

In making this argument, he purposely tried to find a way to justify the use of black militiamen in the pending war. McHenry contended that "the government would find them [African American militiamen] valuable to send into Cuba." Finally, if not to Cuba, then African American militiamen might be sent to southern Florida to "prevent the Spaniards from landing troops in this country." Jackson McHenry's prediction in 1896 that the United States would need trained black militiamen to meet a military emergency two years later was about to be confirmed. McHenry as a result publicly sought a way to incorporate black militiamen within the military structure of the coming war, perhaps anticipating the exclusion of blacks by both the United States and Georgia when the nation mobilized for war with Spain in Cuba.[46]

In March, black militiamen not only attempted to find a way to be included in the coming war but also became the point of some discussion by Georgia's adjutant general. Early in the month, the *Savannah Tribune* published an article confirming the appointment of former militiaman Christopher C. Wimbush as Surveyor of Customs for Atlanta. In April 1898 the First Battalion, the Georgia Artillery, and the Savannah Hussars sponsored a banquet celebrating Lieutenant Colonel John H. Deveaux's appointment as Savannah's Collector of Customs. These political patronage positions were rewards conveyed upon black Republicans for assisting in electing William McKinley as president of the United States, in 1896. The political appointments also reinforced African Americans' leadership capabilities and commitment to serving the nation. Georgia Democrats, however, especially its two U.S. senators, consistently opposed black patronage appointments, highlighting a growing region-wide resistance to African American officeholders. In contradistinction to such opposition, blacks merged politics with militia service as a long-standing tradition among black officers in the Georgia Volunteers, Colored.[47]

The *Tribune* added its voice to the mix, certifying black militiamen's military readiness with three brief articles. The first reminded African Americans of their loyalty, service, and bravery during the Civil War. The bottom line was that black men had "fought bravely then and [would] do the same again whenever the flag of this country is insulted." The second article made the point that young black men had "become enthused with the spirit of patriotism and fostering of companies," as war fever brought younger black men to Savannah's First Battalion. Further, young men "have everything to gain thereby, and [could] do themselves much good by becoming faithful and efficient soldiers." The paper, however, admonished the "large number of others" who had not enlisted in Savannah's First Battalion. Almost in contradiction, the newspaper asserted, "There are half a million colored men available and willing to take up arms in defense of old glory and the National honor." Black men therefore constituted "one potent factor among Americans who can always be safely relied on by the government in cases of emergency." The *Tribune* thereby restated a longstanding black militia tradition of commitment to U.S. citizenship and to the nation's defense.[48]

Pro Rata Funding

From mid-March to the beginning of April, Acting Adjutant General Oscar J. Brown carried on a correspondence with African Americans that both acknowledged the state's decades of neglect of black militiamen and officially rebuffed black efforts to expand the number of African American militia companies to meet the looming war emergency. Brown wrote Captain Jackson McHenry on March 11, 1898, informing him that the state of Georgia would pay "the pro rata amount due your company" for "uniforms [in] the amount of $40.00." This was done because $800 "from the Military fund" allocated by the Military Advisory Board proved "impracticable to encamp" the Georgia Volunteers, Colored. At last it appeared that black militiamen had received financial support from the Georgia Volunteers to advance their training. Since the early 1890s black militiamen had petitioned for "pro rata" funding from militia authorities to fund black encampments. Ironically, even the pro rata funds in 1898 proved inadequate to address the encampment needs of the eleven hundred members of the Georgia Volunteers, Colored. Despite consistent efforts to get the General Assembly and militia officials to allot a fair share to black militiamen, the money in 1898 fell significantly short and continued the inequities between black and white militiamen.[49]

Five days later Governor William Yates Atkinson acknowledged a letter from the Confederate Soldiers Association offering "their services to their native state in case of necessity," namely, war with Spain. Atkinson noted that the adjutant general would keep the letter on file and replied, "Should an emergency arise I feel that the honor and safety of the state could not be entrusted to better hands than those of the veterans of so many battles." At the end of March, however, Acting Adjutant General Brown wrote Lieutenant Colonel Isaiah Blocker concerning exchanging old .50 caliber weapons for .45 caliber "guns [that] are not new but are serviceable." More importantly, however, Brown conceded to Colonel Blocker that it was "well known at this office that little ha[d] been done for the Georgia Volunteers, Colored." Specifically, "the best that ha[d] ever been done [was] to provide arms and equipment." Yet Brown contended, too, that "the white companies [were] still lacking" because "not much more for white organizations" was being done "owing to the limited means at hand." Brown thereby asserted that the legislative neglect had been universal. Neglect continued to the point that none of the militiamen had uniforms. Nevertheless, the story black militiamen would tell discounted universal neglect, as white militia men did receive more than arms and equipment; they had gotten training and were better prepared for the coming emergency.[50]

While Acting Adjutant General Brown and Governor Atkinson politely accepted and filed away former Confederate offers to defend Georgia, Brown in mid-April also filed away black offers of national defense. He additionally claimed that state legal limitations stood as the reason for restructuring, if not rejecting, black efforts to volunteer to fight in the upcoming war with Spain. African Americans from Milledgeville and Thebes, Georgia, endeavored to organize and offer their services "in case of War with Spain." Brown in both cases contended, "Under law, no other companies of colored troops can be organized, as the legal number has been reached." Brown was even more direct in his response to Thebes's black applicants: "Unless there is an unusual demand for troops in case of war no other organizations will be called into service."[51]

In early April the Military Advisory Board convened to plan the year. They faced deciding between undertaking war preparations or a new encampment. War preparation involved spending $42,000 for equipment "to put the militia [a force of 4,500 men including over 1,000 African American militiamen] into service in the field," if the 1896 and 1897 annual reports serve as accurate assessments of the Georgia Volunteers and Georgia Volunteers, Colored, combined troop strength. Board members projected war preparations that would expand the militia to twelve thousand men. Such an expansion was deemed almost immediately possible. Throughout this daylong meeting and the report making recommendations to Governor Atkinson came only one mention of black troops: the potential disbandment of the Bibb County Blues if the company did not improve and meet state requirements. The Board's principal recommendation involved the distribution of new weapons. Should war occur "new arms shall be issued to such of the older companies in the state service as may have demonstrated a proper care of the arms already held by" the established companies. The "intent of this resolution [was] to recognize [the long term] merit in the older companies and thus to stimulate a proper care for the arms."[52]

The implications for black units appeared to be that new weapons were not going to be part of their profile. African American companies had never been considered part of the old company structure dating back to the American Revolution, and they definitely possessed no standing as a mainstream unit in the Georgia Volunteers. While every black unit turned over .50 caliber weapons for serviceable .45 caliber rifles, the general assessment of black militia companies mirrored the problems facing the Bibb County Blues, that is, failure to meet state regulations. At the beginning of April were African American militiamen part of the Georgia Volunteers preparing for war, or were they a reserve force to be utilized only if white troops failed to step forward to meet the emergency?

War

Between April 11 and April 19, 1898, the United States declared war on Spain. The presidential request came on April 11 and the congressional declaration came eight days later. On April 23, the *Savannah Tribune* published the full officer complement of the Georgia Volunteers, Colored, leading the three battalions and six unattached companies that included the Georgia Artillery, the Savannah Hussars, and infantry companies from Rome, Bibb County, Macon, and Colquitt. According to the *Tribune*, "The colored citizens will be quite a factor if hostilities continue any length of time," with Lieutenant Colonel Deveaux commanding all of Georgia's black militia units should the call to serve come. The *Tribune*, like Jackson McHenry, sought to make sure that African Americans had the chance to prove their citizenship as militiamen and soldiers ready to serve the United States at war.[53]

On April 25, 1898, Governor William Yates Atkinson, known to African Americans as the antilynching governor and commander-in-chief of the state militia, called together nine white militia officers for a "council of war." The council included seven regimental commanders and two battalion commanders. Colonel Alexander R. Lawton, leading the First Infantry Regiment of Savannah, headed the list. Second Infantry Regiment Colonel Charles Wylie, representing Macon, also served with Madison's Third Infantry Regimental leader, Colonel Usher Thomason, Valdosta's Colonel James O. Varnadoe, who commanded the Fourth Infantry Regiment,

Atlanta's Fifth Infantry Regiment, led by Colonel John S. Candler, and Waynesboro's Sixth Infantry Regiment, operating under the leadership of Colonel William E. Jones. Colonel W. W. Gordon led the First Calvary Regiment in Savannah. Longtime militia leader and Advisory Board member Colonel William Garrard and Major John M. Barnard, respectively, led battalion-size units: Savannah's First Infantry Battalion and the First Cavalry Battalion. None of the three black battalion commanders—Lieutenant Colonel John H. Deveaux, First Battalion, Lieutenant Colonel Isaiah Blocker, Third Battalion, or Lieutenant Colonel Floyd Crumbly, Second Battalion—received telegraphed orders to attend the war council. The nine white officers were called to decide how to raise the 3,174 troops that President McKinley "asked of Georgia" as the nation mobilized for war against Spain in Cuba. The war council also contemplated not mobilizing the state militia to fulfill the federal request for soldiers.[54]

Atkinson and the war council held several meetings, some of which were done in secret behind closed doors. Their decisions about meeting President McKinley's troop quota and whether to deploy the militia reflected their fear that Spain or pirates might invade Georgia. Given such projections Atkinson and the council decided against sending the Georgia Volunteers to Cuba. They would meet the federal troop quota by asking Georgia's men to individually volunteer. Atkinson, as a result, hoped to keep a significant part of the militia in Georgia to defend the state from a feared Spanish invasion. President McKinley, the *Atlanta Constitution* reported, had a different vision. He hoped that Georgia would send its militiamen because these troops were already trained and armed. The paper speculated that somewhere between a small number to half of the Georgia militia might be used to fill the thirty-one-hundred-man federal levy. Georgia's war council, however, insisted that the state would meet its quota with individual volunteers. They would not go any further nor commit the Georgia militia to combat outside Georgia.

Two days after the initial war council, Valdosta's Fourth Infantry Regiment was designated to remain in Georgia. The war council hoped to use Colonel Vanaradoe's Civil War experience to meet any coastal invasion. Four days later, at the end of April, however, the *Constitution* announced the governor's decision to create two voluntary infantry regiments and two volunteer light artillery regiments to fulfill the nation's war needs while keeping the entire state militia in Georgia. In light of the governor's refusal to allow organized militia companies to go intact to war, militiamen negotiated hard as individual volunteers to find ways to serve under the command of Georgia Volunteer Officers in the new U.S. Volunteer companies. Near the end of May the *Savannah Tribune* announced that Vanaradoe had abandoned his post as the state's defender. He joined the new federal volunteer force as a staff officer for a regular army major general. These individual and official decisions marked the dissolution of the Georgia Volunteers as Georgia's state militia.[55]

With no seat on the war council, black militiamen found their status and presence "ignored." The *Savannah Tribune* also outlined the events that brought black militiamen to their moment of invisibility. According to the *Tribune*, Governor Atkinson and the war council "acted as if there were no colored troops in the state." Black resentment increased because "not only ha[d] the colored troops been ignored in not being ordered to increase enlistment, or to attend the governor's conference, but they ha[d] also been denied the privilege of defending their country." Additionally, "the state [had] done nothing toward fully equipping them." The "guns, etc, given them are second-hand and in some instances unserviceable." Realistic about what they now faced, black militiamen understood how hard it would be to get members of the race to enlist at the state or federal levels, even as white Georgians volunteered to defend their nation. African Americans, despite these setbacks, still hoped to find a way to get the attention of Georgia authorities as well as the McKinley administration.[56]

Searching for Inclusion

Getting the nation's attention was not going to be easy for black Americans. Willard Gatewood has noted the complex emotions, vision, and goals that African Americans wrestled with at the coming of the Spanish-American War, the Cuban War of Independence, and the Philippine-American War. The war of 1898 provided a very public moment for black and white people to establish their identity and self-esteem. Military service provided a way to do both. Fighting, at the risk of dying, for your country was the ultimate avenue to achieve citizenship with all its rights and privileges. Combat service would also allow black men to "achieve the full height of manhood," thereby giving the race an unambiguous standing as true citizens of the nation. The war was, Gatewood contended, the "first time . . . black men were called upon to render military service outside the United States" since they had become citizens after the Civil War. In that context, participation as a citizen in the defense of the nation should result in racism's eradication. War against the Spanish in Cuba provided blacks in general but African American men specifically with a chance to prove their patriotism, demonstrate their military acumen, and gain respect for an entire people. It was for these reasons that Jackson McHenry, the *Savannah Tribune*, Georgia's black militiamen, and African Americans across the United States put so much energy into trying to be a part of the war in Cuba.[57]

This effort continued into May 1898, although by then its success was questionable. The *Savannah Tribune*, nevertheless, devoted page two of its early May editions to critical assessments directed at Governor Atkinson's wartime decisions. Other articles on pages two and three outlined the actions of patriotic black people and the public outings of the Georgia Volunteers, Colored. The *Atlanta Constitution* also recorded national black efforts that did not get reported by the *Tribune*. At the beginning of May the *Tribune* claimed, as other blacks in Georgia had done, that the "colored troops [would] be called out when there [was] real fighting to be done." Additionally, the paper made note that despite their disappointment, black men had not "sulked." Specifically, black men were patriots who continued to be ready to respond to the nation's needs. As proof the *Tribune* made it clear that Georgia's black militiamen were alive and well, with three lieutenant colonels, one major, twenty-two captains, fifty-eight lieutenants, and twelve hundred "of the most loyal and patriotic men that [could] be found anywhere." Black Georgians as a result were ready to defend their homeland. Furthermore, the war had united the nation, bringing to an end the old Civil War sectional divisions of North and South. The Confederacy in Georgia, however, continued to lurk behind the scenes, undermining national unity and the patriotic spirit. Confederate sentiment raised its challenging presence in Gainesville, Georgia, where militiamen who wore a blue uniform during Confederate Memorial Day were refused permission to march in parade where only gray uniforms marked the occasion.[58]

The *Tribune* countered with examples of black loyalty and soldierly actions. Black men of the all–African American United States Army Ninth Cavalry were extolled by "a well known military man" in the May 7, 1898, issue of the *Tribune*. Pointing to the scorn heaped on "the fighting qualities of . . . black boys" in 1866, when Congress created the Ninth Cavalry, this unnamed commentator sought to convey to the broader public that black troops were worthy of the nation's trust as combat troops. The Ninth Cavalry had proved their mettle in 1867, when they confronted Native Americans in combat. This black regular military unit commanded by white officers had not only met the challenge of Native Americans in the West but also confronted and subdued "wilder bandits." Black cavalrymen also were "no parade command." They worked hard in less than desirable Western postings. Eastern military posts held more prestige and were seen by white officers as better assignments than service on the Western frontier. Members of the Ninth Cavalry therefore worked under more pressure owing to the constant combat in the West. As a result, they "never had any but fighting assignments."

Black regular soldiers such as those of the Ninth felt they had been proving their worth as combat soldiers from 1867 to the 1898 War in Cuba; indeed, the *Tribune* declared, "It has been one long fight." With this article, the *Tribune* pointed to black history, a story being erased, but one of black military service of which Governor Atkinson should be aware. Black soldiers in the Ninth Cavalry had given the nation thirty-plus years of consistent combat service defending the nation's interest. Militiaman and *Savannah Tribune* managing editor Solomon C. Johnson placed these articles on page two of the May 7, 1898, edition to promote and prove the merit and character of black men defending the nation. African Americans had proven themselves in the United States Army and as Georgia militiamen. Black soldiers, both regulars and militiamen, were ready to serve in the War in Cuba.[59]

The following week, on May 14, 1898, the *Tribune* again noted that the "colored troops [were] illy armed and equipped by the state, but . . . ready to respond" as national defenders. To prove the race's mettle, black United States Army troops guarded the first prisoners of war under the shadow of "Old Glory . . . in its glory." These black regulars were, however, publicly criticized for "the least wrong," even though their discipline was "among the best," especially in comparison to that of white soldiers, who appeared to "act with impunity." Black regulars had to be on their best behavior. At the same time the all-black Twenty-Fifth Infantry regiment suffered Jim Crow segregation in the United States South as they mobilized and traveled to war in the Caribbean. The *Tribune* quoted a northern newspaper that countered that war was no time for white southerners to practice customary racial segregation simply to uphold southern etiquette. Essentially both the *New York Journal* and the *Tribune* argued that if a man was a "citizen good enough to wear the uniform" of the United States Army, then he was "good enough to ride in any car with anybody." Segregation had no power over patriotism and national service.[60]

The *Tribune* also highlighted Georgia militia activities. Lieutenant Colonel John H. Deveaux dictated "Order No. 4" to First Battalion Adjutant

Solomon C. Johnson, who published the military directive in the *Tribune*. The order set the attitude expected of every First Battalion member in preparation for the May 19, 1898, parade. The parade took on a singular uniqueness owing to the "importance of the situation," namely, the United States at war. As a result, "every [militiaman,] enlisted man and officer [needed] to show his patriotism" by participating in the parade. All of the First Battalion's all-black companies were going to march with .45 caliber secondhand and replacement guns and in regulation uniforms. The war also enhanced militia enlistment; each company was "filled with young blood," ensuring one of the largest assemblies of black militiamen in some time. The *Tribune* also commended the white Irish Jasper Greens for their enthusiastic response to the state's call for volunteers, but this compliment hardly countered its criticism of the state. Irish Jasper Greens's members volunteered by their own admission because "the state ha[d] equipped them and sent them into camps to prepare for such calls" to duty. Georgia had prepared its white militiamen for war and had made them honorable men.[61]

At the end of May the *Atlanta Constitution* reported on black efforts that did not reach the pages of the *Savannah Tribune*. On successive days the *Constitution* presented two articles focused on blacks who sought national authority to clear them for combat in Cuba. The May 25 article detailed the general characteristics of the Georgia Volunteers, Colored, highlighting Lieutenant Colonel Floyd Crumbly's command of the Atlanta-based Second Battalion. This article preceded a much more important discussion two days earlier between black politicians, President William McKinley, and Secretary of War Russell Alger.[62]

Recently appointed register of the treasury, Georgian Judson Lyons, and former Mississippi congressman John Lynch spent a significant amount of time with McKinley and Alger discussing the federalization of black militiamen. Lyons and Lynch hoped that the president might "recognize the services of the colored volunteers by assigning them to one or more of the immune regiments provided for under existing law." Such an appointment would take advantage of the training of black militiamen, especially those who had survived yellow fever, which by implication made them immune to tropical diseases. With this assumed immunity from climatic disease, these soldiers were ready for military service in a tropical climate. Lyons and Lynch acknowledged in their meeting that race served as a major determinant, since white troops resented "the mixing of the two classes of citizens." Furthermore presidential action had become essential, because state governors had ignored the thousands of black volunteers who presented themselves to militia authorities in Georgia, Mississippi, and South Carolina eager and ready to serve.

Willard Gatewood has noted, however, that there were very few African American militia units available for service in the United States. Lyons, probably aware of this, presented Georgia's black militiamen to President McKinley as one of the few trained urban-based black state militias that could be mobilized to meet the war emergency. Georgia's African American militiamen, Lyons contended, could muster at least a regiment and perhaps additional volunteer organized infantry from Atlanta, Augusta, Macon, and Savannah. There were also more specialized cavalry, and the sole artillery companies prepared to depart for Cuba. All that was needed, the two black men argued, was presidential agreement and acceptance of their proposal to recruit, organize, deploy, and incorporate black volunteers within the nation's military. It would not, however, be until the summer of 1898 that the states and Congress created ten immune regiments. The volunteer immune regiments were intended to be manned by those individuals who had been infected with, survived, and apparently attained immunity from yellow fever.[63]

The next month, June 1898, was a complex blend of continuing black protest, criticism of state officials, celebration of inclusion, veneration of black people (especially of soldiers), and war weariness. The *Savannah Tribune* devoted space to each subject, starting with the commemoration of black valor. The newspaper qualified its positive message with the assertion that black invisibility persisted despite courageous acts by black soldiers who had served the nation and continued to do so during the country's time of need. Atlanta's Elder R. E. Hart seven years earlier had publicly sermonized about black military invisibility when he addressed Jackson McHenry's company. In June 1898 the paper noted that the war had made its mark on African Americans, because "[i]n war the colored man is brave. This much is history." Further, during the war in Cuba the black soldier, the paper declared with certainty, "will also distinguish himself," with "heroic deeds on the field of battle." Despite such admirable accomplishments in combat, invisibility would make sure that these deeds would "not be known," because they would "be shielded in mystery" until black soldiers on site survived to tell their story. And yet, who would listen? Getting Georgians and the nation to recognize the valorous deeds of black soldiers was a problem that plagued both black militiamen and African Americans serving as regular troops in the U.S. military.[64]

This conclusion by a newspaper and its editor reflected the ongoing disillusionment and frustration caused by invisibility during the nation's involvement in a global war and imperial expansion. The War of 1898, black people had believed, was the one sure moment when blacks could publicly declare themselves full citizens of the United States. This goal was lost as African Americans watched their citizenship disappear in the wake of American imperial expansion abroad and the rise and legalization of Jim Crow segregation at home while white racial superiority engulfed both the foreign and domestic spheres.[65]

Black Officers for Black Troops

At the beginning of June, the *Tribune* continued to use page two of each edition to promote black soldiers and castigate their detractors. By June it was clear to managing editor and black militiaman Solomon C. Johnson that "colored citizens [had] not received the recognition due them" with regard to the war in Cuba. Specifically only four African American officers had been selected to serve during the conflict, and no black officer had been appointed above the rank of major. White officers received most of the appointments leading black units. Alabama's black militiamen, for example, requested to go to Cuba as an all-black unit, but white officers would command the company. Federal and state authorities prevented the militia's full complement of black officers from commanding African American troops in combat. With this slight against black militia officers and the enlisted militiamen they had led for a significant amount of time, the *Tribune* joined the African American press in a nationwide crusade to insist that black officers should lead black troops.

This demand that authorities respect black capabilities was reinforced a week later. Federal officials authorized the mobilization and mustering in an all-black Georgia immune regiment. The Tenth Volunteer Infantry Regiment, one of four black immune regiments created by Congress and the president during the conflict, was to be a southern unit filled with black southerners. According to the *Tribune*, the communities of Atlanta, Augusta, Macon, and Savannah were projected as possessing the numbers to successfully construct a black regiment. But the new regiment "must have white commanders"; this decision ignored the fact that while blacks wanted to enlist, they "would never do so under the circumstances" proposed.[66]

Rejection

Black enlisted men wanted to be led by African American officers. Black men in Georgia's segregated militia had officered the neglected African American companies for over twenty years, and Alabama's black militiamen were led by black officers before the War of 1898. In another moment of irony white Georgians had campaigned hard to be led by white Georgia militia officers in the new federal volunteer regiments. While former white Georgia militiamen who volunteered to serve in Cuba achieved some success in making this demand for continuity and familiarity, black demands both in Georgia and nationally were characterized as unreasonable or impossible to achieve.[67]

This issue in June 1898 was compounded by the paper's comments on lynching and the total rejection of every black militia company in the Georgia Volunteers, Colored. White lynching bees drew the newspaper's attention and ire while producing a warning about a significant contradiction: as the "war continues, likewise lynching bees." White Georgia, the *Tribune* contended, needed to address the lynching problem by controlling and finding ways of "reform[ing the] . . . class of [white] lawless men" who had "degenerate[d] into cannibals." This juxtaposition between the war to liberate Cubans from Spanish colonial and imperial oppression, on the one hand, and whites lynching blacks in the United States, on the other, was compounded by the *Tribune*'s "foregone conclusion that the services of the entire [First] Battalion . . . will not be accepted at present." Disappointment overwhelmed any celebration in recognition of black men enlisting in the 10th immune regiment. Black hope that participation in the war would draw to them significant attention and positive recognition disappeared when the War Department restricted black volunteer enlistment to just one Savannah company. The various black members of the Georgia Volunteers, Colored, regardless of their limited training and petitions by Judson Lyons and John Lynch, were ignored again not only by the state of Georgia but also by the president of the United States. Both governments ignored African Americans and their desire to defend the nation as a right and duty of citizenship.[68]

Late June and all of July brought shorter articles on the African American press's continuing demand for black officers to lead black enlisted men, with occasional notices from Cuba about successful black regulars' combat operations. These positive moments were overwhelmed by national and statewide war weariness that combined with critiques of American imperial expansion and its racial implications for spreading Jim Crow segregation outside the United States. Specifically African Americans and black Cuban natives were victimized by white men seeking quick access to wealth, generally at the expense of people of color. The *Tribune* also pointed out that the military had a white manpower problem. White men had failed to volunteer in sufficient numbers to meet the troop quotas requested by the War Department. Georgia, for example, furnished only 255 of the 704 men required by the War Department during a second call for troops. White men in North Carolina and Virginia also failed to volunteer in sufficient numbers. The newspaper in response repeated the point that black men were ready, willing, and able to fill the gap "if the authorities would only cast their [racial] feelings aside and fully recognize the colored man as an American citizen."[69]

International Peace and Local Recriminations

The week of August 13, 1898, brought peace between the United States and Spain and recriminations in Georgia over the state's response to the war. At the end of the month the *Savannah Tribune* attacked decisions state leaders made at the beginning of the war. The *Tribune* noted that the war began with the "state organiz[ing] for the purpose of keeping the Negroes from uprising while the war was progressing." This charge contradicted the *Atlanta Constitution*'s April report that Governor Atkinson wanted to keep the militia in Georgia to deter an invasion. According to the *Tribune*, "We assured them [white authorities] then that the colored man was law abiding and had the interest of his country at heart as much as any class of people." Given black people's patriotic commitment, the *Tribune* could not comprehend the decision to keep the Georgia Volunteers in the state. The plan "was useless."[70]

Allen Candler: Reorganizing the Georgia Militia

The end of the war with Spain did not result in great celebration among militiamen of any color. The year ended with a new governor, Allen Daniel Candler, a man scholars have assessed as "bland." Candler's tenure has also been described as a failure. His reign as Georgia's first citizen was assessed more for what he did not do. Candler's governorship in this context came to be noted for its penny pinching and its gutting of public school funding. Candler continued the tradition of being a tool of Georgia's ruling elite, the Bourbon Triumvirate, as well as of lobbyists who had controlled the state since the early 1870s. Born in north Georgia's mountains, Candler was a Civil War veteran who had risen from private to Colonel in the army of Tennessee. In 1864 a battle around Jonesboro, Georgia, took his eye, and Candler pursued a career in education. He became mayor of Gainesville, Georgia, then a member of Congress, and eventually served in the cabinets of Governors William J. Northen and William Yates Atkinson. His primary achievement as governor of Georgia was giving white supremacy a political foundation by "claim[ing] credit for having masterminded the Democratic white primary" and "eliminating black voters from the Democratic primary" as a champion of legalized Jim Crow segregation. Although classified by some scholars as opposed to reform,[71] Candler initiated a house cleaning of the state's militia companies in the wake of the War of 1898.

The war, Candler contended in October 1899, "almost destroyed" Georgia's militia. War caused widespread "withdrawal from companies and regiments," taking the best from the Georgia Volunteers. Georgia's militiamen departed the state militia to volunteer for service in the U.S. military. Racial violence, especially the lynching of Sam Hose in Coweta County, just southwest of Atlanta, during the spring of 1899, convinced Candler that the nation's founding fathers were wise in writing into the Constitution, "A well regulated militia is essential to the peace and security of the state." The war with Spain left "scarcely an efficient company or regiment in the state" at a moment when troops were needed to maintain order between the races. Specifically, 1899 was "a time when a reliable military was more needed for local protection than ever before in our history." The *Atlanta Constitution* additionally noted that Governor Candler wanted "none but efficient officers and men [to] . . . remain in the militia." The future militiaman had to be "thoroughly drilled and disciplined" to produce "the best militia" any Georgia governor had ever commanded since the Civil War. This combination of global war, domestic racial violence, a gutted militia, and the need for new men to man the militia forced Candler to call for a reorganization of the Georgia Volunteers, which one reporter now characterized as the "national guard."[72]

The Georgia Volunteers were almost destroyed by the leaves of absence white officers and enlisted men took from their militia obligations so that they could individually participate in the war with Spain. Their leaves allowed them to become members of three regiments of U.S. Volunteers organized in Georgia to meet President McKinley's troop requests. The First and Second Regiments were completely officered by white Georgia Volunteers. Twenty-three other white militia officers manned the Third Volunteer Regiment. All three white regiments served in the War of 1898. It was this brain drain from the Georgia militia that disturbed Governor Candler. He sought to address the problem by threatening to terminate the leaves of absence. Candler set December 1, 1898, as the final deadline for former militiamen to return to their posts as Georgia militiamen. The governor attempted to force the volunteer soldiers to leave regular army service and return to the state militia. According to the *Atlanta Constitution*, these white regiments continued to be active duty units in the U.S. military, awaiting assignments, deployment, or mustering out as December approached. Additionally, the *Constitution* reported in a footnote that a "number of officers from the colored troops [had volunteered and] joined the United States army," Floyd Crumbly being one of them. These soldiers' commissions, like those of the white officers, were to be filled by new members of the Georgia Volunteers after December 1, 1898, should they not return to duty as members of the white Georgia Volunteers or the Georgia Volunteers, Colored.[73]

Georgia's problems, according to Coweta County's *Newnan Herald*, went beyond a brain drain of experienced Georgia militia officers. The *Herald* contended that an angry Georgia Legislature had "practically abolished the national guard organization, the militia," at the end of 1898. The spring and summer of 1898 also revealed a new and highly negative assessment of white encampments. The encampments had not created well drilled and disciplined soldiers ready "to perform military evolutions in the field upon the tap of a drum, wherever their services became necessary." Encampments were supposed to produce "an organized army" ready to serve and act. In the end when war came "not a single one of these organized bodies were ordered into action." Individuals went off to war, but not one unit that had attended an encampment was ready for the real war. Yet the *Atlanta Constitution* contended, "Georgia is not the only state which suffered . . . the same disregard," whereby the militia was ignored by state administrations when the call for troops came. The *Constitution* joined Candler in calling for a reorganization of Georgia's National Guard, with the aim of creating "a sure enough military" capable of responding when the need arose. In the meantime the paper acknowledged that each Georgia militia company had "declared they were ready and prepared to go to the front and if they did not have the opportunity to do so it was not their fault."[74]

Acting Adjutant General William G. Obear commanded the Georgia Volunteers in November 1898 during John McIntosh Kell's ongoing illness and Oscar J. Brown's leave of absence to become an officer in the U.S. Volunteers. Obear would be given the task of "reorganizing" the Georgia Volunteers in the absence of its former officer corps. He commenced his task with strict orders from Governor Candler that required unwavering adherence. Not only was he commanded to be rigid in dealing with the absent officers, but his mission of getting "the Georgia militia back on its old footing" in reality transformed the militia through a series of extremely rigorous by-the-book inspections. Candler's and Obear's instructions also included the proviso that the inspections be "strict, but fair to all commands alike, whether composed of white or negro troops." Obear went to work with no budget, because the General Assembly's appropriation committee "virtually cut the military money for two years." The *Constitution* asserted, however, that the absence of legislative funding would "not materially affect the militia or the state." The two-year revocation definitively affected encampments. More important was the prediction that "the soldier boys [would] lose interest in the militia." The absence of white enthusiasm would define the state militia and reorganization as the twentieth century dawned and a new militia came into being.[75]

Candler's reorganization therefore posed significant problems, and the Clark Rifles, in Athens, Georgia, provided proof of the fact. In March 1899, at the beginning of Obear's inspection tour, Clark Rifles members assessed the company. They resolved to "make no effort to retain their place in the Georgia militia." While unit members understood the need for inspection, collectively the membership conceded that disbanding, and not improvement, would be the next step. Clark Rifles also had operated without a significant weapons allocation because those arms "had been taken away from them" and the remaining arms were unusable. Given these problems and the failure to spend money on new uniforms Clark Rifle members concluded that Georgia "seems to care very little whether she has any militia or not." Disbanding became a very attractive option.[76]

Three years later, in 1902, Inspector General William G. Obear would deliver his annual report to Acting Adjutant General Phil G. Byrd. Obear's annual report reiterated that white militiamen's despondency was real. His assertions were based on three years of continuous and rigorous inspections since 1899. The absence of state funding combined with these strict inspections to create a dire situation. Georgia's white militiamen desperately needed encampment training; it was the one activity that could end their despondency. Obear's conclusions about encampments contradicted the assertion that the war with Spain had proved encampments a waste of time and money. According to Obear, the absence of encampment opportunities made for a "disinterested" set of white troops who had lost interest in militia service. Encampment, Obear argued, would restore young men's enthusiasm for enlisting in the Georgia militia. Morale, however, had deteriorated so badly by 1902 that Obear lowered his rigid inspection standards out of a "desire to retain organizations in the service." He hoped within the context of reorganization that government, whether state or federal, would see the light in 1903 and "provide the necessary means for a camp." For Obear the need was "so absolutely necessary for the encouragement as well as for the training of the troops." This alone would raise morale.[77]

Obear: The New Militia, the National Guard

But at the end of 1898, Obear adamantly contended that "all of our efforts should be exerted towards reducing the organizations and making better troops of those left in the service." According to Obear, there was a need "to have a thorough renovation, to put in young and active and enthusiastic men." Within the context of this redefinition of Georgia's military, the nineteenth-century militia had "been allowed to drag along in slipshod style without any show of pride in the command of the state." The Georgia Volunteers as a result stood at the end of the nineteenth century at a crossroads of war and change. The militia was characterized as an aged institution in need of an infusion of youthful enthusiasm. To do that required a new image, which would begin with a name change. The Georgia General Assembly on December 20–21, 1898, chose to create a new militia.

The legislature intended, with the name change, to instill in militiamen a new attitude as it sought to implement Governor Candler's demand for a reorganized militia. Reorganization would be an ongoing project from 1898 well into the first decade of the twentieth century. The obsolescence of the Georgia Volunteers required the discarding, disbanding, and termination of companies with long nineteenth-century histories but who at the start of the new century did not measure up to the standard set by Governor Candler and Adjutant and Inspector General Obear. Serving at the governor's direction, Obear truly believed in the mission in 1899:

The reorganization and reduction of the Georgia Volunteers and Georgia Volunteers, Colored, had become a true necessity. In place of the state military came the National Guard. The new guard had to be younger and smaller yet committed to Georgia. Thus the Georgia State Troops and Georgia State Troops, Colored, became the National Guard of Georgia, a new military organization for the state.[78]

Obear began the initial five-month inspection and reorganization tour in Atlanta on March 1, 1899. He inspected twelve companies, including three African American units that Obear intended to review fairly but rigidly. By the end of March Obear was in Columbus, Georgia, a community whose militia units were traditionally attached to regiments and battalions operating out of Atlanta. He "disbanded every company in Columbus," both white and black. Columbus militiamen, similar to their counterparts across Georgia, suffered from an absence of enthusiasm for all things military. According to the *Atlanta Constitution*, the community had been the home to "two fine companies," an African American unit and a white machine gun platoon. The spring of 1899 brought no celebration of militia enlistment in Columbus. Just the opposite occurred: As enlistment terms ended, so, too, did any commitment to renew militia membership. Given the low morale, militia service in Columbus was effectively dead. It had been dying for a while in a sterile environment devoid of militia meetings, an injury capped by officers' resignations "some time ago."[79]

Defining the Militia in White and Black

In the midst of this change in the character of the state militia and of Governor Candler's response to racial violence, the *Savannah Tribune* at the end of March offered its definition of the militia to counter white violence. Following the lynching of Sam Hose in Palmetto, Georgia, in Coweta County, Coweta whites petitioned the Military Advisory Board and the governor for permission to organize a militia company. According to the *Tribune*, the reason Coweta whites sought this company "seem[ed] to be to 'keep the Negroes down,'" even to the point where whites needed "to shoot down colored men," believing that doing so would end assaults on white women. If Georgia permitted such an organization within the state's military, the paper contended, it would be an open invitation for "lynchers to ply their vocation." The paper, nevertheless, offered a counter definition: a "military company . . . organized for the protection of all classes and not to keep any one class down." With this definition the

Tribune added its voice to several other black voices in the 1890s that declared black Georgians citizens of the state who were deserving of all the rights and privileges of that citizenship, including equal representation within the militia. African American militiamen had protected Georgia's citizens regardless of color and did not segregate their devotion to duty and service to one isolated group.[80]

Three weeks later, Savannah's black militiamen endeavored to make that definition a partial reality. During the week of April 15, 1899, the *Savannah Tribune* reported Obear's inspection of the First Battalion. According to the newspaper, Obear conducted "an exhaustive examination under the new regulations." His evaluation "of the condition and drills of the [black] companies was the most rigid ever held in the state." The African American companies, the *Tribune* noted, met the challenge with a "heroic effort" and "hoped they may have made the proper record and average."[81]

Obear's assessment had its impact in Savannah and Macon. Reorganizations were ordered for Macon's Union Lincoln Guards and Savannah's Forest City Light Infantry and Georgia Artillery, three of the longest-serving black militia units. Consolidation into one company was also recommended for the Union Lincoln Guards and Forest City Light Infantry. All three companies unfortunately could not complete the process of reorganization and consolidation in time for the First Battalion's annual May Parade. Only three companies of the former eight-company battalion marched in the May event. Black militiamen viewed this public performance as a vital moment in their existence. The significance of the occasion became evident with "General Order No. 5," which called for the black companies to come to the parade "fully uniformed, armed, and equipped (with leggings)." The units also had to muster at "full enlistment strength"; the assembly was urgent, as it was the first public gathering of the battalion following Inspector General Obear's rigid inspection. In the end, however, the battalion had operated with three fewer companies since the parade in 1898. Two of the three companies ceased to exist as a result of Obear's pre-May inspection: The Lone Star Cadets and the Savannah Hussars, the cavalry company, were ordered to disband in the spring of 1899.[82]

Just after mid-September 1899, Obear submitted additional disbanding recommendations. He called for disbanding sixteen or seventeen black militia companies and twelve white units. This brought to an end five months of inspections wherein Obear met with, inspected, and made decisions concerning ninety-five militia companies. His report to the newly appointed and empowered Military Advisory Board was pivotal to the continued existence of thirty militia companies. The Advisory Board had not met since 1897, now two years before. Governor Candler recalled the board so that this officers' group would make the final decision on disbanding. Black militiamen did not fare well. At the end of the day only three or four African American companies remained out of the twenty-two designated as state-sponsored militia units authorized by the General Assembly's 1880s reorganization and troop limit. Nearly two decades later these units would survive the latest reorganization that created the new black militia: the Georgia State Troops, Colored.[83]

The Advisory Board disbanded sixteen or seventeen black companies based on Obear's unsatisfactory inspections and Governor Candler's directives for reorganizing and creating the Georgia State Troops, Colored. According to the *Atlanta Constitution*, the assessment was not unfair. The state wanted to keep black militia companies in the Georgia State Troops, but the primary reason for Obear's negative evaluation was that "the vast majority of them [were] incompetent on drill and woefully lacking in discipline." Such critical criteria so overwhelmingly defined African American militia companies during the spring to fall inspection tour that even well-liked black militia officers could not persuade the Military Advisory Board to make an exception to what amounted to wholesale disbanding of the Georgia State Troops, Colored. Black officers from Savannah and Atlanta attended the Advisory Board meeting to promote their units as functional and viable. Colonel John H. Deveaux appealed for the continued existence of their commands, joined by Captains W. J. Pickney, L. A. Washington, J. C. Simmons, and Lieutenant P. Y. Giles as the Savannah petitioners. Deveaux also represented the sole cavalry unit, the Savannah Hussars. Political activist and long-time militia company leader Jackson McHenry made the case for Atlanta, yet, despite McHenry's pleadings, the board disbanded his company during the afternoon session. The Advisory Board's actions reflected their adamant commitment to militia reorganization. And so the board went about the process of disbanding underperforming companies, including the Hussars. McHenry "left the capitol disconsolate."[84]

7

THE NEW ERA, 1899–1905

The new Military Advisory Board's work was done by September 1899. Its completion heralded a "new era" for the Georgia militia, which "from this time on . . . [would] be made an honor to the state." Those creating the new militia—Governor Candler, the legislature, Inspector General W. G. Obear, and the Advisory Board—were actively engaged in a moment of transformation. They discarded the nineteenth-century militia for the new century's reorganized state militia, which the local press called the National Guard. From late 1898 to the end of the summer of 1899, however, the *Atlanta Constitution* credited Governor Allen D. Candler for "laboring to raise the standard of the militia." In the *Constitution*'s estimation, Candler had achieved his goal and exceeded it, because he had created a new state militia.[1]

Creating the new militia placed more pressure on black militiamen to perform as close to perfection as they could get. Black militiamen pressed by inspection after inspection sometimes found their units and race championed by white supporters, yet white opponents directly involved in constructing the new-era militia questioned whether African American militiamen were needed in the new militia. The end of the nineteenth century and dawning of the twentieth framed the reorganization for black militiamen as a question of whether to preserve the old or make something new. Whites meanwhile struggled to stabilize and define the new militia. Would the new militia belong to Georgia or to the United States of America?

Savannah's Blacks Resist Segregation One Last Time

Black people in Savannah began September 1899 with reasons to celebrate as well as to despair. The *Savannah Tribune*'s front page on September 16, 1899, noted the U.S. War Department's creation of two volunteer black regiments: the Forty-Eighth and Forty-Ninth, respectively organized in Fort Thomas, Kentucky, and Jefferson Barracks, in St. Louis, Missouri. These regiments would be led by white regular field officers, but company-level line officers were to be "colored men who served in the War with Spain in either regular or volunteers" organizations. Volunteer Captain Floyd H. Crumbly, former lieutenant colonel in the Georgia Volunteers, Colored, was one of the black line officers in the Forty-Ninth Regiment. He led the regiment's recruiting effort in Brunswick, Georgia, along with Lieutenant Pritchard, a regular army officer serving with the all-black Ninth Cavalry. Given the opportunity for black military service in the Philippines, the newspaper anticipated African American volunteers rallying to the call of the army commander leading the force in the Philippines and of President William McKinley. Both regiments mustered 1,350 officers and men per unit, with each organized around twelve companies containing 109 men per company and 3 battalions.[2]

In the same September 1899 edition the *Tribune*'s editor, militiaman Solomon C. Johnson, Blair L. M. Kelley asserts, "demanded a boycott" to contest new attempts to segregate Savannah's streetcars. The Savannah Electric Company and several suburban communities serviced by the company's transit lines sought to make segregated streetcars legal. Johnson in response reminded Savannah's blacks that they had successfully defeated segregated public transportation twenty-seven years earlier with a boycott. He urged blacks to do it again at the end of the nineteenth century. Using the *Tribune* to strike a blow against streetcar segregation, as Deveaux had done nearly thirty years before, Johnson argued that blacks provided a third of the streetcar company's ridership. Blacks rallied in 1899. They organized and successfully boycotted segregated public transit, forcing an end to segregated streetcars by the beginning of 1900. Black people also challenged whites who wished to deny public education to more than three thousand black students. As a result, black people's celebration of the creation of the Forty-Eighth and Forty-Ninth Regiments and of their successful challenge to segregated public transportation was undermined by Jim Crow's ongoing erosion of black rights at the end of the nineteenth century.[3]

It is within the context of reemergent streetcar segregation, public education problems, and the federal creation of two black Volunteer Regiments that Savannah blacks confronted Georgia's decision to disband sixteen black militia companies. The *Tribune* acknowledged that these companies had not been the only units marked for disbanding. There were also twelve white units disbanded for similar reasons, chief among them "deficiency." Macon's Lincoln Guards, nevertheless, survived the disbanding, joining the Colquitt Blues, the Savannah Light Infantry, and the Chatham Light Infantry as the surviving black infantry companies. The Georgia Artillery was retained while the Forest Light Infantry and Union Lincoln Guards were consolidated into one company. According to the *Tribune*'s count, Savannah continued supporting five infantry companies, including one Macon unit and the Georgia Artillery. The disbanded African American companies included the well-regarded Augusta companies, whose record did not preclude these units from being "honorably discharged from the service."

The companies surviving the new era had done well during the spring inspections. They also maintained their traditional activities. The Chatham Light Infantry's picnic for Macon's Lincoln Guards and the Savannah Light Infantry's breakfast and picnic for South Carolina's Capital City Guards continued traditions long established by the units. These events culminated with the Savannah Light Infantry's seventeenth anniversary. By November, however, black Georgians had to mobilize again to challenge streetcar segregation, for the second time in nearly thirty years, and disfranchisement. Former Third Georgia Volunteer Infantry officer and now state representative Thomas W. Hardwick, representing rural Georgia, proposed to disfranchise African Americans. Hardwick's proposal provided one additional sign that the status of black people was deteriorating.[4]

As 1899 came to an end, black Georgians also found that some things affirmed their citizenship. In November Governor Candler approved Company A as a new unit in Savannah's First Battalion. Colonel Deveaux, too, "enlisted a large number of men for the new company" and the Georgia Artillery. W. J. Pickney was elected to command the new company, while J. C. Simmons continued leading the Georgia Artillery. Two weeks later, Deveaux led seventy-two officers and men serving in four companies—the Savannah Light Infantry (25), the Chatham Light Infantry (24), the Colquitt Blues (18), and the Georgia Artillery(5)—to Brunswick, Georgia, for "Negro Day at the Fair," where the units paraded and marched. Their arrival drew at least two ovations from the "great crowd" that followed them from the depot to the fairgrounds, where they received their second ovation. The program organizers made the units feel welcome by catering to their comfort. This event capped the previous week's event, the defeat of Representative Hardwick's disfranchisement proposal. Colonel

John Deveaux and other African American leaders across the state led the resistance. The nineteenth century closed with Deveaux's First Battalion planning another Emancipation Day combined with additional victories over streetcar segregation and disfranchisement.[5]

The Twentieth Century's First Emancipation Day

Emancipation Day in 1900 was the military's day despite additional participation by local civic groups and the Emancipation Association's planning under the leadership of former militia officer Captain L. M. Pleasant. The *Savannah Tribune* devoted considerable attention in its January 6, 1900, edition to "the grandest celebration of Emancipation Day." While the weather forced the program's literary presentations indoors at Second Baptist Church, the First Battalion's companies "turned out strongly." The four-company infantry battalion marched with the Georgia Artillery, which fired a salute. Grand Army of the Republic's Robert G. Shaw Post Number Six marched in the parade with the Georgia State Industrial College for Colored Youth's College Cadets, instructors, and president, R. R. Wright. Georgia State Industrial College was located in a Savannah suburb that had endorsed segregated streetcars in 1899. Emancipation Day in 1900 had a significant meaning for the college's students, faculty, and staff, because black people had successfully ended the threat of segregation.

These groups followed immaculately dressed black militiamen, which the *Tribune* reported as "neat": "The arms were bright, and the marching of the men excellent." Chatham Light Infantrymen had the most participants and the new company A earned "favorable comment" at its first public appearance. The newspaper's praise in 1900 resembled its accolades from the 1870s that elevated the units to equal standing with the state's best white militia companies. Specifically, the First Battalion in 1900 demonstrated a "strength and efficiency" that made it "rank with any [unit] in the state." Its professionalism spoke "well for its officers," especially Colonel John H. Deveaux, who led officers of which "any commander [could] well afford to feel proud."[6]

Captain J. J. Durham, D.D., a chaplin and a new First Battalion officer and major boycott leader, delivered the day's major oration. According to the *Tribune*, Durham's presence and speech held symbolic importance. His appearance and bearing made him "every inch of which he looked," as he stood before the Second Baptist Church audience celebrating the occasion "in the uniform of the soldier." Chaplin Durham "thundered forth facts that were emphatic and worth the telling" about black citizenship. Arguing that policymakers needed to accept black citizenship and the permanence that went with it, Durham asserted that African Americans were "a great potent and increasing factor in all the social, industrial, economical, and political institutions of this country." To discount black citizenship, Durham warned, constituted a costly local, state, and national mistake. The nation paid in "blood and treasure" every time white people viewed black people as "something less than a citizen." Durham's advice to his black audience was to be productive, industrial, intelligent, and useful to their local communities, to the state, and to the nation. Exercising these recommended and individualized traits made a good citizen any person who sought "by all honorable and manly means to live on terms of peace and good will with their white neighbors." They also were the keys to "the future of this country" so that all would be well between the races.[7]

Georgia State Troops: The New-Era Militia versus the Georgia Volunteers

The Georgia State Troops came into existence on February 1, 1900, marking the "open[ing] up of a new era in the life of the military service of Georgia." Governor Candler had implemented what the *Atlanta Constitution* claimed was "the first reorganization [of the Georgia militia] in its history," ignoring the reorganizing ordered by the state legislature in the late 1870s, several times in the 1880s, and most recently in the early and mid-1890s. In 1900 Governor Candler claimed he had insisted on the state military's reorganization "to put the militia on a footing where it [could] respond to a call at a moment's notice." According to this explanation, two years after declaring the militia broken, Candler re-created the militia "in the hope of perfecting the organization." Candler wanted a reliable military that "he could depend [on] at any time." In that context, Governor Candler, with the cooperation of the Georgia Legislature and a set of militia colonels leading five of the state's white regiments, redefined the militia. Specifically, reorganization ended life-time officer's commissions. The late nineteenth-century policy had given officers almost uninterrupted longevity as militia leaders, but Thomas W. Hardwick's military bill, in 1899, ended all late nineteenth-century commissions on February 1, 1900. The bill also called for the election of new officers for all National Guard companies the same day. The newly elected officers at the dawn of the twentieth century served three-year enlistments. With these changes

Georgia's nineteenth-century military, the Georgia Volunteers, "cease[d] to be that only in name," suggesting that the nineteenth-century militia had not been the kind of military institution Candler, the Military Advisory Board, the adjutant general, the inspector general, and the Georgia General Assembly had hoped to construct for the new century. Georgia's leadership began the new millennium arguing that they had created a militia that embraced a level of professionalism able to meet the challenges of the new century. Georgia's new militia had become ready to respond to any emergency.[8]

The new militia's mission and responsibilities involved white militiamen in fifty-nine companies organized under five regiments. These units now covered "every portion of Georgia." This was a change from the previous militia system, in which not all regions were represented on the Military Advisory Board and in which disparities had existed in how the militia mobilized to protect communities in distress. According to the *Atlanta Constitution*, the nineteenth-century militia had unevenly served Georgia's rural and small-town communities, while Governor Candler's twentieth-century militia resolved these regional inadequacies. Equitable militia distribution that met state needs was important, particularly in light of the mob violence and lynchings that continued in the new century. Rural violence required positioning white militia units so that Georgia communities were within "easy access of at least one command."[9]

Candler's reorganization also expanded state allocations to include all militiamen. For the first time state financial support would be allocated for companies renting an armory. Before the 1899 reorganization, nineteenth-century Georgia militia companies and their members had to meet the costs of renting local facilities themselves. Each company purchased, rented, and funded their own armory without state financial support. The twentieth century opened with Georgia's state government taking over responsibility for contracting armory rentals. This policy change was one of several legislative actions aimed at raising state militiamen's morale. Georgia's government also sought to take advantage of federal military reorganization, done in the wake of the Spanish-American War, which continued into the first decade of the twentieth century. Federal officials reorganized the U.S. military as they evaluated the military's performance during the war. Among the policies federal officials hoped to implement was standardized militia training that would be more in line with that of the regular military. Standardization encouraged some officials to more closely incorporate the militia within the national defense system, a thirty-year goal of the National Guard Association (NGA). Georgia also wanted its reorganized militia to be part of the National Guard Association's campaign to integrate the militia into the nation's military and join the National Guard. The new-era militia submitted to federal authority in exchange for more resources, standardized training regulations, and incorporation within a nationalized military structure.[10]

Federal Reorganization

As a result of National Guard lobbying and postwar federal military reorganization, federal allocations to state militias came close to tripling after the war. Georgia's share went from just over $11,000 annually to nearly $30,000. Additionally, Georgia officials may have hoped to improve militia morale and recruitment by increasing the per diem and buying new uniforms. Savannah's main white newspaper acknowledged as much. According to the *Morning News*, the fact that militiamen had to pay for their own uniforms and armory rent kept "a young man from joining" the militia. In the same article, Inspector General Obear noted, "The state should aid [in paying for] everything absolutely necessary" for efficient militia operation. The challenges of insurrection, mob suppression, and state law enforcement demanded a state militia that could mobilize at a moment's notice, which was the governor's new militia standard. Atlanta's primary newspaper and militia organ reinforced the idea. New resources were equally important. In 1900 state resources paid for armory rent and per-diem costs for the first time. Federal money ($27,000 in 1900) went to pay for new uniforms costing an estimated $25,000. Each allocation enabled the "state [to expect] more from the militia than it ever did in the past," as these new measures removed the unnamed issues that had made the nineteenth-century Georgia militia less reliable.[11]

Georgia State Troops, Colored, and Reorganization: A Look Backward and Forward

State reorganization in 1900 had a negative impact on Savannah's First Battalion, Georgia State Troops, Colored. The Hardwick bill restructured Georgia's military organization, transforming the nineteenth-century militia into the new era's twentieth-century militia. The First Battalion's nineteenth-century leadership had included a lieutenant colonel and a major. Under the Hardwick legislation, the highest-ranking battalion commander would be a major. Savannah's black battalion now served as the central organizing unit for Georgia's black militia companies. To address the leadership changes, Savannah's black militiamen attended the First Battalion's board of officers meeting, bringing together "the largest ever" assembly of African American militia members. They met with the understanding that the new militia standards overturned the battalion's leadership structure and thereby forced the membership to make decisions about who would lead the unit and its affiliated companies.[12]

As a result, Lieutenant Colonel John H. Deveaux, the late nineteenth-century black militia leader serving with a lifetime commission and solid credentials as an effective militia leader, could no longer lead the First Battalion. Battalion "sentiment," nevertheless, urged that Deveaux be retained as the unit's leader, thereby challenging the Hardwick reorganization standards, set for implementation on February 1, 1900. This meant that the late nineteenth century's battalion major, William H. Royal, was forced to decide whether he wanted to remain the unit's principal leader, given that Deveaux was heavily entrenched as a Republican Party leader, patronage recipient, and officeholder. Deveaux's political responsibilities extended to state and federal offices in Brunswick and Savannah, respectively. Deveaux also continued leading Georgia's black Masonic order. Royal had effectively led the First Battalion in Deveaux's absence as Deveaux met his political obligations, a circumstance that took the *Savannah Tribune*'s owner away from the militia and provided Royal with increased opportunities to lead the battalion.

Despite having served as de facto battalion leader, Royal resigned his commission, deferring to Deveaux, the battalion's official leader since 1881. On February 1, 1900, black militiamen did not seek new leadership in the context of statewide militia reorganization. They looked back in time, honoring Deveaux's longevity while replacing only those officers who departed the black militia battalion of their own volition. In this way the Georgia State Troops, Colored, held on to the past, while the Georgia State Troops started a new century with a different focus.[13]

Black militiamen did not hold on to every part of the past. At the end of 1900 Deveaux journeyed to Atlanta to consult with Governor Candler, Acting Adjutant General Byrd, and Inspector General Obear. He presented them with a legislative proposal to end disparities between black and white militia officers. Deveaux sought not only to redress his loss of rank owing to the Hardwick reorganization legislation but also to get state recognition for retiring black officers. White officers at the moment of retirement automatically had their names placed on "the retired roll." This was a privilege and honor for long-term militia service that was denied African American officers. Deveaux noted that honorably discharged and retiring black officers were "not placed on the retired roll" despite respected service records. Major Deveaux went to Atlanta carrying the consent of "all of colored military men of the state" who voted to restore his rank because they "want[ed] it to be as heretofore." Based on these contentions he presented Georgia's militia leadership with a bill to remedy the retirement issue, which "they heartily approved." A year would pass, however, before the General Assembly voted to make Deveaux a lieutenant colonel for life.[14]

Black junior officers with commissions dating back to the early to mid-1890s also continued to lead their companies. The Chatham Light Infantry captain, Nelson Law (1896), the Savannah Light Infantry captain, Henry N. Walton (1890), and the Lincoln Guards captain, John "Sandy" Lockhart (1891), were each re-elected for three-year terms commencing February 1, 1900. Under the new Hardwick legislation all officers on February 1, 1900, stood for election and served only three years before having to stand for re-election. Newly elected officers also went before a board of examiners, who administered a written examination to determine the officer's fitness to lead. Those who failed to receive grades above "the percentage required in the examination" left the militia. Black second lieutenant-candidate P. L. Bowers, for example, did not pass. The Military Advisory Board, Governor Candler, and Inspector General Obear "inspected and ushered into the state service" one new black company on February 27, 1900: Atlanta's Fulton Guards. This unit reported to Major John H. Deveaux, who commanded the First Battalion. Additionally, the *Savannah Tribune* reported, "It is the purpose of the state to furnish each company with forty uniforms."[15] The Georgia State Troops, Colored, held on to its highly successful nineteenth-century leadership, challenged and changed retirement list discrimination, secured a new company, and restored Deveaux's lifetime colonelcy. Black militiamen benefited from the new-era reorganization.

In May 1900 Savannah's First Battalion marched in the annual May parade. They proceeded through Savannah's streets led by Captain Henry N. Walton in the absence of Major Deveaux. Despite his absence from this perennial parade, Deveaux had again reorganized the battalion directed by a capable set of officers who molded the unit into a "first class condition in every respect." The First Battalion's companies paraded at full strength, moving with the precision attained only through "much practice." The

Savannah Tribune claimed that the First Battalion "made an appearance that would have done credit to the [United States Army] regulars." Such a positive showing could be attributed to each company's receipt of the first month's armory rent and forty new uniforms. The Georgia State Troops, Colored, had improved in two ways. First, they had made the First Battalion a "first class" organization. Second, white leaders had indicated that parity with white militiamen might be possible, since the state paid for uniforms and armory rent for the entire militia.[16]

The First Battalion's twentieth anniversary added to the impression that the Georgia State Troops, Colored, were approaching parity. They received positive reviews from state authorities. The anniversary parade, inspection, and evaluation in August 1900 could have revived memories of the militia companies of the 1870s, especially the prize drill contest in 1878. In 1878 local white officials, the governor, and militia leaders reviewed the troops and assessed their military skills. These white officials and militiamen made public statements commending black militiamen. In mid-August 1900 Inspector General William G. Obear attended the anniversary event and inspected the entire battalion. His visit contrasted markedly with the Georgia Artillery encampment four years earlier, when no state or militia official came to review the black artillerymen's encampment. The First Battalion's summer activities had generated distinctly positive accolades from black and white observers. They earned the compliments even as the August heat left militiamen prostrate and exhausted. The comments suggested that black militiamen had a positive future despite the recent disbanding.[17]

The *Atlanta Constitution* spelled it out with a headline: the First Battalion's eight black companies "Made A Good Showing." Atlanta's Fulton Guards and seven Savannah companies paraded in Savannah before four thousand black and white excursionists. The sheer size of the crowd overwhelmed local hotels and surprised city officials, and the anniversary proved significant, because the "colored troops made a splendid showing." Inspector General William G. Obear reinforced the *Constitution*'s compliment with his own glowing assessment. According to Obear, the First Battalion's companies "were a credit to themselves and to the state." Further, the battalion had exhibited "great improvement . . . since the reorganization" in 1899.[18]

While Atlanta's press summarized the events surrounding the First Battalion's anniversary, the *Savannah Tribune* endeavored to present a more detailed report, including placing the anniversary in its proper historical context. Twenty years before, black men had petitioned for permission to form a battalion with eight local companies. Atlanta and Augusta also organized separate battalions at about the same time. Over the years the Savannah battalion had lost two units. In 1899 the six-company command lost two more companies, owing to their "ordered disbanding," which also included the "complete disbanding" of two other black battalions, based in Atlanta and Augusta. State-ordered disbanding left only one African American company in Macon and the surviving Savannah units. The black companies in Atlanta, Augusta, Columbus, and Rome were ordered to disband. State militia reorganization placed Macon's lone African American unit and a newly created black Atlanta company (the Fulton Guards) in the First Battalion, reestablishing an eight-company battalion in 1900. The First Battalion's twentieth anniversary celebration was the first opportunity for African American militiamen to present the reorganized battalion to the public.[19]

Members of the newly re-created First Battalion planned an anniversary intended to be "a complete celebration of the day." Their activities went from morning to late at night and were capped by a ball. Inspector General Obear's presence added another layer to the day, even though "Col. Deveaux" knew by the Sunday before the anniversary that Obear would inspect the unit as they marched on their anniversary date. The day of the anniversary celebration, spectators thronged the line of march to the park extension and made favorable comments "about the excellent showing by the battalion." Black militiamen's assessments were harsher; they concluded that their performance "did not come up to that standard" owing to the August heat. Despite heat prostration while marching in review, their inspection by Obear came off favorably.[20]

The crowning moment came when Obear sent a copy of his recorded observations to Deveaux. The *Tribune* included Obear's inspection comments in the anniversary article. According to Obear, Deveaux had mastered a very important element in militia leadership: generating enthusiasm. The First Battalion's members "demonstrated an active interest in their military work." This was evident in several ways: first, their overall performance despite the oppressive heat; second, the fact that "all commands were in line including those from a distance [Atlanta and Macon] who came at their own expense to make the occasion a success"; third, their "hearty support for their commander," Deveaux. Equally vital was the noticeable improvement in the First Battalion's performance. Specifically, the "improvement over last year was very marked and shows that you have taken hold in earnest to make a first class organization of your battalion." Obear hoped "the rate of improvement [would] continue in the future as it ha[d] in the past."[21]

The First Battalion grew by one more fifty-man company, Augusta's Maceo Guard, who joined the battalion in mid-November. Named after the late black Cuban Revolutionary leader, Antonio Maceo, this company became part of a battalion now able to brag that it was "in apple pie order." Additionally, arms and equipment, records, and drill routines and discipline met the state's highest standards. Every company was reported as having achieved a "first-class condition." Savannah's Company "A" also celebrated its first anniversary at the end of November with full ranks of more than eighty men.

Clearly, Deveaux and the battalion's officers had improved the companies' performance, with "good results." The Georgia Legislature "allowed the colored citizens" eight black infantry companies and one artillery company, with five based in Savannah and one each in Atlanta, Augusta, and Macon. According to the *Savannah Tribune*, the expansion to eight companies equaled most of the state's battalion-size units, perhaps giving African American militiamen parity with their white counterparts. Such thinking was especially important given that neighboring South Carolina disbanded Columbia's Capital City Guards owing to a dispute between the African American militia company and white men, who twice drove through the company during a parade. This disbanding in neighboring South Carolina, a renewed black disfranchisement proposal by white militiaman Thomas W. Hardwick, and antiblack lynching violence undermined the positive accolades that defined the First Battalion as a first-class operation.[22]

"A Growing Hostility"

Adding to this concern was the adjutant general's report for January 1, 1899, to October 17, 1900. Adjutant General James G. Roberson's report, Frances Smith has noted, capped "a growing hostility toward Georgia's black militia." This was increasingly evident within the militia's leadership. Roberson favored "disbanding the negro troops" for at least two major reasons. First, he questioned whether black militiamen could "be of any service," especially "from a military standpoint." Specifically should black militiamen be "called into service for quelling riots?" He concluded that they could not be utilized, even if it was "not their fault," yet "this [disqualifying] condition exists." In Roberson's estimation only white troops were trustworthy and capable of putting down lynch mobs, even if the rioters were white. Blacks, the argument went, would not control or arrest black lawbreakers. Given such circumstances, Roberson contended that black militiamen could not be asked to preserve order.

Second, in light of the new spending priorities on equipment and armory rentals mandated by Candler's militia reorganization, Roberson considered African American militiamen a drain on the state's financial resources. Roberson's report initiated a questioning of the status, place, reliability, and continuation of the black militia as a state-funded institution. He recommended "that the General Assembly be asked to pass a law disbanding the Georgia State Troops, colored." In July 1900 Obear added a critical note. He challenged the black militia's fitness when he questioned the battalion adjutant's (probably the *Tribune*'s Solomon C. Johnson) ability to correctly complete militia records, a strange criticism given Johnson's employment and career. That said, Johnson had led the streetcar boycott. Was Obear's criticism aimed at Johnson's highly public political activism?[23]

High and Low Profiles

Nevertheless, Deveaux and the First Battalion's officers successfully spent most of 1900 addressing the nineteenth-century problems of the Georgia Volunteers, Colored, so that the Georgia State Troops, Colored, might earn a respected place within the Georgia State Troops, and Johnson had been part of that reorganization. In 1900, comments concerning the black militia's improvement outweighed the threat of disbandment, because the First Battalion was growing not shrinking. According to Inspector General Obear's estimation, the black companies had significantly improved their performance and the battalion's reputation. Other state officials, however, questioned the capabilities and existence of every black militiaman. Race, not performance, was at the base of this questioning of black worthiness to serve in the new-era militia.

Black and white militiamen took both parallel and diverging paths in 1901. The First Battalion's companies celebrated their respective anniversaries throughout the year. These units also initiated various fundraising and social activities that included picnics, fairs, bazaars, and balls. Each event kept the units in the public eye. Their public presence justified their continued existence and contributions to their local communities. The Chatham Light Infantry, in January and April 1901, respectively, conducted a successful bazaar and commemorated its twenty-ninth anniversary. Savannah's companies also marched in February and May, commemorating Abraham Lincoln's birthday, for which "all our companies paraded," and the annual May parade, in which only four companies participated. The First Battalion's twenty-first anniversary, in August, only mobilized the hosting Savannah companies, the Chatham Light Infantry and the Savannah Light Infantry, and drew solitary guest units from Augusta and Macon. There was no mention of Atlanta's Fulton Guards. Savannah's streetcar company also failed to provide the promised vehicles needed to transport the large crowds to anniversary venues. Despite these problems, the anniversary was "Grandly Celebrated" and the First Battalion still had a future.[24]

The spring of 1901 brought the second presidential inauguration of William McKinley. Thirty Georgia Artillery members with two of the company's cannons marched in the inaugural parade. According to the *Savannah Tribune*, the military outnumbered the civilian inaugural participants 3 to 1. The Georgia Artillery, led by its long serving leader, Captain John C. Simmons, "performed admirably." Marching in the parade's third division the Georgia Artillery was notably sandwiched between northern military units, specifically, the New Jersey National Guard's infantry and artillery and Connecticut's governor, marching with his militia staff. Additionally, Congress was "overwhelmingly Republican from top to bottom" and the president and vice president were "stalwart Republican[s]." Yet only one other Georgian, Atlanta's Republican League leader, J. F. Hanson, marched beside the Georgia Artillery, as Georgia Republicans assumed a low profile.[25]

Military Advisory Board: Debating Disbanding

Immediately following the inauguration parade, a newly appointed Military Advisory Board prepared for its first meeting. The *Atlanta Constitution* claimed that "there were no matters of importance to be considered"; the Advisory Board needed to convene simply to comply with its legal obligations to advise the governor about the militia. The newspaper also noted that the advisory board would "probably be called upon to take formal action" concerning white units, such as admitting four new white companies into the First Infantry Regiment and formalizing the transformation of Savannah's Volunteer Guards from an infantry unit into a heavy artillery battalion.[26]

Rumor also defined the Advisory Board's projected agenda. The *Constitution* wrote, "It was reported around the capitol yesterday that the advisory board would probably also discuss the subject of the negro military companies of the state." Assistant Adjutant General Phil G. Byrd asked for the discussion and called for disbanding the Georgia State Troops, Colored. Byrd was not alone; "many of the state officers of militia would welcome" discussion. Georgia State Troops' officer corps had "various reasons" for disbanding the black militia companies. The proposal sparked statewide debate within the militia hierarchy. Macon's officers had debated the issue "the other day" and decided to support disbandment. The *Constitution*, however, presented only two reasons for disbanding: money and duplication of ranks. One state official pointed to Savannah as the primary example of how duplication harmed the militia. Savannah, a community of "twelve or thirteen companies of white troops," had "more than enough" militia companies. The white units alone were prepared to handle any disturbance. Savannah's five black companies cost the state $62.50 per month in armory rent. Statewide "the total amount paid" African American companies for armory rent was "$100 per month." These costs, measured against the fact that "negro troops . . . [were] considered of little value for duty" because "they are never called upon" to quell disturbances, justified the call for disbandment. There were also a number of potential white companies that could be admitted into service "where . . . needed." But the *Constitution* did not know "whether or not the advisory board [would] take this matter up," declaring, "It remains to be seen."[27]

Candler's Reorganization and Its Costs

Yet the Advisory Board had not yet made the final decision. The militia's uncertainty was reinforced by Governor Candler's continuing reorganization efforts and the state's financial problems. The *Constitution* declared, "Governor Candler is inclined to do everything in his power for the military of the state, but his means are necessarily somewhat limited." The limitations were financial. Obear in late March informed the governor that the execution of one Military Advisory Board recommendation—to supply the state militia with overcoats and blankets—meant spending $76,000. This was "impossible for the governor," yet Candler wanted to give each regiment one hundred overcoats and blankets, limit gun distribution to sixty, and see "the military laws of the state put in proper shape." Each initiative would cost the state resources. By October 1901 the General Assembly was grappling with "a deficiency of about $157,000." Candler recommended, as he did in 1900, a $500,000 reduction in the school fund, hoping to limit this expenditure to a $1 million allocation. It was in this context of state financial concerns that Candler's power and desires for militia reorganization were limited. His objective, nevertheless, was to continue reorganizing the Georgia State Troops by funding such initiatives as supplying overcoats, blankets, and guns and by overhauling the militia code. Candler went ahead with reorganization.[28]

National Guard Association's Vision and National Reorganization

In 1901 state officials seemed to forget about the First Battalion's previous year's achievements. Complimented in 1900 by the inspector general, the First Battalion had met militia standards. Adjutant General Roberson's recommendation to disband all the black militia companies nevertheless gained traction in 1901, when Assistant Adjutant General Byrd and the *Atlanta Constitution* made more public the debate questioning the value black militiamen delivered to the state. Justifying disbandment with financial concerns placed Georgia in line with other states that had similarly cited economic problems as the reason for dismantling their African American militia companies in the late nineteenth century. What ultimately happened reflected the state's increasing commitment to training and equipping the militia and expanding its importance within the national military. The initiative to incorporate the militia within the national military actually began in 1879, when some states (but not Georgia) founded the NGA. The NGA lobbied state and federal governments for more militia funding while promoting the idea that state militias were a significant part of the nation's defense network. This involved redefining the militia from a force for resolving local and state emergencies to "an integral component of the national military force."[29]

Georgia's and other southern states' advocacy of states' rights, especially as they defined who commanded the militia, and the region's commitment to limited government delayed Georgia's committing its militia to a more professionalized organization. The Spanish-American War, the Cuban War of Independence, and the Philippine-American War lay the power and needs of the federal government on the Georgia militia. War in 1898 superseded states' rights, because the president mobilized the nation's military, calling for volunteers to take a leave of absence from the militia for adventure, combat, and service in Cuba, Puerto Rico, and the Philippines.

Federal mobilization for war in 1898, however, had been disorganized. This problem prompted President William McKinley and Secretary of War Elihu Root to reorganize the regular military, opening the way for the National Guard Association to successfully lobby for including state militias in the broader national military reorganization. Georgia's leaders concluded that the war had destroyed the state's military and thereby justified Governor Candler's ongoing reorganization of the militia and its transformation into the twentieth century's Georgia State Troops. The stated purpose of Georgia's reorganization was to create a reliable national guard that met the state's needs in a new century. It also meant that increased federal and state funding empowered Georgia and other state governments to demand more from their militiamen than they had in the nineteenth century. The National Guard Association, representing state militia organizations, encouraged state militiamen to seek regular army training as a significant part of their professionalization. National Guard Association lobbying at the beginning of the twentieth century additionally called for state militias to be incorporated into the nation's military structure. Including the militia within the national military defense system would transform the militia from a mid-nineteenth-century local social club into a twentieth-century federally funded and controlled branch of the U.S. military. The transition entailed the expectation that militiamen would drill, practice, and perform at the same level as the nation's regular military units.

The war had revealed that both state and national military organizations were not ready for the twentieth century. War mobilization problems alerted state and national leaders to the fact that their military organizations were disorganized and unable to meet the challenges posed by the war with Spain, despite victories in the Caribbean and across the Pacific Ocean. The disruptions created the need for standardized training between the regular army, the volunteer units, the immunes, and militiamen, all of which also called for modernizing the nation's military. Meeting this challenge defined early twentieth-century reorganizations of both the state militia and the national military organizations.[30]

National reorganization sparked by the problems that emerged during the Spanish-American War, the Cuban War of Independence, and the Philippine-American War resulted in an increase in state and federal funding for the nation's military. According to Jerry Cooper, Elihu Root and the War Department staff "used federal aid to force compliance [by state militias] with federal [military] regulations." Some states resisted federalization. State militiamen, nevertheless, were becoming National Guardsmen. Some militiamen, however, "clung tenaciously to unit tables of organization that did not conform to Army provisions or were [involved in units] too large for their states to man and fund." Accepting increased federal money at the beginning of the twentieth century gave state militias stability. It also enabled militiamen to fulfill their legally mandated service obligations within their home states. More federal funding also brought new responsibilities outside state boundaries. Militiamen, Cooper noted, "obligated themselves to answer a presidential call subject to court martial, and after 1908, to serve overseas." Federal financial support transformed state militias into military units no longer obligated to state governors only. Militia loyalty and obligation were shifting in the early twentieth century from local and state responsibilities to serving the nation at the behest of the president of the United States.[31] It was this change in the role of the militia that brought about the final chapter of the Georgia State Troops, Colored.

"Stayhereation"

The First Battalion of the Georgia State Troops, Colored, opened 1902 under a new watchword coined by the Emancipation Day orator, Rev. C. L. Bonner, pastor of Savannah's St. Paul Colored Methodist Episcopal Church. Bonner focused his oration on the history and present of African Americans and defined their future as positive. He made this public declaration despite black and white leaders who characterized black status using such negative words as "segregation," "emigration," "expatriation," "colonization," "amalgamation," and "extermination." Each word challenged the place of black people in the United States. While these words came, respectively, from such luminaries as Colored Methodist Episcopal Bishop Lucius Henry Holsey, activist and African Methodist Episcopal Bishop Henry M. Turner, former North Carolina U.S. Senator Marion Butler, Georgia newspaperman and politician John Temple Graves, African American newspaperman and activist T. Thomas Fortune, and South Carolina politician Benjamin Tillman, Bonner countered their collective pessimism by proposing a new word: "stayhereation." This upbeat term meant that black people were here to stay, because African Americans constituted "a separate and distinct race." Bonner declared, "The God that has brought us this far can carry us on."[32] "Stayhereation" revived an argument that the *Tribune* and Deveaux had made in the 1870s, and Bonner endeavored to carry it into the new century: Black people were here, and they were citizens of the nation and the state.

Bonner contended that the past thirty-five years had been characterized by black "prosperity and progress" and that blacks would "surely not relinquish this . . . advancement." But lynching, symbolized by "the dangling rope and sturdy tree," cast a significant shadow over that advancement. At the same time, Bonner declared that "the sun [was] rising" for African Americans because the evidence proved the "advancement and achievements in the past forty years by the Negro here." According to Bonner, a definitive example of black progress was "our own J. H. Deveaux": "[Deveaux] stands so prominent in the state that in the Georgia Legislature, in the presence of Governor Candler, in the face of cheap and narrow Tom Hardwick, a bill passed that broke the record of the state, that conferred a title of 'Colonel' upon this deserving man for life."[33]

Bonner's optimism and the conferral of a lifetime colonelcy upon Deveaux were indicators that stayhereation had some relevancy, especially when it came to shaping the future of the Georgia State Troops, Colored. Inspector General William G. Obear's winter inspection offered further proof that the future was bright for black militiamen. From January 20 to February 8, 1902, and possibly beyond, Obear inspected both black and white militia companies. During these winter days, Obear devoted time enough to inspect every black unit, and only one white unit. According to Obear's report, "Annual Inspection, Colored Battalion," the entire First Battalion had demonstrated "marked improvement since last inspection." All was not perfect, however, and each company received an individualized critique that noted such deficiencies as misplaced property, poor record keeping, overenlistment, too much talking in ranks, and errors in military procedures. Every company lacked ammunition, even though all the battalion's rifles had recently been replaced. Notably, however, Obear observed that the rifles were "very old and badly rust eaten . . . probably totally unserviceable." Obear, nevertheless, paid the battalion a compliment. Despite the fact that their weaponry was unserviceable, black militiamen had made a consistent effort to keep the weapons in a condition that was "very creditable to the men to whom they are entrusted."[34]

Obear also observed that the First Battalion's eight companies had been allocated $1,200 for armory rent, or $150 per unit. In contrast, the eighty-two white companies received $14,208.33, or $173.27 per company, for similar expenses. White units received an additional $5,791.67 for "Riot pay" and other expenses. Divided among the eighty-two white units, this allocation increased their funding by $70.63. The two funding sources gave white companies nearly ninety-four dollars more than the African American companies. Despite this resource disparity, Obear evaluated the First Battalion's eight companies as disciplined across the board. Each unit "was found to be very good." The enlisted "men obey[ed] promptly and cheerfully all orders given them." Obear, nevertheless, criticized one company for having confused drill routines because of talking in the ranks. Overall the inspector general found that "the colored officer as a rule ha[d] learned to wear his authority with the proper dignity" and "in the proper manner" by speaking "only when necessary."[35]

Obear's "Annual Report" to the adjutant general clearly noted that black militia companies at last contained the "Very Best" militiamen. Reflecting the general guiding assumptions surrounding the "reorganization of 1899," African American militiamen in 1902 were a "marked contrast with what existed" before Candler and the Georgia Legislature had changed the Georgia Volunteers into the Georgia State Troops. The early twentieth century's Georgia State Troops, Colored, had in Obear's estimation become "reliable, sober, industrious men." They were men of character because the First Battalion's members were screened and "accepted as recruits." What had changed was the removal of undesirable militiamen. According to Obear, the First Battalion's officers were "on the alert to eliminate such an element from their rolls." Any militiaman not meeting the new criteria did not "long remain in the State Forces." Such concentrated scrutiny had "been done in numerous cases as to enlisted men [and] in one or two as to officers"; any men found lacking were told to leave.[36]

Further, Obear made it clear that the African American militia officers were "educated reliable men." This characterization served as another example that some parts of Candler's reorganization had filtered down to the black units. Candler wanted the new militia to be reliable. Black officers were meeting this standard. More importantly Obear praised the black officers for their demonstrated selectivity. African American officers, despite being nineteenth-century men, carry-overs from the increasingly discredited militia, now "carefully selected" the enlisted personnel. He also noted, "This Department has made its point to exact of the colored troops that none but the best men of their race shall be enrolled as enlisted men or officers." Specifically, the officers had "the respect and confidence of the white people in the cities where they [were] located as well as the colored race." Given that black militiamen were being both monitored by local whites and supervised by state officials, the new selectivity suggested that black militiamen may have been drawn solely from the black elite. Obear suggested that the new black militiaman was selected for his class, familiarity with white people, education, and reliability.[37]

Perhaps unbeknownst to Obear, black militiamen in Augusta's Georgia Infantry in the early 1870s boasted that their members held jobs with white employers. Their behavior reflected the sober and industrious actions of the very best among black Augustans. These African American militiamen made a point of separating themselves from other blacks by class. Further, Savannah's black militiamen in 1878 had endeavored to prove their professionalism and present to such white leaders as Governor Alfred Colquitt clear evidence of their racial progress. They also sought ways to please their white militia counterparts by presenting themselves as military men who had mastered their military training. Having white benefactors and maintaining a polished public persona had been the main goal of many black militiamen in the nineteenth century, especially Savannah's African American companies, which John H. Deveaux and Solomon C. Johnson critiqued in the pages of the *Savannah Tribune*.

Further, elite whites had intervened on behalf of individual black militiamen and on occasion had helped ensure the survival of local African American militia companies. What had been practiced in the nineteenth century as white paternalism was being presented in the early twentieth century as innovative white management of black behavior inside a white institution, ignoring more than two decades of black pride, initiative, professionalism, and responsibility. The militia had been a white institution at its inception. Nineteenth- and early twentieth-century African American militiamen had taken the initiative to make the militia an institution serving black people.

Black militiamen intended to recall and preserve their twenty-year history as state soldiers. They had carved out a history that gave them reason to be proud of their twenty years of learning to be a professional and of taking on the responsibilities of manhood, citizenship, and citizen soldier. Whites at the end of the nineteenth century and start of the twentieth did not take these signs of black progress seriously. The new-era militia erased the black past, a past of service, progress, citizenship, and autonomy. Yet with their achievements and adherence to local etiquette, blacks declared that they had "stayhereation"; they were here to stay.

African Americans: The Enthusiastic Militiamen of 1902

Deveaux entered the twentieth century with nineteenth-century officers who helped him make the First Battalion Georgia State Troops, Colored, a battalion on the rise. What had changed in the new-era reorganization that distinguished it from what black militiamen had sought to achieve earlier in the nineteenth century? Was it white paternal control, with its roots in the nineteenth century? Was it the increased scrutiny of black militiamen by white leaders constructing the new twentieth-century order? In any event, Obear made it clear that the First Battalion had met and exceeded state standards and were ready to serve in the new era as a reliable militia unit. African American militia leaders had achieved this improvement by being more critical of their enlistment practices in one way but not so diligent in another. If Obear's inspection at the beginning of 1902 was correct, then he expected each company to be capped at between fifty-five and sixty enlisted men, because equipment and arms were limited but allocated by the adjutant general and the governor, who intended not to exceed these state and financially imposed parameters. The state at the same time, beginning in the late nineteenth century, had debated how to recruit men, retain them, sustain their enthusiasm and militia membership, and measure the length of an average enlistment.

In 1902 black men in the First Battalion averaged eighty-eight enlistees, "a surplus of thirty-eight men" who could not, under the reorganization, "render sufficient return to the State." The militia company's upper enlistment limit, Obear decided, "should be fixed on the maximum strength" of sixty enlisted men. Despite these problems of overenrollment, Inspector General William G. Obear declared the Georgia State Troops, Colored, a worthy investment at the beginning of 1902.[38]

Near the end of 1902, black men exhibited an enthusiasm for militia membership that exceeded that of whites, who were experiencing a drop in morale owing to an encampment hiatus approaching three years. Obear observed this difference during his inspection tour. Seventy-three percent of the 504 black registered First Battalion members presented themselves for inspection. In contrast, white units mustered no more than 63 percent of their listed troop strength at inspection musters. African American militiamen at the beginning of the twentieth century demonstrated a clearer commitment to militia service than did their white counterparts. They were enthusiastic despite the new era's disbanding policy. Morale among white militiamen had dipped so far that Obear lowered the standards he used to inspect the entire militia. He hoped that white units might be retained and that they would sustain some enthusiasm for the militia until another encampment, funded by state and federal sources, could be organized.[39]

Pivotal Year: 1903

By October 1903 Obear's language and descriptions of African American militia units had changed. In December 1903 Obear recommended disbanding the Georgia Artillery, the Chatham Light Infantry, and the Fulton Guards. According to Obear, the Chatham Light Infantry's officers had "retarded" the company's previous progress, the unit's captain was "not competent," and the lieutenants were "not qualified to be promoted." The central problem was poor record keeping, the very issue with which Obear had assailed Solomon Johnson. Furthermore, the Fulton Guards lacked discipline, did not understand how to drill, and failed guard duty. Most if not all of these deficits had been addressed, at least for the white companies, at the late nineteenth-century encampments. Blacks had been excluded, with one exceptional moment, from such detailed training. Obear also decided that the Chatham Light Infantry and the Georgia Artillery should be consolidated into one unit, thus transforming the artillery unit into an infantry company despite the consistent efforts by the artillerymen to maintain their cannons at their own expense. The inspector general placed all three units on a sixty-to-ninety-day probation with ordered disbandment to follow if the three companies could not get themselves into "better shape."[40]

Obear's accusations of officer incompetence and failed tactics and training significantly contrasted with his previous assessments. Between 1900 and 1902 black officers were described as model leaders who selected the right kind of militiamen and trained them so well that they attained "apple pie order." For two years Obear officially lauded black militiamen as competent and enthusiastic, but Obear's 1903 evaluation reached conclusions that directly opposed those he had made two years earlier. The 1903 inspections made the year a pivotal moment in black militia history.

In January 1903 the adjutant general's office ordered an end to overenlisting. According to the *Savannah Tribune*, some of the First Battalion's companies carried enlistments approaching one hundred members, a reflection of the high level of black enthusiasm for militia service. The state, nevertheless, required all militia companies under guidelines set by the 1899 reorganization to not exceed sixty men. State militia authorities recommended that units discharge overenrolled members. The legislatively imposed reductions lowered the number of black militiamen to four hundred enlisted personnel and twenty-five officers. A week later, a report revealed that the Georgia Artillery had "made phenomenal success and today it is on as solid a basis as any company." Further, a year earlier, Obear had complimented the Georgia Artillery as being "very good," because the company took care of its property, had excellent record keeping, and had discipline in the ranks despite too much talking during drills.

By February 1903 the First Battalion's officers had been reelected, and those who were required to were preparing to take their examinations, indicating that the Georgia State Troops, Colored, continued to have a place within the state militia with state-approved and competent leadership. The new governor, Joseph Meriwether Terrell, issued commissions to black officers whose tenure as militiamen ranged from relative greenhorns, of four years' service, to men who had become officers in the First Battalion back in 1885 and 1886. At the same time Major W. H. Royall retired, earning "the distinction of being the first colored soldier to be placed on the retired list." Royal's retirement brought to an end a twenty-three-year militia career, including eleven years as major of the First Battalion, when Deveaux's political obligations took him away from militia responsibilities. This milestone reinforced among black militiamen, and as Bonner suggested, that the race had advanced and found acceptance as citizens of Georgia. Black people were here to stay.[41]

Federal Reorganization: The Dick Act

By June 1903, however, black citizenship was being called into question. The national debate concerning militia federalization as the National Guard began anew, with Georgians discussing whether to accept congressional passage of the Dick Bill. This bill made the militia an integral part of the nation's defense network. It marked the culmination of the National Guard Association's twenty-four-year lobbying effort to formally incorporate the militia into the structure of the national military. Charles Dick, president of the National Guard Association, commander of the Ohio National Guard with the rank of major general, and Ohio's congressman, chaired in 1903 the House of Representative's Militia Committee. A year earlier, as National Guard Association president, Dick had appointed a NGA committee to draft a bill for Association members to consider during their annual meeting, on January 23 and 24, 1902. The bill addressed the direction and future of the National Guard. Secretary of War Elihu Root, charged by President William McKinley to reorganize the U.S. military after the Spanish-American War, supervised the War Department's own congressional bill, which John K. Mahon notes was based on the National Guard Association's 1902 committee proposal. The U.S. Senate approved the bill on January 21, 1903, creating the Dick Act.

The Dick Act brought to an end more than a century of militia tradition highlighted by the U.S. Constitution's 1792 militia clause. The original clause authorized each state to muster its own militia. The Dick Act initiated a new era in U.S. military traditions and operation: the militia as the National Guard. The National Guard became a reserve force within the nation's regular military defense force. The Dick Act also initially required a state's governor to formally request federal funding for militia operations. When a state requested and accepted federal resources, the governor took a "fateful step." He undermined the state's primary control over the militia. While federal money alleviated some state militia problems, federal funding also "required . . . [a state's] organized militia" to submit to federal military standards, evaluation, and annual inspections. Militiamen additionally had to drill twenty-four times each year, and two-thirds of the militia were expected to turn out for five days of encampment.

By accepting the Dick Act's reorganization initiatives and the federal resources that accompanied the act's passage, a governor relinquished control of his state militia and placed that militia in the hands of the president of the United States. Federalization, especially during a time of war, dissolved any loyalty militiamen owed their state. As federal troops, militiamen became "volunteers," members of the regular military devoid of any association with their home state. This was the very problem that Georgia faced during the Spanish-American War. Georgia's "volunteers" left state militia service to fight in the war as members of three U.S. Volunteer Regiments. As a result, individualized volunteerism terminated the Georgia Volunteer state militia. The militia's demise sparked Governor Candler's 1899 reorganization and the new-era militia: the Georgia State Troops and National Guard.[42]

Dick Act Supporters and Opponents

Almost exactly six months after the Dick Act's passage, Georgians debated whether to accept or resist the act's proposed reorganization. According to the *Savannah Tribune*, white southerners, "especially a few in" Savannah, opposed the Dick Act. Their objection repeated a concern raised in the late 1870s, namely, that the reorganization would give "too much power to the President." A newfound objection in 1903 brought the issue of race to the forefront, because the Dick Act threatened to be "the means of giving colored troops ascendancy over" white troops. The *Tribune* discounted these objections as "assertions . . . for effect only." In contrast, black militiamen, the *Tribune* claimed, would "readily enlist under [the Dick Act's] provisions." Specifically, African American militiamen "endorsed" the act and were "joined by ninety-five percent of the white troops of the state." In 1904 Obear acknowledged that the enlisted men of Georgia's State Troops almost universally embraced the Dick Act and anxiously awaited its rewards, in particular its increased funding.[43]

Unfortunately for African American militiamen, the State Troops' white officer corps did not reflect the sentiments of white enlisted men, who looked to federal funding as a means of alleviating the expense of being a militiaman. White officers had been debating the value of black troops since Governor Candler's reorganization in 1899, even as they embraced segments of the Dick Act four years later. Given the white officer corps' sentiments and use of the Dick Act in setting inspection standards, the existence of the Georgia State Troops, Colored, was in jeopardy. Inspector General Obear attended the First Battalion's successful twenty-third anniversary, but by September 1903, the Georgia Artillery's inspection, although "a creditable one" with "only four men absent," had been followed by "very rigid" inspections of the First Battalion's infantry companies "under the provision of the Dick Bill." Two weeks later, Captain J. C. Simmons, longtime commander of the Georgia Artillery, journeyed to Atlanta hoping to persuade Governor Joseph M. Terrell not to disband the unique company. Simmons came away hopeful, but by April 1904 the sole black artillery company in the United States was no more and two more black companies had suffered a similar fate.[44]

Inspector General William G. Obear's 1903 Annual Report submitted in the spring of 1904 explored the Dick Act's impact on the Georgia militia. Georgia's rank and file militiamen, Obear conceded, had given the Dick Act their "hearty and almost unanimous approval." The "Dick Bill," as

Obear titled it, had garnered widespread acclaim from rank-and-file white and black militiamen because it had "given increased recognition to the State troops in the shape of new arms and equipment and a recognized" public status. The Dick Act was a welcomed new obligation that brought vitally needed resources and an enthusiasm for militia service and that required the Georgia State Troops to make only a few changes to better align themselves with the standard operations of the U.S. military. This included adapting and utilizing the national military's terminology, creating a battalion quartermaster's post, and adjusting roles and positions inside the adjutant general's office.[45]

"Whether the Colored Troops Should Be Retained in the Service or Not"

Black militiamen had embraced the Dick Act as a positive good. They viewed the act as a win for the entire militia. Obear, however, was part of the antagonistic white officer corps that included the adjutant general, a key decision maker. The Georgia State Troops' officers raised the ultimate question associated with the Dick Bill: "the question [of] whether the colored troops should be retained in the service or not." The question forced Obear and the state militia's leadership to face the issue of racial equality among the officer corps. Federalization under the Dick Bill, Obear assumed, "contemplate[d] that they [black militiamen] be put on the same equality in every way with other troops." It also meant ending "discrimination against them to the extent that . . . the colored officer [was] always junior to the white officer regardless of their relative rank." Georgia had codified such racial discrimination within "section 34 of the Military Code," but accepting federal funding and embracing the Dick Bill would force Georgia to repeal section 34. Further, equality, the militia officer corps worried, would have a direct impact on Georgia State Troops' morale, an assertion contradicting the views of the rank-and-file, white, enlisted militiaman.

According to Obear's 1904 annual report, white troops had a definite "lack of interest" in the militia, despite the scheduling of the first encampment since 1897, owing to the Dick Act's largesse. Obear claimed that the Georgia State Troops were not "in a more satisfactory condition." White militiamen performed poorly during their 1903 inspection. Their officers also failed to comprehend why inspections were vitally important to efficient militia operation. White militiamen as a result continued failing fundamental militia duties: drill, sentry duty, and other basic activities defined in their manual of operation and reinforced by encampment training. Troop morale had not improved in spite of the ongoing reorganization and the improved material comforts that came with it.[46]

Persistent low morale among white militiamen caused Obear to fear elevating black militiamen, especially African American officers, to an equal standing with their white counterparts. Retaining black troops and placing them on an even playing field under federal authority was, in Obear's mind, another negative blow to white troop morale. Obear concluded, "It will certainly decrease the enlistment of desirable men in the white organization." Obear came to this conclusion even though he acknowledged the enthusiastic reception of the Dick Act among black and white enlisted men alike. Equality between black and white officers threatened white power, status, and white supervision over the militia. The possibility of black authoritative equality changed Obear's mind. He contended that white men objected to racial equality, especially among militia officers, because white men did "not desire to put themselves in a position where a colored officer may command [them] or demand their salutes in recognition of his rank," respect, and authority automatically due an officer.[47]

Obear also argued that black militiamen had and offered no "practical benefit to the State." He made this assertion despite a very positive assessment of black militiamen. According to Obear, by the spring of 1904, African American militia companies had attained "their highest state of efficiency." They drilled well, were organized and disciplined, and met reorganization standards. The officers and men represented the best African Americans, "but in the very nature of things were they even better than they now are and fully armed and equipped they would be useless as a military unit to the State and a detriment to the other and larger branch of the service." Even though Obear recognized black capabilities, he and the officers of the white Georgia State Troops believed black militiamen "could not be used to suppress [a white] riot." Nor did Obear trust African American militiamen to confront "a mob composed of their own race"; white men's reliability under similar circumstances meanwhile went unquestioned. Finally, black militia companies cost too much. Obear claimed that equipping seven black militia companies would cost the state $20,000. This sum did not include the Georgia Artillery, which required more money on top of an annual outlay of $1,200 from the state's Military

Fund for armory rent. Taken together, Obear asserted, "It is thought by many [that such resources] could be put to better use that can and would be of service to the State when needed."[48]

"The State Has Too Many Organizations"

By the time Obear turned in his 1904 inspection report in January 1905, his frustration with the entire militia had become evident. He concluded that holding every company to the strict efficiency standards had to be the path for restoring militia proficiency, but militia quality continued to lag behind Georgia authorities' expectations, despite increased federal funding and access to training. In Obear's opinion, Georgia had the "right . . . to expect better service from its militia," given the resources being poured into the units from state and federal sources. Obear also noted that state government was "paying armory rent, issuing clothing, and arms and equipment sufficient for [improved] field service." State and federal funding had enabled white militiamen to attend the first encampment since 1897. The encampment had been restricted so that black militiamen, now solely infantry and state naval units, did not receive invitations for training that was intended primarily for infantry units. Given the resources allocated to militiamen by the newly combined governmental sources, Obear concluded, "It cannot be said that the State and United States Governments have not made considerable improvement in their treatment of the militia." In this context of expanded governmental support and voicing the opinions of "Many [militia] officers," Obear repeated a conclusion proposed first in the 1870s and again at the beginning of the 1899 reorganization: "The State has too many organizations."

This time Obear contended that there were too many companies to be supported by the finite governmental resources. His 1905 annual report on the preceding year allowed him to qualify his assertion: "I feel quite sure that it is generally conceded that there are too many inferior organizations in the service." Further, 30 percent of the companies he inspected throughout 1904 failed to muster their full troop complement. Obear expected that at least during the required annual inspection "every man should be present," because inspection was a highly significant moment in a militia unit's existence. To counter the malaise, Obear embraced the possibility of eliminating useless officers and companies. He would be much more rigid with inspection standards and demand efficiencies spelled out by the law. Weeding out the "indifferent and incompetent" benefited the state, Obear claimed, with "the increased efficiency of the troops that remained." As a result, Obear returned to his early-1899 mindset, justifying strict inspections while urging Georgia authorities to adopt an elimination policy. He thereby reversed his thinking on how to maintain the militia Candler and his successors had envisioned. Obear had relaxed inspection standards at the beginning of the new century to keep white units functional, even when they did not meet the efficiency standards and professionalism that new resources had encouraged under his inspection regime. By the end of 1904 Obear was once again imposing strict inspection standards on every company. He returned to what might be described as a color-blind standard of excellence, with stricter standards owing to the acceptance of state and federal funding and to the invitation to join the greater U.S. military.[49]

On April 18, 1904, Obear disbanded Savannah's Chatham Light Infantry and Georgia Artillery. Atlanta's Fulton Guards followed on May 12, 1904. Obear's inspection record for the year indicated that 92.43 percent of the First Battalion mustered for inspection. No black company mustered with less than 86 percent of its enlistment. In contrast, white companies mustered just three percentage points more, with 89.54 percent of their members present at inspection. One unit, the Fourth Infantry regiment, a white unit, mustered only 69 percent of its enlistment. Overall the nine white regimental organizations mustered only 80.15 percent of their numerical strength, compared to the better attendance, by 12 percentage points, by black militiamen. These numbers revealed that the most enthusiastic militiamen in 1904 were African American, yet Obear called the year a failure, because white militiamen were significantly less enthusiastic.[50]

"The Negro Is an American"

The *Savannah Tribune* opened 1904 attempting to reassure African Americans that all was well in the world of the black militiaman. The Emancipation Day oration, delivered by Rev. R. H. Singleton, began with the declaration, "The Negro is an American." Black citizenship had been earned by "the right of primitive settlement" and "the right of inheritance bought by blood," and "however much . . . denied, the right [to be an American] is unquestionably his." Further, Singleton declared, "This is the Negro's country by toil, sacrifice, and bloodshed." African American rights had therefore been earned and "won under God, upon the battle fields of [t]his country." Singleton asserted, "Our fathers fought for the country, and we must be willing to fight. Who would be free himself must strike the blow." Within this context of past and present sacrifice and achievement, black "civil and political rights must be guarded at all times."

Black Americans had survived in the United States, while the Spanish had come and gone. Native Americans, "the first settlers," too, had lost the battle and "gone to his reservation." Black soldiers had given and continued to give their lives for American freedom. Starting with Crispus Attucks, "the first martyr to American Independence, through all the wars of the country to the recent charge up the heights of San Juan [Hill], the Negro's blood ha[d] mingled with that of the white man's to purchase this noble heritage." Finally, black people paid $500 million in taxes to local and national governments. These contributions of both blood and treasure to the nation made them U.S. citizens. Further, black people had worked hard to earn their "God given way to prosperity and peace." At January's end the *Tribune* assured its audience, "There is no necessity for our people to become apprehensive of the disbandment of the colored troops." The newspaper's editor felt that the black companies would be protected by unnamed "fair minded white friends" too numerous to allow disbandment.[51]

Nevertheless, by mid-April the Chatham Light Infantry and the Georgia Artillery, two Savannah companies with substantial traditions dating back to the 1870s, had ceased to exist. The Fulton Guards, a new twentieth-century militia unit, barely survived four years before Obear disbanded the company, in May 1904. On the eve of the 1905 Emancipation Day celebration, only three First Battalion companies—A, D, and F—prepared to march on what some African Americans argued was the most important day in African American history.[52]

A depleted First Battalion devoid of five of its full strength of eight units was not the only noticeable difference on January 1, 1905. Even though the weather proved "pleasant," Emancipation Day brought only hundreds to line Savannah's streets in celebration. In the past Savannah's black infantry performed their Emancipation Day drill before "several thousand." In 1905, when First African Baptist Church opened its facilities for the annual oration, the *Tribune* reported only that Mr. George S. Williams delivered "a practicable" address that stressed how "to act in a manner that will redound to the best interest of the race." The paper printed only these fourteen words commemorating the day of freedom. In contrast, previous Emancipation Day celebrations were reported nearly verbatim. Emancipation Day was a moment when African Americans publicly demonstrated that they had "patriotism and loyalty" and affirmed their citizenship. Yet, in 1905, "the number that participated in the parade was smaller than usual"; black mass participation waned as Jim Crow rose in significance.[53]

"The Colored Troops Need . . ."

The First Battalion's remaining companies practiced drill routines after Emancipation Day in preparation for the year's annual inspection, now dictated by the Dick Act. The Dick Act also had encouraged states to seek out and employ United States Army officers to train and inspect state militiamen. In 1905 the number of regular military officers inspecting the Georgia militia increased from one to five. The presence of the added personnel shortened the three-to-four-month inspection process Obear endured alone to about a month and a half. Army officers, with William G. Obear, inspected the entire militia complement of 4,236 officers and men between February 1, 1905 and April 16, 1905. According to the *Atlanta Constitution*, however, there were "just 4,031 officers and men in the Georgia state militia." This statement ignored "the number of colored troops in the state." The paper contended that "no distinction [was] made between white and colored troops," yet the *Constitution* suggested that just over 4,000 white men alone served "in the Georgia state militia" while 233 officers and men, "the number of colored troops in the state," possessed a different status. Black militiamen appeared to be outside the structure of the Georgia State Troops. The paper in early 1905 acknowledged them as colored troops but made no direct association between them and "the Georgia state militia."[54]

African American militiamen also drilled to learn new tactics, hoping to stave off press and annual inspection reports that suggested that black companies failed to keep up with and meet national military standards now mandated by the Dick Act, army officers, the inspector and adjutant generals, the governor, and the Georgia General Assembly. In February 1905 the *Savannah Tribune* publicly laid out the scope of the pending black militia problems, connecting black militiamen to the decline in African American citizenship. While Inspector General William G. Obear had consistently evaluated First Battalion companies as "more efficient than ever before," a Chatham County white newspaper, *The Press*, in part blamed the Dick Act and black militiamen for failing to meet the militia's efficiency standards. This white newspaper called for reorganizing black militia companies instead of mustering the units out and ending their existence. Further, the paper's editor argued that "the colored troops need encouragement rather than disbanding." According to this account, black militiamen had "repeatedly" been "warned that their commands were not up to standard." Some white companies were just as lax "and the Dick Bill [did] not seem to improve the situation." At the same time, the white editor asserted, "If the colored man is to become a citizen and to share his responsibility," then reorganizing the black militia companies was absolutely necessary. Reorganization would require consolidating the First Battalion's surviving companies and eliminating those units not meeting the new standard. The *Tribune* accepted most of *The Press*'s assertions but objected to the claim "that the colored troops ha[d] 'failed to come up to requirements,'" because the inspector general's reports from 1900 to 1904 had stated the exact opposite.[55]

Link: Disbanding and Disfranchisement

By February 18, 1905, calls for disbanding the surviving black militia companies had gained momentum, reaching what the *Tribune* labeled a "tirade." The "malicious" and "misleading" white press "advised [black militiamen] to surrender their privileges." The paper went even further, additionally demanding that "Negro citizens ... also surrender their elective franchise," thereby connecting militia status and service directly to black citizenship and the vote. The black militia company was again linked to African American political power and autonomy. The white press's demand was a significant proposition that directly connected the black military presence with political power.

Historically states seeking to disfranchise African Americans across both antebellum and postbellum history had combined these efforts with antiblack violence. Black militiamen's presence in at least one instance protected and restored African American suffrage. Rhode Island black militiamen mobilized to put down white labor violence in the early 1840s, receiving in reward a restored franchise—a badge of citizenship denied blacks two decades earlier by white attacks on black homeowners and the community. Antiblack acts of violence in antebellum Rhode Island in 1822, Pennsylvania in the 1830s, and Wilmington, North Carolina, in 1898 were all directly connected with disfranchising black Americans. White Georgians constitutionally disfranchised black Georgians after two related events: the disbanding of the Georgia State Troops, Colored, during the summer of 1905 and the Atlanta race riot, in 1906.[56]

Major W. H. Royal and Captain Sandy Lockhart

Countering white demands that black people relinquish their nineteenth-century military and political gains, the *Tribune* encouraged black people to embrace their pride and promote the African American militia record. To change public opinion black people first needed to stand on their own two feet. Specifically, African Americans should "maintain [their] position to the last." Surrendering military service and voting rights were not acts of manhood or race pride.[57]

Black militiamen had earned the mantle of citizenship for African Americans. Their martial service was their badge of honor. The black militia record proved the quality of the race, because they had accomplished a "great good." Yet the white press had lowered the status of black militia commander Colonel John H. Deveaux to that of a white corporal, while the *Tribune* contended that Deveaux was a proven leader who successfully led black militiamen. He led the companies by molding the First Battalion into an efficient unit "unequaled by many of the white troops." Georgia's black soldiers had also made significant achievements, which were "known" across the state. As proof, the *Tribune* claimed, "Black state troops are made of the same stuff that actuated the movement at Bunker Hill and those who took part in every active event to the last war." With this historical account it was clear that "the Georgia State Troops, Colored, [were] not quitters." Their determination to maintain the black militia companies with no state support or encouragement was commendable. African American militiamen were principled men who possessed the "will" to sustain the militia companies "until they [were] compelled to surrender." When that time came blacks would "not [surrender in] . . . a cowardly" way. In fact, "the Negro troops of Georgia [would] never show the white flag under any circumstances."[58]

In 1905, five black militia companies remained, having survived the 1904 purge. Three companies continued operating in Savannah, with solitary units operating in Augusta and in Macon. Savannah's three companies participated in the funeral proceedings for Major W. H. Royal in early April and marched in the annual May parade. The *Tribune* identified Captain John Sandy Lockhart as one of the best militia officers. Lockhart's unit operated efficiently, causing the paper to wonder whether "the

Legislature [could] afford to do ought against such a class of citizens" by abolishing not only Lockhart's company but all the black militia units. All five black companies, nevertheless, came together in August to celebrate the First Battalion's anniversary.

At the same time, the *Tribune* helped undermine the surviving units, allocating less space to militia activities. Gone were the congratulatory articles that defined the 1870s and 1890s militia as an efficient and professional institution equal in its proficiencies and professionalism to those of its white counterparts. In 1905 the newspaper offered solitary and unique acclaim to Captain Sandy Lockhart, who efficiently and competently commanded the Lincoln Guards. The paper, nevertheless, stopped presenting complimentary accolades and high praise for each unit's military proficiency. Gone, too, were the detailed articles highlighting black militia events. The 1905 coverage was sparse in contrast, with only an announcement of the event and the name of the company. Even Major Royal's funeral received very limited reporting; the funeral procession involved Savannah's three companies and Masonic units marching as an honor guard. The focus was not on Royal the militiaman but on Royal the wealthy and generous businessman who shared his wealth with the African American community.[59]

President Theodore Roosevelt's Inauguration

Captain Sandy Lockhart commanding the Lincoln Guards in Macon, Georgia, petitioned Governor Joseph M. Terrell for permission to take his company to Washington, D.C., for President Theodore Roosevelt's inauguration, in March 1905. Governor Terrell refused the petition for four reasons. First, he wanted to control Georgia's public image. He was concerned about militiamen's behavior when traveling outside the state, because while not officially conducting state business, militiamen represented state government and any misdeeds could embarrass the state. Misbehavior, no matter how minor, the *Atlanta Constitution* reported, "reflected [poorly] on the state's military standing and discipline." Governor Terrell intended to protect his legacy by keeping militiamen from any mischief during his governorship. With this declaration Terrell decided that no state militia unit could venture outside Georgia, even to an encampment, unless their mission was federally sanctioned to "attend army maneuvers."[60]

Second, the governor was not convinced of the Lincoln Guards' readiness. First and foremost, the company did not have "proper equipment." This problem confirmed the long-term neglect that black militia units had suffered and continued to suffer, despite the 1899 reorganization and the endless inspections begun in the 1890s and continuing into the twentieth century. The third reason reinforced the second. According to the *Constitution*, denying the Lincoln Guards' permission to attend the presidential inauguration raised further consideration of William G. Obear's call, in his 1903 and 1905 annual reports, to disband "all of the colored commands." The inspector general had assessed the black units as being plagued by "inexpediency and inefficiency." They cost too much and the resources saved through their disbandment "might be given [to] the white militia organizations that are of some value," making it clear that black militia companies no longer held any purpose in the minds of state officials.[61]

Fourth, public accolades, especially from sources outside Georgia, were showered on Governor Joseph M. Terrell when he denied the Lincoln Guards permission to march in the Republican presidential inaugural parade. Jim Crow segregation, white supremacy, and popular support for these ideologies came from Mississippi Governor James K. Vardaman. Vardaman telegraphed Terrell his congratulations to "the white people of Georgia" and their governor for "refusing to permit the Lincoln Guards" to participate in the presidential inauguration. In Vardaman's estimation, had the Lincoln Guards received permission white Georgians and the state would have been "dishonored" and "embarrassed" and would have invited "the severest condemnation from [northern and southern] negrophiles ... bribed referees ... and political creatures." Terrell, however, had represented "nine-tenths of the decent, liberty-loving, self-respecting white people of the south." Terrell also stood for "the faithful old-guard," the "southern gentlemen" who continued to resist federal impositions on free states and suffer the corruption of bribed officials with federal patronage, continuing white condemnation of the Republican Party as the party of blacks. Vardaman then commended Terrell for challenging the oppressive debauchery of Republican "presidential flattery."[62]

Three Southern Governors and White Supremacy

Vardaman's telegram certified the rising public presence, power, and importance of white supremacy, or as Grace Elizabeth Hale has defined it, the "culture of segregation." While Joseph M. Terrell had not been born and raised as a member of the Civil War generation's old-guard, gentleman plantation owners who Vardaman venerated, Terrell was admitted to Georgia's bar twenty-one years after the start of the Civil War in 1882, just seven years before the dawn of Vardaman-style radical racism. Born on June 6, 1861, Terrell advanced rapidly in Georgia politics, being just twenty-three years old when he was elected to the General Assembly, in 1884. Six years later Terrell won election to the Georgia Senate; two years later he ascended to the Attorney General's office and ten years later, the governorship. As governor of Georgia for two terms at the dawn of the twentieth century, Terrell was noted for his education proposals and support for Progressive legislation that included child labor regulations. Not known as a reformer and considered by some historians as conservative, Terrell held office during the period in which strong public declarations of antiblack rhetoric were acceptable.

But Terrell was no Vardaman. James K. Vardaman joined a cast of "ordinary leaders in their communities" who espoused racism and white supremacy as reflective "of the hearts and minds of [the] people." Radical racists of Vardaman's ilk assumed that blacks did not belong in the South and asserted that the world could not continue with both races competing for space, resources, and freedom in a changing industrialized consumer-focused national culture. According to radical racism theory, as analyzed by Joel Williamson, African American freedom, especially that exercised by the first generation to lead lives free of slavery, such as Tunis Campbell, Cudjo Fye, Corday Harris, and Joseph Morris, created a black "retrograded . . . dangerous beast" who threatened white freedom with assaults on white women and girls. White men needed to remove the threat. As a result, radical racists such as Vardaman projected and called for African American extinction so that whites might create a New South. In such a context, denying publicly active black people access to high-profile public events was one way to undermine black citizenship. Vardaman applauded and reinforced Terrell's decision.

A public declaration of black disfranchisement followed in July 1905. Former Atlanta newspaper owner and rising politician Michael Hoke Smith attacked the black right to vote, and it won him the governorship. According to the *Savannah Tribune*, Smith had not been an opponent of black rights before seeking the governor's seat in 1905. Specifically, Smith was "liberal minded" in his dealings with African Americans, yet the "reverse [was] being proven" as he embraced disfranchisement in hopes of winning the August gubernatorial primary election with the support of now Congressman Thomas W. Hardwick, former Populist Thomas E.

Watson, and *Atlanta Journal* owner James R. Gray. The *Tribune* failed to mention that Smith's campaign manager was a militiaman and state legislator who initiated the call to disfranchise black Georgians and a key leader in reorganizing the new-era militia. That man was Thomas W. Hardwick.[63]

"We Deserve Better Treatment"

Theodore Roosevelt's inauguration included African American military men from the U.S. Ninth Cavalry and black militiamen from Washington, D.C. The Lincoln Guards' reputation in Georgia remained high and was enhanced among blacks when Governor Terrell denied them the opportunity to march in Theodore Roosevelt's inaugural parade. The Lincoln Guards nevertheless continued as "one of the most efficient companies in Col. Deveaux's battalion" and remained a highly functional company. In July the Lincoln Guards excelled by being the first militia unit—black or white—to respond in a riot readiness drill. The black company arrived on the scene before the first white company, the Floyd Rifles. Given such efficiency during the practice drill, the *Tribune* wondered why the Georgia Legislature had convened "to do ought against such a class of citizens."

A month later, in August 1905, the *Tribune* charged that through "the strenuous efforts . . . by a few young officers" who joined forces with "a prejudice[d] set of legislators" the five surviving black militia companies were scheduled to be disbanded. Classified by the paper as "Negro haters," this antiblack coalition "simply took advantage of the [black] troops on account of the power that they held" as militia officers and legislators. With "prejudice . . . in their hearts" Georgia legislators and militia officers ended nearly thirty years of black militia service. African American militiamen had "done so much for the making of this southland a garden spot." In essence black militiamen enabled Georgia to make the claim that it was a state where blacks and whites cooperated. Yet the record of black militia service during those years, as Elder Hart, Maxwell, and George Washington Williams feared, now counted for nothing. According to the *Tribune*, a new white antiblack generation had finally succeeded in passing "class legislat[ion] . . . disbanding the colored troops." White supremacy's victory came in mid-August 1905, just as the First Battalion prepared to celebrate its anniversary.[64]

The five surviving companies, the *Tribune* made plain, had withstood the "severe tests" of multiple inspections. The legislature's "Negro Haters," however, used reports of inefficiency to justify their demands for disbandment, but "each time the prejudice[d] efforts of the Negro Haters were unsuccessful." The unnamed opponents, however, had persistently pursued disbandment and disfranchisement legislation. According to the *Tribune*, disbanding in 1905 ended years of "unquestioned" African American "fealty" and "service." African American citizens had also paid their taxes. White officials additionally ignored the "thousands of dollars [black militiamen had expended] in equipping themselves and coming up to the requirements of the law. Until recently these troops were not molested, especially under the regime of those state house officers who were broad minded and willing to give a helping hand to the race." Despite their efforts to provide a helping hand to forestall disbandment, even these advocates had succumbed. Disbandment "was a direct thrust" against black Georgians' citizenship.[65]

Militiaman and *Tribune* editor Solomon C. Johnson raised some important points, suggesting that in the mind of black militiamen, the disbanding of the Georgia State Troops, Colored, was an antiblack attack by young white militia officers and state legislators. According to this story, African American militiamen had legislative supporters and advocates such as the Chatham County's *Press*'s editor, who had forestalled total disbanding under Governor Candler's new-era reorganization. There were also opponents who publicly emerged with the creation of the new-era militia in the officer corps. Inspector General William G. Obear joined the officer corps in questioning the black militia's value, as his inspection reports went from positive to extremely negative. His inspection evaluations changed with the Dick Act of 1903. In 1905 the *Atlanta Constitution* reported, "Inspector General W. G. Obear was one of the most ardent advocates of the bill disbanding the negro troops of the state." The August 1905 subheadline read: "Abolish Negro Troops." Obear made sure he was "present . . . when the governor signed the bill making it [disbandment] a law." His enthusiasm became even more obvious when he "kept the pen" Governor Terrell used to sign the bill. Obear then placed the treasured souvenir in his desk draw, "with a smile," and declared, "There is the pen that of a truth was mightier than the sword, or, at least, the sword of the colored troops."[66]

Obear's enthusiasm for disbandment was the result of the continuing militia reorganization that brought the militia's officer corps and state legislators together. Working in August 1905 with militia officers including Inspector General William G. Obear, Colonel A. J. Scott, and First Lieutenant of the Sixteenth Infantry United States Army L. S. D. Rucker,

Jr., the General Assembly went about the task of rewriting Georgia's Military Code, a task Governor Candler had asked for six years earlier. The reorganizations prompted by the new era and the Dick Act were long, involved, and ongoing during the twentieth century's first decade. The Georgia Legislature, nevertheless, finished reorganizing the military code at the same time that it disbanded the Georgia State Troops, Colored, in August 1905. Legislators rewrote the code, intending to reshape the Georgia State Troops so that the militia would pass an anticipated United States Army inspection due in three years when "additional elements of the Dick bill went into effect."

The new code reduced the new-era militia to four thousand white officers and men. This new ceiling would allow for every white militiaman to be "fully armed and equipped." Reorganization was also done so that Georgia's white military companies would be part of the newly reorganized U.S. military. This national military expected Georgia's militia to conform to army regulations and structure, which "require[d] that retired officers be commissioned and ma[d]e . . . available for all duties except to command troops" a regulation that had the potential to force white men, especially the officers, to salute and obey black superior officers such as John H. Deveaux or the captains leading the five surviving black companies. Legislators and militia officers, disturbed by racial equality in the new century, concluded that the state and national reorganizations required an all-white militia, a reliable twentieth-century unit. They hoped this militia would be transformed into "the national guard of Georgia." White leaders, using state and national military reorganizations alongside the ideology of the new culture of segregation, carved out a place in the national narrative for Georgia's whites to be American citizens. They were part of a regional effort wherein whites triumphed over people of color as they consolidated the nation-state at the end of the nineteenth century. They used black regulars to defeat Native Americans and then erased the black militia and military record, as whites in the North and the South reconciled as Americans.[67]

Disbanding five black militia companies to reorganize the Georgia State Troops not only ended the First Battalion's existence but also removed the late Major W. H. Royal from the hallowed retired list. Disbandment erased thirty years of service by thousands of black citizens and the communities they served. It also terminated Lieutenant Colonel John H. Deveaux's lifetime commission and brought to fruition the idea that blacks were not citizens and did not contribute to the national narrative. The black Masonic organ, the *Odd Fellows Journal*, reflected on the erasures prompted by reorganization. To bring the Georgia National Guard to life, the *Journal* concluded, required sending Colonel John H. Deveaux, collector of the Port of Savannah, into a respected military retirement, even though Deveaux had kept his companies "in a high state of efficiency" and had earned "a clean and enviable record." In light of these achievements and nearly thirty of years of black militiamen's service and fealty, the Masonic newspaper lamented, "We deserve better treatment."[68]

CONCLUSION

The nineteenth century, scholars now argue, was one of tremendous change. It included debates about citizenship, national belonging, and, I would add, the role of the militia in colonial expansion, revolution, and state formation. This study has been about two groups of people: the white Georgians and the black Georgians involved with the development, evolution, and maintenance of independent and state-sponsored militia companies during the late nineteenth century. It has examined how these Georgians used the militia company to shape and define their freedom, citizenship, and belonging. Their late nineteenth-century endeavors were part of "the problem of freedom" explored by Thomas C. Holt and "the problem of emancipation and its aftermath" examined by Jeffrey R. Kerr-Ritchie.[1] In the context of these scholarly examinations, the militia was more than an early to mid-nineteenth-century social club in the United States, or even the mid- to late nineteenth-century military organization described by militia and military scholars. The post–Civil War militia company was a political organization that sometimes also functioned as a platform for economic autonomy. In this study, economic autonomy directly informed how rural white Georgians linked their militia companies to local prosperity, and how black Georgians organized their militia companies to protect African American land ownership and labor rights.

While, for black Georgians, the independent militia companies served these political and economic functions, they also protected black social rights and empowered African American politicians to defend black people's newly acquired citizenship. Black Georgia's politicians and community organizers such as Tunis Campbell, Cudjo Fye, Todd Norris, Corday Harris, and Joseph Morris used the militia to organize and mobilize black Georgians to defend black autonomy. Black people also utilized the independent militia company to test the parameters of the Civil Rights Act of 1875 in Georgia's small towns. It was one element, for example, in the black effort to secure access to public places for mass political and economic meetings. This, along with land acquisition in the seven counties allegedly involved in the Johnson County Insurrection, was a key black objective. Blacks involved in militia formation also were community builders. Militiamen such as John Deveaux endeavored to create institutions that promoted black citizenship and belonging. For black Georgians, the path to local and national belonging started at the local level, where rural blacks sought to exercise their political and economic autonomy based on the protective promises of the Civil War Amendments and the Civil Rights Acts of 1866 and 1875.

At the same time, racially focused political competitions initiated by white Georgians politicized the militia company. White Georgians in rural and urban communities organized militia companies to physically remove black office holders and contest parallel black militia formation. They made both the white independent and state-sponsored militia companies key instruments for local whites seeking to restore white political and economic dominance. These white militia companies were central players in containing, preventing, and defeating African American political and economic organizing. Black and white people, nevertheless, viewed the independent militia company as a political instrument. The militia company brought like-minded people together for collective action. Both races utilized the independent militia company to define freedom, citizenship, and autonomy.

Black urban, state-sponsored militia companies were not as politicized as were the independent militia units. Yet these militiamen took the lead in organizing public events that displayed African American citizenship, freedom, and national belonging. Black militiamen marched and paraded on Emancipation Day, on the anniversaries of the Thirteenth, Fourteenth, and Fifteenth Amendments, on Abraham Lincoln's birthday, on May Day, and on Independence Day. Each of these days commemorated black freedom in the United States. These were days where black people publicly declared that they were loyal citizens of the nation. Such black public demonstrations of citizenship, manhood, and military proficiency were also intended to prove that African Americans served the nation as responsible citizens. Black state-sponsored militiamen secured African Americans access to contested public places such as parks and city streets. Their public events carved out public space for black celebrations of freedom and citizenship. The state-sponsored companies, like the independent militia units, were closely tied to their local communities. As a result, militiamen were active civic citizens involved in politics, benevolent organizations, and institution building. Militiamen were local citizens with stable employment, which allowed them the time to participate in militia drills, training, fund-raising, institution building, and public celebrations of black history and freedom. Black independent and state-sponsored militiamen were also active members of the Republican Party who recruited and organized both militia companies and large Republican Party events.

Blacks proved their citizenship throughout the late nineteenth century through acts of belonging. Marching militiamen on parade during public events demonstrated their patriotism, citizenship, and commitment to national service. African Americans assumed that their sacrifice as soldiers defending the Union during the Civil War had earned them the right to a protected citizenship. Their postwar celebrations, organized and led by black militiamen, were commemorated as proof that black Americans were loyal national citizens. They pointed to their public patriotism in contrast to the lack thereof among Georgia's whites, who venerated the Confederate past on Confederate Memorial Day and Robert E. Lee's birthday. Black militiamen perfected their military training in 1878 to demonstrate that slavery had been transcended. They wanted whites to see that blacks had developed as men, citizens, and Georgians. Whites commended them, claiming that urban black militiamen were less politicized than African Americans had been ten years earlier. Blacks, nevertheless, organized state-sponsored militia companies in the 1870s as proof of their national loyalty and belonging. They also endeavored to present themselves as contributors to the overall peace and harmony of their local communities. Militia service also allowed black militiamen to train as citizen soldiers who were ready to defend not only the local community but also the nation. This was especially important at the end of the nineteenth century, when black militiamen found that their historical presence was being erased. White people in the North and South reconciled, using the Spanish-American War, imperial expansion, and the triumph of segregation to create a nation for whites only.

The white South had separated from the Union to defend slavery and states' rights. They also revolted to establish a nationalism that would sustain these systems. Wrestling with defeat and seeking acceptance as citizens, white southerners would spend the late nineteenth century contesting federal military and governmental power. The contest was between federal centralization and southern states' rights. White Georgians were actively engaged in this debate. They insisted on state control over the militia but accepted the national government's financial resources to operate the state militia. For nearly two decades Georgia's state militia operated solely on federal resources, even as white militiamen venerated the Confederate past. White Georgians' path to national belonging would be based on whiteness and what Grace Elizabeth Hale has called the "culture of segregation." Segregation, as Nathan Cardon, Hale, and others have noted, was not intended to be a look back in time. Rather, it was the solution for controlling the future, where capital industrialization, urbanization, standardization, governmental centralization, and consumer culture all threatened to create a more inclusive South and nation. Each of these agents of change transcended local traditions. They were national movements that challenged local white political, economic, and social dominance. Segregation, in turn, defined who was an American citizen, giving local whites a system that regulated these changes. It restricted access to the vote, wages, and resources, using race as the primary criteria for inclusion. National citizenship would be for white people only as white southerners regained their place as citizens.

This story was not limited to nineteenth-century Georgians. Militia service and the problems of freedom and emancipation in the Americas had parallels across the Western Hemisphere. This book only hints at the additional stories concerning African-descendant people, the militia, and the problems of freedom and emancipation that Holt, Kerr-Ritchie, and Latin American scholars have described. I have, however, sought, like Kerr-Ritchie and Holt, to establish emancipation and the problem of freedom within a discussion of the United States South generally. This discussion needs new eyes and to tell the story of the South as a component of the broader story of the Western Hemisphere and the problems of freedom and emancipation.

The problems of freedom and emancipation have not been resolved. The promises of freedom, inclusion, and belonging persist in the Western Hemisphere right now. The murder of nine black people at a prayer meeting in Charleston, South Carolina, in June 2015 has brought us, temporarily, together to bring down a flag aimed at opposing civil rights. Yet disenfranchising black citizens is now the aim of various states in the Union. The deaths of young black people in 2014–2015—in Cleveland, Ohio; Detroit, Michigan; Ferguson, Missouri; and Charlotte, North Carolina—and the victims of older violence—in North Charleston, South Carolina; New York City; and Hempstead, Texas—have caused many to ask whether black lives matter. Outside the United States, the Dominican

Republic, in 2015, has returned to a twentieth-century policy that negates the citizenship of its Haitian citizens. This is a short list of the problems of freedom in the twenty-first century. They remind us that black militiamen and African-descendant people, over a hundred years ago now, faced similar challenges, including lynching, disfranchisement, and how to establish their worthiness for belonging. What has changed between then and now? The problem of freedom persists.

NOTES

Preface

1. "Reckoning with State Power: Perspectives On the Atlanta Riot of 1906," Southern Historical Association Meeting, Little Rock, Arkansas, October 30–November 2, 1996, Gregory Mixon, "The Georgia Militia and the Atlanta Riot of 1906," paper presented at SHA 1996.

2. Charles Johnson Jr., *African American Soldiers in the National Guard: Recruitment and Deployment During Peacetime and War* (Westport: Greenwood Press, 1992).

Introduction

1. For Benjamin Davis's philosophy, see *The Atlanta Independent* 1904–1928; Gregory Mixon, "The Making of a Political Boss: Henry A. Rucker, 1897–1904," *Georgia Historical Quarterly* 89 (Winter 2005): 485–504; Gregory Mixon, "The Political Career of Henry A. Rucker: A Survivor in a New South City," *Atlanta History: A Journal of Georgia and the South* 45 (Summer 2001): 4–26; "Captain Jesse Jones," *Atlanta Independent*, May 7, 1904. For the relationship militiamen had with their community during the nineteenth century and how that relationship changed at the end of the nineteenth and beginning of the twentieth century, see Eleanor L. Hannah, "From the Dance Floor to the Rifle Range: The Evolution of Manliness in the National Guards, 1870–1917," *The Journal of the Gilded Age and the Progressive Era* 6, no. 2 (April 2007): 149–177, especially, 155, 157–160, 165, 169–170, 173, 175; hereafter cited as "Dance Floor."

2. "Captain Jesse Jones." For the evolution of the militiaman at the beginning of the twentieth century, see Hannah, "Dance Floor," 173–177.

3. See Leon Litwack, *Trouble in Mind: Black Southerners in the Age of Jim Crow* (New York: Vintage Books, 1998); Steven Hahn, *A Nation Under Our Feet: Black Political Struggles in the Rural South From Slavery to the Great Migration* (Cambridge, Mass.: Belknap, 2003). For the rise of white supremacy, Jim Crow segregation, lynchings, and mob violence and the repression of the black quest for inclusion and citizenship, see Gregory Mixon, *The Atlanta Riot: Race, Class, and Violence in a New South City* (Gainesville: University Press of Florida, 2005).

4. "Captain Jesse Jones."

5. See "An Amusing Book," *Atlanta Constitution*, August 28, 1904; "At Manassas—Lieut. Vanderbilt was Overcome by the Heat," *Atlanta Constitution*, September 8, 1904; "Private Jimmy Writes of Political Dysentery—'The Only Hero Was a Georgia Boy Who

Refused to Salute a Nigger,'" *Atlanta Constitution*, September 11, 1904; Gregory Mixon, "Constructing Atlanta's Auditorium-Armory, 1904–1909: The Public and Private and Race," unpublished manuscript, 1–37, in possession of the author.

6. Theodore D. Jervey, *The Slave Trade: Slavery and Color* (New York: Negro Universities Press, 1969), v–vi, 183–185.

7. For a detailed history of this African American militiaman and his political career, see John David Smith, *Black Judas: William Hannibal Thomas and the American Negro* (Chicago: Ivan R. Dee, 2002).

8. For a discussion of the issues of white and black power after the Civil War, see Henry W. Grady, *The New South Writings and Speeches of Henry Grady* (Savannah: Beehive Press, 1971), 11, 20–24, 47–52, 73–85, 91–92, 95, 99–101, 105, 136–140; Ferald J. Bryan, *Henry Grady or Tom Watson? The Rhetorical Struggle for the New South, 1880–1890* (Macon: Mercer University Press, 1994); Lawrence Friedman, *The White Savage: Racial Fantasies in the Postbellum South* (Englewood Cliffs, N.J.: Prentice-Hall, 1970), chapter 3; Paul M. Gaston, *The New South Creed: A Study in Southern Myth Making* (Baton Rouge: Louisiana State University Press, 1970), 124–125, 130–135, 140; Mixon, *Atlanta Riot*, chapter 1; Ben H. Severance, *Tennessee's Radical Army: The State Guard and Its Role in Reconstruction, 1867–1869* (Knoxville: University of Tennessee Press, 2005), 119; The *Union and Dispatch* was quoting a black man. My thanks go to Mr. Kerry Wilson, who suggested the farmer image.

9. Otis Singletary, *Negro Militia and Reconstruction* (Austin: University of Texas Press, 1957); Otis Singletary, "The African American Militia during Radical Reconstruction," in *Brothers to the Buffalo Soldiers: Perspectives on the African American Militia and Volunteers, 1865–1917*, ed. Bruce A. Glasrud, 19–33 (Columbia: University of Missouri Press, 2011). Hereafter cited as "African American Militia."

10. Singletary, *Negro Militia*, vii.

11. Ibid., vii–viii, 15–16, 35, 145, 151–152; "African American Militia," 20–23, 26. On the evolution of scholarship "focused on the actions of whites and of white institutions in creating and maintaining a system of white supremacy" in contradistinction to black agency, see Evelyn Nakano Glenn, *Unequal Freedom: How Race and Gender Shaped American Citizenship and Labor* (Cambridge, Mass.: Harvard University Press, 2002), chapter 4.

12. Singletary, *Negro Militia*, vii, 4, 15; "African American Militia," 23.

13. Singletary, *Negro Militia*, chapters 3–4, 6–9; "African American militia, 24–27, 30; Glenn, *Unequal Freedom*, 97, 101–102, 105, 111, 116.

14. "African American Militia," 21–22; Singletary, *Negro Militia*, 24–25.

15. Elsa Barkley Brown, "To Catch the Vision of Freedom: Reconstructing Southern Black Women's Political History, 1865–1880," in *African American Women and the Vote, 1837–1965*, ed. Ann D. Gordon, Bettye Collier Thomas, John H. Bracey, 66–98 (Amherst: University of Massachusetts Press, 1997), especially 66–67, 69, 71, 74–76; Jeffrey R. Kerr-Ritchie, *Freedom's Seekers: Essays on Comparative Emancipation* (Baton Rouge: Louisiana State University Press, 2014), chapters 1–2, 6; Jeffrey R. Kerr-Ritchie, *Rites of August First: Emancipation Day in the Black Atlantic World* (Baton Rouge: Louisiana State University Press, 2007), chapters 3–7; Glenn, *Unequal Freedom*, chapter 4, especially 95–96, 127–128.

16. Kerr-Ritchie, *Freedom's Seekers*, 21, 29–30, 32, 39, 44–45.

17. See Severance, 143–145, 176–177, 229–233; Samuel B. McGuire, "The Making of a Black Militia Company: New Bern Troops in the Kirk-Holden War, 1870," *The North Carolina Review* 91, no. 3 (July 2014): 288–322, especially 314–317, 320; James K. Hogue, *Uncivil War: Five New Orleans Street Battles and the Rise and Fall of Radical Reconstruction* (Baton Rouge: Louisiana State University Press, 2006), 192–194; Rebecca J. Scott, "Fault Lines, Color Lines, and Party Lines: Race, Labor, and Collective Action in Louisiana and Cuba, 1862–1912," in *Beyond Slavery: Explorations of Race, Labor, and Citizenship in Postemancipation Societies*, ed. Frederick Cooper, Thomas C. Holt, Rebecca J. Scott, 61–106 (Chapel Hill: University of North Carolina Press, 2000); and Rebecca J. Scott, *Degrees of Freedom: Louisiana and Cuba After Slavery* (Cambridge, Mass.: Belknap, 2005).

18. John K. Mahon, *History of the Militia and National Guard* (New York: Macmillan Publishing Company, 1983), chapters 6–11. See also Hogue, *Uncivil War*, 13, and Scott, *Degrees of Freedom*.

19. Eleanor L. Hannah, *Manhood, Citizenship and the National Guard: Illinois, 1870–1917* (Columbus: Ohio State University Press, 2007), introduction. See also Glenn, *Unequal Freedom*, chapters 1–4, 7. For the white response to capital industrialization during the late nineteenth century and early twentieth century, see Grace Elizabeth Hale, *Making Whiteness: The Culture of Segregation in the South, 1890–1940* (New York: Pantheon Books, 1998), introduction and chapter 3; Nathan Cardon, "The South's 'New Negroes' and African American Visions of Progress at the Atlanta and Nashville International Expositions, 1895–1897," *Journal of Southern History* 80, no. 2 (May 2014): 290; and Glenn, *Unequal Freedom*, chapters 3–4.

20. Roger D. Cunningham, *The Black Citizen-Soldiers of Kansas, 1864–1901* (Columbia: University of Missouri Press, 2008). For Illinois, see Hannah, *Manhood*, and for North Carolina, see Glenda E. Gilmore, *Gender and Jim Crow: Women and the Politics of White Supremacy in North Carolina, 1896–1920* (Chapel Hill: University of North Carolina Press, 1996), 78–80.

21. See Gregory Mixon, "'Merecemos tratamiento mejor': Auge y Caida de las Milcias Negros en el Hemisferio Occidental durante el siglo XIX," ["We deserve better treatment": The Rise and Fall of the Militia in the Nineteenth Century Western Hemisphere] *Boletin Americanista* 64, no. 1 (2014): 55–76; George Reid Andrews, *Afro-Latin America, 1800–2000* (New York: Oxford University Press, 2004), chapters 2–3; Kerr-Ritchie, *Freedom's Seekers*, chapters 1, 2, 6; Kerr-Ritchie, *August First*, chapters 3–7; Roger Norman Buckley, *Slaves in Red Coats: The British West Indies Regiments, 1795–1815* (New Haven: Yale University Press, 1979), chapters 1–2, 4, 6, conclusion.

22. Ben Vinson III, *Bearing Arms for His Majesty: The Free-Colored Militia in Colonial Mexico* (Stanford: Stanford University Press, 2001), 1–2, chapter 6.

23. Ibid., 3, 5, 14–21.

24. Ibid., 27–45.

25. Ibid., 3, 5, 14–21. For black revolts, see the years 1608, 1611–1612, 1624, 1665.

26. Andrews, *Afro-Latin America*, 8–9, 11, 46, 87–89, 94, 107–108; Benjamin Quarles, *The Negro in the American Revolution* (New York: W. W. Norton and Company, 1961), vii.

27. Hendrik Kraay, "The Politics of Race in Independence-Era Bahia: The Black Militia Officers of Salvador, 1790–1840," in *Afro-Brazilian Culture and Politics: Bahia, 1790s to 1990s*, ed. Hendrik Kraay, 30–56 (Armonk, N.Y,: M. E. Sharpe, 1998), especially 30, 37–40, 43.

28. Kraay, "The Politics of Race," 31–32, 40–46, 50–51.

29. Philip A. Howard, *Changing History: Afro-Cuban Cabildos and Societies of Color in the Nineteenth Century* (Baton Rouge: Louisiana State University Press, 1998), 17–48, for the militia and cabildo, and 57–77, for the cabildo; Matt D. Childs, *The 1812 Aponte Rebellion in Cuba and the Struggle against Atlantic Slavery* (Chapel Hill: University of North Carolina Press, 2006), 96–118.

30. Howard, *Changing History*, 73–77; Childs, *1812 Aponte Rebellion*, 6, 9, 11, 13, 15–18.

31. Michele Reid-Vazquez, *The Year of the Lash: Free People of Color in Cuba and the Nineteenth-Century Atlantic World* (Athens: University of Georgia Press, 2011), 117–119; Jane G. Landers, *Atlantic Creoles in the Age of Revolutions* (Cambridge, Mass.: Harvard University Press, 2010), 7–14. See also Childs, *1812 Aponte Rebellion*, 71, 77, 79, 82–96.

32. Reid-Vazquez, *Year of the Lash*, 118–119, 126–129, 132, and chapter 5.

33. Ibid., 142–143.

34. Ibid., 144.

35. See Ada Ferrer, *Insurgent Cuba: Race, Nation, and Revolution, 1868–1898* (Chapel Hill: University of North Carolina Press, 1999); Aline Helg, *Our Rightful Share: The Afro-Cuban Struggle for Equality, 1886–1912* (Chapel Hill: University of North Carolina, 1995). For the evolution of Afro-Cuban status, see Howard, *Changing History*, chapters 7–epilogue. For the "culture of segregation," see Hale, *Making Whiteness*, chapter 3.

36. Robert J. Cottrol, *The Afro-Yankees: Providence's Black Community in the Antebellum Era* (Westport: Greenwood Press, 1982), chapters 2 and 3; Gilmore, *Gender and Jim Crow*, 78–80. For the positive influence of black political power and militia service during the War of 1898, see Hannah, *Manhood*, chapter 5; Eleanor L. Hannah, "A Place in the Parade: Citizenship, Manhood, and African American Men in the Illinois National Guard, 1870–1917." In *Brothers to the Buffalo Soldiers: Perspectives on the African American Militia and Volunteers, 1865–1917*, ed. Bruce A. Glasrud, 86–111 (Columbia: University of Missouri Press, 2011); Cunningham, *Black Citizen-Soldiers of Kansas*, chapter 7.

37. Gilmore, *Gender and Jim Crow*, 80–82.

Chapter 1. The Search for Freedom: Black Militiamen in Nineteenth-Century North America

1. For "claims making," citizenship, and military service, see Ronald R. Krebs, *Fighting for Rights: Military Service and the Politics of Citizenship* (Ithaca: Cornell University Press, 2006), 1–15.

2. For the community building tradition, see Landers, *Atlantic Creoles*, 88–89, 130, 138–148, 154–155; Howard, *Changing History*, 32–35, 73–74; Elizabeth D. Leonard, *Men of Color to Arms!: Black Soldiers, Indian Wars, and the Quest for Equality* (New York: W. W. Norton and Company, 2010), 204–207.

3. Singletary, *Negro Militia*, 9, 11–12, 145; Carole Emberton, *Beyond Redemption: Race, Violence, and the American South after the Civil War* (Chicago: University of Chicago

Press, 2013), 8, 138–140, 162, chapter 6; Russell Duncan, *Entrepreneur for Equality: Governor Rufus Bullock, Commerce, and Race in Post–Civil War Georgia* (Athens: University of Georgia Press, 1994), 40, 43–44, 47–55, 67–73, 117–118, 129–133; Numan V. Bartley, *The Creation of Modern Georgia*, 2nd ed. (Athens: University of Georgia Press, 1990), 32–38, 50–54, 58–72, 81–86; Donald L. Grant, *The Way It Was in the South: The Black Experience in Georgia* (New York: Birch Lane Press, 1993, 91–93, 95–96; Hahn, *Nation Under Our Feet*, 266, 273, 282, 312–313; Emberton, *Beyond Redemption*, chapter 6 and epilogue.

4. Jeffrey R. Kerr-Ritchie, "Rehearsal for War: Black Militias in the Atlantic World," *Slavery and Abolition* 26 (April 2005): 1–34. See also Kerr-Ritchie, *August First*.

5. Kerr-Ritchie, "Rehearsal for War," 12–24.

6. Bernard C. Nalty, *Strength for the Fight: A History of Black Americans in the Military* (New York: Free Press, 1986), 87.

7. Kerr-Ritchie, "Rehearsal for War." For the militia in the Americas, see Gregory Mixon, "'Merecemos tratamiento major,'" 55–76.

8. For a definition of the militia, see James B. Whisker, *The Rise and Decline of the American Militia System* (London: Selinsgrove: Susquehanna University Press, 1999), 7, 11–12, 55, 81, 240–245; Nancy L. Todd, *New York's Historic Armories: An Illustrated History* (Albany: State University of New York Press, 2006), 1; Mahon, *History of the Militia*, 4–5. For antebellum use of the militia, see Samuel J. Watson, *Peacekeepers and Conquerors: The Army Officer Corps on the American Frontier, 1821–1846* (Lawrence: University of Kansas Press, 2013), 143; and Bartley, *Creation of Modern Georgia*, 3, 16–20, 28–29.

9. For a summary of the National Guard Association's ambitions and goals for inclusion within the nation's defense network from 1879 to 1903, see Mahon, *History of the Militia*, chapters 8–10.

10. Emberton, *Beyond Redemption*, chapter 6, also examines the relationship between white antiblack violence, citizenship, power, national reconciliation, and white masculinity and manhood. For the broader parameters of national views of citizenship, civilization, and the place of white versus nonwhite people at home and abroad, see Matthew Frye Jacobson, *Barbarian Virtues: The United States Encounters Foreign Peoples at Home and Abroad, 1876–1917* (New York: Hill and Wang, 2000), 4–5, 8, 180–181, 190–192, 219.

11. Jacobson, *Barbarian Virtues*, 205–223.

12. Emberton, *Beyond Redemption*, chapter 6. For black militia failure, see Singletary, "African American Military," especially 22, 25–27, 30; Singletary, *Negro Militia*, 145–152.

13. Kerr-Ritchie, "Rehearsal for War," 9; Virginia Statutes at Large, 1639; Bradford Chambers, *Chronicles of Black Protest: Compiled and Edited With Commentary* (New York: New American Library, 1968), 37. The Georgia Legislature committed to naturalizing free blacks "as white men . . . with 'all the Rights, Privileges, Powers, and Immunities whatsoever which any person born of British parents' could have." See Winthrop D. Jordan, "Mulattoes and Race Relations in Britain's New World Colonies," in *America Compared: American History in International Perspective*, Volume I: *To 1877*, 2nd ed., ed. Carl J. Guarneri, 93–101 (Boston: Houghton Mifflin, 2005); Christopher C. Meyers and David Williams, *Georgia: A Brief History* (Macon: Mercer University Press, 2012), 34–35.

14. Nalty, *Strength for the Fight*, 6; William T. Allison, Jeffrey Grey, and Janet G. Valentine, *American Military History: A Survey from Colonial Times to the Present*, 2nd ed. (Boston: Pearson, 2013), 2–5; Grant, *The Way It Was*, 6–16. On the West Indian Regiments, see Roger Norman Buckley, *Slaves in Red Coats: The British West India Regiments* (New Haven: Yale University Press, 1979), 24, 39, 41, 55, 65, 68, 74–75, 94–95, 107, 130–139. My thanks go to Jeffrey R. Kerr-Ritchie for bringing this source to my attention.

15. Kerr-Ritchie, "Rehearsal for War," 7–9; Francois Furstenberg, "Beyond Freedom and Slavery: Autonomy, Virtue, and Resistance in Early American Political Discourse," *Journal of American History* 89, no. 4 (March 2003): 1316–1326.

16. Jane G. Landers, "Gracia Real de Santa Teresa de Mose: A Free Black Town in Spanish Colonial Florida," in *A Question of Manhood: A Reader in U. S. Black Men's History and Masculinity volume 1 "Manhood Rights": "The Construction of Black Male History and Manhood, 1750–1870*, ed. Darlene Clark Hine and Earnestine Jenkins, 90–114 (Bloomington: Indiana University Press, 1999); Landers, *Atlantic Creoles*, 7–14, and chapter 4. For additional examples of black militia service in colonial North America and the denial of the right to armed self-defense in the same region, see Ira Berlin, "From Creole to African: Atlantic Creoles and the Origins of African-American Society in Mainland North America," in *How Did American Slavery Begin? Readings Selected and Introduced*, ed. Edward Countryman, 17–84 (Boston: Bedford/St. Martin, 1999); and Cunningham, *Black Citizen-Soldiers of Kansas*, ix–xvi, 6–16, 27.

17. Kerr-Ritchie, "Rehearsal for War," 9–10, 21.

18. Kerr-Ritchie, "Rehearsal for War," 20–21. For resentment toward British emancipation and declarations that it was a failure, see Neville A. T. Hall, "Maritime Maroons: Grand Marronage from the Danish West Indies," in *Origins of the Black Atlantic*, ed. Laurent Dubois and Julius S. Scott, 47–68 (New York: Routledge, 2010); Thomas C. Holt, *The Problem of Freedom: Race, Labor, and Politics in Jamaica and Britain* (Baltimore: Johns Hopkins University Press, 1992), 8, 18–19. For a definition and explanation of public rights, see Rebecca J. Scott, "The Atlantic World and the Road to Plessy v. Ferguson," *Journal of American History* 94, no. 3 (December 2007): 726–733.

19. Kerr-Ritchie, "Rehearsal for War," 21–22.

20. Ibid., 10–14, 18–19, 27–28. For a critique of this idea as overly gendered and too closely associated with martial goals and actions, particularly after the Civil War, see Emberton, *Beyond Redemption*. For an examination of the marginalization of a nonwhite population, masculinity, volunteering, and militia/military service and imperial colonial governance, see Mrinalini Sinha, *Colonial Masculinity: The "Manly Englishman" and the "Effeminate Bengali" in the Late Nineteenth Century* (Manchester: Manchester University Press, 1995), chapter two.

21. Kerr-Ritchie, "Rehearsal for War," 14–19.

22. Ibid. For a broader study of the crowd and American antebellum politics, see David Waldstreicher, *In the Midst of Perpetual Fetes: The Making of American Nationalism, 1776–1820* (Chapel Hill: University of North Carolina Press, 1997). My thanks go to my colleague, Christopher Cameron, for introducing me to this work.

23. Kerr-Ritchie, "Rehearsal for War," 10.

24. Ira Berlin, Barbara J. Fields, Steven F. Miller, Joseph P. Miller, and Leslie S. Row-

land, "The Black Military Experience, 1861–1867," in *Slaves No More: Three Essays on Emancipation and the Civil War*, ed. Ira Berlin, Barbara J. Fields, Steven F. Miller, Joseph P. Reidy, and Leslie S. Rowland, 187–234 (New York: Cambridge University Press, 1992), especially 190, 194. My thanks go to Jeffrey R. Kerr-Ritchie for alerting me to this source.

25. Berlin, Fields, Miller, Miller, and Rowland, "The Black Military Experience," 207, 211, 218.

26. Ibid., 223–226, 229–230, 233.

27. Ibid., 104–105.

28. Berlin, Fields, Miller, Miller, and Rowland, "The Black Military Experience," 230, 190; Elsa Barkley Brown, "To Catch the Vision of Freedom"; Vincent Harding, *There Is a River: The Black Struggle for Freedom in America* (New York: Vintage Books, 1981), chapter 11; Amrita Chakrabarti Myers, *Forging Freedom: Black Women and the Pursuit of Liberty in Antebellum Charleston* (Chapel Hill: University of North Carolina Press, 2011), introduction.

29. Kerr-Ritchie, "Rehearsal for War," 26; Emberton, *Beyond Redemption*, 15–16, 23, 50, 55, 66–67, 76, 83, 87–90.

30. Kerr-Ritchie, "Rehearsal for War," 27; Emberton, *Beyond Redemption*, 138–140; Grant, *The Way It Was*, 91–96, 100–102, 107, 110–111, 119; Bartley, *Creation of Modern Georgia*, 33–36, 64–66, 75–95.

31. William A. Blair, *Cities of the Dead: Contesting the Memory of the Civil War in the South, 1865–1914* (Chapel Hill: University of North Carolina Press, 2004), chapter 5. For blacks drilling, see Executive Department Correspondence, 1-1-5, Box 57, Folder: Report of Outrages, no. 92, 29 September 1868, Calhoun County, Georgia Archives, Morrow, Georgia, hereafter cited as GDAH. Also see the folder for white assaults on blacks.

32. For formal militia service during Reconstruction, see Ben H. Severance, *Tennessee's Radical Army: The State Guard and Its Role in Reconstruction, 1867–1869* (Knoxville: University of Tennessee Press, 2005); Singletary, *Negro Militia*. For black celebration of Emancipation Day, see *Savannah Tribune*, 1876–1900; *Atlanta Independent*, 1905; Blair, *Cities of the Dead*, chapter 5.

33. Minutes—Lincoln Association, April 27, 1872, 1–10; Georgia National Guard Militia, 22-1-10, GDAH.

Chapter 2. "We Called It 'The Band of Brothers'": Black Independent Militia Formation and the Johnson County Insurrection of 1875

1. "Johnson County Insurrection," Jacob N. Blount, Foreman, and John W. Robison, Solicitor General of the State of Georgia, Johnson County Grand Jury Report, Augusta, Georgia, September 15, 1875, 16, 18, Georgia Department of Archives and History, Morrow, Georgia, hereafter noted as "Insurrection." The Georgia Department of Archives and History will hereafter be cited as GDAH. For black control over black labor, see Rebecca J. Scott, "Defining the Boundaries of Freedom in the World of Cane: Cuba, Brazil, and Louisiana after Emancipation," *American Historical Review* 99, no. 1 (February 1994): 70–81.

2. For a general summary of the first Reconstruction government in Georgia, see Bartley, *Creation of Modern Georgia*, 47. See also the Code of the State of Georgia: Re-

vised and Corrected, 4th ed., 1882, all laws passed since 1873, original code, 1858, 1860, 1862, 1873, Taxation, 126; Public Roads, 139–150. For examples of general struggles over local control, see Work Projects Administration, *Washington City Council, The Story of Washington-Wilkes: Compiled and Written by Workers of the Writers' Program of the Work Projects Administration in the State of Georgia* (Athens: University of Georgia Press, 1941), 61–66; Joseph T. Maddox, *Wilkinson County Georgia Historical Collections Revised and Reported 1980* (LaGrange: Family Tree Martha Smith Anderson, 1999), 62, 110–111. For a history of the Ordinary at the county level and some discussion of the county roads, see Bertha Sheppard Hart, *The Official History of Laurens County Georgia 1807–1941* (Atlanta: Cherokee Publishing Company, 1978), 72–74.

3. My thanks go to Mr. Dale Couch, former archivist, GDAH, Jonesboro, Georgia, for suggesting defining this event as a tax revolt.

4. For Louisiana, see Scott, "Fault Lines, Color Lines, and Party Lines," especially 66, 70–83; Scott, *Degrees of Freedom*, chapters 2–3. For Georgia and Union League and rural black self-defense activities, see Hahn, *Nation Under Our Feet*, chapter 6; and Donald L. Grant, *The Way It Was*, chapter 3.

5. For examples of petitions for admission by white and black militiamen, see Georgia National Guard Militia Petitions to Form Militia Companies, Folders 1870–1883, 022–01–010 Volume 17, Georgia National Guard/Defense Adjutant General, GDAH.

6. Kerr-Ritchie, "Rehearsal for War," 9, 18, 19, 24; Howard N. Rabinowitz, *Race Relations in the Urban South, 1865–1890* (New York: Oxford University Press, 1978), xiii–xvi. See also Richard C. Wade, "Foreword," *Race Relations in the Urban South, 1865–1890*, Rabinowitz (New York: Oxford University Press, 1978), ix-xii.

7. Rabinowitz, *Race Relations*, xiv–xv, 332–339, 289.

8. Edmund L. Drago, *Black Politicians and Reconstruction in Georgia: A Splendid Failure* (Baton Rouge: Louisiana State University Press, 1982), 74, 88, 90–94; Grant, *The Way It Was*, 91–93.

9. Grant, *The Way It Was*, 92–96; Hanes Walton Jr., *Black Republicans: The Politics of the Black and Tans* (Metuchen: Scarecrow Press, 1975), 47–48; Frances Smith, "Black Militia in Savannah, Georgia, 1872–1905," (master's thesis, Georgia Southern College, 1981), 9–16.

10. Grant, *The Way It Was*, 96–100; Drago, *Black Politicians and Reconstruction*, 88–90; Walton, *Black Republicans*, 50. Walton notes that "J. E. Bryant, the white Carpetbagger . . . was General Superintendent of the Freedman's Bureau and chief organizer of the black Georgia Equal Rights League."

11. Harry Watkins, Abraham Smith, George Blunt, S. W. Love, Morgan Gale, and 120 others (colored) to Maj Gen'l Steadman, Nov. 5, 1865; and Mingo Williams, Robert Williams, Horace Bailey, Claiborne Cherry, William Isom to Major General Davis Tillson, Acting Assistant Commissioner, State of Tennessee, n.d., Records of the Assistant Commissioner for the State of Georgia Bureau of Refugees, Freedmen and Abandoned Lands, 1865–1869, National Archives Publication M798, Roll 36, "Unbound Miscellaneous Papers," http://www.freedmensbureau.com/georgia/request.htm.

12. Report of Outrages, Gov. Rufus Bullock Correspondence, Executive Department Correspondence 1-1-5, Box 57, Old Location no. 2740–13, Folder October 2, 1868: W. C. Morrill Freedmen's Bureau (Bureau of Refugees Freedmen and Abandoned Lands

Office Agent Division of Americus—Sumter, Schley, and Webster Counties), Agent to Bt Capt M. Frank Gallagher AAAGenl in Atlanta, October 2 & 3, 1868, GDAH; Drago, *Black Politicians and Reconstruction*, 93–96; Grant, *The Way It Was*, 100–102.

13. State of Georgia Bureau of Refugees.

14. Grant, *The Way It Was*, 100; Drago, *Black Politicians and Reconstruction*, 90–93.

15. Grant, *The Way It Was*, 103; Walton, *Black Republicans*, 47–48.

16. State of Georgia Bureau of Refugees.

17. Ibid.; Grant, *The Way It Was*, 100–102.

18. Georgia Archives—Public Reference Service—File II—Tunis Campbell: Black Reconstructionist, Folder: Tunis Campbell (1), United States of America, State of Georgia, McIntosh County, Port of Darien, July 5, 1871, Affidavit of L. B. DeSammes(?),7–11; Affidavit of Hamilton Jackson, n.p.; Affidavit of Joseph P. Gilson; Affidavit of W. R. Pritchard, Dairen, [Georgia], May 20, 1872; Affidavit of James R. Burnett, Sheriff; Affidavit "Executed by Hamilton Jackson, Constable" 3, 5; Affidavit of Lecture (?) Crawford, Anthony Simmons, Sandy Stewart, London Andison (?), James Macmillion (?), Effriam (?) Black to Honorable Senate Committee, May 20, 1872, Darien, McIntosh County, GDAH; Russell Duncan, *Freedom's Shore: Tunis Campbell and the Georgia Freedmen* (Athens: University of Georgia Press, 1986), 29.

19. Affidavit of L. B. DeSammes(?),7–11.

20. Affidavit "Executed by Hamilton Jackson, Constable," 3, 5.

21. Affidavit of Lecture Crawford; Georgia Archives—Public Reference Service—File II—Tunis Campbell: Black Reconstructionist, Folder: Tunis Campbell(1), Affidavit of H. W. Corker, Darien, May 20, 1872, 1–2; Beng Conley, Executive Department, State of Georgia, Atlanta, Georgia, to Hon. T. G. Campbell, Senator 2nd Dist., Darien, Georgia, December 19, 1871, GDAH. Also see E. Merton Coulter, "Tunis G. Campbell, Negro Reconstructionist in Georgia Part I," *The Georgia Historical Quarterly* 51, no. 4 (December 1967): 421.

22. "July 5, 1871," Georgia Archives—Public Reference Service—File II—Tunis Campbell: Black Reconstructionist, Folder: Tunis Campbell(1), Def Affidavit of Allan C. Gould, James Steel, Samuel Patterson, Lecture (?) Crawford; Affidavit of W. R. Pritchard, Dairen, 1st Lieutenant James H. Bradley to Brvt Col. J. H. Taylor Asst. Adjutant General Department of the South, June 13, 1870, Atlanta, Georgia, p. 4; Affidavit of W. R. Pritchard, Dairen, GDAH. For the results of combining religion and politics, see Duncan, *Freedom's Shore*, 44–45.

23. "July 5, 1871;" Def Affidavit of Allan C. Gould.

24. For other efforts by rural African Americans in Georgia, see Hahn, *Nation Under Our Feet*, part II, especially chapter 6, and Jonathan M. Bryant, *How Curious a Land: Conflict and Change in Green County, Georgia, 1850–1885* (Chapel Hill: University of North Carolina Press, 1996). On this issue in the Western Hemisphere, see Scott, *Degrees of Freedom*; Andrews, *Afro-Latin America*; and Reid-Vazquez, *Year of the Lash*.

25. Scott, "The Atlantic World," 726–733, especially 729–730.

26. For a detailed discussion of the "struggle for values," see Scott, "Defining the Boundaries," 70–74, 76–77, 80–81. Also see Leeanna Keith, *The Colfax Massacre: The Untold Story of Black Power, White Terror, and The Death of Reconstruction* (New York: Oxford University Press, 2008), 37, 45, 47–48, 51, 58, 64, 69, 87–89.

27. Adjutant General Miscellaneous Records: National Guard, Box 20, Folder: 22-1-10, GA. Natl Guard Militia & State Troops Petition Chatham Light Inf. at Savannah, April 22, 1872, Muster Roll 1874, Enlistments 1893, 1895, 1900, Enlistment 1896, GDAH; Georgia National Guard/Defense Adjutant General, Box 17, Folder: 22-1-10 Ga National Guard-Militia—Request to Gov. Colquitt to Elect Officers Savannah Hussars 20 Jun. 1877; Minutes—Lincoln Association, April 27, 1872, 1–10, Georgia National Guard Militia, 22-1-10, GDAH. Adjutant General Miscellaneous Records: National Guard, Box 20, Folder: 22-1-10, Ga Natl Guard Militia Petition for Election of Officers For Douglass Infantry at Augusta September 20, 1873, and 22-1-10, Ga Natl Guard Militia Petition for Election of Officers Georgia Infantry (Col.) March 5, 1874, GDAH.

28. "Christian Citizenship," *The [Savannah] Colored Tribune*, 4 March 1876. For a description of Bryant's commitment to and vision for a national Union League and its protection of black political power in the South, see Michael W. Fitzgerald, *The Union League Movement in the Deep South: Politics and Agricultural Change During Reconstruction* (Baton Rouge: Louisiana State University Press, 1989), 235–240.

29. "Christian Citizenship." For a discussion of John Emory Bryant's political career and association with blacks, see Drago, *Black Politicians and Reconstruction*, 28–30, 40, on positive relations with blacks, and 44–45, 53–60, on strained and negative interactions with African Americans that led to Bryant's opposition to black political activity even to the point of joining Conservative Democrats in 1870; by 1877 Bryant was no longer a friend of African American politicians. For similar conclusions about Bryant being first a friend and then a foe of blacks, see Allison G. Dorsey, *To Build Our Lives Together: Community Formation in Black Atlanta, 1875–1906* (Athens: University of Georgia Press, 2004), 124, 127.

30. "Christian Citizenship."

31. Ibid.; "Go to the Exchange and Register," *The [Savannah] Colored Tribune*, July 8, 1876; "Republican National Platform: Declaration of Principles," *[Savannah] Colored Tribune*, July 8, 1876.

32. See Kathleen Ann Clark, *Defining Moments: African American Commemoration & Political Culture in the South, 1863–1913* (Chapel Hill: University of North Carolina Press, 2005), chapter 2. See also William H. Becker, "The Black Church: Manhood and Mission," in *A Question of Manhood: A Reader in U. S. Black Men's History and Masculinity*, Vol. I: *"Manhood Rights: The Construction of Black Male History and Manhood, 1750–1870*, ed. Darlene Clark Hine and Earnestine Jenkins, 322–339 (Bloomington: Indiana University Press, 1999), especially 325–327, 330. For another interpretation of black masculinity, see Riché Richardson, *Black Masculinity and the U. S. South: From Uncle Tom to Gangsta* (Athens: University of Georgia Press, 2007), chapter 1. On black demands and attempts to utilize the levers of governance and white fear, see Landers, *Atlantic Creoles*, chapter 1; Reid-Vazquez, *Year of the Lash*, chapters 4–6; Holt, *The Problem of Freedom*, xvii–xix; Richard Zuczek, *State of Rebellion: Reconstruction in South Carolina* (Columbia: University of South Carolina Press, 1996), 37, 41 48–49, 56–59.

33. Clark, *Defining Moments*, 57, 59, 63–67, 69–71, 80. To examine an additional vision of manhood within the AME Church, see Becker, "The Black Church," 332–336. Clark's chapter in *Defining Moments* also explores the price black men paid as they gendered their history before and during the antebellum and postbellum periods. For an

examination of another dimension of the black vision of freedom, see Brown, "To Catch the Vision of Freedom." For assertions of autonomy and initiative throughout the Western Hemisphere, see Reid-Vazquez, *Year of the Lash*, chapters 5 and 6; Andrews, *Afro-Latin America*, chapter 3; Aline Helg, *Our Rightful Share: The Afro-Cuban Struggle for Equality, 1886–1912* (Chapel Hill: University of North Carolina Press, 1995), chapters 1–4; Ada Ferrer, *Insurgent Cuba: Race, Nation, and Revolution, 1868–1898* (Chapel Hill: University of North Carolina Press, 1999); Christopher Leslie Brown and Philip D. Morgan, *Arming Slaves: From Classical Times to the Modern Age* (New Haven: Yale University Press, 2006), 146–353.

34. "Burke County: [Special Telegrams to the Chronicle and Sentinel]," *Augusta Chronicle and Sentinel*, August 20, 1875.

35. Adjutant General Miscellaneous Records: National Guard, Box 20, Folder: 22-1-10, Ga Natl Guard Militia Petition for Election of Officers For Douglass Infantry at Augusta, September 20, 1873, GDAH.

36. Ga Natl Guard Militia Petition for Election of Officers Georgia Infantry (Col.), March 5, 1874, GDAH.

37. Ibid.; *Roster of Georgia Volunteer Military Organizations*.

38. See the following county histories for black goals and actions, African American institution-building, resurgent white power, Ku Klux Klan activity, the nature of local economic distress, and black and white relations: *Official History of Laurens County*, 56–264; Victor Davidson, *History of Wilkinson County* (Spartanburg: Reprint Company, Publishers, 1978), 205–278; Mary Alice Jordan, ed., *Cotton to Kaolin: A History of Washington County, Georgia, 1784–1989* (Sandersville and Roswell: Washington County Historical Society, Inc., and W. H. Wolfe Associates Historical Publications Division, 1989), 1–78, appendix C; Ella Mitchell, *History of Washington County* (Atlanta: Cherokee Publishing Company, 1924), 9–112, 168–171; Marion Little Durden, *A History of Saint George Parish, Colony of Georgia, Jefferson County, State of Georgia* (Swainsboro: Magnolia Press, 1983), 51–95; Albert M. Hillhouse, *A History of Burke County, Georgia, 1777–1950* (Swainsboro and Spartanburg: Magnolia Press, 1985), 115–160; Angela Lee, *Images of America Burke County Georgia* (Dover, N.H.: Arcadia, 1996), 10–12, 20–21, 43–45, 77, 82, 96–105; Nell H. Baldwin and A. M. Hillhouse, *An Intelligent Student's Guide to Burke County (Ga.) History* (Waynesboro: Nell H. Baldwin and A. M. Hillhouse, 1956), preface–203.

39. For descriptions of black and white confrontations, see Hart, *Official History of Laurens County*, 88–89; Davidson, *History of Wilkinson County*, 273–278; Durden, *A History of Saint George Parish, Colony of Georgia, Jefferson County*, 86–95.

40. Hart, *Official History of Laurens County*.

41. For descriptions of black and white confrontations, see Hart, *Official History of Laurens County*; Davidson, *History of Wilkinson County*, 273–278; Durden, *A History of Saint George Parish, Colony of Georgia, Jefferson County*, 86–95.

42. Davidson, *History of Wilkinson County*, 273–274.

43. Ibid., 273–277.

44. Durden, *A History of Saint George Parish, Colony of Georgia, Jefferson County*, 86–87.

45. Ibid., 87–89; *Sandersville Herald and Georgian*, July-October 1875. For a view of

black expectations, federal power, and African American autonomy, see David Carter, "Romper Lobbies and Coloring Lessons: Grassroots Visions and Political Realities in the Battle for Head Start in Mississippi, 1965–1967," in *Making a New South: Race, Leadership and Community after the Civil War*, ed. Paul A. Cimbala and Barton C. Shaw, 191–208 (Gainesville: University Press of Florida, 2007), especially 196, 204–207. For the pursuit of land in the nineteenth century, see Holt, *The Problem of Freedom*, chapter 2; Landers, *Atlantic Creoles*, chapters 1–3.

46. Hart, *Official History of Laurens County*, 88–89; Davidson, *History of Wilkinson County*, 273–278; Durden, *A History of Saint George Parish, Colony of Georgia, Jefferson County*, 86–95.

47. Davidson, *History of Wilkinson County*, 273–278; Durden, *A History of Saint George Parish, Colony of Georgia, Jefferson County*, 86–95; Hart, *Official History of Laurens County*, 88–89; "Gen. Joseph Morris," *Sandersville Herald and Georgian*, September 9, 1875.

48. Davidson, *History of Wilkinson County*, 275–277; "Gen. Joseph Morris."

49. Davidson, *History of Wilkinson County*, 273–278; Durden, *A History of Saint George Parish, Colony of Georgia, Jefferson County*, 86–95; Hart, *Official History of Laurens County*, 88–89; "The Insurrection (?)," *Sandersville Herald and Georgian*, August 19, 1875.

50. Ronald R. Krebs, *Fighting for Rights: Military Service and the Politics of Citizenship* (Ithaca: Cornell University Press, 2006), 29–38, especially 29–30. Emphasis in original.

51. "Keep Cool," *Sandersville Herald and Georgian*, July 22, 1875.

52. Ibid.

53. Ibid. For Prince Rivers's place in South Carolina history, see Stephen Budiansky, *The Bloody Shirt: Terror After the Civil War* (New York: Plume, 2009), 51–52, 57–64, 242–253.

54. "The Colored 'Mass Meeting,'" *Sandersville Herald and Georgian*, July 29, 1875. For "Sambo dialect" as an attempt to discredit Prince Rivers as an inarticulate black man, see Budiansky, *The Bloody Shirt*, 253. On British policy makers and colored Jamaicans who considered former slaves to be uneducated, uncivilized, and savage, see Holt, *The Problem of Freedom*, chapter 2.

55. "The Colored 'Mass Meeting.'"

56. "Insurrection."

57. "The Negro Insurrection"; "The Negro Troubles," *Savannah Morning News*, August 20, 1875.

58. "Insurrection"; "The Negro Insurrection"; "Negro Troubles." See "Civil Rights Act of 1875," *United Statues at Large* XVIII, 335. http://chnm.gmu.edu/courses/122/recon/civilrightsact.html, accessed June 13, 2008. My thanks go to Ms. Lois Stickell, Reference Librarian, Atkins Library, University of North Carolina at Charlotte, Charlotte, North Carolina. Also see John Hope Franklin, "The Enforcement of the Civil Rights Act of 1875," *Prologue: The Journal of the National Archives* 6, no. 4 (Winter 1974): 225–235; John Hope Franklin, "Race and the Constitution in the Nineteenth Century," in *African Americans and the Living Constitution*, ed. John Hope Franklin and Genna Rae McNeil, 21–32 (Washington, D.C.: Smithsonian Institute, 1995). For a discussion of land and black goals, see John Hope Franklin and Alfred A. Moss Jr., *From Slavery to Freedom: A*

History of African Americans, 8th ed. (New York: McGraw Hill, 2000), 256–260; Hahn, *Nation Under Our Feet*, 128–129; Eric Foner, *Nothing But Freedom: Emancipation and Its Legacy* (Baton Rouge: Louisiana State University Press, 1983), 12–15, 20–21, 31–36. For black self-determination, see Henry Louis Gates Jr., "Behind '40 acres, mule' story," *The Root* in *Charlotte Observer*, January 12, 2013.

59. "Insurrection."

60. Hahn, *Nation Under Our Feet*, 128–129. Also see Foner, *Nothing But Freedom*, 20–36.

61. "Insurrection." For black violence against whites in the context of blacks exercising political power, see Andrews, *Afro-Latin America*, 90–91, 110–111, 113, 131; Landers, *Atlantic Creoles*, 110–111; and Charles Lane, *The Day Freedom Died: The Colfax Massacre, The Supreme Court, and the Betrayal of Reconstruction* (New York: Henry Holt and Company, 2008), 11, 17–21.

62. "Insurrection."

63. Ibid.; "The Negro Troubles." For an examination of African American collective action and goal setting in conflict with white perceptions of black actions, worldview, and collective behavior, see Brown, "To Catch the Vision of Freedom," 66–99; John David Smith, *Black Voices From Reconstruction, 1865–1977* (Gainesville: University Press of Florida, 1997); Scott, *Degrees of Freedom*, chapter 2. For the Haitian Revolution and fears of Haitianization, see Michael A. Gomez, *Reversing Sail: A History of the African Diaspora: New Approaches to African History* (Cambridge: Cambridge University Press, 2005), chapter 6; and Andrews, *Afro-Latin America*, chapters 3–4.

64. "Insurrection," 2–3, 5, 9, 36. For parallels to slave revolts, see Gomez, *Reversing Sail*, chapter 6.

65. "Insurrection," 3–5, 25–27. For slave insurrections and black self-mastery, see Burton, *The Age of Lincoln*, 190, 194–197.

66. "Insurrection," 6–7.

67. Ibid., 8–9. The white response to black militia activity is also explored in Mitchell Snay, *Fenians, Freedmen, and Southern Whites: Race and Nationality in the Era of Reconstruction* (Baton Rouge: Louisiana State University Press, 2007), 4; Scott, *Degrees of Freedom*, chapter 2; Fitzgerald, *Union League Movement*.

68. "Insurrection," 8.

69. Ibid., 15–17, 28, 32.

70. Ibid., 16–18, 24–29.

71. Ibid., 17–19.

72. Ibid., 19–22, 30.

73. Ibid.

74. Ibid., 23–26, 29, 31–43.

75. Governor Executive Department, Governor's Subject Files, 1877–1882, Governor Alfred Colquitt, State of Georgia Executive Minutes, Jan 12, 1877, to July 1881, Reel 1208, Ben W. Fortson Jr., Secretary of State, Executive Department, Atlanta, Ga., Nov. 19, 1879, 601, GDAH.

76. "Gov. Smith described in the [New York] Herald," *Savannah Colored Tribune*, March 4, 1876.

77. Michelle Mitchell, *Righteous Propagation: African Americans and the Politics of*

Racial Destiny after Reconstruction (Chapel Hill: University of North Carolina, 2004), 18–19, 24, 30, 33–35, 38, 45, 47–49, 57. Mitchell notes that "Georgia was particularly fertile ground for emigrationism" to Africa from Reconstruction to the beginning of the twentieth century (46). A generation after the 1875 insurrection, in 1894, "one thousand women, men, and children . . . longed to emigrate" from Laurens County (47–49), and during the same period Washington County blacks, some "250–300 familys," including leaders David Green and J. W. Sessions, pursued emigration "to our Fatherland" (40).

Chapter 3. Creating the Georgia Militia: Blacks and the Road to State Militia Companies, 1865–1880

1. "Affairs in Georgia," *Savannah Morning News*, January 8, 1872; Singletary, *Negro Militia*, 3. For a discussion of how the right to self-defense was and is restricted to white men, of the process African American men followed to carve out definitions of freedom and defense of the black community, and of having a gun as part of white men's personal attire, see Kerr-Ritchie, "Rehearsal for War," 3–9, 11, 26–28; Emberton, *Beyond Redemption*, 149–150, 176.

2. For the James M. Smith inauguration and its importance to white power, see "By Telegraph," *Savannah Morning News*, January 13, 1872, and "The Redemption of Georgia," *Savannah Morning News*, January 23, 1872.

3. Georgia Legislature, 1878–1879, Title X—Military Revised Code of 1873, Organization of Volunteer Troops Number 276, Section II Organization, 103, GDAH. Whites took tentative steps toward recreating the militia, including speculating on the federal response. See "Volunteer Military Companies," and "Volunteer Companies," *Savannah Morning News*, March 16, 1872.

4. On Haitianization, see Andrews, *Afro-Latin America*, 110, 113,131, 142.

5. For the problems of change, see Hale, *Making Whiteness*, 9, 126–139, 148, 167, 200, 221, 229, 231–233, 238.

6. "Volunteer Military Companies," *Savannah Morning News*, March 15, 1872; Ogeechee, "Volunteer Companies," *Savannah Morning News*, March 15, 1872.

7. "Volunteer Military Companies"; Ogeechee, "Volunteer Companies."

8. For New Orleans's and Mobile's militia behavior and vision of power, see Hogue, *Uncivil War*; and Michael Fitzgerald, *Urban Emancipation: Popular Politics in Reconstruction Mobile, 1860–1890* (Baton Rouge: Louisiana State University Press, 2002). For the antebellum role of the militia as a defender of property, as slave management, as race control, and as an antislave insurrection institution, see Joel Williamson, *The Crucible of Race: Black-White Relations in the American South Since Emancipation* (New York: Oxford University Press, 1984), 20–21; and Orville Vernon Burton, *The Age of Lincoln* (New York: Hill and Wang, 2007), 125–126, 130.

9. Mahon, *History of the Militia*, 68.

10. Governor James M. Smith, Executive Department Correspondence, Box 62, Folder August 14, 1872, Henry S. Westmore Ordinary and W. J. Clements to His Ex Gov. Ja M. Smith, GDAH; Governor James M. Smith, Executive Department Correspondence, Box 62, Folder July 8, 1872, William C. Starns and A. Husse (?) to His Excellency Jas. M. Smith, Governor of State of Georgia, GDAH.

11. Savannah Cadets Minute Book and Scrapbook, Box Samuel-Savannah Cadets Miscellaneous Papers No. 677–681, 34-G-6, Folder 1: Savannah Cadets Minute Book 1861–1873, 105, 107, 115–119, 122, 125–126, 137–138, Georgia Historical Society; see 156–171 on preparation for petition for admission to the state militia and guns; hereafter cited as the Savannah Cadets Minute Book.

12. Governor James M. Smith, Executive Department Correspondence, Box 62, Folder July 8, 1872, William C. Starns and A. Husse (?) to His Excellency Jas. M. Smith, Governor of State of Georgia, GDAH.

13. Military Revised Code of 1873, 103; Governor James M. Smith, Executive Department Correspondence, Box 62, Folder August 14, 1872, Henry S. Westmore Ordinary and W. J. Clements to His Ex Gov. Ja M. Smith, GDAH.

14. Governor James M. Smith, Executive Department Correspondence, Box 62, Folder: June 7, 1872, A. T. Harman to His Excellency Jas. Smith; Folder: June 1, 1872, J. M. Smith to Hon. James M. Smith, Governor of Georgia; Folder: July 13, 1872, Thomasville, Georgia, Chas P. Hansell, President to His Ex J. M. Smith Gov of Georgia; Folder: June 11, 1872, Seaborn Reese to Hon. James M. Smith, Governor etc.; and Folder: July 6, 1872, Seaborn Reese to J. W. Warren Secretary, etc., GDAH.

15. Governor James M. Smith, Executive Department Correspondence, Box 62, Folder: July 13, 1872, John L. Culver & Others; and Folder: Short Folder, July 15, 1872, J. R. Murphy to His Excellency Jas. M. Smith, Gov. elect-of Georgia, GDAH.

16. Governor James M. Smith, Executive Department Correspondence, Box 62, Folder: July 20, 1872, E. S. McCandless to Gov James M. Smith; and Folder: June 25, 1872, Augustus Pitehus to His Excellency Governor Smith, GDHA.

17. Governor James M. Smith, Executive Department Correspondence, Box 62, Folder: July 1872, Undated, Savannah Cadets, H. M. Branch and Case H. J. Dickerson to Hon. J. M. Smith, Governor of State of Georgia, GDAH.

18. For an example of white requests for uniform style and color, see Governor James M. Smith, Executive Department Correspondence, Box 62, Folder: June 10, 1872, Joseph Hilton to His Excellency James M. Smith Governor of Georgia, GDAH.

19. For a discussion of white anticipation of black insurrectionary activity and the idea of race war as a means of securing white dominance, see Sidney Herbert, "Trial of Corday Harris," *Savannah Morning News*, September 6, 1875, 1; "Electric Flashes—Negro Troubles Anticipated in Sandersville," *Atlanta Daily Constitution*, July 24, 1875, editorial page; "War of Races!" *Atlanta Daily Constitution*, 20 August 1875, editorial page; "The Black Fiasco—All Quiet on the Front," *Atlanta Daily Constitution*, August 22, 1875; "Peace!" *Atlanta Daily Constitution*, August 22, 1875, editorial page; "The Seminole Negroes—Contemplated," *Savannah Morning News*, September 2, 1875, editorial page. For the right to assemble, see "By Telegraph," *Savannah Morning News*, September 2, 1875.

20. Governor James M. Smith, Executive Department Correspondence, Box 62, Folder: July 11, 1872, Walter H. Johnson to His Excellency J. M. Smith, Governor, GDAH; Adjutant General Miscellaneous Records: National Guard, Box 20, Folder: 22-1-10, GA Natl Guard—Militia, Petition for Election of Officers, Columbus Volunteers (Col.) May 16, 1874, GDAH; "Roster of Colored Companies," *Roster of Georgia Volunteer Military Organizations*, n.p., GDAH.

21. Adjutant General Miscellaneous Records: National Guard, Box 20, Folder: 22-1-

10, GA. Natl Guard Militia & State Troops Petition Chatham Light Inf. At Savannah, April 22, 1872, Muster Roll 1874, Enlistments 1893, 1895, 1900, and Enlistment 1896, GDAH; Savannah Cadets, 155–162.

22. Minutes—Lincoln Association, April 27, 1872, 1–10, Georgia National Guard Militia, 22-1-10, GDAH. On black belief, commitment, and adherence to the law as an important transition from slavery to freedom and how whites contradicted this trend, see Christopher Waldrep, *Roots of Disorder: Race and Criminal Justice in the American South, 1817–80* (Urbana: University of Illinois Press, 1998), 101, 111, 113–114, 119.

23. Adjutant General Miscellaneous Records: National Guard, Box 20, Folder: 22-1-10, Ga Natl Guard Militia Enlistment of Forest City Light Infantry, Co. A., 1st Bn Inf., GA vol.: (Co), Petition for Election of Officers, Forest City Light Infantry, Col.) Co. B, July16, 1874; and Folder: 22-1-10, Ga Natl Guard Militia (Colored), Petition from Savannah Light Infantry & Muster Roll, July 21, 1877, Enlistment of Savannah Light Infantry, GDAH.

24. Frances Smith, "Black Militia in Savannah, Georgia 1872–1905," (master's thesis, Georgia Southern College, 1981), 22. Smith notes that the Hussars—all butchers—participated in Savannah's 1874 Emancipation Day festivities. Sidney Herbert, "Roster of Cavalry Companies," in *Roster of Georgia Volunteer Military Organizations* (Atlanta: James P. Harrison & Company State Printers and Publishers, 1878), Library, GDAH; Georgia National Guard/Defense Adjutant General, Box 17, Folder: 22-1-10 Ga National Guard-Militia—Request to Gov. Colquitt to Elect Officers Savannah Hussars, June 20, 1877, GDAH.

25. Adjutant General Miscellaneous Records: National Guard, Box 20, Folder: 22-1-10, Ga Natl Guard Militia Petition for Election of Officers For Douglass Infantry at Augusta, September 20, 1873, and 22-1-10, Ga Natl Guard Militia Petition for Election of Officers Georgia Infantry (Col.), March 5, 1874, GDAH.

26. For white attitudes about the black militia companies alleged to have been at the heart of the Johnson County Insurrection, see *Sandersville Herald, Atlanta Daily Constitution, Augusta Chronicle and Sentinel,* and *Savannah Morning News,* July 26–October 1, 1875. See also *Savannah Colored Tribune,* March 1876.

27. Adjutant General Miscellaneous Records: National Guard, Box 20, Folder: 22-1-10, Ga Natl Guard Militia Petition to Elect Officers, Atlanta Light Infantry, Aug 27, 1873, Folder: 22-1-10 Ga Natl Guard—Militia, Muster Roll Order for election, Fulton Guards (Col), June 3, 1874, Petition for Election of Officers, Fulton Guards, April 27, 1883, Enlistment of Fulton Guards at Atlanta, 1891, 1892, 1893, Application for reinstatement, Fulton Guards (formerly Co. D, 2nd BN, Ga vol. Inf. Colored), Enlistment of Fulton Guards, Co. B. 1st Bn Inf. Colored at Atlanta, 1900, Enlistment of Non-Commissioned Staff, 2nd Bn (Col) at Atlanta, 1898; Folder: 22-1-10 Ga. Natl Guard, Petition to form Battalion by Atlanta Light Infantry, Washington Guards, Capital Guards, Governors, September 29, 1880, Petition to form Atlanta Washington Guards, May 3, 1877, Petition to form Capitol Guards, Election of Officers & Muster Roll, 1878, Petition from GA. Cadets, 1879, Muster Roll, Gov. Volunteers, 1879, GDAH. The other commanding officers were: Jefferson Murphy, commanding the Atlanta Light Infantry, and Thornton Tuner, commanding the Washington Guards.

28. For Rucker's political career, see Gregory Mixon, "The Political Career of Henry

A. Rucker: A Survivor in a New South City," *Atlanta History: A Journal of Georgia and the South* 45 (Summer 2001): 4–26. For the political activism that black militiamen carried out in 1880, see Walton, *Black Republicans*, 47–55.

29. For militia commitment to separate the institution from party politics, see "The Military Convention," August 28, 1880, Chatham Artillery Records, Ms 966, Chatham Artillery Papers, Scrapbook 1872–1883, Box 37, p. 93, Georgia Historical Society.

30. Hale, *Making Whiteness*, 6–9, 96. On capital industrialization, see also Glenn, *Unequal Freedom*.

31. Hale, *Making Whiteness*, 78, 103.

32. Ibid., 117, 125–35.

33. Ibid., 210, 228–29.

34. Ibid., 6, 15, 128–29, 137–39, 143, 148, 169.

35. Drago, *Black Politicians and Reconstruction*, 52, 120, 126–27, 129.

36. Governor James M. Smith, Executive Correspondence, Box 62, Folder: July 31, 1872, W. F. Cannon, Wilkinson County, GDAH.

37. Drago, *Black Politicians and Reconstruction*.

38. For militia companies and their political links, see Sydney Herbert, *Roster of Georgia Volunteer Military Organizations* (Atlanta: 1878), GDAH, hereafter cited as *Roster of Georgia Volunteer Military Organizations*. For actions of the Jefferson Dragoons, see "Insurrection: All Quiet in Burke, Jefferson and Washington County," *Augusta Chronicle and Sentinel*, August 22, 1875.

39. *Roster of Georgia Volunteer Military Organizations*.

40. *Official History of Laurens County*, 88–89.

41. Davidson, *History of Wilkinson County*, 273–74.

42. Ibid., 275–77.

43. "The Colored 'Mass Meeting,'" *Sandersville Herald and Georgian*, July 29, 1875.

44. Ibid., Hale, *Making Whiteness*, 125.

45. "The Colored 'Mass Meeting'"; "War of Races!" *Atlanta Daily Constitution*, August 20, 1875; "The Negro Troubles," *Savannah Morning News*, August 20, 1875.

46. Hale, *Making Whiteness*, 125–28; Roberta Senechal de la Roche, "The Sociogenesis of Lynching," in *Under Sentence of Death: Lynching in the South*, ed. W. Fitzhugh Brundage, 48–76 (Chapel Hill: University of North Carolina Press, 1997); W. Fitzhugh Brundage, *Lynching in the New South: Georgia and Virginia, 1880–1930* (Urbana: University of Illinois Press, 1993), chapters 1–4.

47. "The Colored 'Mass Meeting'"; "War of Races!"; "The Negro Troubles," *Savannah Morning News*, August 20, 1875; *Atlanta Daily Constitution*, August 20, 1875.

48. "The Colored 'Mass Meeting.'"

49. "The Insurrection (?)," *Sandersville Herald and Georgian*, August 19, 1875.

50. Ibid. On Jerry Waters's name also being Jerry Walters, see the unpaginated preface to the "Report of the Commissioners Johnson County Insurrection." Actual deposition is numbered.

51. "The Insurrection," *Sandersville Herald and Georgian*, August 26, 1875; "By Telegraph to the Morning News," *Savannah Morning News*, August 21, 1875; "War of Races!"

52. "The Insurrection"; Rooster, "Prefactory," "The Negro Insurrection," *Savannah Morning News*, August 23, 1875; "Trial of the Negro Insurrectionists," *Savannah Morning News*, September 3, 1875.

53. "The Negro Insurrection"; "The Negro Troubles."
54. "The Negro Insurrection."
55. Ibid.
56. Ibid.
57. Ibid.
58. "The Insurrection"; preface to "Report of the Commissioners Johnson County Insurrection"; "By Telegraph," *Savannah Morning News*, August 31, 1875.
59. Hale, *Making Whiteness*, 125–37, 143–44.
60. "The Trial of the Negro Insurrectionists," *Savannah Morning News*, September 1, 1875; "Charge of Judge Johnson," *Sandersville Herald and Georgian*, September 2, 1875.
61. "The Trial of the Negro Insurrectionists."
62. Ibid. For Amos T. Ackerman/Akerman's work and outlook on antiblack violence see Charles Lane, *The Day Freedom Died: The Colfax Massacre, the Supreme Court, and the Betrayal of Reconstruction* (New York: Henry Holt and Company, 2008), xvii, 4, 61, 139–40.
63. "The Trial of the Negro Insurrectionists"; "By Telegraph," *Savannah Morning News*, September 1, 1875; "By Telegraph," *Savannah Morning News*, September 2, 1875; "Trial of the Negro Insurrectionists; Sidney Herbert, "Letter From Sandersville," *Savannah Morning News*, September 4, 1875; "Trial of Corday Harris," *Savannah Morning News*, September 6, 1875; For additional defense counsel and prosecutors and a partial list of grand jury members, see "Trial of the Negro Insurrectionists."
64. "Final Presentments of the Grand Jury," *Savannah Morning News*, September 6, 1875.
65. "Insurrection," introduction to John W. Robison Solicitor General of the State of Georgia, "State of Georgia, Johnson County Grand Jury," and "The State against Austin Mason et al.," n.p. On the fear of black oath taking and black violence against whites, the Haitian Revolution, and the Haitianization/Africanization process whereby black people ruled themselves or asserted their autonomy, see Landers, *Atlantic Creoles*, 60–61; Andrews, *Afro-Latin America*, 110, 113, 131; Reid-Vazquez, *Year of the Lash*, 65–67; and Thomas C. Holt, *Children of Fire: A History of African Americans* (New York: Hill and Wang, 2010), 161–67.
66. "The Insurrection: All Quiet in Burke, Jefferson, and Washington County," *Augusta Chronicle and Sentinel*, August 22, 1875; "The Attempted Insurrection," *Augusta Chronicle and Sentinel*, August 24, 1875.
67. "By Telegraph: The Georgia Insurrectionists," *Savannah Morning News*, September 10, 1875.
68. See Georgia, Executive Department Minutes, 1874–1877, microfilm, GDAH, 356, 380, 416–18, 432, 446. Also see "Roster" for a list of the white companies in 1878.

Chapter 4. "Any Person Capable of Doing Military Duty": The Georgia Volunteers, 1878–1890s

1. For the multiple roles of the militia and the relation between the militia and politics, See Bruce E. Baker, *This Mob Will Surely Take My Life: Lynching in the Carolinas, 1871–1947* (London: Continuum, 2008), 17–18, 23, 35–36, 55.
2. Georgia Legislature, 1878–1879, Title X—Military Revised Code of 1873, Organi-

zation of Volunteer Troops Number 276, Section II Organization, p. 103, GDAH; Frances Smith, "Black Militia in Savannah, Georgia, 1872–1905," (master's thesis, Georgia Southern College, 1981), 32–34.

3. Sidney Herbert, *Roster of Georgia Volunteers Military Organizations* (Atlanta: James P. Harrison, 1878), 15–18; Frances Smith, "Black Militia in Savannah," 21–26. For the parameters, regulations, and standards for the Georgia militia, see "Title X Military," in *Acts and Resolutions of the General Assembly of the State of Georgia, 1878–79* (Atlanta: James P. Harrison Public Printer, 1880), 103–114; for parade regulations, see especially 110, GDAH.

4. Frances Smith, "Black Militia in Savannah," 20, 26–28; see Herbert, "State Military Board" and "Military Committees of General Assembly"; "The Military Convention—Address of Colonel Clifford W. Anderson" *Savannah Morning News*, July 17, 1880. The members of the State Military Board were: Col. Clifford W. Anderson, Savannah, Georgia, Board of Officers President; Lt. Col. W. H. Ross, Macon, Georgia; Lt. Col. W. Daniel, Augusta, Georgia; Capt. John F. Wheaton, Savannah, Georgia; Capt. William S. Shepherd, Columbus, Georgia; Maj. W. S. Basinger, Savannah, Georgia; Maj. Thomas F. Jones, Blakely, Georgia; Maj. C. W. Henderson, Atlanta, Georgia; Capt. P. M. B. Young, Cartersville, Georgia. For National Guard Association discussions, see W. Berum Wetmore, Cor. Secretary National Guard Association, "The National Guard Bill in Congress," *United Service: A Quarterly of Military and Naval Affairs* 6 (March 1882): 337. American Periodicals Online, Atkins Library, University of North Carolina at Charlotte, Charlotte, North Carolina, hereafter cited as APOUNCC; Albert Ordway, "A National Militia," *The North American Review* 134 (April 1882): 395, APOUNCC; Charles E. Lydecker, "An Unconstitutional Militia," *The North American Review* 134 (June 1882): 631, APOUNCC; "Our Volunteer Military," *Savannah Morning News*, February 10, 1877.

5. James Michael Russell, *Atlanta, 1847–1890: City Building in the Old South and New* (Baton Rouge: Louisiana State University Press, 1988), 2–7, 10–11, 260–64; "States Rights in Georgia," *Savannah Morning News*, February 7, 1877, 1; Bartley, *Creation of Modern Georgia*, chapters 3 and 4.

6. "Our Volunteer Military."

7. "To Arms! They Come!" *Atlanta Daily Constitution*, November 21, 1878.

8. "The Military Convention—Address of Colonel Clifford W. Anderson."

9. "To Arms! They Come!"

10. "Our Atlanta Letter—This, That and the Other—Matters Worthy of Mention—The Military Commission," *Savannah Morning News*, February 8, 1877; "To Arms! They Come!"; "The Military Convention—Address of Colonel Clifford W. Anderson." The "committee of citizen soldiers" included: General P. M. B. Young (Captain in 1877), of Cartersville, Georgia; Lieutenant Colonel Wilberforce Daniel, of Augusta, Georgia; Colonel Clifford W. Anderson, of Savannah, Georgia; Lieutenant Colonel Ross (Captain in 1877), of Macon, Georgia; Lieutenant Colonel John F. Wheaton, of Savannah, Georgia; Major C. W. Henderson, of Atlanta, Georgia; and Major William Shepherd, of Columbus, Georgia.

11. For General Wayne quote, see Frances Smith, "Black Militia in Savannah," 26; "To Arms! They Come!"

12. Frances Smith, "Black Militia in Savannah," 14–16. For a discussion of this period

and the obstacles to militia formation, see Duncan, *Entrepreneur*, 54–55, 66–67, 6–70, 72–73, 123, 146–47, 199. For the use of black and white militia in support of Radical Reconstruction, see Ben H. Severance, *Tennessee's Radical Army: The State Guard and Its Role in Reconstruction, 1867–1869* (Knoxville: University of Tennessee Press, 2005); for use of black militiamen in South Carolina, see Benjamin Ginsberg, *Moses of South Carolina: A Jewish Scalawag during Radical Reconstruction* (Baltimore: The Johns Hopkins University Press, 2010), 132–37. My thanks go to colleague John David Smith for bringing the Ginsberg book to my attention.

13. Duncan, *Entrepreneur*, 51–52, 69–70, 129–36, 159, 199. See 16 STAT 363 Chapter. 299, 41st Congress, 2nd Session, "An Act: Relating to the State of Georgia, 1870, Approved July 15, 1870." Also note in this Act the 1867 notation "prohibiting the organization, &.c. of the militia" (364). My thanks to Ms. Lois Stickell and Ms. Beth L. Rowe, reference librarians, Atkins Library, University of North Carolina at Charlotte for their assistance; hereafter cited as UNCC. For independent black militia organizations, see Duncan, *Freedom's Shore*, 23, 25, 67–71, 87–88, 109, 113; Ruth Currie-McDaniel, *Carpetbagger of Conscience: A Biography of John Emory Bryant* (New York: Fordham University Press, 1999), 128; Bryant, *How Curious a Land*, 114, 118, 140; Susan O'Donovan, *Becoming Free in the Cotton South* (Cambridge, Mass.: Harvard University Press, 2007), 225–30, 265; James S. Allen, *Reconstruction: The Battle for Democracy* (New York: International Publishers, 1937 reprinted 1963), 7, 12, 92–102.

14. "An Act Relating to the State of Georgia"; Frances Smith, "Black Militia in Savannah," 14; Resurgum, "Georgia Militia to be Reorganized," *Atlanta Constitution*, July 10, 1870, ProQuest Historical Newspapers Atlanta Constitution.

15. Frances Smith, "Black Militia in Savannah," 20. For federal stipulations, see United States War Department, Adjutant General's Office, "General Order 39," March 21, 1873, in Record Group 22, Series 13, GDAH.

16. "Our Atlanta Letter—This, That and the Other—Matters Worthy of Mention—The Military Commission," *Savannah Morning News*, February 8, 1877, 1; "Bank and Bayonet," *Augusta Chronicle*, August 28, 1880; Frances Smith, "Black Militia in Savannah," 14–16, 20, 26–28. For federal stipulations, see United States War Department, Adjutant General's Office, "General Order 39," March 21, 1873, in Record Group 22, Series 13, GDAH. For restrictions on the number of militia units, see John A. Stephens to Parker, Weston, Georgia, November 19, 1884, Adjutant General Letter Book October 8, 1884–September 24, 1886, 27; John A. Stephens AG to Hubbard Cumming, Madison, Georgia, May 7, 1886, Adjutant General Letter Book October 8, 1884–September 24, 1886, 334; John McIntosh Kell, Adjutant General and Inspector General, to L. Comfort, Darien, Georgia, April, 21, 1887, Adjutant General Letter Books, September 24, 1886–August 23, 1887, 230, GDAH. The *Savannah Tribune* noted the evolution of Georgia's militia policies. See *Savannah Tribune*, November 16, 1889, January 23, 1892, and December 3, 1892.

17. For the political takeover, see Walton, *Black Republicans*, chapter 3, especially 50–61. See Capital City Guards Petition, Muster Roll, Election of Officers 1878, Record Group 22-1-10, Georgia National Guard—Militia, Adjutant General Miscellaneous Reports, Box 20, 5259–0710, GDAH. For the members of the militia company and a biographical sketch of "Henry Allan Rucker," see LRAF, Folder: Henry A. Rucker Personal

Correspondence (1904–1908) biographies (n.d.) newspaper clippings, 1970, 1979, Atlanta History Center, Atlanta, Georgia, hereafter cited as AHC. For scholarly work on post–Civil War African American men and their ambitions, see Laura F. Edwards, *Gendered Strife and Confusion: The Political Culture of Reconstruction* (Urbana: University of Illinois Press, 1997), chapters 5, 6; Gilmore, *Gender and Jim Crow*, chapters 1, 2.

18. For Civil War service 13 U.S. Col'd H. Art'y. Union, Pvt, M589 roll 59 African American Civil War Memorial, Civil War Soldiers and Sailors System NPS website, www.civilwar.nps.gov/cwss/Personz_Detail.cfm 8/18/2009; assisted by Ms. Lois Stickell, reference librarian, UNCC. See Capital City Guards Petition, p. 1, for petition signed by Jackson McHenry.

19. "Jackson McHenry," Freedman's Bank Image, series: M816, Roll 6, p. 29, Account 179, Heritage Quest Online, http://persi.heritagequestonline.com/hqoweb/library/do/freedmans/results.image?urn=urn, accessed August 18, 2009; assisted by Ms. Lois Stickell, reference librarian, UNCC; E. R. Carter, *The Black Side: A Partial History of the Business, Religious and Educational Side of the Negro in Atlanta, Georgia* (Freeport, N.Y.: Books for Libraries Press, 1971), 176, 178.

20. Dorsey, *To Build Our Lives*, 93, 100, 122, 131, 136–137, 140–141.

21. Gregory Mixon, "The Political Career of Henry A. Rucker: A Survivor in a New South City," *Atlanta History: A Journal of Georgia and the South* 45 (Summer 2001): 7–9, 17; Walton, *Black Republicans*, chapter 3.

22. Dorsey, *To Build Our Lives*, 122, 133–134; "Henry A. Rucker," 4–23.

23. Dorsey, *To Build Our Lives*, 46, 50, 52, 133; Carter, *The Black Side*, 60–63. For Crumbly's rapid rise through the military ranks, see "Colored Soldiers," *Savannah Tribune*, July 27, 1889. For the Victorio campaign, see Leonard, *Men of Color to Arms!* xii, 55–56, 83–84, 108–112. For a comparison with white entrepreneurs, see Gregory Mixon, "Constructing Atlanta's Auditorium-Amory, 1904–1909: The Public and Private and Race," draft manuscript, 17. For Crumbly's military experiences in the Philippines, see "Captain F. H. Crumbly of the 49th U.S. Volunteers," *Savannah Tribune*, October 14, 1899, and "A Soldier's Letter: Capt. F. H. Crumbly Writes from the Philippines," *Savannah Tribune*, March 17, 1900.

24. Carter, *The Black Side*, 63; John McIntosh Kell Adjutant General and Inspector General to Lt. Colonel Thomas Grant Commanding 2nd Battalion Georgia Volunteers, Colored, January 13, 1891, p. 561, and January 22, 1891, p. 593, Adjutant General Letter Books, July 5, 1890–April 22, 1891, Record Group 22-1-1 Unit 49, GDAH. For Afro-Cuban utilization of the militia, cabildo, and politics, see Howard, *Changing History*, chapters 2, 3; and Reid-Vazquez, *Year of the Lash*, chapter 5. My thanks to my colleague Erika Edwards for alerting me to the Howard monograph and for our discussions about African-descendant people in the Western Hemisphere.

25. For a very brief and general biography of Deveaux, see Charles L. Hoskins, *The Trouble They Seen: Profiles in the Life of Col. John H. Deveaux 1848–1909* (Savannah: Charles Lwanga Hoskins St. Matthew's Church: 1989), 40, 67; Jeffrey Alan Turner, "Agitation and Accommodation in a Southern Black Newspaper: The *Savannah Tribune*, 1886–1915," (master's thesis, University of Georgia, 1993), 5–8. My thanks go to Ms. Laura Acker for bringing this source to my attention. For the discussion on "progress," see "Lincoln, The Martyr, His Memory Honored by Those Whom He Liberated," *Savan-

nah Tribune, February 20, 1892. For Deveaux's vision for the paper and transportation, see *Savannah Tribune*, February 20, 1892. For the role of the periodical in projecting black self-determination, self-reliance, and vision for the race, see Howard, *Changing History*, 137–138, 155, 165–169, 171.

26. *Savannah Tribune*, February 20, 1892; "The Savannah Emeute(?)," *Macon Telegraph*, August 6, 1872; *Macon Telegraph*, August 1, 1872.

27. "Col. Hardeman to the Democracy," *Macon Telegraph*, August 27, 1872. See Holt, *The Problem of Freedom*, 180–181, 202, 207, 215–216, 218, 235; Zuczek, *State of Rebellion*, chapter 3. My thanks go to colleague James Hogue for alerting me to this work. For other examples of black-white conflict over governance and public power as a problem of Western liberalism, Randolph Hohle, *Black Citizenship and Authenticity in the Civil Rights Movement* (New York: Routledge, 2013), 3–4.

28. J. H. Deveaux, "Salutatory," *Savannah The Colored Tribune*, December 4, 1875; Turner, "Agitation and Accommodation," 39–40.

29. Hoskins, *The Trouble They Seen*, 40. Deveaux founded the paper with Louis B. Toomer, Richard White, and Louis M. Pleasant; "The Savannah Tribune," *Savannah Tribune*, November 25, 1876.

30. "Tribute of Respect," *Savannah Tribune*, December 30, 1876.

31. *Savannah Tribune*, December 30, 1876.

32. "New Year's Day," *Savannah Colored Tribune*, January 1, 1876. The idea of hope and a new beginning was reinforced by Cheryl Hicks's presentation at the "Emancipation Proclamation Program," Center City Campus Uptown, University of North Carolina at Charlotte, February 23, 2013. Notes in possession of the author.

33. "Our Position, and Our Duty," Savannah *Colored Tribune*, January 1, 1876.

34. "To the Colored People of Georgia," Savannah *Colored Tribune*, January 1, 1876.

35. Celebration of the 13th Anniversary of the Emancipation Proclamation," Savannah *Colored Tribune*, January 8, 1876. For other public moments where blacks paraded, see Mitch Kachun, *Festivals of Freedom: Memory and Meaning in African American Emancipation Celebrations, 1808–1915* (Amherst: University of Massachusetts Press, 2003), 76, 110. For black men and women's expectations of freedom, see O'Donovan, *Becoming Free in the Cotton South*, 114, 133–134, 138–149, 208. For definitions of equality and citizenship, see Bryant, *How Curious a Land*, 105, 107–109, 117–118.

36. "How to Treat the Colored People," Savannah *Colored Tribune*, January 8, 1876; Kachun, *Festivals of Freedom*, 76. For white resistance and fear of black militia and African American public and private endeavors to define their autonomy, citizenship, and right to act publicly and for the white vision of black freedom, see Bryant, *How Curious a Land*, 100, 105–106, 118–121, 129, 145, and O'Donovan, *Becoming Free in the Cotton South*, 106, 125, 132, 195, 217, 255–257.

37. "The Immortal Emancipator Abraham Lincoln," Savannah *Colored Tribune*, February 12, 1876. For the meaning of public ritual, parading, and Emancipation Day, see Kachun, *Festivals of Freedom*, 48–50, 74, 76.

38. "Briefs," Savannah *Colored Tribune*, July 8 and July 15, 1876; "Chivalric(?)" Savannah *Colored Tribune*, July 8, 1876; "Briefs," Savannah *Colored Tribune*, January 22, 1876; "British Emancipation," *Savannah Tribune*, November 13, 1876; "Lee's Natal Day," *Savannah Morning News*, January 21, 1879; "May Day," *Savannah Morning News*, May 2,

1879; "The Fourth of July," *Augusta Chronicle*, July 3, 1885. For examples of blacks and whites marching segregated in the same event, see "A Community's Heartfelt Tribute," *Savannah Morning News*, January 13, 1879; "Arrival of General Grant: His Reception at Depot," *Savannah Morning News*, January 2, 1880; "Grant's Visit to Savannah," *Savannah Morning News*, January 3, 1880; and "Grant and the South," *Savannah Morning News*, January 6, 1880. For George Washington's birthday parade, see "Washington," *Savannah Morning News*, February 24, 1879. For freedom celebrations and the creation of black militias in the black diaspora, see Kerr-Ritchie, *August First*. For southern whites' abandonment of Independence Day for Robert E. Lee's birthday, see Blair, *Cities of the Dead*, 66–67, 10, 125.

39. For black and white southerners' battle for political power through celebration rituals, see Blair, *Cities of the Dead*, ix, x, 1–2, 7, 9, 14–15, 23–24, 27–28–30, 33–36, 42, 47, 78, 97–98, 108–109. For the issue of black and white manhood, see Blair, *Cities of the Dead*, 6, 79, 85, 99–100, 105, as well as 17–20, 125–126, 140. For the July 4th celebrations and black history, see Blair, *Cities of the Dead*, 164; Kachun, *Festivals of Freedom*, chapters 4, 5; Kerr-Ritchie, *Rites of August*, chapter 6.

40. The Fifteenth Amendment," Savannah *The Colored Tribune*, May 27, 1876.

41. Voters Will be Protected," *Savannah Tribune*, August 26, 1876; Hahn, *Nation Under Our Feet*, 248–249, chapter 3; Dorsey, *To Build Our Lives*, chapters 3–6; Charles L. Lumpkins, *American Pogrom: The East St. Louis Race Riot and Black Politics* (Athens: Ohio University Press, 2008), chapters 1, 2; Brown, "To Catch the Vision of Freedom."

42. "Fair at the First Bryan Baptist Church," Savannah *Colored Tribune*, January 22, 1876.

43. "Grand Anniversary of the Savannah Hussar," *Savannah Tribune*, July 29, 1876 and August 5, 1876. "The Union Lincoln Guards—Flag Presentation," *Savannah Tribune*, August 5, 1876. For a discussion black defense of the Union, see Hahn, *Nation Under Our Feet*, chapter 2.

44. For black women's autonomy, contributions to defining freedom, and cooperation and participation with black militiamen, see Blair, *Cities of the Dead*, 6, 98, 101–104,.

45. Hannah, *Manhood*, 44–58.

46. Ibid., 40–42, 44, 52–53.

47. "The Savannah Hussars late visit to Charleston," *Savannah Tribune*, May 27, 1876. For the value militiamen placed in parading and African Americans placed on public displays of manhood, citizenship, and the place of blacks in defining themselves and their place as equals to whites in the nation, see Hannah, *Manhood*, 18–19, 33, 35.

48. "Briefs," Savannah *Tribune*, January 1, 1876; "In Memoriam," Savannah *Colored Tribune*, January 22, 1876; Hannah, *Manhood*, 21, 35, 42, 44.

49. "Briefs," Savannah *Colored Tribune*, April 8, 1876; "Anniversary Parade," Savannah *Colored Tribune*, May 13, 1876; "Notice," *Savannah Tribune*, August 19, 1876; "The Forest City Light Infantry," *Savannah Tribune*, September 2, 1876; "Relief for Savannah," *Macon Telegraph*, September 20, 1876. For ownership and rental of the Lincoln Guards armory, see "Brevities," *Macon Telegraph*, February 28(?), 1879. For hospital appointment and yellow fever epidemic, see *Savannah Tribune*, September 16 and 23, 1876.

50. "The Chatham Light Infantry," *Savannah Tribune*, July 29, 1876; "Briefs," Savannah *Colored Tribune*, April 29, 1876; "A Grand Pic-Nic," and "We Visited Armory," *Savannah Tribune*, August 26, 1876; "Briefs," *Savannah Tribune*, September 9, 1876. For a discussion of respectable comportment, see Kachun, *Festivals of Freedom*, 237–240.

51. "Lone Star Cadets," and "A Grand Supper," Savannah *The Colored Tribune*, May 13, 1876; "Briefs," Savannah *Colored Tribune*, June 3, 1876.

52. "Chatham County Convention," *Savannah Tribune*, August 12, 1876; "Good Appointment," Savannah *Colored Tribune*, April 15, 1876; "Republican State Convention," Savannah *The Colored Tribune*, May 13, 1876; "Go to the Exchange and Register," Savannah *The Colored Tribune*, July 8, 1876; "Republican District Convention," *Savannah Tribune*, August 12, 1876; "Militia District Mass Meeting," *Savannah Tribune*, August 26, 1876; "To the Republicans of the First District," *Savannah Tribune*, September 16, 1876; "The Recent State Elections," *Savannah Tribune*, November 4, 1876; "The Grand Lodge for the State of Georgia," Savannah *Colored Tribune*, January 1, 1876.

53. "Blood! Iago! Blood!" *Savannah Tribune*, July 15, 1876; "The Hamburg Butchery," *Savannah Tribune*, August 5, 1876. For the details of the Hamburg Massacre, see Hahn, *Nation Under Our Feet*, 302–308, and Budiansky, *The Bloody Shirt*, chapter 6. See also "Acts and Resolutions of the General Assembly of the State of Georgia, 1884–1885," 85, Georgia Legislative Documents, GDAH, neptune3.galib.uga.edu/ssp/cgi-bin/legis-idx.pl?sessionid=7f000001&type=law&byte=571613. For the aftermath of the Hamburg Massacre, see "Chamberlain and Whipper," *Savannah Tribune*, September 2, 1876; "The South" and "Cincinnati's Colored Citizens Resolve," *Savannah Tribune*, September 9, 1876; "General News and Comments," *Savannah Tribune*, August 5, 1876.

54. "General News and Comments," *Savannah Tribune*, July 29, 1876. For South Carolina politics and political players, see Edward A. Miller Jr., *Gullah Statesman: Robert Smalls; From Slavery to Congress, 1839–1915* (Columbia: University of South Carolina Press, 1995), 61. For a discussion of the right to bear arms, of militia service, of the integration of race relations, and of the role of the Second Amendment and militia membership, see H. Richard Uviller and William G. Merkel, *The Militia and the Right to Arms, or How The Second Amendment Fell Silent* (Durham: Duke University Press, 2002), 14–15.

55. "Chamberlain and Whipper"; "General News and Comments," *Savannah Tribune*, August 5, 1876; "General News and Comments," *Savannah Tribune*, July 29, 1876; Miller, *Gullah Statesman*, 61, 104–106, for Edgefield, see Miller, *Gullah Statesman*, 98–103; "South Carolina," Savannah *Colored Tribune*, January 29, 1876. See Zuczek, *State of Rebellion*, chapter 9, to access Chamberlain's impotence.

56. "The Combahee Strike," *Savannah Tribune*, September 2, 1876. For parallel black acts of autonomy in Georgia and white planter response, see O'Donovan, *Becoming Free in the Cotton South*, 112, 132–134, 138–150. For a discussion of Smalls's role in serving both black and white interests during this strike, see Hahn, *Nation Under Our Feet*, 347–350, and Miller, *Gullah Statesman*, 106.

57. "Tunis G. Campbell, Sr.," Savannah *Colored Tribune*, May 13, 1876, 1; "Shocking," Savannah *Colored Tribune*, January 22, 1876; "Georgia Justice," Savannah *Colored Tribune*, January 22, 1876; Duncan, *Freedom's Shore*, 99–109. The *Tribune* reported Camp-

bell to be in his eighties, while Russell Duncan, Campbell's biographer, indicates he was in his sixties during this period.

58. "Tunis G. Campbell, Sr."; "Georgia Justice," Savannah *Colored Tribune*, January 22, 1876; "The Governor Refuses to Pardon Tunis G. Campbell, Sr.," Savannah *Colored Tribune*, May 20, 1876; Duncan, *Freedom's Shore*, 108.

59. Duncan, *Freedom's Shore*, xi, 23–25, 35–36.

60. Ibid. For the importance of land, political rights, and contested definitions of freedom and citizenship between blacks and whites, see Holt, *The Problem of Freedom*, xx, xxii–xxiii, 4, 6, 14, 33, 53, 73–75, 137–139–145, 149, 165, 172, 181–182, 216, 269, 309, and Hannah, *Manhood*, 21, 35.

61. Duncan, *Freedom's Shore*, 30–39, 58, 64–68, 70–71, 87, 114.

62. Ibid., 70–71, 88, 114; Hahn, *Nation Under Our Feet*, 175, 184–185, 195, 239–241, 262. See also "Tunis G. Campbell, Sr. Sent to the Penitentiary," Savannah *Colored Tribune*, January 15, 1876; "Briefs," Savannah *Colored Tribune*, February 5, 1876.

63. For aspects of the multiple roles of the militia and the militia and politics, see Baker, *This Mob Will Surely Take My Life*, 17–18, 23, 35–36, 55.

64. For Aaron A. Bradley's career and political thinking, see Grant, *The Way It Was*, 107. For the emergence of "liberal reformers" and their ongoing opposition to black empowerment, see Nancy Cohen, *The Reconstruction of American Liberalism, 1865–1914* (Chapel Hill: University of North Carolina Press, 2002), 25–43 and chapters 2–4.

65. Grant, *The Way It Was*; For a discussion of black male leaders and the contradictions they wrestled with as they challenged white supremacy, Angela Hornsby-Gutting, *Black Manhood and Community Building in North Carolina, 1900–1930* (Gainesville: University Press of Florida, 2009), 5, 10, 12, 15, 168.

66. Charles L. Flynn Jr., *White Land, Black Labor: Caste and Class in Late Nineteenth Century Georgia* (Baton Rouge: Louisiana State University Press, 1983), 10, 13, 15, 59–60, 82, 93, 101–112. For a study of black freedom in the South and Cuba, see Frederick Cooper, Thomas C. Holt, Rebecca J. Scott, *Beyond Slavery: Explorations of Race, Labor, and Citizenship in Postemancipation Societies* (Chapel Hill: University of North Carolina Press, 2000), chapter 1; Scott, *Degrees of Freedom*, chapter 2; Brown, "To Catch the Vision of Freedom," 66–99; Hahn, *Nation Under Our Feet*, 266; Bess Beatty, *A Revolution Gone Backward: The Black Response to National Politics, 1876–1896* (Westport: Greenwood Press, 1987), 1–4.

67. "Equal Rights at the South," *Savannah Tribune*, November 11, 1876; "The Wilmington, (N.C.) Post," Savannah *Colored Tribune*, April 8, 1876. For black people's commitment to self-defense and group defense, see Hahn, *Nation Under Our Feet*, 276 and chapter 6.

68. "Paddle your own Canoe," Savannah *Colored Tribune*, April 8, 1876; "The Negro's Future" Savannah *Colored Tribune*, June 3, 1876, 1; Beatty, *A Revolution Gone Backward*, 4.

69. "An Address from H. M. Turner, LL. D., to the Colored Republicans of the State," Savannah *Colored Tribune*, April 15, 1876. For a broader exploration of this theme, see Beatty, *A Revolution Gone Backward*, 19–25.

70. "St. Patrick's Day—A lesson for Colored People," Savannah *Colored Tribune*, March 25, 1876.

71. Ibid. See also "Lee's Natal," *Savannah Morning News*, January 21, 1879; "Washington," *Savannah Morning News*, February 24, 1879; "St. Patrick's Day," *Savannah Morning News*, March 17, 1879; "Matters and Things Laconically Noted," *Savannah Morning News*, April 21, 1879, and May 1, 1879; "Prize Drill of the Blues," *Savannah Morning News*, April 29, 1879. For a more detailed study of the intersections between African Americans and the Irish in the post–Civil War South and questions of nationalism, see Snay, *Feninans, Freedmen, and Southern Whites*. For Irish American incorporation into whiteness, see Nell Irvin Painter, *The History of White People* (New York: W. W. Norton, 2010), chapter 14. Holt also examines Irish-Afro-Jamaican comparisons involving peasant proprietorships and access to land. See Holt, *The Problem of Freedom*, chapter 9.

72. Ibid.

73. Flynn, *White Land, Black Labor*, 6, 10, 25–29, 39–50, 52. See also Bryant, *How Curious a Land*, 144–145, 139–150; O'Donovan, *Becoming Free in the Cotton South*, 125–132; Bartley, *Creation of Modern Georgia*, 74–75; and Joseph P. Reidy, *From Slavery to Agrarian Capitalism in the Cotton Plantation South: Central Georgia, 1800–1880* (Chapel Hill: University of North Carolina Press, 1992), 7, 10, 12–13. Hannah connects parading to citizenship, patriotism, and the reciprocal obligation of the supporting community to recognize militia membership as a commitment to political participation. See Hannah, *Manhood*, chapter 2.

74. *Savannah Tribune*, December 23, 1876; "John H. Deveaux," *The New Georgia Encyclopedia* www.georgiaencyclopedia.org/nge/Multimedia.jsp?id=m-10940, accessed February 17, 2010; Lauren Acker, "'AGITATE in a dignified way for your rights': Sol C. Johnson and the *Savannah Tribune*," 1–3, Fourth Annual New Perspectives on African American History and Culture Conference at the University of North Carolina, Chapel Hill, February 26–27, 2010, Panel: "Black Leadership in the Age of Jim Crow," February 27, 2010, Hyde Hall, Chapel Hill, North Carolina.

75. "A Grand Day Among the Colored People," *Savannah Morning News*, May 28, 1878; "The Governor's Volunteers," Atlanta *The Daily Constitution*, June 28, 1879, ProQuest Historical Newspapers Atlanta Constitution, 4; James F. Cook, "Alfred Holt Colquitt 1877–1882," *The Governors of Georgia, 1754–1995*, rev. ed. (Macon, Ga.: Mercer University Press, 1995), 159–162. The other members of the Bourbon Triumvirate were former Confederate General John B. Gordon and Civil War politician and governor and post–Civil War United States Senator, Joseph E. Brown. For Joseph E. Brown, see F. N. Boney, "Joseph E. Brown, 1821–1894," Government and Politics: Governors of Georgia, *New Georgia Encyclopedia* 2013 http://www.georgiaencyclopedia.org/articles/government-politics/joseph-e-brown-1821-1894, accessed April 13, 2014. For Governor Alfred Colquitt and black Georgians, see Grant, *The Way It Was*, 132.

76. "A Grand Day Among the Colored People."

77. Ibid. Hannah contends that physique and manly bearing were universally accepted as key indicators of a militiaman. See Hannah, *Manhood*, 13, 15, 19, 33.

78. "A Grand Day Among the Colored People."

79. Ibid. For Savannah's Mayor's full name, see Frances Smith, *Black Militia in Savannah*, 34.

80. "A Grand Day Among the Colored People." For the May Parade, see *Savannah Tribune*, 1895–1905. For a brief biography of Flipper, who graduated from West Point

and was commissioned in 1877, see Susan Copeland, "Henry O. Flipper (1856–1940)," *The New Georgia Encyclopedia* www.georgiaencyclopedia.org/nge/Article.jsp?id=h-1331&hl=y, accessed September 20, 2010. Flipper published a book in 1878 recounting the discrimination and harassment he experienced during his studies from 1873 to 1877. Also see Leonard, *Men of Color to Arms!* 161–167, 173–176, 181–182, 188–197.

81. Blair, *Cities of the Dead*, 2, 24, 47.

82. Ibid., 2, 24; "A Grand Day"; Hornsby-Gutting, *Black Manhood*, 132, 137–138, 148.

83. "A Grand Day." For a comparison of white elite attendance and speeches at black-initiated public events, see Hornsby-Gutting, *Black Manhood*, 137–138, 148, 150.

84. Hornsby-Gutting, *Black Manhood*, 130–131, 136, 138–139, 148–150; Hannah, *Manhood*, 35–36; Holt, The Problem With Freedom, 273–278.

85. For African American utilization, debate, and notations of their history and memory in the late nineteenth into the early twentieth century, see Hornsby-Gutting, *Black Manhood*, 131, 154, and Kachun, *Festivals of Freedom*, 146, 149–155, 174–175.

86. "A Grand Day."

87. Kachun, *Festivals of Freedom*, 175.

88. "Military Department," Savannah *Weekly News*, April 6, 1878. According to Francs Smith, *Black Militia in Savannah*, 30, Herbert joined the Savannah *Morning News* in 1878. See Herbert, *Roster of Georgia Volunteer Military Organizations*.

Chapter 5. "Be Thou Strong Therefore and Show Thyself a Man": Georgia Volunteers, Colored, 1889–1895

1. Hannah, *Manhood*, 60.

2. William A. Dobak and Thomas D. Phillips, *The Black Regulars, 1866–1898* (Norman: University of Oklahoma Press, 2001), 67–72, 76–77.

3. "Title X, Military," *Acts and Resolutions of the General Assembly of the State of Georgia, 1878–1879* (Atlanta: James P. Harrison, Public Printer, 1880), 103–114; Frances Smith, "Black Militia in Savannah, Georgia 1872–1905," (master's thesis, Georgia Southern College, 1981), 27–36; "Matters and Things Laconically Noted," *Savannah Morning News*, January 27, 1879.

4. "Title X, Military," *Acts and Resolutions of the General Assembly of the State of Georgia, 1878–1879*. For national militia trends, see Jerry Cooper, *The Rise of the National Guard: The Evolution of the American Militia, 1865–1920* (Lincoln: University of Nebraska Press, 1997), 24–25. For federal commitment and challenges to segregation during and immediately after the Civil War, see Dobak and Phillips, *Black Regulars*, xiii–xv, xviii, 44, 48–50, 67–68.

5. Frances Smith, Black Militia in Savannah, 27–28, 39; Adjutant General to A. R. Johnson, Augusta, Georgia, July 14, 1885, Adjutant General Letter Books October 8, 1884–September 24, 1886, Record Group 22-1-1 Accession No. 96-1232A, Box 46, Loc. No. 2971-05, p. 187, GDAH.

6. John A. Stephens to [?] Parker, Weston, Georgia, November 19, 1884, Adjutant General Letter Books, October 8, 1884–September 24, 1886, Record Group 22-1-1 Accession No. 96-1232A, Box 46, Loc. No. 2971-05, p. 37, GDAH; "Title X, Military," 1878–1879, 107–108; "Republican Blues—The Rome Encampment," Savannah *Morning News*, June 5, 1880; Samuel J. Newland, "The National Guard: Whose Guard Anyway?"

Parameters: US Army War College 18, no. 2 (June 1988): 44; Cooper, *Rise of the National Guard*, 15–17, 23–24.

7. Cooper, *Rise of the National Guard*, 15–17, 23–24; Hannah, *Manhood*, 1–2, 5, 9, 13, 15, 17–18, 28, 35, 39, 42.

8. Cooper, *Rise of the National Guard*. The word "integrated" brings into question whether blacks served in black-white units or whether there were all-black companies folded into the overall state military. For examinations of the Negro militia, see Singletary, *Negro Militia*. For black militia and state service during Reconstruction and beyond, see Ben H. Severance, *Tennessee's Radical Army: The State Guard and Its Role in Reconstruction, 1867–1869* (Knoxville: University of Tennessee Press, 2005). For nineteenth century black militias, see Bruce A. Glasrud, ed., *Brothers to the Buffalo Soldiers: Perspectives on the African American Militia and Volunteers, 1865–1917* (Columbia: University of Missouri Press, 2011).

9. Cooper, *Rise of the National Guard*, 23–24; Frances Smith, *Black Militia in Georgia*, 51; "Title XII, Public Defense," *The Code of the State of Georgia* (first edition by R. H. Clark, T. R. R. Cobb and David Irwin; second edition by David Irwin, Geo. N. Lester and W. B. Hill; fourth edition by Geo. N. Lester, C. Rowell and W. B. Hill, 1882), 228; Mahon, *History of the Militia*, 108–110.

10. "The Military Encampment and Convention," Savannah *Morning News*, June 24, 1880–June 29, 1880.

11. Ibid.; Tenth Amendment, United States Constitution; Mahon, *History of the Militia*, 113–114. For the evolution of the national debate on what the militia is, its needs, and the need for governmental support, see Ordway, "A National Militia"; Charles E. Lydecker, "An Unconstitutional Militia," *The North American Review* 134, no. 308 (June 1882): n.p.; and "The National Militia—Preparing a Law to be Operative in All the States," Savannah *Morning News*, January 23, 1879.

For the political use of segregation and the securing of white power through white supremacy and antiblack violence, see John Cell, *The Highest Stage of White Supremacy: The Origins of Segregation in South Africa and the American South* (London: Cambridge University Press, 1982), 2, 12–19, 25, 82–83, 85–87, 91, 103, 106, 147–150, 153, 159–161, 169–170, 175. We should keep in mind, as Cell notes, that the 1890s are regarded as the years of the "legal recognition" of segregation, while its pre-1890s existence marked "no break whatever with southern traditions" that molded the 1890s. Cell also presents the key players who defined segregation and white supremacy, with newspaper editors being important shapers of the New South. For segregation as a response to market capitalism, see Nathan Cardon, "The South's 'New Negroes' and African American Visions of Progress at the Atlanta and Nashville International Expositions, 1895–1897," *Journal of Southern History* 80, no. 2 (May 2014): 287–326. For the culture of segregation, see Grace Hale, *Making Whiteness*. For the relationship between labor, citizenship, capital industrialization, the vote, and segregation, see Glenn, *Unequal Freedom*. For the evolution of segregation, lynching, and antiblack violence, Bartley, *Creation of Modern Georgia*, 81–82, 85–86, 105, 139–140.

12. John McIntosh Kell to Captain J. G. Brahaman, Lawson Light Guards, Eaton, Georgia, May 17, 1887, Adjutant General Letter Books, January 1886–October 13, 1885, Record Group 22-1-1, Accession No. 96–1232A, Unit 47, Location 2971–05, p.

273, GDAH. For the evolution of the Military Advisory Board see "Military Matters," *Atlanta Constitution*, January 7, 1893; "Military Matters," *Atlanta Constitution*, February 17, 1893; "Military Board Named Yesterday," *Atlanta Constitution*, July 2, 1899; and "Advisory Board to Be Summoned," *Atlanta Constitution*, September 3, 1899. *Atlanta Constitution*, 1868–1929, Atkins Library, University of North Carolina at Charlotte, Charlotte North Carolina, hereafter cited as APOUNCC; John McIntosh Kell Adjutant General and Inspector General to Adjutant General James P. Taylor, Nashville, Tennessee, June 14, 1887, p. 338, Adjutant General Letter Books, September 24, 1886–August 23, 1887, Record Group 22-1-1, Accession Number 96–1232A, Unit 47, Location Number 2971-05, GDAH.

13. "The Pipings of Peace—Mr. Harrell Mows Down The Militia," *Augusta Chronicle*, September 4, 1885; "Bank and Bayonet—Important Bills in House and Senate," *Augusta Chronicle*, August 28, 1885; "Our Law Makers—Yesterday's Transactions in the Legislature," *Augusta Chronicle*, August 29, 1885; "Pen Pictures—Our Handsome and Business-like Senator," *Augusta Chronicle*, October 13, 1885; "Constitutionals General Gossip and Editorial," *Atlanta Constitution*, October 10, 1885.

14. "The Legislature: The Full Proceedings of Both Branches Civil Rights and Civil Wrongs," *Atlanta Constitution*, October 11, 1885; "The Legislature," *Atlanta Constitution*, October 13, 1885.

15. "Part I—Public Laws, Title VII, Military, Organization, Government and Discipline of the Volunteer Troops of the State Law Number: No. 355," *Acts and Resolutions of the General Assembly of the State of Georgia, 1884–85, 1884, Volume I*, p. 74, Georgia Legislative Documents, Galileo Digital Initiative Database http://neptune3.uga.edu/ssp/cgi-bin/legis-idx.pl?sessionid=7f000001&type=;aw&byte, accessed May 5, 2010; "Georgia Volunteers," *Atlanta Constitution*, November 12, 1886. For centralization of state militias nationally, see Cooper, *Rise of the National Guard*, 23–24, 26–29, 31, 34, 39–40, 82; Mahon, *History of the Militia*, 109–110; and Ordway, "A National Militia," 398–399.

16. "Georgia Volunteers."

17. Cooper, *Rise of the National Guard*, 29, 31–34, 40–41, 71, 82; Hannah, *Manhood*, 7, 13, 103.

18. "Military Advisory Board," *Atlanta Constitution*, August 20, 1886, Atkins Library, University of North Carolina at Charlotte, Charlotte, North Carolina; Adjutant General John A. Stephens to Lt. Col. A. R. Robinson, Commanding 3rd Batt. Ga. Vol. Colored, August 30, 1886, Augusta, Georgia, p. 444, Adjutant General Letter Books October 8, 1884–September 24, 1886, Record Group 22-1-1, Accession Number 96–1232A, Box 46, Location Number 2971-5; GDAH.

19. For a William H. Woodhouse biography, Frances Smith, *Black Militia in Savannah*, 38–40; Adjutant General John A. Stephens to J. E. T(?) Esquire, La Grange, Georgia, October 1, 1886, Adjutant General Letter Books, September 24, 1886–August 23, 1887, p. 15, Record Group 22-1-1, Accession Number 96–1232A, Box/Unit 47, Location Number 2971–05; Adjutant General John A. Stephens to Hon. R. B. Russell, J. H. Rucker, September 30, 1886, Adjutant General Letter Books, September 24, 1886–August 23, 1887, p. 11, Record Group 22-1-1, Accession Number 96–1232A, Unit 47, Location Number 2971–05; Adjutant General John A. Stephens to Mr. J. B. Holloman(?), July

22, 1886, Gainesville, Georgia, Adjutant General Letter Books, October 8, 1884–September 24, 1886, p. 383, Record Group 22-1-5, Accession Number 96–1232A, Box 46, Location Number 2971–5; Adjutant General John A. Stephens to Lt. Col. J. H. Deveaux, August 9, 1886, p. 384, Record Group 21-1-5, Accession Number 96–1232A, Box 46, Location Number 2971–5, GDAH.

20. John McIntosh Kell to Jn. W. Thompson Esq., Harrison, Georgia, May 5, 1887, p. 268, Adjutant General Letter Books, September 23, 1886–August 24, 1887, Record Group 22-1-1, Accession Number 96–1232A, Unit 47; John McIntosh Kell, Adjutant General and Inspector General to R. M. W. Black, Esq., Sylvania, Georgia, 4/20/1887, p. 243, Adjutant General Letter Books, Record Group 22-1-1, Accession Number 96–1232A, Unit 47; John McIntosh Kell, Adjutant General and Inspector General to W. E. Watkins, Esq., Sandersville, Georgia, May 24, 1887, p. 297, Adjutant General Letter Books, September 24, 1886–August 23, 1887, Record Group 22-1-1, Accession Number 96–1232A, Unit 47; John McIntosh Kell Adjutant General and Inspector General to Capt. Geo. S. Watts, Cuthbert, Georgia, May 25, 1887, p. 304, Adjutant General Letter Books, September 23, 1886–August 24, 1887, Records Group 22-1-1, Accession Number 96–1232A, Unit 47; John McIntosh Kell, Adjutant General and Inspector General to Capt. John Lark, Commanding Augusta Light Infantry(colored), Augusta, Georgia, June 3, 1887, p. 324, Adjutant General Letter Books, September 24, 1886–August 23, 1887, Record Group 22-1-1, Accession Number 96–1232A, Unit 47, Location Number 2971–05, GDAH; "Atlanta Artillery," *Atlanta Constitution*, February 20, 1887; John McIntosh Kell, Adjutant General and Inspector General to L. Comfort(?), Darien, Georgia, 4/21/1887, p. 230, Adjutant General Letter Books, September 24, 1886–August 23, 1887, Record Group 22-1-1, Accession Number 96–1232A, Unit 47, Location Number 2971–05, GDAH.

21. "Military Advisory Board," August 20, 1886.

22. "Military Advisory Board," *Atlanta Constitution*, August 19, 1886, "Article 9—No Title," Atkins Library, APOUNCC; "Public Laws: Title IX. Military, Amending General Law as to Volunteers, Law Number 331," 85–85, Acts and Resolutions of the General Assembly of the State of Georgia, 1886-7, Volume II, Approved October 15, 1887, Georgia Legislative Documents, Galileo Digital Initiative Database.

23. "Military Advisory Board," *Atlanta Constitution*, August 19, 1886; John McIntosh Kell, Adjutant General and Inspector General to Mr. J. B. Monard, Buffalo, New York, October 14, 1890, p. 353, Adjutant General Letter Books, July 5, 1890–April 22, 1891, Record Group 22-1-1, Accession Number 96–1232A, Unit 49, Location Number 2971–03, GDAH. For part of the debate about the constitutionality of "tak[ing] care of her military," see "Georgia Soldiery," *Atlanta Constitution*, July 16, 1889, APOUNCC.

24. For statewide drill competitions, conventions, and encampments, see "Ready for the Contest," *Atlanta Constitution*, May 20, 1889; "A Military Convention," *Atlanta Constitution*, June 27, 1889; "Summer in Augusta," *Atlanta Constitution*, June 8, 1890; "The State Drill," *Atlanta Constitution*, October 22, 1890; "Memorial," *Atlanta Constitution*, July 26, 1887; "Visiting Soldiers," *Atlanta Constitution*, July 14, 1889; "Georgia Soldiery," *Atlanta Constitution*, July 16, 1889; "The Exposition Fairly Booming," *Atlanta Constitution*, July 3, 1890; "The Advisory Board," *Atlanta Constitution*, February 28, 1891; and "Memorial," *Atlanta Constitution*, July 26, 1887, APOUNCC.

25. Cunningham, *The Black Citizen-Soldiers of Kansas*, 30, 95, 151, 179–180; Hannah, Manhood, 196–198, 206–207, 210–212.

26. See "Court and Capitol," *Atlanta Constitution*, July 16, 1887; "Advisory Military Board," *Atlanta Constitution*, November 6, 1887; "Capitol and Customhouse Dots," *Atlanta Constitution*, August 22, 1888. For changes in the Advisory Board tenure in office, frequency of meetings, and board membership, see "Advisory Military Board," *Atlanta Constitution*, November 6, 1887; "The Board to Meet," *Atlanta Constitution*, January 29, 1896; "Advisory Board Meets in April," *Atlanta Constitution*, March 25, 1898; "Military Board Named Yesterday," *Atlanta Constitution*, July 2, 1899; "Advisory Board to be Summoned, *Atlanta Constitution*, September 3, 1899; "New Advisory Board Chosen," *Atlanta Constitution*, March 8, 1901; "Advisory Board Will Meet Soon," *Atlanta Constitution*, March 10, 1901; "Terrell Names Advisory Board," *Atlanta Constitution*, February 11, 1903.

27. For evidence of the politics and benefits involved in attaining a seat on the Military Advisory Board, see "The Official Action," *Atlanta Constitution*, January 17, 1891; "Atlanta and Rome," *Atlanta Constitution*, March 20, 1891; "Into A Regiment," *Atlanta Constitution*, April 9, 1892; "It is Chickamauga," *Atlanta Constitution*, March 29, 1891; "Will Call on the Governor Friday," *Atlanta Constitution*, June 25, 1891; "The Military Spirit," *Atlanta Constitution*, October 24, 1891; "At the Capitol," *Atlanta Constitution*, November 18, 1891; "Georgia Volunteers," *Atlanta Constitution*, January 13, 1892; and "At the Statehouse," *Atlanta Constitution*, January 13, 1893.

28. "The Advisory Board," *Atlanta Constitution*, July 17, 1889; "The Military Advisory Board," *Atlanta Constitution*, November 21, 1889; "The Advisory Board," *Atlanta Constitution*, November 22, 1889; and "The Advisory Board," *Atlanta Constitution*, January 28, 1890. Companies required to "show cause" were white: "Dubignon Volunteers, of Milledgeville, the Spalding Greys, the Hill City Cadets, of Rome, the Quitman Guards, the Hancock Vanguard, Baldwin Blues, Southern Rifles of Talbotton, Constitutional Guards of Taylor county, Griffin Light Guard, Rome Light Guard, Thomson Guards, Tatnall Guards, Wiley Guards, of Pleasant Hill, and the Jackson Artillery, of Albany"; and black: "Georgia Cadets, of Atlanta; Governor's Volunteers, of Atlanta; Washington Guards, of Atlanta; Douglas Light Infantry, of Augusta, and Attucks Light Infantry, of Augusta"; see "The Military Advisory Board." For disbanding companies, "show cause" companies, and the "improved and retained" companies, see "The Advisory Board." The improved and retained companies were white: "Liberty Guards, Hinesville; LaGrange Light Guards, LaGrange; Atlanta Zouaves, Atlanta; Piedmont Rifles, Gainesville; Atlanta Artillery" and black: "Augusta Cadets(c), Augusta; Columbus Volunteers,(c) Columbus; Rome Star Guards(c), Rome; Augusta Light Infantry(c), Augusta."

29. "The Advisory Board," January 28, 1890; "Augusta Gets It," *Atlanta Constitution*, January 29, 1890; and "No New Companies," *Atlanta Constitution*, April 8, 1890, APOUNCC.

30. State Capitol News," *Atlanta Constitution*, March 1, 1890; "Notes from the Capitol," *Atlanta Constitution*, April 3, 1890; "About the Capitol," *Atlanta Constitution*, January 3, 1891; "Some Spicy Bills," *Atlanta Constitution*, November 22, 1890; and "Col. Milledge Talks," *Atlanta Constitution*, January 7, 1891, APOUNCC.

31. "It is Chickamauga," *Atlanta Constitution*, March 29, 1891, and "Will They Get It? *Atlanta Constitution*, June 24, 1891, APOUNCC.

32. "Will They Get It?" June 24, 1891; "Will Call on the Governor Friday," *Atlanta Constitution*, June 25, 1891, APOUNCC. For black political organization in 1890, see Mixon, *Atlanta Riot*, 45–46. The sources did not yield further discussion of the encampment and officers' convention.

33. "Colored Militia," *Atlanta Constitution*, 22 June 1891. For the invisibility of the black body in American history, see Harvey Young, *Embodying Black Experience: Stillness, Critical Memory, and the Black Body* (Ann Arbor: University of Michigan Press, 2010), 132–142.

34. Ibid.

35. "Treat the Negro as a man," and "The great howl by Southern Journals," *Savannah Tribune*, January 19, 1889; "Traits of Colored Soldiers," *Savannah Tribune*, July 13, 1889.

36. "A Good record for the colored troops," *Savannah Tribune*, January 19, 1889.

37. "Colored Soldiers," *Savannah Tribune*, July 27, 1889. For Mizner's career, see Leonard, *Men of Color to Arms!* 122. For discussions of manhood, citizenship, military training, and national defense, see Hannah, *Manhood*, 13, 15–18, 20–21, 35, 42, 44, 62, 103. For positive comments on black military capabilities and service as troops in the United States Army during the nineteenth century, see Dobak and Phillips, *Black Regulars*, 36, 38, 50–51, 62.

38. "The Negro Ye Have With You Always," *Savannah Tribune*, January 26, 1889. For Senator Morgan's political views and military record, see "John Tyler Morgan," *Wikipedia: The Free Encyclopedia*, http://en.wikipedia.org/wiki/John_Tyler_Morgan accessed April 6, 2013.

39. "Emancipation Day!" and "Friends and Fellow Citizens," *Savannah Tribune*, January 5, 1889. Emancipation Day coverage up to this point appears to have not reported on the public address. For black expectations concerning emancipation and afterward, see Joseph P. Reidy, "The African American Struggle for Citizenship Rights in the Northern United States During the Civil War," *Civil War Citizens: Race, Ethnicity, and Identity in America's Bloodiest Conflicts*, ed. Susannah J. Ural, 214–215 (New York: New York University Press, 2010).

40. "Friends and Fellow Citizens." For more on General Hunter's perceptions and comments, see James M. McPherson, *What They Fought For, 1861–1865* (Baton Rouge: Louisiana State University Press, 1994), 66–67.

41. John Hope Franklin, "Stalking George Washington Williams," *Race and History: Selected Essays 1938–1988*, ed. John Hope Franklin, 267–276 (Baton Rouge: Louisiana State University Press, 1989), especially 267, 273; Donald R. Shaffer, *After the Glory: The Struggles of Black Civil War Veterans* (Lawrence: University of Kansas Press, 2004), 180–184.

42. Shaffer, *After the Glory*, chapter 7, especially 169–171, 188; Franklin, "Stalking George Washington Williams," 273.

43. For black citizenship rights, "white civilization," the place of Native Americans in the United States, and the decline of black status, see Leonard, *Men of Color to Arms!* 140, 145–146, 195–197. For protective legislation, see Emberton, *Beyond Redemption*,

5–6, 64 (my thanks to John David Smith for alerting me to this work) and Glenn, *Unequal Freedom*, 84–85.

44. Hale, *Making Whiteness*, 48–50, 53, 73, 76–78, 261–263; Glenn, *Unequal Freedom*, 24, 115.

45. "The Inauguration of President Harrison," *Savannah Tribune*, 9 March 1889; "Friends and Fellow-Citizens," *Savannah Tribune*, January 26, 1889; *Savannah Tribune*, January 19, 1889; "Col. John H. Deveaux," *Savannah Tribune*, March 2, 1889; "The Inaugural Ball," *Savannah Tribune*, February 9, 1889. See *Savannah Tribune*, February 16, 1889, for Atlanta units and the delegation visiting the president-elect, and "Governor's Volunteers," *Atlanta Daily Constitution*, June 28, 1879, ProQuest Historical Newspapers: The Atlanta Constitution (1868–1942), hereafter cited as ACPQUNCC. My thanks to Ms. Lois Stickell, Reference Librarian, Atkins Library, University of North Carolina at Charlotte, North Carolina, for alerting me to the library's access to ProQuest for a second time in December 2010.

46. For an examination of the importance of the local in defining the militia and its activities, see Hannah, "Dance Floor," 149–177. My thanks go to colleague Dr. John David Smith for bringing this article to my attention.

47. "Major John Schwarz Elected Mayor," *Savannah Tribune*, January 19, 1889; "The Mayor and the Military," *Savannah Tribune*, September 28, 1889; Frances Smith, *Black Militia in Savannah*, 38, 41–42.

48. Frances Smith, *Black Militia in Savannah*, 41–42; "Let the Soldiers Turn Out," *Savannah Tribune*, November 2, 1889; "The City's Doors Were Opened," *Savannah Tribune*, November 16, 1889; "Our Military on Parade," *Savannah Tribune*, May 25, 1889; "The Military's Visit to Charleston," *Savannah Tribune*, July 6, 1889.

49. "Gov. Gordon Sent," *Savannah Tribune*, October 5, 1889.

50. "A Quiet Day," *Atlanta Constitution*, October 1, 1889; "Military Matters," *Atlanta Constitution*, October 20, 1889, ACPQUNCC.

51. "The Talk About Abandoning," *Savannah Tribune*, November 23, 1889; "Afro-American League," *Savannah Tribune*, November 9, 1889. For the national efforts at organizing African Americans, see Shawn Leigh Alexander, *An Army of Lions: The Civil Rights Struggle Before the NAACP* (Philadelphia: University of Pennsylvania Press, 2012).

52. "Help the Military," *Savannah Tribune*, December 21, 1889; "The Board of Officers," *Savannah Tribune*, September 7, 1889; "The Military Committee," *Savannah Tribune*, September 21, 1889. It is unclear whether a battalion armory was ever secured or built. Some white units across the state attempted similar fund-raising efforts with limited success. The state at the beginning of the twentieth century began funding militia companies' armory rental bills, and Atlanta, in the wake of the 1906 race riot, built an armory-auditorium/auditorium-armory completed in 1907.

53. Jeffrey R. Kerr-Ritchie, *Rites of August: First Emancipation Day in the Black Atlantic World* (Baton Rouge: Louisiana State University Press, 2007), 166, 180–184.

54. "The Georgia Light Infantry," *Savannah Tribune*, May 25, 1889; "In Honor of Douglass," *Savannah Tribune*, April 6, 1889; "Minister Fred Douglass," *Savannah Tribune*, October 5, 1889; "The Forest City Light Infantry's Bazaar" and "The Bazaar of the Forest City Light Infantry," *Savannah Tribune*, February 16, 1889; "The Georgia Artillery," *Savannah Tribune*, September 7, 1889; "About The Capitol," *Atlanta Constitution*,

May 14, 1891. For additional individual unit activities, see "The 1st Battalion Will Parade," *Savannah Tribune*, August 17, 1889.

55. "Going Into Encampment," *Atlanta Constitution*, June 14, 1890, ACPQUNCC.

56. "The Colored Troops," *Atlanta Constitution*, July 10, 1890; "Colored Companies to Parade," *Atlanta Constitution*, August 14, 1890.

57. Hannah, "Dance Floor," 152, 154–160. See also Hannah, *Manhood*, 104, 107, 109–110, 116, 126–132.

58. "The Full Report," *Atlanta Constitution*, January 17, 1892. See "Colonel Wiley Now in Command," *Atlanta Constitution*, June 24, 1891; "The Governor's Third," *Atlanta Constitution*, July 3, 1891; "It is Very Doubtful," *Atlanta Constitution*, July 3, 1891; "It Will Close," *Atlanta Constitution*, July 4, 1891, for the evolution of the Chickamauga encampment.

59. Hannah, "Dance Floor to Rifle Range," 149–151, 171–177. For fear of federal power in the immediate post–Civil War United States see Emberton, *Beyond Redemption*, chapter 1.

60. Hannah, "Dance Floor to Rifle Range." Also see Hannah, *Manhood*, 109–110, 122–123, 126–133.

61. *Savannah Tribune*, December 31, 1892; "Twenty-Six Years," *Atlanta Constitution*, January 2, 1889.

62. "A New Decade," *Atlanta Constitution*, January 2, 1889. For a parallel study of this dilemma for blacks, their rights, the law, and white resistance to black equality, see Christopher Waldrep, *Roots of Disorder: Race and Criminal Justice in the American South, 1817–80* (Urbana: University of Illinois Press, 1998).

63. *Savannah Tribune*, December 19, 1891; *Savannah Tribune*, December 26, 1891; "Emancipation Day," *Savannah Tribune*, December 12, 1891.

64. "Emancipation Day," December 12, 1891; "Let It Be Celebrated," *Savannah Tribune*, December 12, 1891; "Military Orders," *Savannah Tribune*, December 26, 1891; "Will Celebrate The Day," *Savannah Tribune*, December 19, 1891.

65. *Savannah Tribune*, December 3, 1892; Elsa Barkley Brown, "Negotiating and Transforming the Public Sphere: African American Political Life in the Transition from Slavery to Freedom," *The Black Public Sphere: A Public Culture Book*, ed. Black Public Sphere Collective (Chicago: University of Chicago Press, 1995), 111–115, 118, 120, 123–124, 126, 128–130, 132–134.

66. Brown, "Negotiating and Transforming," 142–145, 149–150. For more recent examinations of this quest to define and defend a respectable womanhood and manhood and for contrasting views of its long-term consequences, see Mitchell, *Righteous Propagation*, chapters 2–5, 7–8; Hornsby-Gutting, *Black Manhood*, introduction and chapter 1; and Bettye Collier-Thomas, *Jesus, Jobs, and Justice: African American Women and Religion* (New York: Alfred A. Knopf, 2010), xx–xxi.

67. Brown, "Negotiating and Transforming"; Mitchell, *Righteous Propagation*, 54–58, 65, 69, 71–75, 79–82, 84–85, 91; Hornsby-Gutting, *Black Manhood*, 18, 20–24, 26–27, 36, 39–40, 47, 51, 58, 167. For the antebellum clash between mass democracy and respectability, see Shane White, "'It Was a Proud Day': African Americans, Festivals, and Parades in the North, 1741–1834," in *The New African American Urban History*, ed. Kenneth W. Goings and Raymond A. Mohl, 17–65 (Thousand Oaks: Sage Publications,

1996), 38, 45–46, 49–51, 56–58. For antebellum and post-bellum disfranchisement, segregation, and antiblack violence, see Julie Winch, *Philadelphia's Black Elite: Activism, Accommodation, and the Struggle for Autonomy, 1787–1848* (Philadelphia: Temple University Press, 1988), chapter 7; W. E. B. Du Bois, *Philadelphia Negro: A Social Study* (New York: Schocken Books, 1967, 1899), 25–31; and Mixon, *Atlanta Riot*, 73–74.

68. *Savannah Tribune*, December 19, 1891; *Savannah Tribune*, December 31, 1892; "Monday Emancipation Day," *Savannah Tribune*, December 31, 1892. For Atlanta's and Augusta's Emancipation Day organizations, see *Savannah Tribune*, November 12, 1892. Brown, "Negotiating and Transforming," 143, notes in the footnotes that the black militia lost some of its public significance as lodge groups such as the Knights of Pythias took over "military ritual" and demonstrations of manhood. This would be evident when the last militia unit in Georgia was disbanded, in 1905, and Emancipation Day became dominated by black fraternal groups in military uniforms.

69. Adjutant and Inspector General John McIntosh Kell to Col. Wm. F. Jones, Comdg, 9th Regt. Ga. Vols., Washington, Ga., May 21, 1891, p. 131–132; Adjutant and Inspector General John McIntosh Kell to Capt. L[?] Stubbs, Comdg Dublin Light Infantry, Dublin, Ga., May 7, 1891, p. 76; Adjutant and Inspector General John McIntosh Kell to Lt. Col. A. R. Johnson, Comdg, 3rd Batt. Ga. Vols, Colored, Augusta, Ga., July 14, 1891, p. 405, VOL1–1706, Defense-Adjutant General—Letter Books—1891 April 23-August 5—"Vol. 8" indexed, 022-01-001, Unit # 50 Consignment 1996-1232A, GDAH. On the improved relationship between the states, local elite, and federal government, see Mahon, *History of the Militia*, 112–115.

70. "Military Inspection," *Savannah Tribune*, January 23, 1892; "Military Inspection," *Savannah Tribune*, February 6, 1892; "All The Companies Inspected," *Savannah Tribune*, February 27, 1892; "Mrs. Felton Aroused," *Atlanta Constitution*, February 16, 1892; Mahon, *History of the Militia*, 114; for a history of Emory Upton, see Mahon, *History of the Militia*, 121. The First Battalion, Georgia Volunteers, Colored, in 1891–1892 were the Forest City Light Infantry, Union Lincoln Guards, Chatham Light Infantry, Savannah Light Infantry, Lone Star Cadets, and Colquitt Blues of Macon.

71. First Lieutenant C. B. Satterlee, "Report of Inspection of the Georgia Volunteers and Georgia Volunteers, Colored, September 25th, 1891, to April 5th, 1892," (Atlanta: Geo. W. Harrison, State Printer and Franklin Publishing House, 1892), 89, 95, Rare Book Collection, Collection number 6600, Wilson Library, University of North Carolina, Chapel Hill, Chapel Hill, North Carolina; "Winding Up," *Atlanta Constitution*, July 4, 1891; "Georgia Militia Is Highly Complimented in Captain Field's Report," *Atlanta Constitution*, October 15, 1891; "Georgia's Militia," *Atlanta Constitution*, November 23, 1891.

72. Satterlee, "Report of Inspection of the Georgia Volunteers and Georgia Volunteers, Colored, September 25th, 1891, to April 5th, 1892," 80; "Georgia's Militia."

73. Satterlee, "Report of Inspection of the Georgia Volunteers and Georgia Volunteers, Colored, September 25th, 1891, to April 5th, 1892," 81–83.

74. *Savannah Tribune*, January 30, 1892; *Savannah Tribune*, January 9, 1892; *Savannah Tribune*, January 2, 1892; "The People's Party," *Savannah Tribune*, February 13, 1892; "The State Militia," *Savannah Tribune*, December 3, 1892. For Woodhouse's original appointment, see "A Colored Colonel," *Atlanta Constitution*, September 8, 11, 1880.

75. "Georgia v. Chile," *Atlanta Constitution,* January 21, 1892; "Our Military," *Savannah Tribune,* December 17, 1892.

76. "Public Affairs: Governor Northen Sends His Message to the General Assembly," *Atlanta Constitution,* October 28, 1892. For a discussion of national turmoil in public confrontations requiring militia mobilizations, see Eric Foner, *A Short History of Reconstruction, 1863–1877* (Philadelphia: Harper and Row Publishers, 1990), chapters 11 and 12; Cooper, *Rise of the National Guard,* chapters 2 and 3; and Mahon, *History of the Militia,* 112–124.

77. "The Military: The Annual Report of the Adjutant General and Inspector General is Out," *Atlanta Constitution,* October 27, 1893; "Our Soldiers," *Atlanta Constitution,* November 20, 1893.

78. N. E. Wooten, Attorney and Counselors at Law, Capt. Comdg, Albany Guards to Hon. W. J. Northen, Governor of Georgia, Atlanta, Ga., Jan 13, 1891, Folder 1–13–1891; Robt B. Wayfor, Jr. Eureka Planter Company, LaGrange, Ga. February 11, 1891, to His Excellency Gov. W. J. Northen, Atlanta, Georgia, Folder 2–11–1891, W. J. McClure, Secretary and Treasurer Eureka Planter Company Manufacturers and Proprietors February 9, 1891; C. V. Truitt Heavy Groceries and Plantation Supplies LaGrange, Georgia, February 9, 1891, F. M. Longley, FM&FP Longley Attorneys-At-Law, LaGrange, Georgia, February 9, 1891; J. E. Dunson, Dunson & Dunson General Supply Merchants, La Grange, Georgia, February 11, 1891, Folder 2–11–1891; Mayor M. J. Colson, Council Chamber, City of Brunswick to Hon. W. J. Northen, October 3, 1891; W. G. Brantley, Attorney at Law, Solicitor General, Brunswick Circuit, Brunswick, Georgia, October 3, 1891; Governor—Executive Dept-Governor's Subject Files 1890–1894—Gov. William Jonathan Northen—January thru December 1891, Consignment 1993–1219A, Unit# 102, 001–01–005, GDAH.

79. W. W. Gordon, W. W. Gordon and Company, Cotton Factors and Commission Merchants, Savannah, Georgia to His Excellency W. J. Northen, Governor of Georgia, Atlanta, Georgia, December 5, 1891; W. W. Gordon to His Excellency, W. J. Northen, Governor of Georgia, Atlanta, Georgia, December 15, 1891; William Garrard, Law Offices of Garrard and Meldrum, Savannah, Georgia, to His Excellency W. J. Northen, Governor of Georgia, Atlanta, Georgia, December 15, 1891, Folder 12-5-1891, Governor—Executive Dept-Governor's Subject Files 1890–1894—Gov. William Jonathan Northen—January thru December 1891, Consignment 1993–1219A, Unit# 102, 001–01–005, GDAH.

80. "At Camp Northen," *Atlanta Constitution,* May 3, 1894; "Too Many Elections," *Atlanta Constitution,* December 3, 1894; "Talk About Georgia," *Atlanta Constitution,* March 15, 1895; "The Governor's Message," *Savannah Tribune,* December 1, 1894; *Savannah Tribune,* December 8, 2011. For denial of the appropriation, see *Savannah Tribune,* December 15, 1894.

81. See "With the Military," *Atlanta Constitution,* July 20, 1894; "Two Changes Made," *Atlanta Constitution,* July 28, 1894; "Expenses of Camp," *Atlanta Constitution,* June 30, 1894; "The Military," *Atlanta Constitution,* October 27, 1893. For the low numbers, see "Georgia's Army," *Atlanta Constitution,* December 30, 1892.

82. "Emancipation Day Celebration," *Savannah Tribune,* January 5, 1895.

83. "Atlanta Exposition—Other Notes," *Savannah Tribune,* April 13, 1895.

84. Ibid.

85. *Savannah Tribune*, April 6, 1895. For the self-sponsored drill competition, see "A Colored Military Encampment," *Atlanta Constitution*, August 31, 1886. Nationally, as states funded their militias, black militiamen got increasingly less access to resources. See Mahon, *History of the Militia*, 111.

86. "Atlanta Exposition—Other Notes."

87. "Aimed at the Guard," *Atlanta Constitution*, April 3, 1895. On black demands for access to an encampment, see "Will They Get It?" *Atlanta Constitution*, June 24, 1891.

88. "Military Inspection," *Savannah Tribune*, May 18, 1895.

89. "Struck Tents," *Atlanta Constitution*, July 1, 1895; "The Negro Battalion," *Atlanta Constitution*, July 9, 1895.

90. "His Annual Message," *Atlanta Constitution*, October 29, 1895; "Governor Atkinson," *Savannah Tribune*, December 7, 1895; "Reward for Lynchers," *Savannah Tribune*, December 7, 1895. According to James F. Cook, Governor Atkinson "was even more hostile to lynching than was his predecessor, Governor William J. Northen." Atkinson "repeatedly condemned the practice and urged the legislature to enact laws against it, but to no avail"; James F. Cook, "William Yates Atkinson, 1894–1898, He died in the prime of life," *The Governors of Georgia: Revised and Expanded*, ed. James F. Cook, 181–184 (Macon: Mercer University Press, 1995).

91. "The Negro at the Exposition," *Savannah Tribune*, November 2, 1895; "Negro Building Opened," *Savannah Tribune*, October 26, 1895; "Sayings about Atlanta," *Savannah Tribune*, December 7, 1895.

Chapter 6. The Road to Disbandment, 1896–1899

1. "The Artillery and the Railroad," *Savannah Tribune*, January 25, 1896; "To Celebrate Emancipation," *Savannah Morning News*, January 1, 1896; "The Colored People's Day," *Savannah Morning News*, January 2, 1896. For the reward and Johnston's claim for Motorman West, see "A Reward for An Artilleryman," *Savannah Morning News*, January 20, 1896.

2. "The Artillery and the Railroad"; "A Reward"; "Police Want the Names," *Savannah Morning News*, January 3, 1896.

3. "The Artillery and the Railroad"; "The Assailant Not Yet Found," *Savannah Morning News*, January 29, 1896.

4. "Kell Disbands Four Companies," *Atlanta Constitution*, April 30, 1896; "Flowers for the Hero Dead," *Savannah Morning News*, April 28, 1896; "The Park Extension," *Savannah Morning News*, April 29, 1896; "Control of Parade Ground," *Savannah Morning News*, April 30, 1896. For the importance of Jim Crow segregation in shaping the lives of white and black people, see John W. Cell, *The Highest Stage of White Supremacy: The Origins of Segregation in South Africa and the American South* (London: Cambridge University Press, 1982), chapters 1, 4, 6, 7, 9; Grant, *The Way It Was*, chapter 5; Crystal N. Feimster, *Southern Horrors: Women and the Politics of Rape and Lynching* (Cambridge, Mass.: Harvard University Press, 2009), chapter 2.

5. "Control of Parade Ground." For the evolution of white attitudes towards blacks in the late nineteenth century, see Emberton, *Beyond Redemption*.

6. "Control of Parade Ground."

7. Blacks in Savannah challenged streetcar segregation with an unsuccessful boycott in 1906. They had earlier successfully contested Jim Crow seating in the 1870s and l899. For a general examination, see Robert E. Perdue, *The Negro in Savannah, 1865–1900* (New York: Exposition Press, 1973), 31–35. For a more detailed exploration of black Savannah's actions against segregated streetcars and the role of the *Savannah Tribune*, see Turner, "Agitation and Accommodation," 25–45. For the culture of segregation and its impact in the 1890s, see Hale, *Making Whiteness*; and Nathan Cardon, "The South's 'New Negroes' and African American Visions of Progress at the Atlanta and Nashville International Expositions, 1895–1897," *Journal of Southern History* 80, no. 2 (May 2014): 287–326.

8. See "Acts and Resolutions of the General Assembly of the State of Georgia, 1884–1885," p. 85, Georgia Legislative Documents, GDAH, neptune3.galib.uga.edu/ssp/cgi-bin/legis-idx.pl?sessionid=7f000001&type=law&byte=571613. For a discussion of the 1891 transportation legislation embracing Jim Crow segregation, see Mixon, *Atlanta Riot*.

9. "The Colored Companies," *Savannah Tribune,* February 15, 1896; "Negro Captains Uneasy," *Atlanta Constitution,* February 11, 1896. The members of the Military Advisory Board for the next three years, from 1897 to 1899, included Captain W. W. Gordon, son of Colonel W. W. Gordon, both of Savannah. Colonel Gordon replaced Col. William Garrard as head of the Advisory Board. Major Jordan F. Brooks was also a Savannah resident. The *Atlanta Constitution,* which has been inconsistent in establishing the rank of some militiamen, also listed Brooks as a captain. See "Etched and Sketched," *Atlanta Constitution,* January 15, 1896.

10. "Want to Enlist," *Atlanta Constitution,* January 23, 1896; "The Board to Meet," *Atlanta Constitution,* January 29, 1896; "Georgia's Army and Navy: Advisory Board to Convene," *Atlanta Constitution,* February 1, 1896; "Meetings," *Atlanta Constitution,* February 5, 1896; "Negro Captains Uneasy"; "The Guard Is In," *Atlanta Constitution,* February 12, 1896. For the Gate City Guard, see "Gate City Guard," *Savannah Morning News*, January 10, 1896, and "Militia of the State," *Savannah Morning News*, January 30, 1896.

11. "The Colored Companies"; "Negro Captains Uneasy."

12. "The Colored Companies."

13. Ibid.; "Colored Troops," *Macon Telegraph*, August 5. 1895.

14. Frances Smith, "Black Militia in Savannah," 40–42; "The Colored Companies."

15. Frances Smith, "Black Militia in Savannah," 42–47. For the police incident, see "Outrageous Assault," *Savannah Tribune,* May 18, 1895.

16. For the relationship between race, costs, and disbandment of black militia units, see Cooper, *Rise of the National Guard*, 23–25, 31, 34, 37, 39–43, 71–72, 137; Mahon, *History of the Militia*, 110–111.

17. "They Will Not Be Disbanded," *Savannah Tribune,* February 22, 1896; *Savannah Tribune,* May 9, 1896; "Colored Soldiers on Serenade," *Savannah Morning News*, March 5, 1896. For the streetcar incident, see *Savannah Tribune,* February 22, 1896; and "A Villainous Affair," *Savannah Tribune,* February 22, 1896.

18. *Savannah Tribune,* February 22, 1896; "To Report To-Day," *Savannah Morning News*, February 21, 1896; "May Week Celebration," *Savannah Morning News*, February

22, 1896. For a discussion of the black male exodus from Georgia, see Grant, *The Way It Was*, 288.

19. "May Week Celebration," *Savannah Morning News*, February 22, 1896; "From State Headquarters," *Savannah Morning News*, April 18, 1896.

20. "Orders Are Out For State Camp," *Atlanta Constitution*, May 14, 1896; "Adjutant Makes a Report on Troops," *Atlanta Constitution*, December 16, 1897; "Money for Soldiers," *Atlanta Constitution*, December 11, 1896. For appropriation levels, see "Acting Adjutant General to Sgt George Freeman, Co. A 1st Batt Infy. G. V. Savannah, Georgia, March 1, 1898," 21-1-1 Adjutant General Letter Book, Box 57, p. 223, GDAH.

21. H. R. Butler, "What the Negro Is Doing: Matters of Interest Among the Colored People," *Atlanta Constitution*, May 10, 1896.

22. Butler, "What the Negro Is Doing," *Atlanta Constitution*, May 10, 1896; H. R. Butler, "What the Negro Is Doing: Matters of Interest Among the Colored People," *Atlanta Constitution*, July 5, 1896; "Money for Soldiers"; "Means More Taxs [sic]," *Atlanta Constitution*, December 5, 1896.

23. "Flag Presentation," *Savannah Tribune*, October 3, 1896; Frances Smith, "Black Militia in Savannah," 67.

24. "Flag Presentation." For a discussion of black and white definitions of freedom and citizenship, see Emberton, *Beyond Redemption*, 23, 28, 54, 58–59, 70, 75, 77; and Nancy Cohen, *The Reconstruction of American Liberalism, 1865–1914* (Chapel Hill: University of North Carolina Press, 2002), 62, 65, 70, 178, 219.

25. "Flag Presentation."

26. Ibid.

27. H. R. Butler, "What the Negro is Doing," *Atlanta Constitution*, December 13, 1896.

28. Ibid.

29. For Forest City Light Infantry, see Adjutant General Miscellaneous Records: National Guard, Box 20, Folder: 22-1-10, Ga Natl Guard Militia Enlistment of Forest City Light Infantry, Co. A., 1st Bn Inf., GA vol: (Co), Petition for Election of Officers, Forest City Light Infantry, Col. Co. B, July 16, 1874, GDAH.

30. H. R. Butler, "What the Negro Is Doing," *Atlanta Constitution*, December 27, 1896. For an assessment of the evolution of relations between the United States and Spain, see Robert L. Beisner, *From the Old Diplomacy to the New, 1865–1900*, 2nd ed. (Wheeling, Ill.: Harlan Davidson, 1986), 115–119, 122–130.

31. "Adjutant Makes a Report on Troops"; "Soldiers in Peace, Soldiers in War," *Atlanta Constitution*, March 5, 1897.

32. "Freedmen's Day," *Savannah Tribune*, January 9, 1897; "Negroes Celebrate," *Atlanta Constitution*, January 2, 1897; "Board to Meet on 25th," *Atlanta Constitution*, February 22, 1897.

33. Talk of the Week with Georgia Volunteer Forces," *Atlanta Constitution*, February 22, 1897; "Talk of the Week with Georgia Soldier Boys," *Atlanta Constitution*, February 27, 1897.

34. "Fair in Progress," *Savannah Tribune*, January 23, 1897; "Military Fair Closed," February 6, 1897.

35. "Military Anniversary," *Savannah Tribune*, April 17, 1897; "Military Parade," *Savannah Tribune*, May 22, 1897.

36. "Military Anniversary"; "Our Amusement Column," *Savannah Tribune*, March 13, 1897; "Our Amusement Column," *Savannah Tribune*, April 17, 2011; *Savannah Tribune*, August 7, 1897. For a very brief discussion of the "ladies branch," see Frances Smith, "Black Militia in Savannah," 53, and for the 1893 reorganization, Frances Smith, "Black Militia in Savannah," 64–66.

37. "To Go in Camps," *Savannah Tribune*, August 7, 1897.

38. "Artillery's Encampment," *Savannah Tribune*, August 14, 1897; "Returned from Camp Kell," *Savannah Tribune*, August 21, 1897; Frances Smith, "Black Militia in Savannah," 49.

39. "Returned from Camp Kell."

40. "Returned from Camp Kell"; Frances Smith, "Black Militia in Savannah," 49. For an example of encampment visits by the governor and militia officials, see "With the Soldiers," *Atlanta Constitution*, June 14, 1896.

41. "The Local Legislature," *Macon Telegraph*, February 24, 1897; "City Items," *Macon Telegraph*, February 28, 1897; "Colored Military Picnic," *Macon Telegraph*, July 18, 1897; "The Fats and Leans," *Macon Telegraph*, August 23, 1897; "Their 'Gala Day' Has Come At Last," *Atlanta Constitution*, July 5, 1897; "Ready for Columbia," and "Military Orders," *Savannah Tribune*, September 4, 1897; "Labor Day Celebration," *Savannah Tribune*, September 11, 1897; "What the Negro Is Doing," *Atlanta Constitution*, October 3, 1897. For the planning process for the Labor Day celebration, see "Our Amusement Column," *Savannah Tribune*, August 7, 1897.

42. Acting Adjutant General Oscar J. Brown to Captain J. Lockhart, Macon, November 6, 1897, p. 65; Acting Adjutant General Oscar J. Brown to Captain P. C. R. Bell, Macon, November 6, 1897, p. 66; Acting Adjutant General Oscar J. Brown to Lt. Col. John H. Deveaux, Savannah, n.d., p. 107; Acting Adjutant General Oscar J. Brown to Captain J. F. Brooks, Savannah, December 9, 1897, p. 109; Acting Adjutant General Oscar J. Brown to Captain Charles M. Tyson, Sandersville, p. 110, 22-1-1 Department of Defense, Adjutant General Letter Book, Volume 20 9/16/1897–4/15/1898, Box 57, GDAH; "Military Notes," *Savannah Tribune*, January 15, 1898; *Savannah Tribune*, April 9, 1898.

43. "Stopped a Funeral Procession," *Atlanta Constitution*, January 17, 1898.

44. "HWG, 'Atlanta Negroes Are Ready to Fight Spain,'" *Atlanta Constitution*, March 6, 1898.

45. "HWG, 'Atlanta Negroes Are Ready to Fight Spain.'" For congressional assumptions concerning black troops and tropical disease immunity, see Willard Gatewood, *"Smoked Yankees" and the Struggle for Empire* (Urbana: University of Illinois Press, 1971), 11.

46. "HWG, 'Atlanta Negroes Are Ready to Fight Spain.'"

47. *Savannah Tribune*, March 5, 1898; *Savannah Tribune*, March 12, 1898; "A Royal Banquet," *Savannah Tribune*, April 9, 1898. For the entire roster of black men serving in the national Congress from the end of the Civil War to 1898, see "Colored Men in the House of Representatives and Senate," *Savannah Tribune*, March 19, 1898.

48. *Savannah Tribune,* March 5, 1898; *Savannah Tribune,* April 2, 1898; Gatewood, "*Smoked Yankees,*" 5.

49. Acting Adjutant General Oscar J. Brown to Captain Jackson McHenry, Com'd'g Co. "B," Batt. Inf. G. V. Colored, March 11, 1898, p. 232, 21-1-1 Adjutant General Letter Books, Department of Defense, Box 57, Volume 20, 9/16/1897–4/14/1898, GDAH.

50. Governor Atkinson to Captain C. A. Withers, Commander Confederate Soldier's Association, Augusta, March 16, 1898; Acting Adjutant General to Lieut. Col. I. Blocker, Ga. Volunteers Colored, Augusta, March 31, 1898, p. 295, 21-1-1 Adjutant General Letter Books, Department of Defense, Box 57, Volume 20, 9/16/1897–4/14/1898, GDAH.

51. Acting Adjutant General Oscar J. Brown to Louis K. Swinton, colored, Milledgeville, April 15, 1898, p. 434; Acting Adjutant General Oscar J. Brown to T. H. McIver, colored, Thebes, April 16, 1898, p. 447, 21-1-1 Adjutant General Letter Books, Department of Defense, Box 57, Volume 20, 9/16/1897–4/14/1898, GDAH.

52. "To Equip State Troops For War," *Atlanta Constitution,* April 6, 1898.

53. Beisner, *From the Old Diplomacy to the New,* 128; "President McKinley's Message," *Savannah Tribune,* April 16, 1898; "The Colored Troops," *Savannah Tribune,* April 23, 1898; Gatewood, "*Smoked Yankees,*" 5.

54. "Governor Calls Conference of Army Officers," *Atlanta Constitution,* April 25, 1898. For Atkinson's relationship with African Americans, see *Savannah Tribune,* August 6, 1898.

55. "Governor Calls Conference of Army Officers"; "Three Majors," *Savannah Tribune,* May 21, 1898; "Capt. Brown and Col. Lawton to Lead Georgia Volunteers," *Atlanta Georgia,* April 26, 1898; "Georgia's Quota of Volunteers Is Being Raised," *Atlanta Constitution,* April 27, 1898; "Call to Troops Has Been Made," *Atlanta Constitution,* April 29, 1898; "State Forces Kept Intact?" *Atlanta Constitution,* May 13, 1898; "Half State Guns Sent to Camp," *Atlanta Constitution,* May 18, 1898.

56. *Savannah Tribune,* April 30, 1898; "Colored Troops Ignored," *Savannah Tribune,* April 30, 1898. For the national neglect of black troops, with exceptions in Alabama, Illinois, Indiana, Kansas, Massachusetts, North Carolina, Ohio, and Virginia, See Gatewood, "*Smoked Yankees,*" 9–10.

57. Gatewood, "*Smoked Yankees,*" 3–17. For the gendered problems posed by military service and the "'obsession with manhood,'" war, and freedom generated during the late nineteenth century, see Emberton, *Beyond Redemption,* 104–105 and chapter 4.

58. *Savannah Tribune,* May 7, 1898.

59. Ibid.

60. *Savannah Tribune,* May 14, 1898; "Exchange Notes," *Savannah Tribune,* May 14, 1898. For similar charges against black soldiers, see Amanda Nagel, "'We Are American Soldiers': Masculinity and Race in the Philippine-American War," paper presented at the 99th Annual Meeting of the Association for the Study of African American Life and History, Memphis, Tennessee, September 23–27, 2014.

61. "To Show Its Strength," *Savannah Tribune,* May 14, 1898; *Savannah Tribune,* May 14, 1898. For a report on the May 19, 1898, parade, see "Annual Parade," *Savannah Tribune,* May 21, 1898.

62. Jos. Ohl, "Georgia Negroes Now Have a Chance to Volunteer," *Atlanta Constitution,* May 24, 1898; "Negro Soldiers Want to Fight," *Atlanta Constitution,* May 25, 1898.

63. Jos. Ohl, "Georgia Negroes Now Have a Chance to Volunteer"; Gatewood, "*Smoked Yankees*," 9–11; Beisner, *From the Old Diplomacy to the New*, 93.

64. "Colored Militia," *Atlanta Constitution*, June 22, 1891; *Savannah Tribune*, June 18, 1898. For the problem of invisibility for U.S. African American regular troops, see Dobak and Phillips, *Black Regulars*, 247–280.

65. Gatewood, "*Smoked Yankees*," 9–11; Turner, "Agitation and Accommodation," 1–12; Beisner, *From the Old Diplomacy to the New*, chapters 4 and 5.

66. Gatewood, "*Smoked Yankees*"; *Savannah Tribune*, June 4, 1898; *Savannah Tribune*, June 11, 1898.

67. *Savannah Tribune*, June 11, 1898.

68. *Savannah Tribune*, June 11, 1898.

69. *Savannah Tribune*, June 18–July 23, 1898. See especially *Savannah Tribune*, June 18, 1898; June 25, 1898; July 2, 1898; July 9, 1898. Also see Gatewood, "*Smoked Yankees*," 7–10.

70. *Savannah Tribune*, August 13, 1898; *Savannah Tribune*, August 29, 1898.

71. James F. Cook, "Allen Daniel Candler 1898–1902," *The Governors of Georgia, 1754–1995* (Macon, Ga.: Mercer University Press, 1995), 185–188; *Savannah Tribune*, November 5, 1898; *Savannah Tribune*, December 10, 1898.

72. "Governor Candler's Annual Message a Meaty Document," *Atlanta Constitution*, October 26, 1899; "Georgia State Militia Will Be Reorganized after Nov. 31st," *Atlanta Constitution*, November 8, 1898; "Advisory Board to Be Summoned," *Atlanta Constitution*, September 3, 1899; "Military Board Convenes Today," September 18, 1899. For use of the term "national guard," see "Unnecessarily Touchous," *Atlanta Constitution*, January 5, 1899.

73. "Georgia State Militia Will Be Reorganized after Nov. 31st"; "Many Officers Have Been Made," *Atlanta Constitution*, June 28, 1898. See "Second Georgia Out," *Savannah Tribune*, November 19, 1898, which reported the mustering out of the Second Volunteer Regiment under the command of Colonel Oscar J. Brown.

74. "Unnecessarily Touchous."

75. "Will Reorganize Militia Tomorrow," *Atlanta Constitution*, November 30, 1898; "Military Board Convenes Today."

76. "Will Reorganize Militia Tomorrow"; "Will Probably Disband," *Atlanta Constitution*, March 30, 1899.

77. Inspector General William G. Obear, "Annual Report," Adjutant General Letter Books—1902–1906, 76–98, "Military Laws and Regulations," pp. 86–87, and "Remarks," p. 90; Volume -1–731 022–01–001 Defense—Adjutant General Letter Books 1902–1906, Unit 62, GDAH.

78. Obear, "Annual Report," Adjutant General Letter Books—1902–1906; *Savannah Tribune*, November 5, 1898; *Savannah Tribune*, December 10, 1898; "Will Reorganize Militia Tomorrow"; "Local Companies Inspected Today," *Atlanta Constitution*, March 1, 1899; "Order of Election Issued Yesterday," *Atlanta Constitution*, January 6, 1900; "Military Forces, Organization of Law Number: No. 131," Acts and Resolutions of the General Assembly of the State of Georgia 1900, Part 1 Public Laws, Title V. Miscellaneous, 1900, Vol. 1, p. 84, GDAH.

79. "Columbus Has No Militia," *Atlanta Constitution*, March 25, 1899.

80. *Savannah Tribune,* March 25, 1899.

81. "The Colored Troops," *Savannah Tribune,* April 15, 1899.

82. "Annual May Parade," *Savannah Tribune,* May 20, 1899; "Troops Paraded," *Savannah Tribune,* May 27, 1899; *Savannah Tribune,* April 22, 1899; "About the Military," *Savannah Tribune,* September 23, 1899; Frances Smith, "Black Militia in Savannah," 74–75.

83. "Advisory Board to Be Summoned"; "Military Board Named Yesterday," *Atlanta Constitution,* July 2, 1899; "Military Board Convenes Today"; "Advisory Board to Meet Sept. 18," *Atlanta Constitution,* September 7, 1899; "The Military Advisor Board Makes Changes in State Militia," *Atlanta Constitution,* September 19, 1899. "Inspector General Obear's Report Is Now Made Public," *Atlanta Constitution,* September 22, 1899.

84. "Advisory Board to Be Summoned"; "Military Board Convenes Today"; "The Military Advisory Board Makes Changes in State Militia."

Chapter 7. The New Era, 1899–1905

1. "The Military Advisory Board Makes Changes in State Militia," *Atlanta Constitution,* September 19, 1899.

2. "Two Negro Regiments," *Savannah Tribune,* September 16, 1899; *Savannah Tribune,* October 4, 1899; *Savannah Tribune,* October 21, 1899; *Savannah Tribune,* October 28, 1899; "About The Military," *Savannah Tribune,* September 23, 1899; Gatewood, "*Smoked Yankees,*" 13–15; Brian McAllister Linn, *The Philippine War, 1899–1902* (Lawrence: University of Kansas Press, 2000), 125.

3. *Savannah Tribune,* September 16, 1899. For education issues, see *Savannah Tribune,* August 5, 1899; Blair L. M. Kelley, *Right to Ride: Streetcar Boycotts and African American Citizenship in the Era of Plessy v. Ferguson* (Chapel Hill: University of North Carolina Press, 2010), 166–172.

4. "About The Military"; "On The Alert," *Savannah Tribune,* November 18, 1899; "Georgia Redeemed," *Savannah Tribune,* December 2, 1899. For the listing of Second Lieutenant Thomas W. Hardwick, Sandersville, Georgia, see "Many Officers Have Been Made," *Atlanta Constitution,* June 26, 1898.

5. "Negro Day at the Fair," *Savannah Tribune,* December 9, 1899; "Georgia Redeemed"; "Military Parade," *Savannah Tribune,* December 16, 1899; "Arranged for Celebration," *Savannah Tribune,* December 23, 1899; "Emancipation Day," *Savannah Tribune,* December 30, 1899.

6. "Freedom's Natal Day Proudly Celebrated," *Savannah Tribune,* January 6, 1900; Kelley, *Right to Ride,* 167.

7. "Freedom's Natal Day Proudly Celebrated."

8. "Georgia Militia Enters New Era with its Reorganization," *Atlanta Constitution,* February 2, 1900; "Colonels to Meet Governor Today," *Atlanta Constitution,* January 4, 1900. For the full text of the Hardwick military bill, see "Order of Election Issued Yesterday," *Atlanta Constitution,* January 6, 1900.

9. "Georgia Militia Enters New Era with its Reorganization." For brief discussions of the South, Georgia, the militia, and lynching, see Cooper, *Rise of the National Guard,* 47–49–53.

10. "Georgia Militia Enters New Era with its Reorganization." Mahon, *History of the Militia*, 118–119, 124, 138–141; Jim Dan Hill, *The Minute Man in Peace and War: A History of the National Guard* (Harrisburg: Stack Pole Company, 1964), chapters 7 and 8; Louis Cantor, "The Creation of the Modern National Guard: Background, Passage, and Legislative Aftermath of the Dick Militia Act of 1903," (master's thesis, Duke University, 1961), 23, 28–31; Cooper, *Rise of the National Guard*, 95–97, 108–110, 128, 130. The National Guard Association, beginning in 1879, conducted a campaign "insisting that the National guard was a natural component of the nation's military force." The NGA also spent the last few decades of the nineteenth century and beginning of the twentieth century "fighting the development of a monolithic military establishment under the control of regular officers." See Mahon, *History of the Militia*, 119.

11. "Georgia Militia Enters New Era with its Reorganization"; "Order of Election"; "Militia to Get a Large Slice," *Atlanta Constitution*, June 29, 1900; "Georgia Militia Will Get $22,000," *Atlanta Constitution*, July 28, 1900; "Inspections Will Proceed," *Savannah Morning News*, May 23, 1899.

12. "State Militia Officers Who Were Re-elected," *Atlanta Constitution*, February 12, 1900.

13. "Military Reorganization," *Savannah Tribune*, January 20, 1900; Frances Smith, "Black Militia in Savannah," 75–76; "Order of Election." The white colonels of the First, Third, and Fourth Regiments were grandfathered in to continue leading their units: Colonel Alexander R. Lawton, Savannah, Georgia, continued leading the First Regiment at this rank as of April 4, 1896; Colonel R. Usher Thomason, Madison, Georgia, continued serving the Third Regiment since attaining that rank on August 26, 1894; Lt. Colonel William E. Wooten, Albany, Georgia, continued leading the Forth Regiment since attaining that rank on December 15, 1898. See "State Militia Officers Who Were Re-elected."

14. "Our Military," *Savannah Tribune*, December 15, 1900; Frances Smith, "Black Militia in Savannah," 76–78, especially 78.

15. Adjutant General Letter book, 1900, 5–607, see 164, 166, 168, 337, Department of Defense, Record Group 22-1-5, Unit Number 7, GDAH; "Military Elections," *Savannah Tribune*, February 10, 1900. For a discussion of the examination process, see "Fifth Regiment Leads the State," *Atlanta Constitution*, March 15, 1900.

16. "Battalion Parade," *Savannah Tribune*, May 26, 1900.

17. "Georgia's Negro Soldiers Parade," *Atlanta Constitution*, August 15, 1900; "Grand Celebration," *Savannah Tribune*, August 18, 1900.

18. "Georgia's Negro Soldiers Parade."

19. "Grand Celebration."

20. Ibid.

21. Ibid.

22. "Stir in Military Circles," *Savannah Tribune*, November 24, 1900; "They Looked Grand," *Savannah Tribune*, December 1, 1900; "Guards Disbanded," *Savannah Tribune*, September 8, 1900; "Hardwick Bill Discussed," *Savannah Tribune*, November 17, 1900. For the impact of Antonio Maceo on the black self-image, see Aline Helg, *Our Rightful Share: The Afro-Cuban Struggle for Equality, 1886–1912* (Chapel Hill: University of North

Carolina, 1995), 65; and "Maceo's Death a Trumpet Call," *Savannah Tribune,* December 19, 1896.

23. Frances Smith, "Black Militia in Savannah," 76–78.

24. For the record of activities, see *Savannah Tribune,* 1901. Also see *Savannah Tribune,* February 16, 1901, and January 19, 1900; "Annual Parade," *Savannah Tribune,* May 25, 1901; "Grandly Celebrated," *Savannah Tribune,* August 17, 1901.

25. "Inauguration Ceremonies," *Savannah Tribune,* March 9, 1901; "Order of Inaugural Parade," *Atlanta Constitution,* March 4, 1901; *Savannah Tribune,* March 16, 1901; *Savannah Tribune,* March 9, 1901.

26. "New Advisory Board Chosen," *Atlanta Constitution,* March 8, 1901; "Advisory Board Will Meet Soon," *Atlanta Constitution,* March 10, 1901.

27. "Advisory Board Will Meet Soon."

28. "Political and Personal," *Atlanta Constitution,* March 26, 1901; "Military Laws Will Be Revised," *Atlanta Constitution,* May 12, 1901; "For Good of the State Militia," *Atlanta Constitution,* March 24, 1901; "Business for Coming Session," *Atlanta Constitution,* October 16, 1901.

29. Mahon, *History of the Militia,* 118–119, 124; Cooper, *Rise of the National Guard,* 24–25, 95.

30. Mahon, *History of the Militia,* 111, 114, 122–123, 138; Cooper, *Rise of the National Guard,* 34, 39–43, 71, 108–111, 123, 129–132, 135–139; Bartley, *Creation of Modern Georgia,* 33–36, 60–68, 74–80, 97, 105, 147–148; "The Command of the Army," *Savannah Morning News,* March 13, 1899; "The Army Bill," *Savannah Morning News,* March 2, 1899. The U.S. military adopted the general staff model in its reorganization and made the militia part of its reserve army.

31. Cooper, *Rise of the National Guard,* 102–132.

32. "Emancipation Address," *Savannah Tribune,* January 18, 1902; "The Day Observed," *Savannah Tribune,* January 4, 1902.

33. "Emancipation Address."

34. Inspector General William G. Obear to The Commanding Officer, First Battalion Infantry, Colored, Savannah, Georgia, January 16, 1902, p. 11; Inspector General William G. Obear to Adjutant General, Atlanta, Georgia, January 18, 1902, p. 14; "Annual Inspection—Colored Battalion," Inspector General William G. Obear to Commanding Officer, First Battalion, Infantry, Colored, Savannah, Georgia, February 5, 1902, 19–20; "Annual Report," Inspector General William G. Obear to Adjutant General, Atlanta, Georgia, February 24, 1902, 39–42, 76–98, especially 39–40, Defense—Adjutant General Letter Books, 1902–1906, Volume 1–731 022–01–001, GDAH.

35. "Armory Rent and Incidentals Expenses," January 15, 1902; "Annual Report," p. 40, Defense—Adjutant General Letter Books, 1902–1906, Volume 1–731 022–01–001, GDAH.

36. "Annual Report," 40.

37. Ibid.

38. Ibid.

39. Ibid., 87–93.

40. William G. Obear to Adjutant General, State of Georgia, Atlanta, Georgia, October 31, 1903, p. 166; William G. Obear to Adjutant General, State of Georgia, At-

lanta, Georgia, December 9, 1903, p. 183, Defense—Adjutant General Letter Books, 1902–1906, Volume 1–731 022-01-001, GDAH.

41. "Military Activity," *Savannah Tribune*, January 10, 1903; "The Georgia Artillery," *Savannah Tribune*, January 17, 1902; "Annual Inspection—Colored Battalion," 20; *Savannah Tribune*, February 28, 1903; "Military Appointments," *Savannah Tribune*, March 7, 1903; "Major Royall Retired," *Savannah Tribune*, March 14, 1903.

42. Mahon, *History of the Militia*, 138–140.

43. *Savannah Tribune*, June 20, 1903; Annual Inspector General Report 1903, William G. Obear to Adjutant General, State of Georgia, Atlanta Georgia, "Result of Inspection," Dick Bill, 201; Defense—Adjutant General Letter Books, 1902–1906, Volume 1–731 022-01-001, GDAH. Obear reported also in 1904 that there was "hearty and almost unanimous approval of the troops of the state."

44. "Locals," *Savannah Tribune*, September 26, 1903; *Savannah Tribune*, October 10, 1903; "Result of Inspection," Dick Bill, 200–201.

45. "Result of Inspection," Dick Bill, 201.

46. Annual Inspector General Report 1903, 202–204, 213; William G. Obear to the Adjutant General, State of Georgia, Atlanta, Georgia, January 15, 1905, p. 219; Defense—Adjutant General Letter Books, 1902–1906, Volume 1–731, 022-01-001, GDAH.

47. Annual Inspector General Report 1903.

48. Ibid.

49. Obear to Adjutant General, January 15, 1905, 219, 233–234. See "New Uniforms for Georgia Soldiers," *Atlanta Constitution*, March 27, 1903.

50. Obear to Adjutant General, January 15, 1905, 238.

51. Emancipation Address," *Savannah Tribune*, January 9, 1904; *Savannah Tribune*, January 23, 1904. On black worthiness for citizenship and freedom's connection to martial sacrifice, resistance, and gender, see Emberton, *Beyond Redemption*, chapter 4; Francois Furstenberg, "Beyond Freedom and Slavery: Autonomy, Virtue, and Resistance in Early American Political Discourse," *Journal of American History* 89, no. 4 (March 2003): 1295–1330; and David Waldstreicher, *In the Midst of Perpetual Fetes: The Making of American Nationalism, 1776–1820* (Chapel Hill: University of North Carolina Press, 1997), chapter 6.

52. "Emancipation Day," *Savannah Tribune*, December 31, 1904.

53. "Our Celebration Day," *Savannah Tribune*, January 7, 1905.

54. *Savannah Tribune*, January 7, 1905; "Inspection Dates Given for All Georgia Troops," *Atlanta Constitution*, December 25, 1904; "'Why Not Murphy Candler,' Asks the Savannah Press," *Atlanta Constitution*, January 5, 1905.

55. *Savannah Tribune*, January 7, 1905; "Good for the Officer," *Savannah Tribune*, February 11, 1905; "Better Militia Service Recommended By Obear," *Atlanta Constitution*, January 19, 1905.

56. *Savannah Tribune*, February 18, 1905; Richard Maxwell Brown, *Strain of Violence: Historical Studies of American Violence and Vigilantism* (New York: Oxford University Press, 1975), 189–190, 205–212; Allen D. Grimshaw, *Racial Violence in the United States* (Chicago: Aldine, 1969), 402–407; Robert J. Cottrol, *The Afro-Yankees: Providence's Black Community in the Antebellum Era* (Westport: Greenwood Press, 1982), 8, 43, 63–64;

Julie Winch, *Philadelphia's Black Elite: Activism, Accommodation, and the Struggle for Autonomy, 1787–1848* (Philadelphia: Temple University Press, 1988), 62–68, 137–138.

57. *Savannah Tribune*, February 18, 1905.

58. Ibid.

59. "Military at Lincoln Park," *Savannah Tribune*, August 5, 1905; "Maj. Royal's Funeral," *Savannah Tribune*, April 8, 1905; "Annual May Parade," *Savannah Tribune*, May 13, 1905; *Savannah Tribune*, July 22, 1905.

60. "Georgia Troops Must Stay Home," February 1, 1905.

61. Ibid.

62. Ibid.; "Thinks Terrell Acted Correctly," *Atlanta Constitution*, January 31, 1905.

63. Cook, *The Governors of Georgia*, 189–191. For radical racism, see Joel Williamson, *The Crucible of Race: Black-White Relations in the American South Since Emancipation* (New York: Oxford University Press, 1984), 111, 115–116, 118, 178; *Savannah Tribune*, July 1, 1905. For generational thinking of white men, see Gilmore, *Gender and Jim Crow*. For the "culture of segregation," Hale, *Making Whiteness*.

64. *Savannah Tribune*, March 11, 1905; "Annual Military Parade," *Savannah Tribune*, March 13, 1905; *Savannah Tribune*, May 20, 1905; *Savannah Tribune*, July 22, 1905; "Military at Lincoln Park," *Savannah Tribune*, August 5, 1905; *Savannah Tribune*, August 12, 1905; *Savannah Tribune*, August 26, 1905.

65. *Savannah Tribune*, August 26, 1905.

66. "Gossip Caught in Capitol Corridors," *Atlanta Constitution*, August 20, 1905.

67. "Negro Troops Out of Service," *Atlanta Constitution*, September 16, 1905; Hale, *Making Whiteness*, 8–9, 20–22, 78, 124, 167. For erasing people of color, disbandment, the lack of recognition, and defining who is a citizen in the United States, see Leonard, *Men of Color to Arms!* 146, 207, 222, 232–233, 238–239, 245.

68. "Gossip Caught in Capitol Corridors"; *Savannah Tribune*, September 16, 1905.

Conclusion

1. See Holt, *The Problem of Freedom*, 3–9; Jeffrey R. Kerr-Ritchie, *Freedom Seekers: Essays on Comparative Emancipation* (Baton Rouge: Louisiana State University Press, 2013), 3.

BIBLIOGRAPHY

Primary Sources

Acts and Resolutions of the General Assembly of the State of Georgia, 1884–1885. Georgia Legislative Documents. Georgia Department of Archives and History, Morrow, Georgia.

Acts and Resolutions of the General Assembly of the State of Georgia, 1884–85, Volume I. Georgia Legislative Documents. Georgia Department of Archives and History, Morrow, Georgia.

Acts and Resolutions of the General Assembly of the State of Georgia, 1886–87, Volume II. Georgia Legislative Documents. Georgia Department of Archives and History, Morrow, Georgia.

Acts and Resolutions of the General Assembly of the State of Georgia, 1900, Part 1, Public Laws, Title V. Miscellaneous, 1900, Vol. 1. Georgia Department of Archives and History, Morrow, Georgia.

Adjutant General Miscellaneous Records: National Guard. Georgia Department of Archives and History, Morrow, Georgia.

Adjutant General Letter Books, October 8, 1884–September 24, 1886. Georgia Department of Archives and History, Morrow, Georgia.

Adjutant General Letter Books, January 1886–October 13, 1885. Georgia Department of Archives and History, Morrow, Georgia.

Adjutant General Letter Books, September 24, 1886–August 23, 1887. Georgia Department of Archives and History, Morrow, Georgia.

Adjutant General Letter Books, July 5, 1890–April 22, 1891. Georgia Department of Archives and History, Morrow, Georgia.

Adjutant General Letter Books, Department of Defense, Box 57, Volume 20, 9/16/1897–4/14/1898. Georgia Department of Archives and History, Morrow, Georgia.

Adjutant General Letter Books, 1900, Unit Number 7. Georgia Department of Archives and History, Morrow, Georgia.

Adjutant General Letter Books, 1902–1906, Unit 62. Georgia Department of Archives and History, Morrow, Georgia.

An Act: Relating to the State of Georgia, 1870. 16 STAT 363 Chapter 299, 41st Congress, 2nd Session.

Atlanta Constitution, 1870, 1880, 1885–1887, 1889–1906.

Atlanta Daily Constitution, 1875, 1878–1879.

Atlanta Independent, 1904–1928.
Augusta Chronicle and Sentinel, 1875, 1880, 1885.
Capital City Guards Petition, Muster Roll, Election of Officers 1878. Georgia National Guard—Militia, Adjutant General Miscellaneous Reports. Georgia Department of Archives and History, Morrow, Georgia.
Carter, E. R. *The Black Side: A Partial History of the Business, Religious and Educational Side of the Negro in Atlanta, Georgia*. Atlanta: The Black Heritage Library Collection, Books for Libraries Press, Freeport, 1894, 1971.
Chatham Artillery Records, Ms 966, Chatham Artillery Papers. Georgia Historical Society, Savannah, Georgia.
Civil Rights Act of 1875. United States Statutes at Large, XVIII.
Conley, Beng. Executive Department. Georgia Department of Archives and History, Morrow, Georgia.
Davidson, Victor. *History of Wilkinson County*. Spartanburg: Reprint Company Publishers, 1978.
Defense-Adjutant General Letter Books, April 23–August 5, 1891, Volume 8. Georgia Department of Archives and History, Morrow, Georgia.
Defense-Adjutant General Letter Books, 1902–1906, Volume 1. Georgia Department of Archives and History, Morrow, Georgia.
Department of Defense, Adjutant General Letter Book, Volume 20, September 16, 1897–April 15, 1898. Georgia Department of Archives and History, Morrow, Georgia.
Folder: Report of Outrages. No. 92, September 29, 1868, Calhoun County, Executive Correspondence. Georgia Department of Archives and History, Morrow, Georgia.
Ga Natl Guard Militia Petition for Election of Officers Georgia Infantry (Col.). Georgia Department of Archives and History, Morrow, Georgia.
"General Order 39," March 21, 1873. United States War Department, Adjutant General's Office. Record Group 22, Series 13. Georgia Department of Archives and History, Morrow, Georgia.
Georgia Archives, Public Reference Service, File II, Tunis Campbell: Black Reconstructionist. Georgia Department of Archives and History, Morrow, Georgia.
Georgia, Executive Department Minutes, 1874–1877, microfilm. Georgia Department of Archives and History, Morrow, Georgia.
Georgia Legislature, 1878–1879, Title X, Military Revised Code of 1873, Governor James M. Smith, Executive Correspondence. Georgia Department of Archives and History, Morrow, Georgia.
Georgia National Guard/Defense Adjutant General. Georgia Department of Archives and History, Morrow, Georgia.
Governor Executive Department, Governor's Subject Files, 1877–1882. Georgia Department of Archives and History, Morrow, Georgia.
Governor James M. Smith, Executive Department Correspondence. Georgia Department of Archives and History, Morrow, Georgia.
Governor Executive Department, Governor's Subject Files, 1890–1894. Gov. William Jonathan Northen, January–December 1891. Georgia Department of Archives and History, Morrow, Georgia.

Grady, Henry W. *The New South Writings and Speeches of Henry Grady*. Savannah: Beehive Press, 1971.
Hart, Bertha Sheppard. *Official History of Laurens County Georgia 1807–1941*. Atlanta: Cherokee Publishing Company, 1978.
"Henry Allan Rucker," Long-Rucker-Aiken Family Papers, Folder: Henry A. Rucker Personal Correspondence (1904–1908), biographies (n.d.), newspaper clippings, 1970, 1979. Atlanta History Center, Atlanta, Georgia.
Herbert, Sydney. "Roster of Colored Companies." In *Roster of Georgia Volunteer Militia Organizations*. Atlanta: James P. Harrison and Company State Printers and Publishers, 1878. Georgia Department of Archives and History, Morrow, Georgia.
Insurrection, State of Georgia, Johnson County Grand Jury. Georgia Department of Archives and History, Morrow, Georgia.
"Jackson McHenry." Freedman's Bank Image, series: M816, Roll 6, p. 29 Account 179. Heritage Quest Online. http://persi.heritagequestonline.com/hqoweb/library/do/freedmans/results.image?urn=urn.8/18/2009.
Jervey, Theodore D. *The Slave Trade: Slavery and Color*. Columbia: State Company, 1925.
Jordan, Mary Alice. *Cotton to Kaolin: A History of Washington County, Georgia, 1784–1989*. Sandersville and Roswell: Washington County Historical Society, Inc., and W. H. Wolfe Associates Historical Publications Division, 1989.
Lydecker, Charles E. "An Unconstitutional Militia." *North American Review* 134 (June 1882): 631. American Periodicals Online. University of North Carolina at Charlotte, Charlotte, North Carolina.
Macon Telegraph, 1872, 1879, 1895.
Maddox, Joseph T. *Wilkinson County, Georgia Historical Collections, Revised and Reported, 1980*. LaGrange: Family Tree Martha Smith Anderson, 1999.
Minutes, Lincoln Association, Georgia National Guard, 22-1-10. Georgia Department of Archives and History, Morrow, Georgia.
Mitchell, Ella. *History of Washington County*. Atlanta: Cherokee Publishing Company, 1924.
National Guard Militia Petitions to Form Militia Companies. Georgia Department of Archives and History, Morrow, Georgia.
Ordway, Albert. "A National Militia." *North American Review* 134 (April 1882): 395. American Periodicals Online. University of North Carolina at Charlotte, Charlotte, North Carolina.
"Report of the Commissioners Johnson County Insurrection," Commission and Board Reports. Georgia Department of Archives and History, Morrow, Georgia.
"Report of Outrages, Gov. Rufus Bullock Correspondence." Rufus Bullock Subject Files. Executive Department Correspondence. Georgia Department of Archives and History, Morrow, Georgia.
Sandersville Herald and Georgian, 1875.
Satterlee, C. B. First Lieutenant. "Report of Inspection of the Georgia Volunteers and Georgia Volunteers, Colored, September 25th, 1891, to April 5th, 1892." Atlanta: Geo. W. Harrison, State Printer and Franklin Publishing House, 1892. Rare Book Collection, Wilson Library, University of North Carolina, Chapel Hill, North Carolina.

Savannah Cadets Minute Book and Scrapbook, Box Samuel-Savannah Cadets Miscellaneous Papers. Georgia Historical Society, Savannah, Georgia.
Savannah Colored Tribune, 1876.
Savannah Morning News, 1872–1875, 1877, 1879, 1880, 1896.
Savannah Tribune, 1876–1905.
Tenth Amendment, United States Constitution.
The Code of the State of Georgia: Revised and Corrected, 4th ed. 1882. Georgia Department of Archives and History, Morrow, Georgia.
13 U.S. Col'd H. Art'y. Union, Pvt, M589 roll 59 African American Civil War Memorial, Civil War Soldiers and Sailors System NPS website, www.civilwar.nps.gov/cwss/Personz_Detail.cfm 8/18/2009.
"Title X, Military." *Acts and Resolutions of the General Assembly of the State of Georgia, 1878–1879*. Atlanta: James P. Harrison, Public Printer, 1880.
"Title XII, Public Defense." *The Code of the State of Georgia*. R. H. Clark, T. R. R. Cobb, and David Irwin; 2nd ed. by David Irwin, Geo. N. Lester, and W. B. Hill; 4th ed. by Geo. N. Lester, C. Rowell, and W. B. Hill, 1882.
Virginia Military Institute Papers, 1863–1870, Section 2. Virginia Historical Society Library and Manuscripts Collections, Richmond, Virginia.
"Unbound Miscellaneous Papers." Records of the Assistant Commissioner for the State of Georgia Bureau of Refugees, Freedmen and Abandoned Lands, 1865–1869, National Archives Publication M798, Roll 36, http://www.freedmensbureau.com/georgia/request.htm.
Wetmore, W. Berum. Corresponding Secretary, National Guard Association. "The National Guard Bill in Congress." *United Service: A Quarterly of Military and Naval Affairs*: 337 American Periodicals Series III Online. University of North Carolina at Charlotte, Charlotte, North Carolina.
Work Projects Administration. *Washington City Council, The Story of Washington-Wilkes: Compiled and Written by Workers of the Writers' Program of the Work Projects Administration in the State of Georgia*. Athens: University of Georgia Press, 1941.

Secondary Sources

Acker, Laura. "'AGITATE in a Dignified Way for Your Rights': Sol C. Johnson and the *Savannah Tribune*." Paper presented at the Fourth Annual New Perspectives on African American History and Culture conference at the University of North Carolina, Chapel Hill, February 26–27, 2010.
Alexander, Shawn L. *An Army of Lions: The Civil Rights Struggle Before the NAACP*. Philadelphia: University of Pennsylvania Press, 2012.
Allen, James S. *Reconstruction: The Battle for Democracy*. New York: International Publishers, 1937, reprint 1963.
Allison, William T., Jeffrey Grey, and Janet G. Valentine. *American Military History: A Survey from Colonial Times to the Present*. 2nd ed. Boston: Pearson, 2013.
Andrews, George Reid. *Afro-Latin America: 1800–2000*. New York: Oxford University Press, 2004.
Baker, Bruce E. *This Mob Will Surely Take My Life: Lynching in the Carolinas, 1871–1947*. London: Continuum, 2008.

Baldwin, Nell H., and Albert M. Hillhouse. *An Intelligent Student's Guide to Burke County (Ga.) History*. Waynesboro: Nell H. Baldwin and Albert M. Hillhouse, 1956.

Bartley, Numan V. *The Creation of Modern Georgia*. 2nd ed. Athens: University of Georgia Press, 1990.

Beatty, Bess. *A Revolution Gone Backward: The Black Response to National Politics, 1876–1896*. Westport: Greenwood Press, 1987.

Becker, William H. "The Black Church: Manhood and Mission." In *A Question of Manhood: A Reader in U.S. Black Men's History and Masculinity*. Vol. 1, *Manhood Rights: The Construction of Black Male History and Manhood, 1750–1870*, ed. Darlene Clark Hine and Earnestine Jenkins, 322–339. Bloomington: Indiana University Press, 1999.

Beisner, Robert L. *From the Old Diplomacy to the New, 1865–1900*. Wheeling, Ill.: Harlan Davidson, 1986.

Berlin, Ira. "From Creole to African: Atlantic Creoles and the Origins of African-American Society in Mainland North America." In *How Did American Slavery Begin? Readings Selected and Introduced*, ed. Edward Countryman, 17–64. Boston: Bedford St. Martin, 1999.

Berlin, Ira, Barbara J. Fields, Steven F. Miller, Joseph P. Reidy, and Leslie S. Rowland. *Slaves No More: Three Essays on Emancipation and the Civil War*. Cambridge: Cambridge University Press, 1992.

Blair, William A. *Cities of the Dead: Contesting the Memory of the Civil War in the South, 1865–1914*. Chapel Hill: University of North Carolina Press, 2004.

Boney, F. N. "Joseph E. Brown, 1821–1894." Government and Politics: Governors of Georgia. *New Georgia Encyclopedia* 2013. www.georgiaencyclopedia.org/articles/government-politics/joseph-e-brown-1821-1894, accessed April 13, 2014.

Brown, Christopher Leslie, and Philip D. Morgan. *Slaves: From Classical Times to the Modern Age*. New Haven: Yale University Press, 2006.

Brown, Elsa Barkley. "To Catch the Vision of Freedom: Reconstructing Southern Black Women's Political History, 1865–1880." In *African American Women and the Vote, 1837–1965*, ed. Ann D. Gordon with Bettye Collier Thomas, John H. Bracey, Arlene Voski Avakian, and Joyce Avrech Berkman, 66–99. Amherst: University of Massachusetts Press, 1997.

——. "Negotiating and Transforming the Public Sphere: African American Political Life in the Transition from Slavery to Freedom." *The Black Public Sphere: A Public Culture Book*. The Black Public Sphere Collective, 111–151. Chicago: University of Chicago Press, 1995.

Brown, Richard Maxwell. *Strain of Violence: Historical Studies of American Violence and Vigilantism*. New York: Oxford University Press, 1975.

Brundage, W. Fitzhugh. *Lynching in the New South: Georgia and Virginia, 1880–1930*. Urbana: University of Illinois Press, 1993.

Bryan, Ferald J. *Henry Grady or Tom Watson? The Rhetorical Struggle for the New South, 1880–1890*. Macon: Mercer University Press, 1994.

Bryant, Jonathan M. *How Curious a Land: Conflict and Change in Green County, Georgia, 1850–1885*. Chapel Hill: University of North Carolina Press, 1996.

Buckley, Roger Norman. *Slaves in Red Coats: The British West India Regiments, 1795–1815*. New Haven: Yale University Press, 1979.

Budiansky, Stephen. *The Bloody Shirt: Terror After the Civil War*. New York: Plume, 2009.
Burton, Orville Vernon. *The Age of Lincoln*. New York: Hill and Wang, 2007.
Cantor, Louis. "The Creation of the Modern National Guard: Background, Passage, and Legislative Aftermath of the Dick Militia Act of 1903." Master's thesis, Duke University, 1961.
Cardon, Nathan. "The South's 'New Negroes' and African American Visions of Progress at the Atlanta and Nashville International Expositions, 1895–1897." *Journal of Southern History* 80, no. 2 (May 2014): 287–326.
Carter, David. "Romper Lobbies and Coloring Lessons: Grassroots Visions and Political Realities in the Battle for Head Start in Mississippi, 1965–1967." In *Making a New South: Race, Leadership and Community after the Civil War*, ed. Paul A. Cimbala and Barton C. Shaw, 191–208. Gainesville: University Press of Florida, 2007.
Cell, John. *The Highest Stage of White Supremacy: The Origins of Segregation in South Africa and the American South*. Cambridge: Cambridge University Press, 1982.
Chambers, Bradford. *Chronicles of Black Protest: Compiled and Edited With Commentary*. New York: New American Library, 1968.
Childs, Matt D. *The 1812 Aponte Rebellion in Cuba and the Struggle against Atlantic Slavery*. Chapel Hill: University of North Carolina Press, 2006.
Clark, Kathleen Ann. *Defining Moments: African American Commemoration and Political Culture in the South, 1863–1913*. Chapel Hill: University of North Carolina Press, 2005.
Cohen, Nancy. *The Reconstruction of American Liberalism, 1865–1914*. Chapel Hill: University of North Carolina Press, 2002.
Collier-Thomas, Bettye. *Jesus, Jobs, and Justice: African American Women and Religion*. New York: Alfred Knopf, 2010.
Copeland, Susan. "Henry O. Flipper (1856–1940)." *The New Georgia Encyclopedia*. www.georgiaencyclopedia.org/nge/Article.jsp?id=h-1331&hl=y, accessed September 20, 2010.
Cook, James F. *The Governors of Georgia, 1754–1995*. Macon: Mercer University Press, 1995.
Cooper, Jerry. *The Rise of the National Guard: The Evolution of the American Militia, 1865–1920*. Lincoln: University of Nebraska Press, 1997.
Cooper, Frederick, Thomas C. Holt, and Rebecca J. Scott. "Introduction." In *Beyond Slavery: Explorations of Race, Labor, and Citizenship in Postemancipation Societies*, ed. Frederick Cooper, Thomas C. Holt, Rebecca J. Scott, 1–32. Chapel Hill: University of North Carolina Press, 2000.
Cottrol, Robert J. *The Afro-Yankees: Providence's Black Community in the Antebellum Era*. Westport: Greenwood Press, 1982.
Coulter, E. Merton. "Tunis G. Campbell, Negro Reconstructionist in Georgia, Part I." *Georgia Historical Quarterly* 51, no.4 (December 1967): 401–24.
———. "Cudjo Fye Insurrection." *Georgia Historical Quarterly* 39, no.2 (September 1954): 213–225.
Cunningham, Roger D. *The Black Citizen-Soldiers of Kansas 1864–1901*. Columbia: University of Missouri Press, 2008.

Currie-McDaniel, Ruth. *Carpetbagger of Conscience: A Biography of John Emory Bryant.* New York: Fordham University Press, 1999.
Dobak, William A., and Thomas D. Phillips. *The Black Regulars, 1866–1898.* Norman: University of Oklahoma Press, 2001.
Dorsey, Allison G. *To Build Our Lives Together: Community Formation in Black Atlanta, 1875–1906.* Athens: University of Georgia Press, 2004.
Drago, Edmund L. *Black Politicians and Reconstruction in Georgia: A Splendid Failure.* Baton Rouge: Louisiana State University Press, 1982.
Du Bois, W. E. B. *Philadelphia Negro: A Social Study.* New York: Schocken, 1967, 1899.
Duncan, Russell. *Entrepreneur for Equality: Governor Rufus Bullock, Commerce, and Race in Post–Civil War Georgia.* Athens: University of Georgia Press, 1994.
———. *Freedom's Shore: Tunis Campbell and the Georgia Freedmen.* Athens: University of Georgia Press, 1986.
Durden, Marion Little. *A History of Saint George Parish, Colony of Georgia, Jefferson County, State of Georgia.* Swainsboro, Ga.: Magnolia Press, 1983.
Edwards, Laura F. *Gendered Strife and Confusion: The Political Culture of Reconstruction.* Urbana: University of Illinois Press, 1997.
Emberton, Carole. *Beyond Redemption: Race, Violence, and the American South after the Civil War.* Chicago: University of Chicago Press, 2013.
Ferrer, Ada. *Insurgent Cuba: Race, Nation, and Revolution, 1868–1898.* Chapel Hill: University of North Carolina Press, 1999.
Feimster, Crystal N. *Southern Horrors: Women and the Politics of Rape and Lynching.* Cambridge, Mass.: Harvard University Press, 2009.
Fitzgerald, Michael W. *Urban Emancipation: Popular Politics in Reconstruction Mobile, 1860–1890.* Baton Rouge: Louisiana State University Press, 2002.
———. *The Union League Movement in the Deep South: Politics and Agricultural Change During Reconstruction.* Baton Rouge: Louisiana State University Press, 1989.
Flynn, Charles L., Jr. *White Land, Black Labor: Caste and Class in Late Nineteenth-Century Georgia.* Baton Rouge: Louisiana State University Press, 1983.
Foner, Eric. *Nothing But Freedom: Emancipation and Its Legacy.* Baton Rouge: Louisiana State University Press, 1983.
———. *A Short History of Reconstruction, 1863–1877.* Philadelphia: Harper and Row Publishers, 1990.
Franklin, John Hope. "The Enforcement of the Civil Rights Act of 1875." *Prologue: The Journal of the National Archives* 6, no. 4 (Winter 1974): 225–35.
———. "Race and the Constitution in the Nineteenth Century." In *African Americans and the Living Constitution*, ed. John Hope Franklin and Genna Rae McNeil, 21–32. Washington, D.C.: Smithsonian Institute, 1995.
Franklin, John Hope, and Alfred Moss. *From Slavery to Freedom: A History of African Americans.* 8th ed. New York: McGraw Hill, 2000.
Friedman, Lawrence. *The White Savage: Racial Fantasies in the Postbellum South.* Englewood Cliffs: Prentice-Hall, 1970.
Furstenberg, Francois. "Beyond Freedom and Slavery: Autonomy, Virtue, and Resistance in Early American Political Discourse." *Journal of American History* 89, no. 4 (March 2003): 1295–1330.

Gaston, Paul M. *The New South Creed: A Study in Southern Myth Making*. Baton Rouge: Louisiana State University Press, 1970.

Gates, Henry Louis. "Behind '40 acres, mule' story." *Charlotte Observer*, January 12, 2013.

Gatewood, Willard. *"Smoked Yankees" and the Struggle for Empire*. Urbana: University of Illinois Press, 1971.

Gilmore, Glenda E. *Gender and Jim Crow: Women and the Politics of White Supremacy in North Carolina, 1896–1920*. Chapel Hill: University of North Carolina Press, 1996.

Ginsberg, Benjamin. *Moses of South Carolina: A Jewish Scalawag during Radical Reconstruction*. Baltimore: Johns Hopkins University Press, 2010.

Glasrud, Bruce A. *Brothers to the Buffalo Soldiers: Perspectives on the African American Militia and Volunteers, 1865–1917*. Columbia: University of Missouri Press, 2011.

Glenn, Evelyn Nakano. *Unequal Freedom: How Race and Gender Shaped American Citizenship and Labor*. Cambridge, Mass.: Harvard University Press, 2002.

Gomez, Michael. *Reversing Sail: A History of the African Diaspora: New Approaches to African History*. Cambridge: Cambridge University Press, 2005.

Grant, Donald L. *The Way It Was in the South: The Black Experience in Georgia*. New York: Birch Lane Press, 1993.

Grimshaw, Allen D. *Racial Violence in the United States*. Chicago: Aldine, 1969.

Hahn, Steven. *A Nation Under Our Feet: Black Political Struggles in the Rural South from Slavery to the Great Migration*. Cambridge, Mass.: Harvard University Press, 2003.

Hale, Grace Elizabeth. *Making Whiteness: The Culture of Segregation in the South, 1890–1940*. New York: Pantheon Books, 1998.

Hall, Neville A. T. "Maritime Maroons: Grand Marronage from the Danish West Indies." In *Origins of the Black Atlantic*, ed. Laurent Dubois and Julius S. Scott, 47–68. New York: Routledge, 2010.

Hannah, Eleanor L. "From the Dance Floor to the Rifle Range: The Evolution of Manliness in the National Guards, 1870–1917." *The Journal of the Gilded Age and Progressive Era* 6, no. 2 (April 2007): 149–177.

———. *Manhood, Citizenship, and the National Guard: Illinois, 1870–1917*. Columbus: Ohio State University Press, 2007.

———. "A Place in the Parade: Citizenship, Manhood, and African American Men in the Illinois National Guard, 1870–1917." In *Brothers to the Buffalo Soldiers: Perspectives on the African American Militia and Volunteers, 1865–1917*, ed. Bruce A. Glasrud, 86–111. Columbia: University of Missouri Press, 2011.

Harding, Vincent. *There Is a River: The Black Struggle for Freedom in America*. New York: Vintage Books, 1981.

Helg, Aline. *Our Rightful Share: The Afro-Cuban Struggle for Equality, 1886–1912*. Chapel Hill: University of North Carolina Press, 1995.

Hicks, Cheryl. "Emancipation Proclamation Program." Presented at Center City Campus Uptown, University of North Carolina at Charlotte, Charlotte, North Carolina, February 23, 2013.

Hill, Jim Dan. *The Minute Man in Peace and War: A History of the National Guard*. Harrisburg: Stack Pole Company, 1964.

Hillhouse, Albert M. *A History of Burke County, Georgia, 1777–1950*. Swainsboro, Ga.: Magnolia Press, 1985.

Hogue, James. *Uncivil War: Five New Orleans Street Battles and the Rise and Fall of Radical Reconstruction*. Baton Rouge: Louisiana State University Press, 2006.

Hohle, Randolph. *Black Citizenship and Authenticity in the Civil Rights Movement*. New York: Routledge, 2013.

Holt, Thomas C. *The Problem of Freedom: Race, Labor, and Politics in Jamaica and Britain*. Baltimore: Johns Hopkins University Press, 1992.

———. "Essence of the Contract: The Articulation of Race, Gender, and Political Economy in British Emancipation Policy." In *Beyond Slavery: Explorations of Race, Labor, and Citizenship in Postemancipation Societies*, ed. Frederick Cooper, Thomas C. Holt, and Rebecca J. Scott, 33–60. Chapel Hill: University of North Carolina Press, 2000.

———. *Children of Fire: A History of African Americans*. New York: Hill and Wang, 2010.

Hornsby-Gutting, Angela. *Black Manhood and Community Building in North Carolina, 1900–1930*. Gainesville: University Press of Florida, 2009.

Hoskins, Charles L. *The Trouble They Seen: Profiles in the Life of Col. John H. Deveaux 1848–1909*. Savannah: Charles Lwanga Hoskins St. Matthew's Church, 1989.

Howard, Philip A. *Changing History: Afro-Cuban Cabildos and Societies of Color in the Nineteenth Century*. Baton Rouge: Louisiana State University Press, 1998.

Jacobson, Matthew Frye. *Barbarian Virtues: The United States Encounters Foreign Peoples at Home and Abroad, 1876–1917*. New York: Hill and Wang, 2000.

"John H. Deveaux." *The New Georgia Encyclopedia*. www.georgiaencyclopedia.org/file/5559.

Johnson, Charles, Jr. *African American Soldiers in the National Guard: Recruitment and Deployment During Peacetime and War*. Westport: Greenwood Press, 1992.

Jordan, Winthrop D. "Mulattoes and Race Relations in Britain's New World Colonies." In *America Compared: American History in International Perspective*. Vol. 1, *To 1877*. 2nd ed. ed. Carl J. Guarneri, 91–103. Boston: Houghton Mifflin, 2005.

Kachun, Mitch. *Festivals of Freedom: Memory and Meaning in African American Emancipation Celebrations, 1808–1915*. Amherst: University of Massachusetts Press, 2003.

Keith, Leeanna. *The Colfax Massacre: The Untold Story of Black Power, White Terror, and the Death of Reconstruction*. New York: Oxford University Press, 2008.

Kelley, Blair L. M. *Right to Ride: Streetcar Boycotts and African American Citizenship in the Era of Plessy v. Ferguson*. Chapel Hill: University of North Carolina Press, 2010.

Kerr-Ritchie, Jeffrey R. "Rehearsal for War: Black Militias in the Atlantic World," *Slavery and Abolition* 26 (April 2005): 1–34.

———. *Rites of August First: Emancipation Day in the Black Atlantic World*. Baton Rouge: Louisiana State University Press, 2007.

———. *Freedom's Seekers: Essays on Comparative Emancipation*. Baton Rouge: Louisiana State University Press, 2014.

Kraay, Hendrik. "The Politics of Race in Independence-Era Bahia: The Black Militia Officers of Salvador, 1790–1840." In *Afro-Brazilian Culture and Politics: Bahia, 1790s to 1990s*, ed. Hendrik Kraay, 30–56. Armonk: M. E. Sharpe, 1998.

Krebs, Ronald R. *Fighting for Rights: Military Service and the Politics of Citizenship*. Ithaca: Cornell University Press, 2006.

Landers, Jane G. *Atlantic Creoles in the Age of Revolutions*. Cambridge, Mass.: Harvard University Press, 2010.

———. "Gracia Real de Santa Teresa de Mose: A Free Black Town in Spanish Colonial Florida." In *A Question of Manhood: A Reader in U. S. Black Men's History and Masculinity*, vol. 1, *"Manhood Rights": The Construction of Black Male History and Manhood, 1750–1870*, ed. Darlene Clark Hine and Earnestine Jenkins, 90–114. Bloomington: Indiana University Press, 1999.

Lane, Charles. *The Day Freedom Died: The Colfax Massacre, The Supreme Court, and the Betrayal of Reconstruction*. New York: Henry Holt, 2008.

Lee, Angela. *Images of America Burke County Georgia*. Dover, N.H.: Arcadia, 1996).

Leonard, Elizabeth D. *Men of Color to Arms!: Black Soldiers, Indian Wars, and the Quest for Equality*. New York: W. W. Norton, 2010.

Linn, Brian McAllister. *The Philippine War, 1899–1902*. Lawrence: University of Kansas Press, 2000.

Litwack, Leon. *Trouble in Mind: Black Southerners in the Age of Jim Crow*. New York: Vintage Books, 1998.

Lumpkins, Charles L. *American Pogrom: The East St. Louis Race Riot and Black Politics*. Athens: Ohio University Press, 2008.

Mahon, John K. *History of the Militia and the National Guard*. New York: Macmillan Publishing Company, 1983.

McGuire, Samuel B. "The Making of a Black Militia Company: New Bern Troops in the Kirk-Holden War, 1870." *North Carolina Review* 91, no. 3 (July 2014): 288–322.

McPherson, James M. *What They Fought For, 1861–1865*. Baton Rouge: Louisiana State University Press, 1994.

Meyers, Christopher C., and Williams, David. *Georgia: A Brief History*. Macon, Ga.: Mercer University Press, 2012.

Miller, Edward A., Jr. *Gullah Statesman: Robert Smalls; From Slavery to Congress, 1839–1915*. Columbia: University of South Carolina Press, 1995.

Mitchell, Michele. *Righteous Propagation: African Americans and the Politics of Racial Destiny after Reconstruction*. Chapel Hill: University of North Carolina Press, 2004.

Mixon, Gregory. "The Georgia Militia and the Atlanta Riot of 1906." Paper presented at the 1996 annual meeting of the Southern Historical Association, Little Rock, October 30– November 2, 1996.

———. "Constructing Atlanta's Auditorium-Armory, 1904–1909: The Public and Private and Race." Unpublished manuscript.

———. "The Political Career of Henry A. Rucker: A Survivor in a New South City." *Atlanta History: A Journal of Georgia and the South* 45 (Summer 2001): 4–26.

———. "The Making of a Political Boss: Henry A. Rucker, 1897–1904." *Georgia Historical Quarterly* 89 (Winter 2005): 485–504.

———. *The Atlanta Riot: Race, Class, and Violence in a New South City*. Gainesville: University Press of Florida, 2005.

———. "Creating the Georgia Militia: Blacks and the Road to State Militia Companies, 1865–1880." Paper presented at the annual meeting of the Association for the Study of African American Life and History, Atlanta Hilton Hotel, Atlanta, Georgia, September 27–October 1, 2006.

———. "Merecemos un tratamiento major": Auge y caida de las milicias negras en el Hemisfero Occidental durante el Siglo XIX" ["We deserve better treatment": The Rise and Fall of the Militia in the Nineteenth-Century Western Hemisphere], *Boletin Americanista* 64, no. 1 (2014):55–76.

Myers, Amrita Chakrabarti. *Forging Freedom: Black Women and the Pursuit of Liberty in Antebellum Charleston*. Chapel Hill: University of North Carolina Press, 2011.

Nagel, Amanda. "'We Are American Soldiers': Masculinity and Race in the Philippine-American War." Paper presented at the 99th Association for the Study of African American Life and History Meeting, Memphis, Tennessee, September 24–27, 2014.

Nalty, Bernard C. *Strength for the Fight: A History of Black Americans in the Military*. New York: Free Press, 1986.

Newland, Samuel J. "The National Guard: Whose Guard Anyway?" *Parameters: US Army War College* 18, no. 2 (June 1988): 44.

O'Donovan, Susan. *Becoming Free in the Cotton South*. Cambridge, Mass.: Harvard University Press, 2007.

Painter, Nell Irvin. *The History of White People*. New York: W. W. Norton, 2010.

Perdue, Robert E. *The Negro in Savannah, 1865–1900*. New York: Exposition Press, 1973.

Quarles, Benjamin. *The Negro in the American Revolution*. New York: W. W. Norton, 1961.

Reid-Vazquez, Michele. *The Year of the Lash: Free People of Color in Cuba and the Nineteenth-Century Atlantic World*. Athens: University of Georgia Press, 2011.

Reidy, Joseph P. *From Slavery to Agrarian Capitalism in the Cotton Plantation South: Central Georgia, 1800–1880*. Chapel Hill: University of North Carolina Press, 1992.

———. "The African American Struggle for Citizenship Rights in the Northern United States During the Civil War." In *Civil War Citizens: Race, Ethnicity, and Identity in America's Bloodiest Conflicts*, ed. Susannah J. Ural, 213–237. New York: New York University Press, 2010.

Richardson, Riché. *Black Masculinity and the U.S. South: From Uncle Tom to Gangsta*. Athens: University of Georgia Press, 2007.

Russell, James Michael. *Atlanta, 1847–1890: City Building in the Old South and New*. Baton Rouge: Louisiana State University Press, 1988.

Scott, Rebecca J. Scott. "The Atlantic World and the Road to Plessy." *Journal of American History* 94, no. 3 (December 2007): 726–733.

———. *Degrees of Freedom: Louisiana and Cuba After Slavery*. Cambridge, Mass.: Belknap, 2005.

———. "Fault Lines, Color Lines, and Party Lines: Race, Labor, and Collective Action in Louisiana and Cuba, 1862–1912." In *Beyond Slavery: Explorations of Race, Labor, and Citizenship in Postemancipation Societies*, ed. Frederick Cooper, Thomas C. Holt, and Rebecca J. Scott, 61–106. Chapel Hill: University of North Carolina Press, 2000.

———. "Defining the Boundaries of Freedom in the World of Cane: Cuba, Brazil, and Louisiana after Emancipation." *American Historical Review* 99, no. 1 (February 1994): 70–102.

Senchal de la Roche, Roberta. "The Sociogenesis of Lynching." In *Under Sentence of Death: Lynching in the South*, ed. W. Fitzhugh Brundage, 48–76. Chapel Hill: University of North Carolina Press, 1997.

Severance, Ben H. *Tennessee's Radical Army: The State Guard and Its Role in Reconstruction, 1867–1869*. Knoxville: University of Tennessee Press, 2005.

Singletary, Otis. *Negro Militia and Reconstruction*. Austin: University of Texas Press, 1957.

———. "The African American Military During Radical Reconstruction." In *Brothers of the Buffalo Soldiers: Perspectives on the African American Militia and Volunteers, 1865–1917*, ed. Bruce A. Glasrud, 19–33. Columbia: University of Missouri Press, 2011.

Sinha, Mrinalini. *Colonial Masculinity: The "Manly Englishman" and the "Effeminate Bengali" in the Late Nineteenth Century*. Manchester: Manchester University Press, 1995.

Smith, Frances. "Black Militia in Savannah, Georgia 1872–1905." Master's thesis, Georgia Southern College, 1981.

Smith, John David. *Black Judas: William Hannibal Thomas and the American Negro*. Chicago: Ivan R. Dee, 2000.

———. *Black Voices From Reconstruction, 1865–1977*. Gainesville: University Press of Florida, 1997.

Snay, Mitchell. *Fenians, Freedmen, and Southern Whites: Race and Nationality in the Era of Reconstruction*. Baton Rouge: Louisiana State University Press, 2007.

Todd, Nancy L. *New York's Historic Armories: An Illustrated History*. Albany: State University of New York Press, 2006.

Turner, Jeffrey Alan. "Agitation and Accommodation in a Southern Black Newspaper: *The Savannah Tribune*, 1886–1915." Masters thesis, University of Georgia, 1993.

Turpie, David C. "A Voluntary War: The Spanish-American War, White Southern Manhood, and the Struggle to Recruit Volunteers in the South," *Journal of Southern History* 80, no. 4 (November 2014): 859–92.

Uviller, H. Richard, and William G. Merkel. *The Militia and the Right to Arms, or How The Second Amendment Fell Silent*. Durham: Duke University Press, 2002.

Vinson, Ben, III. *Bearing Arms for His Majesty: The Free-Colored Militia in Colonial Mexico*. Stanford: Stanford University Press, 2001.

Wade, Richard. "Foreword." In *Race Relations in the Urban South, 1865–1890*, ed. Howard Rabinowitz, ix–xvi. New York: Oxford University Press, 1978.

Waldrep, Christopher. *Roots of Disorder: Race and Criminal Justice in the American South, 1817–80*. Urbana: University of Illinois Press, 1998.

Waldstreicher, David. *In the Midst of Perpetual Fetes: The Making of American Nationalism, 1776–1820*. Chapel Hill: University of North Carolina Press, 1997.

Walton, Hanes, Jr. *Black Republicans: The Politics of the Black and Tans*. Metuchen, N.J.: Scarecrow Press, 1975.

Watson, Samuel J. *Peacekeepers and Conquerors: The Army Officer Corps on the American Frontier, 1821–1846*. Lawrence: University of Kansas Press, 2013.

Whisker, James B. *The Rise and Decline of the American Militia System*. London: Susquehanna University Press, 1999.

White, Shane. "'It Was a Proud Day': African Americans, Festivals, and Parades in the North, 1741–1834." In *The New African American Urban History*, ed. Kenneth W. Goings and Raymond A. Mohl, 17–65. Thousand Oaks, Calif.: Sage, 1996.

Williamson, Joel. *The Crucible of Race: Black-White Relations in the American South Since Emancipation*. New York: Oxford University Press, 1984.

Winch, Julie. *Philadelphia's Black Elite: Activism, Accommodation, and the Struggle for Autonomy, 1787–1848*. Philadelphia: Temple University Press, 1988.

Young, Harvey. *Embodying Black Experience: Stillness, Critical Memory, and the Black Body*. Ann Arbor: University of Michigan Press, 2010.

Zuczek, Richard. *State of Rebellion: Reconstruction in South Carolina*. Columbia: University of South Carolina Press, 1996.

INDEX

Ackerman, Amos T., 120
Act X, 28
Adams, S. H., 253
Adams, W. C., 64
African American Soldiers in the National Guard: Recruitment and Deployment During Peacetime and War (Johnson, C.), ix
African-descendant people: definition of, x; militias, xi–xii; mixed feelings about, 29; stories concerning, 340
African Methodist Episcopal Church (AME), 56–57
Afro-Cubans, 15–19, 146
Age of Revolution, 11, 16, 28, 31
Alger, Russell, 284
AME. *See* African Methodist Episcopal Church
American Revolution: impacts of, 30; legacies dating to, 83; participation in, 29, 227, 279
Americus Light Infantry, 205
Ammunition, 26, 83, 110–11
Anderson, Clifford W.: life and career of, 95, 178–79, 181; reorganization and, 136–37
Anderson, Robert H., 96
Andrews, George Reid: on Western Hemisphere and militia, 13; work of, x
Antebellum period, 8–9, 24–25, 30, 32–34, 36–38, 85
Antiblack violence: in Atlanta race riot, 3; impacts of, 1, 9, 27, 45–48, 173, 194, 230, 253, 261–62, 328
Aponte, José Antonio, 16
Appleton, Mr., 253
Appropriations. *See* Funding and fund-raising
Armory, 220, 301, 302, 305, 308, 310
Arms, right to bear, 20, 28, 30–33, 37, 81, 165, 172–73
Army, United States: history of, 226, 234;

Ninth Cavalry, 282–83, 297, 333; surgeon-general's report, 209; trainers, 27
Articles of Confederation, 193
Atkinson, William Y., 241, 246, 261, 264, 277–83, 288
Atlanta Cadets, 91
Atlanta Constitution: caricatures in, 4, 5, 227; on disbandment, 257–58, 293, 309–10; on funding, 268–69; headlines in, 222, 305; on inspections, 234, 238, 240, 244; on reorganization, 289–90, 300–301; reports in, 110, 200, 203–5, 207, 228, 237, 239, 247, 263, 280, 327, 330, 334; on Spanish-American War, 274, 282, 284, 288
Atlanta Cotton States Exposition, 242–43; Negro Building for, 243, 246–47
Atlanta Independent, 1–3, 2
Atlanta Light Infantry, 98
Atlanta race riot (1906), ix, 3, 127, 329
Attucks, Crispus, 155, 212, 326
Attucks Infantry, 258
Augusta Chronicle and Sentinel, 59
Augusta Light Infantry, 199, 258
Avery, Isaac W., 178–79, 181–82

Baldwin, G. P., 234
Band of brothers, 52, 75
Barnard, John, 239, 280
Bartley, Numan V., 41
Bartow Light Infantry, 106, 124
Bay Springs Volunteers, 124
Beck, William, 56–57
Belcher, E. R., 168
Belcher, L. C., 168
Bell, W. H., 163
Benevolent associations, 54, 83–86
Bentley, M. H., 215, 243

Bibb County Blues, 273, 278–79
Biracial police force, 111
Birmingham mining strike, 245
Black freedom: celebration of, 32, 34, 180, 338; commitment to, 13, 18, 21, 51; essence of, 57; land and, 45, 69; tenets of, 64; white freedom compared to, 53
Black independent militia: band of brothers inside, 52, 75; Civil War rehearsal and, 32–34; historiography of, 6; role of, 8, 22, 24–25, 37–39, 42, 61–62, 126, 170, 338
Black liberty, 172–76
Black masculinity, 54–57, 59
Black militias: African-descendant militias, xi–xii; better treatment for, 333–36; celebrations, 157–58; conflicting images, 4, 4–6, 5; days of freedom with, 154–57; "debt of gratitude" to, 14–15; disbandment of, 19, 21–22, 147; enthusiasm of, 317–18; exclusion of, 201–2, 217, 220, 222; fading, 216–17; funding for, 263–64, 323–24; in Georgia, 24–26, 37–39, 42–43; Hannah on, 187; historiography of, 10–11; hostility toward, 307–8; needs of, 327–28; neglect of, 142, 233, 242, 244–45, 247–48, 255, 259, 267–69, 331; nineteenth-century parallels, 19–20; power, class, race, and leadership in, 142–47; reasons for joining, 8–11, 84; Reconstruction and, 5–6; reimaging, 20–22; rejection of, 287–88; role of, xi–xii, 62–63, 338–39; *Savannah Tribune* on, 155–57, 219, 222, 293–94, 333–35; as team players, 218, 249
Blackness: ties to, 101; whiteness compared to, 92, 104
Black officers, 13, 21, 99, 235; disparities between white and, 216, 286, 303–4, 322–23; *Savannah Tribune* on, 286
Black political power: Campbell and, 48–51, 63–64, 170; impacts of, 67, 108; local memories and, 62–64; beyond McIntosh County, 51–52
Black power: questioning of, 21; "Sambo dialect" description of, 67; white power compared to, 70, 182; white response to, 64–65, 82
Black rights: defense and definition of, 125, 214; demand for, 17; erosion and attack on, 16, 18–20; exercise of, 12–13; states' rights and, 149
Blacks: characteristics of, 1–2; contradictions in life of, 246–48; control over labor of, 6, 29, 40–41, 48–50, 53, 74, 76–77, 101, 126, 157; as criminals and convicts, 242–43, 247; deaths of, 340; Georgia *Code* on status of, 119; making traditions and controlling institutions, 176–77; middle-class, 104, 119, 208, 231–32; out-migration of, 76, 262; Reconstruction and self-defense of, 44–48; stereotypes of, 3, 103, 275; women, 158–60, 230–31; yellow fever immunity of, 275, 284–85
Black state-sponsored militia: Colquitt and, 92, 95–96, 98–99; formation of, 82, 92–101; historiography of, 6; role of, 9, 23–26, 38–39, 42–43, 338–39; roster of, 93; Smith, J., and, 92, 95, 98
The Black Phalanx (Wilson, J.), 213
"The Black Regiment" (Hart, R.), 207–8
Blair, William A., 158–59, 181
Blake, A. A., 266
Blocker, Isaiah H., 237, 244, 257, 266, 277–78, 280
Boletín Americanista, xi
Bonner, C. L., 313–14
Boston Congregationalist, 172
Bourbon Reforms, 12
Bourbon Triumvirate, 178, 289
Bowers, P. L., 304
Bradley, Aaron, 100, 171, 208
Bradley, Mat Jackson, 39
Brain drain, 290
Brantley, Ephriam, 68, 115
Brazilian militia, 14–15
Britain: colonization and, 28–29; emancipation and, 31–32
Brookins, Haywood, 110
Brooks, J. F., 242, 257, 274
Brown, A., 266
Brown, Christopher Leslie, x
Brown, Elsa Barkley: on collective responsibility, 8; on disfranchisement, 230–31; on freedom, 36; work of, 9
Brown, J. A., 168
Brown, Oscar J.: Georgia Artillery encampments and, 273; leave of absence, 291;

on pro rata funding, 277–78; weapons exchanges and, 274
Brown v. Board decision, 7
Bryant, John Emory, 55–56, 59
Buckeye Company, 69
Buckeye Guards, 124
Bullock, Rufus, 89, 140, 170, 202
Burke Cavalry Troop, 205
Burke Dragoons, 107
Burke Hussars, 107
Burke Light Infantry, 205
Butler, Frances, 176
Butler, H. R., 263, 266, 267
Butler, Marion, 313
Butler, Matthew C., 151, 165–66
Butler, Thomas, 168
Byrd, Phil G., 291, 303, 310–11

Cabildo, 15–16, 146
Camilla Massacre (1868), 48, 108
Campbell, Tunis: black political power and, 48–51, 63–64, 170; life and career of, 167–72; policies of, 100, 125, 208, 332, 337
Camp Kell, 272
Canada, 30–32, 34
Candler, Allen, 280, 293; on disbandment, 295; reorganization and, 288–92, 298, 300–301, 310–11, 315, 320
Cannon, W. F., 104–5
Capital City Guards, 142–43, 298, 307
Capital Guards, 98–99
Cardon, Nathan, 340
Carolina Light Infantry company, 162
Carswell, R. W., 77–78
Carter, Edward R., 145–46, 228
Cavalry units, 88–89, 95–96, 106–7, 124; white militias, 106–7, 128, *133–34*
Chamberlain, Daniel H., 166
Chatham Light Infantry: activities of, 92, 94–95, 150, 153, 157, 178–80, 221, 252–54, 261, 270, 298–99; anniversary of, 255, 309; disbandment of, 325–26; Obear's inspections of, 318; responsible citizenship and, 161–63; *Savannah Tribune* on, 162
Chew, E. L., 266
Chicago Tribune, 209
Chickamauga encampment, 224–25
Childs, Matt, x, 15

Chiles, John, 68, 71–74, 115–16, 118
Citizenship: characteristics of, 1–3, 172–74; Civil War and, 35, 41, 101, 191, 339; claims to, xii, 298; definition of, 80; in Dominican Republic, 340–41; freedom and, x, 6, 9–10, 14–15, 22, 38–39, 51; military service as path to, 145; national belonging and, xi–xii, 9, 27, 214, 337; patriotism as declaration of, 59, 327, 339; proof of, 57, 191, 223, 339; responsible, 1, 159, 160–66, 208–11, 338; right to, 20, 30–31, 33, 213, 226, 287, 325–26
Citizen soldiers, 20, 24–26, 136, 187, 190, 339
Civil Rights Act (1875): passage of, 40, 69; support for, 52–53, 68, 75–79, 126; tenets of, 77–78, 80, 337–38; testing parameters of, 337; as unconstitutional, 231
Civil rights movement, 7
Civil War: citizenship and, 35, 41, 101, 191, 339; defeat in, xii, 45, 124, 137, 194; impacts of, 83, 86, 104, 107; involvement in, 265–66, 276; legacy of, xii; rehearsal for, 32–35; uniforms, 94; white power and, 102
Claims making, xii, 64–65 Clark, Kathleen Ann, 56
Clark Rifles, 291
Cleveland, Grover, 155, 214
Cobb, Howell, 139
Code of Georgia. See Georgia *Code*
Cohen, Nancy, 171
Collective responsibility, 8, 122
Colonization: Britain and, 28–29; militias and, xi, 11–14, 16–19, 28–30
Colquitt, Alfred H.: black state-sponsored militia and, 92, 95–96, 98–99; life and career of, 60, 78, 142, 178–81; policies of, 316; on true soldierhood, 178, 181
Colquitt Blues, 178, 260, 298
Colquitt Zouaves, 60
Columbus Volunteers, 92
Combahee Strike, 166
Confederate Memorial Day, 155, 175, 252, 255, 282, 339
Confederate Soldiers Association, 277
Confederate Veterans Association, 252–53
Congressional Reconstruction, 41, 44–45
Conley, Benjamin, 49
Conspiracy of La Escalera (1844), 17, 19

"Conspiracy of La Escalera" (Reid-Vazquez), 16–18
Constitution, Georgia (1868), 52, 135
Constitution, Georgia (1877), 135–36, 178, 181, 183, 195, 218, 228
Constitution, U.S.: creation of, 193–94; militia clause of, 320. *See also specific amendments*
Cooper, Jerry, 191–92, 198, 313
Corker, H. W., 49–50
Cotton, 107
Craft, William, 168
Criminals and convicts, blacks as, 242–43, 247
Crumbly, Floyd H.: in Forty-Ninth Regiment, 297; life and career of, 144–46, 207, 236–37, 244, 247, 266, 290, 297; policies of, 213–14; responsible citizenship and, 209–10; Second Battalion, Georgia Volunteers, Colored, and, 263–64; Spanish-American War and, 275, 280, 284
Cuba: deployment to, 275–76, 280–83, 285–87; disbandment in, 19; nationalism, 19; Spanish-American War and, 19, 280–88
Cuban War of Independence: impacts of, 27, 256; participation in, 1, 19, 20, 191, 311–12
Cudjo Fye Insurrection, 62–63, 106
Cummings, R. G., 258
Cunningham, Roger, x

Darien sailors, 48–49, 170
Davidson, Victor, 108
Davis, Ben, 68, 70, 72, 77, 115–17
Davis, Benjamin, 1
Davis, T. James, 272
Democratic Party: ascendancy of, 64, 81, 108; opposition to, 91; Republican Party shift to, 82, 84, 87, 92, 175–76, 192; role of, 21, 43, 141
Democratic Republicanism, 193
Deveaux, James B., 168
Deveaux, John H.: Atlanta Cotton States Exposition and, 242, 247; as Collector of Customs, 276; companies under, 258–59, 298; on disbandment, 256–61, 295; drill competition and, 179–84; Emancipation Day parade and, 251–52, 299; First Battalion Georgia Volunteers, Colored, and, 190, 223, 236, 244, 299, 304, 306–7, 317, 329; flag presentation and, 264–66; Harrison's inauguration and, 215; on Irish people, 174–75; life and career of, 147–51, 168, 169, 190, 237, 299, 335; lifetime commission of, 303–4, 314, 335; responsible citizenship and, 161–64; retirement of, 336; *Savannah Tribune* and, 148, 150–53, 157, 177, 218, 316; Spanish-American War and, 279–80, 283; weapons exchanges and, 274
Dick, Charles, 319–20
Dick Act (1903), 319–23, 334–35
Disbandment: *Atlanta Constitution* on, 257–58, 293, 309–10; of black militias, 19, 21–22, 147; Candler on, 295; of Chatham Light Infantry, 325–26; in Cuba, 19; defending against, 256–60; Deveaux, John, on, 256–61, 295; disfranchisement and, 328–29; of First Battalion, Georgia Volunteers, Colored and, 258, 261, 335; of Georgia Artillery, 258–60, 318, 325; of Georgia State Troops, Colored, 256, 295, 329, 334–35; of Georgia Volunteers, 3, 140, 238, 293; of Georgia Volunteers, Colored, 256–58, 260, 262; Lone Star Cadets, 294; Military Advisory Board on, 255–59, 268, 295, 309–10; orders and recommendations, 306, 318; road to, 254–56; of Savannah Hussars, 294–95; *Savannah Morning News* on, 261; *Savannah Tribune* on, 258–59, 261–62, 326, 328
Disfranchisement: aim of, 340; Brown, E., on, 230–31; defense, status and, 20–22; disbandment and, 328–29; Jim Crow segregation and, 1, 3, 21
Disroon, Frank, 161
Dominican Republic, 340–41
Dorsette, C. N., 246
Dorsey, Allison G., 144
Douglass, Frederick, 34, 59, 96, 145, 221
Douglass Infantry, 59, 96–97, 177, 179
Dred Scott decision, 33
Drills: competitions, 177–84, 190, 201–2, 305; secret, 38, 68
Dublin Light Infantry, 205
Duncan, Russell, 168–69

Dungee, W. J., 215
Durham, J. J., 299–300

Easley, S. W, Jr., 266–67
Eastman Volunteers, 205
Economic autonomy: exercise of, 24, 51, 61, 338; via land ownership, 63, 76, 126, 337; plan for, 49, 125; platform for, 337; promotion of, 55, 57, 74, 79
Edgefield Advertiser, 67
Eight-hour workday, 171
Ellison, David, 94
Emancipation: Britain and, 31–32; impacts of, xi, 86; problem of freedom and, 337, 340
Emancipation Association, 177, 232, 299
Emancipation Day: Bonner on, 313; celebration of, 38, 56, 150, 180, 185, 212–15, 216, 227–28, 230, 257, 268; First Battalion, Georgia Volunteers, Colored on, 326–27; parades, 153–54, 232, 242, 250–52, 299, 338; *Savannah Tribune* on, 151–54, 176–77, 212–13, 229, 232, 299; twentieth century's first, 299–300
Emancipation Proclamation: commemoration of, 151, 154, 157, 250; reading of, 153, 228; signing of, 38
Emberton, Carole, 35–36
Emergency, mobilization for, 189, 216, 219, 267
Encampments: Chickamauga, 224–25; funding for, 197, 226, 238, 240–42, 262–63, 291–92; Georgia Artillery and, 202, 271–74; of National Guard, 4; white militias and, 128, 191, 201–2, 222, 223–25, 243, 262–63
Enlisted men, jobs of, 147
Equality: promotion of, 201, 226–30; *Savannah Tribune* on, 237
Exclusion: of black militias, 201–2, 217, 220, 222; strong signals of inclusion or, 65

Federal power: presence of, 26; protective umbrella of, 40; role of, 82, 157, 216; states' rights compared to, 187, 234; views on, 71, 84
Federal reorganization, 302, 319–20
Ferguson, Joseph, 92
Ferrer, Ada, 19

Fifteenth Amendment, 78, 156–57, 180; anniversary of, 217, 270, 338
Fifth Georgia Regiment, 238
First Battalion, Georgia Volunteers, Colored: activities of, 99, 199, 217, 220, 222–23, 233, 242, 274, 299; anniversary of, 305–6, 308–9, 330, 333; companies in, 258, 298; Deveaux, John, and, 190, 223, 236, 244, 299, 304, 306–7, 317, 329; disbandment of, 258, 261, 335; on Emancipation Day, 326–27; flag presentation to, 264–66; members of, 272; military fair of, 262, 269–70; Obear's inspections of, 314–15, 317, 325
First South Carolina Volunteers, 66
Fitzgerald, Michael, x
Flags: carrying, 189; presentations, 158–59, 264–66, 273
Flipper, Henry O., 180, 184
Florida, 30, 276
Floyd Rifles, 333
Flynn, Charles L., Jr., 176
Forest City Light Infantry: activities of, 95, 153, 157, 178, 221, 270; command of, 258; reorganization of, 294, 298; responsible citizenship and, 160–63; Satterlee's inspections of, 233
Fortune, T. Thomas, 313
Forty-Eighth Regiment, 297
Forty-Ninth Regiment, 297
Fourteenth Amendment, 78, 180, 338
Fourth Infantry Regiment, 280, 325
Fourth of July (Independence Day), 27, 155, 164–65, 217, 273–74, 338
Franklin, John Hope, 213
Free black society, 57
Free-colored militia, 11–13
Freedmen, attacks on, 45–46
Freedmen's Bureau, 44, 46, 100
Freedom: black militias and days of, 154–57; Brown, E., on, 36; citizenship and, x, 6, 9–10, 14–15, 22, 38–39, 51; commemoration of, 158–60, 185; definition of, 230; emancipation and problem of, 337, 340; militias and Spanish, 17–18, 30; militias as symbol of, 102; *Savannah Tribune* on, 158–59; search for, 23–39. *See also* Black freedom; White freedom

410 · Index

Fugitive Slave Act of (1850), 31, 33, 34
Fulton Guards: activities of, 215, 228, 304, 325–26; members of, 1–3, 98
Funding and fund-raising, 269–71; for armory, 220, 301, 302, 305, 308, 310; *Atlanta Constitution* on, 268–69; for black militias, 263–64, 323–24; for encampments, 197, 226, 238, 240–42, 262–63, 291–92; Georgia General Assembly (Legislature) on, 199, 206, 273, 291; for Georgia Volunteers, Colored, 267, 277–79; for Harrison's inauguration, 215; policies on, 201, 218–19, 223, 237, 240–42, 313, 315; pro rata funding, 206–7, 277–79; *Savannah Tribune* on, 241–42, 270–71; sources, 10, 42, 127, 135, 138, 141–42, 159, 191, 195–98, 201–2, 321; for uniforms, 302, 305; white militias and, 223–25, 268–69
Fye, Cudjo: life and career of, 105, 125, 170; policies of, 90, 100, 208, 332, 337. *See also* Cudjo Fye Insurrection

Gaillard, R. G., 242
GAR. *See* Grand Army of the Republic
Gardiner, John, Jr., 94
Gardner, John H., 163
Garrard, William, 216, 224, 240, 280
Gate City Guard, 257
Gatewood, Willard, 281, 285
Gendered respectability, 230–32
Georgia: black militias in, 24–26, 37–39, 42–43; Constitution (1868), 52, 135; Constitution (1877), 135–36, 178, 181, 183, 195, 218, 228; county control in, 86–92; county government in, 40–41, 108; map of counties and seats, 58
Georgia Artillery, 185; activities of, 242, 261, 270, 279, 298, 309; disbandment of, 258–60, 318, 325; Emancipation Day parade and, 250–51; encampments and, 202, 271–74; at Harrison's inauguration, 215; Obear's inspections of, 318–19, 321; reorganization of, 294; Satterlee's inspections of, 236
Georgia Cadets, 99, 215, 228
Georgia *Code*: black status under, 119; on officers' lifetime commissions, 189; passage of, 40; punishment under, 122; rewriting of, 135–36, 335; section 34 of, 322; on segregation, 192, 194; standards set by, 89
Georgia Equal Rights Association, 46
Georgia General Assembly (Legislature): activities of, 218; on funding, 199, 206, 273, 291; legislation by, 41, 49, 194–96, 238, 254–55; May celebrations and, 262–63; petition to, 266–67; policies of, 189–91; reorganization and, 186–87, 195–97, 200–201, 335; role and vision of, 26, 127, 135–36, 141–42; shabby treatment by, 240–42
Georgia Infantry, 258; in drill competition, 177; members of, 60, 97–98, 316; vision of, 101
Georgia Light Infantry, 199, 221–22
Georgia militia: changing role of, 218–20; creating, 81–125; "new era" for, 296; roster of, 106
Georgia State Industrial College, 299
Georgia State Troops: Georgia Volunteers vs., 186, 300–302, 315; members of, 3; National Guard and, 27, 293; reorganization of, 335
Georgia State Troops, Colored: activities of, 147, 317; development and evolution of, 23, 295; disbandment of, 256, 295, 329, 334–35; Georgia Volunteers, Colored, compared to, 186; members of, 3, 146, 226, 247; reorganization of, 188, 194, 302–7
Georgia Volunteers: activities of, 3, 215; admission to, 44, 61; archival collection on, ix; disbandment of, 3, 140, 238, 293; dissolution of, 281; 1878–1880, 189–93; Georgia State Troops vs., 186, 300–302, 315; members of, 91, 98, 101, 123, 125, 205, 223–24, 227; National Guard and, 135–36, 186, 256, 292–93; new companies and double standard in, 198–200; new vision for, 220; race-neutral clause for, 82; reorganization of, xii, 127, 135–38, 146, 177, 185, 186–88, 192, 194–98, 200, 238–41, 250, 289; roster of, 128, 184–85; Satterlee's inspections of, 233–36, 240; segregation of, 127–28, 139–41, 187–88, 194, 249
Georgia Volunteers, Colored: activities of, 3, 181, 216–17, 279; archival collection on, ix; characteristics of, 284; development and evolution of, xii, 23; disbandment

Index · 411

of, 256–58, 260, 262; funding for, 267, 277–79; Georgia State Troops, Colored, compared to, 186; historiography of, 10; influence on, 249; inspections of, 235–36, 243–46; members of, 39, 44, 123, 177, 185, 273, 287; reorganization of, 196, 239, 241; Second Battalion, 99, 190, 263–64; Third Battalion, 190, 233, 236. *See also* First Battalion, Georgia Volunteers, Colored
Gibbons, Stephen, 261
Gibson, John, 47
Gilbert, G. P., 224
Giles, Philip Y., 262, 295
Gilmore, Asa, 120
Gilson, Joseph P., 49
Glenn, Evelyn Nakano, 214
Gordon, John B., 205, 217–20, 222, 223
Gordon, William Washington, 239–40, 257, 280
Gordon Cavalry, 124
Governor Guards, 215
Governor Smith's Horse Guards, 106
Governor's Volunteers, 99; activities of, 215, 228; members of, 3, 178; twelfth anniversary celebration of, 207–8
Grady, Henry W., 6
Grand Army of the Republic (GAR), 213, 299
Grand juries, 68, 72–78, 109, 114–15, 118–23
Grant, Thomas, 146
Grant, Ulysses S., 47, 76, 78, 155
Graves, John Temple, 313
Gray, James R., 333
Grierson, Benjamin Henry, 210
Griffin News, 241
Gunn Logue Rifles, 124

Hahn, Steven, 70
Haitianization, 82, 122
Haitian Revolution, 35, 52, 72, 116
Hale, Grace Elizabeth: on culture of segregation, 19, 83, 102–4, 331, 340; on railroads, 111; on rewriting history of slavery, 214–15; on Washington County Courthouse, 110
Haley, John, ix
Hamburg Massacre, 151, 164–66, 250
Hammond, Attorney General, 120
Hampton, Wade, 185

Hannah, Eleanor, x; on black militias, 187; on black women, 159; on drill competition, 182; *Manhood, Citizenship and the National Guard: Illinois, 1870–1917*, 9; on motivations for militia participation, 191; on parades, 176, 223, 225; on responsible citizenship, 160–61, 211
Hanson, J. F., 309
Hardeman, T., 149, 218, 223–24
Harding, Vincent, 36
Hardwick, Thomas W., 298, 300, 307, 314, 332–33
Harman, A. T., 89, 106
Harris, Cordy (aka Caudy and Corday): Johnson County Insurrection and, 68, 72–73, 75, 77–78, 112–13, 115, 117–18, 120, 123; life and career of, 65–66, 100, 125, 167; policies of, 332, 337
Harrison, Benjamin, 215–16, 260
Harrison, W. H., 168
Hart, Bertha Sheppard, 62
Hart, R. E., 207–8, 214, 285, 333
Hartridge, Julian, 155
Harvey, W. A., 150–51
Hayes, Rutherford B., 163
Hemphill, W. A., 202–3
Herbert, Sydney: career of, 103, 106, 120–21, 124; Georgia Volunteers roster of, 128; *Roster of Georgia Volunteer Military Organizations*, 184–85; *Savannah Morning News* and, 68, 115
Hicks, Jake, 75, 78, 123
Higginbotham, W. B., 168
Higginson, Thomas Wentworth, 66
A History of Negro Troops in the War of the Rebellion (Williams, G. W.), 213
The History of the Negro Race in American from 1619 to 1880 and *Negroes as Slaves, as Soldiers, and as Citizens* (Williams, G. W.), 213
Hogue, James, 9
Holsey, Lucis Henry, 313
Holt, Thomas C., 337, 340
Holtzclaw, R. N., 203
Home Guards, 107
Hornsby-Gutting, Angela, 171, 182, 231
Hose, Sam, 289, 293
House Bill 5638, 194
Houston, Neal, 120
Howard, Philip, 15–16

Howe Guards, 124
Howell, Clark, 202
Hunter, David, 212

Illinois, 20, 21
Inclusion: in nation building, 11; in Spanish-American War, 281–86; strong signals of exclusion or, 65
Independence, battles and wars for, 11, 14, 30
Independence Day. *See* Fourth of July
Independent militia, xii. *See also* Black independent militia
Infantry companies, 106–7; white militias, 128, *129–32*
Inspections: *Atlanta Constitution* on, 234, 238, 240, 244; of Georgia Volunteers, 233–36, 240; of Georgia Volunteers, Colored, 235–36, 243–46; Military Advisory Board on, 200–201, 243–45; Obear's, 291–95, 304–7, 314–19, 321–25, 327, 334; policies on, 200–201, 222; Satterlee's, 233–36, 238, 240, 243, 245, 257–58, 260; *Savannah Tribune* on, 233, 243, 245
Insurrection, definition of, 119, 122
Integrated state-sponsored militia, 167–72
Irish Jasper Greens, 175, 252, 284
Irish people, 174–75
Israelites, 55

Jack Smith Guards, 106
Jackson, Andrew, 207
Jackson, Louis, 48–49
Jefferson Dragoons, 106
Jefferson Grays, 106
Jefferson Hussars, 106
Jefferson Riflemen, 106
Jefferson Sabres, 106
Jervey, Theodore D., 5–6
Jim Crow segregation: challenges to, 229; disfranchisement and, 1, 3, 21; rise and support of, 10, 19, 21, 143, 254–56, 270, 283, 289
Johnson, Andrew, 40
Johnson, Augustus, 94
Johnson, Charles, Jr., ix
Johnson, Frank A., 151
Johnson, Henry, 97
Johnson, Herschel V., 119, 121–23
Johnson, Solomon C.: career of, 308;
Savannah Tribune and, 177, 218, 220, 272, 283–84, 316, 334; on segregation and, 297
Johnson, Walter H., 92
Johnson County Insurrection (1875): aftermath of, 123–25; conception of, 82; confessions, 68, 114–18; grand juries and, 68, 72–78, 109, 114–15, 118–23; Harris, C., and, 68, 72–73, 75, 77–78, 112–13, 115, 117–18, 120, 123; impacts of, 102, 104, 127, 167–68; involvement in, 41–42, 67–80, 85, 106, 108–25, 133, 190, 338; legacy of, 137–38, 204–6; local memories of, 61–62; Morris, J., and, 72–73, 77, 109–10, 112–13, 116–18, 120–21; reasons for, 53; Rivers and, 77, 110, 112–13, 117, 120–21; *Savannah Morning News* on, 115, 120; Smith, J., and, 110, 115; views of, 97; Walters and, 68–69, 75, 77, 112–13, 115, 117; Washington County Courthouse and, 67–68, 77, 108–14
Johnson Rangers, 106, 124
Johnston, J. H., 250–51
Jones, Charles Colcock, Jr., 104
Jones, F. F., 258
Jones, Jesse: in *Atlanta Independent*, 1–3, *2*; career of, 14
Jones, Ralph, 47
Jones, Robert, 32
Jones, William E., 280

Kansas, 10, 21, 202
Kell, John McIntosh: illness of, 272, 291; life and career of, 199–200, 222–23, 233–34, 238–39; May celebrations and, 262
Kelley, Blair L. M., 297
Kelly, Georgia, 158–59
Kerr-Ritchie, Jeffrey R., x, 8, 9, 337, 340
Kraay, Hendrik, 14
Krebs, Ronald R., 64–65
Ku Klux Klan: opposition to, 62, 64; role of, 24, 61, 108, 140

Lamar, Daniel, 60
Land: acquisition of, 71, 73–74, 78, 123, 126; black freedom and, 45, 69; economic autonomy via ownership of, 63, 76, 126, 337
Landers, Jane, x, 17

Lark, John, 258
Laurens County: Laurens Guards, 106, 124; negro riot (1872), 62, 107; Troup Grays, 124
Law, Nelson, 304
Law, Stetson, 94
Lawton, A. R., 264–66, 269, 279
Leadership: in black militias, 142–47; definition of, 230; in white militias, 201–3
Lee, Robert E., 87, 155, 175, 339
Leonard, Elizabeth, 145
Liberalism, 167–72
Liberty Independent Troops, 87–88, 92
Lincoln, Abraham, 39, 151; birthday of, 154–55, 157, 180, 309, 338; eulogy for, 228
Lincoln Association, 39, 54, 92, 94, 101
Lincoln Guards: activities of, 298; in drill competition, 177; at McKinley's inauguration, 273; at Roosevelt's inauguration, 330–31, 333; weapons exchanges and, 274
Linder, George, 62–64
Local memories, 61–64
Lockhart, John "Sandy" A., 266, 274, 304, 329–30
Logan, George, 46
Lone Star Cadets, 162, 178, 258, 270, 294
Long, James, 81
Long, Jefferson, 100
Louisiana, 43, 52
Loving, John H., 161
Loyalty League, 43, 55, 63, 140
Lynch, John, 284–85, 287
Lynchings: Atkinson on, 246, 261; bees, 287; Hose, 289, 293; policies on, 144, 254; as symbol, 314
Lyons, Judson, 168, 236, 284, 287

Maceo, Antonio, 307
Maceo Guard, 307
Mackenzie, William Lyon, 31
Macon's Lincoln Guards, 161, 273–74, 298
Mahon, John K., 193, 320
Malone, T. H., 266
Manhood: definitions of, 22; demonstration of, 338; disciplined, 160; proof of, 35, 54–57, 159
Manhood, Citizenship and the National Guard: Illinois, 1870–1917 (Hannah), 9
Martin's Battery, 106

Masculinity, black, 54–57, 59
Massachusetts, 34
Mass democracy, 230–32
Mass meetings: involvement in, 105, 230; Republican Party, 65–67, 102
Matthews, Richard W., 97
Maxwell, L. B., 212–15, 333
May celebrations, 262–63
May Day, 155, 175, 180, 294, 304, 338
Mayer, Rube (aka Ruben Mayo), 67, 109
McDaniel, Henry D., 194
McDermott, Police Chief, 251
McGuire, Samuel B., 9
McHenry, Jackson: life and career of, 98–99, 142–44, 207, 215–16, 266–67, 295; at Nashville, Tennessee, centennial celebration, 273; Spanish-American War and, 274–76, 282, 285
McIntosh County: black political power beyond, 51–52; Campbell and black political power in, 48–50
McKinley, William: candidacy and election of, 99, 266, 276; inauguration of, 273, 309; policies of, 284–85, 290, 297, 312, 320
Mercer, George A., 234, 269
Mexico, 11–13
Middle-class blacks, 104, 119, 208, 231–32
Military: clubs, 192; fair, 262, 269–70; reorganization of, 3, 12, 14, 311–13, 320; service as path to citizenship, 145
Military Advisory Board: creation of, 194–95; on disbandment, 255–59, 268, 295, 309–10; on inspections, 200–201, 243–45; lobbying for, 239–40; on militia applications, 204–6; policies of, 198–99, 202–4, 206, 223, 278, 301; report by, 201, 224–25
Military Interstate Association, 262
Militia clause, of Constitution, U.S., 320
Militia district, 66
Militias: Afro-Cubans and, 15–19, 146; during antebellum period, 8–9, 24–25, 30, 32–34, 36–38, 85; applications, 204–6; characteristics of, 2; colonization and, xi, 11–14, 16–19, 28–30; defining in white and black, 293–95; establishment and purpose of, 8–9; historiography of, 6–11; motivations for participation in, 191; as peacekeepers, 9, 31; politics and, 10, 41, 43, 276; during postbellum period, 25, 33, 36–37, 86;

Militias—*continued*
  power and, 41, 43–44, 56, 100; in public life, 162–64; research on, ix; responsibilities of, 12, 85–86; role and function of, 337–40; as social club, 188, 220, 224, 312, 337; in South Carolina, 6, 28, 37, 38, 138, 307; Spanish freedom and, 30; state government relationship to, 43, 56, 84, 137–39, 141, 147, 171, 181, 186–89; as symbol of freedom, 102; Western Hemisphere and, x–xi, 11–15, 340; white freedom and, 26–27, 107; whites and, 32, 84. *See also specific counties, militias and states*
Miller, W. Henry, 97
Mirault, Joseph L., 262, 274
Mirault, Simon, 160–62
Mitchell, Michele, 231
Mizner, J. K., 210
Montgomery Bus Boycott (1955–1956), 7
Moore, W. D., 168
Mooreman, Jake, 68, 70, 72–73, 75–77, 115–18
Morgan, John Tyler, 211
Morgan, Philip D., x
Morris, Joseph: Johnson County Insurrection and, 72–73, 77, 109–10, 112–13, 116–18, 120–21; life and career of, 63–64, 66–68, 100, 125, 208; policies of, 332, 337
Morris, Tobe, 68–72, 115–16
Murkerson, Francis, 68, 72–78, 117, 120
Murphy, J. R., 106
Myers, Amrita, 36

Nashville, Tennessee, centennial celebration, 273
National Baptist Convention, 229
National belonging: based on whiteness, 340; citizenship and, xi–xii, 9, 27, 214, 337; debate about, 188
National Business League, 144
National Guard: direction and future of, 320; encampment of, 4; evolution of, 225–26; Georgia State Troops and, 27, 293; Georgia Volunteers and, 135–36, 186, 256, 292–93; membership of, xii; segregation and, 3; South Carolina, 217
National Guard Association (NGA), 135, 302, 311–13

Nationalism: Cuba, 19; ideology of, 174–75, 339; purveyors of, 148
National militia movement, 188
National reorganization, 197–98, 311–13
Nation building: impacts of, 15, 20, 28, 30, 38, 39; inclusion in, 11; politics and, 55; problems of, 102
Native Americans, 214, 282, 326, 335
Naturalization, 30
Negro Building, for Atlanta Cotton States Exposition, 243, 246–47
"Negro Day at the Fair," 298
Negro militia, 7, 43, 45, 191–92
Negro Militia and Reconstruction (Singletary), 7–8
Negro riot, Laurens County (1872), 62, 107
"The Negro Is an American" (Singleton), 325–27
"The Negro Ye Have With You Always" (*Savannah Tribune*), 211
New Jersey National Guard, 309
Newnan Herald, 290
New South: cooperative relationship in, 250; creation of, 45, 332; foundation for, 194; Jim Crow segregation rise in, 254; Old South and, 38; restructuring of, 188
Newspapers, 83, 103, 124
NGA. *See* National Guard Association
Ninth Cavalry, 282–83, 297, 333
Nordhoff, Charles, 81
Norris, Todd, 62, 64, 100, 125, 208, 337
North Carolina, 10, 20–21, 38
Northen, William J., 146, 207, 237–40, 289

Oaths, secret, 71–73, 98, 117–18
Obear, William G.: on Dick Act, 321–22; inspections of, 291–95, 304–7, 314–19, 321–25, 327, 334; reports of, 302, 315, 321–22, 324–25, 331
Oconee Grays, 107, 124
Oconee Rifles, 124
Odd Fellows Journal, 336
Officers: blacks, 13, 21, 99, 235; disparities between black and white, 216, 286, 303–4, 322–23; election and examination of, 300, 304, 319; lifetime commissions for, 138, 142, 189; whites, 202, 209, 280
Official History of Laurens County Georgia (Hart, B.), 62

Oglethorpe Infantry, 91
Old South, 38
Ordinary (official), 41
Out-migration, of blacks, 76, 262

Parades: Emancipation Day, 153–54, 232, 242, 250–52, 299, 338; Hannah on, 176, 223, 225; policies on, 189, 217; purpose of, 38, 56, 96, 156–58, 176, 231, 252–54, 338; tradition of, 25, 33–34, 255
Parrot guns, 259–60
Paternalism, 62, 103, 107, 123, 182, 253, 316
Patriotism: confirmation and connection to, 156, 159; as declaration of citizenship, 59, 327, 339; proof of, 282
Peacekeepers, 9, 31
Peacock, Captain, 110
Peters, Andrea, 71, 116
Peters, Edward, 202
Philippine-American War: impacts of, 27, 256; participation in, 1, 19, 20, 191, 311, 313
Pickney, W. J., 295, 298
Pinkster and Election Day celebrations, 33, 231
Plantation economy, 19, 83, 124
Pleasant, Lewis M., 163, 168, 236, 299
Pledger, William A., 100, 142, 144, 168, 247
Polhill, J. H., 106
Political clubs, 62–63, 170
Politics: militias and, 10, 41, 43, 276; nation building and, 55. *See also* Black political power
Postbellum period, 25, 33, 36–37, 86
Power: black militias and, 142–47; militias and, 41, 43–44, 56, 100. *See also* Black political power; Black power; Federal power; White power
Presidential Reconstruction, 40, 45
The Press, 327–28, 334
Pritchard, Lieutenant, 297
Profiles, high and low, 308–9
Property, slaves as, 85
Pro rata funding, 206–7, 277–79
Public rights, 52–53; access to, xii; assertion of, 37, 65, 78; defense of, 24, 70
Public space: streetcar boycott and, 148–49; use of, 67, 156–57, 165, 175, 181–82, 230–31, 250, 252, 338

Quarles, Benjamin, 13
Quotas, troop, 280, 288

Rabinowitz, Howard, 45
Race war: images of, 113–14; signs of, 67–68, 105, 109–10, 117, 123; in Wilkinson County, 62
Racial utopia, 111, 121
Radical racism theory, 332
Radical Reconstruction, 7, 41, 45, 81–82, 140
Radical Republican Party, 7–8, 139
Railroads: Hale on, 111; impacts of, 83, 102–3, 124
Rainey, W. H., 167
Reconstruction: black militia and, 5–6; black self-defense and, 44–48; Congressional, 41, 44–45; impacts of, xii, 10–11, 26, 40–41, 51, 61, 67; Presidential, 40, 45; Radical, 7, 41, 45, 81–82, 140; segregation and, 139–41
Redemption, white, 24, 27, 100
Reese, Seaborn, 90
Reid-Vazquez, Michele, x, 16–18
Reilly, Captain, 223
Reilly's bill, Colonel, 218–19
R. E. Lee Volunteers, 90
Reorganization: Anderson, C., and, 136–37; *Atlanta Constitution* on, 289–90, 300–301; Candler and, 288–92, 298, 300–301, 310–11, 315, 320; federal, 302, 319–20; of Forest City Light Infantry, 294, 298; of Georgia Artillery, 294; Georgia General Assembly (Legislature) and, 186–87, 195–97, 200–201, 335; of Georgia State Troops, 335; of Georgia State Troops, Colored, 188, 194, 302–7; of Georgia Volunteers, xii, 127, 135–38, 146, 177, 185, 186–88, 192, 194–98, 200, 238–41, 250, 289; of Georgia Volunteers, Colored, 196, 239, 241; of military, 3, 12, 14, 311–13, 320; national, 197–98, 311–13; *Savannah Morning News* on, 302; state, 197–98
Republican Party: Democratic Party shift from, 82, 84, 87, 92, 175–76, 192; direction of, 56; failure to defend, 34; involvement in, 98–100, 143–47, 163–64, 174, 216, 231, 339; mass meeting, 65–67, 102; Radical, 7–8, 139; rally, 65–67, 102, 106; revolt against, 101; role of, 7–9, 38, 43, 45–47, 52, 112

Republican Union, 62
Responsible citizenship, 1, 159, 160–66, 208–11, 338
Resurgum, 140
Revolts, slavery, 11, 16–17, 30, 72, 122
Rhode Island, 20, 328
Richmond County, 59–61
Richmond Guards, 60
Rights: to bear arms in self-defense, 20, 28, 30–33, 37, 81, 165, 172–73; to citizenship, 20, 30–31, 33, 213, 227, 287, 325–26; voting, 54, 59, 63, 157, 270, 332. *See also* Black rights; Public rights; States' rights
Riots: Atlanta race riot (1906), ix, 3, 127, 329; negro riot (1872), 62, 107; North Carolina (1898), 21; occurrences of, 21, 205, 307–8
Rivers, Prince, 66–67; Johnson County Insurrection and, 77, 110, 112–13, 117, 120–21
Roberson, James G., 307–8, 311
Robison, John W., 72–74, 114
Rogers, R. L., 106
Roosevelt, Theodore, 330–31, 333
Root, Elihu, 312, 313, 320
Roster of Georgia Volunteer Military Organizations (Herbert), 184–85
Royall, William H., 272, 303, 319; funeral of, 329–30; retirement of, 335
Rucker, Henry Allen, 98–100, 142–46, 243, 266
Rucker, Jr., L. S. D., 334
Russell, Daniel, 20
Rutledge, R. N., 261

"Sambo dialect" description, of black power, 67
Sandersville Herald and Georgian, 63, 67, 109, 111–13, 118
Satterlee, Charles B.: at Atlanta Cotton States Exposition, 242; inspections and, 233–36, 238, 240, 243, 245, 257–58, 260
Savannah Cadets, 86–87, 91, 92, 94, 95
Savannah Hussars: activities of, 95–96, 153, 157–58, 178, 242, 279; disbandment of, 258, 294–95; members of, 272; responsible citizenship and, 160
Savannah Light Infantry, 95, 153, 298
Savannah Morning News: on disbandment, 261; on Hamburg Massacre, 165; Herbert and, 68, 115; on Johnson County Insurrection, 115, 120; meeting published in, 86; on reorganization, 302; reports by, 167, 177–79, 181–82, 184; on right to bear arms in self-defense, 81; Savannah Tribune relationship with, 217, 270; on segregation, 251, 253; on states' rights, 193
Savannah Morning Telegraph, 139
Savannah Tribune: articles in, 78, 172–73, 246, 276, 329–30, 332; on Atlanta Cotton States Exposition, 242–43; on black militias, 155–57, 219, 222, 293–94, 333–35; on black officers, 286; on Chatham Light Infantry, 162; Deveaux, John, and, 148, 150–53, 157, 177, 218, 316; on Dick Act, 321; on disbandment, 258–59, 261–62, 326, 328; on Emancipation Day, 151–54, 176–77, 212–13, 229, 232, 299; on equality, 237; on freedom, 158–59; on funding, 241–42, 270–71; on Hamburg Massacre, 164–66; on Harrison's inauguration, 215–16; on inspections, 233, 243, 245; Johnson, S., and, 177, 218, 220, 272, 283–84, 316, 334; "The Negro Ye Have With You Always," 211; reports in, 304, 318, 326; on responsible citizenship and, 160–61, 209; *Savannah Morning News* relationship with, 217, 270; on segregation, 250–52, 296–98; on Spanish-American War, 276–77, 279, 281–88; support from, 167, 229
Savannah Volunteer Guards, 175, 216
Saxton, Rufus, 48
Schwarz, John, 216
Scott, A. J., 334
Scott, Rebecca J., 9
Screven, Colonel, 254
Second Amendment, 165
Second Battalion, Georgia Volunteers, Colored, 99, 190, 263–64
Secret drills, 38, 68
Secret oaths, 71–73, 98, 117–18
Segregation: culture of, 19, 83, 102–4, 125, 250, 254, 331, 335, 340; Georgia *Code* on, 192, 194; of Georgia Volunteers, 127–28, 139–41, 187–88, 194, 249; incidents, 250–54; Jim Crow, 1, 3, 10, 19, 21, 143, 229, 254–56, 270, 283, 289; Johnson, S., on, 297; National Guard and, 3; Reconstruction and, 139–41; resistance to, 296–99; *Savannah Morning News* on, 251, 253; *Savannah*

Tribune on, 250–52, 296–98; streetcars and, 148–49, 297–98
Severance, Ben H., 9
Sharecropping, 104, 145
Sharpshooter, 225–26
Shaw, Robert G., 299
Simmons, Jerry, 68, 115, 120
Simmons, John C., 250–51, 258, 261, 295, 298, 309, 321
Simmons, Robert, 258
Simms, J. M., 153, 168
Singletary, Otis, 7–8, 36
Singleton, R. H., 325–27
Slavery: abolition of, 11, 26, 32; defense of, 339; end of, x, 3, 16, 156, 172, 187, 208; Hale on rewriting history of, 214–15; Nat Turner rebellion, 72, 114; revolts, 11, 16–17, 30, 72, 122; slaves as property, 85; stereotypes of, 117; sugar plantations and, 15–17
The Slave Trade: Slavery and Color (Jervey), 5–6
Slave trade: abolition of, 29; challenges to, 16–17; end of, 16
Smalls, Robert, 166
Smith, Frances, 259–60, 307
Smith, James Milton: black state-sponsored militia and, 92, 95, 98; Cannon's letter to, 104–5; as governor, 81, 87; Johnson County Insurrection and, 110, 115; Richmond County and, 59–61; role of, 64, 89–91, 124, 133, 168
Smith, Michael Hoke, 332–33
Smith, Peter, 97
Smith, Richard, 68–70, 72, 115–16
Smith, Theophilus J., 121–22
Social club, 188, 220, 224, 312, 337
South Carolina: Hamburg Massacre and, 151, 164–66, 250; militia in, 6, 28, 37, 38, 138, 307; National Guard, 217
Southern Historical Association, ix
Spalding, Jack, 202
Spanish-American War (1898): *Atlanta Constitution* on, 274, 282, 284, 288; Crumbly and, 274, 280, 284; Cuba and, 19, 280–88; declaration and history of, 279–81; Deveaux, John, and, 279–80, 283; impacts of, 27, 256, 292; inclusion in, 281–86; McHenry and, 274–76, 282, 285; participation in, 1, 10, 19, 20, 146, 191, 290, 301, 311–12; peace and local recriminations, 288; possibility of, 268–69; problems in, 320; readiness for, 274–77; *Savannah Tribune* on, 276–77, 279, 281–88
Spanish Empire, 12–13, 17–18, 30
Spanish freedom, militias and, 17–18, 30
State reorganization, 197–98
State-sponsored militia, xii; liberalism and integrated, 167–72; prohibition of, 54; as state or federal institution, 193–94. *See also* Black state-sponsored militia; Georgia Volunteers; Georgia Volunteers, Colored
States' rights: advocacy of, 311–12; black rights and, 149; doctrine of, 193–94, 339; federal power compared to, 187, 234; *Savannah Morning News* on, 193; sharpshooter vs., 225–26
Stayhereation, 313–17
Stellarville Cavaliers, 124
Stephens, John A., 198–99
Stereotypes: of blacks, 3, 103, 275; of slavery, 117
St. James Tabernacle, 55, 56
Stone, A. W., 95
Streetcars: incidents, 250–51, 254, 261, 274–75; segregation and, 148–49, 297–98
Suffrage, for women, 171
Sugar plantations, 15–17
Surgeon-general's report, 209
Swayze, J. Clarke, 46
Sylvania Rifles, 199

Tabernacle Guards, 106
Tennessee, 38, 273
Tenth Volunteer Infantry Regiment, 286–87
Terrell, Joseph Meriwether, 319, 321, 330–34
Third Battalion, Georgia Volunteers, Colored, 190, 233, 236
Thirteenth Amendment, 78, 180, 338
Thirty-Third United States Colored Troops (later First South Carolina Volunteers), 66
Thomas, J. S., 239
Thomason, Usher, 279
Thomasville Times, 241
Thompson, John W., 199
Tillman, Benjamin, 313
Tilson, Davis, 46, 48
Toledo Blade, 166
Toombs, Robert, 135
Troop quotas, 280, 288

Troup, Joseph, 47
True soldierhood, 178–79, 181, 264–66
Tucker, Harrison, 68, 77, 112, 115
Turkey Creek Rangers, 124
Turner, Henry M., 59, 100, 153, 168, 173–74, 313
Turner, Nat, 72, 114
Tyler, J., 60

Uniforms: Civil War, 94; funding for, 302, 305; policies on, 191, 259–60, 263, 275, 278, 291; responsibility for, 83; as symbol, 91
Union and Dispatch, 6
Union Cornet Band, 215
Union Delmonico Guards, 153, 178
Union League, 45, 84, 140, 169
Union Lincoln Guards, 157–58, 161, 178, 258, 294, 298
United Daughters of Lincoln, 158–59

Values, struggles over, 53–54
Vanaradoe, Colonel, 280–81
Vardaman, James K., 331–32
Varnadoe, James O., 279–81
Vinson, Ben, III, x, 11–12
Volunteer Regiments, U.S., 320
Voting: first time, 47; rights, 54, 59, 63, 157, 270, 332

Walker, T. G., 258
Wallace, George, 168
Walters, Jerry (aka Waters and Walker), 68–69, 75, 77, 112–13, 115, 117
Walton, A. W., 203
Walton, Henry N., 304
War Department, 141, 287–88, 296, 313, 320
Warthen, William, 110
Washam, R., 266
Washington, Booker T., 144, 242
Washington, Brown, 205
Washington, George, 155, 207
Washington, L. A., 258, 295
Washington County Courthouse: Hale on, 110; Johnson County Insurrection and, 67–68, 77, 108–14; Republican Party mass meeting in, 65–67, 102; as symbol of white power, 67–68, 110, 114

Washington County Dragoons, 113, 124
Washington Guards, 98, 228
Washington Light Horse Guards, 106, 124
Washington Rifles, 106, 110, 113
Washington's Blues, 124
Watkins, William J., 35
Watson, Thomas E., 332–33
Wayne, Henry C., 139
Weapons: distribution of, 26, 42, 90, 278–79; exchanges, 274, 277; parrot guns, 259–60; purchase of, 196; requests for, 106; worn out and obsolete, 235–36, 249, 291, 314
Weedon, Captain, 111
Weldrim, Private, 87, 91, 95, 181–82
West, A. J., 203
Western Hemisphere, x–xi, 11–15, 340
West India Day, 31, 33, 221
Wheaton, John F., 179
White, William Jefferson, 98, 215, 236
White freedom: black freedom compared to, 53; militia and, 26–27, 107
White Leaguers, 48
Whiteman, James E., 230
White militias: cavalry units, 106–7, 128, *133–34*; encampments and, 128, 191, 201–2, 222, 223–25, 243, 262–63; funding and, 223–25, 268–69; infantry companies, 128, *129–32*; leadership in, 201–3; Obear's inspections of, 322–23; resources and development for, 249, 255; role of, 338
Whiteness: blackness compared to, 92, 104; commitment to, 21; counting on, 89; definition of, 103–4; national belonging based on, 340
White officers, 202, 209, 280; disparities between black and, 216, 286, 303–4, 322–23
White power: black power compared to, 70, 182; challenge to, 48, 61, 62, 109; Civil War and, 102; emergence of, 91; links to, 85; mobilization of, 65; Washington County Courthouse as symbol of, 67–68, 110, 114
Whites: on black claims to citizenship, xii; memory, change, and restoration, 101–8; militia and, 32, 84; Redemption, 24, 27, 100; response to black power, 64–65, 82; support from, 1; women, violence against, 117
White space, invasion of, 103

White supremacy: advocates of, 1, 4, 21, 289; challenge to, 147; philosophy of, 2, 143, 181, 255; rise of, 216, 256; triumph of, 26; views on, 331–33
Whitten, Prince, 30, 31
Wight, Edward K., 203
Wight, E. L., 234, 239
Wiley, C. M., 224
Wiley, W. H., 75, 76, 110, 114–15
Wilkinson County, 62
Wilkinson Grays, 107
Wilkinson Rifles, 107
Williams, E. A., 258
Williams, George S., 326
Williams, George Washington, 213–14, 333
Williams, Joseph K., 97
Williamson, Joel, 332
Wilson, Anthony, 196
Wilson, Joseph T., 213
Wimbush, C. C., 98–99, 142–44, 146, 247, 266, 276
Wingfield, James W., 97
Women: black, 158–60, 230–31; suffrage for, 171; white, violence against, 117
Woodhouse, William H.: life and career of, 151, 156, 160–63, 178, 190; rehabilitating image of, 236–37; resignation of, 199
Wooten, N. E., 239
Wright, James, 68–72, 115–16
Wright, R. R., 299
Wright, Tony, 71
Wylie, Charles, 279

Yates, William, 150–51
Yellow fever, 161–62; immunity to, 275, 284–85
Young, Eliza, 115–17

Zion Hope Company, 69

Gregory Mixon is professor of history at the University of North Carolina at Charlotte. He is the author of *The Atlanta Riot: Race, Class, and Violence in a New South City.*

SOUTHERN DISSENT

Edited by Stanley Harrold and Randall M. Miller

The Other South: Southern Dissenters in the Nineteenth Century, by Carl N. Degler, with a new preface (2000)
Crowds and Soldiers in Revolutionary North Carolina: The Culture of Violence in Riot and War, by Wayne E. Lee (2001)
"Lord, We're Just Trying to Save Your Water": Environmental Activism and Dissent in the Appalachian South, by Suzanne Marshall (2002)
The Changing South of Gene Patterson: Journalism and Civil Rights, 1960–1968, edited by Roy Peter Clark and Raymond Arsenault (2002; first paperback edition, 2020)
Gendered Freedoms: Race, Rights, and the Politics of Household in the Delta, 1861–1875, by Nancy D. Bercaw (2003)
Civil War on Race Street: The Civil Rights Movement in Cambridge, Maryland, by Peter B. Levy (2003)
South of the South: Jewish Activists and the Civil Rights Movement in Miami, 1945–1960, by Raymond A. Mohl, with contributions by Matilda "Bobbi" Graff and Shirley M. Zoloth (2004)
Throwing Off the Cloak of Privilege: White Southern Women Activists in the Civil Rights Era, edited by Gail S. Murray (2004)
The Atlanta Riot: Race, Class, and Violence in a New South City, by Gregory Mixon (2004)
Slavery and the Peculiar Solution: A History of the American Colonization Society, by Eric Burin (2005; first paperback edition, 2008)
"I Tremble for My Country": Thomas Jefferson and the Virginia Gentry, by Ronald L. Hatzenbuehler (2006; first paperback edition, 2009)
From Saint-Domingue to New Orleans: Migration and Influences, by Nathalie Dessens (2007)
Higher Education and the Civil Rights Movement: White Supremacy, Black Southerners, and College Campuses, edited by Peter Wallenstein (2008)
Burning Faith: Church Arson in the American South, by Christopher B. Strain (2008; first paperback edition, 2020)
Black Power in Dixie: A Political History of African Americans in Atlanta, by Alton Hornsby Jr. (2009; first paperback edition, 2016)
Looking South: Race, Gender, and the Transformation of Labor from Reconstruction to Globalization, by Mary E. Frederickson (2011; first paperback edition, 2012)
Southern Character: Essays in Honor of Bertram Wyatt-Brown, edited by Lisa Tendrich Frank and Daniel Kilbride (2011)
The Challenge of Blackness: The Institute of the Black World and Political Activism in the 1970s, by Derrick E. White (2011; first paperback edition, 2012)
Quakers Living in the Lion's Mouth: The Society of Friends in Northern Virginia, 1730–1865, by A. Glenn Crothers (2012; first paperback edition, 2013)
Unequal Freedoms: Ethnicity, Race, and White Supremacy in Civil War–Era Charleston, by Jeff Strickland (2015)
Show Thyself a Man: Georgia State Troops, Colored, 1865–1905, by Gregory Mixon (2016; first paperback edition, 2024)

The Denmark Vesey Affair: A Documentary History, edited by Douglas R. Egerton and Robert L. Paquette (2017; first paperback edition, 2022)

New Directions in the Study of African American Recolonization, edited by Beverly C. Tomek and Matthew J. Hetrick (2017; first paperback edition, 2022)

Everybody's Problem: The War on Poverty in Eastern North Carolina, by Karen M. Hawkins (2017)

The Seedtime, the Work, and the Harvest: New Perspectives on the Black Freedom Struggle in America, edited by Jeffrey L. Littlejohn, Reginald K. Ellis, and Peter B. Levy (2018; first paperback edition, 2019)

Fugitive Slaves and Spaces of Freedom in North America, edited by Damian Alan Pargas (2018; first paperback edition, 2020)

Latino Orlando: Suburban Transformation and Racial Conflict, by Simone Delerme (2020; first paperback edition, 2023)

Slavery and Freedom in the Shenandoah Valley during the Civil War Era, by Jonathan A. Noyalas (2021; first paperback edition, 2022)

The Citizenship Education Program and Black Women's Political Culture, by Deanna M. Gillespie (2021; first paperback edition, 2023)

Southern History Remixed: On Rock 'n' Roll and the Dilemma of Race, by Michael T. Bertrand (2024)

Printed in the USA
CPSIA information can be obtained
at www.ICGtesting.com
JSHW080240100224
56852JS00010B/7